Nineteenth Edition

Property and Casualty Insurance

A Guide Book for Agents and Brokers

BY PHILIP GORDIS, C.P.C.U., C.L.U.

President, Philip Gordis Associates, Inc.

Coordinator, Insurance Brokers Courses,
Brooklyn College, Adult Educational Division

26520

Property and Casualty Insurance

A Guide Book for Agents and Brokers

Nineteenth Edition, Revised 1972
Second Printing, December, 1972

PRINTED IN THE UNITED STATES OF AMERICA

Preface

THIS BOOK, now in its nineteenth revised edition, had its beginnings in a set of notes first developed by me for students of the Adult Education Division of Brooklyn College who were preparing for the brokers' and agents' examination given by the Insurance Department of the State of New York. The original notes were steadily expanded and revised to reflect the valuable day-to-day experience in the classroom with these students and those of the New School for Social Research and of Packard Junior College, where I was in charge of similar courses.

The present book, although several times the size of the original notes, still utilizes much the same approach, and follows the basic format of the earlier material. Coverages are analyzed and arranged in a manner designed to make it easier for students not only to understand but also to commit to memory the wealth of detail which a constantly developing insurance business requires. Furthermore, the book emphasizes actual agents' and brokers' practices more than texts geared toward academic students, whose study of insurance is often necessarily of a more general nature.

The gratifying response to this book has made it possible to bring out a newly revised edition almost each year since its publication. Every effort has been made to incorporate into each successive printing the more significant developments that take place within the industry, even though changes continue to proliferate both regionally and nationally, with no apparent concern for the toiling author or the publisher. In the effort to keep the material in line with the rapid changes which these years have produced, I have had assistance from many insurance men on a company and agency level, as well as my colleagues in the brokerage business. To them, and to zealous students who have used the book, I wish to express my sincere gratitude. More particularly, I wish to thank Mr. Willard J. Gentile, Assistant Manager of the New York Compensation Insurance Rating Board, for his many helpful suggestions on Workmen's Compensation insurance; Mr. Davis Quinn, senior underwriter of Chubb and Son, New York City, who reviewed the chapters on Fidelity and Surety; Herbert F. Shaffer, underwriter, U. S. Fidelity and Guaranty Co., who made suggestions for improving the chapters on Burglary and Allied Lines; Roland G. Vogel of the Reliance Insurance Co., who reviewed the chapters on Inland Marine Insurance, and Al P. Clifford of the United States Fidelity and Guaranty Co. who helped in developing much of the material on the new Multiple Peril Policies. In updating the chapters on Fire insurance, Automobile Insurance, Accident and Health insurance and Multiple Perils, I have been given invaluable assistance by George Palmer and Aaron Rennert, two of my esteemed colleagues at Brooklyn College and St. John's University.

I am also deeply indebted to these other authorities who have reviewed selected chapters of the original edition, and have made many valuable suggestions on improving the material: To Sidney Gaines, formerly senior attorney of the New York State Insurance Department, on Reinsurance, Negligence, Contract and Agency; to Frank Swearington, former Indianapolis branch manager of the Travelers, on Fire and Allied Lines; to William H. Rodda, formerly manager, Transportation Insurance Rating Board, on Inland Marine insurance; to Richard R. Bjorness, formerly Ocean Marine Manager in New York City of the Reliance Insurance Co.; to Robert Griswold, retired manager, Aetna Life Group at Indianapolis, and Dallas Carpenter of the same companies, on Burglary and Allied Lines; to Harold F. Gee, retired vice president, Continental Insurance Companies, on Fidelity and Surety, and Robert W. Osler, former president, Underwriters National Assurance Company, Indianapolis, on Accident and Health insurance.

Professor Arthur Secord, at that time supervisor of the Adult Education Division, Brooklyn College and Joseph Goodman, present supervisor, both cheerfully accepted the burden of having the original notes and the early revisions prepared at the college. In this work, Mrs. Rita Basist, who did most of the typing and stencil cutting, rendered invaluable assistance. Mrs. Catherine A. Carroll, my secretary, gave her unstinting cooperation, and her highly competent assistance is most gratefully acknowledged.

Walter Keating, secretary of The Home Insurance Co. in New York, who made many valuable suggestions for the original edition has continued to extend his generous assistance with many revisions of the book made necessary by developments in the insurance business. Some time ago, he assisted in circulating a questionnaire among the State Agents of The Home Insurance Co. in the various states and territories. To him and to those many men, too numerous to list by name, who took time from their busy schedules to complete this rather elaborate questionnaire and to volunteer additional comments, I wish to extend my sincere thanks. In the preparation of this last revision I have again received informed assistance from Walter Keating and his able staff at The Home Insurance Co.

Numerous suggestions for improvements throughout the eighteenth edition were made by my friend and fellow-instructor, the late George Palmer, whose untimely death took from our midst one of the most knowledgeable and acute insurance men and educators I ever met.

In my revision of the last two editions, I have been helped immeasurably by Wallace L. Clapp, Jr., CPCU, Editor of Books and Technical Materials of the Rough Notes Co. In each instance, he prepared for my guidance a painstakingly exhaustive summary of the numerous changes and developments in the insurance business. This analysis not only saved me countless hours of work but helped me incorporate many important changes which might otherwise have escaped my researches.

This book is dedicated to the memory of Clifford L. McMillen, with whom I had the privilege of being associated at the time of his death. For a considerable period, he had been giving substantial financial support to a local university to encourage the spread of insurance education and it was natural to this gracious and generous insurance leader to encourage all who were trying to make a contribution to insurance and insurance education. This book would not have been possible without his encouragement and cooperation.

It must be pointed out that the responsibility for any shortcomings in the material rests solely with the author.

PHILIP GORDIS

August, 1972

Contents

Complete Alphabetical Index at End of Book

1. THE LAW OF CONTRACTS AS IT RELATES TO INSURANCE .... Page 27

The Insurance Contract-Fortuitous Event–Insurable Interest–Risk of Loss
How General Rules of Contracts Apply to Insurance Contracts–Concealment–Misrepresentation–Warranty–Valuable Consideration–Legal in Form–For a Legal Purpose

2. THE FIRE INSURANCE POLICY .... Page 30

Standardization of Fire Policy–The New York Standard Fire Policy
Hazards Covered–Fire and Lightning–Fire–Hostile Fire–Proximate Cause
Hazards Not Covered–Enemy Attack–Action by Our Armed Forces–Insurrection, etc.–Order of Civil Authority–Neglect of Insured–Theft–Explosion or Riot
For How Much–Actual Cash Value–Cost to Repair or Replace –Company May Elect to Repair or Rebuild–Company May Take All Property–No Abandonment Clause–Insurable Interest–Assignment of Policy–Pro Rata Liability
Where Covered–Who Is Insured
Property Not Insured–Uninsurable Property–Excepted Property
Insured's Duties and Obligations–Moral Duties–Concealment, Fraud–Physical Factors–Increase of Hazard–Vacancy or Unoccupancy–Change of Ownership
Requirements after Loss–Duties of Insured to Protect Property –Inventory–Proof of Loss–Duties of Insured When Requested by Company–Appraisal–When Loss Is Payable–When Suit Must Be Brought–Subrogation
Time of Policy
Cancellation–At Company's Request–At Insured's Request
Miscellaneous–Binders–Other Insurance–Concurrency

3. FIRE FORMS .... Page 46

Standardization of Forms–Provisions Common to the Various Forms–Hazards Covered–Debris Removal Clause–Liberalization Clause–Hazards Not Covered–Nuclear Perils–Electrical Apparatus Clause–For How Much–Coinsurance Clause–Average Clause–Reduced Rate Contribution Clause–Three-Fourths Value Clause–Three-Fourths Loss Clause–Pro Rata Distribution Clause Under Blanket Policies–Replacement Cost Coverage–Waiver of Inventory

BUILDING AND CONTENTS FORM (General Property Form) (Page 53) What Is Covered–Building Coverage–Contents Coverage – Stock Coverage – Contents, Except Stock – Improvements and Betterments–Personal Property of Others–Off-Premises Extension – Property Not Covered – Foundation Exclusions Clause–Where Covered–Property Outside Buildings–Alterations and Repairs Clause–Insured's Duties and Obligations–Work and Materials Clause–Breach of Warranty Clause–Vacancy and Unoccupancy–Insured's Warranties–Control of Property Clause–Subrogation–Coinsurance–Mortgagee Clause – Benefits Received

by Mortgagee—Obligations Imposed on the Mortgagee—Loss Payable Clause
DWELLING AND CONTENTS FORM (Page 60)—Dwelling Form—Inherent Explosion—What Is Covered—Outbuildings Coverage—Rent Insurance—Trees, Shrubs, Plants—Electrical Apparatus, Lightning Deductible—For How Much—Deductibles—Insured's Obligations
HOUSEHOLD CONTENTS FORM (Page 61) Hazards Covered —Consequential Loss—What Is Covered—Who Is Insured—For How Much—Where Covered—Contents In Open—10% Away From Premises—Removal Within State—Buildings In Course of Construction—What Is Covered

4. VALUED POLICY AND ANTI-COINSURANCE LAWS .... Page 65

VALUED POLICY LAWS (Page 65)—Total Loss on Real Property—No Depreciation, No Right to Rebuild or Replace—Company May Exercise Option—Depreciation Since Date of Policy—All Losses on Real Property, Total and Partial—Refund of Excess Premiums Paid to Insured by Company
ANTI-COINSURANCE LAWS (Page 67)—Acceptance Optional with Insured—Policies Must Be Clearly Stamped—No Coinsurance on Building Property

5. ADDITIONAL PERILS COVERAGE .... Page 69

EXTENDED COVERAGE ENDORSEMENT (Page 69)—Hazards Not Covered—War, Nuclear Perils—Water Exclusion Clause —For How Much—Apportionment Clause—Coinsurance Clause, Average Clause
Privileges Granted—Vacancy and Unoccupancy—Change of Occupancy
Windstorm and Hail Provisions—Hazards Not Covered—Windstorm and Hail Deductibles
Other Provisions—Smoke—Explosion—Riot, Civil Commotion—Aircraft and Vehicles
VANDALISM AND MALICIOUS MISCHIEF ENDORSEMENT (Page 75)—Deductible
DWELLING BUILDING(S) AND CONTENTS—BROAD FORM—(Page 77) —Hazards Covered—Fire, Lightning—Windstorm, Hail, Explosion, Riot, Civil Commotion, Aircraft, Vehicles, Smoke—Vandalism and Malicious Mischief—Burglars—Falling Objects—Weight of Ice, Snow or Sleet—Collapse—Water Damage—Cracking, Burning or Bulging of Hot Water Systems—Glass Breakage—Freezing of Plumbing, Heating, Air Conditioning or Domestic Appliances—Accidental Injury to Electrical Appliances Hazards Not Covered—Earthquake, Volcanic Eruption, Landslide—Water Damage—Unoccupancy Exclusion—Falling Objects —Outdoor Antenna—Fences, Pavements, Swimming Pools—What Is Covered—Outbuildings, Rental Value—Additional Living Expense—Improvements and Betterments—Trees, Shrubs, Plants, Lawns—Debris Removal—Liberalization Clause—Property Not Covered—Foundation Exclusion Clause—For How Much—Replacement Cost Coverage—Deductible Clause—Waiver of Inventory Clause—Where Covered—Away from Premises—Removal for Preservation or Repair—Removal Within State—When Covered —Other Clauses
DWELLING BUILDING(S) SPECIAL FORM (Page 84)—Hazards Covered—Hazards Not Covered—Earthquake, Landslide, or

Earth Movement—Water Exclusion—Freezing During Vacancy or Unoccupancy — Power, Heating and Cooling Failure — Loss to Fences, Walks by Freezing—Unoccupancy—Theft—What Is Covered—Outbuildings Coverage—Rental Value Coverage and Additional Living Expenses—Trees, Shrubs, Plants and Lawns—Debris Removal—Liberalization Clause—Property Not Covered—Foundation Exclusion Clause—Retaining Walls—Radio and Television Antennas—Farm Property—For How Much—Replacement Cost Coverage—Deductible Clause—Waiver of Inventory of Undamaged Property—Where Covered—Removal for Preservation or Repair —Vacancy and Unoccupancy—Other Clauses

FLOOD INSURANCE (Page 87)

6. BUSINESS INTERRUPTION INSURANCE ....Page 90

Business Interruption Insurance—Hazards Covered—What Is Covered—Additional Time To Replace Stock—Interruption by Civil Authority—Salvage—Expense to Reduce Loss—Electronic Data Loss—Business Interruption Forms—Hazards Covered—What Is Covered—Ordinary Payroll Exclusion—Ordinary Payroll—Limited Coverage Endorsement (B)—Hazards Not Covered—Construction Ordinance—Cancellation of Lease, Order, Contract—Strike Interference—For How Much—Actual Loss Sustained—Endorsement Extended Period of Indemnity—Coinsurance Requirements—Other Clauses

EARNINGS INSURANCE (Page 100)—Monthly Limitation

AGREED AMOUNT FORMS (Page 101)

PREMIUM ADJUSTMENT FORMS (Page 101)

CONTINGENT BUSINESS INTERRUPTION INSURANCE (Page 102)—Off-Premises Power, Light, Heat, Gas, Water Supply Forms

TUITION FEES INSURANCE (Page 103)

7. INSURING OTHER CONSEQUENTIAL LOSSES....Page 104

RENT OR RENTAL VALUE INSURANCE (Page 104)—How Policy is Written

Hazards Covered—Access to Premises—Interruption by Civil Authority—Hazards Not Covered

For How Much—Coinsurance or Contribution Clauses—Monthly Limitation Forms—Rental Value—Dwellings

Special Rent Insurance Forms—Seasonal Property—Fluctuating Rent—Premium Adjustment Form—Buildings in Course of Construction

LEASEHOLD INTEREST INSURANCE (Page 109)

EXTRA EXPENSE INSURANCE (Page 111)

COMBINED BUSINESS INTERRUPTION AND EXTRA EXPENSE (Page 113)—Finished Stock

ADDITIONAL LIVING EXPENSE INSURANCE (Page 114)

SELLING PRICE CLAUSES (Page 114)

MARKET VALUE CLAUSES (Page 115)

POWER FAILURE OR CONSEQUENTIAL LOSS PROVISIONS (Page 115)

CONSEQUENTIAL LOSS AND DAMAGE ASSUMPTION CLAUSE (Page 116)—Clothing Policies

DEMOLITION INSURANCE (Page 117)—Contingent Liability from Operation of Building or Zoning Laws—Demolition Cost Endorsement—Increased Cost of Construction Endorsement—Cost of Reproduction of Records—Fire Department Charges

8. FIRE INSURANCE RATES AND RATE MAKING..Page 121

RATE REGULATION (Page 121)—Rate-Making Organizations—Basic Types of Fire Insurance Rates—General Class (or Minimum Rates)—Construction Types—Approved Roofs—Protected and Unprotected Territory
Specific Rates (Schedule Rates)—Interstate Locations
Other Factors Which Affect Fire Insurance Rates—Term Policies—Installment Payment of Term Premiums—Minimum Premiums—Whole Dollar Premium Rule—Coinsurance, Average Clause, Reduced Rate Contribution Clause Credits—Deductible (Excess of Loss) Fire Insurance—Dwelling Deductibles—Franchise (Disappearing) Deductibles—Reduction in Amount—Flat Cancellation—Loss Constant Rating Factor—Civil Disorder Loadings—Fair Access to Insurance Requirements (FAIR) Plans—Vandalism and Malicious Mischief—Consent to Rate Laws
BEACH PROPERTY INSURANCE POOLS (Page 131)—What Is Covered—Perils Covered—For How Much—Coinsurance—Deductibles—When Covered

9. SPRINKLER LEAKAGE AND WATER DAMAGE INSURANCE ....Page 134

Hazards Covered—Damage by Tanks
Hazards Not Covered—Fire and Lightning—Windstorm, Explosion, Riot, Civil Commotion—Insurrecton, Rebellion, Revolution—Order of Any Civil Authority—Theft—Water—Earthquake, Blasting, Rupture of Steam Boilers or Fly Wheels—War Perils—Nuclear Explosion Clause—Vacancy and Unoccupancy—Alterations and Repairs and Unoccupancy—Alterations and Repairs
What Is Covered—Where Covered—Limits—Coinsurance, Reduced Rate Contribution or Average Clause—Non-Reduction After Loss—Other Clauses and Provisions—Waiver of Inventory or Appraisement Clause—Other Provisions—Alarm or Watchman Service Clause—Insuring Consequential Sprinkler Leakage Losses
WATER DAMAGE INSURANCE (Page 139)
Hazards Covered—Water or Steam Discharge—Rain or Snow Admission—Damage by Tanks
Hazards Not Covered—Seepage, Leakage or Influx of Water—Floods, Inundations—Backing up of Sewers or Drains, Gas, Fumes and Vapors—Failure of Refrigerating or Air Conditioning Systems—Vacancy and Unoccupancy—Aircraft in Motion—Alterations and Repairs
What Is Covered—Where Covered
For How Much—Coinsurance, Reduced Rate Contribution or Average Clause—Deductible Clause
Additional Coverages—Underground Water Supply Mains and Fire Hydrants—Chemical Refrigerant Leakage—Other Provisions

10. PERSONAL CRIME COVERAGES....Page 143

BROAD FORM PERSONAL THEFT POLICY (Page 143)
What Is Covered—Damage to Premises—When Premises are Rented to Another
Hazards Covered—Damage—Vandalism and Malicious Mischief—Hazards Not Covered
Who Is Covered—Death of the Insured—Where Covered
Coverage A—Theft From Premises—Depository, Public Warehouse, Other Occupied Residences—Premises Used as Boarding House or for Business—Removal to Other Premises

Coverage B—Theft Away From Premises—Where Covered—Secondary Residences—Property in the Mails—Theft from Laundry, Cleaner, Dyer, Tailor, Presser—Property of Servants
For How Much—Limitation on Money—Limitation on Securities —Limit of Liability on Jewelry and Furs—Other Insurance—Pair and Set Clause—Deductible—Limitation of Liability on Boats
How Theft Insurance Is Written—Section (a)—Section (b)—Specified Articles—Divided Coverage—100% Blanket Coverage—Limitation of Liability to Limits Under Coverage A—Physicians, Surgeons and Dentists Outside Coverage—Insured's Duties and Obligations
Requirements In Case of Loss—Notice of Loss, Proof of Loss—Examination Under Oath—Submission of Records—Suit Against Company—Settlement of Loss with Others—Reinstatement After Loss—Subrogation—Benefit of Insurance—Cancellation—Term of Policy—Assignment of Policy—Regulation
Rates—Minimum Premiums—Three-Year Policies—Whole Dollar Premium Rule

PERSONAL THEFT POLICY (OR ENDORSEMENT) (Page 153)
Hazards Covered—Hazards Not Covered—What Is Covered—For How Much—Where Covered—Theft from Automobile—Dormitory, Fraternity, Sorority—Hotels, Penthouses—How Personal Theft Is Written—Other Clauses

11. COMMERCIAL BURGLARY POLICIES.................Page 156

OPEN STOCK BURGLARY POLICY (Page 156)
What Is Covered—Damage to Premises—Ownership of Property
Hazards Covered—Robbery of Watchman—Theft Insurance (Mercantile Open Stock Theft)—Hazards Not Covered—Infidelity of Employees—War, Insurrection, Etc.—Fire—Change in Condition of Risk—Records of Insured—Vandalism and Malicious Mischief —Fur Articles—Nuclear Perils—Where Covered—Automatic Insurance on Additional Locations—For How Much—Full Salvage to Insured—Profits Insurance—Jewelry and Pledged Articles—Consequential Loss—Clothing Risks—Coinsurance (Average Clause)—Other Insurance
Insured's Duties and Obligations—Records of Insured—Maintenance of Promised Protection—Insured's Statements—Inspection —Maintenance of Premises
Requirements In Case of Loss—Notice of Loss—Proof of Loss—Inventory of Property Not Stolen or Damaged—Cooperation with Company—Time To Bring Suit—Reinstatement After Loss —Subrogation — Cancellation — Binder Cancellation — Reduction in Amount
Rates—Three-Year Policies—Whole Dollar Premium Rule—Credits
Other Clauses—Assignment—Regulation—Term of Policy

MERCANTILE SAFE BURGLARY INSURANCE (Page 166)
What Is Covered—Damage to Furniture, Fixtures and Property —Damage to Buildings—Ownership of Property—Property Not Covered—Hazards Covered—Hazards Not Covered—Records of Insured—Failure to Maintain Protection—Damage to Property and Premises
Where Covered—Automatic Insurance on Additional Locations
For How Much—Profits Insurance—Pledged Articles—Other Insurance
Insured's Duties and Obligations—Records of Insured—Mainte-

nance of Promised Protection—Insured's Statements—Requirements In Case of Loss
Other Clauses—Subrogation—Cancellation—Binder Cancellation—Assignment—Reinstatement After Loss—Regulation
Rates—Territory in Which Risk Is Located—The Insured's Business—Type of Safe or Vault—Minimum Premiums—Whole Dollar Premium Rule—Credits
How Policy Is Written—Term of Policy

12. ROBBERY COVERAGES ....Page 172

MERCANTILE ROBBERY INSURANCE (Page 172)
What Is Covered—Damage to Premises—Ownership of Property—Property Not Covered
Hazards Covered—Kidnapping Coverage—Show Window Robbery—Damage to Property and Premises—Who Is Covered
Hazards Not Covered—Records of Insured—Failure to Maintain Protection—Infidelity of Employees—Nuclear Perils
Where Covered—Home of Custodian Covered—Show Window Coverage—Automatic Insurance on Additional Locations—For How Much—How Insurance Is Written
Insured's Duties and Obligations—Records of Insured—Maintenance of Promised Protection—Insured's Statements—Requirements in Case of Loss
Other Clauses—Subrogation—Cancellation—Assignment—Reinstatement After Loss—Regulation—Term of Policy
Rates—Interior Robbery—Credits—Messenger Robbery—Credits—Minimum Premiums—Whole Dollar Premium Rule
PAYMASTER ROBBERY POLICY (Page 179)
What Is Covered—Loss of Other Money and Securities—Damage to Premises
Hazards Covered—Robbery from Employees—Damage to Property and Premises
Hazards Not Covered—Records of Insured—Infidelity of Employees—Failure to Maintain Protection, Change in Risk
Where Covered—Automatic Insurance on Additional Locations—Home of Custodian Coverage
Who Is Covered—For How Much
Insured's Duties and Obligations—Records of Insured—Maintenance of Promised Protection—Insured's Statements—Requirements in Case of Loss
Other Clauses—Subrogation—Cancellation—Assignment—Reinstatement After Loss—Regulation—Term of Policy
Rates—Credits—Minimum Premiums
PAYMASTER BROAD FORM POLICY (Page 182)—No Custodian on Duty—Dishonesty of Employees—Loss in Any Exchange or Purchase—War, Revolution, Insurrection, Etc.
FEDERAL CRIME INSURANCE (Page 184)—Residential Coverages—Commercial Coverages—Cancellation

13. BROAD FORM PACKAGE POLICIES..................Page 187

MONEY AND SECURITIES BROAD FORM POLICY (Page 187)
What Is Covered—Money and Securities—Other Property—Damage to Premises—Ownership of Property—Property Not Covered—
Hazards Covered—Money and Securities Coverage—Other Property—Locked Cash Register, Drawer or Box—When Loss Must Be Discovered—Superseded Insurance
Hazards Not Covered—Dishonesty of Employees—Loss in Any

Exchange or Purchase—Records of Insured—War, Revolution, Insurrection, Etc.—Nuclear Perils—Loss by Fire—Money in Vending Machine
Who Is Covered—Where Covered—Loss Within Premises, Coverage A—Premises of Banks and Depositories—Automatic Insurance on Additional Locations—Home of Messenger—Loss Outside Premises, Coverage B
For How Much—Pledged Articles—Other Insurance—Full Salvage to Insured
Insured's Duties and Obligations—Records of Insured—Insured's Statements
Requirements In Case of Loss—Notice of Loss—Proof of Loss—Negotiation of Securities—Cooperation with Company
Other Clauses — Subrogation — Cancellation — Assignment — Regulation—Reinstatement After Loss
How Insurance Is Written—Schedule Policy—Blanket Policy—Existing Insurance
Rates—Loss Within Premises, Coverage A—Credits—Loss Outside Premises, Coverage B—Credits
Minimum Premiums—Loss Within Premises, Coverage A—Loss Outside Premises, Coverage B—Term of Policy
PACKAGE CRIME POLICIES (Page 194)
STOREKEEPERS' BURGLARY AND ROBBERY POLICY (Page 194)
What Is Covered—Ownership of Property—Property Not Covered
Hazards Covered—I. Robbery Inside Premises—II. Robbery Outside Premises—III. Kidnapping—Limitation on Number of Messengers—IV. Safe Burglary—V. Theft of Night Depository or Residence—VI. Burglary of Merchandise—Limitation on Jewelry and Pledged Articles—VII. Damage to Property and Premises—Hazards Not Covered—Dishonesty of Employees—Fire—Where Covered—For How Much—Other Insurance
Other Clauses—Rates—Term of Policy
BROAD FORM STOREKEEPERS POLICY (Page 198)
What Is Covered—Hazards Covered—Money Orders and Counterfeit Currency—Burglary, Robbery of a Watchman—Theft from Residence—Employee Dishonesty—Depositors Forgery—Vandalism and Malicious Mischief—Premises Damage—When Covered
OFFICE BURGLARY AND ROBBERY POLICY (Page 200)
What Is Covered—Property Not Covered—Hazards Covered—I. Robbery Inside Premises—II. Theft Inside Premises—III. Safe Burglary; Burglary—IV. Robbery Outside Premises—V. Theft from Night Depository or Residence—VI. Damage—For How Much—Rates
OTHER PACKAGE CRIME POLICIES (Page 202)—Church Theft
INNKEEPERS LIABILITY POLICY (Page 202)
WAREHOUSEMAN'S LIABILITY POLICY (Page 203)
VALUABLE PAPERS POLICY (Page 203)
ACCOUNTS RECEIVABLE POLICY (Page 204)

14. FIDELITY AND SURETY BONDS.........................Page 206

General Principles of Suretyship—Differences Between Insurance and Suretyship—1, Principal—2. Obligee—3. Surety
FIDELITY BONDS (Page 208)—Features Common to All Fidelity Bonds
What Is Covered—Ownership of Property—Hazards Covered

Who Is Covered—Cancellation of Coverage on Dishonest Employee—Absence of Coverage on Employee Previously Cancelled—When Covered—When Loss Must Occur—When Loss Must Be Discovered—Discovery Period—Superseded Suretyship
For How Much—Penalty of Bond—Amount of Loss—Inventory Shortage Exclusion—Non-Accumulation of Liability—Salvage—Other Insurance—Where Covered—Term of Bond—Cancellation
Insured's Duties and Obligations—Notice of Loss, Proof of Loss—Time To Bring Suit—Cooperation
Regulation—Rates—Term Rates—Whole Dollar Premium Rule—Deductibles—Experience Rating

15. TYPES OF FIDELITY BONDS .... Page 219

Individual Bond—Name Schedule Bond

POSITION SCHEDULE BOND (Page 220)—Automatic Coverage on Newly Created Positions—Additional Occupants of Designated Positions

BLANKET BONDS (Page 223)—Loss by Unidentifiable Employees—Automatic Coverage on Terminated Employees—Discovery Periods—Collusion Losses—Commercial Blanket Bond—Penalty Under the Blanket Position Bond—Inventory Shortage
How Policy Is Written
Rates—Experience Credits—Three-Year Policies—Whole Dollar Premium Rule
Cancellation—Cancellation on Employees Discovered To Have Defrauded—Reinstatement After Loss

DISCOVERY BOND (Page 227)

DEPOSITORS FORGERY BOND (Page 228)—Hazards Covered—Who Is Covered—What Is Covered—Personal Account Forgery—Incoming Check Endorsement—For How Much—Other Insurance—Branch Office Endorsement—When Covered

FAMILY FORGERY BOND (Page 232)

CREDIT CARD FORGERY BOND (Page 232)

BONDS COVERING FINANCIAL INSTITUTIONS (Page 233)

BANKERS BLANKET BOND NO. 24 (Page 233)
What Is Covered—Property Not Covered
Hazards Covered—Fidelity Insuring Clause A—Premises Insuring Clause B—Furnishings, Fixtures or Equipment—Forgery Insuring Clause D—Securities Insuring Clause E—In Transit Insuring Clause C
Hazards Not Covered—Teller's Shortages—Credit Card Exposure—Where Covered—In Transit Insuring Clause C
Who Is Covered—For How Much—Securities—Property Other Than Securities—Court Costs and Attorney's Fees—Property in Custody of Armored Car Service—Chattels Not Specifically Enumerated—Non-Accumulation of Liability—Salvage
When Covered—Retroactive Extension—Term of Bond—Cancellation—Discovery Period
Insured's Duties and Obligations—Notice of Loss, Proof of Loss—Time To Bring Suit
Regulation—Rates—Term Rates—Deductibles

PARTNERSHIP BOND (Page 241)

CHARGE CARD ISSUERS BOND (Page 241)

LABOR ORGANIZATION BOND—CONSOLIDATED FORM (Page 242)

WELFARE AND PENSION PLAN DISCLOSURE ACT PAY-OVER RIDER (Page 242)
COMPREHENSIVE DISHONESTY, DISAPPEARANCE AND DESTRUCTION POLICY (Page 243)
Hazards Covered—Employee Dishonesty Coverage, Insuring Agreement I—Coverage Within Premises, Insuring Agreement II —Coverage Outside Premises, Insuring Agreement III—Money Order and Counterfeit Paper Currency Coverage, Insuring Agreement IV—Depositors Forgery Coverage, Insuring Agreement V—Optional Coverages Available—Open Stock Burglary, Theft—Payroll Robbery
Where Covered—When Covered—Discovery Period—Superseded Suretyship
Regulation—Rates—Term Rates
Insured's Duties and Obligations—Notice of Loss, Proof of Loss—Cooperation of Insured—Time to Bring Suit
BLANKET CRIME POLICY (Page 245)

16. SURETY BONDS ....Page 247

COURT BONDS (Page 247)—Form of Court Bonds—Penalty of Bond—Term of Bond—Fiduciary Bonds and Litigation Bonds
FIDUCIARY (PROBATE) BONDS (Page 248)—Joint Control —Types of Fiduciaries
1. Bonds in Estates of Deceased Persons—Executor's, Administrator's Bonds—Miscellaneous Bonds in Estates of Deceased Persons
2. Bonds in Estates of Minors—Guardian Bond—Guardian Ad Litem Bond—Miscellaneous Bonds in Estates of Minors
3. Bonds in Trust Estates
4. Bonds in Estate of Incompetents
Miscellaneous Fiduciary Bonds
BONDS REQUIRED IN BANKRUPTCY OR LIQUIDATION (Page 251)
Receiver's Bond—Trustee's Bond—Assignee's Bond
LITIGATION BONDS (Page 252)—Collateral
PLAINTIFF'S BONDS (Page 252) Attachment—Replevin—Distraint for Rent—Indemnity to Sheriff—Injunction—Appeal Bond—Plaintiff's—Certiorari Bond—Claimant's Bond—Civil Arrest —Cost—Removal Bond
DEFENDANT'S BONDS (Page 254)—Release of Attachment Bond—Counter Replevin Bond—Distraint for Rent, Defendant's Bond—Injunction, Defendant's Bond to Dissolve—Open Default Bond—Stay of Execution Bond—Mechanic's Lien—Bond to Discharge
CONTRACT BONDS (Page 256)—General Principles of Contract Bonds—Extent of Coverage—Collateral—Retained Percentage—Term of Bond—Bid Bonds
Performance Bonds—Construction Contract Bond—Labor and Material Payment Bond—Supply Contract Bond—Completion Bond
SURETY BOND GUARANTEE PROGRAM FOR SMALL BUSINESSES (Page 258)
LICENSE AND PERMIT BONDS (Page 259)
PUBLIC EMPLOYEES BOND (Page 259)—Faithful Performance
PUBLIC OFFICIAL BOND (Page 260)

U. S. GOVERNMENT BONDS (Page 261)—Alien or Immigration Bonds—Custom House Bonds—Income Tax Bonds—Internal Revenue, Intoxicating Liquor Bonds

MISCELLANEOUS BONDS (Page 263)—Lost Instrument Bonds—Workmen's Compensation Bonds—Financial Responsibility Bonds, Motor Vehicle—Miscellaneous Bonds

17. INLAND MARINE INSURANCE ....Page 266

MARINE DEFINITION (Page 266)

PERSONAL FLOATERS (Page 267)—Features Common to All Personal Floaters—All-Risk Basis—Hazards Covered—Exclusions Common to All Personal Floaters
For How Much—Valued Forms—Where Covered
Requirements in Case of Loss—Notice of Loss, Proof of Loss—Sue and Labor—Benefit of Insurance—When Suit Must be Brought
Other Provisions—Minimum Premiums—Term Policies—Installment Payment of Premium—Other Provisions

INDIVIDUAL PERSONAL FLOATERS (Page 270)

PERSONAL ARTICLES FLOATER (Page 270)
Personal Furs—What Is Covered—Additionally Acquired Property—Who Is Insured—Personal Jewelry—What Is Covered—Pair and Set Clause—Who Is Covered—Cameras and Camera Equipment—What Is Covered—Blanket Insurance—Property Not Covered—Rates—Musical Instruments—What Is Covered—Blanket Insurance—Who Is Covered—Stamp and Coin Collections—What Is Covered—Additionally Acquired Property—Blanket Insurance—Hazards Not Covered—Fine Arts—What Is Covered—Newly Acquired Property—Hazards Not Covered—Breakage of Fragile Articles—Damage Due to Process—Packing—For How Much—Valued Policy—Pair and Set Clause—Where Covered—Property on Exhibition—Other Floaters Available

18. UNSCHEDULED PERSONAL PROPERTY FLOATERS ....Page 275

THE PERSONAL EFFECTS FLOATER (Page 275)—What Is Covered—Property Not Covered—Jewelry and Furs Limitation—Hazards Not Covered
Where Covered—Domicile of Insured—Theft from an Unattended Automobile—Property in Storage—Premises of Schools, Dormitories, Fraternity and Sorority Houses
Who Is Covered—For How Much—Deductible Clause—Term Policies—Automatic Reinstatement of Losses
Special Coverages Available—Contents of Trailer Homes—Exclusion of Theft, Larceny, Mysterious Disappearance, Vandalism—When Loss Is Payable—Other Clauses

PERSONAL PROPERTY FLOATER (Page 279)—What Is Covered—Coverage on Real Property—Vandalism and Malicious Mischief
Property Not Covered—Damage to Electrical Apparatus
Property on Which Limited Coverage Applies—Jewelry and Furs Limitation—Money and Securities Limitation
Hazards Not Covered—Breakage of Fragile Articles—Damage Due to Process—Wear, Tear, Mechanical Breakdown—Insects, Vermin—Dampness of Atmosphere or Extremes of Temperature—Flood, Rising Waters, Underground Waters—Damage by Pets—Property on Exhibition

Who Is Covered—Property of Others Extension—Personal Property of Servants
Where Covered—Secondary Residence Limitation
For How Much—Pair and Set Clause—Scheduled Jewelry and Furs—Scheduled Fine Arts—Additional Coverage on Money—Additional Coverage on Securities—Additional Insurance on Unscheduled Jewelry, Watches and Furs—Fire and Lightning—Residence Burglary and Robbery—Extended or Supplemental Coverage—All Risk Coverage—Secondary Location Additional Amount Endorsement—Boats—Deductible Clauses—Other Insurance
Factors on Which Premium Depends—Credit for Deductible—Minimum Premiums—Term Insurance—Whole Dollar Premium Rule
WEDDING PRESENTS FLOATER (Page 291)
Other Provisions—Non-Reduction After Loss—When Loss is Payable—Other Clauses

19. BAILEES' FORMS .... Page 292

Gratuitous Bailments—Special Situations Which Are Not Bailment—Liability of Bailee for Hire—Liability Assumed by Bailees—Limitation of Liability by Special Agreement—Bailees' Forms
BAILEES' CUSTOMERS FORM (Page 295)
BAILEES' CUSTOMERS FORM B (Page 295)—What Is Covered—Accrued Charges—Property Not Covered—Where Covered—Transit Coverage
Hazards Covered—Hazards Covered While in Buildings—Hazards Covered While in Transit—Hazards Not Covered
For How Much—Requirements in Case of Loss—Notice of Loss—Proof of Loss—Sue and Labor Clause—Adjustment of Loss with Insured or Customer—Insured's Privilege of Adjusting Losses—Right to Institute Legal Proceedings
Other Provisions—Cancellation—How Premium Is Determined—Other Clauses—Term of Policy
BAILEES' CUSTOMERS FORM A (Page 299)
FURRIERS' CUSTOMERS POLICY (Page 299)—What Is Covered—Accrued Charges for Storage or Service—Property Not Covered—Where Covered—Hazards Covered
Hazards Not Covered—Damage Due to Process—Liability for Guarantee of Work to Be Done—Dishonesty of Employees
For How Much—Policy Limits—Excess Legal Liability—Certificates Issued to Customers—How Premium is Determined
Requirements in Case of Loss—Notice of Loss—Proof of Loss—Sue and Labor—Examination Under Oath—When Loss is Payable—Term of Policy
PROCESSORS' FLOATERS (Page 304)
COLD STORAGE LOCKER BAILEE FLOATER (Page 304)

20. OWNERS' COMMERCIAL FLOATER POLICIES.... Page 306

GARMENT CONTRACTORS' FLOATER (Page 306)—What Is Covered—Where Covered
Hazards Covered—Hazards Covered in Transit—Hazards Covered on Premises of Contractors—Optional Additional Coverages—Hazards Not Covered—Garment Contractors All-Risk Floater
For How Much—Coinsurance Clause—Liability of Unnamed Contractors—Reporting Form—Other Provisions—Other Insurance—

Requirements in Case of Loss—Released Bills of Lading or Shipping Receipts—Term of Policy—Other Clauses—How Premium Is Determined

JEWELERS' BLOCK POLICY (Page 314)
What Is Covered—Damage to Premises by Theft—Coverage on Money—Patterns, Molds, Models, Dies—Furniture, Fixtures, Machinery, Tools and Fittings—Tenant's Improvements and Betterments—Property Not Covered—Hazards Covered—Hazards Not Covered—Dishonesty of Insured or Employees—Loss Caused by Delay, Loss of Market, Defective Packing—Corrosion, Dampness, Etc.—Damage Due to Process—Earthquake and Flood Exclusion—Breakage of Fragile Articles—Inventory Shortage or Unexplained Loss—C.O.D. Shipments—Exclusion of Fire Losses—Where Covered—In Transit Coverage—In the Mails—Express Shipments—Railroad, Water or Air Carriers—Motor Carriers or Truckmen—Unattended Vehicle Exclusion—Property in Show Cases of Insured—Property in Show Cases of Other Premises—Property on Exhibition
For How Much—Various Limits in Policy—Liability for Pledged Articles—Other Insurance—Deductible Clause
Insured's Duties and Obligations—Application for Insurance—Records—Protective Devices
Requirements in Case of Loss—Cooperation—Sue and Labor Clause—Adjustment of Loss with Others—Notice of Loss—Proof of Loss—When Suit Must Be Brought—Subrogation—Loan Receipt—When Loss Is Payable
Other Clauses—Benefit of Insurance—Cancellation—Automatic Reinstatement of Losses—Term of Policy

INSTALLMENT SALES FORM (Page 322)—Deferred Payment Merchandise Policy

FLOOR PLAN MERCHANDISE (Page 323)

INSTALLATION FLOATER (Page 323)

IMPLEMENT DEALERS' FLOATER (Page 324)

SALESMEN'S FLOATER (Page 324)

CONTRACTORS' EQUIPMENT FLOATER FORM (Page 325)

FARM EQUIPMENT FLOATER (Page 325)

OTHER COMMERCIAL FLOATERS (Page 325)

21. TRANSPORTATION INSURANCE .... Page 327

COMMON CARRIERS AND PRIVATE CARRIERS (Page 327)—Liability of Common Carriers—Liability of Initial Carrier—Duration of Carrier's Liability—Limitation of Liability of Common Carrier
Regulation of Common Carriers—Compulsory Insurance—Notice of Loss—Time to Bring Suit—Extent of Carrier's Liability

MOTOR TRUCK MERCHANDISE FLOATER—CARRIER'S FORMS (Page 333)—Motor Vehicle Cargo Policy—Legal Liability—What Is Covered
Hazards Covered—Theft Coverage—Terminal Coverage—Hazards Not Covered—Where Covered
For How Much—Limits of Liability—Other Insurance
Compulsory Cargo Insurance—Interstate Commerce Commission Endorsement—How Premium is Determined—Cancellation
Requirements in Case of Loss—Notice of Loss—Sue and Labor—Cooperation in Case of Suit Against Company—When Loss Is Payable

Other Clauses—Subrogation—Term of Policy—Misrepresentation and Fraud—Reinstatement of Losses

TRANSPORTATION INSURANCE (Page 339)—General Principles—When Title to Goods in Transit Passes—F.O.B. Shipments

TRANSPORTATION POLICY—SHIPPERS FORM (Page 341) —Transit Policy

What Is Covered—Property Not Covered

Hazards Covered—Other Perils of Transportation—Theft—While Waterborne

Hazards Not Covered—All-Risk Transportation Endorsement

Where Covered—Transportation Form "A"—Transportation Endorsement "B"—Owner's Goods on Owner's Trucks—Endorsement "C"

For How Much—Limit of Liability—Machinery Clause—Labels Clause—Other Insurance

Impairment of Carrier's Liability—How Premium is Determined

Requirements in Case of Loss—Notice of Loss—Proof of Loss—Sue and Labor Clause—Examination Under Oath—Appraisal—Suit Against Company—When Loss Must Be Paid—Subrogation—Reinstatement of Losses—Benefit of Insurance

Other Clauses—Term of Policy—Cancellation—Misrepresentation and Fraud

MISCELLANEOUS TRANSIT POLICIES (Page 348)—Trip Transit Policy—Department Store Floater—Railway Express Transit Policy

PARCEL POST INSURANCE (Page 348)

What Is Covered—Property Not Covered—Perishable Goods—Requirements on Addressing, Labeling, Wrapping, Postage—Goods on Consignment or Memorandum—Property in Contravention of Postal Regulations

Hazards Covered—Where Covered—Shipments to Transients—For How Much

Requirements in Case of Loss—Notice of Loss—Proof of Loss—Subrogation—Cancellation

How Parcel Post Insurance Is Written

REGISTERED MAIL INSURANCE (Page 351)

22. OCEAN MARINE INSURANCE .... Page 353

General Principles of Marine Law—Liability of Shipowner

When Title Passes From Seller to Buyer—Ex Point of Origin—Ex Dock, Named Port of Importation—F.O.B.—F.A.S.—C. & F.—C.I.F.—Seller as Agent of the Buyer

General Average—Liability for Freight Charges

MARINE INSURANCE (Page 356)—Standardization of Marine Policies

MARINE CARGO POLICY (Page 357)—What Is Covered—Import Duties and Freight Charges—General Average—Sue and Labor, Salvage

Hazards Covered—Perils of the Sea—Fire—Assailing Thieves—Jettison—Barratry of the Master—All Other Perils—Explosion—Latent Defects in Machinery, Hull, Appurtenances (Inchmaree)—Optional Hazards That May Be Added—Hazards Covered on Land—Hazards Not Covered—Dampness, Breakage—Delay, Loss of Market—Acts of War, Confiscation, Detainment, Revolution (Free of Capture, Seizure Clause F.C.&S.)—Strikes, Riots, Civil Commotions—All-Risk Insurance

Where Covered—Marine Extension Clauses—On Deck Shipments

—Type of Vessels on Which Goods Are Carried—Seaworthiness of the Vessel—No Deviation
When Covered—Prompt Attachment
For How Much—Coinsurance—Particular Average—Free of Particular Average American Conditions—English Conditions—With Average — Memorandum Clauses — Abandonment — Machinery or Manufactured Goods—Labels—Other Insurance
Who Is Insured—Insured's Duties and Obligations—Fraud, Concealment—Impairment of Carrier's Liability—Notice of Loss—Subrogation—Benefit of Insurance
Cancellation—How Policy Is Written—Rates
CARGO WAR RISK POLICY (Page 370)
HULL INSURANCE (Page 370)
YACHT POLICY (Page 371)
ALL RISK YACHT POLICY (Page 372)

23. NEGLIGENCE AND OTHER TORTS........................Page 373

Degree of Care Required—Attractive Hazard—Contributory Negligence—Last Clear Chance—Comparative Negligence—Res Ipsa Loquitor
TORTS (Page 376)—Time Limit on Commencement of Actions—Limitations by States—Suits of Spouse Against Spouse—Guest Laws—Survival of Actions After Death—Actions For Wrongful Death—Liability of Employers for Negligence of Employees—Respondeat Superior—Vicarious Liability

24. PUBLIC LIABILITY INSURANCE ....Page 389

What Is Covered—Bodily Injury Liability—Property Damage Liability—Defense of Suits, Supplementary Benefits—Medical Payments Coverage
Hazards Covered—Personal Injury Liability—Medical Payments Coverage—Medical Payments Exclusions—Hazards Covered Under Separate Forms
Hazards Not Covered—Liability Covered Under Workmen's Compensation Law—Liability of Insured to Employees—Liability for Property in Insured's Care—Elevators—Elevator Collision Insurance—Liability Arising Out of Automobiles, Aircraft, Watercraft—War, Insurrection, Revolution, Etc.—Liability Arising Out of Alcoholic Beverages—Professional Service Exclusion—Nuclear Energy Liability—Pollution
For How Much—Defense of Suits, Supplementary Benefits—Medical Payments Coverage Limits—Other Insurance
Who Is Covered—Legal Representatives—Additional Interests—Right of Third Parties—Where Covered
Rates—Deductibles—Three-Year Policies—Medical Payments Coverage
Insured's Statements—Insured's Duties—Notice of Accident—Preventing Further Damages—Notice of Claim or Suit—Cooperation with Company—Inspection and Audit—Settlement of Claim
Other Clauses — Subrogation — Cancellation — Assignment — When Covered

25. BASIC PUBLIC LIABILITY INSURANCE COVERAGES ....Page 404

OWNERS', LANDLORDS' AND TENANTS' LIABILITY INSURANCE (Page 404)
Hazards Covered—Newly Acquired Premises—Newly Added Operations—Grantor's Liability—Structural Alterations—Hazards Not

Covered—Assumed Liability—Vehicles, Aircraft—Watercraft—New Construction or Demolition Operations—Water Damage, Sprinkler Leakage—Professional Service Exclusion
Rates—How Premium is Computed—Policy Limits—Three-Year Policies—Whole Dollar Premium Rule

MANUFACTURERS' AND CONTRACTORS' LIABILITY INSURANCE (Page 411)
Hazards Covered—Independent Contractors—New Construction and Demolition Operations—Newly Acquired Premises—Blasting and Explosion, Collapse, Excavation
For How Much—Rates—How Premium Is Computed—Governing Classification—Executive Officers, Owners, Partners—Standard Exceptions—Clerical, Salesmen, Collectors, and Messengers—Outside—Excluded Occupations

PRODUCTS LIABILITY—COMPLETED OPERATIONS (Page 415)—Hazards Covered—Where Covered—Hazards Not Covered—Equipment Rented to or Located for Use by Others—Damage to Property Out of Which Accident Arises—Assumed Liability—Failure to Perform Function—Withdrawal of Product (Sistership Liability)
For How Much—Rates—How Premium is Computed

CONTRACTUAL LIABILITY (Page 420)—What Is Covered—Hazards Not Covered—Liability to Employees—Liability for Property in Care, Custody, Control—Liability to a Person Not Party to Contract—For How Much—Rates—Three-Year Policies

OWNERS' AND CONTRACTORS' PROTECTIVE LIABILITY INSURANCE (Page 423)
Independent Contractors—Hazards Covered—Hazards Not Covered—Maintenance, Repairs or Alterations—For How Much—Rates—How Premium is Computed

COMPREHENSIVE GENERAL LIABILITY POLICY (Page 426)
What Is Covered—Hazards Covered—For How Much—Rates—How Premium Is Determined

STOREKEEPER'S LIABILITY POLICY (Page 428)—Ineligible Risks—What Is Covered—Hazards Covered—Medical Payments Coverage
Hazards Not Covered—Liability of Insured to His Employees—Liability for Property in Insured's Care—Automobiles, Aircraft, Watercraft—Demolition of Any Building—Products Liability—Completed Operations—Water Damage, Sprinkler Leakage—Liability Arising Out of Alcoholic Beverages—Medical Payments Coverage—For How Much—Rates—How Premium Is Determined

DRUGGISTS' LIABILITY POLICY (Page 432)—Hazards Covered—Equipment Rented to or Located for Use by Others—Assumed Liability—Hazards Not Covered—Violation of a Penal Statute or Ordinance—For How Much—Rates

COMPREHENSIVE PERSONAL LIABILITY POLICY (Page 434)
What Is Covered—Hazards Covered—Persons Covered—Severability of Interests—Medical Payments Coverage—Medical Payments Exclusions—Physical Damage to Property—Liability for Damage to Rented Premises or House Furnishings by Fire, Explosion, Smoke, Smudge
Hazards Not Covered—Business Pursuits—Professional Services—Secondary Residences—Residential Property Rented To Others—Automobiles—War Hazard—Liability to Employees of the Insured

—Liability Assumed Under Contract—Liability for Damage to Property Used or Controlled—Assault and Battery—Watercraft While Away From Premises—Aircraft—Elevators—Nuclear Energy —Medical Payments Coverage

Who Is Covered—Where Covered—Business Property—Cancellation

Rates—Three-Year Policies—Other Provisions—Assignment

FARMER'S COMPREHENSIVE PERSONAL LIABILITY POLICY (Page 443)

PROFESSIONAL LIABILITY INSURANCE (Page 444)

PHYSICIANS', SURGEONS' AND DENTISTS' PROFESSIONAL LIABILITY INSURANCE POLICY (Page 445)—Lloyd's Policy

MISCELLANEOUS MEDICAL PROFESSIONAL LIABILITY POLICIES (Page 447)

LAWYERS PROFESSIONAL LIABILITY INSURANCE (Page 447)

BEAUTY SHOP AND BARBER SHOP LIABILITY POLICIES (Page 448)

MORTICIANS PROFESSIONAL LIABILITY INSURANCE (Page 449)

DIRECTORS AND OFFICERS LIABILITY POLICY (Page 450)—Directors and Officers Liability Coverage—Company Reimbursement Coverage—Extended Discovery Clause—Mini-D. & O. Insurance

DATA PROCESSORS ERRORS AND OMISSIONS INSURANCE (Page 452)

BLANKET CATASTROPHE EXCESS LIABILITY (UMBRELLA LIABILITY) INSURANCE (Page 452)—Commercial Umbrella Policy—Personal Umbrella Policy

26. AUTOMOBILE LIABILITY INSURANCE.............Page 455

Eligibility for Family Automobile Policy—What Is Covered—Financial Responsibility Laws—Hazards Covered—Family Automobile Policy—Loading and Unloading—Trailers—Other Drivers and Interests (Omnibus Clause)—Family Automobile Policy—Severability of Interests—Family Automobile Policy—Other Drivers and Interests (Omnibus Clause) Exclusions—Family Automobile Policy—Drive Other Cars—Drive Other Car Exclusions—Newly Acquired Automobiles—Family Automobile Policy—Temporary Substitute Automobile—Medical Payments Coverage—Medical Payments—Drive Other Cars—Family Automobile Policy—Medical Payments Exclusions—Family Automobile Policy—Uninsured Motorist Coverage—Unsatisfied Judgment Funds—Motor Vehicle Accident Indemnification Corporation

Hazards Not Covered—Public or Livery Conveyance—Liability Assumed by Contract—Family Automobile Policy—Liability of an Insured to His Employees—Liability for Property in Insured's Care—Automobile Death Indemnity—Total Disability Benefits—Nuclear Energy Liability

For How Much—Medical Payments Coverage Limits—Other Insurance—Who Is Insured—Other Drivers and Interests (Omnibus Clause)—Right of Third Parties—Legal Representatives—Where Covered—Rates—Nine-Class Rating Plan—Private Passenger Automobile Classifications—Special Farmer Classifications—Good Student Credit—Driver Course Credit—260-Class Rating

Plans—Merit Rating Plans—Modified 260 Class Plan—Certified Risks Surcharge—Increased Limits—Multi-Car Discount—Fleet Rates—Whole Dollar Premium Rule
Insured's Statements—Insured's Duties—Notice of Accident—Notice of Claim or Suit—Cooperation with Company—Medical Reports—Proof—Payment for Services to Others
Financial Responsibility Laws—Subrogation—When Covered—Cancellation—Cancellation By The Company—Cancellation When Certificate Has Been Filed—Suspension of Insurance—Assignment
MODIFICATIONS OF TORT LIABILITY SYSTEM OF COMPENSATING AUTOMOBILE ACCIDENT VICTIMS (Page 484)
Auto No-Fault and First Party Benefit Laws—Pain and Suffering—No-Fault Protection (Optional)

27. COMMERCIAL AND OTHER AUTOMOBILE LIABILITY POLICIES .... Page 489

COMMERCIAL AUTOMOBILES (Page 489)—Rates—Truckmen Rule—Local Truckmen—Gross Receipts Basis—Long Haul Truckmen—Gross Receipts Basis—Whole Dollar Premium Rule—Insurance Required of Franchised Carriers
PUBLIC AUTOMOBILES (Page 493) — Passenger Hazard — Property of Passengers Hazard—Compulsory Insurance for Public Carriers of Passengers—Insurance Required of Intrastate Carriers
NON-OWNED AUTOMOBILES — EMPLOYERS' NON-OWNERSHIP LIABILITY INSURANCE (Page 496)
Hazards Covered—Hazards Not Covered—Who Is Insured—For How Much
Rates—Class 1 Persons—Class 2—Specific and Blanket Basis—Whole Dollar Premium Rule
MISCELLANEOUS NON-OWNERSHIP LIABILITY (Page 501)
HIRED CARS (Page 501)—Specified Automobile Basis—Cost of Hire Basis
COMPREHENSIVE AUTO LIABILITY POLICY (Page 503)
GARAGE INSURANCE (Page 503)
GARAGE LIABILITY POLICY (Page 503)
What Is Covered—Hazards Covered—Products Liability—Expenses for Medical Services
Hazards Not Covered—Liability of An Insured to His Employees—Elevators—Liability Assumed Under Contract—Products Liability—Liability for Property in Insured's Care—Public or Livery Conveyance—Liability to Employees—Racing or Speed Contest—Expenses for Medical Services (Medical Payments)—Rented Automobiles—Haulaway, Tank Trucks, Tank Trailers, Tractors—Structural Alterations, New Construction or Demolition Operations—Aircraft, Watercraft
For How Much—Deductible—Supplementary Payments—Other Insurance
Who Is Covered—Other Drivers and Interests (Omnibus Clause)—Right of Third Parties—Legal Representatives
Where Covered—Rates—Whole Dollar Premium Rule
AUTO INSURANCE (ASSIGNED RISK) PLANS (Page 513)—Limits of Liability—Eligible Risks—Ineligible Risks—Initial Payment with Application—Rate Surcharges

28. COMPULSORY AND FINANCIAL RESPONSIBILITY LAWS (Motor Vehicle)........Page 517

SECURITY-TYPE LAWS (Page 517)—Accidents—Convictions —Judgments—Proof of Financial Responsibility—Compulsory Laws—Connecticut—Delaware—Florida—Illinois—Maryland—Massachusetts—New York—North Carolina—Puerto Rico—Rhode Island

ANALYSIS OF SECURITY-TYPE LAWS (Page 520-521)

29. AUTOMOBILE PHYSICAL DAMAGE INSURANCE ....Page 523

COMPREHENSIVE PHYSICAL DAMAGE INSURANCE (Material Damage Policy) (Page 523)

Equipment—Sound Reproducing or Recording Equipment—Newly Acquired Automobile—Loss of Use by Theft—Rental Reimbursement—General Average and Salvage Charges—Rented or Borrowed Utility Trailer—Family Automobile Policy

Hazards Covered—Family Automobile Policy—Breakage of Glass and Loss by Missiles, Falling Objects, Vandalism, Contact with Animals, Etc.—Family Automobile Policy—Loss of Use by Theft, Rental Reimbursement—Family Automobile Policy—Loss of Use By Perils Other Than Theft—Rental Reimbursement

Hazards Not Covered—Public or Livery Conveyance—Wear and Tear, Freezing, Mechanical Breakdown, etc.—Damage to Tires—Family Automobile Policy—War, Invasion, Insurrection, etc.—Radioactive Contamination—Loss Due to Conversion, Embezzlement, etc.—Loss to Automobile Subject to Undeclared Bailment Lease, Mortgage, etc.—Family Automobile Policy—Illicit Trade or Transportation

For How Much—Actual Cash Value Basis—Stated Amount Basis—Deductible—Valued Monthly Reduction Basis—Other Insurance

Where Covered

Rates—Private Passenger Vehicles—Fleet Rates—Commercial Automobiles—Insured's Statements

Insured's Duties—Notice of Accident—Notice of Claim or Suit—Cooperation with Company

Other Clauses—Appraisal—Subrogation—Cancellation—Assignment—Family Automobile Policy—When Covered

COLLISION INSURANCE (Page 533)—Family Automobile Policy—Hazards Covered—Drive Other Cars—For How Much—80% Collision Form—Convertible (Retention) Insurance

Rates—Private Passenger Automobiles—Driver Course Credit—Good Student Credit—Multi-Car Discount—Bumper Discount—Merit Rating Plan—Commercial Automobiles—Suspension of Insurance—Whole Dollar Premium Rule

SPECIFIED PERILS AUTOMOBILE INSURANCE (Page 537)

Fire, Lightning, Smoke, Smudge—Transportation—Theft Insurance—Windstorm, Earthquake, Explosion, Hail or Water Damage Insurance—Combined Additional Coverage—Towing and Labor Costs

GARAGE KEEPER'S LEGAL LIABILITY INSURANCE (Page 538)—What Is Covered—Loss of Use By Theft—Defense of Suit—Supplementary Benefits

Hazards Covered—Fire and Explosion—Theft—Riot, Civil Commotion, Malicious Mischief—Collision or Upset

Hazards Not Covered—Employee Dishonesty—Liability for Loss

of Robes, Wearing Apparel, Personal Effects, etc.—Liability for Loss of Automobiles Owned by Insured, Employees, etc.—Liability Assumed Under Contract—Elevator Liability—Racing Contest—War, Revolution Risks—Radioactive Contamination—Defective Parts

For How Much—Pro Rata Liability (Coinsurance)—Deductibles

30. WORKMEN'S COMPENSATION AND EMPLOYERS' LIABILITY INSURANCE..................Page 544

Differences Among State Workmen's Compensation Statutes—Liability Regardless of Fault

CHART ANALYSIS by States of Workmen's Compensation Benefits and Requirements (Pages 548-554)

Exclusive Liability of Employer—Right of Action of Employee Against Third Parties

Compulsory and Elective Type Laws

Who Is Covered—Compulsory Type Laws—Elective Type Laws—Longshoremen's and Harbor Workers' Act—Excluded Employments—Maritime Employment—Occupational Safety and Health Act of 1970 (OSHA)—Voluntary Coverage—Independent Contractors

Methods of Complying With Workmen's Compensation Laws

Methods of Insuring—Penalties for Failure to Comply with Law

What Is Covered—Medical Benefits—Occupational Disease Coverage—Diseases Caused by Ionizing Radiation—Extra Legal Medical Coverage—Indemnity for Loss of Time—Waiting Period—Scheduled Awards—Permanent Total Disability—Death Benefits—Status of Benefits—Employer's Duties—Report of Injury by Employer—Keeping of Accident Reports—Report of Injury by Employees

Minors Under Workmen's Compensation Laws—Extra-Territorial Provisions—All States Endorsement—General and Special Employers—Second Injury Funds

WORKMEN'S COMPENSATION AND EMPLOYERS LIABILITY INSURANCE POLICY (Page 575)

What Is Covered—Insuring Agreement I—Coverage A—Workmen's Compensation Section—Coverage B—Employers' Liability Section—Insuring Agreement II—Defense, Settlement, Supplementary Benefits—Insuring Agreement III—Definitions—Insuring Agreement IV—Application of Policy—Conditions—Inspection and Audit—Premium Determination—Partners or Joint Ventures

Who Is Covered—Hazards Not Covered—Locations Not Described—Domestic and Agricultural Employees—Assumed Liability—Punitive Damages, Illegal Employment—For How Much

How Premium Is Computed—Payroll in Excess of $300 per Week—Board, Lodging, Services—Bonuses, Commissions and Tips—Overtime Pay—Payroll of Executive Officers—Partners—Per Capita Premiums—Governing Classification—Standard Exceptions—Exceptions in Construction or Erection Work—Constant Charges—Loss and Expense Constant—Audit Premiums—Interim Premium Adjustments—Minimum Premiums—Premium Discount—Experience Rating—Interstate Experience Rating

RETROSPECTIVE RATING (Page 590)

Retrospective Plan D—Three-Year Fixed Rate Policies

Insured's Duties—Policy Declarations—Notice of Accident—Notice of Claim or Suit—Subrogation—Cancellation—Assignment—When Covered

UNITED STATES LONGSHOREMEN'S AND HARBOR WORKERS' COMPENSATION ACT (Page 594)

31. DISABILITY INSURANCE ....Page 596

HOSPITALIZATION AND MEDICAL CARE INSURANCE (Page 596)

DISABILITY BENEFITS INSURANCE (Page 596)

INSURANCE AGAINST LOSS OF TIME THROUGH DISABILITY (ACCIDENT AND HEALTH INSURANCE) (Page 596)

Types of Accident and Health Insurance

"Uniform" and "Standard" Provisions—Entire Contract—Changes—Time Limit on Certain Defenses—Grace Period—Reinstatement

COMMERCIAL ACCIDENT AND HEALTH INSURANCE (Page 598)

What Is Covered—Indemnity for Loss of Time—Accidental Death Provisions—Principal Sum—Dismemberment or Loss of Sight Provisions—Capital Sum—Elective Indemnity for Specific Accidents—Double Indemnity for Specific Accidents—Hospital Benefits—Surgical Indemnity Provisions—Nursing Benefits—Blanket Medical Expense Benefits—Non-Disabling Injuries

Hazards Covered—Total Disability—Accidental Bodily Injury—Accidental Means—Partial Disability

Hazards Not Covered—Excluded Conditions—Loss While Engaged in Committing Felony—Loss While Intoxicated or Under Influence of Narcotics

When Covered—Age Limits—Grace Period—Pre-Existing Conditions—Incontestable Clause—Probationary Period—Elimination Period, Waiting Period—Reinstatement After Lapse

For How Much—Accumulations—Pro-Rating for Change to More Hazardous Occupation—Pro-Rating with Other Insurance—Limit on Total Indemnity—Reduction for Misstatement of Age—Confining Clause

Insured's Duties—Application—Notice of Claim—Proof of Loss—Time to Bring Suit—Medical Examination, Autopsy

When Loss Is Payable—Cancellation—Cancellation by Insured

INDUSTRIAL (WEEKLY PREMIUM) ACCIDENT AND HEALTH INSURANCE (Page 608)

NON-CANCELLABLE ACCIDENT AND HEALTH INSURANCE (Page 608)

GUARANTEED RENEWABLE ACCIDENT AND HEALTH INSURANCE (Page 608)

LIMITED TYPE ACCIDENT AND HEALTH INSURANCE (Page 608)

HOSPITAL, SURGICAL AND MEDICAL CARE POLICIES (Page 609)

MAJOR MEDICAL EXPENSE INSURANCE (CATASTROPHE MEDICAL INSURANCE) (Page 610)

What Is Covered—Hazards Covered—Hazards Not Covered—War—Workmen's Compensation—Government Hospital Treatments—Cosmetic Surgery—Pregnancy—For How Much—Deductible—Coinsurance—Time Limit on Claims—Lifetime vs. Per Cause Maximum—Who Is Insured—When Covered—Rates

GROUP ACCIDENT AND HEALTH INSURANCE (Page 613)

WHOLESALE OR FRANCHISE INSURANCE (Page 614)

FRATERNAL ACCIDENT AND HEALTH INSURANCE (Page 614)

DISABILITY PROVISIONS IN LIFE INSURANCE (Page 615)
DISABILITY BENEFITS LAWS (Page 615)
How Administered—What Is Covered—Chart Analysis of State Disability Benefits Laws (Pages 617-619)—Hawaii—Puerto Rico

32. MISCELLANEOUS FORMS OF INSURANCE........Page 621

COMPREHENSIVE GLASS POLICY (Page 621)—Neon Signs, Fluorescent Signs and Lamps
What Is Covered—Blanket Policies—Repairing or Replacing Frames—Boarding Up Openings—Removing Obstructions
Hazards Covered—Hazards Not Covered—Fire—War, Invasion, Etc.—Nuclear Energy—Cracked Glass Endorsement
For How Much—Rates—Term Policies—Minimum Premiums—Whole Dollar Premium Rule
Insured's Duties—Notice of Loss—Proof of Loss
Other Provisions—Reinstatement After Loss—Cancellation—Assignment—Subrogation—Regulation—Time of Policy
BOILER AND MACHINERY INSURANCE (Power Plant Insurance) (Page 625)
BOILER AND MACHINERY POLICY (Page 625)—What Is Covered—Loss on Property of Insured—Expediting Expenses—Property Damage Liability—Bodily Injury Liability—Defense, Settlement, Supplementary Payments—Automatic Coverage—Repair and Replacement—Inspection Service
Hazards Covered—Hazards Not Covered—War Damage Exclusion—Nuclear Energy Exclusion—Fire—Strikes, Riot, Civil Commotion, Vandalism, Malicious Mischief—Combustion Explosion Outside of Object—Indirect Loss—Limited Coverage
For How Much—Repair and Replacement Coverage—Other Insurance, Bodily Injury—Other Insurance, Property Damage Liability
Rates—Three-Year Policies—Premium Discount—Deductibles
Insured's Duties—Inspection—Notice of Loss
Cancellation—Suspension
Other Provisions—Subrogation—Assignment—Regulation—Time of Policy
BOILER SCHEDULE (Page 630)—Fired Vessels and Electric Steam Generators
What Is Covered—Boiler Piping—Furnace Explosion
ELECTRICAL MACHINES SCHEDULE (Page 631)—What Is Covered
REFRIGERATING SYSTEMS SCHEDULE (Page 631)
Contamination—Water Damage
RESIDENCE BOILER SCHEDULE (Page 632)
NON-OWNERSHIP EXPLOSION INSURANCE (Page 632)
INDIRECT DAMAGE COVERAGES (Page 632)—Consequential Damage
USE AND OCCUPANCY INSURANCE (Business Interruption Insurance) (Page 633)—Actual Loss Sustained—Valued Form
OUTAGE INSURANCE (Page 634)

33. TYPES OF INSURERS ....Page 636

Mutual Insurance—Capital Stock Companies—Reciprocals (Inter-

Insurance Exchanges)—Associations (Domestic Lloyds)—State Insurance Funds—Domestic, Foreign and Alien Insurers

REINSURANCE (Page 638)—Types of Reinsurance Agreements—Facultative Basis—Treaty Basis—Retrocession

SELF-INSURANCE (Page 640)

MASS MERCHANDISING (Page 641)

34. PERSONAL MULTIPLE PERIL POLICIES...........Page 642

HOMEOWNERS PACKAGE POLICIES (Page 642)—What Is Covered—Property Not Covered—For How Much

HOMEOWNERS POLICY 1—BASIC FORM (Page 645)—Hazards Covered—Hazards Not Covered—For How Much—Where Covered—Supplementary Coverages—Optional Coverages

HOMEOWNERS FORM 2—BROAD FORM (Page 653)—Hazards Covered—For How Much—Where Covered

HOMEOWNERS FORM 3—SPECIAL FORM (Page 654)—Hazards Covered—For How Much

HOMEOWNERS FORM 4—CONTENTS BROAD FORM (Page 654)—What Is Covered—Hazards Covered—For How Much

HOMEOWNERS POLICY 5—COMPREHENSIVE FORM (Page 655)—Hazards Covered—Property Not Covered—For How Much

CONDOMINIUM PROPERTY INSURANCE (Page 657)

35. COMMERCIAL MULTIPLE PERIL POLICIES......Page 659

SPECIAL MULTI-PERIL POLICY PROGRAM (Page 659)—General Provisions of Special Multi-Peril Policy—Mandatory Coverages—What Is Covered—Extensions of Coverage—Property Not Covered—Hazards Covered—Hazards Not Covered—Where Covered—For How Much—How Policy Is Written—Optional Coverages—Section I - Property Coverage—Section II - Liability Coverage—Section III - Crime Coverages—Section IV - Boiler and Machinery Coverages—When Covered—Rates

OFFICE PERSONAL PROPERTY FORM (Page 667)—What Is Covered—Property Not Covered—Hazards Covered—Hazards Not Covered—For How Much—Where Covered—Other Clauses—Rates

COMMERCIAL PROPERTY COVERAGE (Page 672)—What Is Covered—Property Not Covered—Hazards Covered—Hazards Not Covered—For How Much—Where Covered—Other Clauses

MANUFACTURER'S OUTPUT POLICY (Page 676)—What Is Covered—Property Not Covered—Hazards Covered—Hazards Not Covered—Where Covered—For How Much—How Insurance Is Written—Other Provisions

FARMOWNERS-RANCHOWNERS POLICY PROGRAM (Page 680)—What Is Covered—Hazards Covered—For How Much—Optional Coverages—When Covered

CHAPTER 1

The Law of Contracts As It Relates To Insurance

AN INSURANCE AGREEMENT is a contract, and the rights and obligations of both parties to the contract are determined largely by the general principles which apply to contracts of all kinds.

Generally, a contract is any promise or agreement enforceable by law. Six general rules relating to contracts of *all* kinds are:

1. The parties to the contract must be legally capable of contracting.
2. The contract must be based on an offer by one party and acceptance of that offer in the same terms by the other party.
3. There must be equal knowledge on both sides of all material and relevant facts.
4. The contract must be based on a valuable consideration.
5. The contract must be legal in form.
6. The contract must be for a legal purpose.

All of the above conditions must be present. The absence of even one is fatal to the enforcement of the contract.

THE INSURANCE CONTRACT

Generally, an insurance contract is any agreement under which one party is obligated to make good the loss suffered by a second party through the occurrence of a designated event. The event must be a fortuitous one.

Fortuitous Event—An occurrence which is to a substantial extent beyond the control of either party; happening by chance; accidental; e.g., fire, lightning, windstorm, explosion, flood, etc.

Insurable Interest—The second party, to be entitled to collect, must have an insurable interest in the property at the time of such happening. An insurable interest is any right, title or interest in property such that the holder will suffer a financial loss if the property is destroyed or damaged. Or, conversely, any lawful and substantial economic interest in the safety or preservation of the property from loss, destruction, or damage is an insurable interest.

One need not be the owner of property to have an insurable interest in the property, as, for example, mortgagees, trustees, vendors, lessees, remaindermen, bailees, etc.

Insurable interest must exist at the time the loss occurs. In some states, the law requires that it must also be present when the policy is issued. (This is the general rule in Property insurance, and does not apply to Life insurance.)

Risk of Loss—If a property could never be destroyed, there is no risk; if it must necessarily disintegrate or be destroyed, there is no risk. Between these two extremes is the area of exposure of risk—the area subject to insurance.

HOW GENERAL RULES OF CONTRACTS APPLY TO INSURANCE CONTRACTS

The parties to the contract must be legally capable of contracting. The insurance company is a legal entity capable of contracting through its authorized agents. The individual who enters into the contract with the insurance company must be equally capable. (Thus, contracts entered into by infants are unenforceable.)

The contract must be based on an offer by one party and acceptance of that offer in the same terms by the other party. An individual, or his representative, goes to an insurance company requesting coverage. The Company accepts the risk.

There must be equal knowledge on both sides of all material and relevant facts. The Insured must not conceal or misrepresent any material fact when submitting the risk to the Company. Furthermore, he must comply with all the warranties made by him when the policy is issued throughout the time the policy is in force.

Concealment—Failure to disclose a *material* fact. A material fact is one which, if disclosed, would have caused the Company to decline the risk or to refuse to write it on the same basis.

Concealment does not necessarily have to be concealment of a fact about which a question is asked. A property owner who had served a prison term for arson did not reveal this fact to the Company because he knew he would probably be refused insurance. Though the Company had not asked any questions on this score, the Insured's failure to disclose this fact was held to be Concealment. Similarly, if an owner of property knew that it stood in imminent danger of destruction and applied for insurance on the property without disclosing this fact to the Company, the insurance contract might be held unenforceable because the Insured had been guilty of Concealment.

Misrepresentation—A false statement as to past or present fact made to an insurance Company to induce it to accept a risk. As in the case of Concealment, the false statement must be of a material fact to constitute Misrepresentation.

Misrepresentation is a positive act, as opposed to Concealment, which is a negative act.

Warranty—A provision in a policy which requires the existence of a condition that diminishes the risk of loss.

The Insured might warrant that his premises will be protected by a burglar alarm, or that an Automatic Sprinkler System will be maintained in working order, etc. Conversely, a warranty might provide for the non-existence of a condition that increases the risk of loss; e.g., that premises will not be used for any manufacturing purposes; or that a vehicle will not be used outside of a fifty mile radius, etc. Generally, a warranty in an insurance policy calls for strict compliance on the part of the Insured and any breach will void the contract.

Contract must be based on a valuable consideration. On the part of the Insured, the consideration is his payment of the premium, or his promise to pay, plus other provisions and stipulations. (Failure to pay a premium does not invalidate a policy. It remains in force until canceled.)

On the Company's part, its promise to confer benefit or save the Insured harmless is the consideration.

Contract must be legal in form. A policy is issued. The policy is legal in form, sometimes following lines made mandatory by the State.

Contract must be for a legal purpose. Insurance may not be for a gambling purpose, nor for the benefit of an improper insurable interest, nor for a fraudulent purpose.

FOR FURTHER READING

HUEBNER AND BLACK—Property Insurance
LAVINE—Manual on Commercial Law
MAGEE AND BICKELHAUPT—General Insurance
MEHR AND CAMMACK—Principles of Insurance
MOWBRAY AND BLANCHARD—Insurance

(See Reading List at End of Book)

CHAPTER 2

The Fire Insurance Policy

THE COMPLETE TEXT of the Standard Fire insurance policy of New York is reproduced on the pages that follow.

STANDARDIZATION OF FIRE INSURANCE POLICY

Practically every state in the United States and the District of Columbia uses the Standard Fire insurance policy of New York, or bases its standard Fire insurance policy on this form. While certain provisions of the Fire insurance policy in some states vary from the New York Standard policy, the differences are comparatively minor. Where the variations are more than differences in phrasing and are of practical importance, they are pointed up in the discussion of the appropriate provision.

The New York Standard Fire Insurance Policy was enacted into law in 1943 and is mandatory on all companies writing Fire insurance in the state of New York. It is in use in 45 other states and the District of Columbia.

CALIFORNIA, MAINE, MINNESOTA, TEXAS—While the policies of these states are similar in their broad essentials to the Standard Fire insurance policy of New York, there are differences of some consequence and these will be commented on in the discussions of the individual provisions of the Fire policy.*

HAZARDS COVERED

Fire and Lightning—The basic policy covers *both* perils. Loss or damage caused by lightning is covered, regardless of whether fire ensues or not.

Fire—As used in the Fire policy, *fire* is taken to mean oxidation of a sufficient intensity to produce a visible flame or glow. Destruction or damage or spoilage caused by excessive heat, scorching or blistering, when no fire occurs, would not be covered.

---

*This chapter will analyze the basic policy. Many of the provisions of this policy are modified by the forms which are attached to the contract in order to complete it. Chapter 3 treats these forms and highlights the more important modifications brought into being by specific clauses of these forms.

Hostile Fire—The fire must be "hostile" in order for the loss to be covered.

A friendly fire is one which originates and remains confined entirely within the area for which it was intended; e.g., a fire in a furnace, a fireplace, a stove, etc. A hostile fire is one which escapes from its intended area.

A friendly fire becomes hostile at the moment it escapes from its intended area. For example, a fire escaping through a crack in an oven is a hostile fire, even if only a momentary spurt of flame. Contrariwise, if the fire remains confined within the stove and the stove becomes overheated and the excessive heat blisters the paint on the wall, there would be no coverage under the policy, as the fire was friendly (confined to the area for which it was intended —the stove).

There is no mention of hostile or friendly fire in the policy. The policy merely says "loss by fire" but this is understood and held by the Courts to mean only hostile fire.

LOUISIANA, WISCONSIN—In each of these states, a court decision has held that the policy did not distinguish between "hostile" and "friendly" fires, and that as a consequence, either type of loss would be covered.

Proximate Cause—In addition to the loss or damage caused directly by the fire or lightning, the Fire insurance policy covers loss caused by other occurrences of which fire is the *proximate* cause.

Proximate means very close in space, time, order, meaning, etc. It is the opposite of remote. Proximate cause is defined as the active, efficient cause that sets in motion a train of events which brings about a result without the intervention of any force from a new and independent source. A Federal Court recently defined proximate cause as "that cause which, operating in natural and continuous sequence, unbroken by any completely preceding independent intervening cause, produces the results complained of, and without which the result would not have occurred."

EXAMPLE: A building and machinery used for generating electricity were insured under a Fire insurance policy. A fire broke out in a second building located some distance away which contained the dynamos and the electrical machinery. The fire caused a sudden increase in the pressure on the driving belt of the dynamo, which parted. This caused the fly-wheel to revolve too rapidly and it burst, wrecking the machinery and the building. Although the building was not reached by fire, the jury held that the entire loss was covered under the Fire insurance policy.

EXAMPLE: Fire razed a building. One wall was left standing. Seven days later, the wind blew down the remaining wall. It was held that fire was the proximate cause of the collapse of the wall which had been weakened by the blaze, and the loss was covered under the Fire insurance policy.

On the other hand, if a friendly fire is the proximate cause of damage, there is no coverage under the policy. Thus, if smoke from

No.

Renewal of Number

STOCK COMPANY

COMPANY NAME HERE

INSURANCE IS PROVIDED AGAINST ONLY THOSE PERILS AND FOR ONLY THOSE COVERAGES INDICATED BELOW BY A PREMIUM CHARGE AND AGAINST OTHER PERILS AND FOR OTHER COVERAGES ONLY WHEN ENDORSED HEREON OR ADDED HERETO.

PERIL(S) INSURED AGAINST AND COVERAGE(S) PROVIDED (Insert Name of Each)	AMOUNT	RATE	PREMIUM
FIRE AND LIGHTNING	$	$	$
EXTENDED COVERAGE	x x x x x x x	$	$
		$	$
		$	$
		$	$
		TOTAL PREMIUM	$

In Consideration of the Provisions and Stipulations Herein or Added Hereto AND OF the premium above specified this Company, for the term of from (At Noon Standard Time) to (At Noon Standard Time) at location of property involved, to an amount not exceeding the amount(s) above specified, does insure

and legal representatives to the extent of the actual cash value of the property at the time of loss, but not exceeding the amount which it would cost to repair or replace the property with material of like kind and quality within a reasonable time after such loss, without allowance for any increased cost of repair or reconstruction by reason of any ordinance or law regulating construction or repair, and without compensation for loss resulting from interruption of business or manufacture, nor in any event for more than the interest of the insured, against all DIRECT LOSS BY FIRE, LIGHTNING AND BY REMOVAL FROM PREMISES ENDANGERED BY THE PERILS INSURED AGAINST IN THIS POLICY, EXCEPT AS HEREINAFTER PROVIDED, to the property described hereinafter while located or contained as described in this policy, or pro rata for five days at each proper place to which any of the property shall necessarily be removed for preservation from the perils insured against in this policy, but not elsewhere.

1 No. Item	Amount Fire or Fire and Extended Coverage, or Other Peril	2 Per Cent of Co-Insurance Applicable	Amount Other Peril if Different Than Fire	3 Per Cent of Co-Insurance Applicable	4 DESCRIPTION AND LOCATION OF PROPERTY COVERED Show construction, type of roof and occupancy of building(s) covered or containing the property covered. If occupied as a dwelling state No. of families.

Subject to Form No.(s). attached hereto.

Mortgage Clause: Subject to the provisions of the mortgage clause attached hereto, loss, if any, on building items, shall be payable to:

....

....

Assignment of this policy shall not be valid except with the written consent of this Company.
This policy is made and accepted subject to the foregoing provisions and stipulations and those hereinafter stated, which are hereby made a part of this policy, together with such other provisions, stipulations and agreements as may be added hereto, as provided in this policy.

Countersignature Date Agency at

....**Agent**

Concealment, fraud. This entire policy shall be void if, whether before or after a loss, the insured has wilfully concealed or misrepresented any material fact or circumstance concerning this insurance or the subject thereof, or the interest of the insured therein, or in case of any fraud or false swearing by the insured relating thereto.

Uninsurable and excepted property. This policy shall not cover accounts, bills, currency, deeds, evidences of debt, money or securities; nor, unless specifically named hereon in writing, bullion or manuscripts.

Perils not included. This Company shall not be liable for loss by fire or other perils insured against in this policy caused, directly or indirectly, by: (a) enemy attack by armed forces, including action taken by military, naval or air forces in resisting an actual or an immediately impending enemy attack; (b) invasion; (c) insurrection; (d) rebellion; (e) revolution; (f) civil war; (g) usurped power; (h) order of any civil authority except acts of destruction at the time of and for the purpose of preventing the spread of fire, provided that such fire did not originate from any of the perils excluded by this policy; (i) neglect of the insured to use all reasonable means to save and preserve the property at and after a loss, or when the property is endangered by fire in neighboring premises; (j) nor shall this Company be liable for loss by theft.

Other Insurance. Other insurance may be prohibited or the amount of insurance may be limited by endorsement attached hereto.

Conditions suspending or restricting insurance. Unless otherwise provided in writing added hereto this Company shall not be liable for loss occurring

(a) while the hazard is increased by any means within the control or knowledge of the insured; or

(b) while a described building, whether intended for occupancy by owner or tenant, is vacant or unoccupied beyond a period of sixty consecutive days; or

(c) as a result of explosion or riot, unless fire ensue, and in that event for loss by fire only.

Other perils or subjects. Any other peril to be insured against or subject of insurance to be covered in this policy shall be by endorsement in writing hereon or added hereto.

Added provisions. The extent of the application of insurance under this policy and of the contribution to be made by this Company in case of loss, and any other provision or agreement not inconsistent with the provisions of this policy, may be provided for in writing added hereto, but no provision may be waived except such as by the terms of this policy is subject to change.

relating to the interests and obligations of such mortgagee may be added hereto by agreement in writing.

Pro rata liability. This Company shall not be liable for a greater proportion of any loss than the amount hereby insured shall bear to the whole insurance covering the property against the peril involved, whether collectible or not.

Requirements in case loss occurs. The insured shall give immediate written notice to this Company of any loss, protect the property from further damage, forthwith separate the damaged and undamaged personal property, put it in the best possible order, furnish a complete inventory of the destroyed, damaged and undamaged property, showing in detail quantities, costs, actual cash value and amount of loss claimed; and within sixty days after the loss, unless such time is extended in writing by this Company, the insured shall render to this Company a proof of loss, signed and sworn to by the insured, stating the knowledge and belief of the insured as to the following: the time and origin of the loss, the interest of the insured and of all others in the property, the actual cash value of each item thereof and the amount of loss thereto, all encumbrances thereon, all other contracts of insurance, whether valid or not, covering any of said property, any changes in the title, use, occupation, location, possession or exposures of said property since the issuing of this policy, by whom and for what purpose any building herein described and the several parts thereof were occupied at the time of loss and whether or not it then stood on leased ground, and shall furnish a copy of all the descriptions and schedules in all policies and, if required, verified plans and specifications of any building, fixtures or machinery destroyed or damaged. The insured, as often as may be reasonably required, shall exhibit to any person designated by this Company all that remains of any property herein described, and submit to examinations under oath by any person named by this Company, and subscribe the same; and, as often as may be reasonably required, shall produce for examination all books of account, bills, invoices and other vouchers, or certified copies thereof if originals be lost, at such reasonable time and place as may be designated by this Company or its representative, and shall permit extracts and copies thereof to be made.

Appraisal. In case the insured and this Company shall fail to agree as to the actual cash value or the amount of loss, then, on the written demand of either, each shall select a competent and disinterested appraiser and notify be made by this Company in case of loss, and any other provision or agreement not inconsistent with the provisions of this policy, may be provided for in writing added hereto, but no provision may be waived except such as by the terms of this policy is subject to change.

Waiver provisions. No permission affecting this insurance shall exist, or waiver of any provisions be valid, unless granted herein or expressed in writing added hereto. No provision, stipulation or forfeiture shall be held to be waived by any requirement or proceeding on the part of this Company relating to appraisal or to any examination provided for herein.

Cancellation of policy. This policy shall be cancelled at any time at the request of the insured, in which case this Company shall, upon demand and surrender of this policy, refund the excess of paid premium above the customary short rates for the expired time. This policy may be cancelled at any time by this Company by giving to the insured a five days' written notice of cancellation with or without tender of the excess of paid premium above the pro rata premium for the expired time, which excess, if not tendered, shall be refunded on demand. Notice of cancellation shall state that said excess premium (if not tendered) will be refunded on demand.

Mortgagee interests and obligations. If loss hereunder is made payable, in whole or in part, to a designated mortgagee not named herein as the insured, such interest in this policy may be cancelled by giving to such mortgagee a ten days' written notice of cancellation.

If the insured fails to render proof of loss such mortgagee, upon notice, shall render proof of loss in the form herein specified within sixty (60) days thereafter and shall be subject to the provisions hereof relating to appraisal and time of payment and of bringing suit: If this Company shall claim that no liability existed as to the mortgagor or owner, it shall, to the extent of payment of loss to the mortgagee, be subrogated to all the mortgagee's rights of recovery, but without impairing mortgagee's right to sue; or it may pay off the mortgage debt and require an assignment thereof and of the mortgage. Other provisions

the other of the appraiser selected within twenty days of such demand. The appraisers shall first select a competent and disinterested umpire; and failing for fifteen days to agree upon such umpire, then, on request of the insured or this Company, such umpire shall be selected by a judge of a court of record in the state in which the property covered is located. The appraisers shall then appraise the loss, stating separately actual cash value and loss to each item; and, failing to agree, shall submit their differences, only, to the umpire. An award in writing, so itemized, of any two when filed with this Company shall determine the amount of actual cash value and loss. Each appraiser shall be paid by the party selecting him and the expenses of appraisal and umpire shall be paid by the parties equally.

Company's options. It shall be optional with this Company to take all, or any part, of the property at the agreed or appraised value, and also to repair, rebuild or replace the property destroyed or damaged with other of like kind and quality within a reasonable time, on giving notice of its intention so to do within thirty days after the receipt of the proof of loss herein required.

Abandonment There can be no abandonment to this Company of any property.

When loss payable. The amount of loss for which this Company may be liable shall be payable sixty days after proof of loss, as herein provided, is received by this Company and ascertainment of the loss is made either by agreement between the insured and this Company expressed in writing or by the filing with this Company of an award as herein provided.

Suit. No suit or action on this policy for the recovery of any claim shall be sustainable in any court of law or equity unless all the requirements of this policy shall have been complied with, and unless commenced within twelve months next after inception of the loss.

Subrogation. This Company may require from the insured an assignment of all right of recovery against any party for loss to the extent that payment therefor is made by this Company.

Page 2 of the Standard Fire Insurance Policy of New York

an overheated pan of grease damages property, there is no coverage, since the policy does not cover friendly fire. If, however, the grease itself were to catch fire, any resultant smoke damage would be covered, since the ignited grease is a hostile fire which is covered under the policy and which is the proximate cause of the damage.

HAZARDS NOT COVERED

Certain perils are considered uninsurable and are excluded from coverage in the policy, as follows:

Enemy attack by armed forces, invasion.

Action taken by our armed forces in resisting an attack or an immediately impending attack.

Action taken by our armed forces is excluded only if at the time of an attack or an immediately impending attack. If an American military aircraft on a regular flight or training mission were to crash and start a fire, the loss *would* be covered.

Insurrection, rebellion, revolution, civil war, usurped power.

Order of any Civil Authority—With the one exception given below, any act of the civil authority would be excluded under the Fire insurance policy. If the health authorities were to put the torch to a building because of suspected plague conditions, the resultant fire loss would not be covered. If the police started a fire to halt the march of rioters or escaped criminals, the fire loss would not be covered, etc.

Acts of the civil authority to retard the spread of fire *are* covered. Thus, if the Fire Department ordered a row of houses torn down to break the path of a spreading conflagration, the loss would be covered.

The policy does *not,* however, cover destruction ordered to retard the spread of fire, if the fire originated from a peril excluded under the policy. Thus, if a fire originated from enemy attack (a peril excluded under the policy), any act to retard the spread of this fire would not be covered.

Neglect of the Insured to preserve and protect the property at or after a loss or when the property is endangered by fire.

This exclusion applies only if the Insured fails to preserve the property *at* or *after* a loss. Neglect of the Insured in maintaining his property *prior* to the loss would not prevent his recovering under the policy, unless he wilfully sought to cause the loss.

MINNESOTA—No provision, except that in another section of the policy, REQUIREMENTS IN CASE LOSS OCCURS, the Insured is required to protect the property from further damage (discussed later in this chapter under INSURED'S DUTIES AND OBLIGATIONS).

Theft—The policy does not cover loss due to theft even though it occurs as a result of the confusion which arises during a fire.

MINNESOTA—No provision.

Explosion or riot, unless followed by fire, and then only for the actual fire damage.

If fire precedes an explosion, and the explosion is incidental to the fire, the entire loss is covered.

FOR HOW MUCH

The Fire insurance policy is a contract of indemnity. It is intended to make the Insured whole, to restore him to the position he was in prior to the loss. Under the Fire insurance policy, the Company may indemnify the Insured in one of several ways:

1. Actual Cash Value (Sound Value) at the time of the loss.

Actual Cash Value is usually understood as replacement cost less depreciation. This measure of loss is generally simple to apply in the case of goods held for sale. Thus, merchandise held for sale or goods in process of manufacture will be paid for at the Insured's cost to replace or restore such property in the condition it stood at the time of the loss. This will include the cost of labor and other expenses which have been incorporated in the goods. In the case of personal property or real property, the measure of loss is the same, even though it may be somewhat more complicated to arrive at a figure for their actual cash value.

The actual cash value of property at the time of loss may be more or less than the amount originally paid for the property. Thus, an Insured may have purchased a sofa in 1950 for $300. In 1965, when the sofa is destroyed by fire, the price of a new sofa of the same type is $750. The actual cash value of the property is not $300 (the price originally paid) or $750 (the cost to replace with a new sofa). The Company is liable only for an amount sufficient to replace a sofa of this kind in the condition it stood at the time of the loss—a $750 sofa 15 years old.

(On buildings and dwellings, insurance is available on a replacement basis—Discussed in Chapter 3 under For How Much—Replacement Cost Coverage and in Chapter 5 under Building(s) and Contents—Broad Form—For How Much—Replacement Cost Coverage.)

2. The cost to repair or replace the property with material of like kind and quality within a reasonable time after the loss.

The Company may pay the actual cash value of the property *or* the cost to repair or replace. While these amounts are generally the same, the Company may pay either sum in cases where there is a difference.

3. The Company may elect to repair or rebuild or replace the property destroyed or damaged instead of paying for the loss in dollars. If the Company wishes to exercise this option, it must give notice of its intention to do so within 30 days after it receives Proof of Loss.

4. **The Company may take all of the property** at the agreed or appraised value.

5. **No Abandonment Clause.** Although the Company may elect to take all of the damaged property after a loss, and pay the full value, the Insured does not have the option of turning the salvage over to the Company and insisting upon payment in full. The option to take all of the property is available only to the Company.

EXAMPLE: The Insured carries Fire insurance on his stock of $20,000, which is damaged in a fire. The salvage value of the property after the loss is $12,000. The Company can pay the Insured $8,000, or it can take all of the damaged property, and pay $20,000. On the other hand, the Insured cannot turn over the property to the Company and demand payment of $20,000.

The Company has the choice of indemnifying the Insured for his loss in any one of the four ways discussed above. In no event, however, is the Company liable for more than the interest of the Insured in the damaged or destroyed property.* (See "Insurable Interest" in Chapter 1.)

Insurable Interest—An insurable interest has been defined as a pecuniary interest in property which would be adversely affected by the occurrence of a loss to the property. Or, conversely, as a financial interest in property which furnishes a person with an incentive to preserve the property from loss or damage. Insurable interest can be understood better when it is realized that a Fire insurance policy is a *personal* contract, and insures an individual or a legal entity like a partnership, or a corporation. (In a recent case, the courts said, "A contract of insurance is as much a personal one as is a marriage contract.") The Insured is therefore covered only to the extent of his actual insurable interest in the property.

Insurable interest is present in many situations other than direct ownership. Thus, a mortgagee, bailee, lessee, or a contractor to whom property has been entrusted has been held to possess an insurable interest in property.

---

*In the 23 states listed below, special statutes make it possible under certain circumstances to collect more than the Actual Cash Value of property. In some cases, statutes are in force to prevent or penalize the issuance of overinsurance. These laws and their effect on the Actual Cash Value basis for settlement of losses are discussed in Chapter 4.

Arkansas, California, Delaware, Iowa, Kansas, Kentucky, Louisiana, Massachusetts, Mississippi, Minnesota, Missouri, Montana, Nebraska, New Hampshire, North Carolina, North Dakota, Ohio, Republic of the Phillipines, South Carolina, South Dakota, Tennessee, Texas, West Virginia, Wisconsin.

Assignment of Policy—An Insured who transfers property to another and wishes to assign his insurance to the new owner must obtain the consent of the Company. This requirement is clearly set forth in the basic Fire insurance policy. If the seller assigns his policy to the new owner without the permission of the Company, there will be no coverage under the policy for either party. The new owner will have no protection because the Company did not accept him as an Insured; the former owner cannot collect because he no longer has an insurable interest in the property.

While the policy insures only to the extent of the Insured's insurable interest at the time of the loss, it does not automatically insure every person who has an insurable interest, but only those actually named in the policy, or such others as are included in the policy by policy provision. It is important, therefore, that the policy name as Insureds all persons who have an insurable interest, where such individual is not included in the policy provision; e.g., a Household Fire policy which specifically includes all members of the Insured's household.

Pro Rata Liability—Any policy insuring a given property is liable only for the proportion that it bears to all insurance on the property, whether the other insurance is collectible or not.

EXAMPLE: 3 policies of $5,000 each covering the same property. Loss of $3,000. Each policy pays its pro rata liability, ⅓ of the loss, or $1,000. Assume same set of facts, except that policy in Company C is uncollectible. Policy A still pays only ⅓ of the loss; Policy B also pays ⅓ of the loss. The Company's liability is not affected by the fact that another policy on the property is not collectible.

MASSACHUSETTS—The phrase "whether collectible or not" does not appear in the clause.

WHERE COVERED

The policy covers property while located or contained in the premises described in the policy. It also covers property while removed to any proper place for preservation from an insured peril for five days at each place to which removed. When property is removed for preservation under such circumstances, the coverage at the location to which the property is removed is prorated in the proportion that the value at each location bears to the total value. Thus, if the Insured carries $8,000 of Fire insurance to cover $10,000 of property, and he removes $1,000 of this property to a proper location in order to preserve it from a peril insured against in his Fire policy, 1/10 of the amount of insurance applies for five days to the removed property at the new location.

CALIFORNIA-IOWA—Policy specifies only "fire."

MISSOURI—Policy covers for 30 days.

WHO IS INSURED

In addition to the named Insured, the policy also insures the legal representatives of the Insured—executors, administrators, guardians, etc.

PROPERTY NOT INSURED

Uninsurable Property (which cannot be covered): (a) accounts, (b) bills, (c) currency, (d) deeds, (e) evidences of debt, money and securities.

TEXAS—Policy does not cover accounts, money, currency, securities, deeds or evidences of debt.

Excepted Property (not covered, but may be insured by endorsement): Bullion, manuscripts.

TEXAS—Policy also lists as uninsured, unless specifically named: Cloth awnings, records and books of record, except for their physical value in blank, animals, motor vehicles or aircraft.

INSURED'S DUTIES AND OBLIGATIONS

Moral Duties—The Insured is required to furnish the truth to the Company. Failure to do so may void his policy. (It is a general rule of law that fraud vitiates a contract from its inception.)

Concealment, Fraud—The entire policy is void if, before or after a loss, the Insured has willfully concealed or misrepresented any material fact or circumstance concerning the insurance, or the interest of the Insured, or if he swears falsely. (See also Chapter 1.)

MINNESOTA—After a loss, misrepresentation or concealment must be wilful and intentionally fraudulent in order to void.

Physical Factors—There are certain physical conditions under which the policy will be suspended:

Increase of Hazard—Policy will be suspended only if the increase of hazard is within the control or knowledge of the Insured. Whether the hazard was increased in an individual instance is frequently a question of fact and as such, left to a jury. It is generally held that this clause takes in only *material* increases of hazard, not those which are only temporary or usual to the type of occupancy. On the other hand, it should be understood that the policy may be suspended by an increase of hazard even if the loss does not originate from the increased hazard.

Vacancy or Unoccupancy—If the described building, not merely the premises occupied, is vacant or unoccupied for more than 60 consecutive days, coverage is suspended.

TEXAS—30 days.

Violation of a moral duty voids the policy; violation of a physical "duty" merely suspends it. In the latter case, if the violation ceases prior to the loss, the policy is in full force and effect.

Change of Ownership—TEXAS—The policy is suspended following a change in ownership of the insured property.

REQUIREMENTS AFTER LOSS

The Fire insurance policy imposes a series of requirements on the Insured after he has suffered a loss. Some of these duties fall upon him even though the Company makes no demand for their fulfillment. Others need be met only if the Company makes a formal demand.

Duties That Must Be Met By Insured Even When No Request Is Made

To protect the property from further loss. The Insured is expected to behave as a prudent man would if he had no insurance on the property—to protect openings, dry out building and property, grease machinery, etc. Any expense the Insured undergoes along these lines may be included in the Proof of Loss.

To separate the damaged property from the undamaged.

To put it in the best possible order.

To give immediate written notice of loss to the Company.

CALIFORNIA—Notice is to be given "without unnecessary delay."
MAINE—Notice is to be given "within reasonable time."

To furnish a complete inventory of the damaged, destroyed, and undamaged property, showing in detail quantities, costs, actual cash value and amount of loss claimed.

In Forms covering commercial property, the requirement to furnish a complete inventory of the undamaged property is waived in many states when the loss is below a stipulated amount; most frequently, when less than 2% of the amount of insurance.

This provision and the variations among the states are discussed in Chapter 3 under For How Much—Waiver of Inventory (or Waiver of Inventory and Appraisement) clause.

To furnish Proof of Loss within 60 days after loss—The Proof of Loss is to contain a series of statements signed and sworn to by the Insured on the following points: The time and origin of loss, the interest of the Insured and all others in the property, the actual cash value of each item, the amount of loss, any encumbrances on the property, any other insurance carried, any changes in the title to the property, any changes in the use, occupation, or location of said property, by whom and for what purposes any building was occupied, whether the building stood on leased ground.

ARIZONA—Requirement to file Proof of Loss is waived if the Company fails to furnish forms within 20 days after the Insured makes application for such forms.
LOUISIANA—The Company must furnish blanks for Proof of Loss.
NEW YORK—The Insurance Law requires that the Company furnish forms, and make request for Proof of Loss, and that the Insured have 60 days to file Proof from the date the Company makes such request.
TEXAS—The Insured is given 90 days from the date of the loss to file Proof of Loss.

Duties That Insured Must Meet Only When Requested By Company:

To furnish verified plans and specifications of any building, fixtures and machinery destroyed or damaged.

CALIFORNIA—Such plans must be furnished only if available.

To exhibit all that remains of the property.

To submit to examination under oath.

MAINE—No requirement.

NEW YORK—An Insured who submits to an examination under oath may request that the Company furnish him with a copy of the examination. If the Company does not furnish him with such copy within 10 days, it cannot make use of the examination in any action or proceeding involving the policy.

To produce for examination all books of accounts, bills, invoices and other vouchers, and permit extracts to be made of such records.

Appraisal—If the Insured and the Company fail to agree as to the amount of the loss or the actual cash value, the question may be resolved through special appraisal procedures provided in the Fire insurance policy.

Either party may demand that the differences be submitted to appraisal. Demand must be made in writing. Each party must notify the other of the appraiser he selects within 20 days.

The appraisers must both agree on a disinterested umpire. If they cannot agree within 15 days, either the Insured or the Company may ask a judge of a court of record to appoint an umpire. An award of any two of the three is binding.

Each party pays the appraiser he has chosen, and both parties share the expenses of the appraisal and the umpire.

MASSACHUSETTS, NEW HAMPSHIRE—Loss must be submitted to three "disinterested" men.

MINNESOTA—If either side fails to select an appraiser within the time prescribed, a presiding judge of the district court of the county where the loss occurred may appoint such appraiser upon application of the other party in writing by giving five days' notice in writing to the party failing to appoint. If the appraisers fail to agree on an umpire within 15 days, they may apply to a judge of the aforementioned court.

When Loss Payable—The Company must pay the loss within 60 days after Proof of Loss is received by it and the loss determined either by agreement between the Insured and the Company or by an award arrived at through appraisal (see preceding section).

ARIZONA—If the Company does not pay within this prescribed period, it is liable for an additional 15% plus the reasonable attorney's fees for collecting the loss.

ARKANSAS—Same as ARIZONA, except that the penalty is 12%.

MAINE—Adjustment of loss must begin within 20 days, but no loss which exceeds $100 shall be paid earlier than 45 days after the loss.

MICHIGAN—Company must pay within 30 days.

When Suit Must Be Brought—Suit under the policy must be brought within one year of loss, but not before all the requirements of the policy have been complied with.

ARKANSAS, KANSAS—Within 5 years.
NORTH DAKOTA—Within 3 years.
MINNESOTA—Within 2 years.
TEXAS—Within 2 years and one day after cause of action accrues.

Subrogation—When the Company pays a loss under its policy, it may require from the Insured an assignment of all his rights of recovery against third parties. The Company is "subrogated" to the Insured's claims—it stands in his place.

Thus, an Insured may suffer damage through a fire which is caused or allowed to spread by the negligence of a neighbor. The Company, after it has paid the loss, may sue the negligent neighbor to recover the sums it has paid. Subrogation is an attempt to put the cost for loss on the party who caused the loss.

TIME OF POLICY

The policy attaches at Noon, Standard Time, at the location of the property.

The policy also expires at Noon, Standard Time, on the date shown unless canceled prior to expiration.

EXAMPLE: An Insured carries Fire insurance in Company A which expires on Oct. 1, 1963. He renews the coverage in Company B, effective Oct. 1, 1963. A fire breaks out at 11:30 A. M. on Oct. 1, 1963, and burns for four hours before it is extinguished. Company A is liable for the entire loss.

CANCELLATION

The policy may be canceled by the Insured at any time. The Company may also cancel the policy at any time, except that it is required to give five days' written notice to the Insured. Coverage continues until *midnight* of the 5th day.

CALIFORNIA—Fire insurance policies (as well as certain other forms of insurance) may not be cancelled by the Company except for non-payment of premiums, conviction of the Insured for a crime, fraud, negligence or physical changes in the insured property which render it uninsurable. Furthermore, the Company must give at least 45 days' notice of its intention not to renew a policy. The restriction on cancellation does not apply to personal property used in commercial or industrial enterprises.

MAINE and MINNESOTA—The Company must give ten days' written notice of its intention to cancel a Fire insurance policy.

MASSACHUSETTS—The Company must give twenty days' written notice of its intention to cancel a Fire policy.

NEW YORK—A policy covering dwelling property (other than hotels or motels) or personal property of a non-industrial or non-commercial nature which has been in force for 60 days may not be cancelled by the Company except for non-payment of premium, conviction of a crime arising out of acts which increase the hazards insured against, fraud or material misrepresentation, wilful or reckless acts or omissions which increase the hazards insured against or physical changes in the property which render it uninsurable. Furthermore, the Company must give at least 45 days' notice of its intention not to renew a policy.

WISCONSIN—A policy covering real property for residential purposes used by not more than four families or personal property owned by natural persons or any other risk under a multiple peril policy which develops an annual premium of less than $200 may not be cancelled by the Company after it has been in force for 70 days, except for non-payment of premiums and certain other grounds specified in the policy like material misrepresentation or material change in the condition of the risk. Furthermore, the Company must give at least 30 days' notice of its intention not to renew a policy. The restrictions on cancellation do not apply to loss or damage to property used in a commercial, industrial or professional enterprise.

Cancellation At Company's Request—When a policy is canceled by the Company, the cancellation is made on a pro rata basis. The Insured receives a proportionate share of the premium for the unexpired period of the policy.

NOTE: When the Company cancels a policy, the return premium due the Insured is rounded to the next *higher* dollar. (The entire rule is discussed in Chapter 8 under OTHER FACTORS WHICH AFFECT FIRE INSURANCE RATES—Whole Dollar Premium Rule.)

Cancellation At Insured's Request—When a policy is canceled by the Insured, the cancellation is made on a Short Rate basis. A special table is used under which the Company retains more than the proportionate share of the premium for the time the policy was in force.

EXAMPLE: The Insured buys a Fire insurance policy on January 1, 1961 to expire on January 1, 1962. The premium for the year is $100. On July 1, 1961, the Company cancels the policy. The Company must refund the premium for the unexpired period on a Pro Rata basis. It returns 50% of the premium for the half year. Under the same set of circumstances, if the *Insured* had requested the cancellation, the Company would compute the premium according to a Short Rate table, and would refund a smaller portion of the premium, generally 40% for six months, or $40.

In most territories, a pro rata return premium is allowed when the property is condemned by a Public Authority for demolition or use by the Authority.

Builders' Risk policies may generally be canceled pro rata when the structure is ready for occupancy.

In many jurisdictions, a Fire policy covering stock may be reduced in amount on a pro rata basis up to 50% of the maximum that was in force under the policy at any time.

MISCELLANEOUS

Binders (Not mentioned in the policy)—Immediate coverage on a risk may be obtained under a binder. The binder, which may be written or oral, is a temporary evidence of coverage, pending the issuance of the policy. It is usually written for a period of 15, 30, or 60 days, and remains in force for this period unless canceled. Cancellation of the binder cannot take effect before noon of the business day following the date on which the risk is declined.

NEW YORK— A binder cannot be written for more than 60 days, but extension of the coverage may be provided under a renewal of the binder.

PENNSYLVANIA—A binder is usually written for 30 days.

Other Insurance—Permission to carry other Fire insurance on the same risk is not required. The Company may, however, limit or prohibit other insurance.

TEXAS—Other insurance is not permitted unless the total amount of insurance on each item is shown. (This requirement is waived when the policy is subject to Coinsurance.)

Concurrency—When more than one policy covers on the same risk, it is important that the written portions of all policies read exactly alike, i. e., be concurrent. When the written portions are not alike, the policies are non-concurrent, and considerable difficulties may attend the settlement of a loss on the property. Policies are not deemed to be non-concurrent when only the amounts, rates or period for which they are written differ.

FOR FURTHER READING

ACKERMAN—Insurance
HEDGES—Practical Fire and Casualty Insurance
HUEBNER AND BLACK—Property Insurance
LUCAS—The Standard Fire Insurance Policy of New York
MAGEE and BICKELHAUPT—General Insurance
MOWBRAY AND BLANCHARD—Insurance
POLICY, FORM AND MANUAL ANALYSIS SERVICE
RIEGEL, ROBERT AND MILLER—Insurance

(See Reading List at End of Book)

CHAPTER 3

Fire Forms

THE FIRE INSURANCE POLICY analyzed in Chapter 2 is not complete in itself. As was mentioned, to each policy when issued there is attached an endorsement or rider containing additional provisions which are made part of the policy. This rider is usually referred to as a Form.

The Form contains clauses which alter or modify the basic policy, and adapt it to the type of risk being insured. Thus, there are different Forms for dwellings, commercial buildings, household property, contents of mercantile or manufacturing establishments, churches, apartment houses, etc. Frequently, a single Form is divided into distinct sections with only specific provisions applicable to various classes of property.

In every instance, the attached Form modifies certain conditions of the basic Fire policy. Some clauses broaden the policy by permitting the Insured to do things prohibited to him or restricted by the policy, or by relieving him of certain duties and obligations. Other clauses of the Form act to restrict the coverage under certain conditions or to increase or decrease the extent of the Company's liability for stipulated losses.

This chapter will discuss the more typical Forms which attach to the basic Fire policy. Before the individual Forms are taken up, provisions which are common to all the Forms will be outlined.

Standardization of Forms—While Forms differ in various territories, and more than one Form is often used in the same locality, considerable standardization has been achieved, and certain Uniform Standard Forms are widely used by most companies in any territory. It should be pointed out that there are important variations possible in these Forms. The reader is therefore urged to check local practices in his territory.

PROVISIONS COMMON TO THE VARIOUS FORMS

HAZARDS COVERED

Debris Removal Clause—The policy is extended to cover the cost of removal of insured debris after a loss caused by a peril insured against.

This clause merely *extends* the policy. It does not *increase* the amount of insurance. Thus, if property insured for $10,000 suffers a $10,000 loss, there would be no insurance left, after payment of the direct loss, to cover the cost of removal of debris.

The policy will pay for removal of debris only that proportion of such expense as the amount of the policy bears to all insurance on the property, whether or not such other insurance contains a Debris Removal clause. Thus, if the Insured carries two policies of $10,000 each on the same property, and Policy A contains a Debris Removal clause while Policy B does not contain such clause, Policy A will pay only one-half of the cost of removal of debris after a loss.

Liberalization Clause—Fire insurance policies and endorsements are often broadened by state statute or regulation or by rulings of the rating organization in a given locality. Where such broadening of the policy is granted without additional premium charge, the Liberalization clause extends the broadened coverage to all policies already in force at the time of the change.

FLORIDA, LOUISIANA, MARYLAND, MASSACHUSETTS, NEW HAMPSHIRE, NEW JERSEY, NEW YORK, NORTH CAROLINA, PENNSYLVANIA, SOUTH CAROLINA, WISCONSIN—The Liberalization clause also provides that any change which went into effect within 45 days prior to the inception of the policy will be extended to policies already written.

HAZARDS NOT COVERED

Nuclear Perils—The Form clarifies the fact that the policy is not intended to cover loss caused by nuclear reaction or nuclear radiation or radioactive contamination, whether such loss be direct or indirect, proximate or remote, whether or not contributed to or aggravated by fire, or any other perils insured against by the policy. However, the policy *does* cover direct loss by fire resulting from nuclear reaction or nuclear radiation or radioactive contamination.

Electrical Apparatus Clause—If electrical appliances, devices or wiring are damaged as a result of electrical injury from artificial causes, the policy does not cover unless followed by fire, and then only for the actual loss or damage caused by the fire. But damage to such equipment caused by lightning *would* be covered.

FOR HOW MUCH

COINSURANCE CLAUSE

Average Clause, Reduced Rate Contribution Clause

SINCE MOST FIRE LOSSES are partial in extent, many property owners are inclined to carry only partial insurance on their property, counting on the chance that a fire at their premises would be brought under control before it exceeded the amount of their insurance. Different property owners, if they choose to maintain different amounts of insurance on property of the same value, are then paying different premiums, thus contributing unequally to the general fund out of which all losses must be paid.

Thus, assume two firms, each carrying a stock worth $10,000. A insures his stock for $10,000; B elects to carry only $2,000 of insurance. Each sustains a $2,000 loss by fire. Both Insureds would collect the same amount, $2,000, although one has been paying five times as much premium as the other.

To distribute the cost of insurance more equitably among all policyholders, many Fire insurance Forms contain a clause under which the Insured agrees to maintain insurance of not less than a given percentage of the actual cash value of the property at the time of the loss. These clauses are known variously as Coinsurance clauses, Average clauses, or Reduced Rate Contribution clauses.* A reduced rate is granted the Insured on policies which include a clause of this kind. The amount of the reduction increases with the percentage of coinsurance.

The Form usually stipulates that the printed Coinsurance clause will be applicable only if there is inserted on the first page of the policy a percentage figure under the heading "Percent of Coinsurance Applicable." (See specimen Fire policy reproduced in Chapter 2.)

NORTH CAROLINA—Coinsurance applies except if the word "None" is shown in the Coinsurance column on page 1 of the policy.

In Fire insurance, the most commonly used percentage is 80%, although other percentages are used. The general principle remains the same, regardless of the particular percentage used.

NEW YORK—Optional Coinsurance percentages are permitted on insurance covering *building* property only— 50%, 60%, 70%.

Thus, under an 80% Coinsurance clause, the Insured agrees to carry insurance of not less than 80% of the actual cash value of the property at the time of the loss. If he carries less than this agreed percentage of insurance, he will not be entitled to collect in full for a loss, but will have to bear part of any loss himself. The Company will be liable only for such percentage of the loss as the amount of insurance carried bears to 80% of the actual cash value of the property at the time of the loss. The percentage of loss for

---

***For restrictions on the use of this type of clause in many states, see Chapter 4.**

which the Company is liable under these circumstances may be expressed by the formula: $\frac{C}{R} \times L = A$

where C is the amount of insurance Carried,

R is the amount of insurance Required—the stipulated percentage of the actual cash value of the property at the time of the loss,

L is the amount of the Loss,

A is the Amount for which the Company is liable.

EXAMPLE: Assume property worth $90,000 has been insured for $36,000 in a Fire insurance policy which contains an 80% Coinsurance clause (Average Clause, or Reduced Rate Contribution clause). The Insured suffers a $5,000 loss. The Company is liable only for one-half of the loss, as follows:

$$\frac{C}{R} = \frac{\text{Amount of Insurance Carried}}{\text{Amount of Insurance Required}} = \frac{\$36{,}000}{\$72{,}000} = \tfrac{1}{2} \text{ of Loss}$$

(80% of actual cash value, $90,000)

Generally, no appraisal of the value of the property is made when the policy is issued. No effort is made by the Company to ascertain whether the Insured is living up to his requirements under the Coinsurance clause (Average clause). The practical effects of the clause only make themselves felt when the loss occurs. At that time, the Company determines whether the Insured has complied with the provisions of the Coinsurance clause and, if not, to what extent he will have to bear a part of the loss himself.

The Coinsurance clause takes into account the actual cash value of the property *at the time of the loss.* It is of no significance that the amount of insurance may have been adequate when the policy was issued. If the value of the property has increased, the Insured is obligated to increase the amount of his insurance, in order to comply with the provisions of the Coinsurance clause and avoid being a co-insurer.

The Insured can never collect more than the amount of his insurance. Thus, in the illustration given above, where the insurance on property worth $90,000 stood at $36,000 on the date of the loss, if the Insured sustained a loss of $80,000, he could not collect more than $36,000,—the face amount of his policy.

The effect of the Coinsurance clause on an Insured's recovery will be the same whether he carries one or more policies on the property. Each policy is liable only in the proportion that the amount of insurance in the policy bears to the percentage stated of the actual cash value of the property. Thus, in the illustration used above, where the Insured's property was worth $90,000 if he carried two policies on the property of $18,000 each, each policy would be liable only for ¼ of any loss, as follows:

$$\frac{C}{R} = \frac{\text{Amount of Insurance Carried}}{\text{Amount of Insurance Required}} = \frac{\$18{,}000}{\$72{,}000} = \tfrac{1}{4} \text{ of Loss}$$

(80% of actual cash value, $90,000)

Both policies *together* will be liable for ½ of any loss, the same result as when there was only one policy of $36,000.

The Coinsurance clause percentage is not the maximum percentage of any loss that the Insured may collect. It is merely the minimum amount of insurance which the Insured must carry in order to collect losses in full. If he maintains this required amount of insurance, he will collect on any loss *in full,* up to the face amount of his policy. Furthermore, the Coinsurance clause does not limit the amount of insurance that may be carried. Any owner of property may carry 100% insurance to value. In the event of a loss, he will be entitled to collect 100% of his policy, if the loss is total.

Most states prohibit the use of Coinsurance or Average clauses on certain types of property, most generally on dwellings and household contents. Other States rule that policies containing such clauses must be clearly stamped; others stipulate that the Insured will be entitled to the refund of any excess premium if it is found that he carried *more* insurance than the value of his property. In some States, the use of such Coinsurance or Average clauses is optional and must be accepted by the Insured. These special statutes, as they apply in the various States, will be discussed in Chapter 4.

ARIZONA—The Fire insurance policy limits recovery to the actual cash value of the property at the time of the loss (discussed in Chapter 2 under FOR HOW MUCH). The form attached to the Fire policy provides that the value of stock sold by the Insured but not removed shall be valued at the Insured's selling price.

Three-Fourths Value Clause—In rural areas and other localities where the fire protection is not up to standard, Fire insurance is sometimes written with a Three-Fourths Value clause. Under the terms of this clause, the liability of the Company is limited to not more than three-fourths of the actual cash value of the *property* at the time of the loss.

Three-Fourths Loss Clause—Another type of clause which limits the liability of the Company is the Three-Fourths Loss clause. Under the terms of this clause, the Company is liable for only three-fourths of the amount of any *loss.*

Note that the Three-Fourths Loss clause is different from the Three-Fourths Value clause. Under the Three-Fourths Value clause, an Insured can collect partial losses in full. Under the Three-Fourths Loss clause, the Insured must bear 25% of any loss, no matter how small.

EXAMPLE: An Insured owns a dwelling worth $10,000. Under the Three-Fourths Value clause, he can collect in full for any loss up to $7,500 (if he has at least $7,500 of insurance). On any loss which exceeds $7,500, his recovery will be limited to $7,500. Under the Three-Fourths Loss clause, the Insured will collect only 75% of any loss, no matter how small. If he sustains a $2,000 loss, the Company is liable only for $1,500; on a $4,000 loss, he is entitled to only $3,000; on a $6,000 loss, he can collect $4,500, etc.

PRO RATA DISTRIBUTION CLAUSE UNDER BLANKET POLICIES

Fire insurance policies are sometimes written to cover blanket over two or more locations. A Pro Rata Distribution clause is almost always attached* to such blanket policies. The clause operates to distribute the amount of the policy by providing that insurance attaches in each building or location in the proportion that the values at the location bear to those in all locations covered. The Pro Rata Distribution clause thus limits the Company's liability at each separate location, with only a specific proportion of the policy applying to each location.

EXAMPLE: Values at Location A— $5,000
Values at Location B—$10,000
Values at Location C—$15,000

A Blanket policy of $24,000 with a Pro Rata Distribution clause covers all three locations. The Pro Rata Distribution clause operates to distribute the insurance as follows:

Amount of Insurance Applicable to Location A

$$\frac{\text{Values at Location A}}{\text{Values at All Locations}} = \frac{\$5{,}000}{\$30{,}000}, \text{ or } 1/6 \text{ of } \$24{,}000 = \$4{,}000.$$

Amount of Insurance Applicable to Location B

$$\frac{\text{Values at Location B}}{\text{Values at All Locations}} = \frac{\$10{,}000}{\$30{,}000}, \text{ or } 1/3 \text{ of } \$24{,}000 = \$8{,}000.$$

Amount of Insurance Applicable to Location C

$$\frac{\text{Values at Location C}}{\text{Values at All Locations}} = \frac{\$15{,}000}{\$30{,}000}, \text{ or } 1/2 \text{ of } \$24{,}000 = \$12{,}000.$$

Under the terms of the Pro Rata Distribution clause, if values fluctuate as between the different buildings, the insurance will automatically change. Thus, in the above example, if all the values were to shift to Building A, all insurance would automatically apply there.

If insurance is carried to the full value of all the property, the loss payment will not be limited by the clause. Contrariwise, if property is underinsured, then under this clause, it is equally underinsured at every location. If the owner carries 50% insurance to value, he is 50% underinsured at each location that the policy covers, regardless of how the total value is distributed among the different locations.

Replacement Cost Coverage—In most territories, it is possible to insure on a *replacement cost* basis buildings, improvements and

*In most territories, the Pro Rata Distribution clause is not required on risks which are insured with 90% or higher Coinsurance clauses.

betterments, furniture, fixtures, machinery and equipment, and supplies in connection with such property. This broader coverage does NOT apply to merchandise or household contents, except for governmental, educational, religious and non-profit hospital risks. The contents of these risks may be covered on a Replacement Cost basis, but such broadened coverage is not available on manuscripts; or articles of art, rarity or historical interest.

Replacement Cost coverage eliminates from settlement of a loss any depreciation in the value of the property. The Insured will be collecting "new for old." (Compare this basis of recovery with actual cash value, discussed in Chapter 2 under FOR HOW MUCH.)

No increase in rate develops, but the Insured is required to base his insurance on the *replacement* cost of the structure, and compliance with the Coinsurance clause is based on the higher figure. Policies written on a replacement cost basis usually incorporate an 80% Coinsurance clause, even where the basic (actual cash value) policy is written without Coinsurance requirements.

Replacement Cost coverage policies stipulate that the Insured must replace the property within a reasonable time, if he is to recover for his loss on a replacement cost basis. Courts have held that one year is a reasonable period within which to replace.

NOTE: Replacement Cost coverage on dwellings is discussed in Chapter 5 under DWELLING BUILDING(S) AND CONTENTS—BROAD FORM—FOR HOW MUCH—Replacement Cost Coverage.

NEW YORK—A Fire insurance policy on a *building* may be written with a special endorsement under the terms of which the amount of insurance will increase automatically every three months. The Insured may elect a 1%, 1½% or 2% increase.

The endorsement may not be attached to a policy which covers building and contents as a blanket amount.

The endorsement may be attached at the inception of the policy or at the end of any quarterly period after the policy goes into effect.

Waiver of Inventory (or Waiver of Inventory and Appraisement) Clause—The Fire insurance policy obligates the Insured, after a loss, to furnish a complete inventory of the damage and the *un*damaged property. When the Insured suffers a comparatively small loss, it is felt that it would be a hardship to require an inventory of the *un*damaged property. For this reason, the Form attached to the policy waives the requirement when the loss suffered is below a certain amount. A widely used Waiver of Inventory clause relieves the Insured of the requirement to furnish an inventory of the *un*damaged property when the loss is less than 2% of the amount of insurance.

ARIZONA—The requirement to furnish an inventory of the *un*damaged property is waived only when the loss is both less than 2% of the amount of insurance, and also less than $5,000.

LOUISIANA, MARYLAND, MASSACHUSETTS, NEW HAMPSHIRE, NEW JERSEY, NEW YORK, NORTH CAROLINA, PENNSYLVANIA, SOUTH CAROLINA, TEXAS—The requirement to furnish an inventory of *un*damaged property is waived only when the loss is both less than 5% of the amount of insurance and less than $10,000.

The Waiver of Inventory clause does not release the Insured from any requirements of the Coinsurance clause. While the Insured need not furnish an inventory of the *un*damaged property where the loss is below the stated percentage, the Company is not prevented from showing through other means that the Insured was not carrying sufficient insurance to comply with the requirements of the Average (Coinsurance) clause.

BUILDING AND CONTENTS FORM
(GENERAL PROPERTY FORM)

BUILDINGS AND CONTENTS of a commercial nature are covered in a special Form. (A separate Form applies to dwelling property and household goods.)

WHAT IS COVERED

Section II of the Form makes available seven coverages, as enumerated below.

(A) Building Coverage—This Section applies when the policy to which it is attached covers a building. The Form enumerates a series of items which are covered under the Building policy as pertaining to the service of the building. There are variations in this clause in Forms of the various territories, but basically they all provide coverage for machinery used in servicing the building, plumbing, electric wiring, communication, stationary heating, lighting, ventilating, refrigerating, air-conditioning, and vacuum cleaning apparatus and fixtures, boilers, awnings, signs and metal smokestacks, screens, storm doors, windows, elevators, etc.

(B) Contents Coverage—This section covers furniture, fixtures, machinery and equipment owned by the Insured, stock and other personal property. Coverage under this section is available on the Insured's interest in similar property owned by others to the extent of the value of labor and materials expended on such property by the Insured.

(C) Stock Coverage—Under this section, coverage is afforded for merchandise, materials and stock supplies of every description *owned by the Insured.*

(D) Contents, Except Stock Coverage—This section covers contents, as defined in section (B), except stock owned by the Insured.

(E) Improvements and Betterments—Coverage applies only

when the Insured is not the owner of the building. A tenant who leases premises will often make improvements, additions or changes in the property which will make the premises better suited to his purposes. Most leases provide that the improvements and betterments will become the property of the landlord as soon as they are installed. The tenant retains only the right to enjoy the improvements until the expiration of his lease. In most states, where a lease is silent on this point, the same result would be achieved by operation of law. Some Fire insurance Forms provide coverage under the Equipment item. In most territories, the Forms provide that recovery for loss or damage to such property will be available in one of three ways, discussed below.

1. If repair or replacement of the damaged or destroyed improvements and betterments is made by the Insured within a reasonable length of time, the Insured will be entitled to the actual cash value of the improvements and betterments.

2. If such repair or replacement is not made within a reasonable time, the Company is liable for the proportion of the original cost of the damage improvements and betterments which the unexpired term of the lease at the time of the loss bears to the period from the date such improvements were made to the expiration date of the lease.

3. If repairs or replacements are made without expense to the Insured, the Company has no liability to the Insured.

(F) Personal Property of Others Coverage—At the option of the Insured, the policy may be extended to cover personal property of others while in the care, custody or control of the Insured while on the described premises. This coverage is afforded only if the policy covers such personal property of the Insured's and only if the policy includes a Coinsurance clause of 80% or higher.

Coverage is limited to 2% of the amount of insurance applicable to such items under the policy and to a maximum of $2,000 on each such item.

(G) Off-Premises Extension Coverage—Under this Section, the Insured may apply up to 2% of the amount of insurance applicable to each item of insurance under the policy, but not more than $5,000 to each item, on property (other than merchandise) owned by him while temporarily removed from the described premises for purposes of cleaning, repairing, reconstruction or renovation.

It is important to note that this extension of coverage is not available to loss in transit nor to loss occurring in any premises owned, leased, operated or controlled by the Insured.

PROPERTY NOT COVERED

Foundation Exclusions Clause—The Form excludes brick, stone or concrete foundations, piers and other supports which are below the undersurface of the lowest basement floor, or where there is no basement, which are below the ground; underground flues, pipes, wiring and drains; cost of excavations and similar items. This clause is applied only when the policy is subject to Coinsurance. When a policy on a building or other structure is written without Coinsurance, the foundations are covered together with the building itself.

COLORADO, KANSAS, KENTUCKY, MINNESOTA, NEBRASKA, OKLAHOMA, SOUTH DAKOTA, WISCONSIN — The Form excludes from coverage the following classes of property:

Customers' goods in laundries, dry cleaning establishments where the principal business consists of altering, repairing, servicing or storing of customers' goods, unless specifically covered by endorsement and unless the 90% or higher Coinsurance clause applies to this item;

Personal property of employees unless specifically endorsed and unless the 80% or higher Coinsurance clause applies to this item;

In manufacturing risks, patterns, molds, models and forms unless specifically covered by endorsement and unless the 90% or higher Coinsurance clause applies to this item;

Property of guests;

The Insured's interest in personal property in which others have an insurable interest when the Insured's interest in such property is otherwise specifically covered.

NEW YORK—The Form also excludes foundations of machinery.

WHERE COVERED

Property Outside Buildings—The Form extends the coverage of the basic policy to property on platforms attached to the building, or while located in the open within 100 feet of the building, or in or on vehicles or railway cars in the open within 100 feet.

ALASKA, ARIZONA, CALIFORNIA, MONTANA, NEVADA, OREGON, UTAH—Policy is extended to cover on property, other than merchandise or stock, while temporarily removed from the described premises for purpose of cleaning, repairing, reconstruction or restoration. This extension of coverage is limited to a maximum limit of $5,000 without charge.

ARIZONA—Except for materials intended for use in construction, repair or alteration of a building which are covered while within 100 feet of the building, the form affords coverage for other property while within 50 feet of the building. Property on vehicles or cars is covered while within 300 feet of the building.

NEW YORK—Policy does not cover lawns, roadways or other paved surfaces which are outside of and more than 25 feet from the insured building.

Alterations and Repairs Clause—The policy is extended to cover property in any additions to the premises made by the Insured.

INSURED'S DUTIES AND OBLIGATIONS

Work and Materials Clause—The basic Fire insurance policy is suspended while the hazard is increased by any means within the control or knowledge of the Insured. Thus, an Insured who purchased a Fire insurance policy and subsequently introduced a new machine or process might be held to have increased the hazard and thereby suspended his insurance.

The Work and Materials clause broadens the policy by granting the Insured the right to use the premises for any purpose usual or incidental to his regular business as described in the policy. Under the terms of this clause, the Insured's protection is not affected by his doing anything or using any materials in his occupation, as long as he continues in the business described in the policy.

If the Insured keeps large quantities of prohibited articles, he might still be deemed to have increased the hazard and suspended his policy unless it could be shown that the storage of such quantities of these dangerous articles was usual to his type of occupancy. Thus, a property owner who stored gasoline in his dwelling might be held to have caused the suspension of his insurance because it is not usual to dwelling occupancy to store quantities of gasoline, particularly if gasoline is easily obtainable from nearby filling stations.

Breach of Warranty Clause—If the policy covers two or more buildings, or the contents of two or more buildings, it is provided that the Insured's breach of warranty in any one building shall not prejudice his right to recover for loss in another building where no breach of warranty exists.

Vacancy and Unoccupancy—The basic Fire insurance policy is suspended if the described building is vacant or unoccupied beyond 60 consecutive days (discussed under Insured's Duties and Obligations—Chapter 2). This restriction is often eased by the Form attached to the policy, particularly in areas which are under the protection of regularly manned fire-fighting organizations.

The Form may extend the policy to cover unlimited vacancy or unoccupancy by granting "privilege to be vacant or unoccupied." In some cases, the Form only broadens the policy to allow for three months of unoccupancy, or some other specified period.

In some states, different periods of vacancy and unoccupancy are permitted for different types of operations. The Forms also provide varying periods of permitted vacancy or unoccupancy depending on the proximity of the risk to fire-fighting equipment and fire hydrants. In protected territories, permission is often granted to be vacant or unoccupied without limit of time. School Forms are drawn to extend the 60-day unoccupancy period permitted by the basic policy throughout the vacation period. The reader is urged to check local practice in his area on this important feature of coverage under a Fire policy.

Insured's Warranties—While the Forms attached to the policy generally broaden the coverage of the basic policy in many respects, they may also impose additional requirements on the Insured. Thus, the Insured may warrant that he will maintain a distance of not less than ___ feet between the insured property and any other manufacturing establishment, or that his premises will be patrolled by a watchman at all times when they are not open for business, or that insofar as is under his control, an automatic sprinkler system will be in working order, etc. Such warranties by the Insured call for strict compliance, and a breach may void the coverage.

LOUISIANA—Under Fire policies covering stock, the Insured is required to take a complete itemized inventory of the stock on hand at least once in each calendar year, and unless such inventory shall have been taken at least once in the twelve months preceding the inception of the policy, or within 30 days after its issuance, the policy is null and void. The Insured is further required to keep a set of books which set forth clearly the business transacted, and these books must be kept in a fireproof safe at night, and at all times when the building is not open for business or in some place not exposed to a fire which would destroy the building described in the policy. The Insured's failure to produce such books shall render the policy null and void.

Control of Property Clause—The policy will not be affected by the Insured's failure to comply with any warranty in a portion of the premises over which he has no control.

Subrogation—The basic policy grants to the Company which has paid a loss an assignment from its Insured of all right of recovery the Insured may have against a third party (discussed in Chapter 2 under Duties That Must Be Met By An Insured — Subrogation). The Forms in most states provide that the Insured will not invalidate his insurance by waiving his right of recovery against a third party, provided such waiver is in writing and is executed *prior* to the loss. Where the Form is silent on this score, most companies will agree to permit such waiver.

ARIZONA—The Insured may release or waive his rights of recovery against any third party prior to a loss; after a loss, such release may run only to a third party insured under the policy, or a corporation, firm or entity owned or controlled by the Insured, or which owns or controls the Insured. It is further provided that in all events, the Insured must have waived his entire rights of recovery against the third party.

TEXAS—The provision appears in the basic policy.

Coinsurance—NEW YORK—On buildings, the Insured is offered a choice of Coinsurance percentages—50%, 60%, 70% or 80%.

MORTGAGEE CLAUSE

THE WIDESPREAD PRACTICE of mortgaging real property as security for a loan has brought into use a special clause which may be attached to any Fire insurance policy covering real property—the Standard Mortgagee clause, commonly referred to as the New York Standard Mortgagee clause. All Fire insurance policies provide a space to insert the name of the mortgagee, if any. When the name of a mortgagee is included in the policy, it brings into action the Standard Mortgagee clause which appears in all building Forms, and the provisions of the basic policy on "Mortgagee Interests and Obligations."

MINNESOTA-NEW HAMPSHIRE—The mortgagee's name is inserted in a space provided in the Form attached to the policy.

TEXAS—The basic Fire insurance policy contains a Mortgagee clause.

The Mortgagee clause sets up a separate contract between the insurance Company and the mortgagee. The clause grants the mortgagee specific protection and imposes certain requirements on him.

Benefits Received by Mortgagee

1. Any loss on the property is payable to him, as his interest may appear.

2. If the Company wishes to cancel the policy, it must give the mortgagee separate notice. Furthermore, it must give the mortgagee not less than 10 days' notice, even though the Insured may be entitled to only 5 days' notice.

NOTE: Since the mortgagee usually retains the original policy, the Insured cannot cancel without the mortgagee's consent.

3. The mortgagee's protection will not be affected by any act or neglect of the owner, unless the mortgagee is aware of such actions on the part of the Insured. Thus, an Insured may cause the suspension of his policy by increase of hazard, or by vacancy or unoccupancy of the premises beyond the permitted period. He may neglect to protect and preserve the property from further loss at or after the time of a loss. Under these and similar situations, the Insured may find himself unable to collect under his policy, but any mortgagee named in the policy would still be fully protected to the extent of his interest in the property.

NOTE: If the Company, in a particular loss, claims that it has no liability to the Insured because of some act or neglect committed by him, and the Company pays the *mortgagee* because of the protection afforded him by the mortgagee clause, the Company will be subrogated to the claim of the mortgagee against the owner under its mortgage.

Furthermore, the Company has the option of paying off the balance of the mortgage and receiving a full assignment of the mortgage.

Thus, assume Jones' home worth $20,000 is mortgaged to a bank under an $8,000 mortgage. Jones carries a Fire insurance policy of $16,000 with a Standard Mortgagee clause. A fire breaks out and does $6,000 of damage to the property. The insurance Company will pay $6,000 in a check made payable to the bank and to Jones, as their interests may appear. The bank will either endorse the check over to Jones, who can then use the money to rebuild the property, or will credit him with $6,000 in reduction of his mortgage.

Suppose, however, that Jones had violated the terms of his insurance policy and the Company disclaims any liability to him. Since the Mortgagee clause protects the mortgagee to the extent of his interest, despite any act on the Insured's part, the Company will pay the bank $6,000 in settlement of the loss. The mortgagee will not credit Jones with any of this money, since Jones was not entitled to protection under the policy.

In this type of situation, the insurance Company is legally subrogated to the extent of its payment to the mortgagee and is entitled to recover $6,000 from the owner, Jones, after the bank has received the balance of its money from Jones. Thus, Jones, the owner, loses $6,000, since he had no protection to cover the loss, and settlement is made with the mortgagee bank as though there were a separate contract between the insurance Company and the bank.

4. The mortgagee is protected against voidance of the policy by foreclosure, change in title, or ownership, unless he is aware of such change.

5. If the owner fails to furnish a Proof of Loss within the prescribed time, the mortgagee may file.

6. The mortgagee may sue on the policy in his own name.

Obligations Imposed on the Mortgagee

1. If the Insured fails to pay the premium, the mortgagee shall, on demand, pay the premium; otherwise he forfeits the protection afforded him under the Standard Mortgagee clause.

MINNESOTA-NEW HAMPSHIRE — There is no provision regarding payment of the premium by the mortgagee.

PACIFIC COAST TERRITORY—The Standard Mortgagee clause used in this territory *obligates* the mortgagee to pay the premium, if the Insured fails to do so.

2. The mortgagee is required to notify the Company of any change in ownership, or increase in hazard of which he has knowledge.

3. The mortgagee is required to furnish Proof of Loss, if the Insured fails to do so.

4. The mortgagee is bound by the time to file suit.

5. The mortgagee is bound by the appraisal provisions of the policy.

NOTE: Several cases decided recently indicate that the mortgagee is *not* bound by the appraisal provisions of the policy unless he is actually a party to the appraisal.

6. Where a policy is subject to Coinsurance, the mortgagee is bound by the Coinsurance provisions of the policy.

LOSS PAYABLE CLAUSE

Other clauses are sometimes used under which it is agreed that loss will be payable to a third party instead of the Insured. These clauses read simply, "Loss, if any, shall be payable to----------," or "Loss, if any, shall be adjusted with and payable to---------." Under this type of Loss Payable clause, the mortgagee places himself in the same position as the Insured. He is not immune to acts of the Insured as he is under the terms of a Standard Mortgagee clause.

DWELLING AND CONTENTS FORM

A special Form is used to provide insurance on private dwellings and/or the contents of private dwellings. Household goods in apartment buildings are covered under a Form which provides essentially the same coverage as is afforded under the Dwellings-Contents Form. This section will analyze first the coverage afforded on the dwelling structure, and then the provisions of the insurance on household contents.*

DWELLING FORM

Inherent Explosion—The forms covering dwelling property and the contents of such structures provide coverage (or may be written without extra charge to provide coverage) on loss by explosion in the described building or appurtenant private structure from hazards inherent in the building. However, the Company is *not* liable for loss by explosion of steam boilers, steam pipes, steam turbines, if owned by, leased by, or operated under the control of the Insured.

WHAT IS COVERED

The Dwelling Form covers not only the actual structure but also the building equipment, fixtures and outdoor equipment pertaining to the service of the premises, provided the Insured is the owner of such equipment.

Outbuildings Coverage—The Dwelling Forms also permit the Insured to apply up to 10% of the amount of insurance on the dwelling to cover any other private structure and garage whose use is incidental to the maintenance of the main building.

The extension of coverage does not apply to any structure used for mercantile, manufacturing or farming purposes nor to any structure leased to others.

An exception is made for structures used for private garage purposes and for any other structures rented to a tenant of the dwelling covered under the policy.

Rent Insurance—The Dwelling Forms also permit the Insured to apply up to 10% of the amount of insurance on the dwelling to cover the rental value of the dwelling during such time as it would

---

*In recent years, special package policies for home owners have come into wide use. These are discussed separately in Chapter 34, Personal Multiple Peril Policies.

take to restore the premises to tenantable condition. Rent insurance is available to an owner-occupant of a dwelling, or to an owner who rents to a tenant and who would be deprived of the rental income of the dwelling in the event the premises are rendered untenantable by the damage to or destruction of the premises by an insured peril.

Not more than 1/12 of the said 10% may be applied for any one month during which the premises are untenantable. Thus, under a Fire insurance policy of $24,000 covering a dwelling, the Insured may apply up to $2,400 (10% of the amount of insurance) to cover the rental value of the dwelling, but not more than $200 (1/12 of the amount applicable to rental value) may be collected for any month of untenantability. If the premises were damaged and it would take three months to restore them to use, the Company's liability will be limited to $600 ($200 for each month).

An Insured who requires coverage on outbuildings or rental value loss in an amount in excess of the 10% extensions granted by the Dwelling Form may purchase such additional insurance for an additional premium.

Trees, Plants, Shrubs — The Dwelling Forms exclude trees, shrubs, plants, and lawns. In most territories, the Form provides for covering trees, shrubs, and plants which are not grown for commercial purposes. In wide use are forms which limit coverage as follows: $100 per tree; $10 per shrub; $1.00 per plant.

ARIZONA—The maximum recoverable on any tree, plant or shrub is $100.

MASSACHUSETTS, NEW HAMPSHIRE—The limits are $300 per tree; $25 per shrub; $5.00 per plant.

Electrical Apparatus, Lightning Deductible—NEW YORK—A $50 deductible is applicable to any loss by lightning to electrical appliances, devices, fixtures and wiring covered under the policy.

FOR HOW MUCH

Deductibles—In almost every state, Fire insurance policies covering dwelling property are written subject to a Deductible clause (discussed in Chapter 8 under OTHER FACTORS WHICH AFFECT FIRE INSURANCE RATES—Dwelling Deductibles).

INSURED'S OBLIGATIONS

NORTH CAROLINA—An Insured who owns a dwelling in unprotected territory is required to maintain interior plumbing supplied by water from a continuous source, electric wiring system for lighting, a stipulated type of heating system, continuous mortared masonry or concrete foundation and a telephone. Failure to maintain *all* of these facilities (except if beyond his control) will reduce any loss settlement by 25%.

HOUSEHOLD CONTENTS FORM

As was pointed out above, household goods may be insured

under the Dwelling Form. Such insurance is afforded as a separate item. Tenants who occupy rented quarters, whether in a private dwelling or an apartment building, may insure their household and personal property under a special Household Contents Form.

HAZARDS COVERED

Consequential Loss—The Form extends the policy to cover loss to personal property contained within the described dwelling due to change of temperature as a result of physical damage to the structure or the equipment within or on the premises. Thus, as an example, if a fire damaged the electric wiring of a residence and impaired the flow of electricity to a freezer, the resulting food spoilage would be covered.

WHAT IS COVERED

The Form extends the coverage to all household and personal property such as is usual to the occupancy of the dwelling as a residence, including household and personal property purchased under an installment plan belonging to the Insured, or for which the Insured may be liable. Excluded are aircraft, motor vehicles and boats other than rowboats and canoes.

WHO IS INSURED

All personal property of the Insured such as is usual to dwelling occupancy is covered. The policy also covers property of others for which the Insured may be liable. Furthermore, at the Insured's option, the policy will cover property of a member of the Insured's family, or a servant.

FOR HOW MUCH

In many jurisdictions, Coinsurance is not applicable to household contents. Where a Coinsurance clause does apply to such property, a percentage is stipulated on the first page of the policy.

WHERE COVERED

Contents In Open—The policy is extended to cover such property as is insured while in the open on the premises.

10% Away From Premises—The Insured may apply up to 10% of the amount of insurance to cover property while elsewhere than on the described premises. Coverage is confined to that part of the continental North America included within the United States, Canada and Hawaii. No coverage away from the premises applies to rowboats, canoes, animals or pets.

This extension of insurance is not available for the benefit of any carrier or other bailee. Thus, if the Insured were to lose an article of clothing in a fire at a tailor or laundry, the insurance would not relieve the tailor or laundry of its liability for such loss.

GEORGIA—The 10% Away from Premises extension is world-wide.

TEXAS—Coverage includes Mexico.

Removal Within State—If contents as defined in the policy are removed to another location within the state occupied as the Insured's residence, the policy is extended automatically to cover at the new location, and shall cease to cover at the former location, except that during the period of removal, the policy covers at each location in the proportion that the value of the property at each location bears to the aggregate value at both locations.

BUILDINGS IN COURSE OF CONSTRUCTION

A BUILDING IN COURSE OF CONSTRUCTION may be insured against the perils of fire and lightning under a Fire insurance policy, with a Builder's Risk form attached. The perils of the Extended Coverage endorsement may be added to the policy by endorsement, and the coverage further extended to insure against Vandalism and Malicious Mischief.

Insurance on buildings in course of construction may be provided in one of several ways. While certain risks may call for special treatment, most buildings in process of construction are insured in one of three ways:

1. Builder's Risk Reporting Form (or Automatic Cover clause)
2. Builder's Risk Completed Value Form
3. The regular Building Form may be used to cover a building in course of construction. The form is stamped "Privilege to Complete and Occupy" and the amount of insurance must be increased regularly to keep pace with the increase in the value of the structure as it is being erected.

WHAT IS COVERED

Both Forms cover the structure while in the course of construction, which is understood to include the period up to the time the building is completed. (Under the Completed Value Form, provision may be made for continuing the coverage even after the building is completed, if the permission of the Company is obtained.) If a tenant were to move into a building before it is completed, the policy would provide coverage. Once the building is completed, the Company is to be notified and the rate for the policy adjusted. Privilege is granted to set up and test machinery in the building, and such activity is not construed as occupancy of the building.

The policy covers not only the structure being erected but also materials, equipment, supplies and temporary structures of all kinds used in the construction of the building. In addition, builder's machinery, tools and equipment (unless otherwise insured) are covered under the policy. Such materials and equipment are covered whether within the structure or in the open on the premises, or on sidewalks, streets or alleys adjacent thereto.

FOR FURTHER READING

ACKERMAN—Insurance
HEDGES—Practical Fire and Casualty Insurance
HUEBNER AND BLACK—Property Insurance
MAGEE and BICKELHAUPT—General Insurance
MOWBRAY AND BLANCHARD—Insurance
POLICY, FORM AND MANUAL ANALYSIS SERVICE
RIEGEL, ROBERT AND MILLER—Insurance

(See Reading List at End of Book)

CHAPTER 4

Valued Policy and Anti-Coinsurance Laws

IN ABOUT ONE-HALF of the States, special statutes or regulations are in force which may modify the basis of settlement under a Fire insurance policy or restrict or limit the use of Average or Coinsurance clauses or otherwise act to discourage or penalize insurance companies for over-insurance of property.

This Chapter will discuss these various statutes and regulations as they affect Fire insurance in the separate states.

VALUED POLICY LAWS

THE STANDARD FIRE INSURANCE POLICY used in practically every state of the country limits recovery to the "actual cash value" of the property at the time of the loss, but a number of states have enacted some form of Valued Policy Law under which the Company may be liable for *more* than the actual cash value of the property at the time of the loss. These Valued Policy Laws vary considerably among the different states. Their scope is broad in some states, and comparatively limited in others.

Total Loss on Real Property

The most common form of Valued Policy Law is one which applies only to real property when totally destroyed. Under this type of law, the Company must pay the full amount of insurance on any building which is totally destroyed by fire (and in some cases by other perils). The company cannot limit its liability to the actual cash value of the property at the time of its destruction. Some states permit the Company to show that depreciation had taken place in the value of the property since the date the policy was issued, but the amount of insurance originally effected is presumed to be the actual cash value of the property at the date of the inception of the policy.

In some states, the Company may exercise its option to rebuild or replace the property instead of paying in cash. In such states, the effect of the Valued Policy Law is considerably softened since the Company is not bound to pay the face amount of the policy if it believes that this is more than the value of the property, but can elect to rebuild or replace. In other states, the Company may not exercise its option to rebuild and must actually pay in cash the full amount of the policy in force.

To be considered a total loss, the entire structure need not necessarily be razed to the ground. A part of the building may still be left standing after the fire, but the loss will be considered total if a prudent builder would not use the remaining portion, but would tear down to the foundation before proceeding to rebuild.

No Depreciation—No Right to Rebuild or Replace—In the following states, the Company must pay the face amount of the policy covering any building which has suffered a total loss:

ARKANSAS-SOUTH DAKOTA—applies to fire losses only.
FLORIDA—Every policy shall have endorsed on its face, "It is agreed between the insurer and the Insured that the value of the insured property is $.................... and this estimate shall be binding on both parties as to the value." Applies to fire losses only.
KANSAS—The Company must examine the property and the policy must contain a complete description. The amount of insurance in the policy shall be conclusive as to the value of the property.
MINNESOTA-MISSISSIPPI—applies to fire losses only.
MONTANA—applies to fire, lightning, and tornado losses.
NEBRASKA-NORTH DAKOTA—applies to fire losses only.
NEW HAMPSHIRE—applies to fire loss only. The Insured may receive a lower rate by accepting a Coinsurance clause. The Agreed Amount does not apply to buildings insured blanket with contents or other buildings.
OHIO-SOUTH CAROLINA-TEXAS—The Company must examine the property before issuing policy.

Company May Exercise Its Option to Rebuild or Replace

REPUBLIC OF THE PHILIPPINES—When the Insured desires, he may request and the Company must examine the property. Value is then fixed.
WISCONSIN

Company May Show Depreciation Since Date of the Policy

IOWA-KENTUCKY—applies to fire and storm losses. Also to policies of life or accident insurance on livestock.

All Losses on Real Property, Total and Partial

In six states, the Valued Policy Laws apply to all losses on real property, total as well as partial. In these states, the amount of insurance is presumed to be equal to the true value of the property, and *all* losses are either adjusted on this basis, or the Company held liable for the full amount of any partial loss.

CALIFORNIA—applies to fire losses only. If the Insured desires to have a valuation named in the policy, he may require of the Company that it examine the property and set a value which is then to be fixed. The Company may exercise its option to rebuild or replace.
IOWA—Amount of insurance is prima facie evidence of the insurable value of the property, but the Company may show depreciation from the date of the policy to the date of the loss.

LOUISIANA—The value as assessed, or as permitted to be assessed, is conclusive as to the actual cash value of the property. Company may exercise its opinion to rebuild or replace.
MISSOURI—applies to fire, lightning, and other hazards. Company must examine property and fix a valuation in the policy. The Company may show depreciation since the date the policy took effect.
TENNESSEE-WEST VIRGINIA—within 90 days of the issuance of the policy, the Company shall inspect the structure. If such inspection is not made, the Company must pay on the basis of the insurance in force.

Refund of Excess Premiums Paid to Insured by Company

In five states and territories, the Company is not required to pay the face amount of its policy in the event of total destruction of real property. However, if the actual cash value of the property at the time of the loss is found to be less than the amount of insurance in force, the Company must refund the premiums for the excessive amounts of insurance. One other state declares the issuance of excessive insurance to be illegal.

HAWAII-IDAHO—As above.
MASSACHUSETTS-TENNESSEE—Company must refund premiums for excessive insurance plus interest at the rate of 6% on all current policies as well as any previous expired policies written in the same Company.
NORTH CAROLINA—Company must refund excess premiums plus interest at the rate of 6%.
WYOMING—Requires Certificate of Valuation when policy is issued.

ANTI-COINSURANCE LAWS

ELEVEN STATES prohibit or restrict the use of Coinsurance or Average clauses in Fire insurance policies. In a majority of these states, such clauses may be incorporated in Fire insurance policies on certain types of property, provided the Insured agrees to accept such provision in his policy.

CALIFORNIA - LOUISIANA - MISSOURI - NEW HAMPSHIRE - TENNESSEE-WEST VIRGINIA—While these states do not restrict the use of Coinsurance clauses, it should be noted that their Valued Policy Laws stipulate that total loss of real property be paid in full, and that any partial loss be paid at the actual cost of replacing the damage. For all practical purposes, the Valued Policy Law in these states prevents application of the Coinsurance clause in such losses.

Acceptance of Coinsurance Optional With Insured

INDIANA-IOWA—but not on farm property or dwellings. (In Indiana, Coinsurance clauses may not be used on farm buildings, single family dwellings or household contents.)
KENTUCKY—must be signed by both the Insured and the Company.
MINNESOTA—Insured must make written request, but only when the value of the property exceeds $5,000. If value of the property is below $5,000, and on certain classes, no Coinsurance is applicable.
MICHIGAN-MISSOURI—Insured must make written request.
TEXAS—Coinsurance may be inserted on cotton, grain, or other products in process of marketing, shipping, storing, or manufacturing. The Insured may accept on other property but not on private dwellings or retail stocks of less than $10,000.

Policies Containing Coinsurance Clauses Must Be Clearly Stamped—Florida, Louisiana, North Carolina.

No Coinsurance on Building Property—Arkansas, New Hampshire.

FOR FURTHER READING

HUEBNER AND BLACK—Property Insurance
MAGEE AND BICKELHAUPT—General Insurance
(See Reading List at End of Book)

CHAPTER 5

Additional Perils Coverage

THE BASIC FIRE insurance policy insures against the perils of Fire and/or Lightning. In addition, coverage for a series of other perils may be added by endorsement. Nine additional perils are incorporated in one endorsement which is widely used throughout the United States and Canada. This endorsement, called the Extended Coverage Endorsement (the Supplemental Contract in Canada), provides coverage for loss or damage by any of the following perils:

Windstorm, Hail, Explosion, Riot, Riot Attending a Strike, Civil Commotion, Aircraft, Vehicles, Smoke.

(These may be remembered by the acronym—W. C. Shaver.)

EXTENDED COVERAGE ENDORSEMENT

WHILE SEPARATE INSURANCE against the above listed perils is available, the most common method of covering these perils is by the all-inclusive Extended Coverage Endorsement. In Canada, a similar extension of the Fire insurance policy is widely used—the Supplemental Contract.

Under this endorsement, nine perils are added to the basic Fire insurance policy. The listed perils are substituted for the word "fire" wherever it appears in the policy. The coverage on any of these perils is subject to all the conditions of the basic Fire insurance policy.

NOTE: With the widespread use of the Extended Coverage Endorsement in Fire insurance policies, many Companies now have the provisions of the Endorsement printed in all Fire insurance Forms. The additional coverages do not become operative, however, except when an additional premium for the Extended Coverage Endorsement is shown in the policy.

TEXAS—These perils are covered under a section in the basic policy, Specific Coverage Conditions.

HAZARDS NOT COVERED

War, Nuclear Perils—There is no coverage for loss caused directly or indirectly by (a) hostile or war-like action in time of peace or war, including action in hindering, combating or defending against an actual impending or expected attack; (1) by any government or sovereign power (de jure or de facto), or by any authority maintaining or using military, naval or air forces; or by (2) military, naval or air forces; or (3) by any agent of such government, power, authority or forces. Any discharge, explosion or use of any weapon of war employing nuclear fission or fusion shall be conclusively presumed to be such a warlike action; (b) insurrection, rebellion, revolution, civil war, usurped power, or action taken by governmental authority in hindering, combating or defending against such action.

Water Exclusion Clause—The policy does not cover loss caused by, or contributed to by (a) flood, surface water, waves, tidal water, overflow of bodies of water, or spray from such sources; (b) backing up of sewers or drains; (c) water below the surface of the ground, including that which seeps through sidewalks, driveways, foundations, walls, basement or other floors, or through doors, windows or any other openings in sidewalks, driveways, foundations, walls or floors; UNLESS fire or explosion ensues, and in such event, the Company is liable for the ensuing loss.

NOTE: Insurance against flood, now available in selected areas, is discussed at the end of this chapter under FLOOD INSURANCE.

FOR HOW MUCH

The Extended Coverage Endorsement must be written for the same amount as the Fire insurance policy itself. Furthermore, the rules in practically every state do not allow for cancellation of the Extended Coverage Endorsement without cancellation of the entire policy.

NEW YORK—Such cancellation of the Extended Coverage Endorsement is permitted without cancellation of the basic policy, but must be made on a short rate basis when the Insured requests the cancellation.

The Extended Coverage Endorsement does not increase the amount of insurance of the policy to which it is attached. It merely extends the coverage to include the added perils.

EXAMPLE: An Insured carries a $10,000 Fire insurance policy with Extended Coverage. During a windstorm, a fire breaks out. The fire does $7,000 of damage, and the windstorm does $6,000 of damage, but he cannot collect more than $10,000 under the policy for the entire loss.

Apportionment Clause—The Company, under the Extended Coverage Endorsement, is liable only for the proportion that its policy bears to all *Fire* insurance on the property, whether or not such other Fire insurance contains an Extended Coverage Endorsement.

The Apportionment clause makes it important that *all* the Fire insurance policies covering the same property include the Extended Coverage Endorsement, if one policy is so endorsed.

EXAMPLE: Insured carries three Fire insurance policies of $5,000 each, on the same property. Policies A and B contain an Extended Coverage Endorsement; Policy C does not. The Insured suffers a windstorm loss of $6,000. Policy A is liable for $2,000; Policy B for $2,000.

Furthermore, the Company, under the Extended Coverage Endorsement, is not liable for a greater proportion of any loss or damage than the amount of its policy bears to all insurance which covers in any manner on such peril.

EXAMPLE: Insured carries a $20,000 Fire insurance policy with Extended Coverage on his residence. He also carries a separate Windstorm policy on the residence of $10,000. In the event of loss or damage by windstorm, the Fire insurance policy is only liable for ⅔ of the loss.

Coinsurance Clause, Average Clause—When a Fire insurance policy contains a Coinsurance (or Average or Reduced Rate Contribution) clause, the Extended Coverage is subject to the provisions of such clause.

FLORIDA—Fire insurance on dwellings and other property may be written without Coinsurance. The Extended Coverage Endorsement, when attached to such a policy, is nevertheless subject to Coinsurance.

PRIVILEGES GRANTED

Vacancy and Unoccupancy—The Extended Coverage Endorsement grants privilege to be vacant or unoccupied without limit of time. This privilege applies only to the perils insured under the Extended Coverage Endorsement; it does not extend the time allowed by the basic Fire insurance policy for loss or damage by fire or lightning.

In other words, if the basic Fire insurance policy covering a particular risk provides that coverage will be suspended if the building is vacant or unoccupied beyond 60 consecutive days, this restriction continues to be effective as regards any loss by *fire or lightning,* even though the Extended Coverage Endorsement is attached to the policy. Vacancy and Unoccupancy, however, would not affect recovery for any loss caused by any of the nine perils of the Extended Coverage Endorsement.

Change of Occupancy—In a manner similar to the Vacancy and Unoccupancy privileges discussed in the preceding paragraph, permission is granted the Insured to change the occupancy of the premises without affecting the protection afforded by the Extended Coverage Endorsement.

WINDSTORM AND HAIL PROVISIONS

Hazards Not Covered—While the perils of Windstorm and Hail are brought within the coverage of the policy by the Extended Coverage Endorsement, certain types of Windstorm and Hail losses are specifically excluded. There is no liability for loss caused directly or indirectly by

1. Frost or cold weather.

2. Ice (other than hail), snowstorm, tidal wave, high water whether driven by wind or not.

NOTE: The exclusion applies even if the tidal wave or high water is driven by the wind. Ordinarily, when wind is the proximate cause of a loss, there is coverage. Thus, if the wind were to uproot a tree and cause it to fall on insured property, the resultant damage would be covered. The specific type of losses enumerated, however, are not covered.

There is no liability for damage caused by water, rain, snow, sand or dust to the interior of any building or the property within the building unless the wind or hail first does actual damage to the roof or walls of the building. If such damage to the building is sustained, the policy will pay for loss caused by the water, rain, snow, sand or dust entering through openings made by the wind or hail.

There is no coverage for loss or damage by wind or hail to:

1. Grain, hay, straw or other crops outside of buildings
2. Windmills, windpumps or their towers
3. Crop silos or their contents
4. Metal smokestacks
5. When outside of buildings, awnings or canopies (fabric or slat), including their supports, signs, radio or television antennas including their lead-in wiring, masts or towers
6. Lawns, trees, shrubs or plants.

The property excluded above may be insured as a separate item for an additional premium charge.

Some forms also enumerate as excluded from coverage, unless specifically endorsed for an additional premium, fences, screening and supports enclosing pools, patios, seawalls, greenhouses, hothouses, trellises, pergolas, cabanas, wharves, docks, piers, boathouses, bulkheads or other structures located over water.

In some states, liability for such classes of excluded property is assumed, if the policy is subject to Coinsurance.

Windstorm and Hail Deductibles—The Extended Coverage Endorsement written in many territories includes a Deductible clause applicable in some cases to the perils of Windstorm and Hail only; in others, to all the perils of the Endorsement. (see below). When such Deductible is included, the Insured will have to bear the initial part of any loss (generally $50) caused by windstorm or hail. The Company is liable only for the excess of any loss over the amount of the Deductible, or the applicable limit of liability, whichever is less.

In some states, the inclusion of a Deductible is optional with the Insured and may be removed by payment of an additional premium. In other territories, a Deductible is mandatory, while some states have no provision of this kind. Futhermore, practices vary as to the type of property to which such Deductible applies, some states requiring a Deductible on buildings only, others on both buildings and contents. Some states prohibit Deductibles except on farm property, or permit its use only in certain areas. The reader is urged to check local rules as they apply on this score.

In many jurisdictions, the Windstorm and Hail Deductible on contents applies only when such contents are in the open. It can be seen that for an Insured in such territory whose property is entirely enclosed within a building, the Extended Coverage endorsement *with* Deductible provides no less coverage than without such Deductible.

Almost all states make it mandatory that all Fire policies covering a *dwelling* incorporate a Deductible, applicable either to all the perils of the policy, or those of Windstorm and Hail under the Extended Coverage Endorsement. Such a deductible is usually either for $50 or $100.

OTHER PROVISIONS

Smoke Provisions—While the Extended Coverage Endorsement adds the peril of "smoke" to a Fire insurance policy, only loss by smoke of a specified kind is covered. As used in the Endorsement, it means only smoke due to a sudden, unusual, and faulty operation of a heating or cooking unit when such unit is connected to a chimney by a smoke pipe or by a vent, and while in or on the described premises. Furthermore, smoke from fireplaces or industrial appliances is *not* covered.

To be covered, the loss must be one which satisfies all the conditions stated in the clause. Thus, if the unit is a heating or cooking unit *not* connected to a chimney by a smoke pipe, as a gas range in an apartment, there would be no coverage. If the unit which causes the damage is a heating unit connected to a chimney, but located on a neighbor's premises, there would be no coverage. Any heating unit or cooking unit used for industrial purposes would not be covered, etc.

(Smoke from a hostile fire is covered under the basic Fire insurance policy.)

Explosion Provisions—Under the Explosion provisions of the Extended Coverage Endorsement, the Company is liable for all explosion losses except the explosion, rupture, or bursting of steam boilers, steam pipes, steam turbines or steam engines if owned by, or leased by or actually operated under the control of the Insured. It is stipulated that sonic boom, bursting of moving parts of machinery caused by centrifugal force or mechanical breakdown, electric arcing, water hammer, the bursting of water pipes and bursting due to expansion or swelling of the contents of any building due to water or the rupture, bursting or operation of pressure relief devices are *not* explosions within the meaning of the Explosion provisions of the Endorsement.

Coverage against loss due to sonic boom may be provided by endorsement of the policy under the Sonic Shock Wave Endorsement.

Any explosion other than the kind specifically excluded would be covered; e. g., explosion of gases, gasoline, naphtha or other volatiles, explosion of devices using compressed air, etc.

Only the explosion of the steam or water containing vessel in a boiler is excluded. If the explosion originates in the fire-box or combustion chamber from accumulated gases or unconsumed fuels, the loss is covered, even if the fire-box or combustion chamber is part of a steam vessel.

Only the explosion of steam vessels which are owned by, or leased by or actually operated under the control of the Insured is excluded.

Thus, explosion of a steam boiler located in a neighbor's building, or of a steam boiler in the basement of an apartment house causing damage to an insured's property would be covered, except only if the vessel were owned by, or leased by or actually operated under the control of the Insured.

Riot, Riot Attending a Strike, Civil Commotion Provisions—Riot is excluded under the basic Fire insurance policy except if fire ensues, and then only for the damage by fire. Under the Extended Coverage Endorsement, the policy is extended to cover direct damage caused by riot or civil commotion.

The term "riot" is a statutory one, defined in the laws of each state. A fairly general definition of riot states: "Whenever three or more persons, having assembled for any purpose, disturb the public peace by using force or violence to any other person, or to property, or threaten or attempt to commit such disturbance, or to do an unlawful act by the use of force or violence, accompanied with the power of immediate execution of such threat or attempt, they are guilty of riot."

Civil Commotion is defined as "an uprising among a group of people which occasions a serious and prolonged disturbance and infraction of civil order, not attaining the status of war or armed insurrection."

If damage were caused by one or two persons, or by a large group acting in a manner that was not construed as a riot or a civil commotion, there would be no coverage. Thus, if a group of mischievous boys or vandals defaced or damaged property, there would be no coverage under the Extended Coverage Endorsement.

The coverage is extended to include direct loss caused by striking employees during a sit-down strike, provided the loss is caused by employees of the owner or tenant of the building. Such loss is covered whether or not the striking employees are acting in a riotous manner. Damage caused by persons *other* than striking employees is covered only if the acts constitute a riot.

Under the Riot portion of the Extended Coverage Endorsement, coverage is also afforded for loss from pillage or looting occurring during the riot at the place of the riot.

Loss caused by change in temperature or interruption of operations resulting from riot or strike or occupancy by striking employees or civil commotion is not covered. Thus, if the employees of a greenhouse were to occupy their place of work, any direct damage caused by them *would* be covered, but not loss due to their failure to maintain proper temperatures.

Aircraft and Vehicles Provisions—The Extended Coverage Endorsement affords coverage for loss or damage caused by actual physical contact of an aircraft or vehicle with the property insured under the policy or with the building containing the property. It also covers damage by objects falling from an aircraft. The term "aircraft" includes self-propelled missiles and spacecraft.

Physical contact of the vehicle or aircraft is required, except as to objects falling from aircraft. If a passing truck catapulted a rock into an insured building, there would be no coverage.

PACIFIC COAST, TEXAS—The Extended Coverage Form used in these territories does not require actual physical contact of the vehicle. Any direct damage caused by a vehicle or aircraft would be covered.

Excluded is any loss caused by a vehicle owned or operated by the Insured or a tenant, and damage *to* fences, driveways, walks or lawns, or to trees, shrubs or plants.

Since the Form defines "vehicle" as vehicles running on land or tracks, and not aircraft, the exclusion of damage to fences, driveways, walks, lawns, trees, shrubs or plants does not apply when such loss is caused by aircraft.

The clause specifically excludes loss *to* any aircraft or vehicle or their contents.

VANDALISM AND MALICIOUS MISCHIEF ENDORSEMENT

THE RIOT AND CIVIL COMMOTION provisions of the Extended Coverage Endorsement do not cover damage caused by vandals or by persons acting maliciously. These perils may be insured by attaching a Vandalism and Malicious Mischief Endorsement to a Fire insurance policy. The Endorsement may be attached only to a Fire insurance policy which contains the Extended Coverage Endorsement.

The Endorsement covers all wilful or malicious physical injury to or destruction of insured property, with the following exceptions:

1. Glass which is part of the building (other than glass building blocks) or which is part of an outside structure or sign is not covered.

2. There is no coverage for loss by pilferage, theft, burglary or larceny. An exception is made for damage to a *building*. Wilful or malicious mischief injury to such property is covered, even if committed by thieves or burglars. This exception does not extend to contents or any property other than buildings. (Some Forms do not contain this exception, and the reader is urged to check in his own territory.)

3. No coverage is afforded for loss or damage caused by explosion of steam boilers, steam pipes, steam turbines, steam engines or rotating parts of machinery caused by centrifugal force if owned by, or leased by or actually operated under the control of the Insured.

NOTE: This exclusion is identical with the one spelled out in the Explosion section of the Extended Coverage Endorsement. Explosion of any other kind of vessel, whether caused maliciously or accidentally, would be covered under the Extended Coverage Endorsement.

4. There is no coverage for loss caused by depreciation, decay, deterioration, change in temperature or humidity, or loss of market. These are considered indirect losses and, as such, are not covered.

5. There is no coverage under the Vandalism and Malicious Mischief Endorsement if the premises are vacant beyond 30 consecutive days.

NOTE: Most jurisdictions now restrict unoccupancy as well as vacancy, and unoccupancy beyond 30 consecutive days suspends the coverage of the policy. The restriction on *unoccupancy* does NOT apply to dwellings, nor to certain seasonal risks like schools or canning factories which are unoccupied during periods of non-use which are normal for such operations.

NOTE: The Vacancy *and* Unoccupancy restrictions do not apply to buildings in course of construction. A recent court case held that buildings under *re*-construction are *not* exempt from the restrictions.

It should be noted that the courts usually hold that only a sane, sober person of age can commit malicious mischief. Thus, it is frequently ruled that a child below the age of seven cannot be deemed to have committed malicious mischief.

Deductible—In a number of states, Vandalism and Malicious Mischief is written subject to a mandatory deductible.

ARKANSAS, DISTRICT OF COLUMBIA, ILLINOIS, INDIANA,

KANSAS, MISSOURI, TENNESSEE, VIRGINIA, WISCONSIN—The Endorsement contains a Deductible of 2% of the amount of insurance, with a minimum of $100 and a maximum of $250 on dwellings; a $250 minimum and $2,500 maximum on commercial property.
CONNECTICUT, RHODE ISLAND—Same as ARKANSAS above, except that there is no maximum limit in policies covering commercial risks.
DELAWARE, PENNSYLVANIA—In policies covering owner-occupied dwellings, the Deductible is a flat $50; on all other property, it is 1% of the amount of insurance, subject to a minimum of $100 and a maximum of $1,000.
NEBRASKA, SOUTH DAKOTA—Same as ARKANSAS above, except that the Deductible does not apply to insurance on dwellings.
OHIO—Same as ARKANSAS above except that there is an optional $50 Deductible.
MARYLAND—Same as ARKANSAS above except that the percentage is 1%, subject to a $100 minimum and $1,000 maximum.
MICHIGAN, MINNESOTA—Same as ARKANSAS above except that there is a flat $50 Deductible on dwelling risks.
NEW JERSEY—The Deductible is $100 on dwellings; $10,000 on institutional and manufacturing risks.
WYOMING—A flat $50 Deductible is applied to dwellings; $250 on commercial property.

DWELLING BUILDING(S) AND CONTENTS—BROAD FORM

The Dwelling Building(s) and Contents—Broad Form is available to owners or occupants of private dwellings to cover their building structures or their household contents. This coverage is also part of several of the package Homeowners policies, which are analyzed in Chapter 34.

The Dwelling Building(s) and Contents — Broad Form is attached to the Standard Fire insurance policy. In all, it covers 19 specific perils, including those of the basic Fire policy. The exclusions (discussed below under HAZARDS NOT COVERED) apply differently to the various perils assumed under the policy. For this reason, the 19 hazards are set down in a numbered sequence, and the exclusions which follow refer back to the corresponding perils.

HAZARDS COVERED

(1) Fire and Lightning. (These are the perils of the Standard Fire Insurance Policy discussed in Chapters 2 and 3.)

(2) Windstorm; (3) Hail; 4) Explosion; 8) Riot, Riot Attending A Strike and Civil Commotion; (9) Aircraft; (10) Vehicles; (11) Smoke.

These are the perils of the Extended Coverage Endorsement, discussed at the beginning of this chapter. It is important to note that there are several respects in which the Dwelling Building(s) and Contents—Broad Form is broader than the Extended Coverage Endorsement, as follows:

There is no restriction of damage by vehicles to that caused by actual physical contact of the vehicle with the insured property. Thus, where a passing truck catapults a stone against the Insured's property, the Extended Coverage might be held to provide no coverage since there was no physical contact between the vehicle and the insured property. The Broad Form under discussion would clearly protect against such loss. Furthermore, there is no exclusion of loss by a vehicle owned or operated by the Insured or a tenant, EXCEPT as respects damage caused by such individual to walks, lawns, trees, shrubs and plants. If a person *other* than the Insured or his tenant caused such loss, there would be coverage.

The Dwelling Building(s) and Contents—Broad Form is also less limited as respects the coverage under the Smoke provisions. Under the Extended Coverage Endorsement, coverage on smoke damage is restricted to such as arises from the sudden, unusual and faulty operation of a heating or cooking unit which is connected to a chimney or vent. The offending unit must be on the described premises. There is also no coverage for smoke from fireplaces. Under the Dwelling Building(s) and Contents—Broad Form, any damage by smoke is covered except from agricultural smudging or industrial operations.

(6) Vandalism and Malicious Mischief. (This peril is discussed directly before this section on the Dwelling Building(s) and Contents Broad Form.)

(7) Burglars—This coverage is not to be confused with Theft or Burglary insurance, as it does *not* apply to property taken by the burglars, but only to damage done.

(12) Falling Objects—Damage to property by trees felled by a windstorm would be covered under the basic Extended Coverage Endorsement, since windstorm was the proximate cause of the loss, but there would be no coverage for fall of trees otherwise caused. Under the Dwelling Building(s) and Contents Broad Form, damage by fall of trees would be covered, no matter how caused. There is *no* coverage however for damage to outdoor equipment, fences, trees and similar property.

(13) Weight of Ice, Snow or Sleet— Coverage under this peril is subject to an exclusion for loss to outdoor equipment, fences, driveways, walks, lawns, trees, shrubs and plants or retaining walls and bulkheads not constituting part of the building. There is no coverage for loss of or damage to outdoor radio and television antennas, including their lead-in wiring, masts or towers, outdoor equipment, gutters and downspouts, cloth awnings, fences, lawns, trees, shrubs or plants. Such property is covered however if damaged as a direct result of collapse of the building.

(14) Collapse—This peril is subject to an exclusion applicable to such property as is enumerated under (13) above. Furthermore, there is no coverage for settling, cracking, shrinkage, bulging or expansion.

(15) Water Damage Provisions—The policy covers the perils of accidental discharge of water or steam from within a plumbing, heating or air conditioning system or domestic appliance. The coverage includes any necessary tearing out or replacing of any part of the building covered, but not the cost of repairing or replacing the plumbing, heating or air conditioning systems or appliances, or any part thereof.

(16) Cracking, Burning or Bulging of Hot Water Systems—The basic Extended Coverage Endorsement covers damage by explosion but not when such explosion originates from within steam boilers, steam pipes, steam turbines which are owned, operated or controlled by the Insured or located within the described building.

The Dwelling Building(s) and Contents—Broad Form closes the gap in the Extended Coverage Endorsement and covers *any* explosion originating in steam or hot water systems caused by the pressure of water or steam or by a deficiency of water or steam. It includes losses resulting from the tearing asunder, cracking, burning or bulging of such system. The bursting of a water system by ice is not covered.

The Deductible clause (to be discussed later under FOR HOW MUCH) applies to explosions, but only when the particular loss is NOT covered under the basic Extended Coverage Endorsement. Thus, the explosion of gas accumulated within the fire-box of a heating unit would be covered in full, since this peril is part of the basic Extended Coverage Endorsement.

(17) Glass Breakage Provisions—If glass is broken as a result of fire and lightning, the basic Fire insurance provides coverage. If windstorm, explosion or other peril of the Extended Coverage Endorsement causes breakage of glass, the loss is covered under the Extended Coverage Endorsement. Under the terms of the Dwelling Building(s) and Contents Broad Form, all breakage of glass constituting part of the building is covered, no matter how caused. There is no coverage for glass which is not part of the building like mirrors and other glass objects contained in the building.

(18) Freezing of Plumbing, Heating, Air Conditioning Systems and Domestic Appliances—Coverage is afforded against all loss of this kind, subject only to the exclusions discussed below under HAZARDS NOT COVERED.

(19) Accidental Injury to Electrical Appliances—The policy covers sudden and accidental injury to electrical appliances, devices, fixtures and wiring, except tubes, transistors and similar electronic components resulting from electrical currents artificially generated.

HAZARDS NOT COVERED

GENERAL EXCLUSIONS

As pointed out at the opening of this section on the Dwelling Building(s) and Contents—Broad Form, the policy includes the perils of the Fire insurance policy to which it is attached, and the Extended Coverage Endorsement. Except where indicated to the contrary, all the exclusions basic to those policy provisions apply to the Dwelling Building(s) and Contents—Broad Form.

Several additional exclusions apply to all perils under the Form, as follows:

Earthquake, Volcanic Eruption, Landslide—There is no coverage for any loss caused by, resulting from, contributed to or aggravated by earthquake, volcanic eruption, landslide or any other earth movement. If any such occurrence causes fire or explosion, the Company is liable only for the ensuing loss by the fire or explosion.

Water Damage—All perils are subject to the exclusion of losses due to stipulated sources of water. These are discussed in the opening pages of this chapter under EXTENDED COVERAGE ENDORSEMENT—HAZARDS NOT COVERED—Water Exclusion Clause.

Unoccupancy Exclusion—(applicable to perils 6, 7, 15 and 17)—There is no coverage under any of the four perils enumerated if loss occurs while the building is vacant. Furthermore, if all occupants are away for more than four consecutive days, there is no coverage unless the plumbing, heating and air conditioning systems and domestic appliances have been drained and water supply shut off, OR unless the Insured shall have exercised due diligence with respect to maintaining heat in the building.

Falling Objects—(applicable to peril 12)—There is no coverage for damage to the interior of the building or the property contained in it caused by falling objects unless the building first sustains an actual damage to the exterior of the roof or walls by the falling object. There is, furthermore, no coverage for damage to lawns, trees, shrubs or plants.

Outdoor Antenna—(applicable to perils 12, 13 and 14)—The coverage under these three enumerated perils does not extend to outdoor radio and television antennas including their lead-in wiring, masts or towers, outdoor equipment, gutters and downspouts, cloth awnings, fences, lawns, trees, shrubs or plants. An exception is made for damage to the foregoing classes of property if caused by collapse of a building.

Fences, Pavements, Swimming Pools, etc.—(applicable to perils 13 and 14)—There is no coverage for damage by freezing, thawing or by the pressure of ice or water to fences, pavements, patios, swimming pools, foundations, retaining walls, bulkheads, piers, wharves or docks.

NOTE: The numbering of the perils throughout this section corresponds to those used in the Dwelling Building(s) and Contents—Broad Form.

WHAT IS COVERED

Outbuildings Coverage—Discussed before under DWELLING AND CONTENTS FORM—Outbuildings Coverage.

Rental Value Coverage—The Insured may apply up to 10% of the amount of insurance on the dwelling to cover rental value of the building with respect to a portion of the premises not occupied by him.

Under this extension of coverage, the Company is liable for loss of rental value when access to the premises is prohibited by order of civil authority, to a maximum of two weeks.

Additional Living Expense—The policy is liable with respect to any portion of the building occupied by the Insured for such additional living expenses as he necessarily incurs to continue as nearly as practicable the normal standard of living for his household during the time required, with the exercise of due diligence and dispatch to repair or replace such damaged or destroyed property, or the time required for his household to become settled in permanent quarters. Coverage is also afforded when access to the premises is prohibited by order of civil authority, up to a maximum period of two weeks. No more than 10% of the amount of insurance on the dwelling is available for Additional Living Expense, subject to the further limitation of 10% for the *aggregate* of Rental Value *and* Additional Living Expense.

Improvements and Betterments—If the Insured is not the owner of the premises, he may apply up to 10% of the amount of insurance he is carrying on *contents* to cover improvements and betterments to the premises.

Trees, Shrubs, Plants and Lawns—The Insured may apply up to 5% of the amount of insurance on the dwelling to cover trees, shrubs, plants and lawns, subject to a maximum of $250 on any one tree, plant or shrub. NOTE: The Windstorm and Hail provisions of the Form specifically exclude lawns, trees, shrubs and plants and coverage on such property would be available only under the other 17 perils of the Form.

Debris Removal—Discussed in Chapter 3 under HAZARDS COVERED—Debris Removal.

Liberalization Clause—Discussed in Chapter 3 under HAZARDS COVERED—Liberalization Clause.

PROPERTY NOT COVERED

Foundation Exclusion Clause — Discussed in Chapter 3 under BUILDING AND CONTENTS FORM — PROPERTY NOT COVERED—Foundation Exclusion Clause.

FOR HOW MUCH

Replacement Cost Coverage — Since the Dwelling Building(s) and Contents—Broad Form attached to the Standard Fire insurance policy, it incorporates the "actual cash value" basis of recovery (discussed in Chapter 2 under FOR HOW MUCH—Actual Cash Value).

A second basis for the settlement of loss is available under the policy, but only as respects coverage on the dwelling (not on contents).

When, after a loss, the full cost of repair or replacement to the dwelling is both less than 5% of the amount of insurance *and* less than $1,000.00, the policy will pay the full cost of replacement (without deduction of any depreciation).

Furthermore, if at the time of a loss, the Insured is carrying insurance on the dwelling in an amount not less than 80% of the replacement cost of the structure, the policy will pay the full cost of replacement of any loss, without deduction or depreciation.

If, at the time of a loss, the Insured is not carrying insurance on the dwelling equal to at least 80% of the replacement cost of the building, the Insured's recovery will be limited to (1) the actual cash value of the loss or damage, or (2) the proportion of the full cost of repair or replacement (without deduction for depreciation) of that part of the building damaged or destroyed, which the whole amount of insurance bears to 80% of the full replacement cost of the structure.

EXAMPLE: The Insured owns a private dwelling whose replacement cost is $30,000. The actual cash value of the structure (when deduction for depreciation is taken) is $20,000.00. If at the time of the loss, the Insured is carrying $24,000.00 of insurance (80% of the replacement cost), or more, his loss will be settled on the basis of full replacement cost (without depreciation deduction, or "new for old"). If he is carrying $16,000.00 of insurance, his loss will be settled on the basis of actual cash value. If he is carrying less than $16,000.00 of insurance, and a Coinsurance clause is applicable, his loss will be settled subject to the provisions of the Coinsurance clause, as discussed in Chapter 3 under FOR HOW MUCH—COINSURANCE CLAUSE.

If he is carrying $20,000.00 of insurance on the dwelling (an amount larger than 80% of the actual cash value but less than 80% of the replacement cost), his loss will be settled as follows:

$$\frac{\text{Amount of insurance carried}}{\text{80\% of Replacement cost}} = \frac{\$20{,}000.00}{24{,}000.00} = 5/6 \text{ of loss}$$

The Company is not liable under the Replacement Cost extension of the policy unless and until actual repair or replacement is made.

NOTE: Replacement Cost Coverage is not applicable to carpeting, cloth awnings, domestic appliances, outdoor equipment and roof surfacing.

Deductible Clause—A $50 Deductible applies to all perils of the Broad Form policy but not to the coverage on Rental Value or Additional Living Expense.

Waiver of Inventory Clause—Discussed in Chapter 3 under FOR HOW MUCH—Waiver of Inventory.

WHERE COVERED

Away from Premises—Discussed in Chapter 3 under HOUSEHOLD CONTENTS FORM—WHERE COVERED—10% Away from Premises.

Removal for Preservation or Repair—Instead of the five days' extension granted by the Household Contents Form, the Broad Form covers household goods removed for preservation from perils insured against for 30 days pro rata. Also covered is such property if removed for repairs of damage caused by perils insured against.

Removal Within State—Discussed in Chapter 3 under HOUSEHOLD CONTENTS FORM — WHERE COVERED — Removal Within State. In the Broad Form, the coverage on household property applies only if the removal is to another private residence.

WHEN COVERED

Various restrictions on vacancy and unoccupancy apply to specific coverages under the Broad Form, as outlined above. As respects the other perils, permission may be given for unlimited periods of vacancy and unoccupancy, depending on the protection available to the risk, and the nature of the occupancy, i. e., seasonal, year-round, etc.

OTHER CLAUSES

The Broad Form contains an Alterations and Repairs clause, a Liberalization clause and Mortgagee clauses, similar to those found in the Dwelling and Household Contents Forms.

DWELLING BUILDING(S) SPECIAL FORM

ALL RISK INSURANCE is available to cover private dwellings under the Dwelling Building(s) Special Form. This Form, like the Dwelling Building(s) Broad Form, is attached to the Fire insurance policy. Different from the Broad Form, it cannot be applied to household contents, and may be used only to cover the dwelling structure(s).

HAZARDS COVERED

Where the Broad Form extends coverage of the Fire policy to take in 19 named perils, the Special Form covers against all risks of physical loss, subject only to the stipulated exclusions and limitations.

HAZARDS NOT COVERED

The Special Form does not cover loss caused by:

Wear and tear, deterioration, rust, wet or dry rot, mould, contamination;

Smog, smoke from agricultural smudging or industrial operations;

Birds, vermin, insects or domestic animals;

Mechanical breakdown, settling, cracking, shrinkage, bulging or expansion of pavements, patios, foundations, walls, floors, roofs or ceilings; unless loss from a peril not excluded by the policy ensues, and the Company shall then be liable only for such ensuing loss.

Earthquake, Landslide or Earth Movement — Discussed under DWELLING BUILDING(S) BROAD FORM AND CONTENTS —HAZARDS NOT COVERED.

Water Exclusion—Discussed in the opening section of this chapter under EXTENDED COVERAGE ENDORSEMENT — HAZARDS NOT COVERED.

Freezing During Vacancy or Unoccupancy—Discussed under DWELLING BUILDING(S) AND CONTENTS—BROAD FORM —HAZARDS NOT COVERED—Unoccupancy Exclusion.

Power, Heating and Cooling Failure—Loss caused by the failure of power, heating or cooling apparatus, unless the failure is the result of physical damage to the equipment caused by a peril insured against in the policy. The equipment must be situated on the premises insured in the policy.

Loss to Fences, Walks by Freezing—Discussed under DWELLING BUILDING(S) AND CONTENTS—BROAD FORM—HAZARDS NOT COVERED.

Unoccupancy—If the described building has been vacant beyond 30 days, the policy does not cover loss by vandalism and malicious mischief, theft or attempted theft or glass breakage.

Theft—The Special Form does not cover loss by theft of any property which is not an integral part of the private dwelling or other structure, or from a building in course of construction, unless loss by fire, smoke, explosion, water not otherwise excluded, or glass breakage ensues from the theft or an attempt at theft, in which case, the Company will be liable only for the ensuing loss.

WHAT IS COVERED

Outbuildings Coverage — Discussed under DWELLING AND CONTENTS FORM—WHAT IS COVERED—Outbuildings Coverage.

Rental Value Coverage and Additional Living Expense — Discussed under DWELLING BUILDING(S) AND CONTENTS — BROAD FORM—WHAT IS COVERED.

Trees, Shrubs, Plants and Lawns—While the Special Form provides All Risk insurance, as respects trees, shrubs, plants and lawns, it affords coverage on a named perils basis. The Insured may apply up to 5% of the amount of insurance up to a maximum of $250 on any one tree, shrub or plant for loss to such property if caused by:

- Fire, lightning (the perils of the Fire policy),
- Explosion, riot, riot attending a strike, civil commotion, aircraft, vehicles, smoke other than from agricultural smudging or industrial operations (all the perils of the Extended Coverage except windstorm and hail),
- Vandalism and malicious mischief,
- Collapse of a building,
- Damage caused by theft or attempted theft except with respect to property taken from the premises.

Debris Removal—Discussed in Chapter 3 under HAZARDS COVERED—Debris Removal Clause.

Liberalization Clause—Discussed in Chapter 3 under HAZARDS COVERED—Liberalization Clause.

PROPERTY NOT COVERED

Foundation Exclusion Clause — Discussed in Chapter 3 under BUILDING AND CONTENTS FORM — PROPERTY NOT COVERED—Foundation Exclusion Clause.

Retaining Walls—There is no coverage for loss to retaining walls not constituting part of the building when caused by the pressure of ice or water.

Radio and Television Antennas—There is no coverage for damage by windstorm, hail, ice, snow or sleet to radio and television antennas and aerials, including their lead-in wiring, masts and towers.

ADDITIONAL PERILS COVERAGE

Farm Property—The Special Form does not cover on any farm dwelling or any farm property as defined. The term "farm" is defined as land which is devoted to the production of hay, fruit, or field crops, or the raising or keeping of livestock, poultry or furbearing animals. When the Insured conducts any of the listed operations only as incidental to his dwelling and consumes all the products he raises, the buildings and contents are not considered farm property. Even if incidental amounts of such products are sold, then all farm buildings and outbuildings are considered farm property and are excluded from coverage.

FOR HOW MUCH

Replacement Cost Coverage—Discussed under DWELLING BUILDING(S) AND CONTENTS BROAD FORM—FOR HOW MUCH—Replacement Cost Coverage.

Deductible Clause—A $50 Deductible applies to all losses except by fire, lightning, all the perils of the Extended Coverage Endorsement, sudden and accidental tearing asunder, cracking, burning, or bulging of steam or hot water systems, vandalism and malicious mischief, theft or attempt at theft. An exception is made for appliances for heating water for domestic consumption, and loss to this class of property is subject to the Deductible. Also, in a seasonal dwelling, the Deductible applies to loss by vandalism and malicious mischief, theft or attempted theft.

NEW YORK—A $50 Deductible applies to damage to electrical appliances caused by lightning.

Waiver of Inventory of Undamaged Property — Discussed in Chapter 3 under FOR HOW MUCH—Waiver of Inventory Clause.

WHERE COVERED

Removal for Preservation or Repair—Discussed under DWELLING BUILDING(S) AND CONTENTS — BROAD FORM — WHERE COVERED.

Vacancy and Unoccupancy—If the insured building is vacant or unoccupied, there is no coverage for loss by freezing to plumbing or heating systems or their appliances, or by leakage or overflow of such systems, unless the Insured shall have exercised due diligence with respect to maintaining heat or unless such appliances have been drained and the water supply shut off.

If the property has been vacant beyond 30 consecutive days, there is no coverage for vandalism and malicious mischief.

OTHER CLAUSES

The Special Form contains an Alterations and Repairs clause, a Liberalization clause, Mortgagee clause, No Control clause, similar to those found in the Dwelling and Household Contents Form.

FLOOD INSURANCE

At the opening of this chapter, under EXTENDED COVERAGE ENDORSEMENT—HAZARDS NOT COVERED—Water Exclusion Clause—it was pointed out that the Endorsement specifically excludes loss by flood, surface water, tidal wave, overflow of bodies of water, the backing up of sewers or drains, the seepage of water through sidewalks, driveways, foundations and similar occurrences.

The insurance industry has long struggled with the problem of providing some coverage against losses of this kind but no practical solution appeared to be possible in light of the fact that the flood hazard was confined to certain areas of the country and was so catastrophic in its potential.

Finally, the Federal Government by means of a subsidy established a program under the Housing and Urban Development Act of 1968 to make limited amounts of Flood insurance available to certain classes of risks in specified areas.

The program which is under the supervision of the United States Department of Housing and Urban Development (HUD) is a cooperative undertaking with the Government and the private insurance industry sharing the risk. The insurance carriers have formed the National Flood Insurers Association which has pledged over $42 million in risk capital. The National Flood Insurers Association appoints a servicing company, generally on a state-wide basis, to disseminate information to the public and the insurance industry, to process all policies and to handle claim adjustments. Every licensed broker and agent is authorized to sell Flood insurance.

Briefly, the Act provides for certain insurance facilities against the perils of flood to be made available to communities which agree to undertake certain land use and control measures.

To further spur the purchase of Flood insurance, the Act provides that any property owner who has been eligible for this coverage for at least one year will be restricted in the amount of Federal disaster benefits he may receive after a flood occurring on or after January 1, 1974. Except for individuals in income brackets too low to permit the buying of this insurance, a property owner's disaster benefits will be reduced by the amount of Flood insurance he *could* have purchased.

The Flood insurance program comes into operation in two stages. The Emergency program becomes operative as soon as a community has met the land use control requirements stipulated in the law and is applicable to any properties in existence on that date.

ADDITIONAL PERILS COVERAGE

The Regular program offers Flood insurance at actuarially determined rates after a rate study of the community has been completed. Separate maximums apply under each of the portions of the program, as follows:

Coverage	At Chargeable Rates	At Actuarial Rates (available only under the Regular Program)
Building	$30,000	$30,000
Contents	5,000	5,000

Maximum limits of coverage for dwelling buildings with only one dwelling unit is $17,500. Additional amounts of insurance up to the maximum are available at actuarial rates.

The Flood insurance program was originally designed to be available only to dwellings of not more than four families and certain types of small business firms. Recently, it has been broadened to include all types of general property under a new General Property Program, including buildings, merchandise and stock, furniture and fixtures. Household and personal property in eligible private dwellings may also be covered. As under the basic Fire policy covering a dwelling, appurtenant structures are covered automatically up to 10% of the amount of insurance on the dwelling; tenant's improvements and betterments *may* be covered to an amount equal to 10% of the coverage on contents.

The policy covers losses resulting from (1) overflow of inland or tidal waters, (2) the unusual and rapid accumulation or runoff of surface waters from any source and (3) mudslides caused by accumulation of water on or under the ground.

The policy includes a Debris Removal clause (discussed in Chapter 3 under PROVISIONS COMMON TO THE VARIOUS FORMS—HAZARDS COVERED—Debris Removal Clause). In the Flood policy, the coverage is broader in one important respect. Where the Fire policy will pay for debris removal only if such is made necessary by an insured loss to the property, the Flood policy will pay for the cost of removing debris following a flood even if the insured property sustained no direct damage by flood. Like the clause in the Fire policy, this extension of coverage does *not* increase the amount of insurance under the policy.

The policy does *not* cover water damage resulting principally from causes on the Insured's property or within his control, or from a condition which does not cause general flooding in the area.

A Deductible equivalent to 2% of the amount of the loss on an occurrence basis, but not less than $200, is mandatory.

The Flood insurance policy does not contain a Coinsurance clause.

As might be expected, losses by flood frequently arise concurrently with heavy windstorms or hurricanes. In such cases, it is sometimes difficult to separate the damage by wind from the flood damage. The National Flood Insurers Association has indicated that it will be willing to submit such disputes to arbitration. If the company writing the coverage against windstorm (as under the Extended Coverage Endorsement) and the flood insurers cannot agree on a distribution of the loss, they will be asked to select a third party to arbitrate the question.

FOR FURTHER READING

ACKERMAN—Insurance
DEMAREST—Know Your Fire Insurance and Extended Coverage
HEDGES—Practical Fire and Casualty Insurance
MAGEE AND BICKELHAUPT—General Insurance
MOWBRAY AND BLANCHARD—Insurance
NATIONAL FLOOD INSURERS ASSOCIATION—Manual of Rules and Rates
POLICY, FORM AND MANUAL ANALYSIS SERVICE

(See Reading List at End of Book)

CHAPTER 6

Business Interruption Insurance

THE FIRE INSURANCE POLICY insures against all *direct* loss by fire and lightning. Direct loss is understood to mean not only the damage actually inflicted by the fire or lightning but also any other damage of which fire is the proximate cause. Thus, an Insured is protected for loss caused by water used to extinguish a blaze, or by smoke from the fire, or any directly connected result of fire like the collapse of a structure, or destruction of property caused by efforts to fight the fire, etc.

There is no coverage, however, under the basic Fire insurance policy for indirect or consequential losses. An Insured who keeps perishables under refrigeration may suffer a substantial loss by spoilage when fire damages the wiring which supplies current to the refrigerating equipment. The basic Fire insurance policy will pay for the damaged wiring and fixtures, but not for the consequential spoilage of the food.

Then again, a comparatively minor fire at a milk plant might cause a complete cessation of operation while the health authorities inspected the premises and made necessary tests. The loss of income to the milk producer during the time his plant is closed is not covered under the Fire insurance policy.

The zoning laws in a particular locality may forbid rebuilding a particular structure except with approved, more expensive materials. If fire destroyed a portion of the building, the owner might have to demolish the rest of the property before rebuilding. The basic Fire insurance policy will pay for the damage done by the fire, but not for the portion of the building that must be demolished as a consequence of the fire.

A newspaper whose presses were damaged by fire might go to great extra expense to have the paper printed at some outside printing plant. Its Fire insurance would reimburse the newspaper for the damage to the presses and plant but not for the extra expense to which it is put as a result of the fire. The types of loss outlined are all consequential and indirect, and as such are not covered under the basic Fire insurance policy.

BUSINESS INTERRUPTION INSURANCE

WHILE THE LOSSES CITED ABOVE are somewhat specialized, almost every going business enterprise, after a fire at its premises, may find itself unable to continue in operation and will suffer a total or partial loss of earnings. The basic Fire insurance policy will pay for the damage to the merchandise, equipment and fixtures, but not for the consequential interruption of operations and the loss of earnings.

The insuring clause of the regular Fire insurance policy states that it will indemnify the Insured for direct loss by fire but "without compensation for loss resulting from interruption of business or manufacture." If a business enterprise is compelled after a fire to suspend or curtail its activities, it may stand to lose a great deal more than the value of the property which was destroyed or damaged. During the period of suspension, the firm will lose not only the profits it would otherwise have earned, but will also have to meet certain continuing expenses like taxes, interest on mortgages and other indebtedness, salaries of executives and employees under contract, maintenance expenses, rent (in some instances), advertising, minimum or fixed charges for services and utilities, etc. If a building is damaged or destroyed by fire, the owner may be entitled to full reimbursement under his Fire insurance for the actual damages sustained by the structure but he will almost always lose the rent income he was receiving until the premises are restored to tenantable condition.

In many instances, the loss caused by the interruption of business or manufacture will far exceed the amount of the actual direct damage. A comparatively trifling fire may shut down a business for a protracted period. Sometimes a fire which does practically no damage to the Insured's property creates a bottleneck which brings operations to a complete halt. Thus, when fire destroyed an arcade which provided the only entrance to a large New York theater, the theater was forced to close down. In many manufacturing firms, damage to one piece of equipment may bring the entire plant to a virtual standstill. In other cases, a business may be dependent on special materials which require extensive aging or processing, or must be imported from afar. The destruction of such stock will cause a severe curtailment of production resulting in extensive loss.

Over and above the direct destruction of physical property and the loss of earnings which a fire may cause, a business may find its credit impaired when it faces a protracted period without earnings. Even a business which has been functioning without extensive credit may find it necessary, when it is shut down by a fire, to borrow money to meet continuing expenses. It is fairly evident of course that a business may experience difficulty in obtaining credit at a time when it is not in operation.

A special form of insurance, Business Interruption insurance (formerly commonly called Use and Occupancy insurance), provides coverage on the earnings that are lost to a business through interruption of its normal operations by fire or lightning or other peril. The Business Interruption forms are attached to the Standard Fire policy and afford protection for loss of earnings due to interruption of the business by the perils insured under the basic Fire insurance policy—fire and lightning. Coverage may also be obtained for interruption by any of the perils of the Extended Coverage Endorsement by attaching such endorsement to the Business Interruption policy.

Business Interruption insurance is always in a separate contract; the form is not attached to the policy which insures the stock and/or the fixtures.

HAZARDS COVERED

The Business Interruption policy will indemnify the Insured for loss of earnings during a total or partial suspension of business when such suspension is caused by fire or lightning damage to the premises or the machinery or equipment and, when an Extended Coverage Endorsement is added to the policy, by any of the perils assumed under this endorsement.

WHAT IS COVERED

The Company is liable for the earnings lost to the Insured because of the interruption of business during the period that it would take to "rebuild, repair or replace the damaged property with the exercise of *due diligence and dispatch.*"

In other words, the policy is not liable for the loss for the entire period until the property is actually restored, but only for the time such repairs should normally take. The Insured may not wish to repair the damage, or may prefer not to restore the property in the form it stood at the time of the loss. Nevertheless, the liability of the Company ceases after such time *as would be required* with the exercise of due diligence and dispatch to rebuild, repair or replace.

Once the premises and machinery are restored (or could have been restored), the Company's liability ends, even though it may take additional time for the Insured's volume of sales or production to return to normal. The policy is not liable for reduction in the volume of sales or for loss of customers, good will, contracts, valuable employees, even if such are irrevocably lost to the business.

In some territories, the Business Interruption policy may be endorsed for an additional premium to extend the period of indemnity beyond the date on which premises and equipment are repaired or replaced, and beyond the period which the policy may allow for replacing stock. This is discussed later under Extended Period of Indemnity.

The policy will not pay for any increase in the time to rebuild, repair or replace the property caused by any local or state ordinance regulating construction or repair of buildings, nor for the interference by strikers *at the premises* with the rebuilding or replacing of damaged property. This clause would not exclude delay caused by strikes away from the premises, as at the premises of a firm supplying building materials, or at a company transporting materials to be used in rebuilding.

The measure of loss is the *future* earnings that would have been earned beginning with the date of the loss and ending on the date the damaged building or equipment or machinery could have been restored. While the experience of the business before the loss is taken into account in arriving at the extent of the loss, it is the *future* earnings that are insured.

The period of indemnity is not limited by the expiration of the policy. If the fire (or other insured peril) occurs while the policy is in force, the Insured is entitled to collect for as long as it would take to replace the damage, even though this would extend past the expiration of the policy.

EXAMPLE: The Insured carries a Business Interruption insurance policy which expires on Jan. 1, 1961. On Dec. 25, 1960, his plant burns down. It takes seven months to rebuild the structure and replace the machinery. The Insured is entitled to indemnity throughout this time, even though it extends past the expiration of his policy.

ALASKA, ARIZONA, CALIFORNIA, IDAHO, MONTANA, NEVADA, UTAH—Specified Time Forms are available under which the maximum period of indemnity is limited to a specified number of months.

Additional Time To Replace Stock—After a fire, the Insured may restore his premises and equipment to the condition they were in before the loss but he may still be unable to resume operations because of damage or destruction of his stock. The Business Interruption policy affords protection for any additional period of suspension made necessary by the destruction of stock, with an important exception in the case of manufacturing risks.

The Forms designed for manufacturing risks exclude loss of earnings due to the delay resulting from damage to finished stock.

Coverage on such loss is available under Profits and Commissions policies or Market Value or Selling Price clauses (to be discussed later).

"Finished stock" is defined as stock manufactured by the Insured which in the ordinary course of the Insured's business is ready for packing, shipment or sale.

Interruption By Civil Authority—After a fire, or other insured peril, the authorities may deny access to the damaged premises in order to complete an investigation, make inspections, tests, etc. The policy covers loss of earnings for not exceeding two weeks during such periods of inactivity, when access to the premises is prohibited as a direct result of damage to or destruction of property *adjacent to* the described premises by a peril insured against. It is generally conceded that loss due to shutdown of the insured premises because of the *threat* of damage from an insured peril would not be sufficient to bring in the coverage of this section of the policy.

Salvage—Expense To Reduce Loss—Over and above the indemnity for loss of earnings, the policy will pay for expenses to reduce the amount of loss, but liability for such expenses does not exceed the amount by which the loss is thereby reduced.

EXAMPLE: An Insured's premises are rendered totally unfit for occupancy. His loss of earnings comes to $1,000 per week. By setting up temporary facilities in a neighboring location, he can reduce the weekly loss to $500. The cost of these substitute arrangements comes to $300 per week. The policy will pay these expenses.

Under similar circumstances, an Insured might be able to reduce his loss by $700 through an expenditure of $800 per week. He might consider this good business since it would help him retain his customers. In this instance, the Company is not liable for more than $700 of the additional expenses incurred—the amount by which the loss is reduced.

Electronic Data Loss—The policy contains a limitation on losses resulting from damage to or destruction of media for, or programming records pertaining to electronic equipment. Loss of this kind is covered for no more than 30 days UNLESS other property has been damaged by the same occurrence and more than 30 days is required to restore such other property. This limitation may be extended or deleted entirely by the attachment of the Media for Electronic Data Processing Extension Endorsement for a period of 90 days, 180 days or unlimited time.

BUSINESS INTERRUPTION INSURANCE FORMS

BUSINESS INTERRUPTION insurance is written by attaching a Business Interruption Form to the basic Fire insurance policy. One form, Gross Earnings Form No. 3, is used for mercantile and non-manufacturing risks; risks engaged in manufacture use Gross Earnings Form No. 4.

A non-manufacturing risk differs from a mercantile risk. The latter is a business which derives its earnings from the sale of commodities. A non-manufacturing risk is a service business which derives its major revenue neither from manufacture nor from the sale of products; e. g., hotels, restaurants, theatres, bowling alleys, barber shops, etc.

The amount in a B. I. policy is based on the probable prospective earnings insured under the policy, for one year.

HAZARDS COVERED

Since the Business Interruption Forms attach to the basic Fire policy, they cover the perils of that contract (discussed in Chapter 2). The coverage may be broadened by the inclusion of Extended Coverage and Vandalism and Malicious Mischief (discussed in Chapter 5).

WHAT IS COVERED

The policy covers the ACTUAL LOSS SUSTAINED by the Insured (to be discussed later under FOR HOW MUCH) due to interruption of his business by a peril insured against in the policy. The measure of loss is the length of time as would be required with the exercise of due diligence and dispatch to rebuild, repair or replace such part of the property as has been damaged or destroyed.

NOTE: The period of time for which indemnity will be paid is not limited by the expiration date of the policy. Thus, if an Insured carries Business Interruption insurance in a policy with an expiration date of September 1, 1961, and sustains a loss on August 15, 1961, which it is agreed will require three months to replace or repair, he will collect his loss for the three-month period, even though this carries past the expiration date of his policy.

Ordinary Payroll Exclusion

The Insured has the option of excluding from the coverage any expense of ordinary payroll. This is done by attaching the Ordinary Payroll Exclusion Endorsement (A). The endorsement defines ordinary payroll as "the entire payroll expense for all employees of the Insured, except officers, executives, department managers, employees under contract and other important employees." Excluding such payroll expense may reduce the amount of insurance that must be carried in order to comply with the Coinsurance clause of the policy (discussed later under FOR HOW MUCH).

In calculating payroll expense, an employer may include premiums paid by him for Workmen's Compensation insurance, his contributions to Social Security, Unemployment Insurance, and in states where Non-Occupational Disability insurance is mandatory, the premiums paid by him for such insurance.

Ordinary Payroll — Limited Coverage Endorsement (B)

An Insured may provide coverage for ordinary payroll for a limited period of time. Such a course would be dictated by his need to keep wage workers on the payroll during a relatively short suspension of business, but not otherwise. The Ordinary Payroll — Limited Coverage Endorsement (B) provides coverage for such payroll expense which must necessarily continue during the interruption of business for not exceeding 90 days. (The period may be extended to 120 days, 150 days or 180 days, for an increase in premium.)

HAZARDS NOT COVERED

As mentioned above, Business Interruption insurance is written by attaching a Business Interruption Form to the basic Fire insurance policy. The exclusions of the Fire policy (discussed in Chapter 2 under HAZARDS NOT COVERED) apply to this coverage. In addition, the Form contains several special exclusions.

Construction Ordinance—The policy will not pay for any increase of loss which is due to any local or state ordinance or law regulating construction or repair of buildings or structures.

Cancellation of Lease, Order, Contract — There is no liability under the Business Interruption Insurance Form for the suspension, lapse or cancellation of any lease or license, contract or order.

Strike Interference—The Company is not liable for any increase of loss due to interference by strikers or other persons with rebuilding, repairing or replacing the property or with the resumption of business.

FOR HOW MUCH

Actual Loss Sustained

When a fire (or other peril) interrupts activities of a business, there are almost always certain non-continuing expenses, which the business does not have during the suspension period. Many leases, for example, provide that the tenant is not required to pay rent for any periods during which the premises are unfit for use. In most instances, the Insured is able to reduce his regular payroll until business is resumed. Expenses like telephone, light, heat, power, water, and similar charges may be avoidable during the time the business is not functioning, or may be sharply reduced.

The Business Interruption policy is liable only for the *actual loss sustained,* and will therefore pay the Insured the amount of the gross earnings he would have realized had no loss occurred, *less* the amount of his non-continuing expenses.

Thus, assume an Insured operates a store with average weekly sales of $1,000, and that this gross revenue is normally distributed as follows:

Salaries and other expenses which would continue after a loss	$ 200.00
Cost of merchandise	500.00
Wages and other expenses which would not continue	150.00
Net profit	150.00
	$1,000.00

If a fire causes total suspension of the business for one week, the Insured will be entitled to collect $350.00, arrived at as follows:

Total revenue that would have been realized had no loss occurred	$1,000.00
LESS expenses that do not continue and cost of merchandise	650.00
ACTUAL LOSS SUSTAINED	$ 350.00

It can be seen that if the Insured collects $350, his actual loss sustained, he will be able to pay the expenses that must be met, and will also have the profit he would normally have enjoyed. He is in the same financial position he would have been in had no loss occurred.

The policy, we have seen, covers only such earnings as would have actually been realized by the business had no loss occurred. If there would have been no earnings during a particular period, there is no recovery under the policy.

Thus, if an Insured has a loss at a time when he is not producing or selling, as during a slack season or a strike, or when business is temporarily at a standstill, he is not entitled to any recovery under his Business Interruption insurance.

On the other hand, if the loss occurs when business activity is at a height, the policy will pay the full amount of the *actual loss sustained* during the period of suspension. Furthermore, a plant may sustain a loss when it is in a slack season, but if the period of time required to rebuild, repair or replace would carry into what would normally be the active period, the policy will pay for the loss of earnings during what would have been the "busy" season.

The Business Interruption policy, as pointed out above, pays not only for the loss of *profits*, but also for all loss of earnings. For this reason, a business which is not earning any net profit may still require Business Interruption insurance to cover the expenses which it would have to meet even when loss curtails operations. As a matter of fact, a business which has been operating without profit, or even at a loss, may experience greater difficulty in meeting continuing expenses than one which has been yielding a good profit, and may therefore stand in greater need of Business Interruption insurance than its more fortunate competitor.

It is extremely important to understand that the Business Interruption policy will not necessarily indemnify the Insured for all the loss he may sustain. As was pointed out, the policy covers the

ACTUAL LOSS SUSTAINED, but only for the length of time it would take to restore, rebuild or replace the damaged property. An Insured may find after restoration of his damage that he has lost customers to his competitors which he cannot recover, or that a valuable contract or lease is not being renewed. There is no coverage for any such loss which extends past the time which it would take to rebuild or replace.

Extended Period of Indemnity—As pointed out, the Business Interruption policy provides coverage for such loss as is sustained during the period it would take with the exercise of due diligence to repair, rebuild or replace. The loss of earnings which may continue beyond this point is not covered.

In almost all states, the policy may be extended by payment of an additional premium to cover the ACTUAL LOSS SUSTAINED during such additional time as would be required to restore the Insured's business to the condition that would have existed had no loss occurred. Such coverage is limited to a stipulated number of days beyond the date of completion of repairs.

COINSURANCE REQUIREMENTS

Business Interruption insurance policies contain a Coinsurance clause under which the Insured agrees to carry a minimum amount of insurance. If he carries less than the stipulated amount, he will have to bear a portion of any loss himself. In Business Interruption insurance, the Insured has a choice of four Coinsurance percentages—50%, 60%, 70% or 80%—PROVIDED he does not use either the Ordinary Payroll Exclusion Endorsement (A) or the Ordinary Payroll-Limited Coverage Endorsement (B). It is optional with the Insured which Coinsurance percentage he elects to use in his policy. The Company is liable under its policy for no greater percentage of loss than the amount of insurance carried bears to the stipulated Coinsurance percentage of the gross earnings that would have been earned in the *twelve-month* period following the date of the loss.

If the gross earnings of an Insured (sales less cost of merchandise) in the twelve months after a loss *would* have been $100,000, and he elects to buy Business Interruption insurance with a 50% Coinsurance clause, he must carry at least $50,000 of insurance. If he carries less, he will be a coinsurer and will have to share in any loss.

Thus, if he carried $30,000 of insurance, he would be entitled to receive only 3/5ths of any loss, no matter how small. This same Insured with an 80% Coinsurance clause in his policy must carry not less than $80,000 of insurance; if the Coinsurance percentage is

70%, he must carry at least $70,000, etc.

In some states, a manufacturer insuring under the Gross Earnings Form may deduct the cost of power, heat and refrigeration consumed in production operations, provided these expenses will not continue under contract after an interruption, and provided the policy is written with a Coinsurance clause of not less than 80%.

If either the Payroll Exclusion or Payroll Limitation Endorsement is attached, the Insured must accept a Coinsurance percentage of not less than 80%. Illustrated next is the effect of the Coinsurance requirement under each of the payroll coverages available to an Insured:

Assume a manufacturer has a net sales value of production of $1,000,000 per annum. The cost of the raw materials and supplies consumed directly in converting such raw stock into his finished product comes to $500,000. The Insured's entire ordinary payroll expense is $300,000 per annum. If the Insured elects not to eliminate any of his ordinary payroll, he can use a 50, 60, 70 or 80% Coinsurance clause. The percentage he chooses will be applied to $500,000, his "gross earnings," as defined in the policy (see below).

If he elects to eliminate his entire ordinary payroll, using the Ordinary Payroll Exclusion Endorsement (A), he must use an 80% (or higher) Coinsurance clause. This percentage will be applied to $200,000—his total annual production less the $500,000 of raw materials and less the $300,000 of ordinary payroll.

If the Insured decides to cover his ordinary payroll for a limited period, using the Ordinary Payroll-Limited Coverage Endorsement (B), he must carry at least 80% of $200,000 arrived at as above, *plus* 80% of his payroll for the period of time for which payroll is covered.

> ALASKA, ARIZONA, CALIFORNIA, IDAHO, MONTANA, NEVADA, UTAH—Under the Specified Time Forms available in these states, ten Coinsurance percentages are offered, depending on the period of indemnity chosen. The percentages are 25%, 33%, 42%, 50%, 58%, 67%, 75%, 83%, 92% or 100%.

Certain risks may be eligible for a special form which waives Coinsurance requirements. These forms will be discussed later in the chapter under Agreed Amount Forms.

OTHER CLAUSES

The Business Interruption Forms contain several clauses which are identical with those found in Fire insurance forms covering stock, fixtures, machinery, etc., as discussed in Chapters 2 and 3:

Electrical Apparatus
Alterations and Repairs
Liberalization Clause
Pro Rata Liability.

EARNINGS INSURANCE

This form of Business Interruption insurance is available to any non-manufacturing risk (mercantile and service businesses). It is designed primarily for the small businessman. Recently, a form of Earnings insurance has been introduced which is available to manufacturing risks.

Earnings Insurance is a Gross Earnings Form, similar to the Gross Earnings Forms discussed before. The most important difference between these two Gross Earnings Forms is that Earnings Insurance does not contain any Coinsurance clause. An Insured who does not carry sufficient insurance will not have to share in a loss himself, except if the loss exceeds the amount of his insurance.

Monthly Limitation—Earnings insurance policies do not contain a Coinsurance requirement, but the Insured is limited in the amount he can collect for any single month of business interruption. He is offered a choice of one of three percentages, 16⅔, 25 or 33⅓%. For any period of loss of 30 consecutive days, or fraction thereof, the selected percentage of the amount of the policy is the maximum which is recoverable. Thus, a merchant who is carrying $30,000 of Earnings insurance in a policy with a 25% Monthly Limitation can collect for any shutdown or interruption of 30 consecutive days no more than $7,500; if he had selected the 33⅓% Monthly Limitation, his maximum recoverable loss for any 30-day consecutive loss would be $10,000; under the 16⅔ Limitation, he could collect no more than $5,000. There is no pro-rating for shorter periods of interruption. If the interruption of business does not go beyond one week, or three days, he can still recover up to the amount of the selected Monthly Limitation.

The rate per $1,000 of insurance under this Form is highest with the 33⅓% Limitation, lower for the 25% and lowest for the 16⅔% Limitation.

NOTE: "Gross Earnings" as used in the Business Interruption policy has a very specific meaning, which should be clearly grasped.

In Form No. 3, for mercantile and non-manufacturing risks, "gross earnings" is defined as: Total net sales and other earnings derived from the business *less* the cost of merchandise sold, including packaging materials therefor and materials and supplies consumed directly in supplying the services sold by the Insured and services pre-purchased from outsiders for resale which do not continue under contract.

In Form No. 4, for manufacturing risks, "gross earnings" is defined as the total net sales value of production and the total net sales of merchandise and other earnings derived from the business, less raw stock from which such production is derived and supplies consumed directly in converting such raw stock into finished stock or in supplying the services sold by the Insured and merchandise sold and services purchased from outsiders for resale which do not continue under contract.

AGREED AMOUNT FORMS

As pointed out in the preceding Section, the Coinsurance clause requires of the Insured that he maintain insurance in an amount equal to a given percentage of the loss of earnings that *would have been earned* in the 12-month period following the date of the loss. It is understandably not too simple to keep insurance in line with such a requirement, since it calls for projecting earnings into a future period. Certain types of business enterprises are eligible for a form of Business Interruption insurance with an Agreed Amount Endorsement.

Under this endorsement the amount of insurance required is an agreed amount *in dollars* instead of a *percentage* of the prospective earnings for twelve months following the date of the loss. If the Insured maintains the amount of insurance agreed upon in the endorsement, the Coinsurance clause is waived.

Generally, this endorsement is available for use by all mercantile, non-manufacturing or manufacturing risks written under the Gross Earnings Business Interruption Forms, without restriction as to construction or fire protective devices. It is further provided that only risks which have been in business for at least one year shall qualify for this form of Business Interruption insurance.

The Insured is required to file a statement of his earnings for the past period and an estimate of his earnings for the period covered by the Agreed Amount Endorsement. In some states, the statement must be certified by an auditor.

PREMIUM ADJUSTMENT FORMS

When the Premium Adjustment Endorsement is attached to a Business Interruption policy (Gross Earnings Form only), the Insured is required to file a report of his actual earnings for the last available fiscal period. At the end of each succeeding fiscal year, he files a new statement of the actual earnings for the period. If the amount of insurance he has carried is larger than his actual earnings for the period, he is entitled to a return of most of the excess premium. While this Endorsement does not waive the Coinsurance clause, the Insured can protect himself against its penalty by carrying larger amounts of insurance than appear necessary at the beginning of the year, counting on the fact that most of the premium for the not-needed insurance will be returned to him. The Premium Adjustment Endorsement is available to all risks, although practical considerations generally confine its use to larger Insureds.

CONTINGENT BUSINESS INTERRUPTION INSURANCE

CERTAIN BUSINESS ENTERPRISES are so constituted that they are highly dependent on other firms for their supply of essential materials. In modern industry, it is standard practice to rely on contractors and sub-contractors for parts of the product being assembled or manufactured. Then again, a whole series of selling agencies like commission merchants, brokers, and mail order houses are often dependent on an uninterrupted flow of products from other sources.

The opposite side of the picture is presented by producers whose major output is marketed through one or two large outlets, or whose major production is used in another commodity assembled elsewhere. In both types of situation, interruption of activity at the other location will severely reduce or entirely eliminate the firm's earnings, even though its own premises are completely untouched by the fire or other peril.

Contingent Business Interruption insurance is designed to protect an Insured against losses of this kind. There are two Forms in wide use:

Form No. 1—Contributing Properties Business Interruption—covers when the peril strikes a supplier of materials.

Form No. 2—Recipient Properties Contingent Business Interruption insurance—covers when the peril insured strikes a receiver of material.

It is fairly common for one tenant of a shopping center to be responsible for bringing into the center the majority of the shoppers. If the "magnet" store were struck by fire (or other insured peril) and were unable to continue in its normal operations, the neighboring stores might suffer a severe curtailment of income, even though their own premises were, in fact, untouched by the casualty. Similarly, steps taken to prevent the spread of fire might affect the business of the other stores. The Contingent Business Interruption Form may be endorsed to include this type of contingency loss situation.

Off-Premises Power, Light, Heat, Gas, Water Supply Forms—Another form of Contributing Properties Business Interruption insurance is one designed to indemnify an Insured whose operations are suspended because of the failure or interruption of the supply of power, light, heat, gas or water furnished by a public or private utility company. This insurance may be purchased as a separate policy or may be endorsed on the Business Interruption insurance policy for an additional premium charge.

TUITION FEES INSURANCE

COLLEGES AND OTHER EDUCATIONAL INSTITUTIONS which depend on tuition fees usually require a special form of the Business Interruption insurance policy. Since arrangements for school attendance are usually made for an entire school year, a fire which causes a comparatively short suspension of classes might result in the loss of an entire year's revenue. The Form is also available to camps whose situation is similar to that of educational institutions which make charges for tuition.

Thus, if fire damaged a college or private school building on September 1st, and it took two months to restore the building, most of the students would arrange to attend other schools, and the entire year's income would be lost to the school. Business Interruption insurance, which limits the period of recovery to the time to "rebuild, repair or replace" the property, would not meet the needs of such institutions.

Tuition Fees insurance is designed to meet the needs of schools which depend on tuitions for all or part of their support. The insuring clause does not limit the recovery to the time to rebuild, but to the following period: "From the date of the fire to the day preceding the beginning of the next school year following the day on which the property is restored." It is further provided that coverage will be afforded for losses sustained during the next school year if the property cannot be restored within 30 days of the scheduled opening date.

EXAMPLE: A university suffers damage by fire on August 31, 1953. The premises are restored on November 10, 1953. Tuition Fees insurance will cover the loss of tuition fees until September 24, 1954, the day before the opening of the next school year.

FOR FURTHER READING

ACKERMAN—Insurance
CROUCH—Use and Occupancy or Business Interruption Insurance
HEDGES—Practical Fire and Casualty Insurance
HUEBNER AND BLACK—Property Insurance
KLEIN—Business Interruption Insurance
MAGEE AND BICKELHAUPT—General Insurance
MEHR AND CAMMACK—Principles of Insurance
MOWBRAY AND BLANCHARD—Insurance
POLICY, FORM AND MANUAL ANALYSIS SERVICE
RIEGEL, ROBERT AND MILLER—Insurance
(See Reading List at End of Book)

CHAPTER 7

Insuring Other Consequential Damage Losses

RENT OR RENTAL VALUE INSURANCE

MANY LEASES PROVIDE that a tenant will be relieved of rent during any period that the premises he rents are unfit for occupancy. When the premises are partially unusable, the tenant's rent is reduced proportionately. Where the lease is silent on this question, the law of the state may stipulate that the lease will terminate or the rent abate during such periods. In some states, the tenant has the option of terminating his lease if the premises he rents are rendered untenantable by fire.

In any event, damage to a building which renders it totally or partially untenantable will bring in its wake some loss of rent income. Where the rent need not be continued, the owner of the property suffers a loss of rent income, much like the businessman whose production is interrupted by a casualty at his plant. And like the businessman, the property owner will have to meet certain continuing expenses—mortgage payments, interest on other indebtedness, maintenance costs, salaries, etc. In a similar vein, a general lessee who sub-leases premises to others may also suffer a loss of rental income if the premises are rendered totally or partially untenantable due to fire, or other casualty.

Where the tenant is obligated to continue payment of rent even after his premises are rendered unfit for use by fire or other peril (as is often the case under long term leases), the owner of the property will not suffer any loss of income. The *tenant*, however, will have to pay for other space while he continues rent payment to his first landlord. Damage to the premises, under such circumstances, causes the *tenant* a loss of rent.

When the owner of a building occupies the property himself, he may not actually pay himself rent but, if he loses the use of his premises, it will become necessary for him to rent substitute quarters. Damage to the premises in this type of situation will cause the owner a loss of the rental value of the property, which is equivalent to the rent income he could realize if he were to lease the premises to another.

The basic Fire insurance policy, whether purchased by an owner of property who rents to another, or by an owner who occupies the premises himself, or by a tenant, will pay for the direct damage to the buildings or the contents, but will not pay for the loss of rents or rental value. Such loss is a consequential one, and is not covered under the basic Fire policy.

A special form of insurance, Rent insurance, is used to protect the owner of a building for the loss of rent income after a fire (or other peril). The same form of insurance is used to insure a tenant who leases premises, or a building owner who occupies his own property.

How Policy is Written—Rent insurance forms are attached to the Standard Fire insurance policy. Sometimes this insurance is written as a separate policy, although many Building Forms provide for insuring of rents as a separate item under the policy. In insurance on private dwellings, this coverage is almost always provided in the same policy as covers the structure itself.

HAZARDS COVERED

Although there are several Forms under which Rent insurance is written, all policies provide coverage for loss of rents during the period that the building or a portion of it is rendered untenantable by fire or lightning. (Forms to insure seasonal property, buildings in course of construction, and other special situations will be discussed later under Special Rent Insurance Forms.)

Coverage may also be obtained for rent loss caused by any of the perils of the Extended Coverage Endorsement and by Vandalism and Malicious Mischief by attaching the respective endorsements.

As under the Business Interruption policy, the insured is entitled to indemnity for the rent income lost to him beginning on the date of the fire (or other insured peril) and ending on the day on which the building could, with the exercise of due diligence, be restored to the same tenantable condition as it was in before the loss.

In most territories, the policy may be extended by payment of an additional premium to cover the ACTUAL LOSS SUSTAINED during the time that would be required to restore the Insured's premises to the condition that would have existed had no loss occurred.

EXAMPLE: A building owner may have 100% occupancy before a fire damages his property. It takes six months to complete the repairs (with due diligence and dispatch) but when these repairs are complete, occupancy of the insured building has fallen to 60%, and it is several months before full occupancy is restored.

The policy also covers expenses incurred to reduce a loss, to the extent that the loss is thereby reduced.

There is considerable variation among the various Forms as to whether they cover loss of rents only from rented portions or from rented and vacant premises. The reader is urged to check the Forms used in his territory for their provisions on this score.

Some Rent insurance Forms cover rent lost only for those portions of a building as are actually rented at the time of the loss. Such Forms are in general use in the Southeastern States.

Other Forms, used widely in the Middle West, cover loss of rents on premises whether rented or vacant. However, coverage is provided only for the "actual loss sustained," and the Insured, if he would collect for loss of rents on premises which were vacant at the time of a fire, must be able to demonstrate that the premises would have been rented if the loss had not occurred.

On the Pacific Coast, the Insured is offered a choice of insuring only the rented portions, or both the rented and vacant premises. Coverage on the vacant premises is limited to "actual loss of rental income."

In the East, the forms used cover the rental income of the entire property, whether rented or vacant.

Access to Premises—Interruption By Civil Authority—In most territories, the policy also covers loss of rents during such time as access to the premises is denied by order of a civil authority because of a fire or other peril insured against in the policy, provided the prohibition is the direct result of damage to an *adjacent property*. The maximum period for which indemnity will be paid under this provision is two weeks.

It is important to be clear on the fact that the two-week limit applies only to situations where access to the insured premises is denied because there is damage to *adjacent* property. Where access is denied because of damage to insured property, there is no limitation other than the policy's basic test of the time "it would take with the exercise of due diligence to restore the property to the same tenantable condition it was in before the loss."

HAZARDS NOT COVERED

The Rent insurance policy covers increase in the loss of rents caused by any ordinance or law regulating construction, nor by interference with rebuilding caused by strikers or other persons at the premises.

FOR HOW MUCH

The Rent insurance policy will indemnify the Insured for rents or the rental value lost to him as a result of the peril insured against, less any expenses which do not continue after the loss. While the amount of such non-continuing expenses is not usually as important a factor as it is in Business Interruption insurance, there are always some charges which the Insured will be spared, particularly after a total or substantial loss; e. g., elevator service, maintenance, premiums for insurance, the cost of heat, light, power, etc. The policy may be endorsed to cover the loss of profits on sales in the building of electricity, steam, gas, water, watchman service, Muzak, etc.

Coinsurance or Contribution Clauses—Under Rent insurance, the Insured is required to maintain a definite amount of insurance to be entitled to collect in full for a loss. If he fails to carry the required amount of insurance, he will be a coinsurer and will have to bear a portion of the loss himself. The amount of insurance required is based on the rental value of the insured property for the 12-month period following the date of the loss. In most territories, the Insured is not permitted, in arriving at the amount of insurance, to deduct from his gross annual rent income the amount of any expenses which would not continue after the loss.

The Insured is granted a choice of Coinsurance percentages, usually 50%, 75% or 100%. The Company is liable only for the proportion that the amount of insurance carried bears to the stipulated percentage of the *annual* rental income as would have been realized after the loss, less the non-continuing expenses.

NEW YORK—Three Coinsurance percentages are available—60%, 80%, or 100%.

Note that the 12-month period is applicable only to the Coinsurance clause, and establishes the amount of insurance that needs to be carried in order to avoid being co-insured. There is *no* limit on the period of time for which loss is covered, provided it would require such time to rebuild or restore the property with the exercise of due diligence and dispatch.

Note too that the period of recovery is not limited by the expiration date of the policy.

Monthly Limitation Forms—There is no Coinsurance clause, as such, in the Monthly Limitation Forms, but the Insured can collect only a stated fraction of the amount of insurance for any month in which the premises are untenantable. For periods of less than a month, he is entitled to a proportionate share of the monthly indemnity. Most commonly, the maximum indemnity payable during any one month is 1/12th of the amount of insurance, although, in some territories, 1/9th or 1/6th is used.

The Monthly Limitation Form is not as severe in its effects as the two Coinsurance forms. Under the Monthly Limitation clause, an Insured who is not carrying insurance equal to the annual rental value of his premises will have to contribute to any loss which cuts off the total income from the property. On the other hand, if only a portion of the premises is rendered unfit and the Insured continues to receive rent from some of his tenants, he may not be subject to any penalty.

EXAMPLE: The Insured owns a building which is leased to five tenants, each of whom pays $500 a month. After deducting the expenses which would not continue after a fire, his net annual rent income is $24,000. The Insured elects to carry only $18,000 of Rent insurance, in a policy with a 1/12 Monthly Limitation clause. When a fire breaks out at the building, it damages three of the stores and leaves two intact. The building owner continues to collect $1,000 a month from these two tenants, but receives no rent from the three others. His income is reduced by $1,500 per month. Although the Insured cannot collect more than 1/12 of the amount of his policy for any one month, or $1,500, he will in this case be completely reimbursed for the entire rent income he loses from the three tenants who were burnd out.

Rental Value—Dwellings—The Forms used to insure private dwellings grant the Insured an extension of coverage equal to 10% of the amount of insurance on the structure to cover loss of rental value at the rate of 1/12th per month. These Forms are discussed in Chapter 3 under DWELLING AND CONTENTS FORMS, in Chapter 5 under DWELLING BUILDING AND CONTENTS—BROAD FORM AND DWELLING BUILDING(S) SPECIAL FORM and in Chapter 34 under HOMEOWNERS PACKAGE POLICIES.

For many home owners, this 10% extension will not be sufficient to cover the actual rental value of their homes. Additional insurance on rents may be provided separately. The coverage provided under the Rent item of a Dwelling and Contents policy in a particular territory follows the general provisions of the regular Rent insurance policies used in that territory.

SPECIAL RENT INSURANCE FORMS

Seasonal Property—Owners of seasonal hotels, resorts, camps and similar businesses would not be adequately protected under the regular Rent insurance Forms, which limit recovery to the time to rebuild the property.

For a risk of this kind, the time to rebuild or restore damage caused by a fire or other peril may extend past the opening of the regular season and the rent income for the entire season would be lost. This situation is very similar to the one which faces colleges and other educational institutions which charge tuition fees.

A form specially adapted for this type of risk is used to provide the needed coverage, which does not limit indemnity to the period which would be required to rebuild, replace or restore the property, but to the actual loss sustained under a bona fide written lease.

The policy designates the months of each year which are covered and stipulates a maximum liability per month.

Fluctuating Rent—Premium Adjustment Form— Some property is leased under an arrangement in which the rent is a percentage of the volume of business done by the tenant or of the profit he realizes. Since the rent is not fixed, it would be very difficult to estimate the prospective rental value of the premises.

Rent insurance for risks of this kind is written under a Premium Adjustment Form. The Insured agrees to furnish, within 60 days after the expiration of the policy, a rental income statement. Some forms require that the statement be drawn up by a certified public accountant. If the statement shows that the amount of insurance carried during the term of the policy was greater than was actually required, the Company refunds the premium for such excessive insurance. The form prescribes a minimum retained premium, usually $50, and no premium is refunded which will serve to make the final retained premium less than this amount.

Buildings in Course of Construction—If a building is damaged or destroyed during the course of its construction, the time when the owner will begin to realize income from rents or have use of the premises for his own purposes is delayed. Such loss may be insured under a Rent policy covering the building in course of construction. The form used promises indemnity to the Insured for loss of the rental value of the completed building during the period for which the tenantability of the building is delayed by fire or lightning (or other peril insured). As in all other Rent Forms, recovery is limited to the time it would take, with the exercise of due diligence and dispatch, to restore the structure to the condition it was in on the date of the loss.

LEASEHOLD INTEREST INSURANCE

MANY LEASES CONTAIN a clause which permits the landlord or lessor to cancel the lease if fire destroys or seriously damages the property. This option to cancel becomes operative in some leases only if the premises are rendered totally unfit for occupancy; other clauses stipulate that the premises must be substantially damaged, or more than half destroyed, etc. Such a clause in a lease may create a Leasehold Interest which a tenant will need to insure.

A tenant is said to possess a Leasehold Interest in property when the rent he is paying under a lease is less than the normal rental value of the premises. It can be seen that cancellation of a lease of this kind could subject the tenant to loss because he might have to pay higher rent than under his former lease for similar premises, or even to the same landlord to continue possession of the premises under a new lease. In any event, whether he does in fact have to pay higher rent in new premises or removes to cheaper quarters or even if he retires from business, his Leasehold Interest policy will be liable for the difference between the rent he had been paying and what comparable accommodations would cost at the time of the loss.

There are many situations which create Leasehold Interest. Some of the more common types of Leasehold Interest are:

1. When the tenant occupies premises under a lease entered into before large scale improvement of the neighborhood enhanced the value of the premises and the lease is subject to cancellation in the event of damage to the premises.

2. When the tenant paid a bonus at the time of entering into the lease, and the bonus will be forfeited if the lease is canceled.

3. When the tenant has invested large sums in improvements and betterments of which he plans to enjoy the use until the expiration of the lease and the lease may be cancelled in the event of fire.

4. When a tenant sublets the premises he holds under a lease at a higher figure than he is himself paying for the premises.

Leasehold Interest insurance is designed to protect an individual or firm against losses of the kind outlined above. The policy insures the difference between the actual rent being paid under the lease and the normal rental value of the premises when the premises are damaged by fire and the landlord exercises his option to cancel the lease, or when the lease is cancelled by operation of state law.

The total amount of the policy of course decreases from month to month—a factor which is taken into account in fixing the rate. If a loss results in cancellation of the lease, the Company pays the Insured in a lump sum the discounted value of the leasehold interest for the months remaining in the lease period (except that the first three months of indemnity are paid without discount). The dates of the lease and a copy of the conditions in the agreement relating to fire damage are included in the policy. The interest used most commonly in computing the discounted value of a Leasehold interest is 4%. Thus, if the monthly "profit" which the Insured is enjoying in his rent by virtue of a favorable lease is $500, and the lease has five years to run, the amount of Leasehold Interest insurance required will be based on discounting the future monthly payments of $500 (except for the first three months). The factor for 60 months is 54.4134 which when multiplied by $500 a month will produce a figure of $27,206.70.

If the landlord does not cancel the lease, the policy is liable for the leasehold interest during the period that it takes to rebuild, repair or replace the property.

While less common than the situation in which a tenant has a Leasehold Interest in the premises he rents, a Landlord may find himself in the market for Leasehold insurance if the rent he is collecting from his tenant under a lease is *higher* than he would normally be able to expect in the open market, and a fire would relieve the tenant of his liability to pay rent under his lease. In a situation of this kind, the landlord could purchase a Leasehold Interest insurance policy to cover this exposure.

EXTRA EXPENSE INSURANCE

NEWSPAPERS, MILK DISTRIBUTORS, bakeries, power plants, laundries, food supply houses, banks, hospitals, schools and many other service businesses stand in a special relation to the public which makes it vital for them to furnish their product or service without interruption.

If their premises or equipment are damaged by fire or other peril, there is almost no limit to the extra expense which they would be willing to undergo to obtain substitute facilities or products. The amount of such extra expense may well exceed their total average earnings during a period of suspension, but they will be willing to take this loss in order to retain their customers.

While the regular Business Interruption policy will pay for the extra expense that an Insured undergoes after his operations are interrupted by fire or other insured peril, it will not pay for more than the amount by which such expenditures reduce the loss. The Business Interruption policy will therefore not meet the needs of many service organizations of the type listed above, whose extra expenses after a loss might far outstrip their actual reduction in earnings.

A special form of insurance, Extra Expense insurance, is used to provide for the extra expense necessary to continue doing business during the time it takes to rebuild, repair or replace the property. (This insurance is known in some territories as Additional Charges and Expenses insurance.)

Like the Business Interruption policy, it covers only during the period required with the exercise of due diligence and dispatch to restore the property.

The policy covers the extra expense during the period necessary to rebuild, repair or replace premises or *contents*. There is no time limit on the time to replace stock as in Business Interruption policies. Different from Business Interruption insurance, the Insured cannot collect under an Extra Expense policy unless he actually obtains substitute facilities. Under the Business Interruption policy, the Insured can collect his expenses to reduce the loss, if such can be made, or his actual business loss.

EXAMPLE: A laundry supplying hospitals, hotels and restaurants has a gross income of $100,000, of which $90,000 is used to cover expenses leaving a profit of $10,000. He suffers a severe fire damage at his premises which renders it impossible for him to meet his contracts except by purchasing services from his competitors at a cost of $130,000. His Extra Expense loss would be adjusted as follows:

Income prior to fire, $100,000 ($90,000 expenses; $10,000 profit)	
Cost of purchasing service from competitors	$130,000
Continuing expenses at damaged location	20,000
	$150,000
Less normal operating costs	90,000
Extra Expense claim	$ 60,000

It can be seen that the Insured will be in the same position as he would have been had no loss occurred. He will receive $100,000 from his customers to which he will have to add $30,000 out of his insurance claim in order to pay them the $130,000 he is being charged. He will pay out $20,000 to defray his continuing expenses at his damaged plant and will therefore be left with the $10,000 profit he was earning before the loss.

Maximum percentages of the amount of insurance that may be applied to the loss during various periods of restoration are fixed in the policy. Usually not more than 40% of the policy amount may apply to a loss when the restoration period is one month or less, not more than 80% of the policy for periods longer than one month but not longer than two months; 100% of the policy when the period of restoration is in excess of two months but not in excess of three months, etc.

The percentages stated are the top limits that will be paid *in the aggregate* for losses of specific duration, but these amounts need not be incurred within the specific months within the over-all restoration period. Thus, if the Insured carries $100,000 of Extra Expense insurance, he cannot collect more than $40,000 for extra expenses incurred by him during the first month after the loss. If his policy provides 80% limitation on a restoration period of two months, he can collect up to $80,000 for extra expenses incurred within the first two months after the loss, even if he incurred $70,000 of these expenses within the first month and only $10,000 within the second month.

COMBINED BUSINESS INTERRUPTION AND EXTRA EXPENSE INSURANCE

As was pointed out above under EXTRA EXPENSE INSURANCE, some business enterprises would not be properly protected against interruption of their operations under a Business Interruption insurance policy, and require Extra Expense coverage. In most instances, it will be found, a business will be exposed to an interruption loss which calls for only one of these two forms of insurance. There are businesses however which are exposed to *both* types of loss. A familiar example is the publisher of a newspaper or magazine, usually in a smaller city or town who also offers regular printing services to other businesses. An entrepeneur of this kind will require Extra Expense to cover his newspaper publishing activities, since he will be under great pressure to continue bringing out his paper without interruption. His loss of commercial printing business however will call for a regular Business Interruption policy. Examples of this kind could be multiplied of course in the case of other business enterprises which perform dual roles. In certain instances, careful analysis of a business enterprise's activities will reveal the need for *both* coverages, even when the business engages in only one activity. Thus, in certain large cities, the newspapers have entered into a compact among themselves under which the facilities of the morning papers will be made available to any evening paper whose printing facilities are curtailed due to fire, and vice versa. For the daily editions then, each newspaper would be amply protected if it carried Extra Expense to reimburse it for the extra expense it would be put to in order to produce its regular edition at a plant away from its home base. The special Sunday edition however with its several sections takes almost three days to turn out in its entirety and a fire on Saturday or Friday of any week might well render it impossible to be on the street with the Sunday paper, despite the availability of substitute production facilities at the competitor's plant. To cover this contingency and its severe loss of revenue would call for the purchase of some form of Business Interruption insurance.

Heretofore, risks who were exposed to both types of loss would have to purchase two separate policies, or in some cases, in a combined policy, were required to carry separate amounts of insurance on each exposure. A new form has now been introduced which covers both types of loss in one amount.

The Combined Business Interruption and Extra Expense Insurance policy is essentially the same as the Business Interruption policy discussed in Chapter 6 under BUSINESS INTERRUPTION

INSURANCE FORMS and the EXTRA EXPENSE policy outlined directly above.

The Insured is offered a choice of Coinsurance percentages similar in application to those discussed in Chapter 6 under BUSINESS INTERRUPTION INSURANCE — COINSURANCE REQUIREMENTS *and* a choice of percentage limits of liability as related to the Extra Expense coverage. One percentage is applicable to extra expense when the period of restoration is not in excess of 30 consecutive calendar days; a second, to periods in excess of 30 but less than 60 days; a third to periods in excess of 60 days.

Finished Stock—The policy does *not* cover loss of earnings resulting from damage to finished stock, nor for the time required to replace such stock (see Additional Time To Replace Stock under BUSINESS INTERRUPTION INSURANCE — WHAT IS COVERED in Chapter 6). There is coverage however for any expenses in excess of the normal as are incurred by the Insured in replacing stock to reduce loss of earnings under the policy.

ADDITIONAL LIVING EXPENSE INSURANCE

ADDITIONAL LIVING EXPENSE insurance is essentially Extra Expense insurance applied to dwelling occupancy. The form, which is attached to the Fire insurance policy, provides insurance to reimburse the Insured for additional living expenses necessarily incurred to maintain his normal standard of living. Examples of such expenses are the cost of hotel rooms in excess of normal rent, special transportation, cost of restaurant meals in excess of regular grocery bills, laundry bills in excess of the usual, and similar increased expenses.

This coverage is provided as part of the basic policy under the Dwelling Building(s) and Contents Broad Form and the Dwelling Building(s) Special Form (discussed in Chapter 5) and the Homeowners Package Policies (discussed in Chapter 34).

SELLING PRICE CLAUSES

LOSS OF PROFITS on certain categories of stock may be provided by a Selling Price clause attached to a Fire insurance policy covering the stock of either a manufacturing or a mercantile risk.

When the Selling Price clause is used, the actual cash value basis for settlement of losses is modified and the Insured can collect the price at which the merchandise would have been sold on the date of the loss.

There is an important difference between the Selling Price clause available to manufacturing risks and the one offered to mercantile risks. For the manufacturer, the clause covers all finished stock. For mercantile risks, the clause applies only to finished stock actually *sold* on order but held awaiting delivery.

There is no extra premium charge for attaching this clause to a Fire insurance policy, but the amount of insurance must be increased to comply with any Average Clause or Coinsurance clause in the policy. Thus, an Insured whose stock of 1,000 dresses cost him $10 each to produce must carry not less than $8,000 of Fire insurance, if his policy contains an 80% Coinsurance clause. But if the Selling Price clause is attached to the policy, and the price at which he sells each garment is $15, and if he has actual orders for his entire stock, the amount of insurance he must carry is $12,000—80% of 1,000 garments valued at their selling price of $15 each.

A Selling Price clause does provide protection for the profits on finished stock. The protection, however, is not the equivalent of Business Interruption insurance. Some of the important differences between these different forms of insurance are:

1. Selling Price clause for a mercantile risk covers only goods actually sold on order.

2. No protection is available under Selling Price clauses for more than the stock on hand on the date of the loss. A mercantile risk may suffer damage to the premises which takes so long a time to repair that the firm would have turned over its stock more than once. A manufacturer may suffer damage to his plant or machinery or equipment which prevents his turning out his product. A Selling Price clause grants no coverage for such future production.

3. A Selling Price clause offers no protection for loss of earnings caused by destruction of raw stock, or stocks in process.

MARKET VALUE CLAUSES

In some states, it is possible to have all stock valued at its selling price, whether actually sold on order or not, by attaching a Market Value clause to the policy which insures the stock. Such clauses may be used only when the stock is of a kind which is bought and sold at an established market exchange where the market prices are posted and quoted.

POWER FAILURE OR CONSEQUENTIAL LOSS PROVISIONS

The basic Fire policy will not pay for loss due to spoilage caused by failure of power, heating or cooling equipment unless caused by a peril insured against in the policy. A special clause limits coverage to losses arising from physical damage to such equipment located on the premises where the property is located. This clause is called the Power Failure—Loss Exclusion clause.

Where the power, heating or cooling equipment is housed elsewhere than on the premises where the property is located, a special endorsement, "Power Failure—Loss Assumption Endorsement" must be attached to the policy, if coverage is to extend to loss due to spoilage caused by failure of the equipment. Coverage applies only when there has been physical damage to the equipment from a peril insured against in the policy. An additional premium charge is made for this broadened coverage.

The Power Failure—Loss Assumption Endorsement contains an Apportionment clause identical with the one which is incorporated in the Extended Coverage Endorsement. It is important, therefore, when this endorsement is attached to one policy, that it be attached to all Fire insurance policies covering the same property.

When a Power Failure clause is attached to a Fire insurance policy which includes an Extended Coverage Endorsement, the Insured will be protected for loss or damage to insured property due to interruption or failure of refrigeration when caused by any of the perils assumed under the Extended Coverage Endorsement except that the exclusion of loss due to change of temperature occasioned by riot, civil commotion, or striking employees will still apply, unless otherwise assumed by endorsement.

CONSEQUENTIAL LOSS AND DAMAGE ASSUMPTION CLAUSE

CLOTHING POLICIES

IF, IN A FIRE at a clothing factory, parts of clothing are destroyed and the destruction of these parts of clothing causes a reduction in the value of other parts of clothing, the manufacturer's Fire insurance policy will pay not only for the destruction of the property actually reached by the fire, but also for the reduction in the value of the *un*damaged property.

EXAMPLE: A clothing manufacturer is engaged in making two-piece ladies' suits. The cost of each jacket in the ensemble comes to $40, the cost of the skirt to $25. Assume that this manufacturer has 1,000 such suits in process of manufacture when a fire breaks out at his plant. The fire destroys all the skirts but does no damage to the jackets. It is not possible to match the jackets properly, and they can no longer be made into suits, but must be sold separately for $10 each. The Insured is entitled to collect $25,000 for the destruction of the skirts (1,000 skirts at $25 each) plus $30,000 for the reduction in the value of the jackets (worth $40,000 before the fire, but only $10,000 after the fire).

In other words, the Insured is entitled to reimbursement for the reduction in the actual cash value of *all* the insured property on the premises, whether the fire actually reaches all the property or only part of the property.

The Fire insurance policy is liable, however, only for his loss on property which is contained in the premises described in the policy. If parts of clothing are damaged in a fire at the clothing factory, and this damage causes a reduction in parts of clothing at *other premises,* the Fire insurance policy covering the manufacturer's plant is not liable for the consequential reduction in the value of undamaged parts of clothing located elsewhere.

Thus, in the example used above, assume that the jackets of the two-piece suits being manufactured are being worked on at a contractor's premises, or at a secondary plant of the manufacturer, or at any other location. The fire which breaks out at the manufacturer's plant where the skirts are in process of manufacture causes a consequential reduction in the value of the *un*damaged jackets at the other location, but the manufacturer's Fire insurance policy will *not* pay for this consequential loss.

A Fire insurance policy may be endorsed to bring this consequential loss within the coverage of the Fire insurance covering a clothing manufacturer's location by attaching a Consequential Loss and Damage Assumption clause (for Clothing policies).

The clause extends the policy to cover on the reduction in value of the remaining parts of clothing or parts of suits *wherever located* when the destruction is caused by damage to parts of clothing located on the manufacturer's premises.

There is no charge for adding this Consequential Loss and Damage Assumption clause to the Fire insurance covering a clothing manufacturer, but the Insured will have to carry larger amounts of insurance to comply with the provisions of the Coinsurance clause.

Thus, in the example used above, where the jackets of the two-piece suits are being worked on at other premises, the value of the skirts at the main plant is only $25,000, and the manufacturer could comply with an 80% Average clause in his Fire insurance by carrying $20,000 of insurance. If the Consequential Loss and Damage Assumption clause is attached to his same policies, he will need to carry $52,000 of insurance—80% of the combined value of the skirts at the main plant and the jackets at other locations.

DEMOLITION INSURANCE

CONTINGENT LIABILITY FROM OPERATION OF BUILDING OR ZONING LAWS

SITUATIONS FREQUENTLY ARISE in which zoning laws forbid the erection of structures of certain construction, or for certain occupancies; e. g., a restriction on frame buildings, or multiple dwellings, or factory structures, etc. Generally, these laws were so worded as to apply only to construction begun after the date of the law, and all existing structures were allowed to stand, even though of a type forbidden by the new law. The zoning laws usually stipulate, however, that such structures may not be replaced except in an approved manner after a fire which does a certain amount of damage, usually 50%.

An Insured who owns a building of a class no longer approved may suffer a fire which will destroy a portion of the property and make it necessary for him to demolish the remaining *un*damaged portion. The part of the building that must be demolished is a consequential loss, and is not contemplated in the basic Fire insurance policy, which stipulates in its Insuring clause that it covers "without allowance for any increased cost of repair or reconstruction by reason of any ordinance or law regulating construction or repair."

An owner of property who faces such possible loss may have the Fire insurance that covers his building broadened to cover this hazard, by the attachment of a Demolition Endorsement. The Company will then be obligated to pay not only for any portion of the building actually reached by the fire but also for the portion that must be demolished after a fire. Endorsements of this kind usually include also the cost of the housewreckers' fee.

Although there are several forms under which this insurance can be provided and some variations among the states, the most commonly used endorsements fall into one of the following three groups:

1. Contingent Liability from Operation of Building Laws—The policy is extended to cover loss resulting from the enforcement of a building ordinance or law which necessitates demolition of the undamaged portion of a structure which has sustained a fire. Coverage is extended only to the value of the *un*damaged portion of the structure which must be razed. There is no coverage on the cost of demolishing or of clearing the site, nor for the cost of replacing the building with one which conforms to current building or zoning laws.

2. Demolition Cost Endorsement—This endorsement, which cannot be added to a policy except after the Contingent Liability from Operation of Building Laws Endorsement outlined above has been included, provides indemnity for the cost of demolishing and of clearing the site when such are necessitated by the operation of a building law.

3. Increased Cost of Construction Endorsement (also known

as Excess of Replacement Cost)—This endorsement which may be added to the two preceding extensions of coverage will provide an Insured with the means to repair or replace a building in a manner approved under the current building ordinances.

The form requires that the damaged building must be rebuilt or replaced on the premises. Recovery is limited to such time as would be required with the exercise of due diligence and dispatch to make replacement, but in no event beyond two years unless an extension is granted by the insurer. The coverage is subject to a Coinsurance clause, usually 100% although 80% is permissible in some jurisdictions.

COST OF REPRODUCTION OF RECORDS

THE BASIC FIRE INSURANCE policy will pay for the physical value of any records destroyed in a fire. It will not pay for the cost of reproducing these records.

This protection may be obtained in the basic Fire insurance policy as part of the insurance covering furniture, fixtures and other office supplies and equipment. While no individual amount of insurance need be specified for the cost of reproduction of records, the policy must stipulate that:

"The liability of this company for loss to books of account, abstracts, drawings, card index systems and other records shall not exceed the cost of blank books, blank pages or other materials, plus the cost of labor for actually transcribing or copying said records."

Film, tape, disc, drum, cell or other magnetic recording or storage media foı electronic data processing are not covered beyond the cost of such media in unexposed or blank form.

FIRE DEPARTMENT CHARGES

WHERE PROPERTY IS LOCATED outside of city or town limits, an Insured may be able to avail himself of the fire department facilities of the city or town. If he does call this equipment into play, he is almost always required to pay for this service.

The basic Fire insurance policy will not pay for these charges, which are a consequential loss, but the policy may be endorsed to cover such charges. The endorsement carries a dollar limit of liability, and the Insured should set this amount high enough to cover the maximum charges for which he may be held liable.

FOR FURTHER READING

ACKERMAN—Insurance
HEDGES—Practical Fire and Casualty Insurance
KLEIN—Business Interruption Insurance

OTHER CONSEQUENTIAL DAMAGE COVERAGE

MAGEE AND BICKELHAUPT—General Insurance
MEHR AND CAMMACK—Principles of Insurance
POLICY, FORM AND MANUAL ANALYSIS SERVICE

(See Reading List at End of Book)

CHAPTER 8

Fire Insurance Rates and Rate Making

RATE REGULATION

STATE LAWS or accepted public policy places upon all insurance companies the obligation to charge rates that are adequate, not excessive, and non-discriminatory.

The first requirement, that rates be adequate, is essential if the total premium income of the Company is to be sufficient for it to meet its liabilities and remain solvent. The second condition, that rates should not be excessive, is dictated by the state's function in protecting the public.

Although the insurance business is, for the most part, a private enterprise, its place in the economy of the country is so important that it has come to be looked upon as a quasi-public utility, and the various states exercise considerable control of the rates charged.

The third requirement, that rates be non-discriminatory, actually flows out of the first two requirements. Obviously, if the premium charged an Insured is not to be excessive for the actual risk he presents, and if the total premiums collected by the companies are to be adequate for the safe conduct of their business, each Insured or class of Insureds must be charged a rate which as much as possible reflects the actual hazards of the risk.

While the states (except Texas) do not actually establish Fire insurance rates, they require of the companies that they follow a rating system which is objective and which can be supported by accepted statistical or judgment factors. The state, through its Insurance Department, requires the filing of rates, and retains the power to approve or disapprove individual rates.

TEXAS—A State Commission supervises, and a State Rating Board makes, all rates.

RATE-MAKING ORGANIZATIONS

Establishing rates is a highly technical operation that calls for the services of specialists in making inspections, collecting data, and analysis of the many involved factors that determine the relative hazards of different risks. The cost of such organizations would be prohibitive if each Company were to maintain its own rating unit. The practical method of meeting this problem is for groups of companies to act together and set up a central body to promulgate proper rates. Furthermore, the pooling of experience makes possible more accurate results.

Except for "independent" insurers, most companies are members of, or subscribers to, a central rating organization. The laws of some states make it mandatory that every Company belong to a rate-making body which has been accepted by the state; in some instances, only in a specific organization named by the state. In an effort to encourage freedom of competition on rates, more and more states no longer require the companies within their borders to be members of a rating organization, or permit membership in such associations on an "advisory" basis. The rating organizations are supported by their member companies and by the services they sell to non-member companies.

The state and regional fire rating bureaus for Dwelling and Commercial Fire and Allied Lines of most states have recently been consolidated in one organization — The Insurance Services Office, with its principal offices in New York City.

DISTRICT OF COLUMBIA, HAWAII, IDAHO, LOUISIANA, MISSISSIPPI, NORTH CAROLINA, PUERTO RICO, TEXAS, VIRGINIA, WASHINGTON—In these states, the Property insurance rating bureaus function as independent units.

BASIC TYPES OF FIRE INSURANCE RATES

General Class (or Minimum Rates)—Strictly speaking, no two risks present exactly the same hazards. Even two identical structures will differ as to their contents, their maintenance, the number of occupants, the habits of the tenants, the exposure of the risk to other properties, etc.

Nevertheless, for the majority of risks, it is felt that it would be impractical to try to differentiate between each risk in the group, since they are substantially similar, and since establishing such individual rates would be a tremendous expense that would add to the general cost of all insurance. Such risks are, therefore, rated according to General Class Rates (sometimes known as Minimum Rates).

Into this classification will fall the majority of private dwellings, apartment houses, schools, churches, farms, and some smaller mercantile establishments. This type of risk is rated according to its general class, broken down as to type of construction and territory. Thus, in a given section of a city or town, one base rate will be assigned to all dwellings, a second to apartment houses without stores, a third to apartment buildings with stores, etc. One-story structures will receive another Class Rate; where mercantile establishments are eligible for Class Rates, the type of occupancy will be taken into account. In some cases, the rates will differentiate between those properties with approved roof and those without.

Construction Types—A major factor in General Class Rates is the type of construction. The two chief classes are:

1. Brick—includes buildings of brick, stone, concrete, solid or hollow-concrete block or hollow tile construction and buildings with walls of metal or metal lath and plaster on metal supports.

Types of construction included under the "brick" designation vary. In some states, the definition also lists hollow or solid cement block, corrugated iron on metal frame.

2. Frame—includes buildings of frame, brick filled, or brick and stucco. Some rating organizations also list iron-sheathed frame, brick veneered or brick nogged construction and buildings with walls of metal lath and plaster on wooden supports.

Approved Roofs—A factor that often differentiates dwellings of otherwise similar construction is the type of roof. Generally, an approved roof is one of metal, slate, tile, asbestos, composition shingles, and other grades of composition roofing approved by Underwriters' Laboratories or some other accepted testing organization. Unapproved roofs include roofs of wood shingles, boards and unapproved grades of composition roofing materials like tar paper, etc.

Protected and Unprotected Territory—An important factor in Fire insurance rates is the location of the individual risk. Generally, two broad classifications of risk are designated. Those within an incorporated city or town having a regularly staffed fire-fighting organization, or outside such cities but within a definite number of feet of a fire hydrant, usually 500 or 600 feet, are classed as "protected." All others are classed as "unprotected."

There are numerous other factors that may enter into the establishment of a General Class Rate and important variations in the different territories, but the fundamental characteristic of such rates is that they apply to all properties of a given class or nature.

While the majority of risks fall into the General Class Rate category, such risks account only for a comparatively small part of the total premiums paid for Fire insurance. This is due to the fact that most larger risks are specifically rated.

SPECIFIC RATES (SCHEDULE RATES)

All risks which are not General Class rated are specifically rated.

Each risk is inspected and is measured against a theoretic average. Credit is given for superiorities over this average, like superior construction, high grade maintenance, sprinkler systems, fire extinguishers, sand or water buckets, watchman service, fire doors, and similar private fire protection. Where the individual risk falls below the average, it is surcharged. Such charges will be applied for inferior construction, improper maintenance, extra hazardous materials or processes, exposure to other establishments which present a high degree of hazard, etc.

An Insured whose risk is specifically rated may apply to the Rating Organization for a copy of the schedule, showing in detail how his particular rate is arrived at. He may then take steps to reduce his rate by installing protective devices or otherwise improving the property or its maintenance, and by eliminating hazardous conditions.

Since few Insureds are in a position to analyze a rate schedule, they look to their agent (or broker) to render this important service. The agent may review this schedule with the specialists of the Rating Organization, who will advise him as to the steps that must be taken to obtain a lower rate.

NEW YORK—The Insured must request the schedule in writing from the New York Fire Insurance Rating Organization, but he can instruct them to forward this schedule directly to his insurance representative, who may then present the schedule and discuss it at the Rating Organization on behalf of the Insured.

After the Insured has taken steps to eliminate hazards or otherwise better the risk, a new rate is applied for. The Insured is then entitled to a return premium to reflect the lowered rate.

Helping to reduce Fire insurance rates is an important service an insurance representative renders to his clients, for the following reasons:

1. He helps them save money on their insurance.
2. By decreasing the possibility of fire, he may be safeguarding his clients from loss, since there are almost always consequential losses which cannot be insured against.
3. He aids in preserving property from destruction.
4. He may help save human life.
5. He makes the risk more acceptable to the insurance companies.

INTERSTATE LOCATIONS

Where one Insured owns property located in several states, special rating techniques are applied. These rates are worked out among the various Rating Organizations in the separate states in which the Insured's locations are maintained. Various factors like the number of locations, maximum values at any location and, in some instances, the Insured's past fire losses, are taken into account to arrive at an Average Rate to be used in insuring such risks. For assistance in working out a rate acceptable to all the different rating organizations involved, the Insured may call upon special organizations, like the Multiple Location Service Office, which are organized to provide this specialized service.

OTHER FACTORS WHICH AFFECT FIRE INSURANCE RATES

Term Policies—The term of a policy is the period for which a policy is written, as, the term of the policy is from January 1, 1970, to January 1, 1973. The phrase "term" in insurance is also used to designate policies written for periods in excess of one year. Such policies are spoken of as "term policies."

Fire insurance is often written for periods in excess of one year; usually for three years.

Since the writing of policies is an expense to the Company, a reduction in premium is usually granted on term policies. Generally, such policies are written according to the following rule:

The full annual premium is charged for the first year of the policy period. Only 85% of the regular annual premium is charged for each year of the policy period after the first.

EXAMPLE: A policy with an annual premium of $100.00 will develop a three-year premium of $270.00, as follows:

Charge full annual premium for first year of policy period	$100.00
Charge 85% of annual premium for second year of policy period	85.00
Charge 85% of annual premium for third year of policy period	85.00
THREE-YEAR PREMIUM	$270.00

NOTE: In some states, Fire insurance policies on dwellings are no longer eligible for Term discounts.

Installment Payment of Term Premiums—In most states, plans have been accepted under which the Insured may pay the premium for a three-year policy in three annual installments of 35% of the 3-year prepaid premium.

Minimum Premiums or Amounts—Since the issuance of a policy of any amount calls for certain basic expenses in inspection, rating preparation of the policy, recording, forwarding, etc., it is almost universal practice to charge a minimum premium on all policies. The minimum premium for Fire insurance varies in different rating territories, and the reader is urged to check local practices in his locality. In almost all the states, the minimum premium is at least $25 per policy.

ALABAMA—The minimum is $20 for the first year; $10 thereafter.
ARKANSAS, DISTRICT OF COLUMBIA, WEST VIRGINIA — The minimum is $15.

FLORIDA, GEORGIA—The minimum is $25 for the first year; $10 each additional year.
KENTUCKY—The minimum is $20.
LOUISIANA—The minimum is $25 but $20 for a Deferred Payment Plan installment.
MARYLAND—For the second and third years, the minimum is $20.
MISSISSIPPI—The minimum is $15 for one year, subject to Term discount. For a Deferred Payment Plan installment, the minimum is $25.
NEW JERSEY—The minimum per policy is $15; $25 for a Deferred Payment installment. Plus a $5 flat loading charge on all Dwelling policies.
NORTH CAROLINA—The minimum is $16.
PUERTO RICO—The minimum is $5.
SOUTH CAROLINA—The minimum is $12.50 for the first year; $5 for each additional year.
TEXAS—On 1- and 3-year policies, the minimum is $8; $4 on each Extended Coverage item.
VIRGINIA—The minimum is $15; on each Deferred Payment installment $20.
WASHINGTON—A minimum premium of $5 annually and $15 on 3-year policies is added to all Broad and Special Form Dwelling policies, applicable to each structure and to contents.
WYOMING—$15 for single item 3-year policies and for annual single item building policies. $10 for annual single item contents policies.

The minimum premium for which a Fire insurance policy is written is not necessarily the minimum *retained* premium. No policy will be written for less than the established minimum, but a portion of this premium may be returned to the Insured if the policy is cancelled prior to its expiration.

Whole Dollar Premium Rule—The premium for each policy, and for each separate item insured under any policy, is rounded to the nearer whole dollar. If the computation of a premium develops a figure with 50¢ or more, the premium for the policy (or any separate item insured in the policy) is increased to the next higher full dollar. If the figure is 49¢ or less, the premium is dropped to the next lower full dollar. This method of charging premiums is applied as well to any endorsement of the policy, and to all additional or return premiums.

EXAMPLE: In calculating the premium for a policy, Item 1 covered under the contract develops a charge of $15.60. The premium for this Item is rounded to $16.00. Item 2 of the policy calculates out at $3.40. The charge for this Item is reduced to $3.00. The total premium for the policy is thus figured at $19.00.

Some time later, the Insured adds an endorsement to the policy which calculates out with a premium of $4.50. He is charged $5.00 for this endorsement. He also deletes coverage on some coverage of the policy, and the return premium for this reduction of coverage calculates out at $3.40. He receives a return premium of $3.00.

NOTE: An exception to this rule is made when the insurance company elects to cancel a policy. In such instances, the return premium is always rounded to the next *higher* whole dollar. Thus, if the return premium calculates out at $6.01 when the Company cancels a policy, it must return $7.00 to the Insured.

Coinsurance, Average Clause, Reduced Rate Contribution Clause Credits—Where a policy is written with an Average (Coinsurance) clause, the rate reflects a credit. The credit for such clauses is applied to the "flat rate," which is the rate promulgated without Coinsurance credits. In some territories, particularly rural areas, only flat rates are published, while some territories offer the Insured a choice of a "flat" rate or a Coinsurance rate.

Deductible (Excess of Loss) Fire Insurance—Very large risks, and especially those with a number of diversified locations, can obtain a lower rate for Fire insurance in many states by purchasing their insurance on an Excess of Loss basis. Under this plan, the Insured assumes the initial loss up to a stated amount, usually at least $100,000. The Company is liable only for such portion of any loss as exceeds the deductible amount assumed by the Insured. The insurance provided by the Company is in the nature of catastrophe coverage.

Dwelling Deductibles—In almost every instance, Fire policies covering a dwelling are written with some form of Deductible, applicable to the Windstorm and Hail provisions of the Extended Coverage Endorsement, or to all perils of the policy.

CONNECTICUT, FLORIDA, GEORGIA, LOUISIANA, MONTANA (In certain territories only), NEW YORK, NORTH CAROLINA (in the sea coast areas primarily), SOUTH DAKOTA (only in Rapid City area), TEXAS (beach and sea coast areas), VIRGINIA—A $100 Deductible is mandatory.

MARYLAND—A percentage Deductible applies, subject to a minimum of $100 and a maximum of $1,000.

MARYLAND, MISSISSIPPI, OHIO, OKLAHOMA, WEST VIRGINIA —There is no mandatory Deductible.

ALL OTHER STATES—A $50 Deductible is applicable.

Franchise (Disappearing) Deductibles—This type of clause enables the Insured to collect 111% or 125% of the amount by which his loss exceeds the Deductible. Four separate Disappearing Deductibles are available.

Amount of Deductible	Disappears When Loss Exceeds	Percentage of Excess Over Deductible Which Insured Collects
$ 500	$ 5,000	111%
1,000	10,000	111
3,000	15,000	125
5,000	25,000	125

EXAMPLE: Assume the Insured whose Fire insurance is written with a $1,000 Deductible suffers a loss of $1,300. He will recover 111% (the percentage for policies with $1,000 Deductible) of $300, the excess of the loss over the Deductible, or $333.

If, however, this same Insured's loss were $9,000, he would recover $8,880. Note that in the first instance, the Insured has borne $967 of the loss; but in the latter instance, the Deductible has all but disappeared.

Reduction in Amount—Practices vary as to the method of figuring the premium to be charged an Insured who wishes to reduce his policy during its term. Generally, a Fire insurance policy which covers stocks may be reduced in amount up to 50%, with the return premium computed on a pro rata basis. On Business Interruption insurance and Rent insurance, the maximum reduction permitted pro rata is limited to 25%.

Flat Cancellation—When a policy is returned for cancellation before its inception date, it is cancelled "flat"; that is, without any premium charge. Flat cancellation is sometimes permitted under other circumstances.

In some territories, flat cancellation is permitted on policies returned within 45 days of their effective date.

Loss Constant Rating Factor—In many parts of the country, low-valued dwellings have experienced difficulty in obtaining Fire insurance, since underwriters find the General Class rates applicable to such property inadequate [discussed above under BASIC TYPES OF FIRE INSURANCE RATES—General Class (or Minimum Rates)]. The majority of states now have in operation a special rating plan under which a flat charge is added to the premium developed under the Fire policy. The effect of this charge, usually $6, is to increase substantially the cost per $1,000 of insurance for the smaller policy, with the percentage increase per $1,000 tapering off on policies of larger amount. Below are enumerated the states in which such plans are operative.

ALABAMA, ALASKA, ARIZONA, ARKANSAS, CALIFORNIA, COLORADO, CONNECTICUT, FLORIDA, GEORGIA, IDAHO, ILLINOIS, INDIANA, IOWA, KANSAS, KENTUCKY, LOUISIANA, MAINE, MARYLAND, MASSACHUSETTS, MICHIGAN, MINNESOTA, MISSISSIPPI, MISSOURI, MONTANA, NEVADA, NEBRASKA, NEW MEXICO, NORTH CAROLINA, OHIO, OKLAHOMA, OREGON, RHODE ISLAND, SOUTH CAROLINA, TENNESSEE, TEXAS, UTAH, VERMONT, VIRGINIA, WASHINGTON, WEST VIRGINIA, WISCONSIN, WYOMING.

Civil Disorder Loadings—Almost half of the states of the country require that the rates for commercial properties be increased for the exposure of civil disorder. Generally, a surcharge of 4% is applied in the larger communities (based on population size) and 2% in the smaller towns. Such loadings are now in effect in the following states:

CONNECTICUT, DISTRICT OF COLUMBIA, ILLINOIS, INDIANA, IOWA, LOUISIANA, MAINE, MARYLAND, MASSACHUSETTS, MICHIGAN, MINNESOTA, MONTANA, NEW JERSEY, NEW YORK, NORTH CAROLINA, NORTH DAKOTA, OHIO, PENNSYLVANIA, SOUTH DAKOTA, TENNESSEE, WISCONSIN.

FAIR ACCESS TO INSURANCE REQUIREMENTS (FAIR)

The basic Fire insurance policy does not cover loss caused directly or indirectly by insurrection, rebellion, revolution, civil war or usurped power. Furthermore, there is no coverage, unless added by endorsement for riot, unless fire ensues. Thus, under the basic Fire policy, a loss caused by rioters burning property *is* covered. In any event, since most Fire policies do in fact include an Extended Coverage endorsement, the peril of riot is covered, whether or not fire ensues. Also brought within the coverage of the policy is the peril of Civil Commotion (discussed in Chapter 5 under OTHER PROVISIONS—Riot, Riot Attending A Strike, Civil Commotion Provisions).

It can therefore be understood that the wave of riots that swept across the country during the past few years have resulted in large scale losses to the insurers in the affected areas. Underwriters were forced to refuse to write or severely restrict insurance in urban areas which appeared to be prone to civil disorder.

As a consequence, owners of property in these areas found themselves unable to comply with the requirements of their mortgagees as respects furnishing adequate Fire insurance; lenders in increasing numbers refused to supply funds for property owners in these areas. The already difficult situation in urban areas was severely aggravated.

In an effort to respond to the crisis and forestall a growing demand for assigned risk plans in the Fire insurance field, the companies began to develop urban area inspection plans and special surcharges which would help compensate for the extra hazards of insuring in these areas. These plans included voluntary pools of insurers (as in California after the Watts area riots, or The Boston Plan) to offer insurance on residences, and were broadened over the years. In 1968, the Federal Government, in an Omnibus Housing bill, passed the Urban Property Protection and Reinsurance Act, more popularly known as the Federal riot reinsurance program.

The Act authorized the Department of Housing and Urban Development (HUD) to provide Federal riot reinsurance to any insurer who wishes to purchase it. This coverage became available to most carriers on August 1, 1968. In order for a participating carrier to remain eligible for this reinsurance, it is required to participate in a FAIR plan in each of the states in which it seeks to be reinsured. FAIR plans had to be approved by HUD and by the insurance commissioner of each state.

Basically, a FAIR plan calls for an underwriting association to be established to provide Fire and Extended Coverage insurance to real and personal property risks which cannot obtain coverage in the normal market. The legislatures in the various states have amended the insurance laws of the state authorizing and requiring all companies which write Fire insurance (including Homeowners and Commercial Package policies) to join such underwriting association.

At first, a considerable number of plans were evolved in an effort to comply with the requirements of the Act. Today, most of the states which have FAIR plans base their plans on the 100% reinsurance pool concept. Eligible risks are distributed by a central organization to an individual company which cedes the entire exposure to the pool of insurers which has been established. The pool then parcels out the risk to all the participating companies in the proportion that their total premiums on property in the state bears to all premiums written by the entire pool. The writing company, or servicing company, retains no liability under its policy beyond the percentage that is allocated to it under the above formula.

It should be pointed out that the reinsurance association goes by various names in the several states, e. g., in Illinois, the plan is operated by the Illinois Property Insurance Facility; in New Jersey, by the New Jersey Insurance Underwriting Association; the New York Plan is known as the New York Property Insurance Underwriting Association, Pennsylvania calls its facility the Insurance Placement Facility of Pennsylvania, etc.

A FAIR plan is now in effect in all states except those enumerated below:

ALABAMA, ALASKA, ARIZONA, ARKANSAS, FLORIDA, GEORGIA, HAWAII, IDAHO, MAINE, MISSISSIPPI, MONTANA, NEBRASKA, NEVADA, NEW HAMPSHIRE, NEW MEXICO, NORTH DAKOTA, OKLAHOMA, SOUTH CAROLINA, SOUTH DAKOTA, TENNESSEE, TEXAS, UTAH, VERMONT, WYOMING.

All FAIR plans provide for the placement of Fire and Extended Coverage insurance on all eligible risks, both real and personal. In some states, farm property is also eligible, while a few include risks of a manufacturing nature, provided they are not above a stated size.

All FAIR plans place a maximum limit on the amount of insurance that can be placed. The limits vary among the states, ranging from $100,000 to no maximum on habitational property and from $250,000 to $2,000,000 on commercial property.

There are some differences among the FAIR plans but basically they all provide that every risk submitted will be inspected within a specified number of days after receipt of the application, and that a policy will be issued or a written notice sent to the applicant setting forth either: (a) What steps must be taken by the applicant to bring the property up to acceptable level, or (b) the reasons which make the property uninsurable. It is specifically provided that neighborhood is in itself not a permissible reason to reject a risk.

If the facility does not act within 17 days after receipt of the application, the applicant can obtain a binder.

While a risk may not be declined solely because of neighborhood, area, location or environmental hazards, there are a number of conditions which render risks ineligible under FAIR plans. Basically, these take in risks which are in very poor physical condition, or present an unusually high degree of fire hazard, or whose occupancy is violative of public policy, etc.

Vandalism and Malicious Mischief — Most state FAIR plans have recently been broadened to offer Vandalism and Malicious Mischief coverage under recommendations of the Department of Housing and Urban Development.

Consent to Rate Laws—In practically every state, there is statutory provision for writing insurance for difficult to place risks at higher than Board rates (surcharged rates).

Generally, the insured is required to make written application or indicate his acceptance of the surcharge in rate. The insurance can then be placed in the normal markets and processed through the usual Board channels.

CALIFORNIA, MISSISSIPPI, MISSOURI—No consent to rate law is in effect.

MASSACHUSETTS—The law applies to all forms of insurance other than Workmen's Compensation and compulsory Automobile coverages.

TENNESSEE—The law applies to Automobile and General Liability.

TEXAS—The law applies to Fire and Extended Coverage.

BEACH PROPERTY INSURANCE POOLS

The difficulty of obtaining Fire and Extended Coverage insurance on beach property has prompted six states to enact legislation requiring insurers licensed within their borders to form a pool for writing Fire and Extended Coverage on property in certain designated exposed areas.

In the seventh state, ALABAMA, a pool for the writing of this class of insurance was established by the insurers voluntarily.

NORTH CAROLINA, FLORIDA, LOUISIANA, MISSISSIPPI, SOUTH CAROLINA, TEXAS—Pools for writing insurance on beach property have been established by the companies in response to legislation enacted.

WHAT IS COVERED

Practically all real and personal property in the designated areas is eligible for coverage. Motor vehicles and mobile homes are excluded.

MISSISSIPPI—Mobile homes which comply with stipulated anchoring requirements are eligible for coverage.
NORTH CAROLINA, MISSISSIPPI—Manufacturing risks are not eligible, except that MISSISSIPPI permits the insuring of seafood canneries, bottling works and laundries.
ALABAMA, NORTH CAROLINA—All farm property is excluded.
LOUISIANA—All structures built over water are excluded.

With the exception listed below, newly built structures, those which have been substantially remodeled and the contents of such buildings will not be accepted for insurance unless the construction was in accordance with the Southern Standard Building Code.

SOUTH CAROLINA—The requirement for compliance with the Building Code does not apply to remodeled structures, but the new structure must also comply with the standards adopted by the locality in conjunction with the Federal Flood Insurance Program.

PERILS COVERED

Only Fire and Extended Coverage insurance is available through these pools. Builders Risk forms are also available. There is no provision for writing Business Interruption, Rent insurance or any of the other time element coverages.

FOR HOW MUCH

Generally, the maximum coverage on residential properties (dwelling of four families or less) is $100,000. Commercial risks are eligible for insurance of $500,000.

LOUISIANA—The maximum limit is $1 million.
MISSISSIPPI—The maximum limit does not apply to school property which may be insured in an amount equal to 80% of the actual cash value of the property. Also, if the combined exposure of the owner of a building and the tenant exceeds the maximum limits set forth above, each applicant may obtain insurance equal to the maximum.

Coinsurance—In TEXAS, dwellings are subject to an 80% Coinsurance clause; commercial properties may be written with 50%, 80% or 100% Coinsurance. If a particular property is so large that it cannot comply with the Coinsurance requirement within the maximum limits available through the pool, a no-Coinsurance form, subject to a negotiated rate, may be obtained.

Deductibles—In MISSISSIPPI, a deductible of 1% of the amount of insurance, subject to a $100 minimum, applies when the amount of insurance is $35,000 or less; on policies over $35,000 up to and including $100,000, a 2% Deductible applies; on amounts of insurance over $100,000, the Deductible is 5%. Schools and mobile homes are subject to a special set of Deductibles.

TEXAS—A 1% Deductible, subject to a minimum of $250, is applicable to dwellings; on commercial risks, the Deductible is 2%, with a minimum of $500.

WHEN COVERED

ALABAMA, NORTH CAROLINA—Coverage does not become effective until after an inspection is made and the producer notified that the risk is eligible. The coverage attaches on the day following the date of receipt of the premium. It is possible to have an interim binder issued if the premium is submitted with the application. In such event, the coverage attaches 20 days after the application is received by the underwriting pool.

FLORIDA, LOUISIANA, SOUTH CAROLINA—Same as ALABAMA above, except that there is no provision for issuance of interim binders.

LOUISIANA makes an exception for dwelling risks which may be bound as of the date of the postmark if the application is sent together with a photo of the property and the premium.

MISSISSIPPI—Insurance becomes effective at noon of the day following receipt of the application and premium. The pool is to notify the producer as soon as possible whether the risk is "tentatively" accepted.

TEXAS—Same as MISSISSIPPI except that the pool must notify the producer within 15 days after receipt of the application if it wishes to reject the risk.

FOR FURTHER READING

ACKERMAN—Insurance
HUEBNER AND BLACK—Property Insurance
MAGEE AND BICKELHAUPT—General Insurance
MEHR AND CAMMACK—Principles of Insurance
MOWBRAY AND BLANCHARD—Insurance
POLICY, FORM AND MANUAL ANALYSIS SERVICE
RIEGEL, ROBERT AND MILLER—Insurance

(See Reading List at End of Book)

CHAPTER 9

Sprinkler Leakage And Water Damage Insurance

ONE OF THE MOST EFFECTIVE devices for keeping fires under control and reducing the extent of the damage is the Sprinkler System. A series of pipes is installed along the ceiling or roof of the entire premises. These pipes contain water or, where specially required, some other substance or chemical which will extinguish a fire or keep it under control until the Fire Department arrives.

The pipes which carry the water or other substance are equipped with special valves or heads which open when the temperature in the area gets above a certain point, releasing quantities of water or other fire retardant which blankets the area. In addition, the Sprinkler System is usually equipped with an alarm which goes off when a Sprinkler head opens. To supply the Sprinkler System with the required pressure, a tank is often set up.

Damage caused by the water or other substance released from a Sprinkler System during a fire is covered under the basic Fire insurance policy. The Fire insurance policy does not, however, cover the discharge from a Sprinkler System when no fire occurs. Such leakage or discharge can occur under many circumstances, chief among which are:

1. Break in the pipes caused by freezing.
2. Opening of a Sprinkler head due to overheating.
3. Mechanical injury due to jarring of the Sprinkler System.
4. Corrosion, faulty valves, leaky tanks.
5. Malicious tampering with the system.
6. Improper maintenance.

Damage by leakage of a Sprinkler System can cause considerable loss, and this hazard calls for separate insurance under a Sprinkler Leakage policy. This protection is written in some territories as a separate policy, or under an endorsement to the Fire insurance policy called a Sprinkler Leakage Supplemental Contract. The coverage in either case is the same.

The Insuring Clause of the Sprinkler Leakage policy or the Sprinkler Leakage Supplemental Contract is similar to that of the Fire insurance policy except that the words "Sprinkler Leakage" are substituted for "Fire and Lightning."

HAZARDS COVERED

The Sprinkler Leakage policy covers loss caused by the leakage or discharge of water or any other substance from within any Automatic Sprinkler System.

The policy covers not only the damage to the insured property but also to the system itself when caused by the perils assumed under the policy, freezing and breakage.

Damage may be caused by water or any other substance, e. g., chemicals, anti-freeze mixtures, etc. Only discharge from *within* a Sprinkler System is covered. Loss caused by condensation from outside of sprinkler pipes would not be covered.

The discharge of water need not be from the actual overhead Sprinkler System pipes to be covered under the policy. Also covered is leakage from valves, fittings, tanks, pumps and private fire protection mains connected to the sprinkler system, and non-automatic sprinkler systems, hydrants, stand pipes or hose outlets supplied from an automatic sprinkler system.

Damage By Tanks—The policy also covers damage caused by collapse or fall of a tank which forms part of an Automatic Sprinkler System. Coverage is afforded for the damage by the tank and its component parts and supports, as well as by the water in the tank.

NOTE: Although the policy does cover property of others in the Insured's custody under certain conditions (discussed under WHAT IS COVERED), it does not afford coverage for the legal liability of the Insured, as such. Losses of this kind can prove very extensive, as when the sprinkler system of the Insured is discharged accidentally and the water seeps through the walls or floor of the Insured's premises.

Coverage for such liability is available under special Public Liability policies (or endorsements) discussed in Chapter 25 under HAZARDS NOT COVERED—Water Damage, Sprinkler Leakage.

HAZARDS NOT COVERED

The Sprinkler Leakage policy does not cover leakage of a Sprinkler System caused by:

Fire and Lightning (perils of the basic Fire insurance policy).

Windstorm, Explosion, Riot, Civil Commotion (Some of the perils of the Extended Coverage Endorsement under a Fire policy).

Insurrection, Rebellion, Revolution, Civil War, Usurped Power, or Action by governmental authority in hindering, combating, or defending against such an occurrence.

Order of Any Civil Authority—Neglect of the Insured to use all reasonable means to save and preserve the property at and after a sprinkler leakage loss or when the property is endangered by sprinkler leakage in neighboring premises.

Water except from an automatic sprinkler system.

Earthquake, Blasting, Rupture of Steam Boilers or Fly Wheels.

War Perils—Hostile or warlike action in time of peace or war, including action taken in hindering, combating or defending against an actual, impending or expected attack, (1) any government or sovereign power (de jure or de facto), or by any authority maintaining or using military, naval or air forces; or (2) by military, naval or air forces; or (3) by an agent of any such government, power, authority or forces, it being understood that any discharge, explosion or use of any weapon employing atomic fission or radioactive force shall be conclusively presumed to be such a hostile or warlike action by such government, power, authority or forces.

Nuclear Exclusion Clause—The policy excludes loss by nuclear reaction, radiation or radioactive contamination.

Vacancy and Unoccupancy—Policy is suspended at once if the building is vacant or unoccupied, in contrast with the Fire insurance policy, which allows for 60 consecutive days of vacancy or unoccupancy. This suspending condition is often waived in the Form attached to the policy.

Alterations and Repairs—Policy does not cover loss occurring during and resulting from the making of repairs, alterations or extensions involving a wall or support of a floor or roof after a period of fifteen consecutive days from the beginning of such operations. Similarly, loss caused by installation of or change in an Automatic Sprinkler System is not covered after fifteen days from beginning of such operations.

If coverage is desired during alterations which extend past fifteen days, a Mechanics Permit must be attached to the policy. The permit sets forth the dates of the complete operation for which liability is assumed. An additional premium is charged.

WHAT IS COVERED

A Sprinkler Leakage Form is attached to the Sprinkler Leakage policy. The form gives the exact location of the risk, and describes the type of property covered, and the amount of insurance applying to the various types of property.

Provision is made for insuring one or more distinct classes of property:

Building, additions and extensions, and all permanent fixtures connected with the building or its service and maintenance.

The form includes a Foundations Exclusion clause, which is similar to the one in the Building Form attached to the Fire insurance policy.

Contents—A space is provided to insert a description of the property. The form provides protection on all described property owned by the Insured and his interest in similar property to the extent of the value of labor and materials expended thereon by the Insured.

Improvements and Betterments.

Personal property of employees and members of the firm.

Any other property. An Insured may not wish to insure all contents but may require coverage only on machinery, or only on finished stock, etc.

Insurance may be provided on any one or more items as shown above. Or the policy may be written blanket over several items, with one amount of insurance applying to all such blanketed items; e. g.:

$100,000	On all contents . . .
and	On the interest of the Insured in the improvements and betterments to the building . . .
and	On personal property of employees . . .

If the policy is written with a Coinsurance clause percentage of 25% or higher, and it covers any kind of personal (not real) property of the Insured, coverage is extended to cover similar property of others in the care or custody of the Insured. This extension provides an *additional* amount of insurance for the account of the owner(s) of such property up to a limit of 2% of the amount of insurance, but not exceeding $2,000.

WHERE COVERED

Property is covered while contained in the described premises. There is no extension to property outside of buildings as is provided under Fire insurance forms.

While the property insured must be within the premises, the loss need not be caused by a Sprinkler System within the premises.

SPRINKLER LEAKAGE AND WATER DAMAGE

An Insured may sustain damage to his property from a neighbor's Sprinkler System, and such loss would be covered.

LIMITS

Like the Fire insurance policy, the Sprinkler Leakage policy covers only to extent of the actual cash value of the property at the time of the loss, but not more than the cost to repair or replace the property, and not more than the insurable interest of the Insured in the Property.

Coinsurance, Reduced Rate Contribution or Average Clause— Sprinkler Leakage insurance is almost always written with a Coinsurance clause. The application of such clauses to the Sprinkler Leakage policy is the same as under Fire insurance, except that the Insured is granted a choice of Coinsurance percentages, 5, 10, 25, 50, 80% or higher. It is entirely optional with the Insured what Coinsurance percentage he elects to use.

Thus, a risk with stock worth $1,000,000 could comply with a Coinsurance percentage of 10% by buying $100,000 of Sprinkler Leakage insurance. The rate reflects the Coinsurance percentage, with increased credits granted for higher percentages. Thus, when a 5% Coinsurance Clause is used, the no-Coinsurance rate is reduced by 35%; for the 10% Clause, the credit is 60%; on 25% Coinsurance, the credit is 80%, etc.

Non-Reduction After Loss—Like Fire insurance policies, the Sprinkler Leakage policy is not reduced in amount by any loss.

OTHER CLAUSES AND PROVISIONS

Waiver of Inventory or Appraisement Clause—The requirement after a loss that an Insured furnish an inventory of the *un*damaged as well as the damaged property is waived, as under Fire insurance policies, except that, in Sprinkler Leakage policies, this requirement is waived only when the loss is both less than $2,500 and less than 2% of the amount of insurance.

Other Provisions—With the exceptions of the special provisions and exclusions listed above, the Sprinkler Leakage policy is similar to the Fire insurance policy and contains the following provisions which are identical with those of the Fire insurance policy:

Abandonment — Appraisal — Cancellation — Company Options — Concealment, Fraud — Mortgagee Interests and Obligations — Other Insurance — Pro Rata Liability — Requirements in Case Loss Occurs — Subrogation — Suit — Uninsurable and Excepted Property — When Loss Payable.

Alarm or Watchman Service Clause—A reduced rate is granted to an Insured who maintains an alarm or watchman service. When such credit is allowed, the policy contains a warranty that this service will be maintained insofar as it is under the Insured's control.

INSURING CONSEQUENTIAL SPRINKLER LEAKAGE LOSSES

Like the consequential losses caused by fire, the leakage of a sprinkler system may also cause interruption of business, and other consequential losses. For these hazards, an Insured may obtain protection under Sprinkler Leakage Business Interruption policies, Sprinkler Leakage Rent insurance, Sprinkler Leakage Profits and Commissions insurance, Sprinkler Leakage Extra Expense insurance, etc. Such insurance is provided by attaching the appropriate form to the Sprinkler Leakage policy.

WATER DAMAGE INSURANCE

DAMAGE CAUSED BY WATER used to fight a fire is covered by the basic Fire insurance policy, whether the water comes from a Sprinkler System, a fireman's hose, water buckets, or other source. Also covered would be any other kind of water damage of which fire was the proximate cause. In other words, if a fire burns through a water pipe and the escaping water damages insured property, such loss would come under the Fire insurance policy.

When a Sprinkler System opens *other* than because of fire, the Sprinkler Leakage policy provides coverage for the resultant water damage loss, subject to the policy's exclusions.

In addition to the water damage outlined above, most property is exposed to loss caused by the discharge of water from other sources—plumbing supplies, heating supplies, refrigerating equipment, industrial appliances, etc. These perils may be insured against in a Water Damage policy, designed to provide protection against stipulated types of water damage.

The insuring clause of the Water Damage policy is similar to the Fire insurance policy except that the words "Water Damage" are substituted for "Fire and Lightning."

HAZARDS COVERED

The Water Damage policy covers two groups of perils—the leakage of water or steam from certain sources, and the admission of rain or snow under certain conditions, as follows:

Water or Steam Discharge—The Water Damage policy covers

the accidental discharge, leakage or overflow of water or steam, from within the following sources:

Plumbing systems, plumbing tanks
Heating systems
Elevator tanks and cylinders
Standpipes for fire hose
Industrial and domestic appliances
Refrigerating and air conditioning systems.

Damage is covered only if caused by water or steam, but not otherwise. There is no coverage for damage caused by chemicals, dyes, sprays, anti-freeze mixtures, or any other liquid preparations or substances.

The leakage must originate *within* one of the above sources. As under the Sprinkler Leakage policy, leakage of water due to condensation on the outside of the pipes is not covered.

Rain or Snow Admission—The policy also covers the accidental admission of rain or snow through—

Defective roofs, leaders, spouting
Open or defective doors, windows, skylights, transoms, ventilators

Damage By Tanks—The policy also covers damage caused by collapse of a tank which forms part of a plumbing system.

HAZARDS NOT COVERED

The Water Damage policy contains all the exclusions of the Sprinkler Leakage policy (discussed before under SPRINKLER LEAKAGE POLICY—HAZARDS NOT COVERED).

In addition, the Water Damage policy excludes:

Seepage, Leakage or Influx of Water through building walls, foundations, basement floors, sidewalks or sidewalk lights.

Floods, Inundations, Tide, Rising or Surface Water.

Backing up of Sewers or Drains, Gases, Fumes and Vapors (other than steam).

Failure of Refrigerating or Air Conditioning Systems or equipment to maintain proper temperature.

Vacancy and Unoccupancy—The Water Damage is suspended at once if the building is vacant or unoccupied. Contrast with the Fire insurance policy, which allows for 60 consecutive days of vacancy or unoccupancy.

Aircraft in Motion

NEW YORK—This exclusion has been deleted.

Alterations and Repairs—discussed before under Sprinkler Leakage policy.

WHAT IS COVERED

A Water Damage form is attached to the Water Damage policy. The form gives the exact location of the risk, and describes the type of property covered and the amount of insurance applying to the various types of property.

Coverage may be provided under any one or more of the five items for which space is provided in the form. (See WHAT IS COVERED, under Sprinkler Leakage policy.)

The policy does not cover damage *to* the source of loss. There is no coverage for damage *to* the plumbing, heating, refrigerating system, tanks or any other source of water which may cause a loss under the policy.

The forms used by some companies limit coverage on models, drawings, dies or patterns to 10% of the amount of the policy. Where the Insured requires more protection on such property it can be purchased under Item 5 of the policy.

WHERE COVERED

Property is covered while contained in the described premises. There is no extension to cover property outside of buildings, as is provided under Fire insurance forms.

While the property insured must be within the premises, the water need not originate on the Insured's premises. An Insured whose property was damaged by water from a neighbor's premises would be covered for his loss unless the water seeped through building walls, a type of loss excluded under the policy. If the water entered the Insured's premises through the ceiling or floor, the loss would be covered.

FOR HOW MUCH

Coinsurance, Reduced Rate Contribution or Average Clause—The application of Coinsurance to the Water Damage policy is the same as under Sprinkler Leakage insurance. While the Insured is granted a choice of Coinsurance percentages in Water Damage insurance as in Sprinkler Leakage, a minimum Coinsurance percentage is usually required, depending on the size of the risk. Thus, where the values at risk are under $50,000, the Insured is required to select a Coinsurance percentage of 25% or higher; if his property is worth $50,000 but less than $75,000, he may use 20% Coinsurance or any higher percentage, etc.

Deductible Clause—If the Insured wishes, he may have his policy written with a Deductible Clause, under which he will assume the initial $50, $100, $250, $500 or $1,000 of any loss. A rate credit is allowed for the use of a Deductible Clause.

ADDITIONAL COVERAGES

Underground Water Supply Mains and Fire Hydrants—The basic Water Damage policy excludes loss caused directly or indirectly by breakage or leakage from underground water supply mains and fire hydrants. This coverage may be provided for an extra premium. No special endorsement is required, since the Water Damage Form sets forth this coverage with the proviso that it is to be effective only if an additional premium is inserted on Page 1 of the policy. When no such additional premium is shown, the extra protection of this clause does not apply.

When the policy is broadened to include Underground Water Supply Mains and Fire Hydrants, the water from such sources may enter the building through the building walls, and the exclusion of seepage through building walls does not apply. It will still apply, however, to water from any other source.

Chemical Refrigerant Leakage—The basic Water Damage policy covers only damage caused by water or steam. The policy may be extended to cover also the accidental discharge or leakage of the chemical refrigerant from any refrigerating or air conditioning system. No endorsement is needed to broaden the policy, as this added coverage is included in the Water Damage Form, to be effective when an additional premium is inserted.

Other Provisions—The other provisions of the Water Damage policy are identical with the Sprinkler Leakage policy. The reader should refer to the Sprinkler Leakage portion of this chapter, beginning with Non-Reduction After Loss.

FOR FURTHER READING

ACKERMAN—Insurance
HEDGES—Practical Fire and Casualty Insurance
MAGEE AND BICKELHAUPT—General Insurance
POLICY, FORM AND MANUAL ANALYSIS SERVICE
RIEGEL, ROBERT AND MILLER—Insurance

(See Reading List at End of Book)

CHAPTER 10

Personal Crime Coverages

MOST PROPERTY is exposed to the threat of loss from casualties which are not the result of human agency, such as fire, windstorm, water damage, explosion, etc. In addition, the property owner faces a very real threat of loss due to the activities of criminals. Statistics indicate that the number of burglaries, robberies and thefts in this country actually greatly exceed the number of fires.

This chapter will discuss two forms of insurance made available to protect householders against loss or damage caused by theft.

BROAD FORM PERSONAL THEFT POLICY

THE POLICY AFFORDS coverage under two broad sections, each of which is distinct from the other. Coverage A pertains to loss from the Insured's premises and extends to depositories, warehouses or certain occupied dwellings. Loss *away* from the Premises is available under Coverage B of the policy, which is optional with the Insured.

WHAT IS COVERED

The Broad Form Personal Theft policy may be used to cover almost every type of property owned by individuals. This includes personal effects, household furniture and equipment, radios, television sets, books, real property and other property incidental to the use and maintenance of the home.

Several classes of property are specifically excluded from the coverage of the policy, as follows:

Aircraft, automobile, trailer, motorcycle, or any equipment of such

Animals and birds

Articles carried or held as samples or for sale or delivery after sale.

Damage to Premises—The Broad Form Personal Theft policy

also covers damage to the premises and to the insured property by theft or attempted theft.

When Premises Are Rented to Another—If the Insured rents his premises to another for use as a private residence, the policy will cover the Insured's property left on the premises, but not money, securities, jewelry, or watches. The policy will not, however, cover any property belonging to a guest, or to the tenant. There is no coverage for any loss committed by the tenant or members of his household or his employees.

HAZARDS COVERED

The Broad Form Personal Theft policy covers almost every loss due to the unlawful taking of property. The word "Theft" is defined broadly as "any act of stealing" and would therefore take in burglary, larceny, pilferage, etc. Mysterious disappearance (except of a stipulated class of property discussed below under HAZARDS NOT COVERED) is also covered as an insured peril.

The term "mysterious disappearance" has given rise to many thorny situations, with courts in different jurisdictions giving varying interpretations to the term. Put as simply as possible, most decisions appear to see the peril as falling somewhere between an "all-risk" approach where the mere loss of property would suffice to establish a loss and the burden on the Insured of demonstrating by a preponderance of evidence that there was an actual theft. Thus, it has been held that an Insured under a Broad Form Theft policy was *not* covered for the loss of his watch which slipped from his wrist while he was out fishing, since there was no element of "mystery" to the loss. On the other hand, the loss of luggage after it had been checked with the airline was held to be covered under the terms of "mysterious disappearance."

Damage—The policy also covers all damage to the insured property and to the premises caused by theft or an attempted theft. This coverage will apply to damage caused to fences, trees, shrubbery, plumbing fixtures, garages and other structures on the premises, and all real and personal property covered under the policy. Thus, whether the property is actually taken or merely damaged, the loss is covered, as is any damage to the premises. This feature of the policy provides important protection to an Insured, for the damage done by thieves in their search for valuables is often very extensive.

Vandalism and Malicious Mischief—The Broad Form Personal Theft policy also covers damage by Vandalism and Malicious Mischief to the interior of any part of a building occupied by the Insured, and to insured property therein. Loss is covered only if caused to the *interior* of the building, and if the Insured owns the building or is liable for the damage. This is *additional* protection, since it covers acts of vandals or malicious persons even where there was no effort or intent to commit theft.

When coverage is purchased under Coverage B—Theft Away From Premises, insured property is covered against loss or damage by vandalism or malicious mischief anywhere in the world (discussed below under WHERE COVERED — Coverage B — Theft Away From Premises).

A Broad Form Personal Theft policy may be written to cover only against burglary. The premium for a policy so limited is 20% lower than for the regular policy.

HAZARDS NOT COVERED

The Broad Form Personal Theft policy does not cover:

Loss by mysterious disappearance of a precious or semi-precious stone from a setting in a watch or piece of jewelry. Note that *theft* of a stone would be covered.

Theft, attempted theft, vandalism or malicious mischief, committed by an Insured. Since the policy defines "an Insured" to include any person while a member of the named Insured's household, theft committed by such person would not be covered. Theft by a residence employee or a non-relative of the Insured who pays board *would* be covered.

Loss *sustained* by boarders or anyone not related to the Insured who pays board or rent to the Insured.

Loss due to war, whether declared or not, invasion, civil war, insurrection, rebellion or revolution.

Loss caused by nuclear reaction, radiation or radioactive contamination.

WHO IS COVERED

The Broad Form Personal Theft policy covers the loss of property from the premises by theft, whether the insured is the owner of the property or not. It will therefore cover all members of the Insured's household, whether related to him or not, and, at his option, his guests and servants. One specific exception to this broad protection is that the policy does not cover a person not related to the Insured who pays board or rent to the Insured.

If a loss occurs at a portion of the premises not occupied exclusively by the Insured's household, the insurance applies only to property owned by or used by a permanent member of the Insured's household or by a residence employee. Thus, if a guest was to leave some of his property in a vestibule or corridor which was occupied by the Insured in common with others, there would be no coverage.

Death of Insured—If the Insured dies, the policy automatically covers the spouse if resident in the same household. Also covered are the Insured's legal representatives.

WHERE COVERED

As pointed out at the beginning of the analysis of this policy, coverage is afforded separately for loss from the premises and for loss away from the premises. Individual amounts of insurance may be purchased by an Insured under each of the Coverages, and a policy may be written covering only under Coverage A — Theft from the Premises. These sections of the policy are discussed separately below.

Coverage A—Theft from Premises

The policy covers property anywhere on the premises. The word "premises" is used very broadly and is defined to include the grounds, garages, stables, and other outbuildings incidental to the described residence. It would therefore include tool sheds, guest houses, storage sheds, etc. A policy covering an Insured in an apartment house would afford coverage for loss of property in a basement storage bin, public corridors, roof areas, etc. The policy further extends "premises" to include certain designated areas which are not on the Insured's own premises, as discussed later.

Depository, Public Warehouse, Other Occupied Residences—In addition to the premises which the Insured designates in the policy, he is also covered for loss of property which he has placed for safekeeping within any bank, trust or safe deposit company or public warehouse.

The policy also covers loss of property from within any other occupied dwelling which is *not* owned, or occupied by, or rented to the Insured. The policy would not cover any secondary residence owned or occupied by or rented to the Insured unless designated in the policy.

The Premises coverage, Coverage A, applies to losses of insured property from within a safe deposit company, bank, trust company, warehouse and other occupied dwelling, but only if such is located within the United States, District of Columbia, Virgin Islands, Puerto Rico, Canal Zone or Canada.

Premises Used as Boarding House or for Business—If the premises, or any portion thereof, are used for a boarding or lodging house, or for business or professional services, the Insured must declare such use to the Company, which may then extend the policy for such uses. A higher premium is charged for such occupancies. Otherwise, the policy would not cover such premises.

Removal to Other Premises — If the Insured moves to other premises which he intends to occupy permanently as his private residence, the policy covers loss of insured property while in transit, at the new premises, and at the old premises. When the moving is completed, the coverage ceases to apply to the old premises. This extra protection during moving of an Insured's residence is afforded only for 30 days. There is no additional premium for this coverage during the removal period.

Coverage B—Theft Away from Premises

As pointed out above, the Broad Form Personal Theft policy may be written to include coverage for loss of property sustained away from the premises. A separate amount of insurance must be purchased under Coverage B to provide such coverage (except from depository, public warehouse or occupied dwellings which are covered as part of the Premises coverage, discussed above under Coverage A).

The policy may be written with Coverage A—Theft from Premises, only.

Basically, the coverage on property away from premises under Coverage B is the same as that provided under Coverage A for the premises. There are several special provisions that apply to Coverage B, as set forth next.

Where Covered—While the Premises Coverage A is confined to loss sustained within the United States, District of Columbia, Virgin Islands, Puerto Rico, Canal Zone or Canada, Coverage B is world-wide.

Secondary Residences—Coverage B does not extend to property in any dwelling owned or occupied by or rented to the Insured *except* when he is temporarily residing therein. There is no coverage for such locations which are unoccupied or which are permanently occupied, and these would require designation as additional premises.

If the property is placed in an occupied dwelling which is *not* owned or occupied by or rented to the Insured, such location is covered as part of the Premises Coverage, Coverage A.

Property in the Mails—The policy specifically excludes property in the mail.

Theft from Laundry, Cleaner, Dyer, Tailor, Presser—There is no coverage for theft of an Insured's property from a laundry, cleaner, dyer, tailor or presser, except when such theft is effected by robbery (holdup) or by breaking and entering of the premises.

Property of Servants—Property of servants is covered under Coverage B, Theft Away from Premises, only if at the time of the actual loss they are engaged in the employment of the Insured and the property is in their custody or at a temporary residence of the Insured or of a permanent member of his household.

FOR HOW MUCH

The Company is liable for not more than the actual cash value of the property at the time of the loss, nor for more than it would take to repair or replace the property with other of like kind and quality. The Company may pay for the loss in cash or may repair or replace the property.

No Coinsurance clause is included in the Broad Form Personal Theft policy. The Company is liable for the full amount of any loss, as described above, subject to certain important limits which apply to specific classes of property. The basic policy limits the amount of insurance on several types of property, and these are discussed below.

In additional, there are two ways in which a Broad Form Personal Theft policy may be written and under each form the insurance applicable to jewelry and furs differs. Each of these two types of Theft insurance will be discussed separately.

Limitation on Money—The Broad Form Personal Theft policy will not pay more than $100 for any loss of money. This limit is part of the basic policy and is the same in any Broad Form Personal Theft policy, regardless of its amount. The limit may be increased by endorsement and the payment of an additional premium.

Limitation on Securities—The policy will not pay more than $500 for loss of securities and stamps in current use. This limit may also be increased by endorsement.

Limit of Liability on Jewelry and Furs—The Company may or may not be liable up to the full extent of its policy for loss of jewelry and furs. As mentioned, this will depend on the form in which the Broad Form Personal Theft policy is written.

Other Insurance—The Broad Form Personal Theft policy does not cover property insured under any other policy which describes the property specifically. It therefore will not apply to any article insured under a Jewelry Floater, Fur Floater, Camera Floater,

Musical Instrument Floater, and similar policies which itemize each article insured.

If the Insured or a permanent member of his household has other policies covering the property which do not specifically describe the articles covered (like a Fire insurance policy), the Broad Form Theft policy will act as excess insurance, paying only such amount of any loss as exceeds the amount of the other insurance.

Thus, assume an Insured carried $3,000 of insurance on his household property in a Fire insurance policy with an Extended Coverage and a Vandalism and Malicious Mischief endorsement. He also carries $1,000 of Broad Form Theft insurance. Vandals do $3,500 of damage to his household goods. The Fire insurance policy will pay up to its $3,000 limit and the Broad Form Theft policy will be liable for the balance of the loss, $500. On the other hand, if the damage amounted to $2,500, the Fire insurance policy would be liable for the entire loss.

There is no coverage, even as excess insurance, under a Broad Form Theft policy on any property otherwise insured which is not owned by the Insured or a permanent member of his household. Thus, a guest's property which is insured under any other policy would not be covered under the Broad Form Theft policy of the host.

Pair and Set Clause—The policy stipulates that it will give consideration to the importance of an article which is lost from a set, but that the loss will not be considered a total loss.

Deductible—A $15 Deductible clause may be incorporated in the policy which will be written at a discount of 15% from the usual rates, applicable to the first $1,000 of coverage. In many states, a mandatory $100 Deductible applies separately to Coverages A and B.

Limitation of Liability on Boats—There is no limitation of liability on boats which are on the premises and the full amount of insurance applicable to Section A will apply to the loss. Under Section B, Theft Away from Premises, however, the Company's liability for loss of boats is limited to $500.

HOW THEFT INSURANCE IS WRITTEN

For purposes of Broad Form Personal Theft insurance there are two broad groups of property, as follows:

Section (a) Jewelry and furs which include jewelry, watches, necklaces, bracelets, gems, precious and semi-precious stones, articles of gold, platinum, and furs, and articles containing fur which represents their principal value.

Section (b) All property other than of the kind described above under Section (a).

Specified Articles—Under a Broad Form Personal Theft policy, it is possible to insure by endorsement specified articles which are listed and described individually with a dollar value set alongside each article. Any type of property may be insured under this section, jewelry or otherwise. Silverware, stamp and coin collections may be insured as a group, as may linen, liquor and food.

Broad Form Theft policies may be written in one of two ways:

1. **Divided Coverage**—A separate amount of insurance is effected on the class of property described in Section (a) and a separate amount for Section (b). No itemization is required of the property in either group. A dollar amount is set to cover all property in the group; e. g., $1,000 on Section (a), $2,000 on Section (b).

The total amount of insurance under such a policy is $3,000, but only $1,000 may be collected for loss of jewelry and furs, while not more than $2,000 will be applicable to loss of other property.

Thus, if the Insured suffers a theft in which the criminals make off with $1,300 of jewelry and $400 of clothing, he can collect only $1,400—$1,000 for the jewelry and $400 for the "other property," even though he has a total of $3,000 of insurance under the policy.

2. **100% Blanket Coverage**—The entire policy amount is applicable to any loss, regardless of the type of property involved. Section (a) and Section (b) property are combined and are covered by the one amount. Thus, under a $1,000 Broad Form Theft policy written on a 100% Blanket basis, loss of *any* property is covered up to $1,000.

The $100 limitation on money and the $500 limitation on securities applies under either of the two types of Broad Form Theft policy.

Regardless of its amount or the form on which written, the policy provides no coverage on money, securities, jewelry, watches, necklaces, bracelets, gems, precious and semi-precious stones, and articles of gold and platinum which are stolen from the premises after the Insured has rented the premises to another.

The $100 limitation on money, and $500 limitation on securities applies equally to Coverage A and Coverage B.

Limitation of Liability to Limits Under Coverage A—Coverage B must be written on all articles of jewelry or furs which are specifically insured under Coverage A. It may also be written, at the option of the Insured, to cover on a Blanket basis all property of the Insured, whether Section (a) or Section (b) property.

When written on a Blanket basis, Coverage B will apply to Section (a) or Section (b) up to the amount applicable to such property under Coverage A. Thus, assume an Insured buys a Broad Form Theft policy on a Divided Coverage basis writen as follows:

COVERAGE A		COVERAGE B	
Section (a)	$1,000	Blanket	$2,000
Section (b)	3,000		
Specific (c)	750	Specific	750

Though the amount of Blanket insurance under Coverage B is $2,000, only $1,000 of this coverage will apply to jewelry, watches or furs, since that is the limit applicable to this property under Coverage A.

Physicians, Surgeons and Dentists Outside Coverage—Surgical, medical and dental instruments, apparatus, medicines, drugs and books, including the bag or case in which such equipment is carried, may be insured against loss away from the premises under Coverage B by any doctor or dentist whose residence or office is insured under Coverage A.

INSURED'S DUTIES AND OBLIGATIONS

While a written application is not usually required, the Insured is asked whether within the past five years he has sustained any loss or received indemnity for loss by burglary, robbery, theft or larceny. He must also state whether an insurance Company has declined to issue or cancelled a policy of this kind within the past five years. These statements are made part of the basic policy, which provides space for the declarations.

REQUIREMENTS IN CASE OF LOSS

Notice of Loss—Proof of Loss—The Insured is required to give notice of loss as soon as practicable to the Company or its agent, and also to the police. Proof of Loss must be filed within four months after the loss is *discovered.*

Examination Under Oath—Submission of Records — The Company may require the Insured or any other person making claim under the policy to submit to examination under oath, and to produce for examination all records which have any bearing on the loss. The Insured is expected to cooperate with the Company in all matters relating to the loss. As in other forms of insurance, he is expected to behave as a prudent man would if he had no insurance to cover the loss. He may be asked to prosecute a residence employee who has been guilty of theft, make eevry effort to recover the property, make known a reward offer, etc.

Suit Against Company—The Insured cannot institute a suit against the Company until he has complied with all the conditions of the policy and until 90 days have elapsed from the date on which he filed a Proof of Loss with the Company, nor later than two years from the date of the occurrence giving rise to the claim.

Settlement of Loss with Others—The Company may settle a loss for property stolen from the premises with the Insured or, if the property belonged to another, with that person.

Reinstatement After Loss—The Broad Form Personal Theft policy is not reduced by the amount of any loss, and the full limit of liability is available after a loss occurs, but only for losses which occur after the Company has received notice of the earlier loss. The policy *is* reduced for any losses which occur before notice is given.

By way of illustration, assume an Insured carries a Broad Form Personal Theft policy of $1,000 on the 100% Blanket Form. Thieves get into his residence on January 15 and make off with $600 of personal property. He does not report this loss to the Company until January 30. If he was to suffer a second theft on January 25, the amount of insurance available to cover this loss would only be $400, even if the loss was not discovered until after January 30, since the policy is reduced by the amount of the first loss.

Similarly, in the above case, after the Insured had reported the $600 loss to the Company on January 30, and he then discovers a loss which took place on January 5, the amount of insurance available for this loss of January 5 is only $400.

Subrogation—See Chapter 2.

Benefit of Insurance—See Chapter 11.

Cancellation—See Chapter 2.

A binder for a Broad Form Personal Theft policy may be cancelled by the Company, but such cancellation does not take effect until noon of the third business day.

Term of Policy—The policy runs to noon, Standard Time.

Assignment of Policy — Assignment of the policy is not valid without the consent of the Company.

Regulation—Practically every Company writing Theft insurance uses the rates and policies established by the Insurance Rating Board and there is almost complete standardization of the field.

RATES

Rates for Theft insurance are based on the territory in which the Insured's residence is located.

Yachts and railroad cars may be written as private residences.

In Theft insurance, any building which houses more than four families takes the apartment house rate, which is higher in each instance than the corresponding private, two, three or four family dwelling rate.

Rates depend on the territory in which the risk is located. Territorial multipliers or factors are applied to a master table to arrive at rates for the individual states. Each state has its own territorial divisions.

Rates for Broad Form Personal Theft insurance are highest for the first $1,000 of coverage under any of the forms; each additional $1,000 is written at successively lower rates, with the lowest rate applying to the 6th and all subsequent amounts of insurance.

Minimum Premiums—In each territory, the minimum premium is the premium for $1,000 of insurance, but not less than $15.00.

NEW YORK—A minimum premium of $10 applies.

For Blanket Coverage B, the minimum premium is also the premium for $1,000 of insurance and is in addition to the minimum premium for Coverage A. In addition, the annual premium for $1,000 of coverage is the minimum *retained* premium, whether the policy is carried for one year or less.

Three-Year Policies—The three-year rate is 2.7 times the annual. The three-year premium may be paid in installments.

Whole Dollar Premium Rule—discussed in Chapter 8 under OTHER FACTORS WHICH AFFECT FIRE INSURANCE RATES —Whole Dollar Premium Rule.

PERSONAL THEFT POLICY

(PERSONAL THEFT ENDORSEMENT)

DESIGNED FOR THE smaller household, to whom the premium for a Broad Form Personal Theft policy might prove prohibitive, the Personal Theft policy is somewhat more limited in scope than the Broad Form Personal Theft policy, although it is patterned on the broader form of coverage.

The policy may be written as a separate contract, or by endorsement on a Fire insurance policy covering household property.

The Personal Theft policy (or endorsement) follows the Broad Form Personal Theft policy very closely, and the discussion of this newer form will base itself on that of the broader policy analyzed above pointing up only the differences between the two policies.

HAZARDS COVERED

The Personal Theft policy is identical with the Broad Form Personal Theft policy except that mysterious disappearance is not included as an insured peril.

HAZARDS NOT COVERED

The Personal Theft policy is identical with the Broad Form Personal Theft policy.

WHAT IS COVERED

There is no coverage on boats, either on or off premises.

FOR HOW MUCH

Different from the Broad Form Personal Theft policy, which is available in two forms with optional Coverage B (Away From Premises), the Personal Theft policy is a package policy with one amount of insurance applying both on and off the premises.

The policy distinguishes between Section (a) and Section (b) property exactly along the lines of the Broad Form Personal Theft policy when written on a Divided Coverage basis, and may be extended to include specific coverages.

WHERE COVERED

As pointed out above under FOR HOW MUCH, the Personal Theft policy does not distinguish between on-premises and off-premises coverage. A single amount of insurance applies both on and off premises.

Theft From Automobiles—The basic provisions of the Personal Theft policy are the same as under a Broad Form Personal Theft policy. Under the Personal Theft policy there is no coverage, however, for loss of property left unattended in any automobile, motorcycle or trailer, other than a public conveyance, unless the loss results from forcible entry of which visible marks are left on the exterior of the vehicle.

Dormitory, Fraternity, Sorority—The Personal Theft policy does not cover loss from a dormitory, fraternity or sorority house.

Hotels, Penthouses—The Personal Theft policy is not available to Insureds who reside in hotels or penthouses or on premises which are used in whole or in part for professional or business occupancy, nor where more than two boarders or lodgers, other than relatives of the Insured, live with the Insured.

How Personal Theft Policy Is Written—The Personal Theft policy is written for fixed amounts with the various limits described in the preceding paragraph. The premium for increased amounts of insurance reduces substantially in each successive bracket.

Other Clauses—The Personal Theft policy parallels the Broad

Form Personal Theft policy in most of its basic provisions on Insured's Duties and Obligations, Requirements in Case of Loss, Subrogation, Benefit of Insurance, Cancellation, Assignment of Policy, Regulation and Rates. As in the case of the Broad Form Personal Theft policy, rates are based on territory, and are further subdivided for private and two-family dwellings, and apartments and flats. Territorial multipliers or factors are applied to a master table with each state having its own territorial divisions. As pointed out before under WHERE COVERED, the policy is not available for Insureds who reside in hotels or penthouses.

FOR FURTHER READING

ACKERMAN—Insurance
GEE—Agent's Casualty Guide
HEDGES—Practical Fire and Casualty Insurance
KULP AND HALL—Casualty Insurance.
MAGEE AND BICKELHAUPT—General Insurance
MEHR AND CAMMACK—Principles of Insurance
POLICY, FORM AND MANUAL ANALYSIS SERVICE
RIEGEL, ROBERT AND MILLER—Insurance

(See Reading List at End of Book)

CHAPTER 11

Commercial Burglary Policies

OPEN STOCK BURGLARY POLICY

THE STANDARD POLICY to insure commercial property against loss by burglary is the Open Stock Burglary policy. Also known as Mercantile Open Stock Burglary, this insurance can be used to cover any type of business enterprise, including manufacturers, wholesalers, jobbers, retailers, service businesses, processors, etc. As will be shown, the policy covers not only the stock of a business enterprise but also its fixtures, machinery, equipment, and the premises itself.

WHAT IS COVERED

The policy covers merchandise, furniture, fixtures and equipment. No itemization of the property insured is required, the Insured merely stating in the Declarations of the policy the nature of the business being conducted at the premises.

The Open Stock Burglary policy does *not* cover money or securities or manuscripts, records or accounts. The amount of insurance on jewelry and pledged articles is specially limited in the policy, and these limitations are discussed later under FOR HOW MUCH. There is also a restriction for loss of furs by "window-smashing," and this exclusion is discussed under HAZARDS NOT COVERED.

Damage to Premises — The policy also covers damage to the premises caused by burglary or an attempted burglary, provided the Insured is the owner of the premises or is liable for the damage.

Ownership of Property—The policy insures all property on the premises designated, whether the Insured owns such property or not. It covers property held by the Insured in any capacity, whether he is legally liable for the property or not. In addition to paying for loss to such property, the Company will pay the cost of defending any suit brought by persons whose property has sustained any loss or damage by burglary while in the hands of the Insured.

The policy stipulates that insurance does not apply to the interest of any other person or organization in any property unless such interest is included by the Insured in his Proof of Loss. This clause permits the Insured to choose what third party claims should be made against his policy.

HAZARDS COVERED

The coverage of the Open Stock Burglary policy is confined strictly to the peril of "burglary" and one specific form of robbery, discussed directly below under Robbery of Watchman. The policy defines "burglary" as the felonious abstraction of property from within the premises by any person or persons making felonious entry into or exit from the premises by actual force and violence when the premises are not open for business, of which there shall be visible marks made upon the exterior or interior of the premises at the place of such entry or exit by tools, explosives, electricity or chemicals.

All the conditions spelled out must be satisfied for the loss to come within the coverage of the Open Stock Burglary policy. The premises must be closed, entry or exit must be made by force, and marks of violence must be left upon the exterior or interior of the premises at the point of entry or exit. If any one of these conditions is not satisfied, there is no coverage.

Thus, if entry is made into the premises without use of force, there is no coverage even if after entering, the criminals tear open closets, desks, inside rooms, chests, etc. If entry is gained by means of a pass-key, or if the premises are left open, or if a thief gets himself locked inside the premises before closing and leaves the premises without forcibly breaking out, or if property is carried out when the place is open for business, or if a holdup is perpetrated —all these and similar losses are NOT covered.

NEW YORK—Forcible exit from the premises is not covered under the basic policy. This coverage may be added by endorsement of the policy for an additional premium.

Robbery of Watchman—While the policy is designed to cover the peril of burglary, as defined, it is extended to cover loss caused by the robbery (holdup) or attempted robbery of a watchman employed exclusively by the Insured while on duty within the premises, while the premises are not open for business.

Theft Insurance (Mercantile Open Stock Theft)—An Open Stock Burglary policy may be extended by the addition of a Mercantile Open Stock Theft Endorsement to cover the perils of robbery, theft and larceny. Coverage under this endorsement is subject to a $50 Deductible, which will apply to any perils assumed under this endorsement, but not to the coverage of the basic Open Stock Burglary policy. Thus, robbery of a *watchman,* which is a peril assumed under the basic Open Stock Burglary policy, would not be subject to the Deductible, where robbery of other employees would fall within the Deductible provision.

Larceny is a broad term that takes in almost every unlawful taking of property. When the Theft Endorsement is added to the Open Stock Burglary policy, the policy covers during all hours of the day and night, whether the premises are open for business or not. An additional premium of 15% is charged for this endorsement for wholesale, manufacturing and warehouse risks; 45% to others. (Risks rated as jewelers or those who deal in furs and pelts pay a higher premium for the Theft Endorsement.)

NEW YORK—The charges for this endorsement are 40% for wholesale and manufacturing risks; 75% to others.

Mere disappearance is not covered. There must be some evidence of theft. Inventory shortages are not covered except where there is evidence of theft, and then only for such loss as exceeds the Insured's average inventory shortage during the five years preceding the loss.

There is no coverage for loss caused by an employee (discussed directly below under HAZARDS NOT COVERED—Infidelity of Employees).

Also excluded is loss by parting with title to or possession of property through any fraudulent scheme, trick, device or false pretense. This exclusion may be removed for an additional premium of 5%.

HAZARDS NOT COVERED

Infidelity of Employees—The Open Stock Burglary policy does not cover any burglary which the Insured, any associate in interest, or any servant employee causes, or in which such person acts as accessory. This exclusion will apply even if such person does not actually himself participate in the crime, and regardless of whether he is actually working at the time or personally benefits from the crime. Thus, if an employee assists outsiders to perpetrate a burglary, out of a grudge he bears his employer, the loss is not covered.

It is important to remember that the exclusion of employee dishonesty continues to apply, even if the policy is broadened by the addition of a Theft endorsement.

War, Insurrection, Etc.—The policy does not cover loss due to war, whether declared or not, civil war, insurrection, rebellion or revolution, or to any act or condition incident to any of these situations.

Fire—The policy will not cover any burglary during a fire in the premises. If the fire is in another part of the building, the policy will cover. Loss by fire, even if caused by a burglary, is not covered, except for the damage to a safe or vault.

Change in Condition of Risk—The policy does not cover loss occurring while there is any change in the condition of the risk. However, if the protection promised by the Insured is not maintained for reasons which are beyond his control, the coverage of the policy may not lapse.

The situation differs with the type of protection promised. If the protection warranted in the policy is of equipment or services *other* than an alarm system, the policy will be available for the loss but in amount reduced to what the premium paid would have purchased without the discounts granted the Insured for the promised protection.

If an alarm system was warranted, and the system is not in working order for reasons beyond the Insured's control, a watchman must be provided during the entire period when the premises are closed for business and the alarm is not working. In such event, the policy will provide a reduced amount of coverage as under the circumstances discussed in the paragraph directly above.

EXAMPLE: Insured carries $5,000 of Open Stock Burglary insurance. The basic rate for his trade group in his territory is $15 per $1,000 of insurance. He warrants that a burglar alarm will be in working order and receives a 40% discount. He pays $9.00 per $1,000, or $45 for the policy. At closing time, the Insured discovers that the alarm is out of order. He is required to place a watchman on the premises when closed for business, and this watchman must be additional to any already declared in his policy. If he complies with this stipulation, he will have $3,000 of insurance available to cover a loss—the amount of insurance that his $45 premium would purchase without any credits for protection.

Records of Insured—The Insured is required to keep records in such a manner that the Company can accurately determine the amount of loss.

Vandalism and Malicious Mischief—The policy does not cover loss caused by vandals or malicious persons who are not attempting to perpetrate a burglary.

Fur Articles—The Open Stock Burglary policy specifically excludes loss of furs or articles in which fur represents the principal value when such property is stolen from a show window in the premises by a person who has broken the glass from outside the premises, unless such articles are specifically covered.

Nuclear Perils—The Open Stock Burglary policy does not cover loss caused by nuclear reaction, radiation or radioactive contamination.

WHERE COVERED

Coverage is afforded for loss from the premises, which is defined as the interior of that portion of the building at the location designated and described in the Declarations, as occupied by the Insured in his business. By a special endorsement, it is possible to broaden the defintion of "premises" to include the grounds, provided these are entirely enclosed by a fence or wall.

Property in outside show cases (those not opening into the interior of the premises) is covered for loss by burglarly but only up to $100, and only if such show case is located inside the building line of the building containing the premises, or is attached to the building. The $100 limitation applies separately to each show case or show window.

When an Insured operates from more than one location, each location may be separately insured, or a Blanket policy may be written to cover in one amount over all his locations.

Automatic Insurance on Additional Locations—New locations which the Insured adds after his policy is issued may be insured automatically, provided the Insured notifies the Company of the acquisition of the new location within 60 days after he occupies such new premises. This automatic coverage for new locations must be endorsed on the policy, as the basic policy not so endorsed does not provide for this automatic protection.

FOR HOW MUCH

The Open Stock Burglary policy is not liable for more than the actual cash value of the property at the time of the loss or the cost to repair or replace such property. The Company may pay the loss in cash, or may actually repair or replace the property lost or damaged.

Full Salvage to Insured—The policy provides that if any of the property is recovered after a loss, it shall first go to reimbursing the party who effected such recovery, with the balance applied as if the recovery had been made before the loss occurred, and the loss readjusted accordingly. Thus, assume an Insured who carries $5,000 of Open Stock Burglary insurance suffers a $7,000 burglary. The Company pays its full limit under the policy, $5,000. The Company pursues the criminals and is able to recover $3,000 of the stolen property. If its expenses in making this recovery came to $250, it would be entitled to repayment for these expenses. The balance of $2,750 would be applied as though it had been recovered before the loss. The Insured would receive $2,750, and his loss re-adjusted as though it had been $4,250. It can be seen that the effect of the clause is to use any salvage that may be recovered first to make the Insured whole, after payment of expenses of the recovering party. The Company is entitled to retain only any excess left after its Insured is fully indemnified.

Profits Insurance — An Open Stock Burglary policy covering a manufacturer, processor or converter may be endorsed for an additional premium of 33⅓% to cover not only the actual cash value of stolen property but also the loss of profits. The protection covers loss of profits on raw material, material in process and finished merchandise. The Profits insurance of the Open Stock Burglary is akin to the Profits and Commissions Fire insurance policy in that it covers loss of profits on merchandise, but not any loss due to interruption of future production.

Jewelry and Pledged Articles—The Company's liability for any single article of jewelry, or article containing one or more gems, or watch, or precious or semi-precious stones is $50. On any article held by the Insured as a pledge or as a collateral for a loan, the maximum liability is $50, or the value of the article as recorded by the Insured when he made the advance, or, when there is no such record, the amount of the unpaid balance due the Insured, whichever is least.

Consequential Loss—Clothing Risks—When parts of clothing are lost or damaged, it often happens that remaining parts of the garments are reduced in value. This consequential loss may be insured by endorsement under the Open Stock Burglary policy. When the policy is so endorsed, it will pay not only for the parts of the clothing stolen or damaged, but also for the consequential reduction in the parts of the clothing not taken by the burglars.

Where the other parts of the clothing are on the insured premises, there is no charge for the endorsement. Where the parts of clothing are located elsewhere than on the insured premises, an additional premium of 25% is charged.

Coinsurance (Average Clause)—The Open Stock Burglary policy contains a Coinsurance clause. The clause is similar to the Average clause or Coinsurance clause of the Fire insurance policy, in that the Insured is required to maintain a minimum amount of insurance, based on the values at risk. If he fails to maintain this required level of insurance, he will be a coinsurer, and will have to carry a portion of any loss he suffers. (See Chapter 3.)

In Burglary insurance, the required percentage of insurance to value varies with the territory in which the risk is located, ranging from 40% to 80%. Furthermore, an additional factor enters into the Coinsurance provision of the Open Stock Burglary policy — a Coinsurance Limit.

Each trade is listed in the Burglary manual with a definite Coinsurance limit, which is a ceiling on the amount of insurance required by the particular trade. If the Insured carries this stipulated amount of insurance, he is deemed to have complied with the Coinsurance requirement of the policy, regardless of the value of the property he is insuring. These Coinsurance Limits range from $2,000 to $60,000. To comply with the Coinsurance requirements, an Insured need carry only the given percentage of the actual cash value of his property, *or* the Coinsurance Limit, *whichever is less.*

EXAMPLE: A jobber of tobacco products in Brooklyn carries a stock of $40,000. The Coinsurance percentage for this territory is 80%. Based on this percentage, he would have to carry at least $32,000 of Open Stock Burglary insurance in order to avoid being coinsured. But the Coinsurance Limit for jobbers of tobacco products is shown in the manual as $7,500. If this Insured carries $7,500, he is considered to be adequately covered as regards the Coinsurance requirements. Looked at another way, when the Insured carries insurance equal to or larger than the Coinsurance Limit for his trade, the Coinsurance clause is rendered inoperative. The Coinsurance percentage for the territory is stated in the policy Declarations, as is the Coinsurance Limit.

The Insured must not necessarily carry insurance equal to the Coinsurance Limit to comply with the Coinsurance requirements of the clause. He can comply with the conditions of the Coinsurance clause by carrying the stated percentage of the values at risk. Thus, if the tobacco jobber mentioned above had a stock of $5,000, he could be adequately insured, as regards the Coinsurance clause, with $4,000 of insurance—80% of the actual cash value of the property. If his stock was $3,000, $2,400 of insurance would suffice, etc.

The Coinsurance Limit is not a limit on the amount of insurance that may be carried. Thus, the tobacco jobber with a $40,000 stock might feel that he is exposed to a loss far in excess of the Coinsurance Limit for his trade. He may prefer to be fully covered and carry $40,000, or any amount of insurance from $7,500 to $40,000.

Furniture, fixtures, equipment and machinery are not subject to Coinsurance and the value of this property need not be taken into account in determining the amount of insurance to carry in order to comply with the Coinsurance clause. If however the Insured is not carrying sufficient insurance in terms of the value of the merchandise he holds, the deficiency will be applied to the adjustment of any loss involving furniture and fixtures.

Jewelry, watches, necklaces and articles containing one or more gems, precious and semi-precious stones and pledged articles are not subject to Coinsurance, and the value of such property may be excluded in arriving at the amount of insurance required. The value of property in outside show cases not opening directly into the Insured's premises may also be omitted in applying the Coinsurance clause.

Other Insurance—The Open Stock Burglary policy does not afford any coverage on property which is specifically described and enumerated in any other policy. It will apply, as excess insurance only, to property insured in a Blanket, non-specific way, provided the Insured owns such property or is legally liable for it.

INSURED'S DUTIES AND OBLIGATIONS

Records of Insured—Discussed before under HAZARDS NOT COVERED.

Maintenance of Promised Protection—Discussed before under HAZARDS NOT COVERED.

Insured's Statements—The Insured is required to describe accurately the business he conducts and to declare any other business which he conducts at the premises. If the Insured carries any other insurance on Burglary, Robbery or Theft, he must set forth the existence of such other policies. He must declare any losses he has sustained within the past five years by burglary, robbery or theft, and whether any insurance Company has declined to issue or cancelled any insurance of this kind within the past five years.

Inspection—Maintenance of Premises — The Company has the right to inspect the premises of the Insured at any reasonable time, and to require the Insured to make the premises reasonably secure.

REQUIREMENTS IN CASE OF LOSS

Notice of Loss—Proof of Loss—The Insured must give notice of loss as soon as practicable. In actual practice, any written notice of loss is considered acceptable. The police must also be notified immediately. Proof of Loss must be furnished within four months of the date of discovery of the loss.

Inventory of Property Not Stolen or Damaged—As under a Fire insurance policy, the Insured may be asked to furnish a complete inventory of all articles not stolen or damaged. This requirement is not waived, regardless of the amount of the loss.

Cooperation with Company—The Company may request of the Insured that he render every assistance in his power to facilitate investigation or adjustment of any claim under the policy. He is to produce any and all books, vouchers and papers that may have any bearing on the loss. He is to submit himself and any associates to examination under oath and to interrogation and, as far as he is able, any employee or servant.

Time to Bring Suit—Suit against the Company by the Insured may not be commenced until 90 days after filing of the required Proof of Loss, and not later than two years after the date on which the loss or damage occurred.

Reinstatement After Loss—The Open Stock Burglary policy is reduced by the amount of any loss until the premises are restored to the same condition of safety as existed immediately preceding the loss. An exception is made for an Insured who maintains within the premises at all times when they are closed for business a watchman. In this case, there would be no reduction in the policy amount, except that the Insured is generally required to add an extra watchman until the premises are restored.

Subrogation—Discussed in Chapter 2.

Cancellation—Discussed in Chapter 2.

Binder Cancellation—Discussed in Chapter 17 under Cancellation.

Reduction in Amount—The amount of insurance under an Open Stock Burglary policy may be reduced by the Insured on a pro rata basis up to 50% of the maximum that has applied at any time under the policy. This rule applies on one-year policies and on policies written for longer than one year, cancelled after the first year. On policies which are written for longer than one year and are being reduced during the first year, the earned premium is computed according to the pro rata percentage of the annual premium.

RATES

Open Stock Burglary rates are based on two factors:

1. The territory in which the risk is located.
2. The trade classification of the Insured's business.

There are nine trade group classifications into which fall the 400 odd trades listed in the manual. If an Insured carries more than one type of merchandise, the governing factor is the kind of business conducted. For example, a shoe store carrying an incidental line of hosiery and ladies' purses is classified as "boots and shoes."

Generally, the entire risk is rated under one classification. There are certain exceptions, like textile firms, which carry several different kinds of goods, and firms which carry furs and other types of wearing apparel, and these may be divided for purposes of rate according to the type of merchandise insured.

As in Broad Form Theft insurance, rates reduce for each successive higher bracket. In Open Stock Burglary, however, the rates step down for each successive $5,000 of insurance after the first until $20,000 is reached after which the rates are constant.

Territorial multipliers or factors are applied to a master table with each state having its own territorial divisions.

Three-Year Policies—Discussed in Chapter 10 under Rates.

Whole Dollar Premium Rule—Discussed in Chapter 8 under OTHER FACTORS WHICH AFFECT FIRE INSURANCE RATES —Whole Dollar Premium Rule.

Credits—A discount from the regular rate is allowed if the Insured employs a private watchman. A 30% discount is allowed if the watchman makes rounds and signals to a central alarm station outside the Insured's plant or to a police station, at least once every hour while the premises are closed; 15% is allowed for a private watchman who does not signal to an outside station but registers at least once an hour on a watchman's clock, while 10% is allowed for other watchman service.

To qualify for such discounts, the watchman must be employed exclusively by the Insured. No discount is allowed for a watchman who patrols a building in which the Insured maintains only a portion. The Burglary manual lists certain specific buildings (mostly in New York) where a discount is granted to the tenants of a building which is patrolled by a watchman, even though the watchman is not employed exclusively by the Insured. In addition, the watchman must be on duty at all times when the premises are not open for business, including Saturdays, Sundays and any other day when the premises are closed. If the watchman is on duty at all times except during the daytime of a day when the premises are closed, one-half of the above discounts will apply.

A discount is allowed if the premises are protected by an approved burglar alarm system. Discounts depend on the type of system and whether the Insured occupies the grade floor or floors above the grade floor, and range from 15% to 70%.

In addition to the above discounts, certain risks qualify for discount on the basis of Secondary Iron Work, if such is approved by the Insurance Rating Board.

Any of the above discounts will apply against the basic premium for Open Stock Burglary. These protection services will not reduce the rate for the Theft Endorsement, as the risk of loss under this endorsement is not reduced by the maintenance of such protective devices.

OTHER CLAUSES

Assignment—Assignment of the policy is not valid except with the written consent of the Company. If the Insured dies or is adjudged bankrupt or insolvent, the policy covers the legal representatives (excutors, administrators or receivers), provided notice is given to the Company within 60 days after the date of death or adjudication.

Regulation—Most companies writing Open Stock Burglary insurance use the rates and policy provisions established by the Insurance Rating Board. While there is no standard policy, as such, the provisions of policies written by the great majority of companies are uniform, though the arrangements of the policy provisions may vary somewhat.

Term of Policy—There is no standardization on this point, some Open Stock Burglary policies attaching at 12 noon, Standard Time, and others at 12:01 A. M.

MERCANTILE SAFE BURGLARY INSURANCE

SAFE BURGLARY INSURANCE is provided under the Special Coverage policy which is designed to make available Safe Burglary, Mercantile Robbery, Paymaster Robbery, Paymaster Broad Form and over 20 other forms of Crime insurance. Each of these coverages is provided by a separate endorsement of the Special Coverage policy. Safe Burglary insurance will be treated in this chapter; the several forms of Robbery insurance in Chapter 12. While each of these coverages is strictly an endorsement of the Special Coverage policy to which it must be attached rather than an individual policy, the word "policy" will be used to designate the Special Coverage policy with the particular endorsement.

WHAT IS COVERED

The Mercantile Safe Burglary policy covers the loss of money, securities and other property, with certain few types of property excepted. Note that the policy covers money and securities. Contrast with the Open Stock Burglary policy, which covers merchandise, furniture and fixtures, but not money or securities.

A Mercantile Safe Burglary policy may be written to cover only securities at a 50% reduction in rate. It may also be written to cover only merchandise, or merchandise and securities only at a 25% discount.

The Safe Burglary policy covers loss of property only from within the insured safes or vaults (discussed below under Hazards Covered and Where Covered). Also covered is damage to such property caused by safe burglary as well as the felonious removal of the safe. In addition, the policy covers damage to furniture, fixtures and equipment *outside* of the safe when caused by safe burglary or attempted safe burglary. There is no coverage for damage to property outside of the safe, however, except when the burglary is directed at the safe.

Damage to Furniture, Fixtures and Property—The policy also covers damage by safe burglary or attempt at such burglary to furniture, fixtures, equipment and other property *outside* the safe or vault.

Damage to Building—If the Insured owns the building containing the premises, or is liable for damage to it, the Mercantile Safe Burglary policy will also pay for any damage to the building caused by safe burglars.

Ownership of Property—Discussed under Open Stock Burglary policy.

PROPERTY NOT COVERED

The Mercantile Safe Burglary policy does not cover manuscripts, records or accounts.

HAZARDS COVERED

The coverage of the Mercantile Safe Burglary policy is confined strictly to the peril of burglary. The policy defines burglary exactly as the Open Stock Burglary policy. While the policy does not limit its coverage to hours when the premises are closed for business, it does provide that, at the time of the loss, all doors of the safe and vault must be duly closed and *locked* by all combinations and time locks. To come within the meaning of safe burglary, the entry into the safe must be made by force and violence of which there shall be visible marks upon the exterior of all doors of the safe (or any vault containing such safe) if entry was made through such doors; if entry was not made through the doors, the marks of force or violence must have been made on the top, bottom or walls of such safe or vault (or any vault containing such safe) through which entry was made. If entry to the safe was gained by manipulation of the combination without forcible entry as described, there would be no coverage.

While the safe or vault must be entered forcibly, it is not necessary that the premises be entered by force, except that if premium credit has been allowed for an alarm protecting the premises, then the premises must be *burglarized.*

There is no stipulation, as there is in the Open Stock Burglary policy, that loss occurring *during* a fire will not be covered.

There is no provision for broadening a Mercantile Safe Burglary policy to cover other perils besides burglary.

HAZARDS NOT COVERED

Records of Insured—Discussed above under Open Stock Burglary.

Failure to Maintain Protection — Discussed above under Open Stock Burglary.

Damage to Property and Premises — Discussed above under Open Stock Burglary.

WHERE COVERED

The Insured is required to list the safes which he wishes to have insured. If the safe is within a vault, he must describe and designate the vault. The insurance is then arranged with a specific amount of protection applying either to the vault, if any, or only to the safe. If the safe contains a chest, the insurance may apply to the entire safe, whether within the chest or not, or only within the chest. Where the situation requires, the Insured may specify one amount of insurance for the chest, and a second amount to apply anywhere within the safe.

The Safe Burglary policy covers loss of property only from *within* the part of the safe or vault designated in the policy while the safe is located in the premises, or while located elsewhere after removal from the premises by burglars. As in the Open Stock Burglary policy, premises means only the interior of that portion of the building occupied exclusively by the Insured in conducting his business. A Mercantile Safe Burglary policy may be endorsed to cover also in a night depository safe located in a bank or trust company, in addition to the Insured's premises.

Automatic Insurance on Additional Locations—Discussed under Open Stock Burglary policy.

FOR HOW MUCH

The Mercantile Safe Burglary policy covers to the extent of the actual cash value of the property but for not more than the cost of repairing or replacing the stolen or damaged property. The Company may pay for the loss in cash or may actually repair or replace the loss or damage.

Profits Insurance — Discussed under Open Stock Burglary. In

Safe Burglary insurance, the additional premium for this extension is 25%.

Pledged Articles—Like the Open Stock Burglary policy, on any article held by the Insured as a pledge or as collateral for a loan, the Safe Burglary policy will pay no more than the value of the article as recorded by the Insured at the time of making the advance. If no record exists, the Company's liability is limited to the unpaid balance due the Insured.

There is no Coinsurance clause in the Mercantile Safe Burglary policy, nor any limitation on articles of jewelry.

Other Insurance—Discussed before under Open Stock Burglary policy.

INSURED'S DUTIES AND OBLIGATIONS

Records of Insured—Discussed under Open Stock Burglary policy.

Maintenance of Promised Protection — Discussed under Open Stock Burglary policy.

Insured's Statements — Discussed under Open Stock Burglary policy.

REQUIREMENTS IN CASE OF LOSS

All the requirements of the Open Stock Burglary policy apply equally to the Mercantile Safe Burglary policy. The Safe Burglary policy also calls for reasonable evidence of the commission of a felonious act, as contemplated under the policy.

OTHER CLAUSES

Subrogation—See Chapter 2.

Cancellation—See Chapter 2.

Binder Cancellation—See Chapter 10.

Assignment—Discussed under Open Stock Burglary policy.

Reinstatement After Loss—Discussed under Open Stock Burglary policy.

Regulation—Discussed under Open Stock Burglary policy.

RATES

The rates for Mercantile Safe Burglary insurance are based on three factors:

1. **Territory in which the risk is located.**

Territorial multipliers or factors are applied to a master table to arrive at the rates for the individual states. Each state has its own territorial divisions.

2. **The Insured's business.**

While there are five trade groups, most risks fall into the lowest rated group, with only about 30 special businesses rated in one of the higher classifications.

3. **Type of safe or vault.**

Each safe or vault to be insured is rated according to its construction. There are eight classifications, ranging from those bearing the label, "Underwriters' Laboratories, Inc. Inspected Torch, Explosive and Tool Resisting Safe," to one which is merely of fireproof iron or steel construction.

Minimum Premiums—The annual minimum premium for Mercantile Safe Burglary insurance is $10 for the first location and $8 for each additional location.

Discussed in Chapter 10 under BROAD FORM PERSONAL THEFT POLICY—RATES—Three-Year Policies.

Whole Dollar Premium Rule—Discussed in Chapter 8 under OTHER FACTORS WHICH AFFECT FIRE INSURANCE RATES—Whole Dollar Premium Rule.

Credits—Special discounts are granted for watchman service, alarm systems, relocking devices and tear gas systems. These credits range from 5% to 70%.

When an Insured's premises are continuously open for regular business 24 hours a day, and the Insured carries Robbery insurance, a 50% credit is granted from the Safe Burglary rate. Credits are also granted if the total insurance applying to all safes and vaults in one location is divided so that not more than 50% of the amount applies to any single safe or vault. A smaller discount is allowed where not more than 75% applies to any one safe or vault.

HOW POLICY IS WRITTEN

When the Insured has more than one safe on his premises, he may apply a separate amount of insurance to each safe, or may insure two or more safes blanket, with one amount of insurance applying over all his safes. When such blanket insurance is written, the average rate of the various types of safe is applied to the entire amount of insurance.

When the Insured operates from more than one location, it is also possible to insure all his premises under one blanket policy.

Term of Policy—Most Safe Burglary policies are written to attach at 12 noon, Standard Time, at the location of the premises, for a period of one or three years.

MERCANTILE SAFE BURGLARY POLICY

FOR FURTHER READING

ACKERMAN—Insurance
GEE—Agent's Casualty Guide
HEDGES—Practical Fire and Casualty Insurance
KULP AND HALL—Casualty Insurance
MAGEE AND BICKELHAUPT—General Insurance
MEHR AND CAMMACK—Principles of Insurance
POLICY, FORM AND MANUAL ANALYSIS SERVICE
RIEGEL, ROBERT AND MILLER—Insurance

(See Reading List at End of Book)

CHAPTER 12

Robbery Coverages

ROBBERY INSURANCE for business risks is provided under the Special Coverage policy, which is designed to make available Safe Burglary, Mercantile Robbery, Paymaster Robbery, Paymaster Broad Form and over 20 other forms of Crime coverage. Each of these coverages is provided by a separate endorsement of the Special Coverage policy. Safe Burglary insurance was covered in Chapter 11; this chapter will analyze several forms of Robbery insurance. While each of these coverages is strictly an endorsement of the Special Coverage policy to which it must be attached rather than an individual policy, the word "policy" will be used to designate the Special Coverage policy with the particular endorsement.

MERCANTILE ROBBERY INSURANCE

WHAT IS COVERED

The Mercantile Robbery policy covers money, securities and other property. A Robbery policy may be written to cover securities only at a 50% reduction in rate.

Damage to Premises—If the Insured is the owner of the premises, or is liable for damage to the premises he occupies, the Mercantile Robbery policy will pay for damage to the premises caused by robbery or attempt at robbery.

Ownership of Property—The policy is identical with the Open Stock Burglary policy on this score.

Property Not Covered—The Mercantile Robbery policy is identical with the Safe Burglary policy on this score.

HAZARDS COVERED

The coverage of the Mercantile Robbery policy is limited strictly to the peril of robbery. Robbery is defined in the policy as the felonious and forcible taking of property in one of the following ways:

1. By violence inflicted upon a custodian or by putting him in fear of violence.

The robber need not necessarily be armed, nor is it required that he openly threaten the custodian of the property. It has been held that a robber who looked menacingly at his victim had placed him in fear of violence.

2. From one who has been killed or rendered unconscious by injuries inflicted maliciously or sustained accidentally.

The policy will cover taking of property even if the custodian never became aware of the holdup because he was knocked unconscious or killed without warning. It also covers if the custodian of the property suffers an accidental injury, and the property is subsequently taken from him.

3. By any other overt felonious act committed in the presence of the custodian of the property of which he is actually cognizant, provided such act is not committed by an officer or employee of the Insured.

This will include all taking of property even where no violence is inflicted or threatened, provided the custodian is aware of the criminal act being perpetrated. Thus, if a salesgirl sees someone snatch an item from the counter and dash out of the store, the loss would be covered under the Mercantile Robbery policy. There is no coverage for the loss caused by shoplifting, sneak thievery or any other taking which is not overt (open) and known to the custodian.

Kidnapping Coverage—The Robbery policy is divided into two separate sections, one covering inside the premises and a second covering outside the premises (to be discussed under "Where Covered" later). When coverage is purchased to cover inside the premises, the policy also covers stealing of property from within the premises by thieves who compel a custodian or messenger who is outside the premises to admit them into the premises, or to furnish them with the means to open the premises.

The custodian or messenger does not actually have to admit the criminals. Frequently, the robbers will overpower a custodian at his home or on the road and compel him to give up the keys to his place of business. While he is kept powerless by one of the group, the others loot the place. Such loss comes under the Kidnapping coverage of the Interior Robbery (Robbery Inside Premises) policy.

Show Window Robbery—Under the Inside the Premises section of the policy, there is coverage also for the stealing of property from within a show window in the premises by a person who breaks the glass of the window from the outside, while the premises are open for business.

There is no stipulation in the basic policy that the premises must be open for business except as regards stealing from a show window. However, since the basic policy covers only robbery, there must be a custodian or messenger on the premises, or access to the premises must be given by such person.

If the show window is broken into when the premises are closed for business, the Open Stock Burglary policy would apply.

Damage to Property and Premises—Like the Open Stock Burglary and Safe Burglary policies, the Robbery policy also covers damage caused by the peril insured against — by robbery or attempted robbery. Also covered is damage to the premises, if the Insured is the owner of the premises, or is responsible for the damage. While the damage done by robbers is not usually as extensive as that which attends most burglaries, it often reaches a sizable figure, as when robbers tear out wiring and telephones, or rip open cabinets, drawers and containers.

WHO IS COVERED

Under the Inside the Premises section (Interior Robbery), the policy covers robbery from a custodian only. The policy defines a custodian as the Insured or partner or officer of the Insured, or any other person who is regularly employed by the Insured and authorized to have custody of the insured property. The policy may be endorsed to cover a person not in the regular employ of the insured but who is duly authorized to have the care and custody of the insured property.

Specifically excluded from the definition of "custodian" is any person while acting as a watchman, porter or janitor. The policy may be endorsed to cover such individuals.

Under the Robbery Outside Premises section, the policy covers robbery from a messenger only. Messenger is defined in the policy exactly as custodian, except that there is no restriction on watchmen, porters or janitors.

HAZARDS NOT COVERED

Records of Insured—Discussed under Open Stock Burglary policy.

Failure to Maintain Protection—The Mercantile Robbery policy, like the Open Stock Burglary, does provide coverage for losses which occur while any promised protection is not maintained, but on a reduced basis. Under the Mercantile Robbery policy, if the Insured fails because of an unforeseen contingency beyond his control to maintain any service or perform any act promised by him in the policy, the insurance will not be forfeited, but the Company's liability for any loss occurring under these circumstances will be reduced. The Company will be liable only for the amount of insurance that would have been purchased by the premium paid at the rate which would have been charged if no protection had been promised.

EXAMPLE: The Insured operates a retail liquor store in New York County and carries $10,000 of Robbery Outside Premises insurance for which the rate is $5 per $1,000 before any discount. Since the Insured agrees in his policy to provide a private conveyance for the exclusive use of the messenger during his entire trip, he receives a 10% discount. His premium for the $10,000 policy is therefore reduced from $50 to $45. On the day of the robbery, his messenger starts out for the bank in the private passenger automobile provided for the trip, but the vehicle breaks down, and the messenger is forced to complete his trip on foot. He is intercepted and robbed of $10,000.

Although the policy is not forfeited by the fact that the loss occurred when the promised service was not maintained, the amount of insurance available for the loss is reduced to $9,000—the amount of insurance that would have been purchased by the $45 premium at the full rate without discount ($5 per $1,000).

It is important to understand that this is true only if the failure to maintain the service or protection is beyond the Insured's control. If, in the case in point, the Insured had directed the messenger to proceed to the bank on foot because he wished to use the automobile himself, the policy would not cover the loss in any degree.

Infidelity of Employees—The Mercantile Robbery policy does not exclude loss caused by an employee of the Insured or an associate in interest, if such loss is caused by violence or the fear of violence inflicted on a custodian, or by killing or rendering the custodian unconscious. If the loss is caused by other overt act as defined in the policy, there is no coverage if caused by any officer or employee of the Insured.

Nuclear Perils—Discussed in Chapter 11 under OPEN STOCK BURGLARY—PERILS NOT COVERED—Nuclear Perils.

WHERE COVERED

As mentioned above, the Mercantile Robbery policy consists of two separate sections, one covering Robbery Outside Premises (Messenger Robbery) and another covering Robbery Inside Premises (Interior Robbery). Each section is independent of the other, and the Insured is free to purchase any amount of insurance under either portion of the policy, or to insure under only one section of the policy.

The Robbery Outside Premises coverage is confined to the United States and Canada.

The Robbery Inside Premises coverage is limited to the interior of that portion of any building designated by the Insured in his policy.

The definition of premises may be amended by endorsement to take in the entire plot of grounds on which the office or store is located, for an additional premium of 50%. This coverage is very valuable for gasoline stations, beer gardens and similar risks whose operations are not confined to the interior of any portion of a building.

The Robbery Outside Premises coverage does not cover loss from the home of a messenger when such home is located in a building where the messenger collects rents. (Coverage for this exposure may be obtained under a special Home of Custodian Coverage endorsement, discussed next.)

Home of Custodian Coverage—A Robbery Outside Premises policy may be extended by endorsement to cover in the home of a messenger or custodian. This coverage is available in two forms, for the extra premium shown:

1. Burglary, robbery, theft or larceny................$5 per $1,000
2. Burglary only ....$4 per $1,000

Show Window Coverage—As discussed under Perils Covered—Show Window Robbery, the Interior Robbery policy covers stealing of property from a show window in the premises when the window is broken by someone outside of the premises. A Robbery policy may be written as limited to show window robbery only, without any coverage on other robbery.

Automatic Insurance on Additional Locations—Discussed under Open Stock Burglary policy.

FOR HOW MUCH

The entire section under the Safe Burglary policy—For How Much—applies to the Mercantile Robbery policy.

HOW INSURANCE IS WRITTEN

Under the Messenger Robbery coverage, the Insured is required to indicate the number of Messengers who will have custody of insured property and the amount of insurance applying to each. A Blanket policy may be written to cover all the messengers of one risk. Under such Blanket policy, one amount of insurance is applied to any single loss, regardless of the number of messengers involved. When an insured operates more than one location, he may insure each location separately in a schedule policy, or may purchase a Blanket policy to cover all his locations.

INSURED'S DUTIES AND OBLIGATIONS

Records of Insured—Discussed under Open Stock Burglary policy.

Maintenance of Promised Protection—See Hazards Covered.

Insured's Statements—Discussed under Open Stock Burglary policy.

Requirements in Case of Loss—All the requirements of the Open Stock Burglary policy apply equally to the Mercantile Robbery policy.

OTHER CLAUSES

Subrogation—See Chapter 2.

Cancellation—See Chapter 2; Binder Cancellation—See Chapter 2.

Assignment—Discussed under Open Stock Burglary policy.

Reinstatement After Loss—The Mercantile Robbery policy is fully reinstated after a loss without any additional premium.

Regulation—Discussed under Open Stock Burglary policy.

Term of Policy—Discussed under Safe Burglary policy.

RATES

Interior Robbery (Robbery Inside Premises)

Interior Robbery rates are based on three factors:

1. The territory in which the risk is located. Territorial multipliers or factors are applied to a master table to arrive at rates for the individual states. Each state has its own territorial divisions.

2. The Insured's business.

There are five classes. Most businesses are in the lowest rated group, with some thirty odd trades falling into one of the two higher rated classifications.

3. The number of custodians who are on duty.

If only one custodian is on duty at all times, the higher rate is used. When a custodian and at least one other employee are on duty at all times, a lower rate is granted.

Credits — Credits are granted for bandit-resisting enclosures, alarm systems, tear gas systems, and the employment of full-time guards who have no other duties on the premises. When two or more locations of a risk are scheduled (not blanket) under an Interior Robbery policy, a 10% discount applies to all locations except the one which carries the highest premium.

Messenger Robbery (Robbery Outside Premises)

Messenger Robbery rates are based on three factors:

1. The territory of the location from which the Messengers operate. Territorial multipliers or factors are applied to a master table to arrive at rates for the individual states. Each state has its own territorial divisions.

2. The number of Messengers who will have custody of the property. The rate for each Messenger other than the one requiring the largest premium is 50% of the rate for the first.
3. The number of guards who accompany the Messenger.

As used in the Messenger Robbery portion of the policy, a guard is defined as a male person not less than 17 nor more than 65 years of age who accompanies the Messenger at the direction of the Insured. A driver of a public conveyance or a taxi is not considered a guard.

The age limitations may be deleted at no extra charge, if the guard is specified by name.

Credits—The Messenger Robbery policy allows a discount for any of the following:

1. If the property is conveyed in a locked messenger safe or chest.
2. If the property is conveyed in a satchel or wallet lined with steel or wire mesh and attached by a steel or wire strap to the Messenger or the vehicle in which the property is conveyed.
3. If the property is conveyed in an approved messenger protection bag.
4. If the property is conveyed in a locked safe or in locked metal boxes which are chained together and weigh 500 lbs. or more (a lower credit for weight of 250 lbs. or more).
5. If a private conveyance is provided for the exclusive use of the Messenger and his guards throughout the trip. A higher discount applies if the conveyance is an armored car constructed of bullet proof steel and bullet proof glass with securely locked doors.
6. If the property is conveyed from one portion of the building to another without the Messenger leaving the building.

The rates for Robbery insurance do not decrease as the amounts of insurance are increased. The premium for $5,000 of insurance is exactly five times as large as for $1,000 of insurance.

Minimum Premiums—As mentioned, the Messenger and Interior Robbery sections of the policy are each subject to a minimum premium. There is no standard minimum premium applicable to all Robbery policies, and different minimum premiums apply in the various territories.

Whole Dollar Premium Rule—Discussed in Chapter 8 under OTHER FACTORS WHICH AFFECT FIRE INSURANCE RATES—Whole Dollar Premium Rule.

PAYMASTER ROBBERY POLICY

FOR MANY BUSINESSES, the principal exposure to robbery is represented by the payroll funds brought into the premises, usually on one day of the week. Except for this money, there is almost no cash used in the business, and little chance that any merchandise would be taken by robbery. A special form of Robbery insurance, the Paymaster Robbery policy, is available to cover such risks and the premium for this policy is lower than for the regular Mercantile Robbery policy. Like the Mercantile Safe Burglary policy and the Mercantile Robbery coverage, this insurance is written by endorsement to the Special Coverage policy.

The Paymaster Robbery policy differs from the Messenger and Interior Robbery policies in that it applies primarily to loss of payroll funds.

WHAT IS COVERED

The Paymaster Robbery policy covers only money and checks intended solely for the Insured's payroll. It also covers the wallet, bag, satchel, safe or chest in which such property is contained. There is one exception to this restriction.

The Paymaster Robbery policy does not cover other property like the Mercantile Robbery policy. There is only limited coverage for loss of securities, as discussed below.

Loss of Other Money and Securities—Up to 10% of the amount of a Paymaster Robbery policy may be applied to loss of money and securities not intended solely for the payroll of the Insured, when caused by robbery or attempted robbery of a messenger *outside* of the premises while such custodian is engaged in his duties in connection with the payroll. This coverage will apply also to the wallet, bag, satchel, safe or chest in which such property is contained.

This provision does not increase the amount of insurance. Under a $2,000 Paymaster Robbery policy, up to $200 may be applied to cover the loss of securities or money not intended for the Insured's payroll, but the maximum loss payable under the policy is $2,000. Thus, if the Insured's messenger was held up and robbed of $1,800 of payroll funds and $400 of other cash or securities, the Insured could collect only $2,000 for the entire loss.

As will be discussed below, the Paymaster Robbery policy covers loss occurring both Inside the Premises and Outside the Premises. However, the coverage on money and securities not intended for the Insured's payroll applies only to loss sustained *outside* the Insured's premises.

Damage to Premises—Discussed under Mercantile Robbery policy.

HAZARDS COVERED

The Paymaster Robbery policy covers loss by Robbery only, and defines robbery exactly as the Mercantile Robbery policy. It also provides identical Kidnapping coverage. The policy may be broadened to take in additional perils besides robbery, and this broader form is discussed below under Paymaster Broad Form policy.

Robbery from Employees—The Paymaster Robbery policy also covers loss by robbery of money or checks from any of the Insured's employees on the day or night on which they are paid, provided there is at the same time a robbery from the paymaster or an attempted robbery.

This coverage applies only inside the premises. The policy would cover loss only of money received by the employee as wages or salary, and not any other money or property he may have with him. To be covered, the robbery from the employee must take place at the same time as there is a robbery or attempt at robbery from a custodian of the payroll. If the payroll had been completely distributed and robbers subsequently held up some of the employees, the employees would not be covered under the Paymaster Robbery policy.

Damage to Property and Premises—Like all the Burglary and Robbery forms discussed previously, the Paymaster Robbery policy covers damage caused by the peril insured against.

HAZARDS NOT COVERED

Records of Insured—Discussed under Mercantile Robbery policy.

Infidelity of Employees—Discussed under Mercantile Robbery policy.

Failure to Maintain Protection — Change in Risk — Discussed under Mercantile Robbery policy.

WHERE COVERED

The Paymaster Robbery policy is not divided into individual sections covering separately Inside the Premises and Outside the Premises. The basic policy covers loss both inside the premises or outside the premises, provided the loss is sustained within the United States and Canada.

A Paymaster Robbery policy may be written to cover loss of payroll funds only inside the premises. This form of Paymaster Robbery insurance is generally required by firms which have their payroll delivered by armored car services, which assume responsibility for the safe delivery of the funds.

While the basic coverage of the policy applies both on and off the premises, the extension of 10% to cover money and securities not intended solely for the Insured's payroll applies only to loss sustained outside the premises.

If an employee is sent to the bank to withdraw $3,000 for the payroll and $200 for the petty cash fund, and is robbed while en route to his place of employment, the policy will cover (up to the limit of the insurance in the policy). Once he reaches his employer's premises, there is no coverage for any funds other than those intended for the payroll.

Contrariwise, the coverage for robbery from employees applies only *inside* the premises.

Automatic Insurance on Additional Locations—Discussed under Open Stock Burglary policy.

Home of Custodian Coverage—Discussed under Mercantile Robbery policy.

WHO IS COVERED

Except for the protection available to employees under certain conditions, the Paymaster Robbery policy only covers robbery from a custodian while engaged in any of his regular duties in connection with the payroll. "Custodian" is defined as the Insured or a partner or officer of the Insured, or any other person who is in the regular employ of and duly authorized by the Insured to have the care and custody of the insured property, excluding any person while acting as a watchman, porter or janitor.

FOR HOW MUCH

The Company is liable under the policy only to the extent of the actual cash value of the stolen or damaged property, but for no more than the cost to repair or replace the property. The Company may pay for the loss in cash or may actually repair or replace. Since most losses under Paymaster Robbery policies involve cash, there is usually little problem in determining actual cash value. There are no Coinsurance requirements.

INSURED'S DUTIES AND OBLIGATIONS

Records of Insured—Discussed under Open Stock Burglary policy.

Maintenance of Promised Protection—Discussed under HAZARDS COVERED.

Insured's Statements — Discussed under Open Stock Burglary policy.

Requirements in Case of Loss—All the requirements imposed by the Open Stock Burglary policy apply equally to the Paymaster Robbery policy (see entire section under Open Stock Burglary policy —Requirements in Case of Loss).

OTHER CLAUSES

Subrogation—Discussed in Chapter 2.

Cancellation—See Chapter 18 under Safe Burglary policy.

Assignment—See Chapter 18 under Open Stock Burglary policy.

Reinstatement After Loss—The Paymaster Robbery is identical with the Mercantile Robbery policy on this score.

Regulation—Discussed under Open Stock Burglary policy.

Term of Policy—Discussed in Chapter 18 under Safe Burglary policy.

RATES

The rating factors for Paymaster Robbery policy are the same as for the Messenger Robbery portion of a Mercantile Robbery policy.

Although there are the same number of rating territories for Paymaster Robbery insurance as for Messenger Robbery policies, the rating territory for a particular risk is not necessarily the same under both forms of insurance.

Credits—The Discounts in the rate for Paymaster Robbery policies are the same as under Messenger Robbery insurance.

Minimum Premiums—The minimum premium for Paymaster Robbery insurance policies depends on the territory in which the risk is located. In almost every case, the annual minimum premium is $10 for the first messenger. A separate minimum premium applies to each messenger insured under the policy, except that the minimum premium for each messenger after the first is only $4 per year.

PAYMASTER BROAD FORM POLICY

THE BASIC PAYMASTER ROBBERY POLICY covers only against loss by robbery or attempted robbery. A much broader form of insurance is available to cover wrongful abstraction, disappearance and actual destruction of the insured property, which has been held to include damage to the property. This virtually All Risk insurance, Paymaster Broad Form policy, like the Paymaster Robbery policy, is written by endorsement to the Special Coverage policy. While it covers wrongful abstraction and disappearance of the property, it is subject to the following exclusions:

No Custodian on Duty—The Broad Form policy does not cover loss sustained inside the premises except when a custodian is on duty.

For an additional premium, the Paymaster Broad Form policy may be extended to cover when a custodian is not on duty. A specific amount of insurance established for the "absent custodian" coverage, and this protection may be purchased in a lesser amount than the amount of insurance under the basic Broad Form coverage.

Thus, an Insured whose payroll is $10,000 may find that only $9,000 of this sum is usually distributed on the regular payday, while the balance is customarily left overnight in the safe for absent employees. He can cover this entire risk by buying a $10,000 Paymaster Broad Form policy, extended to cover for $1,000 when a custodian is not on duty

If the only property an Insured keeps in his safe which is subject to the threat of stealing is payroll funds, a Paymaster Broad Form policy, with coverage applying when a custodian is not on duty, will take the place of a Safe Burglary policy. Actually, the coverage provided will be broader than under a Safe Burglary policy, since the latter calls for *burglary* of the safe, as defined, while the Paymaster Broad Form policy covers all wrongful abstraction.

Dishonesty of Employees — The Broad Form policy specifically excludes any dishonest act of the Insured or of any officer, employee, partner, director, trustee, or authorized representative of the Insured. The exclusion does *not* apply to losses by robbery or safe burglary, provided such loss is not committed by the Insured or a partner.

Loss in Any Exchange or Purchase—The Paymaster Broad Form policy excludes loss caused by or contributed to by the giving or surrendering of any money or securities in any exchange or purchase. The intent of this clause is to exclude such loss as the Insured might suffer if he gave too much change to a customer, or if he made change of a counterfeit bill, or if he refunded money for merchandise which a customer fraudulently claimed he purchased in the store, and other similar swindles.

The exclusion is limited, however, to losses sustained in the course of an exchange or purchase. If an employee surrendered money to a person who fraudulently represented himself as a messenger from another department of the business, or as as a messenger from a bank, the policy would cover such loss as wrongful abstraction.

War, Revolution, Insurrection, Etc.—While the Paymaster Broad Form policy covers actual destruction of the insured property, as by fire, explosion, flood, etc., it excludes loss caused by war, invasion, insurrection, rebellion, hostilities, revolution, or military or usurped power. Also excluded is loss caused by nuclear reaction, radiation, or radioactive contamination.

FEDERAL CRIME INSURANCE

Individuals and businesses located in high crime areas often find it impossible to obtain insurance against crime losses. To make coverage against these perils available to risks in such high crime areas, the Federal Government under Title VI of the Housing and Urban Development Act of 1970 has begun to offer Crime insurance in designated states where the Federal Insurance Administrator determines that there is a critical shortage of insurance facilities.

CALIFORNIA, INDIANA, MICHIGAN, OREGON—Crime insurance coverages are available through plans run under the state pools.

NEW JERSEY—Residential burglary and robbery and commercial crime coverages are available through the New Jersey Underwriting Association.

WISCONSIN—Dwelling and business properties may obtain insurance against crime (and glass breakage) through the state's FAIR plan.

Presently, the Federal Crime Insurance program is operative in the following states:

CONNECTICUT, DISTRICT OF COLUMBIA, ILLINOIS, MARYLAND, MASSACHUSETTS, MISSOURI, NEW YORK, OHIO, PENNSYLVANIA, RHODE ISLAND.

In these states, any property owner or businessman or tenant may apply for Crime insurance. He is required to complete an application and to prepay the six-months' premium with the application. Furthermore, he must install and maintain in working order certain protective devices, e.g., a resident must equip all doors with a dead bolt, or a self-locking dead latch with certain minimum specifications. The requirements for commercial enterprises are more elaborate than for residential properties and vary with the type of business.

The coverages available differ under the Residential and the Commercial policies.

RESIDENTIAL COVERAGES

The Residential Policy covers against burglary, which means stealing from a locked premises which has been forcibly entered with marks of violence left at the point of entry, and larceny incidental to such burglary.

The policy also covers loss by robbery (discussed at the beginning of this chapter under MERCANTILE ROBBERY POLICY —HAZARDS COVERED).

Like other burglary and robbery policies, there is coverage for damage to the premises committed during a burglary or robbery or attempt at these crimes.

The policy covers against loss of all personal property including jewelry. The policy is subject to a deductible of 5% of the amount of the loss, or $75, whichever is higher. The maximum amount of insurance available under the program is $5,000. Loss of Money is covered up to $100. The policy is extended to cover burglary from an enclosed storage compartment of an automobile.

COMMERCIAL COVERAGES

A commercial risk may purchase up to $15,000 of burglary insurance, or robbery insurance, or a combination of both. The policy also covers theft from a night depository and burglary of a safe, subject to a $5,000 limit on loss from a safe which is not rated as Class E or better.

The Commercial policy is subject to a deductible which varies with the gross receipts of the business:

Gross Receipts	Deductible	
Less than $ 25,000	$ 50	or 5% of the
$ 25,000 to 49,999	75	Amount of the
50,000 to 99,999	100	Loss Whichever
100,000 to 299,999	150	Is Greater
300,000 or over	200	

For all non-profit risks or public property risks, the deductible is $100 or 5% of the amount of the loss, whichever is greater.

Cancellation—Federal Crime insurance will not be denied to any eligible Insured, nor will a policy be cancelled, regardless of the number of claims submitted.

On the other hand, failure to comply strictly with protective requirements or making of false statements as respects such devices will result in cancellation of the policy or denial of coverage. It will also result in denial of claims under the policy.

An Insured who makes intentionally false statements in his application for insurance, or in the presentation of a claim is liable to criminal prosecution.

FOR FURTHER READING

ACKERMAN—Insurance
GEE—Agent's Casualty Guide
HEDGES—Practical Fire and Casualty Insurance
KULP AND HALL—Casualty Insurance
MAGEE AND BICKELHAUPT—General Insurance
MEHR AND CAMMACK—Principles of Insurance
POLICY, FORM AND MANUAL ANALYSIS SERVICE

(See Reading List at End of Book)

CHAPTER 13

Broad Form Package Policies

MONEY AND SECURITIES BROAD FORM POLICY

COMPREHENSIVE INSURANCE on loss of all money and securities is available to almost every commercial enterprise in the Money and Securities Broad Form policy. As will be indicated in the discussion that follows, the policy also provides coverage on loss of other property, although on a more limited basis.

WHAT IS COVERED

The policy divides itself into sections, one applying to money and securities, and the second to other property. The coverage on these two groups of property is quite different, as will be shown under HAZARDS COVERED.

Money and Securities—The Money and Securities Broad Form policy covers *all* loss of money and securities, whether intended for the Insured's payroll or otherwise. In this respect, the policy is similar to the Mercantile Robbery policy.

The policy may be written to cover securities only at a 30% reduction in rate.

Other Property—The policy also covers other property. The coverage on this property is more limited than that which applies to money and securities, and the differences will be discussed later under HAZARDS COVERED.

Damage to Premises—If the Insured is the owner of the premises or is liable for damage to the premises he occupies, he will be covered under a Money and Securities policy for the damage to the premises caused by certain perils.

Ownership of Property—Discussed under Open Stock Burglary policy.

Property Not Covered—The policy specifically excludes loss or damage to manuscripts, records and accounts.

HAZARDS COVERED

While the Money and Securities Broad Form is an individual form of insurance, it may prove helpful in understanding its provisions and remembering its terms to think of the policy as made up of two parts:

1. On money and securities, the broad coverage of the Paymaster Broad Form policy with "absent custodian" coverage, but applying to *all* money and securities.
2. On other property—a combination of the Safe Burglary and Mercantile Robbery policies.

It is important to be clear on the difference in coverage for loss of money and securities as opposed to other property. On money and securities, the coverage is practically all-risk, both on and off the premises. On the loss of other property, or damage to such other property, the coverage includes essentially the perils of Robbery and Safe Burglary only.

The coverage is broadened on this class of property while it is on the premises of the home of a custodian, as discussed later in this chapter under WHERE COVERED—Home of Messenger.

Thus, there is no coverage for burglary or theft of merchandise *except* if taken by holdup or from within a closed and locked safe. For such coverage, the Insured must look to an Open Stock Burglary policy. A Money and Securities Broad Form policy may have Open Stock Burglary or Open Stock Theft insurance added, subject to all the rules and rates of such insurance. The Open Stock Theft extension can be purchased only in conjunction with the Open Stock Burglary coverage.

Money and Securities Coverage—The Money and Securities policy covers loss of all money and securities caused by actual destruction, disappearance or wrongful abstraction. This is virtually all-risk insurance and would cover destruction of insured property by fire, flood, windstorm, malicious mischief, etc.

Other Property—The Money and Securities Broad Form policy also covers loss of property other than money and securities, but only when the loss of such property is caused by Robbery and Safe Burglary. "Robbery" is defined exactly as under the Mercantile Robbery policy and includes kidnapping losses, and stealing from a show window by a person who has broken the glass from the outside when the premises are open for business, as well as damage to insured property and premises caused by robbery or attempt at robbery.

The policy also covers loss of property other than money and securities when caused by safe burglary, which is defined exactly as under a Safe Burglary policy, and damage caused by such burglary or attempted burglary.

Locked Cash Drawer, Cash Box or Register—The policy covers loss of a cash drawer, cash box or register if taken from the premises, as well as damage to such property.

When Loss Must Be Discovered — Since the policy covers all wrongful abstractions of money and securities, whether committed overtly or in stealth, it frequently happens that a loss is not discovered until some time after it has happened. To be covered, the loss must occur while the policy is in force and, furthermore, must be discovered within 12 months after the policy terminates. In other words, after a Money and Securities Broad Form policy is terminated, there is a 12-month Discovery Period, after which time losses are cut off and no recovery is possible.

Superseded Insurance—The policy contains a special clause which picks up any losses which would have been paid under a prior policy of this kind except for the fact that the Discovery Period of the former policy has run out. A full discussion of this clause and of Discovery Periods will be found in Chapter 14 under WHEN COVERED, Discovery Period and Superseded Suretyship (Indemnity Against Loss Under Prior Bond).

HAZARDS NOT COVERED

Dishonesty of Employees—Discussed under Paymaster Broad Form policy.

Loss in Any Exchange or Purchase—Discussed under Paymaster Broad Form policy.

Records of Insured—The Insured is required to maintain his records in such a manner that the Company can accurately determine the amount of a loss. Furthermore, the policy does not cover loss of manuscripts, books of account or records.

War, Etc.—The policy does not cover loss caused by war, whether declared or not, invasion, insurrection, rebellion or revolution, or to any act or condition incident to any of these perils.

Nuclear Perils—There is no coverage for loss caused by nuclear reaction, radiation, or radioactive contamination.

Loss by Fire—The policy does not cover loss by fire to property *other* than money, securities, a safe or vault. This exclusion applies even if a peril insured under the policy contributes to the loss by fire, as when a fire is set by persons seeking to effect a crime.

Money in Vending Machine—Except where the money deposited in coin-operated machines or vending machines is recorded continuously on a recording instrument, the policy does not cover loss of money in such devices.

WHO IS COVERED

The coverage for loss of money or securities or of other property when *outside* the premises applies only when such property is being conveyed by a messenger, which is defined exactly as under a Robbery policy.

WHERE COVERED

Like the Mercantile Robbery policy, the Money and Securities Broad Form policy is divided into two sections:

Coverage A—Loss Within Premises,

Coverage B—Loss Outside Premises.

Each section is independent of the other, and separate amounts of insurance may be applied to each, or insurance purchased to cover only under one section of the policy. Each section of the policy is separately rated, and individual minimum premiums apply.

Loss Within Premises—Coverage A.—The policy covers loss sustained within the premises, which is defined as the interior of that portion of any building occupied solely by the Insured in conducting his business. Risks like gasoline stations, beer gardens and others whose business is not conducted entirely within a building may have the definition of premises broadened (discussed in Chapter 12 under MERCANTILE ROBBERY POLICY—WHERE COVERED).

Premises of Banks and Depositories—Coverage A also applies within any banking premises or similar recognized place of safe deposit.

Automatic Insurance on Additional Locations—Discussed under Open Stock Burglary policy.

Home of Messenger—As was pointed out above under HAZARDS COVERED, the coverage on money and securities is virtually all-risk, whereas other property is covered basically only against the perils of robbery and burglary. Under Coverage B, the policy provides insurance for loss occurring from the residence of a messenger. As respects such premises, the policy is broadened to cover against any loss by *theft.*

A special rule applies to real estate risks, which must cover as an additional location the home of a messenger, making his residence an insured building.

Loss Outside Premises—Coverage B—The geographical limits of the Money and Securities Broad Form policy are the United States, District of Columbia, Virgin Islands, Puerto Rico, Canal Zone, and

Canada, and there is no coverage for losses occurring outside these territories. Coverage also extends to loss of money and securities while being conveyed by an armored motor vehicle company. Also covered is loss from within the living quarters of any messenger, except in case of a real estate risk.

FOR HOW MUCH

The Money and Securities Broad Form policy covers to the extent of the actual cash value of the property, but for no more than the cost to repair or replace lost or damaged property. The Company may pay for the loss in cash or may actually repair or replace the loss or damage. There is no Coinsurance clause in the policy.

It is important to understand that one dishonest act or a *series of related* acts at the premises are considered as arising out of one occurrence, and the entire loss would be subject to the policy limit.

Pledged Articles—Discussed under Mercantile Safe Burglary policy.

Other Insurance—If the Insured carries other insurance which covers in any manner a loss which comes under a Money and Securities Broad Form policy, the latter policy will act as excess insurance only, and will pay only after all other insurance has been exhausted, and only for such amount as exceeds the amount recoverable under the other policies.

Full Salvage to Insured—After a loss, it is often possible to recover some of the stolen or lost property from the individuals who caused the loss, or from others. The Money and Securities Broad Form policy provides that any such recovery shall first be applied to fully Indemnify the Insured, with the insurance Company retaining only such balance as remains after the Insured has been made whole. The Company may deduct the expenses it undergoes in collecting such salvage.

EXAMPLE: The Insured carries a $5,000 Money and Securities Broad Form policy. In a robbery, he loses $7,000. The insurance Company pays the Insured the limit of its policy, $5,000. Sometime later, the robbers are apprehended, and $3,000 of the stolen money recovered. Of this $3,000 of salvage, the Insured is entitled to $2,000, which sum will make his entire loss good. The Company retains only the balance of the sum recovered, $1,000 (and is also entitled to be reimbursed for any expenses it has been put to in recovering the salvage).

INSURED'S DUTIES AND OBLIGATIONS

Records of Insured—Discussed under HAZARDS NOT COVERED.

Insured's Statements—Discussed under Open Stock Burglary policy.

REQUIREMENTS IN CASE OF LOSS

Notice of Loss—Discussed under Open Stock Burglary policy.

Proof of Loss—The Insured is required to file within four months.

Negotiation of Securities—The Insured is required to take all reasonable means to prevent the negotiation, sale or retirement of any securities stolen or lost.

Cooperation with Company—Discussed under Open Stock Burglary policy.

OTHER CLAUSES

Subrogation—See Chapter 2.

Cancellation—See Chapter 2.

Assignment—Discussed under Open Stock Burglary policy—Assignment.

Regulation—See Chapter 11.

Reinstatement After Loss—Discussed under Open Stock Burglary policy.

HOW INSURANCE IS WRITTEN

As mentioned before, the Money and Securities Broad Form policy consists of two optional insuring sections, one covering losses within the premises and the second for losses outside the premises. Each section of the policy is separately rated and is subject to its own minimum premium.

Both sections of the policy may be written on a Schedule or a Blanket basis.

Schedule Policy—When the Insured operates from more than one location, he may purchase a Schedule policy covering each of the premises with a separate amount of insurance. Under Coverage B (Loss Outside Premises), the Insured is required to specify the number of Messengers and the amount of insurance which applies to each.

Blanket Policy—All the locations of one Insured may be covered under a Blanket policy, under which the amount of insurance applies to all locations.

Blanket insurance may also be written under Coverage B (Loss Outside Premises). The entire amount of insurance under such a policy applies to all Messengers of the same risk.

Existing Insurance—It often happens that an Insured who wishes to purchase the Money and Securities Broad Form policy is already carrying individual Robbery and Safe Burglary policies. Since the Money and Securities policy includes the perils covered under these separate policies, the Insured will not need them. If, however, the Insured requests cancellation of the existing policies, such cancellation will be made on a short rate basis.

To avoid this penalty, it is provided that the Insured may continue his existing policies and receive a credit on a pro rata basis for the unearned premium, provided these policies have been in force for at least 60 days. (The procedure for continuing existing insurance parallels the provision in Personal Property Floater, discussed in Chapter 18.)

RATES

Loss Within Premises—Coverage A—The rates for Loss Within Premises coverage under a Money and Securities Broad Form policy are based on three factors:

1. The Insured's occupation. There are 11 classes.
2. The type of safe or vault on the Insured's premises, if any.

Safes are classified as fireproof, semi-burglarproof, burglarproof or double burglarproof.

3. The territory in which the Insured's premises are located.

Territorial multipliers or factors are applied to a master table to arrive at the rates for the individual states. Each state has its own territorial divisions.

Credits—Reductions in rate are granted if the Insured employs watchmen to patrol his premises exclusively, for guards who will be on duty at all times when the premises are open for business and will have no other duties but guarding the premises, for push button robbery alarm systems, and burglar alarm systems.

Loss Outside Premises—Coverage B—The rates for Loss Outside Premises coverage are based on three factors:

1. The territory of the location from which the Messengers operate. Territorial multipliers or factors are applied to a master table to arrive at the rates for the individual states. Each state has its own territorial divisions.
2. The number of Messengers insured under the policy. The rate for each Messenger after the one requiring the largest premium is 50% of the rate for the first.
3. The number of guards who accompany the Messenger. A guard is defined exactly as in a Mercantile Robbery policy.

Credits—Reductions in rate are granted if the Messenger uses a private conveyance provided for his exclusive use throughout his trip. A larger discount applies if the conveyance is an armored car. Other discounts are allowed if the insured property is conveyed in an approved messenger protection bag or in a locked messenger safe or chest or in a satchel or wallet lined with steel or wire mesh and attached by steel or wire strap or chain to the Messenger or the vehicle in which the property is conveyed. Where the Messenger conveys property only within the building containing the insured premises, a further discount is made available.

If the policy is written on a Blanket basis, it will not include any warranties by the Insured as to any such forms of protection *inside* the premises. Failure by the Insured to maintain a device *inside* the premises, even though he has been allowed a credit, will not breach his policy, nor will there be any reduction in the amount of coverage available to him in a loss.

Rates for Money and Securities Broad Form insurance do not decrease as the amount of insurance is increased. The premium for $5,000 of insurance is exactly five times as large as for $1,000 of insurance (but see Minimum Premiums directly below).

MINIMUM PREMIUMS

Loss Within Premises—Coverage A—Annual minimum premium is $38.00 for the first location, and $15 for each additional location.

NEW YORK—Annual minimum premium for the first location is $37.50.

Loss Outside Premises—Coverage B—Annual minimum premium is $13.00 for the first Messenger, and $5.00 for each additional Messenger.

NEW YORK—Annual minimum premium for the first Messenger is $12.50 and $4.50 for each additional messenger.

Term of Policy—The policy attaches at 12 Noon, Standard Time, at the place the insurance is effective.

PACKAGE CRIME POLICIES

THERE ARE a number of special package crime policies which combine a series of perils, each for a stated amount. Generally, the same amount of insurance is applicable to loss by any of the designated perils. Below are discussed several of the more popular policies of this kind.

STOREKEEPERS' BURGLARY AND ROBBERY POLICY

AS ITS NAME INDICATES, this policy is designed for retail establishments of a store nature, but most Companies will write the policy for almost every mercantile risk. The form is especially useful for the smaller risk that requires protection against loss caused by criminals, but is not in a position to meet the premiums required by the Coinsurance requirements of the Open Stock Burglary policy and the minimum premiums for Messenger Robbery, Interior Robbery and Safe Burglary insurance, or the Money and Securities Broad Form policy.

In the one policy, for a comparatively modest premium, the Insured is covered up to the limits of the policy for the perils of the Interior Robbery policy, the Messenger Robbery policy, the Safe Burglary, and the Open Stock Burglary policy, including damage caused by an insured peril, and theft from a night depository or residence of a custodian.

WHAT IS COVERED

The Storekeepers' Burglary and Robbery policy is divided into seven sections, each covering a specific type of loss. The kind of property insured differs somewhat under some of the perils insured, and these will be discussed directly below under Perils Covered.

Ownership of Property—Discussed under Open Stock Burglary policy.

Property Not Covered—The policy specifically excludes the same types of property as are excluded under the Safe Burglary policy. It also excludes personal effects.

HAZARDS COVERED

I. Robbery Inside Premises.

II. Robbery Outside Premises.

III. Kidnapping.

Under the three Insuring Agreements listed above, the policy covers loss of money, securities, merchandise and, where applicable, furniture, fixtures and equipment. Protection is afforded for loss caused by the perils insured under Messenger and Interior Robbery policies.

Limitation on Number of Messengers—The Insured is required to state in his policy that no more than two Messengers will have custody of insured property at one time. If, at the time of the loss, it is found that more than two Messengers did have insured property in their custody, these coverages are entirely void. If the Insured does employ the services of more than two Messengers at the same time, such additional Messengers may be insured under the policy at the regular Messenger Robbery rates.

IV. Safe Burglary—Under Insuring Agreement IV, the policy covers loss of money, securities and merchandise. Protection is afforded for loss caused by the perils insured under a Mercantile Safe Burglary policy (discussed in Chapter 11 under Mercantile Safe Burglary—Perils Covered). In addition, the policy covers up to $50 on loss of money when caused by burglary of the *premises.* This limit may be increased for an additional premium.

V. Theft of Night Depository or Residence—Under Insuring Agreement V, the policy covers loss of money and securities from the night depository of a bank or from the residence of a custodian or Messenger, but only when caused by theft of the bank night depository or the residence. Only money and securities are covered, and only against theft.

Coverage is afforded for theft of the residence of a custodian or Messenger, but not for any other residence. Messenger and custodian are defined as under a Mercantile Robbery policy. If a custodian or Messenger leaves money at a friend's residence, there is no coverage.

VI. Burglary of Merchandise—Under Insuring Agreement VI, the policy covers loss of merchandise, furniture, fixtures and equipment caused by burglary, which is defined as under an Open Stock Burglary policy and includes robbery of a watchman (discussed in Chapter 11 under OPEN STOCK BURGLARY POLICY—HAZARDS COVERED). It is important to point out that there is no Coinsurance clause in the Storekeepers' Burglary and Robbery policy.

There is no coverage for loss of money from the premises by burglary, and loss of such property is covered only when caused by robbery, safe burglary or by burglary of a night depository or the residence of a custodian or Messenger.

A Storekeepers' Burglary and Robbery policy written for a risk which stores oil or gasoline in containers outside the premises may be extended to cover loss of such property by burglary. The coverage applies only to loss from containers connected to locked pumps. An additional premium of $5 is charged for this extension.

Limitation on Jewelry and Pledged Articles—Discussed under Open Stock Burglary policy.

The limitation applies to each article of the kind described. If the burglars made off with three watches, the Insured could collect up to $150 for the loss.

The $50 limitation on any article of jewelry applies only under the Insuring Agreement covering burglary of a store, and would not apply to losses by robbery or safe burglary.

VII. Damage to Property and Premises—Like all Burglary and Robbery forms discussed in the preceding chapters, the Storekeepers' Burglary and Robbery policy covers damage to all insured property caused by burglary or robbery, or any attempt at such crimes. If the Insured owns the premises, or is liable for the damage, the policy also covers damage to the premises.

HAZARDS NOT COVERED

Dishonesty of Employees—The exclusion is similar to the one found in the Open Stock Burglary policy (discussed in Chapter 11 under PERILS NOT COVERED), except that it does not apply to the perils of Safe Burglary (Insuring Agreement IV) and Robbery (Insuring Agreements I and II).

Fire—Discussed in Chapter 11 under OPEN STOCK BURGLARY POLICY—HAZARDS NOT COVERED.

WHERE COVERED

Insuring Agreements I (Robbery Inside Premises), III (Kidnapping), IV (Safe Burglary), VI (Merchandise in Store) and VII (Damage) cover loss within the premises, which is defined as the interior of that portion of the building which is occupied solely by the Insured in conducting his business. Excluded is any show case or show window which does not open directly into the interior of the premises and public entrances, halls and stairways.

Under Insuring Agreements I and II covering Robbery, the policy is broadened to include the space immediately surrounding such building, provided such space is occupied by the Insured in conducting his business. By endorsement, the policy may be extended to cover gasoline or oil in containers connected to locked pumps outside the premises. The territorial limits of the policy are the United States, District of Columbia, Virgin Islands, Puerto Rico, Canal Zone and Canada.

FOR HOW MUCH

The basic Storekeepers' Burglary and Robbery policy provides $250 of insurance on *each* of the seven Insuring Agreements. It is important to understand that the Insured can collect up to $250 for loss due to any of the perils insured. If burglars break into the Insured's store and carry off $200 of merchandise and do $150 of damage to the furniture and fixtures, the entire loss is covered. If the same burglary also resulted in loss of $250 of money and securities from within a locked safe, the policy would be liable for this sum too. The maximum liability of the policy in any one loss is actually 7 x $250, or $1,750, although it is very unlikely that one loss could involve all seven Insuring Agreements.

The Insured may purchase any number of additional Storekeepers' Burglary and Robbery policies, thereby increasing the limits of liability under all coverages, including the $50 limitation on jewelry. The full premium is charged for each additional policy purchased on this basis.

It is also possible to purchase one, two or three additional units at a reduced rate. Such additional units will increase the limits of liability under each Insuring Agreement, but not the $50 limitation on jewelry. No more than three additional units may be purchased at this reduced rate, and the total maximum insurance under each of the Insuring Agreements cannot exceed $1,000.

The Company is liable to the extent of the actual cash value of the property lost or damaged, but for no more than the cost to repair or replace. The Company may pay the loss in cash or may actually repair or replace.

Other Insurance—The Storekeepers' Burglary and Robbery policy does not afford any coverage on any property which is specifically described and enumerated in any other policy. It will apply, as excess insurance only, to property insured in a Blanket, non-specific way, provided the Insured owns such property or is legally liable for it.

OTHER CLAUSES

The Storekeepers' Burglary and Robbery policy is the same as the Open Stock Burglary policy in the following respects:

Insured's Statements, Records of Insured and Regulation.

Rates—The rates for all types of businesses are the same, and vary only with the territory in which the risk is located. Territorial multipliers or factors are applied to a master table to arrive at the rates for the individual states. Each state has its own territorial divisions. The policy may be written for three years at 2.7 times the annual rate.

Term of Policy—The policy attaches at 12 o'clock Noon, Standard Time, at the Insured's place of business.

BROAD FORM STOREKEEPERS POLICY

Broader coverage than is afforded under the Storekeepers' Burglary and Robbery policy is available in a Broad Form Storekeepers policy. This policy is a package policy, patterned on the Storekeepers' Burglary and Robbery policy. It packages nine perils which will be analyzed below. Since the policy parallels the Storekeepers' Burglary and Robbery policy, this section will discuss only the differences between the policies, and should be read together with the preceding analysis of the Storekeeper's Burglary and Robbery policy.

The Broad Form Storekeepers policy is available only to single-location risks which do not customarily employ more than four persons. Since it includes coverage on employee dishonesty, it is sometimes considered as a "baby" Comprehensive 3-D policy, discussed in Chapter 15.

WHAT IS COVERED

Where the Storekeepers' Burglary and Robbery policy covers money, securities, merchandise, furniture, fixtures and equipment, the Broad Form Storekeepers policy covers money, securities and *other property.*

HAZARDS COVERED

Where the Storekeepers' Burglary and Robbery policy covers essentially the perils of robbery, safe burglary with limited coverage on burglary of premises, theft of night depository and residence of custodian, the Broad Form Storekeepers policy covers actual destruction, disappearance or wrongful abstraction of money and securities, and covers other property against the perils of robbery and safe burglary. (The insuring clause is identical with the Broad Form Money and Securities policy.)

Loss away from the premises provides the same coverage as is afforded under the Money and Securities Broad Form, i. e., on money and securities protection against the perils of actual destruction, disappearance or wrongful abstraction and on other property against the peril of robbery or attempted robbery.

There is a limit of $50 on loss of contents of a show window or show case not opening directly into the interior of the premises and damage to such show case. There is also a limit of $50 on any one article of jewelry

Money Orders and Counterfeit Currency—The Broad Form Storekeepers policy covers loss due to the Insured's acceptance of any post office or express money order if such money order is not paid upon acceptance, and of counterfeit paper currency of the United States or Canada. Such loss is payable only if the money order or currency was taken in an exchange for merchandise, money or services, and would not cover if taken merely for purposes of cashing.

Burglary, Robbery of Watchmen—The Broad Form Storekeepers policy provides coverage up to the limits purchased for loss due to burglary or robbery of watchman. In this respect, the policy affords coverage similar to the Open Stock Burglary policy discussed in Chapter 11, except that there is no Coinsurance clause in the policy.

Theft From Residence—The policy covers loss from the residence of a messenger or custodian of money and securities when caused by theft.

Employee Dishonesty—Coverage is afforded for loss caused by any employee, whether acting alone or in collusion with others. In this respect, the policy is similar to the blanket Bonds discussed in Chapters 14 and 15.

Depositors Forgery—The coverage is identical with that of the Depositors Forgery Bond discussed in Chapter 15.

Vandalism and Malicious Mischief—Where the Storekeepers' Burglary and Robbery policy covers only damage due to burglary, robbery, safe burglary or attempts to commit these crimes, the Broad Form Storekeepers policy covers these perils as well as vandalism and malicious mischief following burglarious entry into the premises.

Premises Damage—A separate section of the policy applies to damage to the premises and to insured property.

WHEN COVERED

The Broad Form Storekeepers policy contains a 1-year Discovery Period. This feature is discussed in Chapter 13 under MONEY AND SECURITIES BROAD FORM—HAZARDS COVERED.

OFFICE BURGLARY AND ROBBERY POLICY

SIMILAR TO THE Storekeepers' Burglary and Robbery policy is the Office Burglary and Robbery policy, a package policy sold to individuals or firms occupying business or professional offices which are not on the same plot of ground where the Insured has merchandise which is sold or manufactured, or held for cleaning, repairing, processing, storage or distribution.

The policy may be sold to businesses which sell merchandise, but to cover only offices which are not adjacent to the place where the merchandise is sold. The policy would not in any event cover property held for sale. It is intended primarily for professional offices and service businesses, and there are a considerable number of risks which are ineligible for coverage under the policy, regardless of where the office is located, as follows:

Amusement parks, auctioneers, banks, bowling alleys, clubs, coal dealers, dairies, garages, hotels, ice dealers, ice cream manufacturers or dealers, loan companies, lumber yards, money exchanges, offices in which tickets are sold for travel, amusement or recreation, pawn brokers, pool rooms, rental agencies (except real estate), restaurants, theatres and a series of risks enumerated in the Burglary manual as Class 2, Class 3 or Class 4 occupancies.

WHAT IS COVERED

The Office Burglary and Robbery policy covers money, securities, furniture, equipment and other articles, but does not cover merchandise held for sale or samples, or property held by the Insured as bailee.

The type of property covered varies somewhat under some of the Insuring Agreements and the differences will be discussed below under HAZARDS COVERED.

Property Not Covered—Discussed under Safe Burglary policy.

HAZARDS COVERED

The Office Burglary and Robbery policy is very closely patterned after the Storekeepers' policy. It contains six Insuring Agreements.

I. Robbery Inside Premises—Only loss of money and securities is covered under this section of the policy, which also includes the peril of kidnapping (discussed in Chapter 12 under MERCANTILE ROBBERY INSURANCE—PERILS COVERED—Kidnapping Coverage).

II. Theft Inside Premises—Coverage under this section extends to office equipment only. Manuscripts, books of account and records are excluded. Gold, platinum and other precious metals are not covered, except that for a dentist, the policy may be endorsed to cover precious metals used in his practice.

III. Safe Burglary; Burglary—Safe Burglary coverage extends to money and securities (discussed in Chapter 11 under Mercantile Safe Burglary Insurance). In addition, this section provides $100 of coverage for money and securities for loss by burglary of the *premises*. This coverage is part of the limit under the section, and does not serve to increase the amount of coverage under the section. Thus, if an Insured who has purchased an Office Burglary and Robbery policy with a limit of $250 applicable to each Insuring Agreement were to suffer a loss in which burglars took $200 from the safe and $150 from a drawer, he can collect only $250 for the entire loss.

IV. Robbery Outside Premises.

V. Theft from Night Depository or Residence—Discussed under Storekeepers' Burglary and Robbery policy.

VI. Damage—Damage to money, securities and office equipment by robbery, theft, safe burglary or attempt thereat are covered, both inside and outside the premises. The policy stipulates that damage to premises is covered only if the Insured is the owner of the premises, or liable therefor.

FOR HOW MUCH

Like the Storekeepers' Burglary and Robbery policy, the Office Burglary and Robbery policy is written with $250 of coverage applicable to each Insuring Agreement.

There is no limit, however, to the number of additional policies that may be purchased at 50% of the basic premium for the initial policy.

RATES

Rates for all risks eligible for the Office Burglary and Robbery policy are the same, $14 country-wide.

OTHER PACKAGE CRIME POLICIES

Church Theft—Any house of worship is eligible for a Church Theft policy, which covers all church property—including money, securities, furnishings, musical instruments, hymn books, scrolls, gold, silver and plated ware, stained and art glass, altar vessels, etc., and may be extended to cover the personal property of the clergyman conducting the service.

INNKEEPERS LIABILITY POLICY

Although this policy is usually written by the Burglary department of insurance companies, it is a form of Liability insurance and as such applies only to the loss of or damage to guests' property for which liability is *imposed on the Insured by law.*

The policy covers such liability for injury to, destruction of, or loss of property belonging to the Insured's guests while the property is within the Insured's premises. (A more limited form of coverage, Hotel Safe Deposit Box Legal Liability is available to cover only when loss occurs from the hotel safe deposit boxes on the premises).

The insurance company's liability under the Innkeepers Liability policy is limited to $1,000 for loss of the property of any one guest. For all losses during the policy period, liability is limited to $25,000. Both these limits may be increased for an additional premium.

Loss assumed by the hotel by contract or agreement is not covered except if such assumption of liability has been entered into before the loss in a written agreement. The policy does not apply to loss of or damage to automobiles, their equipment or property in any automobile. Similarly, there is no coverage on property in the Insured's custody for laundering or cleaning.

The policy does not apply to property which a guest holds for sale or delivery or for exhibition. Liability for damage from spilling, upsetting or leakage of food or liquid is not covered, unless specifically endorsed for an additional premium.

Like all Liability policies, the policy also covers the cost of defending a suit (discussed in Chapter 24 under WHAT IS COVERED—Defense of Suits, Supplementary Benefits).

WAREHOUSEMAN'S LIABILITY POLICY

Like the Innkeepers Liability policy, the Warehouseman's Liability policy is also generally written by Burglary departments of insurance companies. It is a Liability policy however covering liability *imposed on the Insured by law* arising out of his activities as a bailee. As bailee for hire, he is charged with extending better care to the property entrusted to him than to his own goods.

The policy covers the Insured's liability arising out of almost every situation. Excluded from coverage are only the following types of losses:

Liability arising from fire or sprinkler leakage;
Liability assumed by the Insured under a contract;
Loss of money, securities or perishables.

The policy, like all Liability policies, covers the cost of defending suits (discussed in Chapter 24 under WHAT IS COVERED—Defense of Suits, Supplementary Benefits).

The policy is written with a limit on merchandise, and subject to this limit, to an aggregate limit on all personal property. It is always written with a Deductible. The Insured is offered a choice of Deductibles—$50, $100, $250, $1,000, $5,000 and $10,000.

VALUABLE PAPERS POLICY

Many individuals and business firms have in their possession valuable papers and documents whose destruction would prove very costly. Some examples of such property are records, customers' lists, maps, drawings, abstracts, deeds, documents, etc. Virtually all-risk protection is available for such papers in a Valuable Papers policy, which excludes only losses due to the perils of war, invasion, rebellion, etc., and wear, tear, gradual deterioration, vermin and inherent vice. Loss from errors or omissions in processing or copying is not covered except when due to fire or explosion, and in such event, only for the loss due to the fire or explosion. Policies issued to libraries exclude loss caused by failure of borrowers of books or other valuable papers to return them.

Each paper may be insured specifically, or a Blanket policy may be written to cover all "valuable papers." Outside the premises, coverage is limited to 10% of the amount of insurance applying under both the Blanket and the specific coverages of the policy, or $5,000, whichever is less.

Articles insured under the Blanket portion of the policy are covered for their replacement cost. Scheduled items are covered on a valued basis—the Company will pay the amount set alongside the particular property, even though it is not possible to replace it with other of like kind and quality. It can be seen that it is important that all material which cannot be reproduced or duplicated be scheduled.

ACCOUNTS RECEIVABLE POLICY

Accounts receivable records are insurable under a special policy, the Accounts Receivable policy, which covers loss suffered by the Insured due to his inability to collect sums due him because of loss of, or damage to, records of accounts receivable on the premises.

The coverage is virtually all-risk and covers loss due to destruction of records of accounts receivable from any cause, except:

War, insurrection risks;

Nuclear reaction, nuclear radiation or radioactive contamination;

Electrical or magnetic injury, disturbance or erasure of electronic recordings other than by lightning;

Fraudulent acts by the Insured, a partner, director or trustee.

It is important to be clear on the fact that the policy does not cover loss arising out of the Insured's inability to collect from customers as such, but only when due to physical damage or destruction of the bookkeeping records. Accounting errors, cycle billing imbalances and inventory shortages are not within the intent of the coverage.

The basic policy covers only when the records are kept on the insured premises. In addition, the Insured is required to keep the records in a safe or vault or other designated "receptacle" when they are not being worked on. The type of safe or vault or other receptacle is specified in the policy.

An exception is made for situations where the Insured removes the books of account to preserve them from a threatening peril. Notice of their removal under these circumstances must be given to the Company within ten days. For an additional premium, off-premises and branch office coverage may be added.

FOR FURTHER READING

ACKERMAN—Insurance
GEE—Agent's Casualty Guide
HEDGES—Practical Fire and Casualty Insurance
KULP AND HALL—Casualty Insurance
MEHR AND CAMMACK—Principles of Insurance
POLICY, FORM & MANUAL ANALYSIS SERVICE
RIEGEL, ROBERT AND MILLER—Insurance

(See Reading List at End of Book)

CHAPTER 14

Fidelity and Surety Bonds

GENERAL PRINCIPLES OF SURETYSHIP

ALTHOUGH FIDELITY BONDS and Surety Bonds are generally considered as separate divisions of the bonding business, the term "Surety" actually covers all bonds and takes in a wide variety of such forms, including Fidelity Bonds, which insure against employee dishonesty, various bonds which guarantee performance like Bid Bonds and Construction Contract Bonds, a host of Court Bonds covering Fiduciaries, as well as Litigation, License and Permit Bonds, and other Miscellaneous Bonds.

The word "surety" is also used to designate the Company that writes the Bond. Companies which confine themselves to the bonding business are sometimes incorporated as the ________ Surety Company or Corporation, and other insurance Companies which started in the bonding business are still titled as Surety Companies, even though they write many forms of insurance besides Surety. On the other hand, many Companies whose names make no reference to Surety operate active bonding departments.

Many obligations between two parties are still guaranteed by personal suretyship; that is, when an individual lends his name or credit to such obligations. A fairly common example of personal suretyship is an individual's acting as co-maker on a loan which a friend is making from a bank or other lending institution. The type of suretyship, however, with which insurance men are generally concerned is Corporate Suretyship, provided by bonding Companies or insurance Companies, and some of the more widely used Bonds written by such Corporate Sureties will be considered in these chapters.

DIFFERENCES BETWEEN INSURANCE AND SURETYSHIP

While it is true that a Bond, like an insurance policy, is purchased to protect against loss, there are certain differences between the principles of insurance and suretyship, and these differences are outlined below.

Generally, the purpose of a Bond is to guarantee the performance by one party of an obligation to another. A Bond, then, is always a 3-party agreement among the following parties:

1. **Principal**—One who undertakes to perform, to fulfill a contract, or meet an obligation; e. g., a Contractor agrees with a real estate corporation to erect a building according to specifications; a Public Official promises the people of a city that he will perform the duties of his office faithfully; a Guardian pledges to the Court that he will guard carefully the property belonging to a minor and will use this money solely for the benefit of the minor; an employee, in accepting employment, inferentially agrees with the employer that he will perform the duties of his employment honestly, etc.

2. **Obligee**—The second party to the contract or agreement with the Principal. The Obligee expects the Principal to perform on his obligation; e. g., a real estate corporation which hires a Contractor to erect a building, the city which appoints or elects a Public Official, the minor who expects his interests to be protected by his Guardian, an employer who looks to his employee for honest performance of his duties, etc.

3. **Surety**—One who guarantees the performance of the obligation of the Principal to the Obligee; e. g., an Insurance Company or a Bonding Company which writes a Bond, a co-maker on a loan, or a person putting up bail, etc. If the Principal fails in his promised performance, the Surety will fulfill the obligation or indemnify the Obligee.

The Principal is the one who may cause a loss under a Bond.

The Obligee is the one who collects under a Bond, and is similar to an Insured under a policy.

The Surety pays or makes good, like an Insurance Company after a loss.

If the Principal fails to perform according to his agreement with the Obligee, the Surety will step in to complete the obligation of the Principal or will indemnify the Obligee, but it will then look to the Principal for repayment.

Theoretically, the Surety does not anticipate any losses, except if the Principal is insolvent and cannot repay the Surety, or if the Principal is a bad moral risk that attempts to defraud. Basically, then, bonding differs from insurance in that it sells the Surety's name and credit rather than collect premiums from a group of Insureds to pay losses.

In actual practice, it will be seen that many types of Bonds are more akin to insurance, and that the difference is more theoretical than real. It is necessary, however, to understand the basic differences between the two forms of protection, outlined as follows:

Insurance	Suretyship
The insurance Company assumes the entire risk.	Theoretically, the Surety assumes no risk, except the moral hazard.
A two-party contract between the Insured and the Company.	A three-party contract among the Principal, the Obligee and the Surety.
No collateral contract is involved.	Guarantees a collateral contract.
Usually no salvage is recoverable.	Salvage is a very important factor.
Rates are based on the law of averages.	Premiums are primarily service fees.
Losses are paid from the premiums collected.	Losses are paid from the Principal's resources as well as the Surety's.
Consideration for the insurance policy is the premium.	Consideration for the Bond is the agreement of the Principal to perform and to indemnify the Surety if he fails.
The Company may cancel the policy at any time.	No cancellation privileges, in most instances.
No Discovery Period to report losses after termination of policy.	Generally a Discovery Period, and it to run for many years.

FIDELITY BONDS

As MENTIONED BEFORE, Fidelity bonding is one branch of the Surety business. Like all Bonds, a Fidelity Bond guarantees a collateral contract between two parties. While employees are seldom asked to enter into a written agreement to perform their duties honestly, such agreement is implied in all contracts of employment. The Fidelity Bond guarantees this honest performance.

As under all Bonds, after the Surety pays a loss under a Fidelity Bond, it is entitled to collect from the employee who caused the loss. Since the employee often cannot make full restitution, the Surety suffers actual loss, and the Fidelity Bond is more akin to insurance than other Bonds which anticipate few losses. In light of this fact, it is becoming increasingly common for Companies to speak of Fidelity Bonds as Dishonesty insurance.

Fidelity insurance is a necessary part of the insurance program of almost every business which wishes to be fully protected against loss. Where Burglary, Robbery and Theft policies protect against acts of criminals, Fidelity Bonds protect against the actions of those within an Insured's organization who are in a position of trust, and are often better situated to cause large scale losses than outsiders.

Many businesses actually present comparatively little exposure to loss by criminal acts of outsiders but, in almost every instance, such enterprises are exposed to loss by employee dishonesty. That many employers who carry all forms of Burglary and Robbery insurance are inadequately protected against the hazards of employee dishonesty, or are completely uninsured, can be seen in the fact that in an average year an estimated $100,000,000 is taken from employers by persons in positions of trust, of which sum only about $15,000,000, or about 15%, is covered by insurance.

FEATURES COMMON TO ALL FIDELITY BONDS

WHAT IS COVERED

The Fidelity Bond covers an employer against the loss of *any* kind of property, whether real or personal, including bullion and manuscripts, trees and shrubbery, automobiles, aircraft, boats and animals.

Ownership of Property—The Insured need not necessarily be the owner of the property. The Fidelity Bond will cover him for loss of any property in which he has a financial interest or any property for which he is legally liable, and also for any property held by him in any capacity, whether he is legally liable for the property or not.

HAZARDS COVERED

The Fidelity Bond covers all fraudulent or dishonest acts of employees. The Insuring clause is very broad, and takes in almost every form of unlawful taking of property by an employee, whether such is technically a larceny or embezzlement under the laws of the state. Some Bonds specifically mention forgery, theft, wrongful abstraction, wilful misapplication, and any act of fraud or dishonesty. Such losses are covered whether the employee acts alone or in collusion with others. Also covered is any inventory shortage which the Insured-employer can conclusively prove was due to fraud or dishonesty on the part of an employee or employees. Such loss is no longer an inventory shortage, but actually an embezzlement loss. To prove "conclusively" that a loss of this kind is due to a dishonest employee is of course sometimes difficult. The intent of the coverage is to protect against loss through dishonesty and not loss through inventory shortage.

There must be dishonest intent on the employee's part. Unauthorized application of an employer's funds would not be covered unless the employee was consciously acting in a dishonest way. Thus, if a cashier pays out money to a person who falsely represents himself as entitled to receive such money, or if an employee pays a bill which he was not authorized to pay, the resulting loss to the employer would not be covered. Nor will a Fidelity Bond pay for loss caused by an employee's mistake or lack of judgment where there was no intent on his part to commit fraud.

The employee need not actually commit the fraud himself, or personally take part in the act of stealing for the loss to come within the coverage of a Fidelity Bond. If an employee aids outsiders to deprive his employer of money or property, the Fidelity Bond will cover. Thus, a night watchman might arrange to leave a door open, or otherwise give access to thieves, without himself taking part in the actual theft, and such loss would be covered. Losses of this kind, when an employee of the Insured is an accessory, are specifically excluded under the Open Stock Burglary policy (discussed in Chapter 11 under OPEN STOCK BURGLARY POLICY —PERILS NOT COVERED—Dishonesty of Employees), and the Fidelity Bond closes a gap in the protection afforded by such policies.

An employee need not necessarily profit personally from the dishonest act for the loss to come under a Fidelity Bond. Thus, if an employee aids in perpetrating a dishonest act for the benefit of another, or acts out of a personal grudge against his employer, such losses would be covered under a Fidelity Bond, even though the employee might never receive any share of the loot.

It is important to understand that the Bond covers only *direct* losses. Consequential losses, such as interruption of business, are not losses contemplated under the Bond. Thus, if an employee were to steal a machine worth $1,000 and it took three days to replace the machine during which time there was a production loss of $5,000, only the loss of the machine would be covered—$1,000.

WHO IS COVERED

The various forms of Fidelity Bonds differ as to the employees who are covered, some insuring only certain named individuals, some covering all occupants of named positions, and others covering all employees of a firm without reservation. (These different Bonds will be discussed separately in Chapter 15 under Types of Fidelity Bonds.)

Even where the Bond includes all employees of a risk, coverage is afforded only for losses caused by employees who are in the regular employ of the Insured and whom the Insured compensates by salary, wages or commissions, and whom the Insured has the right to govern and direct in the performance of their duties. The Bond specifically excludes brokers, factors, commission merchants, consignees, contractors or other agents or representatives.

If the Insured is a partnership, the Fidelity Bond will not, of course, cover defalcations committed by any of the partners, since they are not employees, but employers. A corporation, by contrast, is a distinct legal entity; all its officers are employees of the corporation and, as such, a Bond covering all employees of a corporation will protect against fraud committed by an officer. Specifically excluded, however, are directors or trustees of the Insured-corporation unless they are also officers or employees in some other capacity.

Under Fidelity Bonds which cover all employees of a firm, it is possible to specifically exclude officers of a corporation.

Cancellation of Coverage on Dishonest Employee—Any employee who is discovered to have committed any fraudulent act is immediately excluded under the Bond from any further coverage on future acts. If the Bond covers only this one employee, the entire Bond is terminated. If more than one employee is covered, or if the Bond covers all employees, the Bond continues in full force on the other employees, but not on the one whose dishonest act was discovered.

Committing a dishonest act does not itself exclude the employee from further coverage. The fraud must be *discovered*. In other words, assume Jones, a bookkeeper, dips into his employer's till for the first time on November 1, 1951, and then again, before this first theft is discovered, on December 15, 1951, at which time both thefts are discovered. The Bond is available for both dishonest acts of Jones. After the loss is discovered, however, in this case on December 15, Jones is no longer covered under the Bond.

Note too that coverage ceases whether or not the discovered loss is reported to the Surety. Thus, if an employer wishes to spare his employee and does not report the loss, any subsequent larcenies committed by this employee would not be covered. Note too that the coverage on a dishonest employee whose act is discovered is completely cancelled, not merely reduced in amount.

Absence of Coverage on Employee Previously Cancelled—The Bond also often excludes from coverage any employee on whom coverage was cancelled by *any* Fidelity insurer and not reinstated, whether because he was discovered to have committed a dishonest act, or for other reasons, unless the present Surety specifically agrees in writing to include such employee.

EXAMPLE: Jones, a bookkeeper, is bonded to his employer, the Roberts Co., under a Fidelity Bond issued by the Sterling Surety Co. In 1945, Jones is discovered to have defrauded his employer of $1,500, and this loss is paid by the Sterling Surety Co. Coverage under the Bond is cancelled for any future acts of Jones. In 1950, the Roberts Co. replaces the Bond in the Merit Surety Co., which writes a Blanket Bond covering all employees of the Company. Jones, who is still employed by the Roberts Co., is not covered under the new Bond, since coverage on him had been cancelled under a previous Bond.

The cancellation as to a particular employee must have occurred under a Bond issued for the same Insured-employer or a predecessor in interest. In the above case, if Jones had been fired by the Roberts Co. in 1945, when his dishonesty was discovered, and was subsequently employed by another employer, he *would* be covered under the Bond carried by this new employer. This will be true, however, only if the new employer has no knowledge of the dishonest act committed by his employee.

WHEN COVERED

Since most of the losses which fall under Fidelity Bonds are committed in stealth, it can readily be seen that many of these dishonest acts may not be discovered for some time after they are committed. (A study made by Bonding Companies reveals that the average loss develops over a period of three years before detection.) It is important, therefore, to be clear on the fact that a loss, to be covered under a Fidelity Bond, must satisfy two elements of time—it must have been caused during certain periods, and must also be discovered within certain time limits, as discussed below.

When Loss Must Occur

1) while the Bond was in force,

OR

2) while a prior Bond was in force, subject to certain conditions (to be discussed under Superseded Suretyship).

When Loss Must Be Discovered

1) while the Bond is in force,

OR

2) after cancellation of the Bond, within the specific Discovery Period granted by the particular Bond (discussed below).

Discovery Period—Most Fidelity Bonds provide an additional period *after cancellation* for the Insured to discover losses caused while the Bond was in force. This additional time for discovering of losses is known as the Discovery Period, and varies from six months to three years, depending on the particular Bond.

While a Bond is in force, losses do not have to be discovered within any given time after they occur. Fidelity Bonds are continuous until cancelled, and any loss which occurs while the Bond is in force and is discovered while the Bond is in force will be paid, no matter how long the loss took to come to light. The Discovery Period (also known as a Cut-Off Clause) only begins to run after a Bond is *cancelled.*

The Discovery Period does not extend the Bond to cover any

losses except those which occur when the Bond is in force. (This rule is substantially modified under most Bonds which replace others, as will be discussed later under Superseded Suretyship, but the basic coverage of the Bond applies only to losses actually sustained during the term of the Bond.) The Bond does not apply to losses caused before the Bond took effect or after it has been cancelled.

Thus, assume the Roberts Co. buys a Fidelity Bond covering all its employees on January 1, 1948. This Bond is cancelled on January 1, 1950. Two months later, within the Discovery Period, the employer finds that a cashier had defrauded him of $3,000 in 1947, $3,000 in 1948, $3,000 in 1949 and $3,000 in 1950. The first fraud which occurred in 1947 is not covered, since it took place before the Bond took effect. The losses of 1948 and 1949 are covered, since they took place while the Bond was in force and were discovered within the Discovery Period. The loss caused in 1950 is *not* covered, since it took place after the Bond was *cancelled,* even though within the Discovery Period.

Discovery Periods under individual and schedule Bonds are not standardized, ranging from six months to three years. Under Blanket Bonds, the Discovery Periods are standardized, and these are discussed under the particular Bond in Chapter 15.

The Discovery Period also comes into play when a Bond is reduced in amount. During the Discovery Period, the employer can recover the old amount of insurance. After the Discovery Period has run, he can recover no more than the reduced penalty.

Superseded Suretyship (Indemnity Against Loss Under Prior Bond)—As pointed out above, the basic Insuring Clause of a Fidelity Bond covers only those losses which are sustained while the Bond is in force. Most Bond forms now include a Superseded Suretyship clause (Indemnity Against Loss Under Prior Bond clause).

Under this clause, the Bond picks up losses which were sustained under a prior Bond and would have been paid by the earlier Bond except for the fact that they were not discovered within the prior Bond's Discovery Period. Superseded Suretyship thus provides a bridge of continuity of coverage from the old Bond to the new one replacing it. The replacing (superseding) Bond agrees to pay such losses, subject to certain limits.

EXAMPLE: The Insured buys a Fidelity Bond on January 1, 1940, from the Ajax Surety Co., which he carries until January 1, 1946. This Bond has a 24-month Discovery Period. On January 1, 1946, he cancels this Bond and replaces it as of the same date in the Solid Surety Co. On July 1, 1949, it is discovered that an employee had committed a fraud against his employer during the month of January, 1944. This loss was caused while the first Bond was in force, but the 24-month Discovery Period allowed by this earlier Bond has run out, and the Bond is not liable for the loss. Under the Superseded

Suretyship clause, the replacing Bond in the Solid Surety will be available for this loss, even though it was not written until 1946, nearly two years after the fraud was committed.

The Superseding Suretyship clause of a Bond will go into operation only if the replacing Bond is substituted for the previous Bond on the very same day as the prior Bond was cancelled. There must be no break in the continuity of the two Bonds, not even for one day, otherwise there is no superseding suretyship.

The replacing Bond which picks up losses under its Superseding Suretyship clause is liable only for the amount that the former Bond would have paid, or the amount that it would itself pay for the loss if it had been effective when the loss occurred, *whichever is less.*

EXAMPLE: Under the set of facts given in the example used above, assume the first Bond in the Ajax Surety Co. had been written with a penalty (limit of liability) of $10,000, while the replacing Bond in the Solid Surety was written for $20,000. Assume too that the loss discovered in July, 1949, to have been committed by the employee in 1944 came to $15,000. Although the second Bond's penalty is $20,000 and is available up to this sum for losses which occur while it is in force, it is liable under the Superseded Suretyship clause only for $10,000, the earlier Bond's lesser limit. Similarly, if the penalty of the first Bond had been $20,000, while the replacing Bond was written for $10,000, the Surety's maximum liability for the loss described above would be $10,000, since that is the lesser of the two amounts.

The provision in the Superseded Suretyship clause, limiting liability to the lesser of the two amounts available under either Bond, will apply also when the form of coverage provided under one Bond is more limited than under the other. (An example of the operation of the clause under such circumstances will be found in Chapter 15 under the Blanket Position Bond—Collusion Losses.)

FOR HOW MUCH

Penalty of Bond—The maximum liability of the Surety for any single loss under a Bond is referred to as the penalty of the Bond, which is equivalent to the amount of insurance under an insurance policy.

Amount of Loss—Dishonest employees almost always commit a series of thefts or embezzlements before they are detected. It is important to understand that all the separate acts of fraud are combined at the point of discovery and considered as one loss. The penalty of the Bond is the maximum amount available for any single loss, regardless of the number of individual fraudulent acts actually committed before detection.

EXAMPLE: Assume Smith, a paymaster, is bonded to his employer under a Bond which has been in force since 1935. The penalty of the Bond is $5,000. On November 15, 1950, the auditors in checking the firm's books discovered that Smith had embezzled $2,000 in 1948. Further check of the payroll records reveals that Smith had also taken $4,000 in 1943, and $2,000 in 1945. All three thefts of Smith are combined and the loss considered as $8,000. Thus, in this case, although no single fraud committed by Smith amounted to more than $4,000, the $5,000 Bond is not sufficient to cover the entire loss.

Inventory Shortage Exclusion—Loss based entirely on shortage of inventory is not covered under a Fidelity Bond. The employer must be able to prove that the loss was caused by the dishonesty of an employee. This exclusion is discussed more fully in the next chapter under Blanket Bonds—Inventory Shortage.

Non-Accumulation of Liability—The penalty of a Fidelity Bond is not increased, regardless of the number of years the Bond has been in force. Thus, in the example used directly above, in which paymaster Smith helped himself to his employer's money in three separate years, not more than the penalty of the Bond is available for the entire loss. The Insured-employer cannot contend successfully that the penalty of the Bond should be made available for each year separately.

Salvage—Fidelity Bonds contain a Full Salvage clause. If the Insured sustains a loss which exceeds the amount of coverage under his Bond, he is entitled to any recoveries (salvage) up to the point where he is fully reimbursed for his loss. Balance of the salvage, after the Insured has been made whole, goes to the Surety company.

EXAMPLE: Superior Mfg. Co. carries a Fidelity Bond with a penalty of $5,000 covering all its employees. Larkin, a stock clerk, makes off with $9,000 of his employer's merchandise. The Surety Company pays the employer the penalty of its Bond, $5,000. Some time later, Larkin is apprehended, and $3,000 of the stolen money is recovered. This entire sum must be turned over to the employer, Superior Mfg. Co. Similarly, if the salvage were $4,000, it would all belong to the Insured. Only salvage in excess of $4,000 would be retained by the Surety Company, for when $4,000 had been turned over to the employer, he would have been made whole. The Surety is not entitled to any reimbursement from the Insured for its expenses in recovering salvage unless these are of an unusual nature, such as exceed the regularly allocated claim expense.

Other Insurance—If the Insured carries any other insurance which covers a loss recoverable under a Fidelity Bond, the Bond acts as excess insurance only over such other insurance, and will pay only after the limit of liability under the other policies has been exhausted, and only for the excess over such amount.

WHERE COVERED

The standard Blanket Fidelity Bonds cover loss caused by employees while engaged in the service of their employer within the United States of America, Canada, Puerto Rico, the Canal Zone and the Virgin Islands, and elsewhere for a limited period.

TERM OF BOND

As mentioned above, the term of a Fidelity Bond is continuous. The policy contains no expiration date, and remains in force until formally cancelled. Premiums for the Bond are figured for one year or for three years, and the employer is required to pay further premiums on the premium anniversary of the date of the Bond.

Fidelity Bonds attach at 12:01 A.M.

Cancellation—While many Surety Bonds may not be cancelled, Fidelity Bonds may be cancelled by the Surety or the employer, like other insurance policies. If the Surety wishes to cancel a Fidelity Bond, it usually must give at least 15 days' notice to the Insured. The return premium to which the employer is entitled will be computed on a short rate basis, if the cancellation is effected at his request. If the Company initiates the cancellation, the cancellation is figured pro rata.

Coverage on any employee who is discovered to have committed a fraud terminates immediately upon discovery of the loss (discussed above).

INSURED'S DUTIES AND OBLIGATIONS

Notice of Loss—Proof of Loss—The employer is required to give notice of any dishonest act on the part of an employee at the earliest practical moment, but in any event, usually not later than 15 days after he discovers such act. Proof of Loss usually must be filed within four months after discovery of the dishonest act.

Time to Bring Suit—Under the Blanket Bonds, the Insured may not bring suit against the Surety Company before two months have elapsed from the date of his filing of a Proof of Loss. Such suit usually must be brought within 15 months after the date of the discovery of the dishonest act which caused a loss under the Bond.

Cooperation—The employer must render every assistance to facilitate the investigation and settlement of the loss.

REGULATION

Most Surety Companies are members of the Surety Association of America. This organization has the following purposes:

1. To classify risks, promulgate rates for the various classifications, and to file these rates for its members with the various State Insurance Departments.
2. To establish standard forms, wherever feasible.
3. To collect data and act as a clearing house on all matters pertaining to suretyship.

4. To establish and regulate ethics and practices in the Bonding business.

All Fidelity Bonds are standardized except the Individual and Schedule Bonds.

RATES

Rates for Fidelity Bonds depend on the number of employees and the amount of coverage applicable to each employee, the type of position held by the bonded employee, and the type of Bond. (A full discussion of the rating of Blanket Bonds will be found in Chapter 15 under BLANKET POSITION BOND—How Policy Is Written.) Rates for Fidelity Bonds also depend on the class of business. Most classes of business fall within one group; certain classes are surcharged because of poor experience, e. g., hotels, chain stores, amusement enterprises, etc. Others receive a credit, e. g., hospitals, colleges, libraries, charitable institutions.

As the amount of the penalty under a Fidelity Bond is increased, the basic rate per $1,000.00 of coverage decreases.

Term Rates—While the Fidelity Bond is usually continuous, premiums are shown for a three-year period. The three-year premium is 2.7 times the annual, if paid in advance. The three-year premium may also be paid in three annual installments for an additional 5% carrying charge. The installments are calculated at 35% of the three-year premium.

Whole Dollar Premium Rule—Discussed in Chapter 8 under OTHER FACTORS WHICH AFFECT FIRE INSURANCE RATES —Whole Dollar Premium Rule.

NEW YORK—Applies to all Bonds other than State Liquor License Permit Bonds.

TEXAS—Rounding to the nearest higher dollar begins with premiums with 51¢ or more.

Deductibles—Deductibles ranging from $50 to $500 may be included in all Fidelity Bonds. The Deductible may apply to all employees or only to certain classes of employees. Thus, the Insured may provide that the Deductible will apply only to Class B employees, or to all special Class A employees, or to all employees in a particular position. It cannot be applied only to individuals in a class unless the entire class is included.

Experience Rating—Schedule Bonds with a total liability of $100,000 or more and *all* blanket Fidelity Bonds, regardless of size, are experience rated to a maximum credit of 50% or a maximum debit of 50%.

FOR FURTHER READING

ACKERMAN—Insurance
CRIST—Corporate Suretyship
GEE—Agent's Bonding Guide
HEDGES—Practical Fire and Casualty Insurance
HUEBNER AND BLACK—Property Insurance
POLICY, FORM AND MANUAL ANALYSIS SERVICE
RIEGEL, ROBERT AND MILLER—Insurance

(See Reading List at End of Book)

CHAPTER 15

Types of Fidelity Bonds

AS INDICATED in the previous chapter, there are several types of Fidelity Bonds, designed for the needs of different employers. The basic Insuring Clauses of these Bonds are very similar, but they differ as to the number or kind of employees covered. The more widely used Fidelity Bonds and the purpose for which each is designed will be discussed below, together with any differences in coverage that appear in any one Bond. In all cases, the remarks on any of these Bonds are to be read together with the general discussion on Bonds which makes up Chapter 14.

INDIVIDUAL BOND

THE INDIVIDUAL BOND is used when an employer wishes to bond a single employee. The employee is named in the Bond, and coverage applies only to him. If the named employee leaves the Insured's employ, the Bond is terminated and will not apply to any new employee who may replace the former holder of the position, unless specifically written into the Bond.

Individual Bonds are not standardized, and different Surety Companies' forms may vary on some of the basic provisions. Almost always, the Bond contains a Discovery Period, but these range from six months to three years. The Discovery Period begins to run from the date the Bond is cancelled, or the date the bonded employee leaves the Insured's employ.

Since coverage on any employee who is discovered to have committed fraud is cancelled as of the date of discovery of the crime, the Individual Bond terminates when the designated employee is caught in a fraudulent act.

Some Individual Bonds have a Pro Rata Salvage clause instead of a Full Salvage clause. Under the Pro Rata type of clause, any salvage recovered by the Surety is shared pro rata between the Insured-employer and the Surety Company on the basis of their respective shares of the loss.

NAME SCHEDULE BOND

NAME SCHEDULE BOND is similar to the Individual Bond except that it bonds several employees. As under the Individual Bond, each employee who is bonded must be named in the Bond. A specific penalty is established for *each* employee, and this penalty may be different for the several employees; for example:

John Smith, President	$ 5,000.00
Mary Doakes, Cashier	30,000.00
William Jones, Bookkeeper	10,000.00

Although the Name Schedule Bond requires the Insured to specify the position held by each employee, the Bond will follow the employee regardless of the work he is doing. In promulgating a rate for the Bond, the Surety naturally takes into account the position occupied by the employees to be placed under Bond, since obviously the risk may vary with the position filled.

The Name Schedule Bond is not standardized and the forms used by different Sureties may vary somewhat. Some Name Schedule Bonds require the employer to notify the Company when he shifts a bonded employee to a new position, and to pay any additional premium as may be required by the increased exposure.

Some Surety Companies also issue an Automatic Name Schedule Bond. This form is identical with the Name Schedule Bond except that it also provides automatic coverage for anywhere from 30 to 120 days on newly assigned employees who occupy the same or similar positions to those occupied by the employees named in the Bond.

POSITION SCHEDULE BOND

THE POSITION SCHEDULE BOND does not mention any employee by name. It covers the position or positions listed, with a specific penalty applying to each position. The number of occupants of each position must be stated in the Bond. For example:

1 Bookkeeper	$15,000.00
2 Cashiers	5,000.00
5 Sales clerks	2,000.00

The limit of liability (penalty) of the Bond stated alongside each position is available for each occupant of the position. Thus, in the example used, *each* of the sales clerks is bonded for $2,000.

Under the Position Schedule Bond, it does not matter who fills the bonded position, or how often the person filling any position is changed.

The employer may add or eliminate any positions by requesting an endorsement for such changes from the Surety.

The coverage on any employee, regardless of the position he occupies, terminates when he is discovered to have committed a fraud or other dishonest act. The other occupants of the position continue covered under the Bond.

Automatic Coverage on Newly Created Positions—The Position Schedule Bond is not a standardized form, and there is considerable variation among the different Companies.

Many Position Schedule Bonds provide for temporary automatic coverage on newly created positions. A widely followed practice on this score is to provide that any newly created position in the continental United States or Canada shall be covered automatically for the first 30 days after it is created. The limit of liability applicable to such automatically covered newly created positions will be equal to the smallest amount for which any position of that class is then covered in the Bond but, in any event, for not more than $5,000.

If the Bond does not recite any position of a class similar to the one newly created, the new position will be covered for the largest amount for which any position is then covered, but not more than $5,000 in any event.

If the employer fails to notify the Surety within 30 days of the creation of a new position in his firm (or other number of days specified in the Bond), the coverage on this position becomes void from the beginning.

Automatic coverage on newly created positions, such as may be provided under a particular Position Schedule Bond form, is not to be confused with automatic coverage on additional occupants of a position already listed in the Bond (discussed below).

Additional Occupants of Designated Positions—Some Position Schedule Bonds provide that additional occupants of a position listed in the Bond will be covered automatically, and the Insured becomes liable for the appropriate additional premium to cover such extra employees.

A great many Position Schedule Bonds do not provide for such automatic coverage. When an employee holding a position listed in the Bond causes a loss and it is found that there were more occupants of this position than were designated in the Bond, the limit of the Company's liability for the position is reduced. Under such circumstances, the Company will be liable only for the proportion of the liability listed for the position as the number of persons designated bears to the actual persons occupying the said position.

$$\frac{\text{Number of Employees Specified in Bond for Position}}{\text{Number of Employees Actually Occupying Position}} \times \text{Penalty of Bond for Position}$$

EXAMPLE: The Insured buys a Position Schedule Bond, written as follows:

2 bookkeepers	$ 5,000
2 cashiers	12,000
1 comptroller	20,000

The Insured increases his staff by adding one cashier, but fails to notify the Surety. If a cashier causes a loss under the Bond, the Surety's liability for this loss is limited to $8,000, arrived at as follows:

$$\frac{\text{Number of Cashiers Stipulated in Bond}}{\text{Number of Cashiers Actually Employed}} = \frac{2}{3} \times \text{Penalty for Position} = \frac{2}{3} \times \$12{,}000 = \$8{,}000$$

The reduced indemnity available for loss caused under the above conditions will apply whether the individual causing the loss is the new employee or one of the older ones who was in the Insured's employ when the Bond was issued. It will apply equally if the Insured, at the time he buys the Bond, lists a smaller number of employees in a given position than actually fill the position. For this reason, the Position Schedule Bond is not suitable for the employer who wishes to insure a position, but cover only some of its occupants. Fidelity insurance under such circumstances presents underwriting problems, but might be arranged on a Name Schedule form.

Indemnity will be reduced only when there are extra occupants of the position held by the person causing the loss, and will not be affected by additions to other positions. Thus, in the example used above, if the Insured had not added a fifth cashier, but had increased the number of bookkeepers, and one of the cashiers had caused the loss, the full penalty of the Bond would be available for such loss.

Some Position Schedule Bonds read differently on the manner in which losses will be treated, when the number of persons in a position exceeds the number stipulated in the Bond. The clause used in such policies provides that the Surety will be liable only for that portion of any *loss* that the number of employees stated as holding a designated position bears to the number of employees actually employed in that position. Under this clause, which is more akin to a Coinsurance Clause, the employer must share in any loss, no matter how small, when he fails to cover all holders of a position.

Thus, in the example used above, in a clause of the kind under discussion, the Surety is liable only for 2/3rds of the *loss*. If the loss caused by the cashier was $9,000, a Bond of this kind would be liable for only $6,000. (This same loss under a Bond of the kind discussed directly above would be covered for $8,000.)

Position Schedule Bonds which provide for automatic coverage on newly created positions may also stipulate that if all positions of any class are not covered when a loss occurs, the Surety's liability for any occupant of a position of the class shall not exceed the quotient resulting from dividing the sum total of the amounts carried on such positions by the number of such positions.

BLANKET BONDS

MORE AND MORE, employers are turning to Bonds which cover all employees of the firm without exception. These Blanket Bonds cover everyone in the Insured's employ when the Bond is issued, and also all new employees, whether in the same or similar positions, or in newly created positions—automatically and without notice to the Surety. The employer is completely safeguarded up to the penalty of his Bond, against a loss caused by *any* employee.

There are two Blanket Bonds in wide use today—the Commercial Blanket Bond and the Blanket Position Bond. These two Blanket Bonds are identical on all but a few points and will be discussed together in this section. Only those features which are unique in these Bonds are analyzed below. The reader should also refer to the Chapter 14 for a fuller discussion of the basic provisions of all Fidelity Bonds.

Loss by Unidentifiable Employees—Under the Individual Bond or Name Schedule Bond, it is essential, of course, that the employer be able to point to the employee who caused the loss, if he would collect under the Bond covering such employee. Under the Position Schedule Bond, it is necessary at least to establish that the loss was due to the actions of individuals in the bonded positions.

Under the Blanket Bonds, it is not necessary to identify the employee or employees who were guilty of the dishonest act. If the employer can show that he was defrauded by his employees, he can collect, even though he cannot actually identify the specific individuals who caused the loss.

EXAMPLE: Auditors discover that a series of bank deposit slips have been falsified, causing loss to the employer. It is not possible to determine which cashier was guilty of altering the deposit slips, or whether the fraud was accomplished by one of several other office workers who had made deposits on occasion. It is clear, however, from all the circumstances that the loss was caused by employee dishonesty. Under the Blanket Bond, the loss would be covered, up to the penalty of the Bond.

Automatic Coverage on Terminated Employees—The coverage of a Blanket Bond is extended automatically on former employees for 30 days after their employment has terminated. This extension does not apply when the Bond is cancelled in its entirety, or to employees whose individual coverage has been terminated.

Discovery Periods—The Commercial Blanket Bond has a 1-year Discovery Period; the Blanket Position Bond has a 2-year Discovery Period.

Collusion Losses—The chief difference between the Commercial Blanket Bond and the Blanket Position Bond is the manner in which they apply to collusion losses (losses which are caused by several employees acting together).

The Commercial Blanket Bond does not differentiate between losses caused by one employee and losses caused by several employees acting in collusion. Regardless of the number of employees involved in a single loss, the Commercial Blanket Bond is available up to its penalty for any single loss. Thus, under a $10,000 Commercial Blanket Bond, the employer cannot collect more than $10,000 for any single loss, whether it is the work of one employee or several employees acting in collusion.

Under the Blanket Position Bond, the full penalty of the Bond is available for each employee involved in a fraud. Under a $10,000 Blanket Position Bond, if three identified employees acting in collusion cause a loss of $30,000, the full loss is covered. The maximum liability of the Surety under a Blanket Position Bond is the penalty multiplied by the number of employees working for the Insured. A $10,000 Blanket Position Bond written for an employer of 500 workers could theoretically be called on in a single loss for $5,000,000.

If the employer cannot identify the individuals who participated in the larceny or fraud, recovery is limited to the penalty of the Bond.

In the preceding chapter, under WHEN COVERED—Superseded Suretyship (Indemnity Against Loss Under Prior Bond) is discussed. It is pointed out that a replacing Bond, which picks up losses that occurred during the term of a prior Bond, is liable only for the lesser of the amounts that would be available for the loss under either Bond. This applies not only when the penalty of the respective Bonds is different, but also when the coverage on a particular loss is more restrictive in one of the Bonds. Under the same set of facts as is used in Chapter 14 to illustrate this clause, assume the first Bond which the Insured carried in the Ajax Surety Co. from January 1, 1940, to January 1, 1946, was a Blanket Position Bond with a penalty of $10,000, and that the replacing Bond in the Solid Surety Co. is written for the same penalty, but on a Commercial Blanket Form.

The loss, which is discovered on July 1, 1949, after the Discovery Period of the Blanket Position Bond has run out, involves two employees acting in collusion, and comes to $18,000. Although the loss occurred while a Blanket Position Bond was in effect, and such Bond is ordinarily available in a collusion loss of this kind for $20,000, the replacing Bond is only liable for $10,000, the maximum which it would itself have paid for such loss, if it had been in force at the time.

Similarly, if the Commercial Blanket Bond had come first, and had been replaced by a Blanket Position Bond, the superseding Bond would only pay $10,000 for the loss—again the lesser of the amounts available under either Bond.

Inventory Shortage—Most Insureds who deal in merchandise will develop inventory shortages. Such shortages can be due to many causes, only one of which could be dishonesty of the Insured's employees. The Insured must be able to prove that the shortage is due to the dishonesty of one or more of his employees. Until the inventory shortage is distilled down to a provable fidelity loss, the Bond is not intended to provide coverage. A specific stipulation appears in the Bond which indicates that there is no coverage for any loss the proof of which, either as to its factual existence or as to its amount, is dependent upon an inventory computation or a profit and loss computation—and that inventory records will neither be presented nor accepted as proof of loss under the Bond.

HOW POLICY IS WRITTEN

Both Blanket Bonds are written with one amount applying to all employees. Where an employer wishes to provide increased indemnity on an individual, or several individuals or on any positions, the Surety will issue the Bond with the named positions written for larger amounts. The minimum amount for which a Commercial Blanket Bond may be written is $10,000. Larger amounts may be written, in multiples of $2,500 up to $25,000. Above $25,000, increases come in multiples of $5,000. There is no maximum limit to the amount of the penalty under a Commercial Blanket Bond, except that each Company is limited to the amount it can write in any one Bond by virtue of its capital and surplus. Blanket Position Bonds may be written with a penalty as low as $2,500, but for no more than $100,000.

RATES

For either of the Blanket Bonds, an application is required on which the employer is required to enumerate the *number* of his employees whose regular duties include the handling of money, securities or merchandise, e.g. executive officers, managers, bookkeepers, auditors, stock clerks, etc. These are classified as Class 1 employees.

The number of Class 1 employees determined in this manner is then subtracted from the total number of the Insured's employees. Of the remainder, 5% of the first 100 employees and 1% of the excess over 100 are added to the number of Class 1 employees to arrive at the premium for the Bond, which is based on the number of Class 1 employees so arrived at.

EXAMPLE: An Insured operates a business with 950 employees. Of these, 50 are engaged in handling money, securities or merchandise. Of the remaining 900 employees who are not so engaged, 5% of the first 100 (or 5) plus 1% of the remaining 800 (or 8), a total of 13, are added to the 50 Class 1 employees, and the premium charge made for 63 Class 1 employees.

Once a Blanket Bond is written, the premium is fixed for the premium period of the Bond (one year or three years, as the case may be). The employer does not report any additions to his payroll, nor is he required to pay for such increases in his staff. On the first or third anniversary of the Bond, depending on the premium period, the Surety requests a new application, and computes a new renewal premium to reflect the changed employment picture of the risk.

An exception to this rule is made if the Insured merges or consolidates his business with another during the term of the Bond. He is then required to notify the Company of any additions made to his staff as a result of the merger or consolidation, and must pay an additional pro rata premium for these individuals.

Experience Credits—As indicated in Chapter 14, the employer's past experience with dishonesty in his organization is taken into account when the Bond is being rated. Credits are allowed for a loss history which is better than average, and a debit applied for risks with poor experience.

Three-Year Policies—Basic premiums are shown for three-year policy periods. A one-year policy may be written for 35% of the premium shown in the manual.

Whole Dollar Premium Rule—Discussed in Chapter 8 under OTHER FACTORS WHICH AFFECT FIRE INSURANCE RATES—Whole Dollar Premium Rule.

CANCELLATION

In addition to the usual provisions for cancelling a Bond in its entirety, the Surety may cancel the coverage on any employee. The employer must receive not less than 15 days' notice.

Cancellation on Employee Discovered To Have Defrauded—Like all Fidelity Bonds, coverage is cancelled automatically on any employee discovered by the Insured in a fraudulent act, whether committed before or after the date of employment by the Insured. The Blanket Bond continues on all other employees.

REINSTATEMENT AFTER LOSS

Blanket Bonds are automatically reinstated to their full penalty after a loss, and the employer is not required to pay any additional premium. This restoration applies to any losses as may occur after the first loss (Prospective Restoration) and to any undiscovered losses which had occurred prior to the loss, but during the term of the Bond (Retroactive Restoration). This restoration applies, of course, only to acts of employees other than the one discovered in a dishonest act on whom coverage is cancelled.

If an employee is discovered in a dishonest act, coverage ceases for any future acts of this employee, but not necessarily on dishonesties which he has already perpetrated, which have not yet been discovered. In such an instance, after an employee has been discovered in a loss, the Bond is reduced by the amount of such loss as respects any loss which has already occurred but which is discovered subsequent to the discovery of the first loss. This reduction in amount will also apply to any other undiscovered loss in which this employee was acting with any other employee.

EXAMPLE: On August 1, 1957, auditors discover that A had defrauded his employer of $6,000 in 1956. Two months later, they discover that A had previously stolen $10,000 in 1954. For this $10,000 loss the Bond will respond but only for such amounts of the penalty as has not been used up to pay the first discovered loss of $6,000. This reduction will apply not only to losses that A had previously committed but any losses in which A was involved in collusion with others.

DISCOVERY BOND

As DISCUSSED ABOVE, all Fidelity Bonds allow the Insured some additional period after cancellation to discover losses which occurred while the Bond was in force. This period is known as the Discovery Period.

It is important to understand that the Discovery Period will not bring within the coverage of the Bond any losses other than those which actually were caused while the Bond was in force, or while a prior superseded Bond was in force. Any undetected frauds which had already been committed when the Bond is effected will not be covered, even if they are detected while the Bond is in force.

A long-established employer who is purchasing a Fidelity Bond for the first time may wish to be protected against such old undiscovered losses which may turn up at some later date. A special Bond, the Discovery Bond, is designed for this purpose. Under a

Discovery Bond (not to be confused with a Discovery Period), the employer will be entitled to indemnity for any losses *discovered* while the Bond is in force, regardless of how long ago the frauds were actually committed.

The Discovery Bond will be liable only for losses discovered while the defrauding employee is still in the Insured's employ. A 12-month Discovery Period may be added to a Discovery Bond for an additional premium of 10%. Under such Discovery Period, the employer will be covered for any losses discovered within 12 months after a defrauding employee has left the firm's employ.

Superseded Suretyship is not available on any Fidelity Bond which supersedes a cancelled Discovery Bond.

DEPOSITORS FORGERY BOND

DESPITE THE LARGE AMOUNT of currency in use in everyday business, the bulk of payments made in industry and commerce are in the form of checks, drafts, and similar orders to pay. For this reason, almost all businesses (and many individuals) are exposed to the threat of serious loss through the forgery or alteration of such instruments.

The most widely used form of written order to pay is, of course, the check or draft drawn on a bank in which the drawer maintains an account. Under many conditions, the bank which pays a forged check is obliged to indemnify the depositor, but this liability is far from absolute. There are many situations in which the bank is held free of liability to its depositor, and the latter must himself bear the loss.

Thus, the laws of many states require that the depositor discover the forgery within a given period of time and report it to the bank; otherwise the depositor is barred from recovering. Then again, if the depositor fails to exercise reasonable care in drawing a check, or is otherwise negligent, as in his supervision of the employees entrusted with drawing checks, he may by his actions have relieved the bank of any liability for its paying out a forged check.

Where a firm uses mechanically reproduced signatures on its checks, it is generally required to release the bank for any liability in paying out checks which bear signatures similar to the facsimile signatures in general use. Then again, when an instrument is made payable to a fictitious or non-existing person, and the maker of the instrument is aware of the fact that the payee is fictitious or non-existent, the check or draft is generally held payable to any bearer.

CALIFORNIA, GEORGIA, IDAHO, ILLINOIS, LOUISIANA, MASSACHUSETTS, MISSOURI, MONTANA, NEW MEXICO, WISCONSIN

—A check payable to a fictitious or non-existent payee may be deemed payable to the bearer, if the fictitious nature of the payee is known to an employee or agent of the maker who supplied the name of the payee. Under this rule, the maker of the check may not himself be aware of the fact that the payee was fictitious, but the check may nevertheless be payable to the bearer and require no endorsement.

A frequent source of loss for which the bank may not be liable is the giving of checks to an imposter. Such acts, even though fraudulent, are not considered forgeries, and the bank is usually not liable for paying out the instrument. The rules governing a bank's liability in such cases are somewhat complex, and differ among the states. Generally, when a check is delivered to an imposter as a payee, and the person drawing the check believes that the check will be paid upon the endorsement of the person to whom he delivers the check, and the imposter does actually endorse the check in the name he is assuming, the act is not considered a forgery.

Thus, in a recent case in New Jersey, a charitable lady received a telephone call from a person reputedly soliciting funds for disabled soldiers. The person used the name of a well-known, civic-minded citizen who was known by reputation to the lady, but asked that the check be drawn to the order of his secretary, one Henry Williams—since he did not wish to receive any publicity himself for the work he was doing. Some time later, the alleged secretary called and identified himself as Williams, and received a $500 check from the lady. The telephone call, of course, had been made by an imposter. It also turned out that there was no such person as Williams. The lady sued the bank which had paid out the $500 check, contending that the fraud was a forgery and the bank therefore liable. The courts held that the endorsement of the check, even though by an imposter, was genuine, and that the bank was free of any liability in this case.

While there is no hard and fast rule, generally, when the drawer of the check deals with the imposter in a face-to-face transaction, the fraud is not considered a forgery.

Insurance against the loss caused by alteration of a written order to pay, whether such act constitutes a forgery under the laws of the particular state or not, is provided under a special Bond, the Depositors Forgery Bond.

HAZARDS COVERED

The Depositors Forgery Bond covers any loss caused to the Insured by forgery or alteration of any check, draft, promissory note, bill of exchange, or similar promise, order, or direction to pay a sum of money. The Bond covers whether such instrument was drawn by the Insured or is purported to have been drawn by the Insured.

Loss is covered whether the altering of the instrument is a forgery under the laws of the state or not. Included is loss due to paying out check or draft to a fictitious payee, or an imposter.

Mechanically reproduced facsimile signatures are treated the same as handwritten signatures.

While the Depositors Forgery Bond is usually considered along with Fidelity Bonds, it is not limited to dishonest acts of employees, but covers forgery or alteration of orders to pay, *no matter by whom committed.* It will therefore cover such losses, whether caused by an employee or an outsider. It is important, however, to be clear on the fact that Fidelity Bonds, do *not* exclude loss caused by an employer by his employee's forgery. Such loss would be covered under a Blanket Position Bond, Position Schedule Bond, or other similar Bond, as well as under a Depositors Forgery Bond.

Coverage of employees may be excluded under the Depositors Forgery Bond at a premium discount of 50%.

The basic Depositors Forgery Bond covers only instruments issued by or purported to have been issued by the Insured. It does not cover incoming checks. Such coverage may be endorsed on a Depositors Forgery Bond, although it is written very sparingly by most Surety companies. (This extra protection will be discussed under WHAT IS COVERED.)

WHO IS COVERED

The Depositors Forgery Bond covers the named Insured for any loss sustained by him due to forgery or alteration as described. In addition, the Bond covers the Insured's bank for any loss suffered by the bank in paying, cashing, or taking for collection any instrument made or drawn or purported to be drawn by the Insured. The bank is covered at the option of the Insured, who has a choice of including the bank's loss on his own proof of loss at the time of making claim.

The bank is treated as an additional Insured under the Bond. If the loss has already been paid to the Insured by the bank, the Bond will reimburse the bank. If the loss has not been paid by the bank, the Surety will indemnify the Insured but, regardless of whether the bank is liable for the particular loss, the Surety Company cannot recover from the bank.

WHAT IS COVERED

As discussed above, the Depositors Forgery Bond covers loss

by alteration of checks, drafts, promissory notes, bills of exchange or similar promise to pay.

The Depositors Forgery Bond covers only written orders to pay *a sum of money,* like checks, drafts, promissory notes, etc. It does not cover forged or altered orders to pick up merchandise, warehouse receipts, bills of lading and similar orders. Protection is available under a special option to cover loss due to the forgery of credit cards.

Also covered under the Bond are court costs and attorney's fees and similar legal expenses as may be incurred by the Insured or the bank (an additional Insured) in defending an action brought to enforce collection by any party. The Underwriter must give his written consent to the defense of the suit.

Personal Account Forgery—The Depositors Forgery Bond may be extended to cover the personal account of an officer of the insured corporation or of a partner. This extension does not increase the amount of the Bond.

Incoming Check Endorsement—Coverage may also be extended to include insurance for the personal checking account of officers or partners of the Insured. The basic Depositors Forgery Bond covers only instruments issued by the Insured or those purported to have been issued by the Insured. *Incoming* checks and other instruments are not covered.

Such incoming instruments received by the Insured in direct face-to-face exchange with the Insured's customers for goods or services may be covered by endorsement. There is no coverage for checks received in payment of a bill when credit has been extended. Under the Incoming Checks Endorsement, the Company's liability is limited to 75% of any loss, and the Insured must in all instances bear 25% of the loss himself.

FOR HOW MUCH

The Depositors Forgery Bond is liable for the loss actually sustained by the Insured up to the penalty of the Bond. Court costs and attorney's fees, however, are payable over and above the amount of the Bond penalty.

Other Insurance—The Depositors Forgery Bond acts as primary insurance. In other words, if the Insured carries a Fidelity Bond as well as a Depositors Forgery Bond, and an employee commits forgery, the Depositors Forgery Bond will pay for the loss up to its penalty. If the penalty of the Depositors Forgery Bond is not large enough to cover the entire loss, the Insured may look to the Fidelity Bond for the balance.

Branch Office Endorsement—If the Insured operates branch offices, these are included automatically, without additional premium charge. The amount of coverage is *not* increased, however; the insurance is merely extended. In the event of a loss involving both the principal office and a branch office, the Bond will not pay more than its basic amount.

WHEN COVERED

The Depositors Forgery Bond contains a 12-month Discovery Period. For losses to be covered under the Bond, they must occur during the time the Bond was in force, and must be discovered either during the term of the Bond or within 12 months after termination of the Bond. The Bond also contains a Superseded Suretyship clause (Indemnity Against Loss Under Prior Bond).

FAMILY FORGERY BOND

A SPECIAL FORGERY BOND, the Family Forgery Bond is available to cover losses sustained by private individuals due to forgery or alteration of written instruments. The Family Forgery Bond covers the head of a household and his spouse and all children who reside permanently at the Insured's address. The coverage under the Family Forgery Bond is similar to the Depositors Forgery Bond, but it also covers incoming checks and losses sustained by giving of any value or the extension of credit on account of any stock certificate or any negotiable instrument, interest coupon, money order or mortgage. It also covers if the instrument is lost or stolen. The Family Forgery Bond also covers acceptance in good faith of any counterfeit paper currency up to $50 in any one loss, or $100 in the aggregate.

CREDIT CARD FORGERY BOND

The widespread use of credit cards has brought into being a new Forgery Bond, the Credit Card Forgery Bond.

The Bond covers loss sustained by an Insured through forgery or alteration of any written instrument required in conjunction with any credit card issued to the Insured or to any partner, officer or employee of the Insured or to Insured's spouse or any child living with the Insured.

The Bond covers court costs and attorney's fees in connection with any lawsuit, and these costs are payable over and above the amount of the Bond. In most other respects the Credit Card Forgery Bond is very similar to the Depositors Forgery Bond.

The Insured is required to comply fully with the provisions, conditions and other terms under which the credit card is issued.

The Credit Card Forgery coverage may be written by endorsement to a Homeowners Policy, a Depositors Forgery Bond, a 3-D policy, Blanket Crime Policy or a Family Forgery Bond.

Rates are based on the amount of coverage, and the number of card holders for each Insured. As under the Depositors Forgery Bond, forgery by employees of the Insured may be excluded, and a discount granted.

Under an amendment to the Federal Truth in Lending Law, as of Jan. 25, 1971, the maximum liability of a card holder is limited to $50 for any one card. In view of this limitation of liability, the demand for this Bond may decrease except for Insureds who have a number of cards, and who are interested in the Defense and Depositors Forgery features of the contract.

BONDS COVERING FINANCIAL INSTITUTIONS

SPECIAL BOND FORMS are made available to Commercial Banks, Commodity Brokers, Credit Unions, Federal Home Loan Banks, Federal Savings and Loan Associations, Finance Companies, Foundations and Endowment Funds, Investment Banking Houses, Investment Trusts, Mutual Savings Banks, Savings and Loan Associations, and similar institutions.

Most banks are currently insured under one of the Blanket Bond forms designed for such institutions. In widest use by banks are three forms: Bankers Blanket Bond No. 2, Savings Banks Blanket Bond No. 5, and Bankers Blanket Bond No. 24. The Bankers Blanket Bond No. 24 is the broadest of the three forms, and is fast replacing the more limited Form No. 2. It is not available to savings banks, which insure under Savings Banks Blanket Bond No. 5. This Form is somewhat more limited than the Bankers Blanket Bond No. 24, which is analyzed next.

BANKERS BLANKET BOND No. 24

THE BANKERS BLANKET BOND is a package policy designed to provide commercial banks in a single contract with protection against a wide variety of hazards. Although it is known as a Bond, the policy, as will be shown, is considerably broader than Dishonesty insurance. The Bond contains five separate Insuring Clauses, as follows:

1. Fidelity Insuring Clause
2. Premises Insuring Clause

3. In Transit Insuring Clause
4. Forgery Insuring Clause
5. Securities Insuring Clause.

WHAT IS COVERED

The Bankers Blanket Bond specifically enumerates over 50 types of items (listed below), including money, coin, stamps, precious metals, jewelry, valuable papers and documents of various kinds. Loss of such property is covered whether the Insured is the owner of the items or is holding the property in any capacity, and whether liable for the property or not. As respects property of others being held by the Insured, the Bond stipulates that such loss must be included in the Insured's Proof of Loss, at his option.

As used in the Bond, "property" means money (i.e. currency, coin, bank notes, Federal Reserve notes), postage and revenue stamps, U. S. Savings stamps, bullion, precious metals of all kinds and in any form and articles made therefrom, jewelry, watches, necklaces, bracelets, gems, precious and semi-precious stones, bonds, securities, evidences of debt, debentures, scrip, certificates, receipts, warrants, rights, transfers, coupons, drafts, bills of exchange, acceptances, notes, checks, withdrawal orders, money orders, travelers' letters of credit, bills of lading, abstracts of title, insurance policies, deeds, mortgages upon real estate and/or upon chattels and upon interests therein, and assignments of such policies, mortgages and instruments, and other valuable papers, including books of account and other records used by the Insured in the conduct of its business, and all other instruments similar to or in the nature of the foregoing, in which the Insured has an interest or in which the Insured acquired or should have acquired an interest by reason of a predecessor's declared financial condition at the time of the Insured's consolidation or merger with, or purchase of the principal assets of, such predecessor or which are held by the Insured for any purpose or in any capacity and whether so held gratuitously or not and whether or not the Insured is liable therefor, and chattels which are not hereinbefore enumerated and for which the Insured is legally liable.

On chattels, other than those which are enumerated, the Bond covers only such items for which Insured is legally liable, and the Bond is liable only for the first 60 days after the Insured becomes aware of the fact that he has become liable for the safekeeping of such chattel. However, regardless of how long held by the Insured, the Bond is liable for loss to such chattels caused by the dishonest acts of its employees.

The Bankers Blanket Bond also provides coverage against stipulated perils for loss of furnishings, fixtures or equipment in the Insured's office, as well as damage to such property by an insured peril, provided the Insured is the owner of or legally liable for the items. Also covered are any court costs and reasonable attorney's fees in any suit or legal proceeding brought against the Insured to establish his liability for a loss which would constitute a claim under the Bond.

Property Not Covered—The Bankers Blanket Bond specifically excludes loss through paying of forged or altered travelers' checks except if due to employee dishonesty.

HAZARDS COVERED

Fidelity Insuring Clause—(A)—The Bankers Blanket Bond covers any loss caused by employee dishonesty, whether committed by an employee alone or in collusion with others. Coverage is afforded for such loss to property (as defined) held by the Insured for any purpose or in any capacity, whether the Insured is liable for such property or not. The Bond covers on a "discovery" basis, i.e., any loss discovered within its term even if the loss was actually sustained before the inception of the contract. By endorsement, it is possible to convert the Bond to cover on a "loss sustained" basis.

Premises Insuring Clause—(B)—The Bond also covers loss or destruction of property caused by robbery, burglary, theft, false pretenses, misplacement, or mysterious unexplainable disappearance. Also covered is loss of property while in the possession of a customer who is on the Insured's premises, whether or not the Insured is liable for such loss. Coverage extends to loss by robbery of a customer who is transacting business at an outside window or other similar facility provided by the Insured bank or who is in any building, driveway or parking lot or similar facility maintained by the Insured as a convenience for its customers.

Loss or damage from any of the named perils is covered, whether caused by the Insured's employees or otherwise. This coverage makes the Bankers Blanket Bond considerably broader than the usual Fidelity Bond, since the latter covers only employee dishonesty.

Furnishings, Fixtures or Equipment—Under the Premises Insuring Clause (B), the Bankers Blanket Bond also covers loss of or damage to furnishings, fixtures, supplies or equipment within any of the Insured's offices by larceny, burglary, theft, robbery or attempt thereat, as well as by vandalism and malicious mischief to the *interior* of such office. Such loss is covered, provided the Insured owns the property or is liable for it.

Forgery Insuring Clause—(D)—The Bond contains a very inclusive Forgery insuring clause, which covers any loss through accepting, cashing or paying forged or altered checks, drafts, acceptances, withdrawal orders, letters of credit, money orders and similar instruments, by forgery or alteration of checks, drafts, acceptances, withdrawal orders or receipts for the withdrawal of funds or property, certificates of deposit, letters of credit, warrants, money orders and similar instruments as well as the extension of credit by the bank in relying on such forged or altered instruments, or on telegraphic, cable or teletype instructions or advices sent by a person purporting to be a customer of a banking institution, the transfer or delivery of any property, and the payment of forged or altered promissory notes.

The Bankers Blanket Bond may be written to eliminate entirely any coverage under Insuring Clause D. This Insuring clause may also be written in an amount different from the basic Bond.

Securities Insuring Clause—(E)—The Bankers Blanket Bond also covers loss sustained by the bank in purchasing, selling, delivering, extending credit, assuming liability or otherwise acting upon any securities, documents or written instruments which prove to have been forged or counterfeited, raised or otherwise altered, or lost or stolen.

This section also covers loss through the Insured's paying or redeeming or witnessing any signature on United States Savings Bonds, Series A to K inclusive which have been forged, counterfeited, raised or otherwise altered, or lost or stolen. Also loss through the receipt of counterfeit currency of the United States or Canada.

Coverage under this Insuring Clause is limited to the forgery or alteration of securities, documents or other written instruments. Specifically excluded is the alteration of checks, drafts or money orders (covered under the Forgery Insuring clause of the Bond).

The Bankers Blanket Bond may be written to eliminate entirely any coverage under Insuring Clause E. This Insuring clause may also be written in amount different from the basic Bond.

In Transit Insuring Clause—(C)—This coverage is discussed below under Where Covered.

HAZARDS NOT COVERED

The Bankers Blanket Bond does not cover loss due to military, naval, or usurped power, war or insurrection unless such loss occurs in transit and then only if the transit had been initiated before the Insured knew of such occurrence.

The Bond does not cover loss resulting from payments made or withdrawals from a depositor's account by reason of uncollected items of deposit having been credited to the depositor's account, unless the depositor or his representative is within the office of the Insured at the time such payment or withdrawal is made, or unless such loss is covered under Insuring Agreement (A).

There is no coverage for loss of property in customers' safe deposit boxes unless caused by dishonest act of a bank employee in such circumstances as would make the bank liable therefor.

The Bond does not cover loss caused by any director of the bank except if he is an employee or official of the bank or while acting as a member of any committee duly elected by a resolution of the Board of Directors to perform specific as distinguished from general duties.

The Bond does not cover loss sustained by the Insured in any loan transaction except if effected through employee dishonesty or forgery as covered under the Forgery Insuring clause or through the forgery or alteration of securities as covered under the Securities Insuring clause. (Both clauses are discussed above.)

The Bond excludes loss, in time of peace or war, directly or indirectly caused by the effects of nuclear fission or fusion or radioactivity. The exclusion does *not* however apply to loss caused by the industrial use of nuclear energy.

Teller's Shortages—The Bankers Blanket Bond does not cover any shortage in the cash handled by a teller which is due to error, and any shortage which is not in excess of the normal shortage in the teller's cash is presumed to be due to error.

If a teller develops a shortage which is excess of normal, and there is reasonable evidence that the loss was due to misplacement or mysterious unexplainable disappearance, the loss may be covered under Insuring Clause B, unless that clause has been written to exclude by rider loss due to misplacement.

The entire "teller's shorts" exclusion may be deleted from the policy for an additional premium.

Credit Card Exposure—A special rider may be attached to the Bankers Blanket Bond which excludes losses sustained by the bank through fraud arising out of its credit card business. A separate Bond, the Charge Card Issuers Bond (discussed briefly directly after this section on the Bankers Blanket Bond) is available to insure this exposure.

WHERE COVERED

In Transit Insuring Clause—(C)—The Bankers Blanket Bond

covers loss of property through robbery, larceny, theft, hold-up, misplacement, mysterious unexplainable disappearance, or if lost or otherwise made away with, as well as damage or destruction of such property while in transit anywhere in the custody of a bank employee or partner of the Insured or person acting as messenger, or while in the custody of an armored motor vehicle. In the last case, the Bankers Blanket Bond acts as excess over any other coverage available for the loss, or the amount which the bank collects under its contract with the armored car company.

This coverage is world-wide, and is virtually all-risk. There is no coverage, however, for loss due to riot or civil commotion or loss due to military, naval or usurped power, war or insurrection, UNLESS when such transit was initiated, there was no knowledge of such riot, civil commotion, military, naval or usurped power, war or insurrection on the part of the person who initiated the transit.

The Bond covers loss to insured property while lodged or deposited within any offices or premises located anywhere. (See Premises Insuring Clause B, discussed above under PERILS COVERED.)

NOTE: The Bond does not cover loss of property in the mails or with a carrier for hire, except if with an armored car company.

WHO IS COVERED

The Bond automatically covers all nominees organized by the Insured-bank for the purpose of handling certain of its business transactions, provided such nominees are composed exclusively of its officers, clerks or employees.

The Bond may be endorsed to cover as employees attorneys who are retained to perform legal services for the Insured and the employees of such employees. There is no charge for adding this rider to a Bankers Blanket Bond.

FOR HOW MUCH

The liability of the Surety for any one loss does not exceed the amount of the Bond, even though the loss may come under more than one Insuring Clause.

EXAMPLE: A bank carries a Bankers Blanket Bond in the amount of $100,000. In a burglary, $40,000 of damage is done to the premises and the vaults, and $90,000 of currency stolen. The liability of the Bond for this entire loss is limited to $100,000—the penalty of the Bond.

Securities—The Surety is obligated to settle any loss of securities in kind. For purposes of loss payment, the value of securities is set at their value on the day preceding the loss. The Insured has the option under this Bond of accepting payment in cash equal to the cost of replacing the securities.

Property Other Than Securities—The Surety is not liable for more than the actual cash value of the property at the time of the loss or the cost to repair or replace, whichever is less. The Surety may elect to actually replace or repair the loss.

Court Costs and Attorney's Fees—Court costs and attorney's fees are covered over and above the amount of the Bond, and with out limit.

Property in Custody of Armored Car Service — The Bankers Blanket Bond, as it applies to loss of property in the custody of an armored motor vehicle company, acts as excess only over the amount received by the Insured under his contract with the armored car company, or the amount of insurance carried by the company for its customers' benefit, or any other insurance in force for the benefit of the customers of the armored car company.

Chattels Not Specifically Enumerated—On any chattel which is not specifically listed in the clause defining property (discussed before under WHAT IS COVERED), the Bankers Blanket Bond acts as excess only over any insurance effected by anyone other than the Insured.

Non-Accumulation of Liability—See Chapter 14.

Salvage—See Chapter 14.

WHEN COVERED

Retroactive Extension—The Bankers Blanket Bond No. 24 is written on a full discovery basis. It covers any loss coming within its terms which occurred while the Insured was carrying similar insurance and which is discovered while the Bond is in force. The superseded Suretyship coverage of this Bond is broader than under ordinary commercial Fidelity Bonds in that it extends the amount of the new Bond retroactively to cover losses which were covered under the old Bond but were not discovered during the term of the former instrument.

Term of Bond—Like all Bonds, the Bankers Blanket Bond is continuous, and remains in force until cancelled.

Cancellation—The Bankers Blanket Bond may be cancelled by the Surety by giving not less than thirty days' notice to the Insured. The Insured may cancel the Bond at any time. As under most other forms of insurance, if the cancellation is made at the request of the Insured, the Surety is entitled to retain the short rate percentage of the premium for the period the Bond was in force. If the Surety initiates the cancellation, the cancellation is effected pro rata.

The Bond contains a special Cancellation provision, which stipulates that the Bond will be cancelled immediately if the Insured bank is taken over by a receiver or liquidator, or if the bank is taken over by another institution, when the earned premium is figured on a pro rata basis.

Discovery Period—Different from the Blanket or Schedule Fidelity Bonds, the Bankers Blanket Bond does not contain any Discovery Period. When the Insured cancels the Bond, he may purchase one-year Discovery coverage for 25% of the last annual premium at the time of cancellation.

INSURED'S DUTIES AND OBLIGATIONS

Notice of Loss—Proof of Loss—The Insured is required to give notice of loss within a reasonable time after discovery of loss. Proof of Loss must be filed within 120 days after a loss is discovered.

Time to Bring Suit—If the Insured desires to institute a suit against the Surety, such suit must be instituted within 24 months after he discovers the loss for which he wishes to claim. Different from the Fidelity Bonds discussed previously, there is no period which must elapse before the Insured can commence a suit.

REGULATION

Most companies writing Bankers Blanket Bonds are members of the Surety Association of America. The functions of this organization are discussed in Chapter 8 under Regulation.

The Bankers Blanket Form No. 24 and others which are designed for financial institutions were developed by the Surety Association of America, working with the American Bankers Association.

RATES

Rates for the Bankers Blanket Bond depend on the following factors:

1. The number of employees.

2. The form in which the Bond is written, i. e., whether it includes Insuring Clause D, Insuring Clause E, etc.

3. The number of branches operated by the bank.

4. The loss experience of the bank. (All Blanket Bonds are experience rated.) For each bank, a basic unit of coverage is set up, depending on the size of the bank. A primary portion of the basic premium thus arrived at is then subject to a debit or credit, depending on the experience. The modification can vary from a credit

of 50% to a 50% debit. The excess amount over the basic unit is *not* subject to experience modification.

5. The size of the bank in terms of its volume of deposits, the amount of loans and discounts made by the bank, etc.

Term Rates—See Chapter 14.

Deductibles—Under Bankers Blanket Bonds No. 2, 5, 22 and 24, the Insured may purchase coverage at a lower rate by including a Deductible clause. Deductibles range from $100 to $1,000.

PARTNERSHIP BOND

LEADING STOCK EXCHANGES require the bonding of partners to the partnership (in excess of the defaulting partner's interest in the firm). The rules of these particular exchanges prescribe the amount of the Form No. 14 Bond and the amount of the Partnership Bond, depending on the size of the partnership. The amount of the Partnership Bond required is the same as for the Blanket Bond No. 14, for which minimums are also set by the exchanges.

CHARGE CARD ISSUERS BOND

Commercial banks are exposed to large scale loss through their credit card business. A special Bond, the Charge Card Issuers Bond, is available to protect the bank against losses caused by lost, stolen or counterfeit credit cards.

The Bond is written with several dollar limits. First, an overall or aggregate limit of $500,000 or $1,000,000 will apply to *all* losses within the period for which the Bond is written. The payment of any loss under the Bond, it can be seen, will reduce the amount available for any subsequent losses during the term of the contract.

A second limit is established as a maximum on loss per card. It is important to understand that this limit applies to all losses stemming from all credit cards in the same series. The Bond defines "per card" as "all cards with the same identifying numbers or letters."

A Deductible is mandatory under the Bond. There is a range of Deductibles, but these are not optional with the Insured. Instead, they depend on three provisions of the Bond, to wit:

1) 200% of the total average annual adjusted loss for the three year period ending 90 days prior to the date the Bond attaches;

2) The amount determined by multiplying the average number of accounts per month during the past twelve months, or the num-

ber of accounts at the beginning of the year, if the latter is higher, by a Deductible charge in a special table.

3) $25,000.

The highest figure of the three stipulations above will apply.

The insured bank must absorb 20% of any loss which exceeds the Deductible, with the insurer paying 80% of such excess.

LABOR ORGANIZATION BOND—CONSOLIDATED FORM

THE LABOR-MANAGEMENT REPORTING AND DISCLOSURE ACT OF 1959 requires that union officials and employees be covered for faithful performance of their duties. Under the Law as recently amended, a more limited form of Bond, the Fraud or Dishonesty Coverage, will fulfill the statutory requirements for bonding. The Labor Organization Bond—Consolidated form can be issued on a name schedule basis or on a form similar to the Blanket Position Bond, the latter with or without excess indemnity on certain positions.

Union pension and welfare funds or plans are subject by law to the same Bond coverage.

The penalty of the Bond must be equal to at least 10% of the funds handled by the employee, but not more than $500,000.

WELFARE AND PENSION PLAN DISCLOSURE ACT PAY-OVER RIDER

WHERE THE FUNDS of an employee welfare or pension or profit-sharing plan are administered by an officer, employee or administrator of the Plan, the Welfare and Pension Plans Disclosure Act requires that a Fidelity Bond be issued to cover against loss by embezzlement. The Bond must be in an amount equal to at least 10% of the assets administered, subject to a minimum of $1,000 and a maximum of $500,000.

A Plan may carry its own Bond, or may be named as an additional Insured under the employer's Bond. No additional premium is charged for adding a plan to the employer's Bond, but where a plan is so named, the Bond must carry a special "pay-over" rider, which provides that the Plan have priority over the employer in any loss. If the same employee or employees commit a fraud both against the Plan and the employer, the full penalty of the Bond will be applied first to indemnify the Plan, with the employer's protection limited to the balance remaining after the Plan has been made whole. In light of the fact that in a situation of this kind the employer's coverage may be seriously depleted, it is often advisable to have the Plan carry its own Bond, or to substantially increase the penalty of the employer's Bond.

It is estimated that some 60,000 welfare and pension and profit-sharing plans are subject to the bonding requirements of the Welfare and Pension Plans Disclosure Act.

COMPREHENSIVE DISHONESTY DISAPPEARANCE AND DESTRUCTION POLICY

A COMPREHENSIVE POLICY insuring against a wide variety of losses due to crime is available to all business enterprises (except for certain financial institutions which are eligible for a Bankers or Brokers Blanket Bond). The Comprehensive Dishonesty, Disappearance and Destruction policy, also referred to as the 3-D or C. D. D. D. policy, is a package policy which covers losses due to the dishonesty of employees as well as outsiders. In this respect, it is similar to the Bankers Blanket Bond No. 24, which was discussed earlier. (The coverage is also included, by some Companies, as part of a package policy, usually at a discount from the separate rates for the individual coverages.)

The basic policy contains five separate Insuring Agreements, and coverage may be provided under any or all of these sections. Furthermore, different amounts of insurance may be purchased under the various Insuring Agreements. Essentially, the Comprehensive Dishonesty, Disappearance and Destruction policy combines a Blanket Fidelity Bond, a Broad Form Money and Securities policy, Safe Deposit Box coverage and Depositors Forgery insurance. Each of these Insuring Agreements will be discussed below. In addition, the Insured may, at his option, add Open Stock Burglary, Theft, or Paymaster Robbery insurance.

HAZARDS COVERED

Employee Dishonesty Coverage—Insuring Agreement I—Under this section, the Insured may provide coverage against the dishonesty of all his employees exactly as under a Blanket Fidelity Bond Two forms are available:

Form A—Provides the coverage of a Primary Commercial Blanket Bond.

Form B—Provides the coverage of a Blanket Position Bond.

Coverage Within Premises—Insuring Agreement II—The coverage under this section is similar to the Loss Within Premises section, Coverage A, of a Money and Securities Broad Form policy. (See Chapter 13.)

Coverage Outside Premises—Insuring Agreement III—The coverage under this section is similar to the Loss Outside Premises section, Coverage B, of a Money and Securities Broad Form policy. (See Chapter 13.)

Money Order and Counterfeit Paper Currency Coverage—Insuring Agreement IV—Under this section, the Insured may obtain coverage against loss caused by his accepting in good faith any post office or express money order in exchange for merchandise, money or services. Also covered is loss due to acceptance of counterfeit United States currency in the regular course of business.

Depositors Forgery Coverage—Insuring Agreement V—Under this section, the Insured may insure against loss due to forgery. The coverage is identical with that of the Depositors Forgery Bond.

OPTIONAL COVERAGES AVAILABLE

Open Stock Burglary—Theft—Although the Insured has the option of purchasing or omitting insurance under any of the Insuring Agreements outlined above, the Comprehensive 3-D policy is drawn with these provisions as part of the basic policy. In addition, coverage may be added by special endorsement on Open Stock Burglary, and this coverage may be further extended to cover also against Theft, Larceny and Robbery.

Payroll Robbery—If the Insured requires additional insurance to cover his payroll, he may purchase coverage to apply inside and outside the premises, or inside the premises only. The coverage is similar to the Paymaster Broad Form policy.

WHERE COVERED

The Comprehensive 3-D policy provides blanket insurance on all the premises occupied by the Insured. The policy may also be written to apply only to designated locations.

WHEN COVERED

Discovery Period—Under the 3-D policy, the Discovery Periods are the same as under the separate policies which make up the several agreements.

If the policy is written on Form B, which provides coverage under Insuring Agreement I on a Blanket Position Bond basis, the Discovery Period under this Insuring Agreement is 24 months, in line with the provision in the Blanket Position Bond. The Discovery Period for losses under any of the other Insuring Agreements remains 12 months.

Superseded Suretyship (Indemnity Against Loss Under Prior Bond)—Discussed in Chapter 14.

REGULATION

Since the 3-D policy combines Fidelity insurance with Money

and Securities Broad Form protection, the policy is under the jurisdiction of both the Surety Association of America and the Insurance Rating Board.

RATES

The premium for a 3-D policy is the sum of all the premiums that would be developed for the various coverages under separate policies. Each Insuring Agreement is also subject to the minimum premiums applicable to the individual policy.

Term Rates—The policy may be written for three years at 2½ times the annual premium. Insuring Agreements II, III, and IV premiums must be paid in advance; Insuring Agreements I and V may be paid in annual installments of 50%, 30% and 20% for an additional charge of 5% added to the three-year premium.

INSURED'S DUTIES AND OBLIGATIONS

Notice of Loss—Proof of Loss—The Insured is required to give notice of any loss as soon as practicable, but in any event not later than 15 days after he discovers the loss. Proof of Loss must be filed within four months of discovery.

If the loss is due to an occurrence which comes under Insuring Agreements II, III or IV, notice must also be given to the police authorities.

Cooperation of Insured—The Insured is obligated to render every assistance to the Company to facilitate the investigation and adjustment of any claim under the policy. Any expenses incurred will be borne by the Company.

Time to Bring Suit—At least 90 days must elapse after filing of Proof of Loss before the Insured may bring a suit against the Company, but the suit must be commenced within two years from the date on which the loss was discovered.

BLANKET CRIME POLICY

This policy is closely patterned on the Comprehensive DDD, discussed directly above. The Fidelity coverage under this policy is always written on the Commercial Blanket basis, similar to Form A of the Comprehensive DDD policy.

The Blanket Crime policy is available only with a single limit of liability applicable to all coverages. The *rate* for the policy, however, is based on the actual exposures presented by the risk. If the exposure on one coverage of the policy is low, the Insured will pay only for the actual risk at the time the policy is written. He will nevertheless have the benefit of the amount of the policy for this as well as other coverages of the policy.

Under the Blanket Crime policy, Theft coverage of office equipment may be purchased as an optional coverage. Open Stock Burglary insurance, which is offered as optional coverage under the Comprehensive DDD may not be added to the Blanket Crime policy.

FOR FURTHER READING

ACKERMAN—Insurance
CRIST—Corporate Suretyship
GEE—Agent's Bonding Guide—Broad Form Crime Insurance Primer
HEDGES—Practical Fire and Casualty Insurance
MAURICE—Checks Payable to Fictitious Payees
MEHR AND CAMMACK—Principles of Insurance
POLICY, FORM & MANUAL ANALYSIS SERVICE
RIEGEL, ROBERT AND MILLER—Insurance

(See Reading List at End of Book)

CHAPTER 16

Surety Bonds

As POINTED OUT at the beginning of Chapter 14, the several branches of the bonding business are generally grouped under two broad headings—Fidelity Bonds and Surety Bonds. While the former are more akin to insurance, Surety Bonds follow more strictly along the lines of Suretyship, in which the Surety merely lends its name and credit to guarantee an obligation between two parties.

An almost endless variety of different contracts, judicial proceedings and licenses are guaranteed by Surety Bonds, and Surety companies write hundreds of different types of Bonds to meet these needs. These Bonds fall into one of the following groups:

1. Court Bonds
2. Contract Bonds
3. License and Permit Bonds
4. Public Official Bonds
5. Federal Bonds
6. Miscellaneous Bonds.

COURT BONDS

IN ALMOST EVERY PROCEEDING conducted in a court of law or equity, some form of Bond may be required by the Court. Court Bonds are of two kinds—Fiduciary Bonds and Litigation Bonds. Below are set down some of the features common to Court Bonds and several examples of Bonds of each type.

FORM OF COURT BONDS

The Court Bond is almost always a brief instrument which merely recites the obligation or court action being undertaken and binds the Fiduciary (or Litigant) and the Surety to the Court. The form of Bond is usually prescribed by the Court or by statute, and the actual forms are obtained from the Court.

Penalty of Bond—The penalty (amount) of the Bond required is also set by the Court. Frequently, the Court demands a Bond with a penalty of twice the amount of the estate being handled or the amount at risk. (In a few special cases, the Bond may be written for an open penalty, with no top limit to the Surety's liability.)

Term of Bond—Court Bonds are continuous instruments, and remain in force until the obligation is completely fulfilled or the litigation completely closed. These Bonds are not subject to cancellation, except with the consent of the Court.

While the term of a Court Bond is continuous, premiums are payable annually. The initial premium charged when the Bond is issued is the minimum retained premium, and no refund is made even if the case is closed before the end of the year. If the Bond is still required after the year has elapsed, a renewal premium is charged which is equivalent to the full first year's premium. If the Bond should terminate during the second or any subsequent year, the Surety will refund the unearned premium on a pro rata basis, subject to a minimum premium of $5 for the year in which cancellation takes place.

FIDUCIARY BONDS AND LITIGATION BONDS

Court Bonds are of two kinds—those required of Fiduciaries, which are known as Fiduciary Bonds, and those required of parties to a court action, called Litigation Bonds (or Judicial Proceedings Bonds). Each of these groups of Court Bonds is discussed separately below.

FIDUCIARY (PROBATE) BONDS
(Surrogate Bonds)

GENERALLY SPEAKING, a Fiduciary is an individual (or a firm) appointed by a Court to hold, control or manage the property of others; e. g., executors, administrators, guardians, receivers, etc. The Fiduciary has a very high responsibility to perform his duties faithfully and may be held liable if there is any loss to the property entrusted to him.

When the Court appoints a Fiduciary, it almost always requires that he post a Bond to cover his activities. Since most Fiduciaries are appointed in probate proceedings, Probate Bonds are the largest class of Fiduciary Bonds.

The Fiduciary Bond guarantees that the Fiduciary (the Principal) will faithfully perform the duties of his trust. If he fails, the Court will look to the Surety to make good on the loss. The form of the Bond to be posted is generally prescribed by the Court, which also fixes the penalty for which the Bond is to be written. In some states, the penalty of the Bond is required to be equal to the size of the estate being administered, in others the Bond must be for twice the amount.

Joint Control—Because the handling of an estate is a complicated and involved legal matter, the Surety in many Fiduciary Bonds asks for joint control of the assets entrusted to the Fiduciary. All the funds of the estate are kept in a joint account, and disbursements made only upon the signatures of both the Fiduciary and the Surety. If there is a Safe Deposit Box, it is opened only when both the Fiduciary and a representative of the Surety are on hand.

Types of Fiduciaries—There are many situations in which Fiduciaries are appointed to administer the property of others. Some common examples of such relationships are:

1. In the estates of deceased persons
2. In the estates of minors
3. In trust estates
4. In the estates of incompetents
5. In bankruptcy or liquidation cases
6. In miscellaneous related cases.

Below will be set down some of the basic principles surrounding these various types of Fiduciaries and the Bonds used in such cases.

BONDS IN ESTATES OF DECEASED PERSONS

Executor's Bond, Administrator's Bond—An executor is a person (or corporation) named in a will to administer the estate of a deceased person and supervise the distribution of the assets to those entitled to receive them. When a person dies without leaving a will, the Court appoints an administrator, whose functions are the same as those of the executor. The executor or administrator is a Fiduciary, and is generally required to post a Bond covering the faithful discharge of his duties. The Bond required of an executor is called an Executor's Bond; the administrator furnishes an Administrator's Bond. The Principal under the Bond is the executor or the administrator, as the case may be; the Obligee is the State or the Court for the benefit of beneficiaries and creditors.

Miscellaneous Bonds in Estates of Deceased Persons—In addition to the Executor's Bond and the Administrator's Bond outlined above, special bonds are required of an administrator or executor appointed to succeed an administrator or executor who has died, resigned, or been discharged before the administration of the estate has been completed (Administrator de bonis non, Administrator cum testamento annexo, de bonis non). When a will is contested or where there are other circumstances which delay the qualification of an executor, a special Bond is required of the person or persons charged with preserving the assets of the estate (Administrator Pendente Lite). A separate Bond is required by the Court when it grants authority to sell real estate belonging to an estate.

BONDS IN ESTATES OF MINORS

Guardian Bond—When it becomes necessary to administer property belonging to a minor, the Court appoints a Guardian. The Court will require the Guardian to post a Guardian's Bond to guarantee the faithful performance of his duties as Guardian. The Guardian is the Principal under the Bond; the State is the Obligee for the benefit of the minor, but the minor's property, if not his person, is regarded as a ward of the State and the Guardian acts on behalf of the State, through his appointment by the court.

Guardian Ad Litem Bond—When pending litigation prevents the appointment of a Guardian, a Guardian ad Litem Bond is required of the Guardian appointed under these conditions.

Miscellaneous Bonds in Estates of Minors—When a Guardian wishes to sell real estate belonging to a ward, he must post a special Bond. Other situations which call for Bonds in the estates of minors are the appointment of special Guardians or temporary Guardians.

BONDS IN TRUST ESTATES

Instead of providing that after his death his assets be distributed to named persons, an owner of property may direct that the property be held in trust for those persons, either for a given period of years, or until their death, at which time the property is to be distributed, or held in trust for others to be distributed at a still later date. By creating a trust, the owner of property can defer the final disposition of his property to an indefinite date in the future.

When the trust is set up under the terms of a will to take effect at death, it is known as a Testamentary Trust. Trusts may also be created to take effect during the lifetime of the creator of the trust (inter-vivos trusts). In either case, the property is turned over to a trustee who is charged with a high degree of care and responsibility. The trustee, the Principal, will in many cases be asked to furnish a Trustee's Bond to guarantee the faithful discharge of his duties.

BONDS IN ESTATE OF INCOMPETENTS

When a person is not competent to handle his own affairs, the Court may appoint a Committee to protect his interests. Under such circumstances, a Committee Bond is required to guarantee the faithful performance of those charged with protecting the incompetent's interests. Similar to this type of Bond are those required of conservators, curators, or custodians in related situations.

MISCELLANEOUS FIDUCIARY BONDS

Special Bonds are required of conservators or liquidators of financial institutions, insurance companies, savings and building and loan associations, creditors' committees, stockholders' committees, appraisers, marshals; masters, referees, trustees or commissioners for the sale of real estate or other property in partition, foreclosure, reorganizations, etc. A surviving partner may be required to post a Bond guaranteeing that he will wind up the affairs of the former partnership honestly and protect all interests. A Bond may be required of an estate to guarantee that all inheritance, estate or transfer taxes will be paid, or of a trustee or custodian appointed by the Court.

BONDS REQUIRED IN BANKRUPTCY OR LIQUIDATIONS

When a business finds itself in financial difficulties, it may voluntarily enter a petition of bankruptcy. On the other hand, even if an individual does not wish to file a bankruptcy petition, his creditors may apply to the Court and have bankruptcy proceedings instituted. In the latter case, a Petitioning Creditors' Bond may be required of the creditors. This Bond guarantees that the petitioning creditors, the Principal, will reimburse their debtor, the Obligee, for any loss caused him by their action, if it is found that he was not in fact insolvent.

Receiver's Bond—When a petition of bankruptcy is filed, the Court appoints a receiver to take over temporary control of the debtor's business and administer it. A Receiver's Bond will be required of this individual, the Principal, to guarantee the faithful discharge of his trust.

Trustee's Bond—If, after further hearings by the Court, it is determined that the debtor is indeed bankrupt, a trustee in bankruptcy is appointed. The trustee in bankruptcy takes over the business and is in full charge of its liquidation. Generally, the trustee in bankruptcy is the same person who was originally appointed as a receiver, but a new Bond is now required—a Trustee's Bond.

Assignee's Bond—A debtor may find himself unable to repay his creditors, but may wish to avoid bankruptcy. He will therefore offer to make an assignment of his assets to his creditors. If this offer is acceptable to the creditors, they will apply to the Court to have an assignee appointed. The assignee, the Principal, will be required to post an Assignee's Bond to guarantee his faithful discharge of his duties.

NOTE—The Assignee Bond arises from action in State courts, bankruptcy in Federal courts. Hence, Assignee's acts may be overruled if creditors force bankruptcy on the Assignee.

LITIGATION BONDS

WHILE LITIGATION BONDS are Court Bonds, they are very different in purpose from the Fiduciary Bonds discussed above. Where the Fiduciary Bond is designed to guarantee the honesty and devotion to trust of a person charged with administering the property of others, the Litigation Bond is required of a person who wishes to bring an action at law or equity.

In the action he is instituting, he may seek to tie up the assets of the other party, or to restrain the other from doing something which he claims is unfair to him. If the case is ultimately decided against the person who is bringing the action, his antagonist may maintain that the action injured him and caused him to suffer damages. The Bonds required in litigation guarantee that the contestant in a court case will pay any such damages. A Bond may also be required of litigants to assure their paying of court costs.

A Bond may be required either of the plaintiff (person bringing the action) or of the defendant, and these Bonds are usually classified under these separate headings.

Collateral—Under Suretyship, the Surety anticipates no losses, and will refrain from issuing a Bond unless it is entirely satisfied that the Principal will be able to make good any losses he may cause. For this reason, it may, where it feels it necessary, require of the Principal that he put up collateral to further implement his promise. The collateral required is almost always cash or Government securities.

PLAINTIFF'S BONDS

Attachment Bond—A plaintiff bringing an action may apply to the Court for permission to have the sheriff or marshal take or tie up the property of the defendant, alleging that the defendant is likely to remove the property or conceal it. Similarly, if the defendant is a non-resident of the state in which the action is being brought, the plaintiff may ask for attachment of the property in order to be assured that he will be able to collect if he is sustained in the court action. If the case is decided *against* the plaintiff, the defendant may have a claim against the plaintiff for damages suffered by him while his property was tied up. A (Plaintiff's) Attachment Bond will therefore be required of the plaintiff who is seeking to attach the defendant's property. The Bond guarantees that the plaintiff, the Principal, will pay any damages caused the defendant by the attachment if it turns out to have been unjustified.

Replevin Bond—Plaintiff's Bond to Secure—This Bond is similar in scope and purpose to the Attachment Bond described directly above, except that it is used when a plaintiff is suing to recover specific property rather than to collect a sum of money. A merchant who has sold goods on installments and wishes to retake the property will apply to the Court for a Writ of Replevin. This writ will give him the right to retake the property before his case against the purchaser goes to trial. It may turn out that the Court will uphold the purchaser, and the plaintiff will have to return the property together with any damages he may have caused the defendant. A Replevin Bond is required of the person or firm seeking to recover property of this kind. It guarantees that the plaintiff in the action, the Principal, will return the reclaimed property and pay any damages that may have been caused its rightful owner.

Distraint for Rent—This Bond is similar to a Replevin Bond, except that it is required of a landlord who, in an action for rent, seeks to have personal property of his tenant seized.

Indemnity to Sheriff Bond—A sheriff or a marshal who is asked to execute a process of a Court like a dispossess action may be held liable for damages if the action turns out to have been unjustified. The sheriff may under such circumstances require a Bond from the person making request for execution of the process. This Bond is known as an Indemnity to Sheriff Bond. Under the Bond, the person seeking execution of the process is the Principal, the Sheriff is the Obligee.

Injunction Bond—Plaintiff's Bond to Secure—When one person seeks to restrain another from doing something, he applies to a court of equity for an injunction. The Court, before it grants the injunctive relief requested, may require of the person making the request that he post a Bond guaranteeing the payment of any damages for which he, the Principal, may be held liable to the defendant, if it is ultimately decided that the injunction was unjustified.

Appeal Bond—Plaintiff's—When a litigant has been denied the remedy he sought and wishes to appeal, he may be asked to post a Bond for the payment of the costs on appeal. If in the judgment or decree, his opponent was granted affirmative relief, a Bond to stay execution may be required.

Certiorari Bond—A superior Court may order an inferior Court to certify and return to it the court record of a case so that it may review the proceedings. A Certiorari Bond may be required to guarantee payment of costs in the appellate court. When the Bond includes guarantee of payment of a judgment, it is treated as an Appeal Bond.

Claimant's Bond—While two parties are contesting in the courts over property, a third party may request release of the property to him, claiming that he is its rightful owner. The claimant may be required to furnish a Claimant's Bond to guarantee he will redeliver the property if directed to do so by the court.

Civil Arrest Bond—A Bond may be required of a person who asks for the arrest of another. The Bond, which is known as a Civil Arrest Bond, guarantees that the person asking for the arrest to be made, the Principal, will pay costs and any damages which the defendant may sustain, if it is finally decided that the arrest should not have been made.

Cost Bonds—A Cost Bond guarantees the payment of court costs by a person who institutes an action, and is almost always required of a person who wishes to commence an action in a state of which he is not a resident.

A Removal Bond—A Removal Bond, which is similar to the Cost Bond, is required when a case is removed from one State Court to another, or when a case originally brought in a State Court is removed to Federal Court. The Bond guarantees the payment of court costs by the litigant, the Principal, if it is found that the case was improperly removed to the new court.

DEFENDANT'S BONDS

In many cases, the defendant is required to post a Bond to counter the action or charges brought against him by the plaintiff. Several of the more widely used Defendant's Bonds are listed below. It can readily be seen that most of these Bonds are merely the reverse of corresponding Plaintiff's Bonds.

Release of Attachment Bond (also known as Attachment Bond—Defendant's Bond to Discharge or Release)—After an attachment has been issued, the defendant (the one whose property has been attached) may ask to have his property released from attachment until the case is tried. The defendant in this instance, the Principal, may be required to post a Release of Attachment Bond guaranteeing payment to the plaintiff of any judgment that may finally be entered against him. The action is sometimes called a garnishment and the Bond to release such property a Garnishment —Bond to Discharge or Release.

Counter Replevin Bond (Also known as Redelivery Bond—Defendant's Bond to Recover Property Replevined)—When property has been replevied, the defendant may regain possession of the property by posting a Counter Replevin Bond which guarantees that he will redeliver the property if ordered to do so by the Courts, and otherwise comply with the Court's orders. The Defendant is the Principal in this instance.

Distraint for Rent—Defendant's Bond—Much the same as the Counter Replevin Bond discussed directly above, the Distraint for Rent—Defendant's Bond is designed for a tenant who wishes to retake personal property which has been taken by a landlord for payment of rent. The Bond guarantees that the tenant, the Principal, will surrender the property if the landlord successfully sustains his case in the courts.

Injunction—Defendant's Bond to Dissolve—When an injunction has been granted, the person enjoined may seek to have the injunction dissolved. While the case is being tried, the defendant may continue with the actions which were enjoined. If he loses his case, and the plaintiff demonstrates that he is in fact entitled to enjoin him from the actions in question, the defendant may be liable for the damages suffered by the plaintiff during the time the action had been pending. A Bond may therefore be required of a defendant, the Principal, who seeks to have an injunction dissolved. The Bond guarantees his payment of any damages he may cause the plaintiff.

Open Default Bond—When a judgment has been entered by default, as when the defendant failed to appear, the case may under certain conditions be reopened by the defendant. An Open Default Bond will usually be required of the defendant, the Principal, to guarantee that he will pay the judgment if it is finally decided that he was actually liable.

Stay of Execution Bond—A sheriff, who has been ordered by a Court to levy against a defendant's property, will delay executing the writ only if a Stay of Execution Bond is posted by the defendant, the Principal. This Bond is used when the defendant expects to win a counter suit.

Mechanic's Lien—Bond to Discharge—When a building owner wishes to be discharged from a mechanic's lien, pending final determination of his liability, he will be required to post a Bond guaranteeing payment of any amount that may finally be found due the claimant with interest and costs. When a Contract Performance Bond has been issued, the rate for this Bond is reduced by 50%.

CONTRACT BONDS

CONTRACT BONDS are used in a wide variety of undertakings to guarantee the satisfactory completion or performance on an underlying contract between two parties. They are very widely used in the fields of construction, repair, maintenance, and supplying of materials or equipment. These Bonds are occasionally demanded and prescribed by the person or firm who is awarding the contract. In most cases, they are prescribed by statute. Their general purpose is to guarantee that a contractor or supplier will fulfill his commitment according to specifications. Many of these Bonds are therefore known as Performance Bonds.

GENERAL PRINCIPLES

Extent of Coverage—In writing a Contract Bond, the Surety undertakes to guarantee not only the character of the Principal, but also the fact that his capital and capacity are adequate for the type and volume of work undertaken. For this reason, Contract Bonds are often thought of as underwriting the three C's of the Principal—his Character, Capacity and Capital.

As in all other Surety Bonds, the Surety must be entirely satisfied that the Principal will be able to perform on his contract. The Surety anticipates no losses, and the premium being charged is more in the nature of a service fee for the lending of its name and credit.

Collateral—If the financial statement submitted by an applicant for a Contract Bond does not reveal sufficient liquid assets to warrant issuance of the Bond, the Surety may ask, as further support for the underwriting of the instrument, that the Principal post additional collateral, or that the principals of the corporation agree to be personally liable for any loss sustained in connection with the undertaking. For posting certain types of collateral, which are enumerated in the Manual, the Principal is granted a reduction in premium. If the collateral is a security or a debt obligation, any dividend yield, or interest, as the case may be, is paid to the Principal.

Retained Percentage — Frequently, the Obligee contracts to make payment in installments to the Principal as the work progresses. The Surety, to implement its margin of safety in underwriting the Contract Bond, may demand that the Obligee hold back 10% of the payments due the Principal at all times. In this way, there is an extra "cushion" which the Surety may call on in the event of a default in performance by the Principal.

Term of Bond—Contract Bonds are written for the term of the contract and cannot be cancelled during their term. The initial premium usually covers a period of two years, however, and a renewal premium charged at the end of that time if the contract has not been completed. The premium for the third and any subsequent year is reduced by 50% and applies only to the still to be completed work.

BID BONDS

It is fairly common for firms or individuals who wish to erect or reconstruct structures or make installations or repairs to announce the work being contemplated and ask contractors to submit their bid for the work. In public works of all kinds, like the erection of buildings, hangars, military installations, roads, etc., it is almost universal to open the work to public bidding. The bidders are required to submit their bids in sealed form by a given date and hour. All bids are opened at the appointed hour and the contract is awarded to the lowest bidder.

In almost every contract for public works, the bidders are required to accompany their bids with a Bid Bond. (This requirement is not imposed as widely by private builders.) The Bid Bond guarantees that the bidder, if awarded the contract, will enter into the contract and furnish the prescribed Performance Bond and Payment Bonds, as may be required.

If the bidding contractor fails to sign the contract, or is unable to furnish a Performance Bond (and Payment Bond, if stipulated), the contract may then be awarded to the next lowest bidder. The Surety on the Bid Bond of the defaulting bidder, the Principal, will usually become liable for the difference between the bid of its Principal and the next lowest bid.

The Surety under a Bid Bond is *not* obligated to furnish a Performance Bond for its Principal, if he is awarded the contract. If the Principal, after having been awarded the contract, cannot furnish the required Performance Bond, the Surety on the Bid Bond will become liable as discussed above, but it need not itself furnish a Performance Bond.

PERFORMANCE BONDS

A Performance Bond may be required of a contractor to guarantee that he will faithfully perform on his contract and complete the work undertaken according to the terms and specifications of the contract.

Construction Contract Bond—This Bond is designed for use when the work contracted for forms part of, or will become attached to real property. Under this Bond, the Surety guarantees that the contractor will faithfully and honestly perform the work undertaken in accordance with the specifications and contract price. The Bond may also be written to include the terms of a Labor and Material Bond and a Maintenance Bond, each of which is discussed directly below.

Labor and Material Payment Bond—The Labor and Material Payment Bond guarantees that a contractor, the Principal, will pay all bills for labor and materials in connection with a contract. The Obligee, the individual or owner who is expecting performance by the contractor, is assured that the completed work will be free of mechanics' liens or other liens.

The Labor and Material Payment Bond may be written as a separate Bond, or the guarantee incorporated in the Construction Contract Bond (discussed directly above).

Maintenance guarantees for periods up to one year are generally included in the Construction Contract Bond. If a maintenance agreement is required for a period in excess of one year, a separate Maintenance Bond is usually issued.

Supply Contract Bond—The Supply Contract Bond is similar to the Construction Contract Bond in that it guarantees a contract. Where the Construction Contract Bond guarantees work which is part of real property, a Supply Contract Bond guarantees a contract to supply goods or materials. The Bond guarantees that the Principal will furnish the Obligee with the goods contracted for according to the specifications of the contract.

Completion Bond—A Completion Bond guarantees to a lender of money, the Obligee, that the Principal, the borrower, will use the money in accordance with the terms of the contract, and complete the work undertaken on or before the agreed upon date. It is usually associated with construction work which is being financed in whole or in part by a lender.

SURETY BOND GUARANTEE PROGRAM FOR SMALL BUSINESSES

Small businessmen and contractors who require bonds on a contract but cannot obtain such from a Surety company on the basis of their own financial strength are eligible for a guarantee by the Small Business Administration of the U. S. Government.

The Small Business Administration will guarantee up to 90% of the loss under a bond issued by any Surety company on the Treasury Department's list of approved Sureties. The contractor or other small businessman applies to a Surety company in the regular way for a bond on the usually issued form.

Contract bonds of $500,000 or less are eligible for the Small Business Administration's guarantee, and there is no limit to the number of bonds that can be guaranteed, even for the same contractor.

Any construction firm whose gross annual volume did not exceed $750,000 for the past fiscal year is considered eligible. Other maximums are established for different industries and businesses.

LICENSE AND PERMIT BONDS

UNDER STATE LAWS, municipal ordinances or other regulations, persons who apply for a license to engage in numerous business or professional activities are required to post a Bond. These License or Permit Bonds are designed to indemnify the governmental agency against liability arising from its having issued a license to a business, professional person, artisan, etc. Some License Bonds are written on a broader basis, and give to third parties the right to recover in their own name for loss or damage caused by breach of obligations of the Principal. Most License Bonds are filed for a specific term concurrent with the license which they support.

License Bonds required by the Federal Government are generally considered as a separate section of the bonding business, under the classification Federal Bonds.

Some examples of License and Permit Bonds required by states, counties, cities, towns, villages or other municipalities are those issued to:

> Abbatoirs, assayers, auctioneers, bail bondsmen, blasting, boarding houses, boiler operation, business brokers, detective agencies, employment agencies, hack drivers, hoisters, house wreckers, junk dealers, pawnbrokers, peddlers, plumbers, public accountants, stationary engineers, street obstructions, theatres, ticket brokers, travel bureaus, etc.

PUBLIC EMPLOYEES BOND

Blanket Bonds are also available to cover Civil Service type employees of political subdivisions—cities, towns, villages, boroughs, school districts, fire districts, etc. The Public Employees' Blanket Bond may be used to cover public employees who are not required by *law* to post a Bond. Generally, all workers in public service other than tax collectors and treasurers come within this group.

The Public Employee Bond is an exception to the general rule that Surety Bonds are non-cancellable. The Surety may cancel this form of Bond by giving not less than 30 days' notice to the Insured.

The minimum amount for which this Bond may be written is $10,000.00. Different from other Surety Bonds, the Public Employee Bond is eligible for experience rating.

There is *no* cumulative liability under these Bonds.

The Bond provides that suit by the Insured must be brought within three years.

Like the Blanket Bonds covering regular commercial risks, there are two forms of Public Employee Bonds. The Public Employee Honesty Blanket Bond is similar to the Primary Commercial Blanket Bond in that the Insured can collect no more than the penalty of the Bond for any loss, regardless of the number of employees who acted collusively. By contrast, the Public Employee Blanket *Position* Bond covers on each employee up to the full penalty of the Bond. It is identical on this score with the Blanket Position Bond, discussed above.

Faithful Performance—Public employees may also be covered under broader forms of coverage which will apply not only to dishonesty but also to failure to perform faithfully or to account properly for monies. These Bonds will therefore cover all forms of loss, even when there was no dishonest intent. Thus, a treasurer might deposit public funds in a bank without having checked whether the bank complied with the State laws as respects depositories. If the bank were unable to meet its obligations, and the municipality suffered loss, the Bond would pay.

Like the Public Employee Honesty Bonds, the Faithful Performance Bonds are available under two forms—Public Employees Faithful Performance Blanket Bond and Public Employee Faithful Performance Blanket Position Bond. The difference between these forms is in their treatment of collusion losses.

PUBLIC OFFICIAL BOND

Public officials who handle money are generally bonded. The Public Official Bond is classed as a Surety Bond, but is actually closer to a Fidelity Bond, because the greatest hazard it covers is fidelity—loss due to dishonesty of the public official.

Different from a Fidelity Bond, the liability under a Public

Official Bond is statutory, and guarantees performance by the official of all his obligations under the law. The public official is generally held liable at law for the faithful accounting for all monies received by him. If for any reason, he cannot turn over all the money received by him in any capacity, he is held personally liable. If he cannot make good, the Public Official Bond must, whether or not the official was dishonest.

Some examples of situations in which a Public Official Bond will have to pay even though there was no dishonest act on the part of the Principal are:

1. Embezzlement or other dishonest act by a subordinate. (To insure himself against this hazard, the public official may obtain a separate Fidelity Bond covering the subordinate.)

2. Burglary, robbery, disappearance, destruction of or damage to the funds. (This exposure may be covered under policies like Money and Securities Broad Form, Safe Burglary, Messenger and Interior Robbery, etc.)

3. In some states, loss of money placed in a bank which becomes insolvent. In some instances, liability of this character may be avoided if the Obligee (the state, county or municipality) officially designates a bank to act as depository and the public official uses the designated bank.

4. In some states, a public official may be held personally liable for uncollected taxes that he fails to report within a stipulated time after default.

Due to the statutory nature of the Public Official Bond, no exclusions of specific hazards incorporated in the Bond would be valid.

The Bond which is generally written for the term of the elected or appointed office of the official is non-cancellable during its term. Within a few months after the term of office ends, an audit is made of the public official's accounts, and if these are found in order, written evidence thereof from the Obligee to the Surety is considered sufficient to permit the Surety to cancel its Bond. Even though the Surety may have cancelled its Bond with this kind of "termination evidence" as its basis, it may still be held liable for a loss discovered several years later. There is generally no limit to the Discovery Period in these Bonds. Any limit on time to sustain a claim would be found in the law itself. It should be remembered that there is little uniformity of practice in the more than 116,000 political jurisdictions of the United States.

U. S. GOVERNMENT BONDS

NUMEROUS DEPARTMENTS of the Federal Government, including the Departments of Agriculture, Interior, Treasury, Navy, War,

Commerce, Post Office, require their officers and employees to post a Bond guaranteeing the faithful performance of the duties of their office.

A second group of Federal Bonds are those required of persons or corporations who are not employed by the government to guarantee an obligation they have to the government. In this latter group are Immigration Bonds, Internal Revenue Bonds, Intoxicating Liquors and Industrial Alcohol Bonds, and Custom House Bonds. Each group is discussed briefly below.

Alien or Immigration Bonds—Aliens admitted to this country for temporary periods, like students, temporary laborers, tourists, or hospital patients, may be required to post a Bond guaranteeing that they will leave the country on or before the expiration of their temporary visa.

Custom House Bonds—Custom House Bonds guarantee compliance with the tariff laws of the United States or with Custom House regulations concerning the handling of goods subject to import or export duties. The Bond guarantees that the Principal will pay any additional duty as may be required, if the appraisal on which original duties were based proves to have been improper.

Income Tax Bonds—When the liability of a person or firm for income tax is under dispute, or when payment of the tax has been deferred because the taxpayer is unable to meet his obligation, an Income Tax Bond may be required to guarantee that the taxpayer, the Principal, will pay his taxes to the government, the Obligee, when due.

Internal Revenue Bonds—Intoxicating Liquor Bonds—Various Bonds are required by the Internal Revenue Bureau of manufacturers, processors, dealers, distillers, rectifiers, brewers and transporters of industrial alcohol, alcoholic products and intoxicating liquors, and of certain dealers in tobacco products, oleomargarine and gasoline.

In general, Internal Revenue Bonds guarantee that the dealer, manufacturer, exporter or transporter, as the case may be, will comply with all laws governing the handling of the product, and that he will pay to the government, the Obligee, all taxes imposed.

In certain cases, when tobacco, liquors and some other commodities are stored in bonded warehouses, the government will defer collecting the tax until the goods are actually ready for use. The government, the Obligee, will require of the distiller or other dealer, a Bond guaranteeing the payment of the tax as well as his compliance with all laws. Similarly, when goods subject to domestic taxes are manufactured for export, the manufacturer, the Principal, will be required to post a Bond guaranteeing to the government, the Obligee, the payment of all taxes if the product should ultimately be sold on the domestic market.

MISCELLANEOUS BONDS

In addition to the numerous Bonds which fall into one of the groupings discussed above, there are several hundred miscellaneous Bonds written by Surety companies. In this group are various Bonds required by law as well as many which guarantee voluntary undertakings.

Lost Instrument Bonds—A Lost Instrument Bond, also known as a Lost Securities Bond, may be required of an individual or firm which has lost, misplaced, or accidentally destroyed securities, documents or other valuable papers, and wishes to have a duplicate issued. Such Bonds are often required before issuing a duplicate of a lost life insurance policy, membership certificates in Boards of Trade and Stock Exchanges, government checks and money orders, warehouse receipts, pawn tickets, steamship tickets, common stocks, etc.

The Bond guarantees that the Principal, the one to whom the duplicate is being issued, will reimburse the issuer of the instrument, the Obligee, if the original instrument subsequently turns up and its holder is able to establish a claim for payment under the instrument.

Lost Instrument Bonds are written with a fixed penalty or an Open Penalty. The Open Penalty is often used when a certificate of common stock is lost, since this type of security has no fixed market value, and it is therefore impossible to determine what the market value will be when the lost certificate turns up. In some cases, the Bond covering a lost certificate of common stock is written with a fixed penalty, but the penalty is usually set high enough to take care of all but the most unusual fluctuations in the price of the security.

Workmen's Compensation Bonds—Every state imposes on an employer some responsibility to provide some benefits to workers injured as a result of an occupational accident. The employer is also required to secure the payment of these benefits by providing a policy of Workmen's Compensation insurance.

In the majority of states, an employer who can meet certain standards is permitted to self-insure the benefits required under the Workmen's Compensation Law. To guarantee that the benefits to which an employee may become entitled will actually be available to him, the states will require a self-insuring employer to post a Self-Insurer Bond. Such Bonds are required of *all* self-insuring employers in the following states:

ARKANSAS, CALIFORNIA, COLORADO, CONNECTICUT, DISTRICT OF COLUMBIA, FLORIDA, GEORGIA, ILLINOIS, IOWA, KENTUCKY, LOUISIANA, MARYLAND, MASSACHUSETTS, MISSISSIPPI, MISSOURI, NEW MEXICO, NEW YORK, NORTH CAROLINA, OHIO, RHODE ISLAND, SOUTH CAROLINA, TENNESSEE, UTAH, WEST VIRGINIA.

In 14 states, the employer who wishes to self-insure under the Workmen's Compensation Law is required to file a Bond only if the agency administering the Workmen's Compensation Law is not satisfied with his financial solvency. The states in which this less stringent requirement prevails are:

DELAWARE, INDIANA, KANSAS, MICHIGAN, MINNESOTA, MONTANA, NEBRASKA, NEW HAMPSHIRE, NEW JERSEY, OKLAHOMA, PENNSYLVANIA, SOUTH DAKOTA, VERMONT, WISCONSIN.

In these states, even when an employer is not required to post a Self-Insurer's Bond at the time of self-insuring, he may have to post a Bond to guarantee payment of a specific award to a worker who has become entitled to benefits under the Workmen's Compensation Law.

CALIFORNIA—A special Bond is available to guarantee the payment of Unemployment Compensation Disability benefits.
NEW JERSEY, NEW YORK—Bonds are available to cover the employer's liability under the non-occupational Disability Benefits Laws recently enacted.
WYOMING—Out-of-state employers in extra hazardous employment are required to post a special form of Workmen's Compensation Bond.

Financial Responsibility Bonds — Motor Vehicle — In many states, owners and/or operators of motor vehicles involved in an accident must prove their financial responsibility before being permitted to continue operating their vehicle. Evidence of financial responsibility can usually be brought in the form of a Bond filed with the state motor vehicle agency. In addition, many states require of public truckmen, transportation companies, freight forwarders, and others who carry passengers or cargo for hire, the posting of a Bond to guarantee their ability to meet claims for their liability to the public.

Miscellaneous Bonds—As pointed out above, the variety of Surety Bonds is almost as great as the variety of business enterprises, licenses, permits and services of our economy. By way of suggesting the broad scope of the Surety field, there are listed below a sampling of other Bonds which are found under the Miscellaneous heading:

Insurance Agents—Indemnity Bond; Aid Associations, Children Placed With; Alien Income Tax; Armories, Use of; Auto Tours, Foreign; Average Daily Balance Adjustment, Depository Bonds; Bill of Lading, Delivery of Freight Without; Blue Sky Bonds; Insurance Brokers; Buildings, Use of; Butchers, Packers and Stockyards, Act of 1921; Children, Support of; C. O. D. Shipment; Concessionaires'; Convict Lease; Cotton Seed Samplers; Dealers Indemnity to Warehousemen; Return Cotton Samples; Demurrage Bonds; Grain Elevators; etc.

FOR FURTHER READING

ACKERMAN—Insurance
CRIST—Corporate Suretyship
GEE—Agent's Bonding Guide
HEDGES—Practical Fire and Casualty Insurance
LEVINE—Manual on Commercial Law
MACKALL—Surety Underwriting Manual
MEHR AND CAMMACK—Principles of Insurance
MOWBRAY AND BLANCHARD—Insurance
POLICY, FORM AND MANUAL ANALYSIS SERVICE
RIEGEL, ROBERT AND MILLER—Insurance

(See Reading List at End of Book)

CHAPTER 17

Inland Marine Insurance

INLAND MARINE INSURANCE had its origin in Transportation insurance and some element of transportation is still present in most Inland Marine insurance policies. The field has broadened considerably, however, and it now takes in a great variety of risks in addition to shipped goods. Policies are issued to cover all types of personal and business property which are subject to risk of loss in more than one location.

Since such movable property is known as "floating property," the word "Floater" is often used in place of "policy"; e. g., Fur Floater, Camera Floater, Musical Instrument Floater, Silverware Floater, Personal Property Floater, etc. The field has been extended too to cover not only movable property but also the instrumentalities of transportation like bridges, tunnels, etc.

Marine Definition—In order to describe the kind of risks which may be classified as Marine, Inland Marine or Transportation insurance, the National Association of Insurance Commissioners adopted the Nation-Wide Marine Definition. Within certain limitations, the following types of risk are contained in the Definition: Imports; exports; domestic shipments; bridges, tunnels and other instrumentalities of transportation and communication. The current Definition, which was adopted in 1953, has been adopted with a few minor changes by all states *except* COLORADO, HAWAII, IOWA, MONTANA, NEW MEXICO, TENNESSEE, TEXAS and the DISTRICT OF COLUMBIA.

Many floaters are written on all-risk basis (to be discussed later). For this reason, the Inland Marine branch of many insurance companies is also known as the All-Risk Department.

Since there are close to 100 different Floaters, including an endless variety of tailor-made forms, it will be impossible to cover more than a few of the more widely used forms. These forms are fairly representative of the field and they present the basic characteristics of Inland Marine insurance.

For purposes of discussion, the Floaters to be analyzed will be divided into two broad groups: Personal Floaters and Commercial Floaters.

PERSONAL FLOATERS

FEATURES COMMON TO ALL PERSONAL FLOATERS

All-Risk Basis—Most Personal Floaters are written on an all-risk basis. The insuring clause does not specify perils that are insured against but agrees to cover against "all risks of loss or damage except as hereinafter excluded."

Actually, no Floater covers all risks, as all insurance policies must exclude certain perils. Nevertheless, the Floater coverage is usually broader than any specified perils policy, no matter how many individual risks are assumed under the latter. Furthermore, there is less possibility of dispute under all-risk insurance as to whether a particular loss comes within the coverage of the policy. Where the Insured, under a specified perils policy, must prove that his loss was caused by one of the named perils, under a Floater, for all practical purposes, the burden is on the Company to demonstrate that the particular loss was due to an exclusion stated in the policy.

Hazards Covered—As stated above, the Floater covers all risks of loss or damage except those specifically listed as exclusions. The exclusions are usually few in number, some common to all Floaters, and some applicable only to the type of property covered.

Exclusions Common to All Personal Floaters—The Personal Floaters all exclude perils of the following types:

- Gradual deterioration, wear and tear.
- Insects, vermin, inherent vice.

  Inherent vice is a condition in the property itself which causes it to spoil, break, become defective, or destroy itself.
- Hostile or warlike action in time of peace or war, including action taken in hindering, combating or defending against an actual, impending or expected attack; action by an agent of a government, power, authority or forces; any weapon of war employing atomic fission or radioactive force whether in time of peace or war.
- Nuclear reaction or nuclear radiation or radioactive contamination, whether such loss be direct or indirect, proximate or remote or is caused by, contributed to, or aggravated by the perils insured against in the Floater. However, there is coverage for direct loss by fire resulting from such causes. Insurrection, rebellion, revolution, civil war, usurped power, or action taken by

governmental authority in hindering, combating or defending against such occurrence.

- Seizure or destruction under quarantine or customs regulations.
- Confiscation by order of any government or public authority.
- Risks of contraband or illegal trade.

FOR HOW MUCH

When applying for most Personal Floaters, the Insured is required to list each article to be insured, giving a complete description of the item and the amount of insurance to apply. Before issuing the policy, the companies usually request evidence of the existence of the article and verification of its value. This requirement may be satisfied by submitting a bill of sale, an appraisal by a recognized expert or a previous policy listing the item.

The basic policy limits the Company's liability to the actual cash value at the time of the loss or the amount it would cost to repair or replace the property with other of like kind and quality. The amount of insurance shown in the policy alongside any article is therefore the maximum amount an Insured can collect, subject to the limitation of actual cash value. Thus, if an Insured covered a diamond ring under a Jewelry Floater for $1,500 and, at the time of loss, the ring were found to be worth $2,000, he could collect no more than $1,500, the amount stated in the policy. On the other hand, if this same ring were found to be worth only $1,200 at the time of loss, he could not collect more than $1,200, even though the amount of insurance shown in the policy for this item was $1,500.

Valued Forms—In certain instances, Floaters may be written on a valued basis, and in such cases, the amount of insurance shown after each article is agreed for the purpose of insurance to be the value of the article. Since this basis of settlement does not allow for any depreciation, it is contrary to the basic insurance principle that an Insured is not supposed to benefit from a loss, but is only supposed to be put back in the same financial position he was in prior to the loss. For this reason, Valued policies are issued only infrequently except on fine arts which, because of the unique nature of the property, are universally written on a valued basis.

WHERE COVERED

The Personal Floaters are almost always world-wide, covering loss or damage sustained anywhere in the world.

REQUIREMENTS IN CASE OF LOSS

Notice of Loss—Proof of Loss—The Insured must give notice of any loss as soon as is practicable. He is required to file a Proof of Loss within 90 days of the loss. Some forms say "immediate notice."

Sue and Labor—The Sue and Labor clause imposes two separate requirements on the Insured.

First, it requires that he may make every effort to save and preserve the property from further loss. This requirement is similar to one which appears in the Fire insurance policy.

He must do what he can to assist in recovering the property. The Company will reimburse the Insured for any expense he incurs in these efforts, up to a limit which depends on the amount of insurance in the policy. (It is not entirely clear, when the Insured sustains a total loss, whether he is entitled to recover such expenses over and above the amount of the policy, although most authorities hold that he is.)

Benefit of Insurance—Bailees (persons to whom property is entrusted, like tailors, laundries, repair shops, common carriers, etc.) often insert in the receipt they issue a stipulation that any insurance carried by the owner of the property will be for their benefit as bailee. Thus, if an Insured gave a suit to the cleaners and the suit was lost or damaged, and the Insured collected from his insurance company, the tailor would not have to make good the loss. This would defeat the insurance Company's right of subrogation. To counteract such provisions, the Floater expressly provides that the insurance afforded will *not* insure directly or indirectly to the benefit of any carrier or bailee.

When Suit Must Be Brought—Suit against the Company cannot be commenced after twelve months from the date of the loss.

KANSAS, NEBRASKA—Insured may bring a suit at any time within 5 years of the date of the loss.

OTHER PROVISIONS

Minimum Premiums—With few exceptions, the minimum premium for all floaters is $25.

KANSAS, MARYLAND, NORTH CAROLINA, PUERTO RICO, TEXAS —The minimum is $15.

Term Policies—Most Personal Floaters may be written for a period of three years. The three-year premium is 2.7 times the annual.

PUERTO RICO—The three-year premium is 2½ times the annual.

TEXAS—The three-year premium is 2.78 times the annual.

Installment Payment of Premium—An Insured may take advantage of reduced rate for the three-year policy, but spread his premium over the three years. The Insured pays 35% of the three-year premium at the beginning of each year of the policy period.

This plan is not used in LOUISIANA or WISCONSIN.

Other Provisions (discussed in Chapter 1)—Appraisal—Cancellation—Examination of Records—Subrogation.

INDIVIDUAL PERSONAL FLOATERS
PERSONAL ARTICLES FLOATER

Nine classes of personal property are insurable under the Personal Articles Floater: Furs, jewelry, cameras, musical instruments, fine arts, stamp collections, coin collections, silverware and golfer's equipment. Separate rates are promulgated for each class of property, but one minimum premium, $15, is applicable to the entire policy, regardless of the number of classes of property insured or the term of the policy.

PERSONAL FURS

What Is Covered—Any article of fur, or article trimmed with fur in which fur represents the principal value. All articles to be insured must be specified, except that a fur ensemble, like a coat and matching muff, may be insured as a group, with one dollar value.

Additionally Acquired Property—If, during the term of the policy, the Insured acquires additional items of the kind already insured under his Floater, such property is covered automatically, provided he notifies the Company within 30 days of its acquisition, subject to the following limits. The Company is not liable for more than 25% of the amount of insurance already covering on the particular class of property (jewelry, furs, cameras, etc.) or $10,000, whichever is less. The Insured is required to pay an additional premium for the coverage extended to the new property from the date of its acquisition.

Who Is Insured—One policy may be issued to insure all fur items belonging to members of the same family who reside together.

One policy may not insure related persons who do not reside together, nor members of the same household who are not related. Servant's property may not be insured in the same policy as covers members of the family.

PERSONAL JEWELRY

What Is Covered—Any article of jewelry may be insured. The policy may also cover silverware, plated ware, pewterware, toilet articles, cigarette cases, trophies, etc. Jewelry may be insured separately, or together with furs.

Additionally Acquired Property—discussed under PERSONAL FURS.

Pair and Set Clause—Where articles insured are part of a pair or set, and the Insured loses one article of the set, the policy will pay for the reasonable and fair proportion of the total value of the set, giving consideration to the importance of said article or articles, but without considering the loss to be a total loss.

Who Is Covered—Same provisions as under PERSONAL FURS just discussed, except that engagement rings and wedding rings may be insured in the name of two interested individuals, even though they do not reside together and are not related.

CAMERAS AND CAMERA EQUIPMENT

What Is Covered—Cameras, projection machines, sound equipment and similar articles may be insured. Also films, telescopes, binoculars, microscopes and similar equipment used in photography.

Additionally Acquired Property—discussed under PERSONAL FURS.

Blanket Insurance—While each major item to be insured must be separately listed and described, the Insured may purchase additional insurance to cover blanket over the miscellaneous small items of related equipment. Customarily, such Blanket insurance may not exceed 10% of the total amount of insurance on scheduled items, but this limit may be increased when circumstances warrant. Such Blanket insurance is often used to insure filters, sunshades, meters, and similar miscellaneous smaller items that would be cumbersome to schedule in the policy.

Property Not Covered—Television cameras and equipment, coin operated devices, or camera property for the account of dealers.

Rates—In most states, there are three sets of rates, applying to motion picture producers, other commercial risks and non-commercial risks.

MUSICAL INSTRUMENTS

What Is Covered—All musical instruments may be covered under the policy. Radios, television sets and record players are not eligible for insurance under this policy. In addition, the Floater may insure instrument cases, strings, wind instrument reeds, amplifying and similar equipment which is used in connection with musical instruments.

Additionally Acquired Property—discussed under PERSONAL FURS.

Blanket Insurance—10% Blanket insurance may be provided exactly as under CAMERAS, discussed above.

Who Is Covered—The Floater contains a warranty that the Insured will not be engaged in playing for remuneration any musical instrument insured under the policy. This warranty may be deleted for an additional premium.

It is not necessary that the Insured be a professional, full-time musician for the exclusion to be operative. If he plays an instrument insured under the policy for remuneration at any time during the policy period, the insurance is void.

STAMP AND COIN COLLECTIONS

What Is Covered—The Floater is designed to cover all philatelic and numismatic property. In addition to stamps and coins, the policy will cover reprints, covers, books, pages and mountings as well as medals, paper money, tokens of money, coin albums, containers, frames, display cabinets, etc.

Additionally Acquired Property—Different from the coverage on jewelry, furs, cameras and musical instruments, the Floater does *not* provide any insurance on newly acquired property except in so far as they receive protection under the unscheduled portion of the policy (discussed below under Blanket Insurance).

Blanket Insurance—Blanket insurance is provided on all philatelic and numismatic property. However, not more than $250 is recoverable for any unscheduled stamp, coin, pair, strip or other individual article. Furthermore, there is a limit of $1,000 on all unscheduled numismatic property. In addition, coverage on the Blanket basis is subject to 100% Coinsurance. Since the Floater does permit for scheduling individual items as under a Fur or Jewelry schedule, it is important that valuable articles should be treated in this manner.

Hazards Not Covered—In addition to the perils listed above under Exclusions Common To All Personal Floaters, the Floater excludes:

Fading, creasing, denting, scratching, tearing, thinning, transfer of colors.

Dampness, extremes of temperature.

Damage sustained from handling or while being worked upon.

Theft from an unattended automobile except while in the custody of railroad express or armored car companies or while being shipped by insured or registered parcel post (may be deleted for an additional premium).

Mysterious disappearance of unscheduled items unless they are mounted in a volume and the page to which they are attached is lost.

FINE ARTS

What Is Covered—The Floater is designed to cover works of art or rarity, and articles of historical value. It is used to insure paintings, pictures, tapestries, and other bona fide works of art like valuable rugs, statuary, marbles, bronzes, antique furniture, rare books, antique silver, manuscripts, porcelains, rare glass, bric-a-brac, and similar property.

Blanket Insurance—Discussed under CAMERAS—Blanket Insurance, above.

Newly Acquired Property—Fine Arts items acquired during the term of the policy are covered automatically, subject to a limit of 25% of the amount already covered on Fine Arts, exclusive of the new acquisitions, for which coverage the Insured agrees to report the newly acquired items within 90 days of their acquisition, and to pay a premium thereon from acquisition. If the Insured fails to report the new acquisition by the 90th day, the automatic coverage ceases.

HAZARDS NOT COVERED

Breakage of Fragile Articles—In addition to the exclusions listed under Exclusions Common to All Personal Floaters, the Floater excludes the breakage of statuary, marbles, glassware, bric-a-brac, porcelains and similar fragile articles, *unless caused by*:

Fire, lightning
Windstorm, cyclone, tornado, explosion, aircraft
Malicious damage
Flood, earthquake
Collision, derailment or overturn of a conveyance
Theft or attempted theft.

The breakage of any articles other than of the kind listed is covered under the policy, no matter how caused. The breakage of articles of the kind listed is covered only if caused by one of the occurrences designated.

This exclusion may be deleted for an additional premium charge.

Damage Due to Process—The Floater does not cover damage resulting from any repairing, restoration or retouching process.

Packing—The Floater stipulates that the Insured will have all packing or unpacking of insured property done by competent packers.

FOR HOW MUCH

Valued Policy—Fine arts are almost always written on a Valued basis. The value set alongside each item is agreed upon as its actual cash value for insurance purposes, and losses are adjusted on this basis.

Pair and Set Clause—Under this Floater, when the Insured loses one article which is part of a set or pair, the Company will pay for the value of the entire set and take the remaining items. (Contrast with the Pair and Set clause discussed under PERSONAL JEWELRY.)

The Fine Arts Floater is liable for the full value of the set, if one part of the set is lost.

WHERE COVERED

Property on Exhibition—The Floater does not cover property while on fair grounds or on the premises of any national or international exposition. Coverage for such locations may be added by endorsement.

There is no exclusion of coverage for property on exhibition other than as indicated above. Coverage under the policy is limited, however, to the Continental United States and Canada.

OTHER FLOATERS AVAILABLE

As MENTIONED at the opening of this chapter, Inland Marine insurance takes in a great variety of property, and there are Floater forms designed to cover many different types of special property which are not fixed in location. Examples of other property which may be covered under such forms are:

Outboard Motors, Wedding Presents, Physician's and Surgeon's Equipment, Radium, etc.

FOR FURTHER READING

ACKERMAN—Insurance
HEDGES—Practical Fire and Casualty Insurance
HUEBNER AND BLACK—Property Insurance
MAGEE AND BICKELHAUPT—General Insurance
MEHR AND CAMMACK—Principles of Insurance
POLICY, FORM AND MANUAL ANALYSIS SERVICE
RODDA—Marine Insurance: Ocean and Inland

(See Reading List at End of Book)

CHAPTER 18

Unscheduled Personal Property Floaters

MOST FLOATERS COVERING PERSONAL PROPERTY insure specific articles which are named and described in the policy with a verified value in dollars set alongside each item.

There are several Floaters which provide coverage on personal property which does not have to be scheduled. In such policies, the full amount of insurance is applicable to all personal property of the Insured, or to the type of personal property described; e. g., Tourist Baggage Floater, Personal Effects Floater, Personal Property Floater and Wedding Present Floater.

In this chapter, two of the more widely used Floaters which insure unscheduled property will be analyzed—the Personal Effects Floater and the Personal Property Floater.

THE PERSONAL EFFECTS FLOATER

THE PERSONAL EFFECTS FLOATER was originally known as the Tourist Floater and is still sometimes referred to by that name. It is not to be confused, however, with the Tourist Baggage Floater, a more restricted Floater which is still on the market.

WHAT IS COVERED

The Personal Effects Floater covers on any and all personal effects such as are usually carried by or worn by tourists and travelers. One amount of insurance is specified in the policy, and the entire amount will apply to losses of such personal effects.

PROPERTY NOT COVERED

While the policy covers *all* personal effects as are usually carried by or worn by tourists, it specifically excludes coverage on the following types of property:

Automobiles, automobile robes, motors, motorcycles, bicycles, boats or other conveyances, and appurtenances or equipment pertaining to such items.

Accounts, bills, currency, deeds, evidences of debt, letters of credit, passports, documents, notes, securities, railroad tickets, other tickets, and money.

Household furniture, including contents of trailer homes, animals.

Salesmen's samples, physicians' and surgeons' instruments, merchandise for sale or exhibition, theatrical property of any kind.

Artificial teeth or limbs, contact lenses.

The Personal Effects Floater does not cover any property which is otherwise insured. Thus, a camera being carried by the Insured would be covered under the Personal Effects Floater, but not if such camera were insured under a Camera Floater.

Jewelry and Furs Limitation—While the Personal Effects Floater covers jewelry and furs which are not specifically insured in other policies, the amount of coverage on jewelry, watches, or articles consisting in whole or in part of gold, silver or platinum, and on furs, is limited to 10% of the amount for which the policy is written or $100 *on any one such article,* whichever is less.

HAZARDS NOT COVERED

The Personal Effects Floater is an all-risk policy, and contains the basic exclusions of all Personal Floaters.

In addition, the policy specifically excludes damage to articles of a brittle nature, unless such breakage is caused by fire, theft, or an accident to a conveyance. The breakage of articles which are not of a brittle nature is covered no matter how caused.

WHERE COVERED

While the coverage of the Personal Effects Floater is worldwide, the policy differs from other Floaters, in that it specifically excludes certain types of premises, as follows:

Domicile of Insured—There is no coverage for loss sustained on the premises of the Insured's domicile. Domicile is a somewhat broader term than residence, and has been defined by the courts as the place where an individual has "his permanent home and principal establishment, to which, whenever he is absent, he intends to return."

The exclusion applies to the "premises of the domicile," and would therefore apply not only to losses from within the Insured's home but also from the grounds and other buildings.

ARIZONA, COLORADO, DELAWARE, DISTRICT OF COLUMBIA, FLORIDA, IDAHO, ILLINOIS, IOWA, KANSAS, MARYLAND, MICHIGAN, MISSOURI, MONTANA, NEBRASKA, NEVADA, NEW HAMPSHIRE, NEW JERSEY, NEW MEXICO, NEW YORK, NORTH CAROLINA, NORTH DAKOTA, OHIO, OKLAHOMA, OREGON, PENNSYLVANIA, SOUTH CAROLINA, TENNESSEE, TEXAS, UTAH, VER-

MONT, WASHINGTON, WEST VIRGINIA, WISCONSIN—In these States, the Personal Effects Floater may be extended to cover the domicile of the Insured for an additional premium of 25%, subject to a minimum premium of $10 for this coverage. The coverage is extended to cover *personal effects* in the Insured's domicile. It does not cover household furniture, which is excluded in the basic policy.

If the policy is extended to cover the Insured's domicile, it becomes subject to a 100% Coinsurance clause, except that the Coinsurance Clause does not relate to jewelry, watches, articles of gold, silver or platinum, or to furs. Thus, if an Insured's personal effects are worth $5,000 exclusive of jewelry, watches and furs, he must carry at least $5,000 of insurance in a Personal Effects Floater which is endorsed to cover his residence, otherwise he will have to bear a portion of the loss himself.

Theft from an Unattended Automobile—The Personal Effects Floater does not cover theft from an unattended automobile or a compartment, unless such automobile is equipped with a fully enclosed body or compartment, and *then only* if all doors and windows of the automobile or the compartment are securely locked, and *then only* if the theft is caused by violent, forcible entry of which there shall be visible evidence, and *then only* for an amount not in excess of 10% of the amount of the policy, or $250 in any one loss, whichever is less.

This exclusion may be deleted by the payment of an additional premium of $10.

The exclusion does not apply to property while in the custody of a common carrier. Thus, if an Insured's property is being moved by a truckman, and there is a theft from the truck, the Insured would be covered under his Personal Effects Floater, regardless of whether the truck was closed or not.

Property in Storage — The Personal Effects Floater does not cover property while in storage, except at points and places en route during travel.

Premises of Schools, Dormitories, Fraternity and Sorority Houses—The Personal Effects Floater does not cover loss sustained on the premises of schools, colleges, dormitory or fraternity houses except by fire. This exclusion would apply to any loss of property while at a school, even if a day school. It does not, however, exclude loss suffered by students while traveling to or from school, or loss sustained by a student in a rooming house.

Coverage for such excluded premises may be obtained for an additional charge of 25c per $100, with a minimum of $5 for this extra coverage. The additional premium must be paid on the total amount of insurance under the policy. In other words, if a Personal Effects Floater is written for $1,000, the additional premium for extending the policy to cover premises of schools must be paid for the full $1,000 of insurance. (In this case, the additional premium would be $5 rather than $2.50 because of the minimum premium applicable to this endorsement.)

WHO IS COVERED

The Personal Effects Floater covers personal effects owned, used or worn by the Insured and his spouse and their unmarried children permanently residing together. It would not cover property belonging to other relatives of the Insured, nor property belonging to any married children of the Insured, even though they reside with him. It would not cover property of unmarried children of the Insured who maintain a permanent residence elsewhere.

It is possible to insure under the Personal Effects Floater other persons permanently residing with him. An additional premium of $5 is made for each additional individual to be insured. Each such person must be specifically named in the policy.

FOR HOW MUCH

The Company is liable for not more than the actual cash value of the property at the time of the loss, or the cost to repair or replace the property. There is no Coinsurance clause in the policy, except if endorsed to cover the domicile, and the Insured can collect the full amount of any loss up to the face amount of his policy, regardless of how much insurance he has been carrying.

Deductible Clause—The Personal Effects Floater may be written at a lower rate with a $25 Deductible Clause.

Term Policies—Different from other Personal Floaters, the Personal Effects Floater may not be written for more than one year.

Automatic Reinstatement of Losses — The Personal Effects Floater is reduced by the amount of any loss payment. However, all losses are reinstated automatically and the Insured is required to pay an additional premium on a pro rata basis to the expiration of the policy for the amount of insurance reinstated.

SPECIAL COVERAGES AVAILABLE

Contents of Trailer Homes—The Personal Effects Floater may be extended for an additional premium to cover the furniture and furnishings of an automobile trailer home.

Exclusion of Theft, Larceny, Mysterious Disappearance, Vandalism—An Insured who carries Broad Form Personal Theft insurance may have his Personal Effects Floater endorsed to exclude loss or damage by theft, larceny, burglary, robbery, mysterious disappearance, vandalism and malicious mischief. A policy so endorsed is written at a 50% reduction rate.

When Loss Is Payable—All losses must be paid by the Company within 30 days after acceptance by the Company of satisfactory Proof of Loss.

Other Clauses—Discussed in Chapter 2: Appraisal—Cancellation—Fraud, Concealment—Examination Under Oath; **Discussed in Chapter 17:** Benefit of Insurance—Notice of Loss, Proof of Loss—Sue and Labor Clause—When Suit Must Be Brought.

PERSONAL PROPERTY FLOATER

THE PERSONAL PROPERTY FLOATER, another Personal Floater that covers unscheduled property on an all-risk basis, is the most important Personal Floater in terms of the premium volume it develops. (This policy is sometimes known as the Householders' Comprehensive policy.)

While it is similar in name to the Personal Effects Floater discussed before, it is entirely different in its purpose and scope. It is important that the reader distinguish carefully between the two forms and their designations.

WHAT IS COVERED

The Personal Property Floater covers all personal property owned, used or worn by an Insured. This takes in not only personal effects but also all household property—furniture, kitchen equipment, food, liquors, sports equipment, books, radios, television sets, musical instruments, etc. One amount of insurance is specified in the policy to cover all unscheduled property and the entire amount of insurance is applicable to loss of any personal property.

Personal property is distinguished from real property, the latter being the ground and objects attached to the ground. Personal property is anything which is not real property, and will therefore take in all movable property.

In addition, there are instances where property attached to the land or to the building may be classified as personal property. Although the line of demarcation is somewhat involved, and is differently applied in various states, generally, fixed property is classified as personal property when its attachment is of a temporary character and its removal will not destroy the article or damage the building.

The property need not be owned by the Insured to be covered. The policy covers all property used by the Insured and would therefore apply to borrowed or rented property.

Coverage on Real Property—While the Personal Property Floater is designed primarily to cover personal property, it will also cover certain property which may be classed as real property. The policy is extended to cover *any* property which is not specifically excluded against loss by theft or attempted theft. Thus, theft, or damage by attempted theft, to trees, shrubbery, or fixtures attached to the building would be covered, as would damage by thieves to the building itself.

If the Insured has made improvements, alterations or additions to a building or unit in a condominium he occupies, the Personal Property Floater will cover such property against the perils of fire, lightning (the perils covered by the Fire insurance policy), windstorm, cyclone, tornado, hail, explosion, riot, riot attending strike, smoke, damage by vehicles or aircraft (the perils of the Extended Coverage Endorsement). This coverage is limited to 10% of the amount of insurance on unscheduled property, and does not apply to any building owned by the Insured.

ALABAMA—No coverage is extended to improvements and betterments. TEXAS—Coverage is afforded on fixtures installed by the Insured but only in premises not owned by any person whose property is insured by the policy.

Vandalism and Malicious Mischief—The policy is also extended to cover damage to the interior of the Insured's residence by vandalism and malicious mischief.

PROPERTY NOT COVERED

While the Personal Property Floater covers all personal property, it specifically excludes:

Automobiles, motorcycles, aircraft, boats and other conveyances, or their equipment or furnishings, except when such equipment is actually removed from the conveyances and is on the Insured's premises.

Bicycles, tricycles, carriages, invalid chairs and similar equipment are not excluded.

Coverage on boats may be provided (to be discussed later under Additional Coverages Available).

Animals.

Property of any government or any subdivision thereof.

Property pertaining to the business, profession or occupation of the Insured, except that professional books, instruments and other professional equipment are insured while actually in the Insured's residence.

Damage to Electrical Apparatus—Loss or damage to electrical apparatus caused by electricity other than lightning is not covered unless fire ensues and then only for the damage by the fire.

PROPERTY ON WHICH LIMITED COVERAGE APPLIES

Jewelry and Furs Limitation — While the Personal Property Floater insures all personal property, coverage on unscheduled jewelry, watches and furs is limited to $250.* This $250 limitation applies to any single loss, regardless of how many individual pieces of jewelry or watches or furs are lost. Thus, if the Insured loses three watches worth $100 each in a theft, the maximum liability of the Company for the entire loss is $250.

The Personal Property Floater, however, is so designed that an Insured may also cover any items of jewelry or furs by scheduling these items in the policy (discussed later under FOR HOW MUCH). When such property is scheduled in the policy, the limit of the Company's liability is the amount stated alongside the item. The $250 limitation does not apply to such scheduled items.

It is also possible to increase the $250 limitation on *unscheduled* jewelry, watches and furs.

Money and Securities Limitation—The limit of liability on loss of money, including coin collections, is $100. The limit of liability on loss of accounts, bills, deeds, documents, evidences of debt, letters of credit, notes, passports, railroad and other tickets, securities, stamps, including stamp collections, is $500.

NOTE: These limits may be increased by endorsement (to be discussed later).

HAZARDS NOT COVERED

The Personal Property Floater is an all-risk policy, designed to give the broadest possible protection to an Insured on all his personal belongings. Like other all-risk Floaters, it contains certain basic exclusions and several other exclusions which are made necessary by the all-inclusive scope of the policy.

> FLORIDA: Policy may be written to exclude loss or damage to unscheduled property in any residence in the State when damage is caused by windstorm, cyclone, tornado, rain, high water or tidal wave.

Breakage of Fragile Articles—The Personal Property Floater does not cover breakage of certain types of fragile articles except when the breakage results from designated perils. The intent of the policy in this respect is to exclude the accidental knocking over or

---

*Under the Transportation Insurance Rating Bureau (Mutual) form, the $250 limitation does not apply to Fire, Lightning and the perils of the Extended Coverage Endorsement.

dropping of fragile articles, but not breakage caused by major casualties. Losses caused by marring or scratching are treated similarly.

There is no coverage for breakage (or marring or scratching) of eye glasses, glassware, statuary, marble, bric-a-brac, porcelains or similar fragile articles unless such articles are broken as a result of:

Fire, lightning
Windstorm, explosion, falling aircraft, rioters, strikers
Earthquake, collapse of buildings, flood
Accident to conveyances
Theft or attempted theft
Vandalism and malicious mischief and other similar casualty.

Jewelry, watches, bronzes, cameras and photographic lenses are specifically exempted from this exclusion, and breakage of any such article is covered, regardless of how caused, and despite the fact that such articles might be "similar fragile articles."

Contrast the breakage exclusion of this policy with that of the Personal Effects Floater. Note that the Personal Effects Floater does not limit the exclusion to certain types of property, but excludes any article of a brittle nature.

A brittle article which is not similar to those enumerated above would be covered under the Personal Property Floater but not under the Personal Effects Floater.

Note, too, that the Personal Effects Floater covers breakage of brittle articles only when caused by fire, theft, or an accident to a conveyance, while the Personal Property Floater lists fourteen perils which might cause breakage which would be covered, and states further that breakage caused by a casualty *similar* to those listed would also be covered.

Damage Due to Process—The Personal Property Floater does not cover damage to property resulting from being worked on in the course of any refinishing, renovating or repairing. Jewelry, watches and furs are excepted from this exclusion and damage to such property in the course of being worked upon *would* be covered.

Wear, Tear, Mechanical Breakdown—The policy does not cover loss arising from wear, tear, deterioration or mechanical breakdown or inherent vice.

Insects, Vermin—Like most floaters, the Personal Property Floater does not cover loss due to insects or vermin.

Dampness of Atmosphere or Extremes of Temperature — The Personal Property Floater does not cover loss or damage caused by dampness of the atmosphere or extremes of temperature, unless caused by rain, snow, sleet, hail, bursting of pipes. As under the breakage exclusion discussed above, the intent of the policy is to cover such loss when caused by a casualty or catastrophe but not for day-to-day conditions against which the Insured can protect.

Flood, Rising Waters, Underground Waters—The Personal Property Floater does not cover loss caused by flood, surface water, waves, tidal water or tidal wave, overflow of streams or other bodies of water, or spray from any of the foregoing, all whether driven by the wind or not;

Nor for loss caused by water which backs up through sewers or drains;

Nor for loss from water below the surface of the ground including that which exerts pressure on or flows, seeps or leaks through sidewalks, driveways, foundations, walls, basement or other floors or through doors, windows or other openings in such sidewalk, driveways, foundation, walls, or floors.

It is important to understand that there is no coverage for losses caused by or *contributed to or aggravated by such perils.* An exception is made for *ensuing* fire or explosion and such losses would be covered even if contributed to by one of the excluded perils. Furthermore, the exclusions do not apply to loss by theft. While the clause excludes considerable types of loss, it does not exclude all water damage. Thus, damage by the overflow or discharge of water from plumbing systems, heating systems, etc., are covered, subject only to the preceding exclusion of dampness of the atmosphere.

Damage by Pets—The Personal Property Floater does not cover loss caused by animals or birds owned by or kept by an Insured or a residence employee of an Insured.

Property on Exhibition—Discussed in Chapter 17 under FINE ARTS.

WHO IS COVERED

The Personal Property Floater covers the property of the Insured and all family members of the same household. It will therefore cover property of children, married or unmarried, who reside with the Insured. It will not cover property of children or other relatives who maintain separate residence, as such individuals are not members of the Insured's household.

Children away at out-of-town schools have been held to be members of the Insured's household, and loss of their property would be covered. Similarly, it is probable that the property of a son at an Army camp would be covered, since he has made no change in his permanent residence.

Property of Others Extension — While the policy only covers property of the Insured and members of his family of the same household, the Insured has the option of extending his policy to cover the property of others who suffer loss at his premises. No special request for this extension need be made by the Insured, as this coverage is part of the basic policy. For all practical purposes, the property of any persons is covered while on the premises of the Insured, except that such persons have no direct claim against the Company, but must make such claim through the Insured, and at his option.

Personal Property of Servants—The Personal Property Floater is further extended to cover property of the Insured's servants while they are engaged in the service of the Insured and while such property is in their custody. As in the case of the Property of Others Extension, a servant has no direct claim against the Company, but must make his claim through the Insured, and at his option.

WHERE COVERED

Like most Personal Floaters, the Personal Property Floater provides world-wide coverage. There is one limitation in the policy as it applies to secondary residences of the Insured.

Secondary Residence Limitation—While the Personal Property Floater covers for its full amount any personal property at the Insured's principal residence or anywhere else in the world, only 10% of the amount of insurance on unscheduled property may be applied to personal property ordinarily situated throughout the year at residence other than the Insured's principal residence.

In other words, an Insured who purchases a Personal Property Floater of $10,000 on unscheduled property can collect up to $10,000 for loss or damage to property sustained at his principal residence or while traveling anywhere in the world. If he maintains a secondary residence, however, only $1,000, 10% of the insurance on unscheduled property, applies to personal property which is ordinarily situated throughout the year at such other residence.

This limitation applies only to property *ordinarily situated throughout the year* at such secondary residence. Any personal property which the Insured brings with him for a temporary period or vacation (e. g., fishing tackle, personal clothing, luggage, etc.) would be covered by the full amount of insurance exactly as it would if it were in his principal residence.

The 10% limitation on secondary residences may be increased by endorsement (to be discussed below).

FOR HOW MUCH

The Personal Property Floater is not liable for more than the actual cash value of the property, nor for more than it would cost to repair or replace the property with other of like kind and quality. There is no Coinsurance clause in the policy, and all losses will be paid in full, up to the amount of insurance, regardless of how much insurance the Insured has been carrying, subject to the limitations stipulated in the policy for money, securities, unscheduled jewelry, watches and furs.

The Company makes every effort, however, to have the Personal Property Floater written in an amount which reflects the values at risk and will require at least 80% insurance to value. The Insured is required to complete an application for the policy, in which he estimates the value of his personal property, broken down into 15 classifications, as follows:

DECLARATIONS OF THE INSURED

The following are the approximate values of the unscheduled personal property, other than jewelry, watches and furs, as estimated by the Assured, at the time of issuance of this policy:	Wherever Located	(Of which the following amounts involve personal property ordinarily situated throughout the year at residences other than principal residence)
(a) Silverware and pewter	$	($)
(b) Linens (including dining room and bedroom)	$	($)
(c) Clothing (men's, women's, children's)	$	($)
(d) Rugs (including floor coverings) and draperies	$	($)
(e) Books	$	($)
(f) Musical instruments (including pianos)	$	($)
(g) Television sets, radios, record players and records	$	($)
(h) Paintings, etchings, pictures and other objects of art	$	($)
(i) China and glassware (including bric-a-brac)	$	($)
(j) Cameras and photographic equipment	$	($)
(k) Golf, hunting, fishing and other sports and hobby equipment	$	($)
(l) Refrigerators, washing machines, stoves, electrical appliances and other kitchen equipment	$	($)
(m) Bedding (including blankets, comforters, covers, pillows, mattresses, and springs)	$	($)
(n) Furniture (including tables, chairs, sofas, desks, beds, chests, lamps, mirrors, clocks)	$	($)
(o) All other personal property (including wines liquors, foodstuff, garden and lawn tools and equipment, trunks, traveling bags, children's playthings, miscellaneous articles in basement and attic) and professional equipment, if any, covered under paragraph 6(b)	$	($)

FLORIDA—When the policy does not exclude windstorm and hail losses, the windstorm and hail coverage on unscheduled property is subject to an 80% Coinsurance Clause.

NEW YORK—In Bronx, Kings, New York and Queens Counties of the City of New York, the Company is not liable for loss to unscheduled property for more than the amount set alongside the applicable class of property in the Declarations by the Insured. While no Coinsurance

Clause is applicable, an Insured cannot collect more than these amounts. An exception is made for property acquired subsequent to the inception of the policy. Such property is covered up to $2,500 or 10% of the amount of insurance declared in the policy, whichever is less. Thus assume an Insured lists $5,000 as the value of his furniture under Item (n) of the Declarations at the time he applies for a Personal Property Floater. At the time of the loss, it develops that the loss to furniture which the Insured owned when he bought the policy was $6,000. He cannot collect more than $5,000 for this property, since this was the amount declared by him as applicable to furniture. If in the same loss, there was damage to furniture which he acquired *subsequent* to the inception of the policy, he can collect for such loss, over and above the $5,000 declared by him for the furniture item. Recovery on such newly acquired property is limited to 10% of the amount of insurance on unscheduled property, or $2,500, whichever is less.

Pair and Set Clause—The Pair and Set Clause in a Personal Property Floater is identical with the one used in the Personal Articles Floater (see Chapter 17).

Scheduled Jewelry and Furs—Jewelry, watches and furs which are not scheduled in the policy are insured for no more than $250 in any one loss. In addition to this $250 of blanket insurance in the basic policy on unscheduled jewelry, watches and furs, the Insured may schedule any article of jewelry or fur. Each article to be scheduled is listed and described in the policy exactly as it would be in a Jewelry or Fur Floater, and a value set alongside the item. The rates charged for such scheduled items and the coverage provided are exactly the same as in separate Floaters on such property.

Scheduled Fine Arts—While there is no limitation in a Personal Property Floater on the amount of insurance applicable to fine arts, and such property is insured along with other personal property, an Insured may prefer to schedule his fine arts in his Personal Property Floater. Such an approach will be indicated when the Insured wishes to have broader protection against the risk of breakage than is provided under the basic Personal Property Floater on unscheduled property. By scheduling his Fine Arts, he is in a position to extend the coverage on breakage, exactly as would be possible under a separate Fine Arts Floater. Then again, in some cases it may prove cheaper to schedule fine arts than to include them with all the unscheduled property.

Additional Coverage on Money—The $100 limitation on loss of money, including coin collections, may be increased by an amount not exceeding $400 for an additional annual premium of $2.70 for each $100 of additional insurance.

Additional Coverage on Securities—The $500 limitation on accounts, bills, deeds, documents, evidences of debt, letters of credit, notes, passports, railroad and other tickets, securities, stamps, including stamp collections, may be increased by an amount not exceeding $500 for an additional annual premium of $1.80 for each $100 of additional insurance.

Additional Insurance on Unscheduled Jewelry, Watches, Furs—The basic Personal Property Floater coverage on unscheduled jewelry, watches and furs, is limited to $250 in any one loss involving such property. It is also possible to schedule property of this kind. In either case, such items are covered on an all-risk basis.

It is also possible under a Personal Property Floater to provide additional coverage on unscheduled jewelry, watches and furs, in the Insured's principal residence. Such additional coverage is available either on all-risk basis, or on a specified perils basis. These different coverages are discussed below.

Fire and Lightning—Unscheduled jewelry, watches and furs may be covered against the perils of fire and lightning only for an amount in excess of the $250 of all-risk insurance provided by the basic Personal Property Floater.

Residence Burglary and Robbery—An optional increase of coverage on unscheduled jewelry, watches and furs is available to cover such property over and above the basic $250 of all-risk coverage against the perils of burglary and robbery within the Insured's residence.

Extended or Supplemental Coverage—Broader Coverage on unscheduled jewelry, watches and furs is available to cover against loss by windstorm, hail, explosion, riot, riot attending a strike, civil commotion, aircraft, vehicles and smoke (the perils of the Extended Coverage Endorsement of the Fire insurance policy discussed in Chapter 5) and vandalism and malicious mischief. This added coverage can be purchased only in conjunction with the additional Fire and lightning coverage.

All Risk Coverage—The Insured may also increase the amount of insurance on unscheduled jewelry, watches and furs over the basic $250 provided by the Personal Property Floater on an all-risk basis. While $750 of such additional coverage is available, the basic limit of $250 *per article* still applies.

KANSAS—Not applicable.

The extensions of coverage on unscheduled jewelry, watches and furs, on securities, and on money (discussed in the preceding paragraphs) do not increase the amount of insurance of the policy; they merely extend the coverage. Thus, if an Insured purchases a Personal Property Floater with $5,000 of insurance on unscheduled property, he will have $100 to cover money, $500 to cover securities and $250 to cover unscheduled jewelry, watches and furs. Increasing the amount of insurance on these types of property does not increase the amount of the policy above $5,000, and the Insured cannot collect more than $5,000 in any loss.

ARIZONA, CALIFORNIA, IDAHO, MONTANA, NEVADA, OREGON, WASHINGTON—In these States, the Personal Property Floater may also be extended to cover unscheduled jewelry, watches and furs against the peril of earthquake.

Secondary Location Additional Amount Endorsement — While the Personal Property Floater provides world-wide coverage, it limits to 10% the amount of insurance on property ordinarily situated throughout the year at any secondary residence or residences of the Insured. If an Insured keeps property at a secondary residence whose value is more than 10% of the insurance he carries on his principal residence, he may have this 10% limitation eased, and apply for additional insurance on such secondary locations.

This additional insurance is all-risk insurance and provides the same coverage on property in the secondary residence as it does in the main residence. While it is all-risk in scope, it is not blanket insurance covering any additional residence, but only those named in the endorsement.

Boats—Boats are excluded in the basic Personal Property Floater except for the equipment or furnishings when actually removed from the boat and kept on the premises of the Insured's residence. It is possible to provide coverage on boats specifically under the Personal Property Floater, but only on boats not powered by inboard motor. Coverage is available up to a maximum of $500 per boat against the perils of fire, lightning, explosion, smoke, riot, riot attending a strike, civil commotion, aircraft and other falling objects, vandalism and malicious mischief, collapse of a building, theft and collision, upset or overturning of land vehicles. This extension of coverage also applies to direct loss by windstorm or hail, to rowboats and canoes while on the Insured's premises and to any property described in this extension of coverage while within a fully enclosed building.

Deductible Clauses—While the Personal Property Floater may be written without a Deductible Clause, it is almost universal for companies to require the inclusion of a $50 Deductible.

In a Personal Property Floater, the Deductible Clause does *not* apply to any loss caused by:

Fire, lightning (the perils of the Fire insurance policy)

When the Deductible is applicable to a loss, the amount of the Deductible is to be deducted from the amount of the loss or the limit of liability for given property, whichever is less.

Assume an Insured who carries a Personal Property Floater with a $50 Deductible loses $165 in cash. Since the loss was not caused by a peril specifically exempted (Fire or Lightning), the Deductible will apply. The limit of liability on money in the basic policy is $100. The amount of the Deductible, $50, must be deducted from the limit of liability in this case, and the Insured is entitled to collect $50. On the other hand, if he had lost $65 in cash, the Deductible would be deducted from the amount of the loss, and he would be entitled to collect $15.

If more than one item of property is lost or damaged in one casualty, the Deductible is deducted from the total amount of the loss, and not from each individual item of property.

Other Insurance—The Personal Property Floater replaces all insurance required by an Insured on his personal property. An Insured who purchases a Personal Property Floater will often have other insurance on his personal property; e. g., Fire insurance on his household property, Residence Theft insurance, a Personal Effects Floater, Jewelry Floater, Camera Floater, etc. The Insured may cancel all such existing policies, but he will then be subject to the short rate penalty.

To avoid such penalty, an Insured may continue his existing policies until their expiration. These policies will continue to cover the Insured property exactly as they did before the Insured purchased his Personal Property Floater and will be liable for any loss covered under the policies. The Personal Property Floater will be liable only for losses which are not covered under the specific policies, and for the excess of any loss over the amount of insurance in the basic policies, but not exceeding the amount which would otherwise be collectible. As each specific policy expires, the coverage is automatically picked up by the Personal Property Floater. The Insured is required to list each policy he plans to continue, and he receives a credit for the unearned premiums on such policies.

EXAMPLE: On January 1, 1961, the Insured applies for a Personal Property Floater in the amount of $5,000 on unscheduled property. He has been carrying a Fire insurance policy on his household contents in the amount of $4,000 which attached on January 1, 1960, and will expire on January 1, 1963. He lists this Fire policy in his application for the Personal Property Floater, and receives a credit in his premium for the full unexpired period of the Fire insurance policy.

On March 15, 1961, he suffers a fire loss at his home which does $4,500 of damage. The Fire insurance policy will pay the first $4,000 of the loss, since that is its maximum liability, and the Personal Property Floater will pay the excess over this amount, the other $500. If the loss had amounted to $2,000, the Fire insurance policy would be liable for the entire loss, the Personal Property Floater would pay nothing.

On the other hand, if the fire occurs on January 2, 1963, the Personal Property Floater will be liable for the entire loss, since the Fire insurance policy will have expired. Similarly, if there is any loss by a peril not insured under the Fire insurance policy, as by theft, explosion, or earthquake, the Personal Property Floater is liable for the loss.

FACTORS ON WHICH PREMIUM DEPENDS

When items are scheduled in the Personal Property Floater, the regular Floater rates applicable to the type of property are used; e. g., Fur Floater rates, Jewelry Floater rates, Fine Arts Floater rates, etc.

The rates for the Unscheduled Property coverage under a Personal Property Floater is made up of two factors:

1. The Contents Fire insurance rate at the Insured's residence, plus

2. A loading charge which depends on the territory.

ALABAMA, FLORIDA, GEORGIA, LOUISIANA, MISSISSIPPI, NORTH CAROLINA, PUERTO RICO, SOUTH CAROLINA, TEXAS (on Deductible policies only), VIRGINIA—The windstorm rate is added to the premium for unscheduled property.

In 30 states, one loading charge applies to all locations in the state. In the other states, different loading charges are applied, depending on the county. Generally, one loading charge is applicable to the county or counties which include the larger city or cities, and a second loading charge is used in the balance of the state; e. g., in Alabama, a higher rate is used in Jefferson County, with a lower rate for the balance of the state.

KENTUCKY—The State is divided into three rate groups.
NEW YORK—Each of four counties of New York City is separately rated, with a fifth rate for Staten Island and the balance of the State.

Credit for Deductible—A credit is allowed on the rate for unscheduled property when a Deductible clause is used in the policy, with larger credits applying to the higher Deductibles, and specified maximum and minimum credits, as follows:

Amount of Deductible	CREDIT—% of premium for unscheduled Property	One-Year Policy		Three-Year Policy	
		Minimum Credit	Maximum Credit	Minimum Credit	Maximum Credit
$50.00	40%	$20.00	$50.00	$60.00	$150.00

Minimum Premiums — Minimum premiums are established for the unscheduled portion of all Personal Property Floaters, and no policy is issued for less than these prescribed minimums. No credit, whether for existing insurance or for use of a Deductible clause, or otherwise, can serve to reduce any premium for the unscheduled portion of the policy below the required minimum. The minimum premium varies with the Deductible Clause used.

Term Insurance—The Personal Property Floater may be written for one year or for three years. The three-year premium is written at a discount, and may be paid in one sum, or in three annual installments. The discounts and the installment plans are discussed in Chapter 17 under FEATURES COMMON TO ALL PERSONAL FLOATERS—Term Policies.

Whole Dollar Premium Rule—Discussed in Chapter 8 under OTHER FACTORS WHICH AFFECT FIRE INSURANCE RATES—Whole Dollar Premium Rule.

WEDDING PRESENTS FLOATER

The Wedding Presents Floater is designed to cover wedding presents on a blanket basis. It is subject to the basic conditions of the PERSONAL FLOATERS discussed in Chapter 17 and should be read together with the discussion in that chapter under FEATURES COMMON TO ALL PERSONAL FLOATERS. The Floater covers all presents except realty, animals, automobiles, motorcycles, aircraft, bicycles, boats or other conveyances or their appurtenances, money, notes, securities, stamps, accounts, bills, deeds, evidences of debt, letters of credit, passports, documents, railroad or other tickets. It is written on all-risk basis, subject to exclusions which are essentially the same as those of the Personal Property Floater (discussed earlier under PERSONAL PROPERTY FLOATER—Hazards Not Covered). In addition, it is provided that no insurance under the Wedding Presents Floater will be granted beyond 90 days from the date of the wedding.

OTHER PROVISIONS

Non-Reduction After Loss—The payment of loss to unscheduled property does not reduce the amount of the Personal Property Floater.

> ALABAMA—Policy is reduced after loss payment in excess of $250.00. It may be endorsed to provide for automatic reinstatement of such losses with an additional premium to be charged.

When Loss Is Payable—All adjusted claims must be paid within 60 days from the time Proof of Loss is accepted by the Company.

Other Clauses—Discussed in first half of this chapter under Personal Effects Floater—Other Clauses.

FOR FURTHER READING

ACKERMAN—Insurance
DAYNARD—Paths and Bypaths in Inland Marine Insurance
HEDGES—Practical Fire and Casualty Insurance
MORTIMER—Adjusting Practices, Inland Marine and Transportation Insurance
POLICY, FORM & MANUAL ANALYSIS SERVICE
RODDA—Marine Insurance: Ocean and Inland

(See Reading List at End of Book)

CHAPTER 19

Bailees' Forms

A BAILEE IS AN INDIVIDUAL (or a concern) who has temporary custody of the property of others. The property has been turned over to the bailee by its owner for some specific purpose, as for safe-keeping, repair, renovating, remodeling, processing, delivery, storage, etc. The owner has no intention of effecting any transfer of the property, which he expects to have returned to him.

The bailee is the individual (or concern) to whom the property is entrusted; the bailor is the owner of the property.

The contract between the bailor and the bailee is the Contract of Bailment. The actual property which the bailor turns over to the bailee is referred to as the bailed property.

There are, of course, an almost endless number of situations in which bailment occurs, ranging from the day-to-day occurrences—like giving clothes to be laundered or cleaned or jewelry to be repaired, to the more specialized bailments which are part of many business operations—like turning property over to transportation companies, warehousing of goods, sending textiles to be dyed, machine parts to be fabricated, and similar operations.

All bailments of the kind outlined are entered into for the mutual benefit of the bailor and the bailee. The bailor looks to the bailee to perform a function which will benefit the bailor, while the bailee performs in order to be paid for his services. Such bailment is generally referred to as "bailment for hire."

Gratuitous Bailments—Bailment is also entered into for the sole benefit of the bailor (owner), or solely for the benefit of the bailee. An example of such bailment would be the leaving of a pet with a friend. Such bailment is gratuitous, and is solely for the benefit of the bailor. Gratuitous bailment also occurs which is solely for the benefit of the bailee, as when an individual borrows his friend's car for a week-end.

While individuals who are involved in gratuitous bailment situations sometimes require insurance to cover the property in their custody, these situations do not bulk large in the insurance covering bailed property. The large majority of insurance policies set up to cover bailed property develop in those bailments entered into in the course of business. These bailments are for mutual benefit —bailments for hire.

Special Situations Which Are Not Bailment—One must not arbitrarily assume that bailment always arises when one individual has in his custody the property of others. Thus, an individual may take over property under a conditional sales contract which provides that title to the property will not pass until certain conditions are fulfilled, as, for example, until all installments are fully paid. In such cases, the seller will continue to own the property during a period when the purchaser has it in his custody, but there is no bailor-bailee relationship.

Similarly, an individual may entrust his property to another without creating a bailment relationship, if the owner retains control of the manner in which the property is to be handled. If a home owner calls a carpenter in to make certain repairs, or takes a piece of furniture to the carpenter for repairs, but stays with the carpenter and instructs or directs him in the work being done, there is no bailment. Similarly, a laundress who washes clothes under the direction of the lady of the house is not a bailee. In these situations, the work is being done by a person acting as the servant of the owner.

On the other hand, if the laundress takes the clothes to her home, or if the carpenter performs his work at his shop without the direct supervision of the owner, they would be bailees. The distinguishing feature of bailment is that the owner gives up his control of the property and completely relinquishes it to the bailee.

Liability of Bailee for Hire—A bailee for hire is charged with taking ordinary and reasonable care of the property bailed to him. He is expected to take such care of the property bailed to him as a prudent man would of his own property. His liability for such goods does not go beyond such duty. For the bailee to be held liable for loss or damage to the property, it must be established that he was negligent or careless in caring for the property.

The degree of care which is expected of a bailee will vary with different kinds of property. Thus, a jeweler will be expected to take more precautions against theft with a fine diamond than a refinisher with an ordinary piece of furniture but, in each case, the bailee will not be liable unless he has failed to take the care which is reasonable for the particular property.

As a practical matter, when property in the custody of a bailee suffers loss or damage, the bailee is usually charged with the burden of proving that he was free of negligence, since the owner of the property cannot be expected to know very much about the conditions surrounding the loss.

Special insurance policies are made available to bailees to cover their liability to customers. This type of policy provides protection to the bailee by agreeing to indemnify him for any loss or damage to property in his custody for which he is legally obligated to his customers.

Liability Assumed by Bailees—Under modern business conditions, it has become customary for bailees to voluntarily assume complete responsibility for the goods entrusted to them, or to accept responsibility for at least certain losses which are not the result of their negligence.

Thus, a furrier may advertise that he is responsible for all loss or damage to coats stored with him, or that he will be responsible for fire, theft, moths, and other stated perils. Even where the bailee does not expressly stipulate that he will be liable for losses of this kind, he may find it necessary to make good to his customers for any loss or damage to their property, if he is to continue to enjoy their patronage.

It can be readily seen that the assumption of liability for damage to goods in the care of a bailee, whether expressed or implied, exposes him to the threat of large scale loss. Such losses may be insured under special Bailees' insurance policies, which are broader than those designed to cover only the bailees' liability under the law. These broader policies actually insure the customers' goods while in the hands of the bailee.

Limitation of Liability by Special Agreement — While a bailee may assume liability for loss or damage to property in his custody even when he has not been negligent towards the property, he may also enter into a special agreement with the owner of the property limiting his liability to an agreed maximum.

Thus, a shipper of goods may agree with the carrier that he will be entitled to not more than $50 per package if the package is lost. A lady may store her fur coat and agree that she will accept $100 in full settlement of any claim she may have against the fur storer, etc. Such agreements are generally held to be valid, if the bailee grants the bailor a lower rate for his services than he would if the limitation of liability was not incorporated in the contract of bailment.

On the other hand, it is generally considered as against public policy for a bailee to enter into any agreement which contracts away his liability for his own negligence, and any such agreement is generally held to be invalid.

Bailees' Forms—While special situations arise in business which call for tailor-made forms, the majority of bailees can make use of one of several widely used insurance policies adapted to the particular needs of their business. Some examples of policies of this kind are the Dyers' and Cleaners' Form, Laundry Form, Furriers' Customers Custody Rider, Jewelers' Block Policy, Garment Contractors' Floater, Processors' Floater, Cold Storage Locker Floater, etc.

This chapter will discuss several of the more widely used Bailees' insurance forms. Many of the Bailees' insurance policies are known as Floaters because they cover property which moves from one location to another. Such policies come within the Inland Marine or all-risk branch of the insurance business, but they are not usually written on an all-risk basis, and insure only against perils specifically named in the policy.

BAILEES' CUSTOMERS FORM

THERE ARE SEVERAL FORMS of Bailees' Customers insurance designed for use by laundries, tailors, rug cleaners, upholsterers, and similar enterprises. While there are no standard forms, and no standardization of rates, the forms used by most companies follow a general pattern. Basically, the insurance may be written under one of two forms: Form A—All-Risk, and Form B—Named Perils.

A typical form of each type will be discussed in this section but it should be remembered that the coverage for any individual risk may be broadened or restricted.

BAILEES' CUSTOMERS FORM B
(Named Perils)

WHAT IS COVERED

The Bailees' Customers Form covers all lawful goods which are the property of others accepted by the Insured for cleaning, laundering, pressing, dyeing, repairing or alteration. The policy does not cover any property belonging to the Insured whether for his own use, or for sale.

Accrued Charges—In addition to coverage on the actual property of customers, the Insured is protected against the loss of unpaid charges for services, which he cannot collect because of the destruction of or damage to the property on which he has performed such services.

PROPERTY NOT COVERED

The Bailees' Customers Form does not cover goods held for storage or goods for which a storage charge is made. Goods held by the Insured without instructions from the owner to hold on storage are not considered as being held on storage.

Some companies will cover goods being held for storage by separate endorsement which sets forth specific limits of liability at each location where such property is being held.

WHERE COVERED

The Bailees' Customers Form covers goods while on the premises occupied by the Insured, or while at branch stores, or while in the custody of the Insured's collecting agents, or while being transported to and from customers, or between the Insured's premises and his branch stores or agents.

Some companies will also grant coverage for unnamed locations which the Insured may rent, own, or control. Such automatic coverage is usually allowed for 72 hours from the time the Insured acquires such new premises, after which time he must report them to the Company and have them specifically named in the policy.

Transit Coverage—As indicated earlier, the Bailees' Customers Form covers customers' goods while in transit. Such coverage is confined to the United States and Canada. The policy covers such goods whether being transported by the Insured or by a common carrier.

The policy does not cover any property shipped in the mails, unless so endorsed.

HAZARDS COVERED

The Bailees' Customers Form is not all-risk insurance, but insures only against specific perils named in the policy. When a customer's property is damaged or destroyed by a peril insured against, the Bailees' Customers Form pays for such loss, regardless of the bailee's liability. The policy differentiates between goods on the premises of the Insured, his agents or branch establishments, and while in the course of transit.

Hazards Covered While in Buildings—Customers' property while within a building is generally insured against the following perils:

1. Fire
2. Windstorm, and hail, cyclone, tornado

   The Windstorm provisions of the policy are broader than those of the Extended Coverage endorsement. In the Bailees' Customers Form, rain or snow driven by the wind will be covered, whether the wind has made a break in the walls or roof of the premises, or not.
3. Explosion

   All explosion is covered, whether of a steam boiler or otherwise.

4. Aircraft and objects falling therefrom
5. Motor vehicles except those owned or operated by or for the Insured or by or for any custodian of the property
6. Smoke when due to the unusual faulty operation of a stationary heating furnace, excluding, however smoke from industrial apparatus

   If the Insured is unable to identify his goods, the policy covers such loss, even though the goods are not destroyed or damaged, but such confusion is covered only if it arises as a result of a peril insured against.
7. Strikers, locked out workmen or persons taking part in labor disturbances. This coverage is not applicable to any claims for delay, deterioration, loss of market, etc.

   This clause may be cancelled by either party on five days' written notice.
8. Sprinkler Leakage
9. Earthquake
10. Flood, meaning rising of rivers and streams
11. Theft, including burglary and hold-up
12. Collision of the vehicle on which the property is being carried
13. Confusion of goods resulting from any of the above perils. If the Insured is unable to identify his goods, the policy covers such loss, even though the goods are not destroyed or damaged, but such confusion is covered only if it arises as a result of a peril insured against.

Hazards Covered While in Transit—Most Bailees' Customers policies stipulate that insured property will be carried on trucks of the closed body type equipped with suitable locks and that loss will be covered only while the property is within the closed vehicle and is stolen by forcibly breaking into the vehicle. There is coverage too if the entire vehicle is stolen.

If goods are left overnight on motor vehicles, the coverage applies only if such vehicles are locked in the Insured's private garage or in a building occupied by the Insured.

HAZARDS NOT COVERED

The Bailees' Customers Form contains certain basic exclusions found in all Floaters (see Chapter 17). In addition, the policy does not insure against the following perils:

The policy does not cover loss arising directly as a result of any dishonest act on the part of the Insured, any of his employees or of his bailees.

Unless specifically endorsed, the policy does not cover loss while the property is in the custody of any other bailee.

FOR HOW MUCH

The Bailees' Customers Form covers for the actual cash value of the property at the time of the loss. The policy also pays for any labor or service charges accrued.

The policy contains a maximum limit of liability above which the Company is not liable in any single loss. A separate limit of liability is established for the premises of the Insured as listed in the policy, for each of the branch stores or agencies listed, for any other location not named, and while in transit on any one vehicle. In addition, the policy contains a combined limit for any one casualty, regardless of how many locations are involved.

REQUIREMENTS IN CASE OF LOSS

Notice of Loss—The Insured is required to give immediate notice of any loss to the Company or its agent. In addition, the Insured agrees, in the case of theft, to notify the Police Department.

Proof of Loss—Proof of Loss must be filed within four months of the date of loss.

Sue and Labor Clause (see Chapter 17).

Adjustment of Loss with Insured or Customer—The Company may adjust the loss with and pay it to the Insured *or* to the customer or customers whose property sustained loss.

Insured's Privilege of Adjusting Losses—The Company specifically grants to the Insured the right to adjust any loss in which the aggregate amount of all claims does not exceed $100.

Right to Institute Legal Proceedings—The Insured agrees, after collecting a loss from the Company, to institute a suit, at the expense of the Company, against any other bailee, carrier of goods, or other party who may be liable for the loss.

OTHER PROVISIONS

Cancellation—The Insured or the Company may cancel the policy at any time, but *either* party must give fifteen days' notice to the other party of its intention to cancel. When the cancellation is effected at the Company's request, it is figured on a pro rata basis when, at the request of the Insured, the cancellation is short rate.

How Premium Is Determined—The rate for any individual risk is left entirely to the judgment of the underwriter. Except for very small risks, which are written for a flat premium, the Bailees' Customers Form is written on a reporting form basis. The initial premium collected when the policy is issued is merely a deposit premium. Each month, the Insured reports to the Company the monthly total of gross receipts, and pays the required premium based on the rate used in the policy.

Other Clauses—The Bailees' Customers Form is attached to a basic Inland Transportation policy which contains other clauses common to Inland Marine insurance (see Chapter 17).

Term of Policy—The policy attaches at 12 Noon, Standard Time, at the place the insurance is effected.

Except for smaller risks written on a flat premium for a one-year period, the Bailees' Customers policy is continuous, until cancelled. Policies of this kind, which bear no expiration date, are known as Open Forms.

BAILEES' CUSTOMERS FORM A
(All-Risk)

As indicated at the beginning of this section of Bailees' Customers policies, some companies issue the coverage on an all-risk basis.

A separate limit of liability is established to cover goods while on the premises of the Insured and a second limit applies to property in transit. This form is usually written with a Deductible clause.

Like all all-risk policies, there is no mention of specific perils. All risks of physical loss or damage are assumed, subject only to the stated exclusions.

The Bailees' Customers policy contains the exclusions that are common to all floaters (discussed in Chapter 17 under EXCLUSIONS COMMON TO ALL PERSONAL FLOATERS.) Additionally, the policy also excludes:

Property belonging to the named Insured or its affiliates

Goods held for storage (discussed above under BAILEES' CUSTOMERS POLICY—FORM B—PROPERTY NOT COVERED)

Damage sustained due to any process while actually being worked upon and resulting therefrom, except for loss by fire.

Loss while goods are in the custody of any other bailee.

Loss due to dishonesty of the Insured, his employees or of persons to whom the property is entrusted.

FURRIERS' CUSTOMERS POLICY

THE FURRIER WHO ACCEPTS furs for storage or repair is a bailee like the tailor, laundry, cleaner, and other bailee who insures under the Bailees' Customers policy. The furrier's business usually differs, however, in several respects from those of other bailees. First, a large portion of the furrier's business may consist of storing of customers' property. Secondly, the articles with which the furrier deals are of high value, and very susceptible to loss or damage, with the result that owners of furs expect very broad protection on their property.

A special form of insurance—the Furriers' Customers policy—is available to furrier-bailees to cover customers' goods in their custody. Like the Bailees' Customers policy, this insurance covers more than the furrier's liability to his customers for loss or damage to their property. It actually covers the property of the customers.

WHAT IS COVERED

The Furriers' Customers policy covers two types of property:

1. Furs and Articles Trimmed with Fur—Any customer's fur or article trimmed with fur may be covered under the policy, whether it is accepted by the Insured for storage or for being worked on (cleaning, repairing, remodeling, altering, glazing, etc.).

2. Garments Other Than Furs—The Furriers' Customers policy will also cover customers' garments which are not made of fur, but such property is insured if accepted for storage only. In other words, the policy does not cover clothing other than furs which are accepted by the Insured for processing. Such items require separate insurance under a Bailees' Customers policy.

Where an Insured operates a cleaning establishment and a storage plant, and accepts both furs and other wearing apparel for cleaning and storing, he will need both forms of insurance.

The policy covers only such customer's property for which the Insured has issued a written receipt.

The Furriers' Customers policy covers goods received by the Insured from customers and also any property which is under a contract of sale to the Insured's customers. This latter group would take in a fur coat sold by the Insured on a "layaway" plan where the purchaser agrees to leave the garment with the furrier until certain payments have been made.

Although the policy is sold primarily to furriers and fur storage concerns, it is also available to laundries, cleaners, banks and other bailees who accept furs for storage.

Accrued Charges for Storage or Service—If the property in the Insured's custody is damaged or destroyed, he may be unable to collect the unpaid charges for services performed by him or for the storage. Even when the Insured has collected such charges in advance, he may have to refund them to his customers. Such accrued charges can make up a substantial loss, if not insured. Different from the Bailees' Customers policy, the basic Furriers' Customers policy does not cover these charges, unless endorsed with an "Accrued Storage and Service Charges Endorsement."

Property Not Covered—Any property owned by the Insured, a subsidiary, or affiliate.

Where Covered—While on the premises described in the policy, and while in transit to or from the Insured's customers or to another location for storage, repairs or alterations. Such coverage is confined to the United States and Canada.

Hazards Covered—The Furriers' Customers policy is an all-risk policy. It is therefore considerably broader than the forms used for insuring other bailees, and will cover mysterious disappearance, water damage, dampness, chemical damage and any other peril not specifically excluded.

HAZARDS NOT COVERED

The basic exclusions found in all Floaters appear in the Furriers' Customers policy (see Chapter 17).

Damage Due to Process—Like other Floaters, the policy does not cover loss or damage caused by any work performed on the insured property. It will, however, pay for such damage if caused by fire or explosion, but not otherwise. Thus, if the Insured was cleaning a coat and the cleaning fluid damaged the coat, the policy would not cover; if the fluid was inflammable and the coat caught fire, the policy would cover.

Liability for Guarantee of Work to Be Done—The policy specifically excludes any liability which the Insured may assume when he guarantees the result of work he undertakes to do. Thus, if the Insured accepts a coat for dyeing, and guarantees the shade he will achieve, he may be held liable if he fails to achieve the promised result. The policy will not pay for such liability.

Dishonesty of Employees—While the policy will pay for loss caused by the dishonesty of the Insured's employees, it will apply only as excess over any insurance covering employee dishonesty.

Thus, assume a furrier carries a Blanket Position Bond which covers up to $5,000 loss caused by the dishonesty of any employee. His messenger absconds with a fur coat worth $7,500. The policy will pay $2,500, the excess of the loss over the policy covering employee dishonesty. If the coat was worth $4,000, the policy would pay nothing.

If, on the other hand, the furrier had no insurance covering employee dishonesty, the policy would pay the entire loss, subject to its limit of liability. (Contrast with the Bailees' Customers Form, which excludes any loss caused by dishonesty of the Insured's agents or employees, whether otherwise insured against or not.)

FOR HOW MUCH

Like the Bailees' Customers Form and the Fire insurance policy, the policy is not liable for more than the actual cash value of the property at the time of the loss, or the cost to repair or replace with like kind and quality, whichever is less. In addition, the Furriers' Customers policy contains another limitation of liability which is of the utmost importance.

As mentioned before, the Furriers' Customers policy does not cover any property unless the Insured has issued a written receipt for the item. The policy is not liable for more than the amount stipulated in the receipt issued by the Insured, regardless of the actual cash value of the property at the time of the loss.

The Insured is required to keep an accurate record of all the receipts he issues. The policy stipulates further that the customer accepts the receipt issued by the Insured as correct in all respects unless he notifies the Insured in writing within 10 days of any error.

Policy Limits—In addition to the limit per article, as stated in the receipt, the policy contains a maximum limit for each of the premises used for storage as listed in the policy, for locations not used for storage, for other unnamed premises, and for property in transit. In addition to these separate limits, the policy contains an aggregate limit for any one loss, regardless of how many locations are involved.

Excess Legal Liability—Generally, a furrier or other bailee who issues a receipt to a customer will not be liable for more than the amount stated in the receipt. The Furriers' Customer policy which provides coverage up to the amount stated in the receipt therefore affords the coverage required by the furrier.

There are situations, however, when the bailee may be held liable for *more* than the value stated in the receipt he has issued. Generally speaking, the limitation of liability will hold except when the bailee is guilty of gross negligence or willful wrongdoing, or any act which is tantamount to conversion.

Other related situations may also subject the bailee to liability in excess of the value stipulated in the receipt. Thus, a furrier may accept a fur coat for storage but fail to turn it over to the storage facilities because he wishes to show it as a sample to a prospective customer. If the coat is stolen, the owner may be able to prove that his property did not receive the protection it would have had in the storage facilities, and the furrier may be held liable for the full value of the stolen property.

The liability of an Insured in excess of the amount stated in the customer's receipt may be insured under an endorsement to the policy. This endorsement, called the Furriers' Customers Excess Legal Liability Endorsement, may be written for bailees who issue receipts to garment owners and for bailees who issue receipts to other bailees. The endorsement contains a limit per article, and a limit for all loss or damage sustained in any one casualty.

Certificates Issued to Customers—In all states except California, District of Columbia, Massachusetts, New York, Ohio and Virginia, provision is made for the policy to cover property even when not in the custody of the Insured. Permission is granted the Insured to issue certificates under his Furriers' Customers policy to cover furs wherever located. In effect, these certificates act as Fur Floaters for the owner of the property when the insured items are not in the furrier's custody. The customer pays an extra premium for such certificates, but this extra premium is lower than would be charged for a regular Fur Floater.

How Premium Is Determined—The premium for a Furriers' Customers policy is made up of the basic Fire insurance rate for the vault's contents of the risk, plus a loading charge which varies from ½¢ to 6¢ per month per $100 of insurance, depending on the construction of the vault, and the protective devices installed.

Like the Bailees' Customers Form, the Insured is required to report to the Company each month the values at risk. In the case of the Furriers' Customers policy, the Insured reports the total amount of values stated in all receipts outstanding on the last day of the previous month. The Company computes the premium by multiplying the amount of these values by the rate for the risk, and the Insured pays premium accordingly.

An exception is made for furriers carrying policies of less than $100,000 which do not provide for the issuance of certifications, certificates or special Fur policies through the fur storers. Such risks are not required to file reports monthly.

REQUIREMENTS IN CASE OF LOSS

Notice of Loss—The Insured is required to give immediate notice of loss to the Company.

Proof of Loss—The Insured is required to file Proof of Loss within 90 days of the date of the loss.

Sue and Labor—See Chapter 17.

Examination Under Oath—See Chapter 2.

When Loss Is Payable—See Chapter 18.

Term of Policy—The policy attaches at 12 Noon, Standard Time, at the place the insurance is effected. Like the Bailees' Customers Form, the Furriers' Customers policy is continuous until cancelled. Policies of this kind which bear no expiration date are known as Open Forms.

PROCESSORS' FLOATERS

COUNTLESS INDUSTRIES engaged in the manufacture of a product depend on outside plants and contractors for some service or operation on the product. Where the manufacturer turns his property over to another enterprise for processing or fabricating, he is entering into a bailor-bailee relationship.

The liability of such bailees is identical with that of any other bailee, and is limited only to loss caused by their negligence. However, business practice in many cases dictates that the bailee insure the property being entrusted to him against loss even when not due to his negligence. The processor, bleacher, sponger, shrinker, leather tanner, nickel plater, engraver, or other bailee requires insurance to cover customers' goods in much the same way as the laundry, tailor, furrier or other bailees who insure under Bailees' Customers Forms. Such insurance is afforded under a Processors' Floater.

The Processors' Floater is usually written on a specified perils basis and insures against fire, lightning, sprinkler leakage, windstorm, cyclone, tornado, riots, strikes, burglary and holdup. Like the Bailees' Customers Form, the policy covers the unpaid accrued charges for labor performed on the property which is rendered uncollectible by destruction of the goods.

COLD STORAGE LOCKER BAILEE FLOATER

THE GROWING USE of frozen foods has produced a new kind of bailee, who operates a cold storage locker in which he stores food belonging to others. A special Floater, the Cold Storage Locker Bailee Floater, is issued to such bailees to cover their customers' property.

The Cold Storage Locker Bailee Floater is written either on an all-risk basis, or to insure against specified perils. Generally, the latter policy covers against fire, lightning, windstorm and hail, explosion other than boiler explosion, riot, civil commotion, aircraft and vehicles, earthquake, collision of the conveyance on which the property is being carried, and theft. The policy also covers confusion of goods when due to a peril insured against, a provision identical with the one of the Bailees' Customers policy. The policy also covers spoilage of the stored food caused by the destruction of the refrigerating equipment.

The policy contains a limit of liability per locker and an aggregate limit for an entire casualty.

FOR FURTHER READING

ACKERMAN—Insurance

DAYNARD—Paths and Bypaths in Inland Marine Insurance

LAVINE—Manual on Commercial Law

MORTIMER—Adjusting Practices Inland Marine and Transportation Insurance

POLICY, FORM AND MANUAL ANALYSIS SERVICE

RODDA—Marine Insurance: Ocean and Inland

(See Reading List at End of Book)

CHAPTER 20

Owners' Commercial Floaters

IT IS FAIRLY STANDARD PRACTICE for bailees to carry some insurance on customers' property which is in their custody. In some industries, however, it is more usual for the *owner* of the property, the bailor, to insure his goods while it is in the hands of the bailee. A very popular form of insurance of this kind is that which shippers carry on goods they have turned over to transportation companies.

For some industries where work is regularly done at outside facilities, like the garment industry, special forms have been devised. In the jewelry business, one policy covers the Insured's directly-owned property, the property which he holds as bailee, and that which he entrusts to others. The Garment Contractors' Floater and the Jewelers' Block policy will be discussed in this chapter, as well as special forms used by installment sales firms to insure their property while it is in the hands of customers.

GARMENT CONTRACTORS' FLOATER

GARMENT MANUFACTURERS customarily send out an important part of their work to be done by outside contractors and subcontractors. Not only are specialized operations done by outsiders like pleaters, buttonhole makers, embroiderers and the like, but often the actual sewing and finishing of the garments are done at other plants. While the manufacturer sometimes requires the contractors to insure the goods, it is more usual for the manufacturer to buy the insurance. A special policy, called the Garment Contractors' Floater (although it is purchased by the manufacturer) is used to provide this coverage.

WHAT IS COVERED

The Garment Contractors' Floater covers garments, parts of garments, materials, supplies and containers for such property. Any such property is insured, whether manufactured or in the process of manufacture. The policy covers not only the property of the named Insured but any property held by him in trust or on commission, or on consignment, or on which he has made advances.

WHERE COVERED

The basic policy does not cover property on the premises of the Insured. Coverage is afforded only when away from the Insured's premises, within the United States and Canada.

The Garment Contractors' Floater, except when written on a Gross Sales basis, may be extended to cover on the Insured's premises.

The policy is made up of two sections:

1. On Premises of Contractors — The policy covers property which is temporarily held at the premises of contractors or subcontractors for work to be performed on it. Coverage would not apply if the property was at the contractor's premises for any other reason.

Thus, if the manufacturer had stored goods at a contractor's, there would be no coverage. The policy covers the property insured while on the premises of any contractor, even if not named in the policy. Coverage on such unnamed locations is limited to a percentage of the total amount of insurance.

The policy specifically excludes certain types of processors of textiles. Throwsters or other yarn processors, weavers, finishers or other cloth finishing works, printers, dyers, spongers, shrinkers, tanners or testing houses are not deemed to be contractors for purposes of this insurance. Such operators may be insured under a Processors' Floater.

2. Transit Coverage—Also covered is the Insured's property while in transit between his premises and his contractors and subcontractors and mills and suppliers. The policy specifies the various types of transportation which are covered, as set forth below. Covered is all property while in due course of transit in the custody of:

1. Railroad or railway express company
2. Public or private truckmen, land transfer or other land transportation carriers
3. Air transportation carriers
4. On trucks owned or operated for the Insured or his contractors
5. Messengers.

A separate limit of liability may be set up for each of the different methods of transportation.

Like the Bailees' Customers Form and the Furriers' Customers policy, there is no coverage on property shipped through the mails.

HAZARDS COVERED

As mentioned above, the Garment Contractors' Floater is made up of two sections—while in course of transit, and while on premises of contractors. The coverage under each of these sections differs considerably.

In transit, the property is covered against all risks; while on the premises of contractors, the coverage is on a specified perils basis.

The policy may be extended to cover on an all-risk basis on the premises as well as in transit, and this form of coverage is discussed separately below under GARMENT CONTRACTORS ALL-RISK FLOATER.

Hazards Covered in Transit—While property is in transit between the Insured's premises and those of his contractors or suppliers, it is covered against all risks of loss or damage from any external cause, except those specifically excluded.

Hazards Covered on Premises of Contractors—While on the premises of contractors or subcontractors, the property is covered against seven types of perils. These are basic to the policy. In addition, coverage may be provided for four more types of perils, which are known as Optional Additional coverages. The basic policy covers:

1. Fire and lightning. (The perils insured under a Fire insurance policy.)

2. Windstorm, hail, smoke, vehicles and aircraft. (These are some of the perils of the Extended Coverage Endorsement, but note there is no coverage for explosion, riot, civil commotion.)

3. Sprinkler leakage. (The coverage is very similar to that provided by a Sprinkler Leakage policy.)

4. Water damage. (The policy covers any physical contact with water, and is therefore considerably broader than a Water Damage policy.)

At the opening of this section on the Garment Contractors' Floater, it was pointed out that the basic policy does not cover loss on the Insured's premises, except where the policy is specifically extended to bring in such premises. When a Garment Contractors' Floater is extended to cover on the Insured's premises, the coverage on Water Damage *on the Insured's premises only* is more limited than for damage on the premises of contractors. Other than on the Insured's own premises, the policy covers any loss to property caused by its actual contact with water. On the Insured's own premises, the following exclusion becomes applicable: There is no coverage for loss contributed to or aggravated by flood, surface water, waves, tidal water or tidal wave, overflow of streams or other bodies of water, or spray from any of the foregoing, all whether driven by wind or not; water which backs up through sewers or drains; water below the surface of the ground including that which exerts pressure on or flows, seeps or leaks through sidewalks, driveways, foundations, walls, basement or other floors or through doors, windows, or any other openings in such sidewalks, driveways, foundations, wall or floors UNLESS loss by fire or explosion ensues, and the Company shall then be liable only for such ensuing loss. This exclusion does NOT however apply to property in course of transit or loss arising from theft.

5. Burglary, meaning felonious entry into the premises by force and violence when the premises are not open for business, and of which force and violence visible marks are left.

If thieves entered the premises through a window, door or transom which had been left open, or by use of a pass-key, there would be no coverage. Similarly, there is no coverage for theft during the time the premises are open, nor for mysterious disappearance, pilferage, etc.

6. Holdup, which means the forcible taking of property by violence, or other felonious act committed in the presence of a custodian of the property. Thus, if a criminal in the presence of an employee were to snatch a suit or bolt of cloth, the policy would cover. On the other hand, if the theft were committed furtively without the custodian becoming aware of the act, the loss would not be covered.

7. Boiler explosion, originating within steam boilers, pipes, fly wheels, engines and machinery connected therewith. No other type of explosion is covered. Note that this is the direct opposite of the explosion coverage granted by the Extended Coverage Endorsement.

Optional Additional Coverages—Four additional coverages may be covered under the policy at the option of the Insured. The policy provides space for inserting the word "covered" alongside any of these perils, and no coverage is effective unless the word is inserted, and the additional premium for the peril paid. The Optional Additional coverages are:

1. Theft. When this coverage is added to the policy, it will take in the type of otherwise excluded losses outlined above under No. 5.

2. Strikes, riots, malicious mischief and explosion. The coverage on explosion excludes the explosion of steam vessels, and is similar on this score to the Extended Coverage Endorsement. Note, however, that the basic policy covers steam boiler explosions.

3. Consequential damage to garments. This coverage is similar

to that provided by a Consequential Loss and Damage Assumption Clause—Clothing Policies discussed in Chapter 7.

4. Consequential damage to garments, including broken lots, size or color ranges. This coverage *includes* the coverage granted under No. 3 above. In addition to covering parts of garments depreciated by loss to related parts from an insured peril, the Insured is also protected, if as a result of insured loss or damage, he is unable to make up a full lot or range of sizes or colors, provided he customarily sells his garments in lots or ranges of sizes or colors. It should be noted, however, that this coverage does not extend to complete undamaged garments located elsewhere than at the location where the physical loss or damage occurs.

The Insured agrees to make a bona fide effort to replace the lost or damaged property, and no claim is payable until 21 days after the loss.

When coverage under either of the two Consequential Damage clauses is purchased, consequential losses are insured when caused by any of the perils of the Garment Contractors' Floater, including any optional additional coverages which may have been added to the policy.

HAZARDS NOT COVERED

The Garment Contractors' Floater contains the exclusions common to all Floaters (see Chapter 17). The policy also excludes:

1. Delay or loss of market. Thus, while the Insured would be covered for a direct damage to his goods in transit, he would not be covered for a delay in making delivery.
2. Chafing, rubbing.
3. Dishonest acts of employees.

Note: The policy does not cover either infidelity of the Insured's employees, *or* of contractors or their employees.

GARMENT CONTRACTORS' ALL-RISK FLOATER

As was pointed out, the basic Garment Contractors' Floater provides coverage on property while on premises, only against certain specified perils. In the states enumerated above, it is possible to extend the policy cover on an *all-risk* basis. When so endorsed, the entire sections of the policy which spell out the coverages provided and the exclusions which are incorporated are deleted (as discussed directly above under HAZARDS COVERED and HAZARDS NOT COVERED). In their place, the policy insures against all risk of direct physical loss of or damage to the property covered subject to the exclusions of the basic policy and the following:

Sabotage, theft, conversion or other act or omission of a dishonest character by the Insured or his employees or by any person to whom the insured property is delivered or entrusted to for any purpose. An exception is made for loss which occurs while the property is deposited for safe custody or while in the custody of a carrier for hire or a porter not on the Insured's payroll.

Delay, loss of market, gradual deterioration, chafing, rubbing, insects, vermin and inherent vice.

Loss resulting from the property being worked upon except if fire or explosion ensues, and then the Company is liable only for loss due to the fire or explosion.

Mysterious disappearance or unexplained loss or shortage disclosed on taking inventory.

Hostile or warlike action in time of peace or war, any weapon of war employing atomic fission or radioactive force, insurrection, rebellion, revolution, civil war.

Seizure or destruction under quarantine or Customs regulation, confiscation by order of any government or public authority, contraband or illegal trade.

Nuclear reaction or nuclear radiation or radioactive contamination except that direct loss by fire resulting from nuclear reaction is covered.

FOR HOW MUCH

The Garment Contractors' Floater is liable for loss or damage up to the actual cash value of the property at the time of the loss, but for not more than the cost to replace the property. The value of the labor performed is considered in arriving at the value of the damaged article.

The policy may be endorsed to cover the price at which the goods would have been sold instead of the actual cash value. (See Chapter 7—Selling Price Clauses.)

Coinsurance Clause—The Garment Contractors' Floater is written with a 100% Coinsurance clause. The Insured is required to carry insurance equal to the total value of his goods on the premises of *all* his contractors. If he fails to maintain such insurance to value, he will be coinsured, and will have to bear a portion of any loss himself.

Liability of Unnamed Contractors—As mentioned before, the policy covers property while on the premises of any contractors or sub-contractors. A maximum limit of liability is inserted alongside each of the contractors named in the policy. In addition, the policy provides coverage for the premises of contractors not named in the policy. A limit of liability is inserted to apply to any such unnamed location, but this limit of liability may not exceed 25% of the total amount of insurance carried, or $25,000, whichever is less.

The Insured need not, therefore, specify any contractor to whom he has entrusted his goods, if the value of such goods does not exceed 25% of the amount of insurance and is not over $25,000. If the values at any contractor's premises go above this 25% figure, or over $25,000, he must specify the particular contractor and set the limit of liability high enough to cover the property. Thus, assume a clothing manufacturer sends his garments to be processed at four contractors, where the values are as follows:

Contractor A—$15,000
Contractor B—$30,000
Contractor C—$20,000
Contractor D—$15,000

To comply with the Coinsurance clause, he carries $80,000 of insurance—100% of the values at *all* contractors. The limit of liability for unnamed contractors is set in the policy as $20,000—25% of the amount of insurance, the maximum permitted. Contractors A, C and D do not have to be named in the policy, since the limit for unnamed contractors is high enough to cover the total values of the manufacturer at these premises. Contractor B, however, must be specifically named in the policy, and the limit of liability for this location established at not less than $30,000.

It is important to understand that the Coinsurance clause requires that the Insured carry 100% of the values he has at risk at *all* contractors, whether named or unnamed.

Reporting Form—The Garment Contractors' Floater may be written for a flat annual premium, or on a Reporting Form based on gross sales. The rate for the Reporting Form is arrived at by calculating the flat annual premium by the Insured's gross sales for the 12 months immediately preceding the application for the policy. The policy may be set up on a monthly, quarterly or semi-annual reporting basis, and the Insured is required to report the total amount of gross sales for the particular reporting period established in his policy by the 30th day of the succeeding period. The Coinsurance clause does not apply to policies written on a gross sales Reporting basis. The Reporting Form policy is subject to a deposit premium against which the premium earned for each reporting period is applied. When the deposit premium has been fully earned, the Insured pays an additional premium at the rate named, for each successive period.

It is important to note that the Insured is required to give an accurate record of all property on the basis of the Valuation clause of the policy—actual cost plus labor, since losses will be settled on this basis.

The Reporting Form is subject to a minimum premium of $500.

OTHER PROVISIONS

Other Insurance—If there is in force at the time of the loss any other insurance, whether in the name of the Insured or of any contractor, the Garment Contractors' Floater is liable only as excess insurance, and will pay only the excess of any loss over the amount of such other insurance.

The manufacturer may carry Garment Contractors' Insurance in more than one Company, but such other insurance of this kind must be noted on the policy.

Requirements in Case of Loss—The Insured is required to use all reasonable means to save and preserve the property at the time of and after any loss. The policy does not cover any loss caused by the Insured's neglect in this respect.

Released Bills of Lading or Shipping Receipts — The Garment Contractors' Floater insures goods while in transit. Like other forms of Transit insurance (to be discussed in the next chapter), the policy does not cover if the Insured accepts a receipt from a shipper which limits the carrier's liability to less than the full value of the goods shipped. The Garment Contractors' Floater grants permission specifically to the Insured to accept such limited receipts, provided that certain minimum valuations are declared.

Term of Policy—The policy attaches at 12 Noon, Standard Time, at the place where the insurance is effected. The policy may not be written for more than one year.

Other Clauses—

Benefit of Insurance—Discussed in Chapter 17.
Cancellation—Discussed in Chapter 2.
Examination Under Oath—Discussed in Chapter 18.
Fraud, Concealment—Discussed in Chapter 2.
Notice of Loss, Proof of Loss—Discussed in Chapter 17.
Right to Institute Legal Proceedings—Discussed in Chapter 19.
When Loss Is Payable—Discussed in Chapter 18.
When Suit Must Be Brought—Discussed in Chapter 17.

How Premium Is Determined—The garment manufacturer is required to submit an application in which he sets forth the approximate values he estimates will be a risk during the next 12 months at various contractors. A rate is then promulgated, based on the data submitted. This rate remains in effect for one year. When the policy comes up for renewal, the Insured again submits a breakdown of the different locations he plans to use. If there has been a material change in the locations at which property will be covered, the rate may be changed.

While the application submitted enumerates the contractors which the manufacturer expects to use, he is not held to these locations, and may, subject to the limit for unnamed locations, ship goods to any other contractor.

JEWELERS' BLOCK POLICY

THE JEWELER'S BUSINESS differs in several respects from most other businesses. The property he deals in is usually small in size but of great value, and therefore peculiarly susceptible to loss. In addition, the average jeweler is engaged in several types of activity. For one thing, he usually conducts a mercantile business, selling at retail. In this connection, he may also have one or more outside salesmen who travel for him. He will usually accept jewelry and watches from private persons for repair, renovating or remodeling. In addition, he will often have in his possession property belonging to other dealers for which he may be held liable as a bailee. He may also give out property on consignment to dealers or private persons.

There is available to jewelers a special form of insurance which covers all the various types of property at risk against almost every type of loss or damage. The Jewelers' Block policy is one of the broadest forms of insurance in the Inland Marine field, and has several features which are unique to the policy.

In the one policy are incorporated basic insurance on the Insured's own stock both on and off the premises, Transportation insurance, insurance on the Insured's liability as a bailee, and insurance on customers' goods.

WHAT IS COVERED

The Jewelers' Block policy covers all jewelry, watches, precious and semi-precious stones, precious metals and alloys and other such stock which is usual to the Insured's business.

This property may be owned by the Insured, or by others who entrust their property to the Insured, or by other dealers from whom the Insured receives such property.

The property is insured on the Insured's premises, or in the hands of other dealers, salesmen, or customers, or when deposited for safekeeping, or in the course of transit.

Damage to Premises By Theft—If the Insured owns the building or is legally liable for damage to it, the policy covers damage by theft to the premises. This extension of coverage is limited to 10% of the amount of insurance applicable to the premises, and does not increase the amount of insurance under the policy. This coverage does not apply to glass, or ornamentation or lettering on such glass.

Coverage on Money—The policy may be endorsed for an additional premium to cover money when stolen by breaking into a safe or vault.

Patterns, Molds, Models, Dies—As indicated above, the basic policy covers specifically enumerated types of property. It may be extended to cover by endorsement patterns, molds, models and dies used in the Insured's business against the perils covered in the basic contract, or specifically only against the following:

Fire, lightning

Perils of the Extended Coverage Endorsement

Vandalism and malicious mischief

Earthquake, flood

Sprinkler leakage.

ARIZONA, CALIFORNIA, IDAHO, MONTANA, NEVADA, OREGON, UTAH, WASHINGTON, HAWAII—When the policy is endorsed to cover earthquake, this coverage is subject to a Deductible of 5% of the amount of insurance applicable.

TEXAS—Coverage may be provided only against sprinkler leakage and flood.

Furniture, Fixtures, Machinery, Tools and Fittings—The Jewelers' Block policy may be extended by endorsement to cover furniture, fixtures, tools, machinery and fittings against the perils insured in the basic policy. Such property is insured only while on premises described in the policy.

Tenant's Improvements and Betterments—If an Insured who is *not* the building owner has made improvements and betterments to the property he rents, he may cover them against the perils assumed in the basic policy.

PROPERTY NOT COVERED

The policy does not cover goods sold on the installment plan after it leaves the Insured's custody.

It does not cover property while worn by the Insured, members of his family, firm, or employees, servants, messengers or other persons in the jewelry business, including their families, firm members, employees, servants and messengers.

HAZARDS COVERED

The Jewelers' Block policy is an all-risk form. It does permit the Insured to exclude the perils of Fire and Lightning and receive a reduction in premium.

HAZARDS NOT COVERED

As pointed out under HAZARDS COVERED, the Jewelers' Block policy is an all-risk policy (or may be written to exclude the perils of Fire and Lightning). All loss or damage is covered except for perils specifically excluded. Like all all-risk policies, the contract spells out several exclusions, dictated by the special nature of the property insured.

1. Dishonesty of Insured or Employees—There is no coverage for loss caused by dishonesty of the Insured or any of his employees or any person to whom the property is entrusted.

The policy will pay, however, for loss caused by dishonesty when the property is in the custody of the U. S. mails or any carrier which is covered under the policy. It will also cover loss by dishonesty when the property has been deposited for safe-keeping, or loss caused by a porter or other person helping the Insured or an employee of the Insured.

2. Loss Caused by Delay, Loss of Market, Defective Packing.

3. Corrosion, Dampness, Etc.—The policy does not cover loss due to corrosion, rust, dampness of the atmosphere, freezing or extremes of temperature.

4. Damage Due to Process—This exclusion will apply whether the damage is sustained during the Insured's work on the property or during work done by others to whom the Insured has entrusted the property.

This exclusion takes in all damage, and is more restrictive than the exclusion in the Furriers' Customers or Bailees' Customers Form.

5. Earthquake and Flood Exclusion—Loss or damage caused to the property when on the Insured's premises by earthquake or flood is not covered, except for an additional premium.

ARIZONA, CALIFORNIA, IDAHO, MONTANA, UTAH, NEVADA, OREGON, WASHINGTON, HAWAII—Coverage on earthquake is subject to a Deductible of 5% of the amount of insurance applying to this peril.

6. Breakage of Fragile Articles—The policy does not cover the breakage of articles of a brittle or fragile nature unless caused by one of the following perils:

Fire and lightning
Windstorm, explosion, riot, civil commotion, aircraft, vehicles
Persons taking part in labor disturbances
Flood, earthquake
Burglary or theft
Accident to a conveyance on which the property is being carried.

Breakage caused by one of the above perils is covered only if the peril is insured in the policy. Thus, if the policy has been endorsed to cover earthquake on the Insured's premises, breakage caused by earthquake will be covered. If the Earthquake Endorsement has not been added to the policy, breakage of fragile articles on the Insured's premises will not be covered, but breakage of an article in transit due to earthquake will be covered, since the basic policy excludes earthquake losses only when sustained on the premises.

7. Inventory Shortage or Unexplained Loss—C.O.D. Shipments—The policy does not cover any mysterious disappearance or unexplained loss. Nor does it cover any shortage which may be claimed by a person who receives a package in good order with the seals unbroken. Furthermore, if a package is sent C. O. D. with the right of the addressee to inspect the package before delivery, the policy does not cover.

NOTE: This clause would not exclude losses caused by sneak thieves, or any disappearance of property. The Insured is required, however, to show some evidence of theft.

Exclusion of Fire Losses—As was pointed out above, the Jewelers' Block policy may be specifically endorsed to exclude the perils of Fire and Lightning at any of the premises designated in the policy. In this way, an Insured who carries specific Fire insurance may continue his Fire insurance policy and avoid duplication of coverage.

Similarly, if the Insured wishes to rely on the Fire insurance policy of dealers or others to whom he entrusts his property, he may exclude from his Jewelers' Block policy the perils of fire and lightning at those premises. A reduction in rate is allowed when these perils are excluded from the policy.

WHERE COVERED

The general coverage of the policy takes in the states of the United States, the District of Columbia, Puerto Rico and Canada.

The property is covered while in transit or on the Insured's premises or on other premises, subject to certain special exclusions and limitations:

In Transit Coverage—Damage to property in course of shipment is covered only under the conditions set forth below. It is important to be clear on the fact that any other types of carriage or shipment are *not* covered. Separate limits are designated in the policy for each specific type of transit which is covered.

In the Mails—Coverage is afforded only for shipments by first class registered mail.

Express Shipments—The provisions of the section covering shipments via express are fairly involved, and the reader is referred to the actual policy conditions for a detailed analysis of this coverage. Briefly, the Jewelers' Block policy affords coverage only for railway express shipments, including air express, but any package worth $1,000 or more must be sealed with wax or lead. Furthermore, all express shipments must be declared to the express company at not less than 25% of their value.

In other words, if the Insured ships via railway express a package worth less than $1,000, no special requirements are imposed on him.

Railroad, Water or Air Carriers—Coverage is afforded only for shipments of this kind through the carrier's regular passenger transportation or baggage service.

Motor Carriers or Truckmen—These types of carriage are covered only if they operate *exclusively* as a customer parcel delivery service; or if armored car service; or if a parcel transportation or baggage service of passenger bus lines.

Unattended Vehicle Exclusion—There is no coverage under the policy for loss of property while in or upon an automobile, motorcycle or any other vehicle, unless there is in or upon the vehicle at the time of the loss an employee of the Insured or other person whose sole duty is to guard the vehicle.

NOTE: Theft from an automobile left in a parking lot which was attended at all times has been held to be excluded, as the attendant was not engaged solely in attending the vehicle and was not in the vehicle at the time of the loss.

Property in Show Cases of Insured—The basic policy does not cover loss of property from the show windows of the Insured's premises when caused by thieves who have smashed or cut such windows.

This coverage may be provided under a Show Window Display Endorsement, for which an additional premium is charged. The Endorsement establishes separate limits for any one window and for all windows, when the premises are open for business, and separate limits when the premises are closed.

Property in Show Cases of Other Premises — Unless endorsed specifically, the policy does not cover *any* loss or damage to property exhibited by the Insured in show cases other than at his premises, regardless of how caused. If exhibited by others (as by one of the Insured's dealers) the policy would provide coverage.

Property on Exhibition—There is no coverage for loss sustained at any exhibition promoted or financially assisted by any public authority or trade association. The exclusion does not apply to any private exhibition or showing.

The premises of exhibitions promoted by a public authority or trade association may be insured by endorsement.

FOR HOW MUCH

The Company is not liable for more than the actual cash value of the property at the time of any loss, nor for more than the cost to repair or replace lost or damaged property.

In addition, liability for any loss does not exceed the lowest figure placed on such property in any of the Insured's stock inventories, stock books, stock papers, or lists.

There is no Coinsurance clause in the policy. However, since the policy is issued only to persons who complete a fairly comprehensive application which sets forth the exact amount of the Insured's inventories, the premium is based on the total values at risk at the time the policy is issued. If, however, the Insured's stock increases after the policy is issued, he is fully covered up to the limit of liability stated in the policy.

Various Limits in Policy—One limit of liability applies to property at the Insured's premises. A separate amount of insurance applies to property shipped in the mails, by railway express, deposited in a safe deposit company or bank, or left for safe-keeping with other dealers. A third limit is applicable to any shipment by registered first class mail to any one addressee on any one day. A fourth limit is established for shipments by customer parcel delivery service and other transportation service of railroads, water or air carriers and passenger bus lines. A fifth limit may be inserted to apply to property elsewhere than listed above or otherwise excluded.

Liability for Pledged Articles—On pledged articles (on which the

Insured has made advances), the Company's liability is limited to the amount of the unpaid balance plus interest due.

Other Insurance—The Jewelers' Block policy is liable only as excess insurance when there is any other insurance on the property.

Deductible Clause—A Deductible clause is available to the Insured, and a reduction in rate is offered for the use of such clause. The insured has a choice of amounts for the deductible: $500, $1,000, $2,500, and $5,000.

INSURED'S DUTIES AND OBLIGATIONS

Application for Insurance—The Insured is required to submit a fairly comprehensive application in which he sets forth the exact amount of his inventories during the past 12 months, broken down as to the various types of stock carried, the proportion of stock that will be kept in safes, the names of all salesmen and the amount of jewelry each carries, the names and addresses of all persons who have more than $5,000 of property in their possession, etc.

The application also gives a complete history of all losses suffered by the Insured within the five years preceding the date of the application, the type of records kept by the Insured, and a detailed description of all safes, vaults and other protective devices maintained.

The application must be signed by the Insured, and becomes part of the policy. All statements contained in the applications are in the nature of warranties.

Records—The Insured is required to maintain a detailed record of his inventory and a separate listing of all travelers' stocks.

Protective Devices — The Insured is required to maintain any watchman service or other protective devices which he describes in his application.

REQUIREMENTS IN CASE OF LOSS

Cooperation—A high degree of cooperation is expected from the Insured after a loss, and he must, as far as is within his power, cause all other persons interested in the property and members of their household and employees to submit to examination under oath. The Insured must also submit to examination under oath and must produce all books of account, bills, invoices and other vouchers which will help in proving the loss.

Sue and Labor Clause—See Chapter 17.

Adjustment of Loss with Others—In case of loss involving property of others held by the Insured, the Company may adjust the loss with the Insured or directly with the owner of the property.

Notice of Loss—Proof of Loss—The Insured must give immediate notice of anything likely to result in a claim under the policy to the Company or its agent. Proof of Loss must be filed within 60 days of the loss.

When Suit Must Be Brought—See Chapter 17.

Subrogation—Loan Receipt—Like almost every form of insurance, the Jewelers' Block policy contains a Subrogation clause under which the Insured agrees to turn over to the Company any right of action he may have against a third party for any loss which he has collected from the Company.

The Subrogation clause incorporated in the Jewelers' Block policy also stipulates that the Insured will, if requested by the Company, execute and deliver a customary form of loan receipt, upon receiving payment of a loss.

This method of adjusting losses is widely used in Inland Marine insurance. When the Company is presented with a loss by the Insured which it believes it may be able to recoup from a third party, it does not actually pay the loss, but merely advances the money to the Insured as a loan, for which the Insured furnishes a loan receipt.

When this is done, the Company is not subrogated to the Insured's rights against the third party, since it has not *paid* the loss. The Insured receives the money from the Company as a loan which is repayable to the extent that he collects from third parties, and he must proceed in his own name against such parties.

When Loss Is Payable—The Company must pay any loss within 60 days after satisfactory Proof of Loss is received. The No Abandonment Clause is included in this provision.

OTHER CLAUSES

Benefit of Insurance—See Chapter 17.

Cancellation—See Chapter 2.

Automatic Reinstatement of Losses—The Jewelers' Block policy is reduced by the amount of any loss. Any rewards paid for the recovery of the property are to be included in the amount of the loss. Provision is made for the automatic reinstatement of any losses, but the Insured becomes liable for the pro rata premium covering any reinstated amount of insurance.

Term of Policy—The Jewelers' Block policy is written only for one year. The Insured is required to submit a new application for the policy each year, and the premium is adjusted accordingly. The policy attaches at Noon, Standard Time, at the place the policy is issued.

INSTALLMENT SALES FORM

(Deferred Payment Merchandise Policy)

FIRMS THAT SELL MERCHANDISE on installments retain a financial interest in the property until it is fully paid off, usually under a conditional sales contract, and title to the goods remains in the hands of the seller until the merchandise is fully paid for. The customer is therefore not a bailee, but the merchant is in the position of other bailors in that he has relinquished physical custody over property. While he does not, like a bailor, expect the return of his property, he relies on his right to repossess to safeguard his money. If the property is damaged or destroyed, he may suffer a financial loss.

A special form of Inland Marine insurance is used to protect those who sell goods on deferred payments. The policy describes the type of goods principally sold by the Insured and covers all such property in which the Insured has a financial interest through a lease or an installment sales plan.

The policy contains a maximum liability on property sold to any one customer, and another limit of liability for all losses in any single casualty.

The policy insures against specified perils. The usual perils covered are fire and lightning, the collision, derailment or overturn of vehicles, collapse of bridges, marine perils while on ferries, and may be extended to cover windstorm, explosion, riot, civil commotion, damage by vehicles and aircraft, and smoke. Theft is sometimes added to the coverage afforded during transit and, in some cases, burglary of the Insured's premises.

The policy covers from the time the property is sold, and includes the period when the property is still in the seller's hands prior to delivery, during transit to the purchaser's premises, and while in the purchaser's physical custody until fully paid off.

Three forms of Installment Sales insurance are available:

1. Single Interest Form—Covers the interest which the Insured has in the property; namely, the unpaid balance only.

2. Dual Interest Form—Covers the interest of both the seller and the purchaser. In the event of loss, the Insured is paid by the Company to the extent of the unpaid balance, and the purchaser's loan is fully paid off.

3. The third form is a single interest form like the one described

above. The purchaser receives no benefit under the policy. The Company pays the seller the amount of his unpaid balance, but the Insured must continue his efforts to collect from the purchaser, and the Company is entitled to any payments received by the seller. Its liability is therefore limited to such amounts as the Insured is unable to collect.

The policy generally contains three limits: On any one article, on any casualty, and on any one purchaser's premises.

The policy is written on the Open Form, and is continuous until cancelled by the Company or the Insured. Cancellation notice of 15 days is required from either party. Like the Furriers' Customers policy, the premium is based on the monthly reports filed by the Insured.

FLOOR PLAN MERCHANDISE

MANY DEALERS, especially in the automobile and household appliance business, obtain their merchandise under a "floor plan." The dealer borrows money from a lending institution and secures the loan by encumbering the merchandise he purchases. While this transaction is not an installment sale, the Inland Marine insurance field has been extended in almost every state and territory of the country to provide coverage on such property.

Floor Plan Merchandise insurance may cover only property which is specifically identifiable, and not a general stock of merchandise.

The coverage is written on an all-risk basis, subject only to the exclusions set forth in the policy.

Like the Installment Sales Floater, the Floor Plan Merchandise policy may be written to cover the interest of the dealer alone, or the interest of both the dealer and the lending institution, or to cover only the lending institution's interest.

INSTALLATION FLOATER

CERTAIN EQUIPMENT is sold with the understanding that the seller will install the property before its acceptance by the buyer. The installation may be fairly involved and may take days or even weeks to complete. Typical installations of this kind are those of large presses, elevators, air conditioning or sound proofing, generators, power lines, etc.

During the installation, the property is still at the risk of the seller, since the purchaser does not take over the property until it is fully installed. The regular Fire and Theft insurance policies of the owner of the property will not cover once this property is removed from his plant or warehouse.

The Installation Floater is designed to cover during installation until the job is completed and the purchaser accepts the property.

IMPLEMENT DEALERS' FLOATER

FARM EQUIPMENT AND MACHINERY dealers make it a practice to demonstrate their equipment on the premises of a prospective purchaser, and often to leave the equipment for a trial period. The policies covering the dealer's property on his premises will not apply to such loss. The Implement Dealers' Floater is made available to cover such property as a dealer has away from his premises.

SALESMEN'S FLOATER

SAMPLES CARRIED by salesmen may present a great exposure to loss. Such property may be insured under a Salesmen's Floater, which covers the samples while en route to the Insured's salesmen, and while in the hands of the salesmen anywhere within the continental limits of the United States and Canada.

The policy does not cover the merchandise while it is on the premises of the Insured, whether at his factory, or offices, or showrooms. Such coverage may be provided by endorsement for an additional premium.

The policy is available on an all-risk basis or on a specified perils basis. Coverage is usually granted on a specified perils basis against the risks of:

Fire and lightning
Windstorm, cyclone, tornado, explosion
Earthquake, flood
Collision or overturn of conveyances on which the merchandise is being carried
Theft of an entire trunk or shipping package but only while checked in a hotel
Sinking, stranding, fire or collision while being carried on a ferry including General Average or Salvage Charges (discussed in Chapter 22).

Some companies will include theft from an automobile, but will almost always limit the coverage to such loss from attended automobiles, or to unattended automobiles of a closed body type when securely locked.

The policy contains a limit per salesman, a second limit for property in transit, and a limit for all loss in any single casualty.

CONTRACTORS' EQUIPMENT FLOATER FORM

THE CONTRACTORS' EQUIPMENT FLOATER is designed for contractors who use heavy equipment of all kinds — road builders, mining contractors, bridge and tunnel builders, etc. It is used to insure bulldozers, tractors, power-driven shovels, concrete mixers, pile drivers, portable tool houses, scaffolding and similar equipment.

Each article to be insured is scheduled in the policy, with a value alongside, exactly as under personal Floaters like Jewelry-Fur, Camera, Musical Instrument, etc. Blanket insurance may be provided to cover small items, but the Blanket portion of the policy is subject to 100% Coinsurance. The policy is not used to cover automobiles and trucks.

The policy is written on a specified perils basis. Generally, the following perils are assumed under the basic policy:

Fire and lightning

Windstorm, cyclone, tornado, hail and explosion other than of a steam boiler

Collision, derailment or overturn of land conveyances on which the property is being carried (This does not cover collision of the equipment itself.)

Collapse of bridges

Sinking, stranding, fire or collision of any ferry, including General Average and Salvage Charges (Chapter 22).

The following perils may be added for an additional premium:

Riot, civil commotion, and strikes

Theft (written with a $25 Deductible)

Collision of the equipment itself.

In addition to the exclusions common to other Floaters, the Contractors' Equipment Floater specifically excludes loss or damage occasioned by the lifting of any weight which exceeds the registered lifting capacity of the machine.

FARM EQUIPMENT FLOATER

MODERN FARMING techniques call for the use of heavy machinery. A special Floater is used to cover such equipment. The Farm Equipment Floater parallels the Contractors' Equipment Floater above.

OTHER COMMERCIAL FLOATERS

IN ADDITION to the commercial Floaters and special policies which have been analyzed or commented on in this and the preceding chapter, there are many other similar forms designed for other specialized business operations. Some examples of such special forms are Floaters covering the following varied types of property:

OWNERS' COMMERCIAL FLOATERS

Coin-operated machines, cotton, equipment dealers, films, dealers in furs, morticians' equipment, musical instrument dealers, physicians', surgeons' and scientific instruments, signs, theatrical property, wool, etc.

FOR FURTHER READING

ACKERMAN—Insurance
DAYNARD—Paths and Bypaths In Inland Marine Insurance
HEDGES—Practical Fire and Casualty Insurance
HUEBNER AND BLACK—Property Insurance
MEHR AND CAMMACK—Principles of Insurance
MORTIMER—Adjusting Practices, Inland Marine and Transportation Insurance
RIEGEL, ROBERT AND MILLER—Insurance
RODDA— Marine Insurance: Ocean and Inland

(See Reading List at End of Book)

CHAPTER 21

Transportation Insurance

THE BASIC FORM OF INLAND MARINE insurance is the Transportation Form, out of which were developed most of the policies now classed as Inland Marine insurance. Transportation policies are used to insure an owner of goods for loss or damage to the goods he ships via rail, Railway Express, public truckmen, air freight, or on his own trucks, as well as the carrier for his liability to the shipper for such losses.

The transportation industry is one of the largest in the country, and Transportation insurance makes up a very important part of the Inland Marine insurance business. For the insurance man who may be called on to arrange insurance for a shipper, or a receiver of goods, or for the carrier himself, it is important to have an understanding not only of transportation insurance forms but also of some of the basic elements of transportation law, the customs of the trade and the regulations of the Interstate Commerce Commission and Public Service Commissions.

COMMON CARRIERS AND PRIVATE CARRIERS

THE LIABILITY OF A COMMON CARRIER is very substantially different from that of private carrier, and it is therefore essential to be clear on the characteristics of each type of carriage.

Generally, anyone is classed as a common carrier who holds himself out to the public as a carrier of goods for hire. The important distinguishing feature of a common carrier is that he does not discriminate between customers, but offers his services to all as they come. He may limit his carriage to certain products which he is especially equipped or accustomed to handle, he may refuse to transport dangerous materials or perishables, he may operate only within a very restricted area, but within these restrictions, he offers his services to all at more or less established rates. Nor is it essential that the carrying of goods be his exclusive occupation. A person whose principal occupation is farming may solicit his neighbors and offer to carry their produce to market on his truck, and his relationship to these people is that of a common carrier.

An individual or concern which works for only one firm or for a limited number of companies under regular long-term contracts is not classed as a common carrier. Such operations are known as contract carriers. Similarly, a firm which carries only its own goods is not a common carrier even if *on occasion* it does carry the goods of others for hire.

Freight forwarders do not actually carry goods on their own conveyances and are not carriers. They merely accept goods for packing, crating and forwarding, but they have long assumed the obligations of common carriers, and sign for the property in their own name. Their situation may therefore be considered together with those of common carriers.

Liability of Common Carriers—All carriers of goods for hire are bailees and have a duty towards the property entrusted to their care. There is, however, a very striking difference between the liability of a common carrier and that of a private carrier. The *private* carrier's liability to the shipper is that of an ordinary bailee who is charged with exercising reasonable care to preserve from loss the property bailed to him. He is liable only if he has been negligent towards the property. (See Chapter 19 under Liability of Bailees.)

The *common* carrier, however, is liable for the safe delivery of the goods under all but a very few situations. He stands in the position of an insurer of the goods, and his liability for loss or damage to the goods he carries is almost absolute, regardless of whether he has been negligent or not. Generally, he is responsible for the safe delivery of the goods in his care unless he is prevented from making such delivery by one of the following five factors:

1. An Act of God. An Act of God is one which is no way attributable to human agency; e. g., lightning, earthquake, tornado, etc. Even under these circumstances, the carrier may be held liable, if his negligence contributed to the loss. Thus, if a truckman failed to take reasonable precautions to get his truck out of the path of a flood, or if a ferryman started across a river during a storm in a vessel unfit for such stress, they may be held liable for the loss. In effect, the exemption from liability for an Act of God is modified by the condition that the loss must not be contributed to by the negligence of the carrier.

2. An act of the public enemy. This refers only to a nation at war with the Insured's country. Rioters or mobs are not public enemies, nor are thieves or robbers within the meaning of the exemp-

tion. Loss caused by rioters or other such agencies would be the liability of the carrier.

3. An act of the public authority. When goods are taken from the carrier by valid legal process; e. g., foodstuffs suspected of contamination are seized by the public health authorities.

4. An act of the owner-shipper. If the shipper had so packaged or disguised valuable goods that they appeared of little value, or if he had meddled with the goods, or improperly packed them, or misdirected the shipment, the carrier may be free of liability for loss to the property.

5. Inherent vice of the goods. Inherent vice is a quality in the goods themselves which causes them to spoil or disintegrate without any external cause. Thus, skins improperly cured, dressed or dyed may be said to be possessed of inherent vice. Opals commonly contain inherent defects which develop without their being subjected to any external cause. The common carrier is not liable for damage to such goods provided the inherent vice is the immediate, proximate cause of the damage. Spoilage of perishable foods might, however, be the carrier's liability if the spoilage could have been prevented by proper refrigeration during transit. On the other hand, fruit which must be picked on a certain date may be possessed of inherent vice, if not so picked, or if delivered to the carrier after damage by hailstorm.

Unless the loss is due directly to one of the five exempted causes listed above, the common carrier is liable. He is not relieved of liability because he was overwhelmed and robbed by superior force, or because the goods were damaged in a fire absolutely beyond his control, or in a collision in which he was not at fault, or as a result of the negligence of third parties, or in any manner other than those specifically exempted. The shipper, to establish his right to indemnity from the carrier, need only prove his surrender of the goods to the carrier. The carrier must pay for the loss or damage, or prove that it arose from one of the exempted causes.

While it is customary to embody the contract between the shipper and the carrier in some written form, no receipt, or bill of lading or other agreement is necessary to make the carrier liable.

Liability of Initial Carrier—It is standard practice in modern transportation for a carrier to accept goods for shipment to points beyond the limits of its own lines, and arrange with other carriers to complete the transportation. Sometimes, the complete trip involves a chain of carriers.

The initial carrier who accepts goods from the shipper for through carriage becomes liable for loss or damage to the goods, not only during the time it has the goods in its custody but until the goods are delivered to their destination. The initial carrier is considered the principal who assumes liability for all the acts of the other carriers, who are his agents.

Duration of Carrier's Liability—The carrier is liable for the goods from the time he receives them until they are delivered to their final destination but, under different conditions, his liability for the goods may vary sharply.

If the carrier receives only part of a shipment which he holds while the balance is being prepared, or if the owner must still do something to the goods before they are ready for shipment, or maintains some control over the goods, or has not furnished instructions to the carrier, the carrier's liability is that of a warehouseman only, responsible only for his own negligence like an ordinary bailee.

On the other hand, if the goods are delivered to the carrier in a state ready for immediate shipment, it does not matter whether he holds them for his own convenience while awaiting shipment. His liability as a carrier has commenced. If the goods, while in transit, are temporarily stopped by the carrier, as for transfer to another conveyance, the period is considered incidental to transit, and the carrier's liability continues unabated. However, if the goods are halted in their transit by the order of the shipper, the liability of the carrier becomes that of a warehouseman.

Similarly, the liability of the carrier as a carrier terminates when the goods are delivered to their final destination, provided the carrier has nothing further to do to complete the delivery. If the consignee is offered the goods, it is his duty to remove them promptly. If he fails to do so, or requests the carrier to hold the goods or make delivery elsewhere, the liability of the carrier becomes that of warehouseman only.

In the case of rail shipments, the consignee must be given notice of the arrival of shipment and reasonable time to pick up the goods. Usually 48 hours is allowed to the consignee, after which time the carrier holds the goods as warehouseman.

It should be noted that goods need not necessarily be delivered physically to the consignee to constitute delivery. The customs and usage of a particular business may be such as to constitute constructive delivery when goods are placed at a point where it is customary to deposit them, or when deposited at a point specifically designated in the contract. Carload shipments to private railroad sidings are usually considered delivered when placed on the siding.

There are important differences in some of the states as to what constitutes delivery, and the reader should check with legal counsel in his state or the legal department of the insurance company on the rules applicable in his territory.

For the carrier to become liable, he must take custody of the property. Merely setting the goods out to be picked up by the carrier prior to notifying him of such action will not make the carrier liable for loss to the goods.

Similarly, when the shipper surrenders the goods to someone fraudulently posing as an agent of the carrier, it has been held that the goods did not come into the custody of the carrier, and that no liability was assumed by him. But when the carrier delivered goods to an imposter, the courts have held that no valid delivery had been made and the carrier was liable for the loss.

LIMITATION OF LIABILITY OF COMMON CARRIER

While the liability of a common carrier is almost absolute, he may enter into special arrangements with the shipper under which his liability will be limited to an agreed maximum. The usual method is for the shipper to declare the goods at a value which is below their true value, as for example, $50 per package, or 50¢ per pound. Agreements of this kind will be binding, provided they are accepted by the free choice of the shipper, and are clear and explicit. In interstate commerce, such agreement must be in writing and must appear on the bill of lading.

For such limitations to be valid and enforceable, the carrier must offer the shipper the unrestricted right to choose the valuation he wishes to declare on his goods, and a graduated set of freight rates based on different valuations. If the shipper elects to declare the goods at their full value, the carrier must accept the goods. If a lower valuation is acceptable to the shipper, he must receive a lower freight rate. Unless the carrier actually makes such varying freight rates available to his customers, the agreement limiting his liability will be held invalid.

It is not permissible to limit recovery on livestock, which must be shipped at their full value. The exception applies to cattle, goats, horses, mules, sheep and swine.

REGULATION OF COMMON CARRIERS

All common carriers who operate across any state line are subject to regulation by the Interstate Commerce Commission. This includes carriers who transport goods between any one state and an adjoining foreign country. Air freight carriers are subject to similar regulation by the Civil Aeronautics Board. Where a carrier's operations are confined within the boundaries of a state, he is not subject to the Interstate Commerce Act, but the majority of states have enacted Motor Carrier Acts which are closely patterned on the Federal act. Usually the state acts exempt carriers who operate exclusively within a city or town, but these carriers are subject to local police regulations.

Every motor carrier who wishes to engage in interstate hauling must obtain a certificate from the Commission. Before issuing such certificate, the Commission will inquire into the applicant's ability to perform the service he proposes to undertake and to conform to the requirements, rules and regulations of the Commission. The trucker must also demonstrate that the service he wishes to provide is required by public convenience or necessity.

Under the regulations of the Interstate Commerce Commission, or most state agencies covering intrastate carriers, the carrier is required to file a tariff, a set of rules and rates under which he operates. The tariff will prescribe certain commodities which may not be shipped by the particular form of carriage, and will classify all acceptable goods with the rates for each class. It also specifies the rules governing limitation of values and the charges for values declared in excess of standard values.

Compulsory Insurance—Every motor common carrier who operates in interstate commerce is required to carry insurance covering his liability to his customers. Exempted from the requirement are only carriers of certain commodities which are not exposed to serious loss, like ashes, concrete, corn cobs, cottonseed hulls, garbage, ice, iron ore, lumber, salt in bulk, scrap iron, slate, stone, etc.

Notice of Loss—Time to Bring Suit—The Interstate Commerce Commission also establishes certain minimum periods which must be allowed for filing of claims and bringing of suits against the carrier. No contract between a shipper and a carrier will be held valid which provides a shorter period than nine months for filing of a claim by a shipper, or for less than two years for bringing a suit.

Extent of Carrier's Liability—Except for limitations on liability agreed upon between shipper and carrier, the carrier is liable for the full amount of the loss or damage, usually computed as the market value at the point of destination. Where there is no established market price on particular goods, the invoice price between the buyer and seller usually controls. The carrier may deduct cash discounts only if he pays the loss within the established cash discount period. Trade discounts may usually be deducted by the carrier, since the shipper would not ordinarily have received the amount of such discounts.

MOTOR TRUCK MERCHANDISE FLOATER—CARRIER'S FORM

(Motor Vehicle Cargo Policy — Legal Liability)

THERE ARE NO STANDARD FORMS for Transportation insurance and the underwriter is free to provide any coverage he deems advisable, and at a rate within his discretion. Through the years, there has evolved a more or less standard policy in use by most companies for most risks. This form will be analyzed next, but the reader should know that policies in this branch of insurance may be tailored to the requirements of an individual risk.

The high degree of liability of a common carrier to his customers imposes a serious possibility of loss on such carriers. Motor common carriers may insure their liability under a Cargo policy (Motor Truck Merchandise Floater—Carrier's Form). This insurance is required by carriers not only to protect them against loss but also because shippers usually refuse to entrust their property to uninsured carriers. Furthermore, Cargo Liability insurance of certain minimum amounts is made mandatory on all common carriers who operate in interstate commerce.

WHAT IS COVERED

The Cargo policy does *not* insure the customers' goods. It covers only the legal liability of the truckman for loss or damage to customers' goods being carried by him. If the goods are lost or damaged, and the carrier is held legally liable, the policy will pay, subject to its exclusions and limits of liability. Contrariwise, if there is a loss to such property which is not the liability of the insured motor carrier, there is no coverage under the policy. The Cargo policy does not, however, cover the truckman's liability for *all* losses, but only for certain stated perils.

The policy specifically excludes liability for loss or damage to:

Accounts, bills, currency, deeds, evidences of debt, money, securities (the property excluded under the Fire insurance policy), notes and similar valuables.

Jewelry, precious stones, or other similar valuables.

Livestock, except when death is caused by a peril insured against, or when such peril makes destruction necessary.

Eggs, except where they amount to more than 50% of each insured shipping package, and then for no more than $200 for all loss on one truck.

HAZARDS COVERED

As pointed out above, the Cargo Liability policy is not standardized. Some carriers offer an all-risk form, while others write a named perils policy. The named perils policy does not cover the truckman for all losses he may be held legally liable for. Certain specific perils are stipulated in the policy and only the truckman's liability for a loss by these perils is covered. The policy covers the following perils:

Fire, lightning
Cyclone, tornado, and internal explosion of the conveyance
Flood, collapse of bridges
Perils of the sea while on ferries only (discussed in Chapter 22).
Overturning of the motor vehicle
Collision.

Coverage on collision losses may vary. Generally, the policy covers only collision of the vehicle with other objects but not with the road or earth surfaces, curbing, railroad rails or ties. The policy usually excludes also collision with any stationary object while backing to load or unload, but not while in the course of normal driving. Furthermore, underwriters usually specifically exclude damage by collision *to* the property being carried which extends beyond or above the vehicle, except when the vehicle itself is involved in the collision.

Several of the perils listed above as covered are Acts of God (flood, cyclone, tornado), but losses so caused will be covered only if the Insured is legally liable therefore.

Theft Coverage—Insurance against theft is sometimes added to Cargo policies. The Theft Endorsement is almost always written to cover only theft of an entire shipping package, and excludes pilferage; i. e., theft of some of the contents of a package. The intent under a Theft Endorsement is to cover only when there is some evidence of theft, and many companies seek to make this clear by specifically excluding under the theft coverage "mysterious disappearance, shortage or misdelivery unless there is evidence that a theft has occurred." Theft by any of the Insured's employees is specifically excluded.

Terminal Coverage—A common carrier is liable for goods in his custody until he delivers them to their final destination. In the course of transit, it often becomes necessary for the truckman to place the goods on a loading platform or in a depot or terminal while awaiting loading, transshipment or unloading. The carrier is liable for loss to the goods during such intervals.

The basic Cargo Liability policy covers the truckman only while the property is contained in or on the described vehicles. To protect the truckman for loss in a terminal, the policy may be written to provide coverage while the property is temporarily removed from or awaiting loading on any truck insured under the policy, or on loading platforms or in depots, terminals, etc. The policy usually limits such coverage to 24, 48, or 72 hours, but may be extended to cover longer periods if required by the Insured.

HAZARDS NOT COVERED

The policy contains the usual exclusions of other Floaters (discussed in Chapter 17). In addition, there is no coverage under the Cargo policy for any of the following perils, regardless of the Insured's liability for such losses:

Loss caused by wet or dampness, or by being spotted, discolored, mouldy, rusted, frosted, rotten, soured, steamed or changed in flavor except if as a direct result of a peril insured against.

Loss caused by delay or loss of market.

Neglect of the Insured to use all reasonable means to save and preserve the property at or after the occurrence of any disaster insured against.

Loss caused by strikes, lockouts, labor disturbances, riots, civil commotions or any persons taking part in such occurrences.

Dishonest acts of the Insured's employees.

WHERE COVERED

The Cargo policy covers only when the property is in or on vehicles owned, operated or contracted for by the Insured. The Insured is required to list in the policy all motor vehicles which he operates, and coverage applies only to those vehicles. A limit of liability is set in the policy for each truck.

Permission is given the Insured to substitute a vehicle for any of the vehicles described in the policy. The Insured must report such substitution to the Company as soon as practicable (some policies stipulate within 72 hours) and to pay any additional premium that may be required.

The automatic coverage on substitute vehicles will apply only to vehicles substituted for insured vehicles which are withdrawn from use. It will not cover additional vehicles which the Insured acquires after the policy is issued. Such vehicles must be added to the policy by specific listing. Larger risks are sometimes written without requiring listing of each individual truck.

Coverage on property in course of transit while temporarily detained on platforms, or in terminals or depots may be provided under the policy.

The coverage of the policy extends only within the limits of the United States and Canada.

FOR HOW MUCH

The policy covers to the extent of the Insured's liability, but for no more than the actual cash value of the property at the time of the loss. In addition, Cargo insurance is usually subject to a 100% Coinsurance clause, under which the Company's liability for any loss is limited to the proportion that the amount of insurance on the vehicle involved bears to the Insured's total liability for all goods on the particular truck.

The amount of insurance that must be carried on any vehicle to comply with the Coinsurance clause is based on the extent of the Insured's liability on the particular truck, not the actual value of the goods being carried. Note too that the amount of insurance required is based on the liability for all goods on the truck, not merely that of the individual owner involved in the loss.

Thus, assume a truckman carried on one of his trucks merchandise from five separate concerns. For purposes of the example, assume that the merchandise of *each* shipper consists of four packages worth $250 each, a total of $1,000 for each shipper. Each of the shippers agrees to value his own shipment at $50 per shipping package, a total of $200 per shipment. The trucker's liability to *each* shipper is therefore $200; to all five shippers whose property is on the truck, the liability is $1,000. The truckman, to comply with the 100% Coinsurance Clause, must carry not less than $1,000 of insurance, the amount of his liability for *all* goods carried on the truck.

If he carries less than this amount of insurance, he will have to bear a portion of any loss himself. Thus, if in the above example, he were to carry $500 of insurance, the Company would be liable for only one-half of any loss—the proportion that the amount of insurance carried, $500, bears to the required $1,000 of insurance, 100% of the liability for all goods carried on the particular truck.

Limits of Liability—In addition to a limit per truck, the Cargo policy carries a limit of liability for any one loss, regardless of the number of vehicles involved. An Insured who operates ten trucks might require a limit of $2,000 per truck, if that is his maximum liability on any one truck. In arriving at an adequate limit of liability for any one loss, he must take into account the number of his trucks which may be exposed to the same casualty. If five of his trucks are on occasion housed in one location or transfer point, he will require $10,000 to cover the maximum exposure to loss in any single casualty.

Other Insurance—If there is any other collectible insurance covering in any manner the liability of the Insured, the present policy is null and void to the extent of such other insurance.

Shippers usually carry direct insurance on their goods in transit. The Other Insurance clause of the Cargo policy does not apply to such shipper's insurance, as this does not cover the liability of the truckman.

COMPULSORY CARGO INSURANCE

As indicated above, motor common carriers are required by the Interstate Commerce Commission to prove their ability to meet their obligations to the public they serve. Each carrier is required to furnish security of not less than $2,500 on any one vehicle, and not less than $5,000 for the aggregate loss in any one casualty. The truckman may comply with the security requirements of the Commission by posting a bond, qualifying as a self-insurer, or purchasing a Cargo Liability policy of at least these minimum amounts.

Interstate Commerce Commission Endorsement — The Cargo Liability policy carried by a motor common carrier must include a special endorsement which makes the insurance Company liable for $2,500 on any one truck and $5,000 in any single casualty for *all* loss for which the carrier is legally liable.

This endorsement, up to the limits stated, broadens the policy and makes it virtually an all-risk policy. Under the terms of the endorsement, the policy becomes liable for any loss for which the carrier is liable, even if the peril is not otherwise insured under the policy, or even if the peril is one specifically excluded. A policy so endorsed will be responsible for loss caused by dishonesty of the carrier's employees, for pilferage, for breakage even when due to carelessness, for damage by water, and any other loss except those few for which the common carrier is not liable.

When the insurance Company pays a loss under the terms of the I. C. C. endorsement which it would not otherwise have been liable for, it is entitled to reimbursement from the Insured. The effect of the endorsement is therefore to guarantee the solvency of the common carrier up to $2,500 per vehicle and $5,000 for any one loss.

When the insurance Company pays a loss under the terms of the notice, the endorsement may not be cancelled except by giving 30 days' notice in writing to the Interstate Commerce Commission.

Motor common carriers are also required to carry Public Liability insurance of certain minimum amounts (to be discussed in Chapter 28).

How Premium Is Determined—As discussed earlier, there is no standardization of rates or forms for Transportation insurance, and each risk is rated according to the judgment of the underwriter, who takes into account the area in which the Insured operates, the type of commodity carried, the kind of trucks to be insured, the protective devices installed on the trucks or terminals, the previous loss experience of the Insured, and his level of efficiency. The financial solvency of the Insured is another factor of great importance in underwriting a risk.

In addition, the rate will reflect the radius of the Insured's operations, with the lowest rate granted for local haulers who confine their operations within a fifty-mile radius, a higher rate for the intermediate hauler whose trucks cover no more than a 200-mile radius, and the highest rate for long-haul truckers who cover distances in excess of 200 miles.

Cancellation—The Cancellation clause of the Cargo policy is identical with that of the Fire insurance policy.

The Cargo Liability policy also includes a clause providing for automatic cancellation if the premium is not paid to the Company or its agent within 60 days after its inception date. Such cancellation will go into effect at 12 Noon of the 60th day.

REQUIREMENTS IN CASE OF LOSS

Notice of Loss—Proof of Loss—See Chapter 17.

Sue and Labor—See Chapter 17.

Cooperation in Case of Suit—The Insured may be asked by the Company to aid in securing information and evidence and the attendance of witnesses. The Insured may be required to defend in his own name any suit brought against him, but will be defended by counsel which the Company will furnish.

Suit Against Company—See Chapter 17.

When Loss Is Payable—Loss under the policy is payable within 60 days after satisfactory Proof of Loss has been received by the Company.

OTHER CLAUSES

Subrogation—See Chapter 2.

Term of Policy—The policy attaches at Noon, Standard Time, at the place the policy is issued. Cargo Liability insurance is written for one year.

Misrepresentation and Fraud—See Chapter 2.

Reinstatement of Losses—The Cargo policy is reduced by the amount of any loss payment, but such reduction is automatically reinstated. The Insured agrees to pay an additional premium on a pro rata basis for such reinstatement.

TRANSPORTATION INSURANCE

GENERAL PRINCIPLES

AS DISCUSSED EARLIER, the liability of a common carrier is very broad. It is not, however, absolute, and there are certain perils for which the carrier is not responsible. Owners who ship their property may wish to be insured for *all* loss to such property, whether the trucker is liable for the loss or not. Furthermore, even if the truckman is liable in a loss, he may not be in a position to meet his obligations, particularly if the loss is large.

Then again, a shipper's business may require that he be reimbursed for any loss without delay, and he may therefore prefer not to have to wait upon the outcome of his litigation or negotiations with the carrier. Lastly, the owner may ship under special agreements with the carrier which limit the latter's liability to a stated amount. Despite the fact that the shipper has agreed to this lower valuation to enjoy a reduced freight rate, he may wish to be in a position to recover the full amount of any loss.

Many businesses, therefore, purchase Transit policies to cover their goods while in transit. Such policies are used to cover property of the shipper or consignee (the receiver) while in the custody of a common carrier, or while shipped on the owner's trucks. A basic Transportation form is used, and the appropriate form attached.

When Title to Goods in Transit Passes—The question of when title to goods passes from seller to buyer is often a fairly technical one. Nevertheless, the insurance man who would understand and work with Transit insurance must have a grasp of some of the elementary aspects of this subject, for the location of the title to the goods in transit will often control the settlement of losses. If title to the goods has passed to the consignee at the time of the loss, claim for such loss must be made under the consignee's policy, while a contrary situation will exist if the seller has retained title to the goods in transit.

A few general rules will be set down, but it should be emphasized that these are to be used only as a broad guide to the question.

Individual cases which appear to present any complications should be referred to legally trained individuals in the field.

Generally speaking, title to property at any moment depends on the mutual intent of buyer and seller. Where the contract between the parties is silent on the point, the question of title will depend on the nature of the goods and the stated terms of sale. Different status is afforded to "ascertained" goods, which are goods in a completed state ready for delivery, "unascertained" goods, which are part of a larger quantity and require sorting out, and "fungibles," which are goods of such a nature that any part is indistinguishable from any other part, like coal, spices, wines, etc.

Usually, the contract of sale contains some specific reference to the point at which title is intended to pass. In land transportation, the term most frequently encountered is F. O. B.

F. O. B. Shipments—The term F. O. B. means "free on board" and implies that the seller will deliver the goods at his expense to a designated point. Thus, F. O. B. Point of Shipment means that the goods will be delivered by the seller to the initial carrier, and that title to the property will pass to the buyer at this point. F. O. B. a stated location will effect transfer of title to the buyer when the goods are delivered by the seller at his expense to the stated location. Sometimes a contract of sale may designate F. O. B. on board certain freight cars at a given point. Or a buyer may enter into a contract for purchase of certain property F. O. B. the buyer's city, and title to the goods will remain in the seller until the goods reach the designated city.

A contract of sale may call for goods to be shipped via a named carrier. If the seller ships via another carrier, title to the property will remain with the seller until the goods are delivered to the designated carrier or to the buyer.

The question of title is not dependent upon the date of payment for the goods. Thus, where goods are delivered to the initial carrier under an F. O. B. Point of Shipment contract, title passes to the buyer, even though payment by the buyer is due at a later date.

There are many factors that may modify the rules of thumb cited above. Thus, when a seller, who has not been authorized by the buyer to declare the goods at less than their full value, nevertheless makes such shipment, title does not pass to the buyer upon delivery to the carrier as it would if the goods had beeen fully declared to the carrier, or if the buyer had authorized the use of a lower valuation. Similarly, title to goods may not pass from seller to buyer if the quantity delivered differs from that called for by the contract of sale. In sales on approval, title does not pass to the buyer until he has indicated his approval, or holds the goods without indicating his acceptance or rejection past a reasonable time or agreed trial period. Other special situations develop when the consignee has the right to inspect goods before accepting them, under "On Sale or Return Contracts," when goods are rejected and returned, etc.

TRANSPORTATION POLICY — SHIPPER'S FORM (TRANSIT POLICY)

THERE ARE NO STANDARD FORMS or rates for Transportation insurance, whether covering shipper, consignee or carrier. Policies may be tailored to meet the requirements of any individual risk, and rates may vary for similar insurance in different companies. This section will analyze several forms which have been widely followed by most companies and may be considered fairly basic. It should be remembered, however, that any individual policy may be broadened or restricted, in the discretion of the individual underwriter.

WHAT IS COVERED

The policy covers all goods and merchandise, and containers therefor, as are usual to the Insured's business, whether such property is owned by the Insured, or held by him in trust, or on commission, or on consignment, or on which he has made advances. The policy will also cover goods sold but not delivered.

PROPERTY NOT COVERED

Most Transit policies exclude loss or damage to: Accounts, bills, currency, deeds, evidences of debt, money, securities and notes.

The policy does not cover shipments that have been refused or returned by the receiver.

Usually, export and import shipments are excluded. (This coverage is provided under the Ocean Marine policy, to be discussed later.)

Some forms provide that import shipments will come under the Transit policy after the Marine policy on such goods ceases to cover.

HAZARDS COVERED

Transit policies are often written on a specified perils basis. Many companies will write a broader policy on an all-risk basis, and this form will be discussed later.

The basic policy usually covers the following perils:

Fire, lightning
Cyclone, tornado, flood

Collision, derailment or overturn of a vehicle.

As used in this policy, the term "collision" is broader than in the Cargo Liability policy, which generally excludes collision with stationary objects while backing, and with the road or earth surfaces, curbing, railroad ties, etc. There is no coverage, however, for loss caused by the coming together of cars during coupling.

Other Perils of Transportation — This coverage takes in any losses which are due directly to transportation, like contamination of goods by other goods being carried, or sudden stopping of the vehicle. It does not cover losses *during* transportation unless due directly to the transportation.

Theft, but only of an entire shipping package.

While waterborne, against loss caused by fire and perils of the sea, including general average and salvage charges.

Transit policies are written under several forms to cover different methods of carriage (discussed under WHERE COVERED). The perils covered under the several forms will usually differ in some respects, reflecting the varying hazards that face different carriers.

HAZARDS NOT COVERED

The Transit policy excludes the perils excluded under most Floaters and incorporates most exclusions in the Cargo Liability policy. In addition, the Transit policy specifically excludes the following perils:

Loss by breakage, leakage, marring or scratching unless caused by fire, lightning, cyclone, tornado, flood, collision and/or derailment and/or overturning of the vehicle, or while waterborne, by the vessel being burned, sunk, stranded or in collision.

Loss or damage caused by capture, seizure, arrest, restraint, detainment, preemption, requisition or nationalization, or the consequences of any attempt thereat.

All-Risk Transportation Endorsement—Policies are sometimes issued to cover property in transit on an all-risk basis. Such policies do not specify perils insured against but cover all risks of loss or damage subject to stated exclusions, which are similar to those listed under Perils Not Covered.

WHERE COVERED

Transit policies are written to cover the property of the Insured from the time the goods leave the factory, store, or warehouse at the initial point of shipment, until they are delivered to the store or warehouse at the destination point, all while in due course of transportation. The policy also covers property on docks, wharves, piers, bulkheads, depots, stations, and on platforms, but only when in the custody of a common carrier incidental to transportation. It may be extended to cover for 90 days after reaching the consignee; or for 120 days if the merchandise has been forwarded on consignment.

Coverage applies to property only while within the United States and Canada. Different forms are attached to the basic Transportation policy to provide coverage on various types of carriers.

Transportation Form "A"—This form provides coverage for loss to property while in the custody of any of the following:

1. Any railroad or railroad express company.

2. Any regular coastwise ship lines between inland Atlantic Coast and Gulf ports. The policy usually excludes the Great Lakes, the Mississippi and Ohio Rivers and their tributaries, any canal, and the Pacific Coast.

3. Any public truckmen, land transfer or land transportation companies, provided these carriers are used in connection with railroad and steamer shipments, as described above.

Transportation Endorsement "B"—This form is identical with the Form "A" except that it does not cover any coastwise ship lines as outlined under No. 2 above.

Neither of the two forms discussed above cover loss or damage to property while in the hands of motor common carriers except when such are used in connection with railroad or steamer shipments, but either form may be extended to cover goods while in the custody of truckmen who are common carriers, or while in the hands of any truckman.

Many businesses ship large quantities of merchandise via motor truck common carriers directly to their customers, and for such firms this extension of coverage is of great importance.

Where required by the Insured's operations, the policy may also be written to cover property in the custody of air carriers, the Insured's messengers, or in taxicabs and similar conveyances. Usually, a comparatively low limit of liability will be assigned to these forms of carriage.

Where a shipper also uses his own trucks, the policy must be endorsed to cover property so carried. When a shipper's own trucks provide the sole method of transportation, or a large part of the carriage used, a special form is used.

Owner's Goods on Owner's Trucks—Endorsement "C" — When an owner ships his merchandise on his own trucks, a special form is attached to the Transportation policy, usually known as Transportation Endorsement "C."

Under this form (also referred to as Owner's Goods on Owner's Trucks), the Insured is required to list each truck with an amount of insurance applicable to the truck.

In addition to the property specifically excluded under the other Transportation policies previously discussed, the policy generally excludes loss to jewelry, precious stones and similar valuables, letters of credit, passports, documents, railroad or other tickets, bullion, notes, manuscripts, mechanical drawings, dies or patterns.

Only 10% of the amount of insurance applicable to any truck will apply to loss of wines, spirits, other alcoholic beverages, cigars, cigarettes, tobacco, furs and silk. Loss or damage to paintings, statuary, or other works of art is covered only if absolute total loss and only if caused by fire or lightning, but in no event for more than $250 in any one casualty.

The policy contains the exclusions found in other Transit Forms. It also excludes loss arising out of the dishonesty of the Insured's employees.

FOR HOW MUCH

Transit policies usually stipulate that goods shipped for the Insured's account shall be valued at the actual invoice cost, plus such costs and charges as may have accrued. Goods which have been sold by the Insured will be valued at the amount of the Insured's selling invoice plus any prepaid freight. If goods are not shipped under invoice, they are valued at the actual cash market value at the point of destination on the date of the loss.

Some policies do not contain any clause defining the amount of the loss. Such policies would be liable for the actual amount of any loss at the time and place of the loss.

Limit of Liability—Except for the form used to insure goods carried on an owner's trucks, the Transit policy does not contain any limit of liability for loss on any one vehicle. A limit of liability is established only for the aggregate losses in any one casualty. Different maximums payable for any loss may be set for the various forms of carriage covered in the policy. Thus, the policy may be written with a maximum liability of $100,000 for loss or damage to property in the custody of a motor common carrier, and $10,000 while in the custody of the Insured's messengers, or in taxicabs, etc.

Machinery Clause — When the property shipped is a machine which consists of several parts, and one part of the machine is damaged, the Company is liable only for the value of the part damaged.

Labels Clause—If the labels or wrappers of shipped goods are damaged, the policy will pay only for the cost of new labels or wrappers, and the cost of reconditioning the goods.

Other Insurance—If there is other insurance covering the property, the Transit policy is liable only for any excess of the loss over the amount of such other insurance.

This clause is held to be operative only when there are other policies covering the same interest, and does not apply to insurance carried by others who have an interest in the property.

IMPAIRMENT OF CARRIER'S LIABILITY

When it is remembered that a common carrier's liability is so broad as to cover practically every loss to property in his custody, it can readily be understood that the Company's right of subrogation is of great importance in Transit policies. When the insurance Company pays a shipper for loss to his property in transit, it takes over any right the shipper may have to collect the loss from the carrier.

Since the carrier is liable for the majority of losses to property in his custody, the insurance Company can expect in most instances to be reimbursed for the money it has paid to its Insured. Except for the several Acts of God insured against under the Transit policy, for which a carrier is not liable, the Transit policy acts essentially as a guarantee of the carrier's solvency. The Company, in deciding upon a rate for a Transit policy, takes this factor into account.

The situation is entirely different under the special Transit Forms used to insure a business which ships on its own trucks. Here, there is no possibility of recouping any losses paid, since there is no carrier involved. The rate for such Transit policies must necessarily be substantially higher than for those issued to a shipper who ships via common carrier.

A somewhat similar situation develops with shippers who employ common carriers and agree to release them from liability above a stated amount. Under such circumstances, the insurance Company would still pay the shipper the full amount of his loss, but would take over only the shipper's limited rights against the carrier. The Company could, therefore, expect only partial repayment of the loss paid.

In light of the above, the insurance Company guards its right of reimbursement from the carrier very zealously. The basic Transit policy contains a clause which voids the policy if the Insured enters into any agreement which limits his right to recover for any loss from a carrier, bailee or other party.

A shipper may obtain the permission of the insurance Company to enter into such arrangements limiting the carrier's liability. This permission is expressly endorsed on the Transit policy, and it is extremely important that the Shipper's Transit policy contain this privilege, when he makes such shipments.

Generally, the Company agrees to the Insured's limiting the carrier's liability to a given minimum, as $50 per package or shipment. Sometimes the policy provides that the Insured may accept released bills of lading without stipulating any minimum valuation. Such permission is usually modified by the condition that the Insured will not enter into special arrangement with the carrier without the consent of the Company. The word "special" in this connection means other arrangements which are not customary and usual to the Insured's business.

HOW PREMIUM IS DETERMINED

As previously discussed, there are no standard rates for Transit policies of any kind. Each risk is submitted to the underwriters, who take into account the nature of the commodity shipped, the manner in which it is packed and handled, the kind of carriers used, the distance the goods are usually sent, and the kind of arrangements entered into between the Insured and his carriers.

The premium for a Transit policy is based on the total amount of all shipments made under the policy, and is arrived at by multiplying the rate per $100 of shipments times the volume of shipments.

Smaller risks whose shipments are maintained at a fairly even level throughout the year are usually written for a flat annual premium. If the volume of shipments tends to fluctuate throughout the year, the policy may be written on an annual reporting basis.

The Insured pays a premium at the inception of the policy, which is based on the estimated volume of shipments for the coming year. At the end of the policy year, the Insured reports to the Company the value of all shipments that actually moved under the policy, and the premium is adjusted accordingly. The Insured receives a return premium if the deposit premium paid by him was excessive, or pays an additional premium if the actual shipments exceeded his initial estimate.

Larger risks are written on a monthly reporting basis. The mechanics of arriving at the final premium are the same as under the annual reporting policy just described, except that the Insured is required to forward *monthly* reports of the shipments made by him under the policy.

REQUIREMENTS IN CASE OF LOSS

Notice of Loss—The Insured is required to give immediate notice of any loss or damage that may become a claim under the policy.

While the Insured-shipper must give immediate notice to the insurance Company of any loss, he cannot be limited to less than nine months in giving notice to any common carrier.

Proof of Loss—The Insured must file Proof of Loss within four months from date of loss.

Sue and Labor Clause—See Chapter 17.

Examination Under Oath—See Chapter 2.

Appraisal—See Chapter 2.

Suit Against Company—Action against the Company cannot be commenced until the Insured has complied with all the requirements of the policy, but not later than twelve months after the happening of the physical loss or damage out of which the claim arose.

While the Insured must bring a suit against the Company within twelve months of the date of the happening, he cannot be restricted to less than two years to institute a suit against a common carrier in interstate commerce.

When Loss Must Be Paid—All losses under the policy must be paid within 30 days after satisfactory Proof of Loss is submitted to the Company.

Subrogation—See Chapter 2.

Reinstatement of Losses—The policy provides for automatic reinstatement of losses paid. The Insured is required to pay an additional premium on a pro rata basis for such reinstatement. This clause does not apply to policies written on a reporting basis.

Benefit of Insurance—See Chapter 17.

OTHER CLAUSES

Term of Policy—The policy attaches at Noon, Standard Time, at the place the policy is issued. Policies are written for one year, or on an open basis with no expiration date.

Cancellation—The policy may be cancelled by the Insured or the Company. Usually the Company is required to give not less than 15 days' notice in writing, though some policies provide for 10 days.

The Transit policy also provides for automatic cancellation if the premium is not paid within 60 days after the inception of the policy.

Misrepresentation and Fraud—See Chapter 2.

MISCELLANEOUS TRANSIT POLICIES

TRIP TRANSIT POLICY

A POLICY COVERING A SINGLE SHIPMENT may be required by firms or individuals who do not make regular shipments. The Trip Transit policy, which follows the regular Transit Forms closely, is designed for such purposes.

A Trip Transit policy may be written to cover property in temporary storage, and is often so written for private individuals who send their furniture and household goods to a storage location before moving.

DEPARTMENT STORE FLOATER

Department stores can cover their goods in transit under a form especially designed for their business. The policy is broader than the usual Transit policy. It covers property while in the hands of common carriers, truckmen, on the Insured's own trucks, and in the custody of messengers.

RAILWAY EXPRESS TRANSIT POLICY

Business concerns which make all their shipments via Railway Express are eligible for this special Transit policy which is broader than the policies usually issued to shippers who use other common carriers.

PARCEL POST INSURANCE

IT IS IMPORTANT to be clear on the fact that the United States Government is not a common carrier, and is not liable for property entrusted to its Post Office unless the shipments are sent by registered mail or insured parcel post.

While a shipper could protect himself against loss or damage to mail shipments by insuring each package with the Post Office, most businesses find it more convenient and more economical to buy an insurance policy to cover all their parcel post shipments. Since regular Transit policies exclude property shipped through the mails, a separate policy is required.

WHAT IS COVERED

The policy covers all property the Insured sends through the mails which is usual to his business, subject to certain property which is specifically excluded.

PROPERTY NOT COVERED

The Parcel Post policy does not cover any of the following types of property:

Accounts, bills, currency, deeds, evidences of debt, money, securities, and notes.

Perishable Goods—There is no coverage on perishables except against the risk of fire, theft, pilferage, or non-delivery.

Requirements on Addressing, Labeling, Wrapping, Postage — There is no coverage on packages which do not contain a stipulation, "Return Postage Guaranteed."

The policy does not cover:

Packages which are insufficiently or improperly addressed, improperly wrapped or packed, or on which the postage has not been fully paid.

Any package which shows on the outside the nature of its contents, except when such description is required by the Postal Laws, or except in the case of books, which may be shipped at a reduced rate if marked as such.

Goods on Consignment or Memorandum—There is no coverage for any package sent on consignment, memorandum or approval except if sent to fill an order or to persons to whom the Insured has previously sold merchandise.

Property in Contravention of Postal Regulations — The policy contains a warranty that the Insured will comply with the General Parcel Post Act of 1912 and its amendments. The policy would therefore not cover inflammables or other property prohibited by the Postal Laws.

HAZARDS COVERED

The Parcel Post policy is an extremely broad form of insurance. It insures the safe arrival of the property contained in any package in the custody of the Post Office. It covers all loss or damage to such property from any external cause, subject to the exclusion of the types of property enumerated above under Property Not Covered and the perils excluded under all Floaters (discussed in Chapter 17).

The non-delivery of a package will establish a claim under the Parcel Post policy. There is no need for the Insured to show any presumption of theft.

While the policy covers all loss or damage, such loss must be due to an external cause. Inherent vice of an article would not be covered.

WHERE COVERED

Property is covered from the time it passes into the custody of the Post Office until its arrival at the address to which it is destined. Coverage is afforded only within the Continental United States, the Dominion of Canada, and Alaska. The policy may be endorsed to cover shipments to foreign countries for an additional premium.

Property is insured only from the time it comes into the custody of the Post Office. This is usually understood to mean only when the property is turned over to the Post Office, and would not include packages left outside of Post Office collection boxes. There is no coverage for loss of any property which is in the custody of a messenger on his way to the Post Office.

Shipments to Transients—The Parcel Post policy does not cover shipments by ordinary (uninsured or unregistered) mail to transients at hotels. An exception is made for property shipped to the Insured's salesmen at hotels.

FOR HOW MUCH

The Company is not liable for more than the actual cash value of the property at the time of the loss, nor in any event for more than $100 on any package shipped by ordinary parcel post or unregistered mail, or $500 on any package shipped by registered mail or insured parcel post.

Furthermore, when the Insured ships via insured parcel post, he agrees to carry with the government not less than the following amounts of insurance:

On any package worth $100 or less, 50% of the actual values of the package.

On any package worth over $100, at least $50 of insurance.

REQUIREMENTS IN CASE OF LOSS

Notice of Loss—The Insured is required to give immediate notice of any claim under the policy. He must also submit the receipt issued by the Post Office, if any, and the original wrapper, if such can be located.

Proof of Loss—The Insured must submit Proof of Loss within four months of the date of the loss.

Subrogation—The insurance Company is subrogated, after it pays a loss under the policy, to any claim the Insured may have against third parties. In actual practice, the insurance Company is seldom in a position to be reimbursed for a loss except when caused by a third party other than the Post Office. The Company is entitled, however, to receive the amount of any insurance carried by the Insured with the Post Office.

Cancellation—The Company must give 15 days' notice in writing of its intention to cancel a Parcel Post policy. Cancellation of the policy will not affect any shipments already in the mail. The Company is entitled to a minimum retained premium in the event the policy is cancelled, and these are discussed below under each of the forms of Parcel Post insurance.

HOW PARCEL POST INSURANCE IS WRITTEN

Parcel Post insurance is written on an *open* form, with no expiration date. The initial premium is a deposit premium based on an estimate of the Insured's volume of mail shipments. Additional premiums are charged as warranted by the volume of shipments made. In most companies, the annual minimum premium is $50. In the event of cancellation, the Company will refund the unearned portion of the minimum premium, but it is permitted to retain 1/12th of the minimum premium for each month the policy has been in force.

The policy may be extended to cover incoming and returned shipments. The rate for such return shipments may vary from that charged for regular outgoing shipments. Generally, an additional minimum premium of $5 is charged for the extension to cover incoming shipments. This minimum is over and above the $50 minimum for the basic policy.

REGISTERED MAIL INSURANCE

BANKS, INSURANCE COMPANIES, investment houses, mutual funds, trust companies, and other institutions which are mainly of a fiduciary character are eligible for Registered Mail insurance, which covers bonds, stocks, other securities, stamps, checks, drafts, warehouse receipts, bills of lading, and similar valuable papers, bullion, platinum, and other precious metals, currency, coin, jewelry, watches, necklaces, bracelets, gems and stones, precious and semiprecious.

The policy is very broad in scope, and covers not only while the property is in the custody of the Post Office but also while in the hands of messengers or delivery service to or from the Post Office. Coverage may be provided for Continental United States alone, or for all of North America and between points in North America and elsewhere in the world. Also covered are shipments by express, and air mail and air express shipments may be covered.

FOR FURTHER READING

ACKERMAN—Insurance
DAYNARD—Paths and Bypaths in Inland Marine Insurance
GWERTZMAN—The Law of Transportation In Its Relation to Transportation Insurance
HEDGES—Practical Fire and Casualty Insurance
HUEBNER AND BLACK—Property Insurance
MAGEE AND BICKELHAUPT—General Insurance
MEHR AND CAMMACK—Principles of Insurance
POLICY, FORM & MANUAL ANALYSIS SERVICE
RIEGEL, ROBERT AND MILLER—Insurance
RODDA— Marine Insurance: Ocean and Inland

(See Reading List at End of Book)

CHAPTER 22

Ocean Marine Insurance

GENERAL PRINCIPLES OF MARINE LAW

INSURANCE ON OCEAN-GOING VESSELS and cargoes is probably the oldest form of property insurance in the world. The Marine policy used today to protect shipowners and all those who have an interest in property shipped across the seas is nearly three hundred years old and, except for minor modifications, is substantially the same in its provisions and language as it was in the 17th Century.

Inland Marine insurance, discussed in the preceding chapters, developed out of Ocean Marine insurance, and many of the features of these newer policies will be found in the basic Marine policy. Some understanding of basic law and customs and usages in the trade are essential to an understanding of Marine insurance, and a few of these general principles are outlined below.

Liability of Shipowner—Generally, a steamship company is responsible for damage to the cargo in its custody only when due to its negligence in loading, stowing or unloading the vessel. It is not responsible for loss or damage caused by perils of the sea or errors of navigation or direction of the ship. Whether it is responsible for loss due to a ship's unseaworthiness is often a close question. Usually, the shipowner is not liable for such loss unless he failed to take reasonable precautions to make the vessel seaworthy.

These very general rules of liability may be modified considerably by the contract between the shipper and the steamship-carrier. Under almost every circumstance, however, it is certain that one whose goods move across the seas will find himself exposed to the possibility of severe financial loss. This risk the exporter, importer or lending institution will wish to transfer to a risk-bearing insurance Company.

The shipowner, too, under modern conditions where the value of a single ocean-going vessel runs into millions, is dependent on insurance to protect his investment.

The same basic Marine policy is used to protect both these interests, with the shipper's form known as a Cargo policy, the shipowner's as Hull insurance.

WHEN TITLE PASSES FROM SELLER TO BUYER

The question of when title to goods in transit passes from seller to buyer is of considerable importance in determining the insurance that may be required under different conditions. As indicated, location of title depends on the mutual intent of the buyer and seller. In foreign trade, where buyer and seller are separated by great distances and the movement of goods may involve various forms of carriage stretching over a period of months, the question is understandably even more complex than in the usual land transportation.

The insurance man who arranges insurance for exporter, importer, shipowner, forwarder or commission agent must therefore have same understanding of the terms of sale most frequently encountered in contracts of international trade.

Ex Point of Origin—Such agreements which may designate a factory, warehouse assembling plant or similar location require the seller to place the goods at the buyer's disposal on a given date, or within a stated period. The goods come under the buyer's interest at that point and will be at *his* risk thereafter, whether he actually takes physical possession or not. In such agreements, the buyer requires insurance attaching at the time and place designated.

Ex Dock, Named Port of Importation—Under such agreement, the seller must pay all charges for delivering the goods to the named import port with duty paid. The seller must procure and pay for Marine insurance, including War Risk insurance, and is responsible for the goods until they are deposited at the named port and the free time allowed thereafter expires.

F. O. B. (Free on Board)—Such agreements may specify F. O. B. a designated ship, railroad car, or other carrier. Title to the goods passes when the goods are actually loaded on the designated carrier, after which point they are at the risk of the buyer.

F. A. S. (Free Along Side)—Such agreements require the seller to deposit the goods alongside a named vessel or on a designated dock. The seller is responsible for the property until so delivered, after which time the buyer's risk commences.

C. & F. (Cost and Freight) Named Point of Designation—Under such agreements, the seller includes in his price the cost of transportation to the designated point, but not the cost of insurance, which is to be arranged for by the buyer. It should be noted that the seller is responsible for the goods only until they are delivered to the ocean carrier or, if so required by the bill of lading, when delivered on board.

C. I. F. (Cost, Insurance and Freight)—Under such contract, the selling price includes the cost of the goods, the shipping charges and Marine insurance. While the seller must provide and pay for the Marine insurance, the goods are at his risk only until delivered to the carrier, as under C. & F. agreements discussed above. The seller is also obligated to procure War Risk insurance, but this insurance must be paid for by the buyer.

Seller as Agent of the Buyer—In actual practice, arrangements are often entered into under which the seller will obtain the shipping space for the buyer and arrange the insurance. The terms of the contract may be F. O. B. the vessel, and title to the goods may pass to the buyer at that point. Nevertheless, the seller may arrange to cover such goods under a policy endorsed to cover "for the account of others from which written instructions to insure them have been received."

GENERAL AVERAGE

When a ship is in danger at sea, it often happens that the master can extricate the vessel from her predicament by a voluntary sacrifice of a portion of the cargo, or by intentional damage to the ship's machinery or equipment. A familiar example of such action would be the deliberate throwing overboard (jettison) of some of the cargo or equipment to lighten a vessel which is stranded.

Such losses are known as General Average. Other General Average situations will arise when a fire breaks out in the hold of a ship and orders are given to wet down all the cargo in the hold to retard the spread of the blaze.

In General Average, the voluntary sacrifice of the goods of some of the owners benefits all whose cargo is on the ship and the shipowner whose vessel may be saved by such action. Similarly, if the master, in an effort to save the ship from destruction, works his engines in a manner for which they were not intended, or cuts away masts or spars or otherwise damages his ship or its machinery, the sacrifice is for the common good of all and we have a General Average situation. Extraordinary expenses incurred to safeguard the voyage or the ship, like salvage, towing, putting in at a special port, also come under General Average.

While the laws of various countries and even of the different states of the United States are not unanimous on what constitutes General Average, they are in general agreement on certain broad principles, which may be stated as follows:

1. There must be imminent peril to all the interests involved—cargo, hull and freight.

2. The sacrifice must be voluntary; the special expense incurred must be reasonable.

3. The efforts must result in preservation of part of the venture. If the sacrifice is fruitless, and the entire project is lost, there is no General Average.

4. None of the persons interested in the venture shall have contributed to the loss by his fault.

Under the laws of every country, a General Average loss is apportioned and shared among *all* who benefited by the sacrifice (averaged out). The owner of the property whose goods were jettisoned or wetted down, the shipowner whose machinery was damaged, are to be reimbursed by *all* who were benefited by the voluntary sacrifice. This includes the other cargo owners, the vessel itself, and the freight charges being earned.

No special agreement is necessary to make one liable for General Average losses. This principle is firmly established in the marine law of every country of the world, and contribution in General Average is required whether one is insured or not. (Marine insurance actually developed out of this original attempt to share losses among all involved in a shipping venture, and General Average is found in codes of law which antedate the Christian Era by 1,000 years.)

Liability for Freight Charges—Under the basic form of contract entered into by a shipowner, he is not entitled to receive freight charges unless his voyage is completed exactly according to plan. This rule holds even if he is prevented from fulfilling his mission by reasons beyond his control. It can be seen that a shipowner can undergo great expense in undertaking a voyage, and may actually complete the better part of the trip, and nevertheless be left without any compensation for his expenses or the margin of profit on which he counted. (The above rule holds in England and the United States. It is not applied as stringently in other European countries.)

MARINE INSURANCE

As pointed out, the Marine policy which is used to insure cargo owners and shipowners is essentially the same. The Cargo policy will be analyzed first, and any difference in the Hull insurance policy pointed up directly thereafter.

Standardization of Marine Policies—There is no regulation of Marine insurance forms or rates and each underwriter is free to negotiate any contract he deems advisable with an Insured. Policies may be restricted or broadened in any manner that is agreeable to underwriter and Insured. Despite the absence of any statutory policy, during the centuries that Marine insurance has been written, there has evolved a complete terminology which is basic to all Marine insurance forms.

The language used in modern policies is virtually the same as was employed three hundred years ago, and much archaic language will be found in these contracts. While this phraseology may sometimes give rise to ambiguity, it should be remembered that every word of the policy has been subjected to voluminous interpretation by the courts during these past centuries, and that as a consequence, the application of the policy to present day conditions is fairly well worked out.

While the basic provisions of Marine insurance policies are virtually uniform, the format of the policies used by different companies is varied, and clauses will appear in completely different positions in the different policies. Some companies' policies are drawn with qualifying paragraphs running alongside the insuring clause, while others will incorporate these same provisions in succeeding sections of the policy.

MARINE CARGO POLICY

WHAT IS COVERED

MARINE POLICIES may be arranged to cover the movement of any type of legal goods. The property insured is not itemized in the policy, which is written to cover "goods and merchandise."

Certain types of property are not included under the general category of "goods and merchandise" and these should be specifically described; e. g., livestock, frozen foods, refrigerated meats, poultry, game, etc. Neither are specie, bullion, securities, and similar property generally considered as within the meaning of "goods and merchandise," and it is advisable to mention them specifically also.

Import Duties and Freight Charges—The Marine policy may be written to cover not only the value of the goods shipped but also import duties and freight charges. Thus, a shipper who is required by the terms of his contract with the shipowner to absolutely prepay freight charges, without any right to reimbursement if the voyage is not completed, stands to lose not only the goods he ships but also the freight charges advanced. The amount of such freight may be added to the valuation placed on the goods and so insured. Freight may also be insured by the shipowner who may stand to lose all his expected revenue if the voyage is not completed.

Where import duties have been paid by an importer, who subsequently finds that the goods have sustained partial damage, he will suffer a loss, in part at least, of such duties. The policy may be written to cover the duty that will be due, which is insured as a separate item. In the event of loss or damage to the goods, the Insured is paid by the insurance Company for the damage and for the duties paid by him, and he agrees to make efforts to secure refund of the duty on the damaged goods.

General Average—The Marine policy, whether it covers a cargo or a vessel, also covers the General Average charges for which the Insured may become liable.

Sue and Labor—Salvage—The Sue and Labor clause found in Inland Marine insurance was taken over by those policies from the Marine (Ocean) policy. As pointed out in that discussion, the Insured is obligated to take all possible means to preserve the property from further loss and to seek its recovery. The policy will reimburse the Insured for any expenses undertaken by him in fulfillment of these duties.

In Marine insurance, Sue and Labor expenses often reach sizable figures. A wide variety of expenses may need to be incurred to save a ship or its cargo from a threatening peril, or to preserve property after the vessel has been prevented from completing its voyage in the appointed time. Thus, where a vessel was forced by a storm to put in at a port of refuge, and the captain compelled to purchase extra quantities of feed for the insured cattle on board, this expense came within the Sue and Labor clause. A ship may need to be raised or towed to drydock for emergency repairs, cargo damaged in a storm may need to be hauled to an inland point to be dried out, repacked or treated, cargo may have to be loaded on another ship, etc.

The captain of the vessel acts as agent of the cargo owner and is empowered to take all reasonable means and incur any necessary expense to preserve the property in transit. Sue and Labor expenses are payable under the policy only when incurred to preserve the property from a peril insured against.

Sue and Labor charges are payable over and above the amount available under the policy for a total loss.

HAZARDS COVERED

The Marine policy may be tailored to cover any perils that the Company may wish to assume. Some underwriters will consider certain commodities for all-risk insurance. Generally, the Marine policy covers specified perils, which are usually the following:

Perils of the Sea—Under this coverage come all perils which are peculiar to transportation and which could not be prevented by any reasonable efforts of man. Typical perils of the sea are sinking, stranding, heavy weather, collision with other vessels or submerged objects, damage by sea water when caused by an insured peril, as from opening of seams of the vessel by stranding, etc.

If the tarpaulin of a hatch is ripped off by a storm, and rain damages the cargo, the loss is considered to be due to a peril of the sea. If a sling reloading cargo during a heavy storm breaks because of the storm, the resultant loss of cargo would be covered. Lightning is a peril of the sea.

It is important to understand that a peril of the sea must be fortuitous; that is, due to an uncontrollable action of the sea, not within the control of any persons. Thus, if rain seeps through a tarpaulin not damaged by the action of the sea, there is no coverage. Similarly, a loss caused by a hose negligently allowed to play on cargo would not be covered.

Fire—While fire is not a peril of the sea, the policy covers this risk of loss. There is no coverage against fire which is due to inherent vice of the goods. Thus, certain commodities, like coal or burlap if loaded in a damp condition, may burn spontaneously, and such loss is not covered.

Combustible cargoes are sometimes accepted for insurance with special coverage against spontaneous combustion, but this peril must be specifically assumed by the policy.

Assailing Thieves—Petty thievery is not covered under the policy, but only theft accompanied by violence.

Jettison—Jettison (throwing overboard) of cargo is covered when done to preserve property from loss. There is no coverage for goods surrendered to the seas because they have spoiled; e. g., foodstuffs, plants, hides, etc.

Barratry of the Master—Barratry (violation of trust) of the master is covered, provided it is not done with the connivance of the shipowner. If the master commits barratry in conspiracy with one of the cargo owners, any loss suffered by other owners is covered under their policies.

All Other Perils—The policy covers "all other perils which shall come to the hurt, detriment or damage" of the goods. While this clause would appear to make the policy cover against all risks, this is definitely not the case. As used in the policy, it means only perils of a character similar to those insured. Thus, when a vessel was shored up on heavy supports in a repair dock, and a heavy wind blew down the supports, the damage to the vessel was held covered.

An opposite conclusion was reached when the supports of a vessel were swept away by incoming tide, since those who put the vessel up at that point should have been aware of the fact that the tide would come in, and this loss was not a peril of the sea.

Explosion—Most Marine policies specifically cover the risk of explosion, whether on land or sea.

Latent Defects in Machinery, Hull, Appurtenances (Inchmaree)—Most Marine policies are extended to cover damage caused by bursting of boilers, breakage of shafts or through any latent defect in the machinery, hull or equipment, and through faults and errors in navigation or management of the vessel. (This clause is known as the Inchmaree clause, from a celebrated court case involving a vessel of that name.)

Optional Hazards That May Be Added—Where acceptable to the Insured and the Company, other perils may be added to the policy for an additional premium. Often added to the policy are theft (where no assailing thieves are involved), pilferage, non-delivery, fresh water damage, contact with other cargo, breakage, leakage, hook hole damage, spoilage of refrigerated goods because of breakdown of refrigerating equipment, and sweat damage (condensation from bulkheads, other cargo, etc.). Other perils insured are damage caused by fuel oil or oil carried as cargo, chafing or rubbing of the cargo, taint damage due to contact with other cargo or from taking on odors from other goods, overheating of cargo placed too close to the engine rooms, loss due to bad stowage, etc.

Hazards Covered on Land—As will be discussed under WHERE COVERED, the Marine policy is almost always written to cover on land during the course of transit of the property. The policy lists a series of perils which are insured on land, generally the following:

Fire, lightning, sprinkler leakage

Cyclone, hurricane, earthquake, flood, collapse or subsidence of docks and wharves

Collision, derailment, overturning or other accident to conveyances.

HAZARDS NOT COVERED

The basic policy excludes certain perils, most of which may be insured against by specific endorsement. The old language of the Marine policy is carried over and exclusions are phrased as "warranted free from."

Dampness — Breakage — The basic policy excludes damage to goods from dampness, change of flavor, or being spotted, discolored, or musty unless caused by actual contact of the sea water due to a peril of the sea.

Breakage is covered only if caused by sinking, stranding, collision of the vessel, or by fire.

Delay—Loss of Market—The Marine policy does not cover loss caused by delay or loss of market unless specifically endorsed. Losses of this kind are considered to be incidental to business and are seldom assumed by the underwriter, except on certain special commodities like meatstuffs, where coverage may be granted for spoilage due to delay when caused by a fortuitous event like storm, fire, lightning, etc.

Acts of War, Confiscation, Detainment, Revolution (Free of Capture, Seizure Clause—F. C. & S.)—The policy does not cover loss caused by capture, seizure, arrest, detainment, confiscation, preemption, requisition or nationalization, whether in time of peace or war. Also excluded is loss or damage due to any hostilities or warlike operations, and damage caused by any weapons of war employing atomic or nuclear fission and/or fusion or other reaction or radioactive force or matter.

This exclusion will take in embargoes or other measures which interfere with the free flow of trade, and all warlike acts, revolutions, insurrections and similar occurrences.

The clause makes it clear that collision, explosion, stranding, heavy weather or fire will be excluded only if directly caused by a hostile act. Contact with a mine or torpedo is specifically excluded, and shippers are subject to this peril even in times of peace, and frequently insure their cargo under War Risk policies.

While most other forms of insurance do not assume the risks of war, Ocean Marine underwriters will cover this peril for an additional premium. The coverage is almost always written in a separate policy.

Strikes, Riots, Civil Commotions—The basic policy excludes loss or damage caused by or resulting from strikes, lockouts, labor disturbances, riots, civil commotion or the acts of any persons taking part in such disturbances.

Coverage on these perils and on certain losses caused by vandalism, malicious mischief and sabotage are usually assumed by the Marine policy under an S. R. & C. C. Endorsement. The endorsement covers damage, theft, or pilferage by strikers, rioters, persons taking part in civil commotion, and persons acting maliciously. The coverage does not take in delay, deterioration or loss of market caused by such persons, but only such direct damage as they may cause. Any damage caused by weapons employing atomic energy is excluded.

Limited coverage is granted within the continental United States and Canada for vandalism, sabotage and malicious mischief. Protection is afforded for loss caused by agents of any government, provided they are acting in secret and not in connection with any military operation in the country in which the property is situated. As under the Strikes and Riots coverage discussed above, there is no protection for loss caused by any weapon employing atomic energy.

All-Risk Insurance—As mentioned, underwriters will consider certain commodities for all-risk insurance. Most manufactured goods can usually qualify for this broad coverage. Flour, hides and skins are examples of other products which are frequently insured on an all-risk basis. The all-risk policy is written to insure against all risks of physical loss or damage from an external cause, irrespective of percentage. The policy contains certain exclusions, usually the F. C. & S., S. R. & C. C. perils and loss due to delay or loss of market (discussed directly above).

WHERE COVERED

While Marine policies are sometimes arranged to insure goods only while on the high seas, the Marine policy is usually written on a "warehouse to warehouse" basis. Under the one policy, the property is covered from the moment it leaves the shipper's premises until delivered at the warehouse of the consignee named in the policy. After the goods leave the ship, the coverage on land is limited to 15 days or, if the destination to which goods are being shipped is outside the limits of the port, to 30 days.

It can be seen that the Marine policy may cover a shipment in course of transit over many inland miles before being loaded on a vessel; then, while on the vessel and, after arrival at the port, over inland routes to the premises of the consignee. (The basic terms of the coverage differ somewhat when the property is on land than when on the high seas, as outlined before under Hazards Covered. Where the policy extends to "All Risks," these conditions apply Warehouse to Warehouse.)

It is important, however, to understand that the coverage applies only while the goods are in *due course of transit*. The progress of the goods must be continuous and move in the ordinary course of transit. Thus, if a shipper who had sold goods in Chicago bound for London were to order the shipment halted when it reached New York because he did not care to complete the shipment, or had received a cancellation of the order, the policy would cease to cover, as the goods would no longer be in the course of transit.

Under modern conditions, it is sometimes necessary for the shipper to halt the forward movement of goods to repack, relabel or permit examination to buyers or banks, and the policy may be extended to cover during such periods.

Marine Extension Clauses—Marine policies today are commonly endorsed with the "Marine Extension clauses." These clauses broaden the policy to take in deviation, delay, forced discharge, reshipment and transshipment, by eliminating the requirements that the ordinary course of transit be maintained continuously. The clause also eliminates the 15 or 30-day limit after goods are discharged from the vessel. It is agreed that no such interruption or suspension of transit will be covered unless beyond the control of the Insured.

On Deck Shipments—The Marine policy usually states that it covers "shipments *under* deck." Whether there is a specific exclusion or not, the Marine policy does not cover any shipments carried *on* the deck of a vessel, unless notice is given to the underwriter of such stowage of goods.

An exception to this well-established rule of Marine insurance is made for goods which are required by law or shipping custom to be carried on deck. In such cases, where the practice is firmly established, the underwriter may be presumed to know of such usage, and the policy held to cover even when the owner did not give notice.

Some policies grant coverage for on-deck shipments of a limited amount against certain stated perils.

Type of Vessels on Which Goods Are Carried—The Marine underwriter usually inserts a clause in the policy specifying that the goods are insured only while shipped via iron or steel steamers. Generally, the policy excludes all sailing vessels.

Seaworthiness of the Vessel—Seaworthiness of the vessel is one of several implied (not expressed) warranties in a Marine policy. These warranties developed out of court decisions affecting Marine insurance, and are as binding on the Insured as any written into the policy. All Marine policies are subject to the implied warranty of seaworthiness, which requires that the ship be suitably constructed, properly equipped, manned, fueled and provisioned for the type of voyage being undertaken, or for the separate parts of such voyage. Thus, a vessel fit to navigate a bay or river or coastwise might not be fit to make a transatlantic crossing; certain ships may be safe for one cargo but not for another, etc.

Since under modern trade conditions the shipper seldom has any knowledge of the fitness of the ships on which he relies to carry his goods, most Marine policies, in a special clause, admit the seaworthiness of the vessel.

No Deviation—Another warranty is that of "no deviation," implied in all Marine policies. Under this doctrine, once the risk has commenced, there must be no substitution in the voyage, or deviation from the agreed or usual course, no matter how slight, except when made necessary by stress of weather or unavoidable accident, or by circumstances over which neither the shipowner nor the master has any control, or to save human life whether on the insured vessel or another, or to obtain medical or surgical relief for persons on board.

Any other deviation will void the policy, even if the original course is thereafter resumed. Where the deviation is very slight, as for one hour or for a mile, it has been held that the policy is merely suspended during the deviation, and continues in effect when the deviation terminates. This is the exception, however, and generally any unexcused deviation will void the policy, even if the original course is subsequently resumed.

Because modern shippers are seldom in a position to exercise any control over the navigation of the vessel on which their goods is placed, it is customary to insert in Marine policies a clause which states that the insurance will not be voided by deviation of which the Insured has no knowledge, or by any unintentional error in description of the vessel, voyage or interest or interruption in the ordinary course of transit.

The Insured is required under this clause to notify the Company of any deviation of which he becomes aware, and to pay such additional premium as may be required to cover the added risk.

WHEN COVERED

Prompt Attachment—As discussed before, the Marine policy is usually written on a "warehouse to warehouse" basis. The insurance need not attach from the time the policy is written, but may be issued to cover a prospective voyage.

There is, however, another implied warranty in Marine insurance which may affect the coverage — the implied warranty of prompt attachment.

Unless permission is specifically granted by the Company to extend the period, it is assumed that the voyage will be commenced within a reasonable time and, if not so begun, the policy will be void. This warranty has become firmly rooted in Marine insurance, since the risk of loss in a particular voyage may vary sharply during different times of the year and the Company should know when the goods will be moved.

FOR HOW MUCH

Marine insurance is written on a *valued* basis. The valuation to be placed on the goods is agreed upon between the Insured and the Company at the time the policy is written or the shipment made. This valuation will be binding on both parties in the event of loss, and neither party can reopen the question except if fraud can be demonstrated.

There are several popular Valuation clauses in use, but most commonly the policy agrees to value the goods "at invoice cost plus 10% plus freight." Where goods are subject to fluctuations in price, the policy may agree to value the goods at the highest market value which was attained during any point in the voyage.

Coinsurance—While there is no Coinsurance clause as such in Marine policies, the settlement of losses is based on the agreed valuation of the goods. In the event of a partial loss, then, the Insured's recovery is measured by the extent of damage to the goods. Thus, assume an Insured ships 100 cases of merchandise which are agreed to be valued at $150 each. They are received at their destination in a damaged condition. The extent of the deterioration in their value is first to be determined. If the market value of each case in sound condition is $200, and their value in the damaged state is $100, the Insured is entitled to one-half of the insured value of the goods, or $75 per case. The formula may be expressed as follows:

$$\frac{\text{Depreciation}}{\text{Sound Market Value}} \times \text{Insured Value}$$

Particular Average—In the insurance sense, Average means loss less than total. Particular Average refers to loss which affects only a particular interest, as opposed to General Average which affects all interested in the voyage. Except on certain all-risk policies, all Marine policies contain some "Average" clause which limits recovery on most partial losses. There are several types of "Average" clauses, and these are described below.

Free of Particular Average (F. P. A.) American Conditions—This clause reads, "Free of Particular Average (unless General) or unless caused by stranding, sinking, burning or collision with another vessel."

Under the terms of this clause, total destruction of a cargo would be covered, no matter how caused, but partial losses will be covered only if caused by one of the designated perils of the sea. This is the most restrictive form of Average clause in use.

Free of Particular Average (F. P. A.) English Conditions—This clause reads, "Free of Particular Average (unless General) or unless the vessel be stranded or craft be stranded, sunk, burnt, on fire or in collision with another vessel."

This clause is essentially the same as the American Conditions clause above except that, under the English conditions, the policy will pay partial losses whether caused *by* the designated perils of the sea or occurring *after* such peril has happened. Thus, under the English conditions, if the vessel has stranded, the warranty is open thereafter during the voyage and all partial losses will be paid, even if they are in no way traceable to the stranding or any other peril of the sea.

The English type of clause, F. P. A. E. C., is usually used on under-deck shipments, while the American conditions are usually applied to on-deck shipments.

With Average (W. A.)—Less restrictive than either of the F. P. A. clauses described above is the With Average clause, which reads, "Subject to Particular Average if amounting to 3% (unless General), or the vessel or craft is stranded, sunk, burnt, on fire or in collision."

Under this clause, all partial losses are covered if they exceed 3%, and smaller losses if caused by one of the designated perils. Other percentages may be provided and some policies contain a clause setting forth varying percentages for Particular Average losses on different commodities.

Average clauses may also include other perils in addition to those designated in the quoted clause, such as theft, pilferage, non-delivery, breakage, fresh water damage, sweat damage, etc.

Memorandum Clause—The Particular Average percentages may differ for various commodities, based on their estimated susceptibility to damage. Some commodities will be listed as Free of Particular Average, others if under 20%, 10%, 7%, 3%, etc. An excerpt from a typical Memorandum clause reads:

> "It is also agreed that bar, bundle, rod, hoop and sheet iron, wire of all kinds, tin plates, steel, madder, sumac, wicker-ware and willow, salt, grain of all kinds, tobacco, fruits, cheese, dry fish, hay, vegetables, rags, bags, household furniture, skins and hides, musical instruments, looking glasses and all other articles that are perishable in their own nature are warranted by the Insured free from Average unless General; hemp, tobacco stems, matting and cassia, except in boxes, free from Average under 20% unless General; sugar, flax, flax-seed and bread are warranted by the Insured free from Average under 7% unless General; and coffee in bags or bulk, pepper in bags or bulk, and rice, free from Average under 10% unless General . . ."

The phrase "unless General" appears after all Particular Average percentages to indicate that any loss which is sustained by a particular interest for the good of all is a General Average loss, and is not subject to Particular Average. In other words, if a portion of the cargo of a particular owner is jettisoned to lighten the ship, such loss comes under General Average and is not subject to the Particular Average percentage.

The Particular Average clause is *not* a Deductible. Once the loss exceeds the stated percentage, the entire loss is payable. Assume a shipment of $100,000 is made subject to Particular Average, if amounting to 3%. If the cargo sustains damage (other than by a peril designated in the clause) of less than $3,000, the policy pays nothing. If the loss is $3,000 or more, the policy is liable for the entire loss. This type of clause is known as a Franchise clause.

Unless the Franchise clause is modified by some qualifying language, the Average clause is applied to the value of the entire shipment. When the value of a single shipment is very high, the clause may be drawn to apply to a unit or part of the shipment, as to each lot, or to 25 bags, or to a dollar amount, as to each $10,000, etc.

Abandonment—When a heavy loss is suffered by a vessel or its cargo, the cost of salvage may appear so high that it is not prudent to try and make repairs or save the property. Such losses are deemed constructive total losses, and the Insured may tender abandonment of the property to the Company. If the Company accepts the abandonment, it pays the Insured for the total value of the goods or the vessel, as the case may be, and takes any salvage that remains.

In Marine insurance, it is optional with the Insured whether he wishes to abandon. The Company cannot insist upon taking the insured property and paying for a total loss. This is in direct contrast to the rule in Fire insurance, where the *Company* has the option of taking all of the property and paying for a total loss.

The Insured agrees not to abandon insured property in case of capture or seizure until after 90 days after the property is condemned. In case of blockade, the Insured agrees not to abandon the property but to proceed to the nearest port where he is to end the voyage.

Machinery or Manufactured Goods—If one part of a shipped machine is damaged, it may render the entire machine useless. Similarly, manufactured goods which consist of several parts may be received with one part damaged and the entire product may not be of any value.

The Marine policy stipulates that the Company's liability will be limited to the value of the lost or damaged part or, at the Insured's option, to the cost of repairing or replacing the part.

Labels—Discussed in Chapter 21 under TRANSPORTATION POLICY — SHIPPERS FORM — FOR HOW MUCH — Labels Clause.

Other Insurance—It frequently happens that the same shipments are insured by more than one person. Under American practice, the policy which was effected first is primary, and the second policy is liable only for any excess of the loss over the amount of the primary policy. The English rule is different on this score, and either policy may be collected from, with the companies then working out their respective shares of the total liability.

WHO IS INSURED

Any person who has a valid insurable interest in the property may insure under a Marine policy. This interest may be that of ownership or any other interest which will be impaired because of loss or damage to the goods. Thus, an agent who will upon delivery of the goods become entitled to a commission, no matter how small, is deemed to possess an insurable interest which he may insure.

INSURED'S DUTIES AND OBLIGATIONS

Fraud, Concealment—The rule requiring an Insured to disclose all material facts to the underwriter is very strictly construed in Marine insurance. Where, in other forms of insurance, the policy is voided only if the Insured *wilfully* conceals or misrepresents a material fact, in Marine insurance such failure will void the contract whether it is intentional or otherwise. Generally, if the concealment is not intentional, it will void the policy as regards any losses arising from the concealed facts; if the concealment is intentional, the entire policy is void from its inception.

Impairment of Carrier's Liability—The Marine policy forbids the Insured to enter into any agreement with the shipowner or anyone else in charge of the vessel which would limit or impair his right to recover from such parties for any loss caused to the goods, except that privilege is usually given to ship goods under released or limited bills of lading.

Notice of Loss—All claims for loss or damage must be reported promptly to the Company or its agents. Proof of Loss and bills of expenses are to be approved by an agent of the Company.

Subrogation—After the Company has paid a loss, it is subrogated to any right the Insured may have to proceed against third parties. This right is of considerable importance in Marine insurance, since it may be possible to recapture substantial sums from third parties who were at fault. Thus, collision losses are often recoverable from the other ship when it was at fault; indemnity may sometimes be had from plants or facilities which explode and damage ships and cargoes; Governments whose actions cause damage to a ship may offer reimbursement, etc.

Benefit of Insurance—See Chapter 17.

Cancellation—Marine policies may be cancelled by the Insured or the Company. Either party is required to give 30 days' notice to the other party.

How Policy Is Written—A Marine insurance policy may be written to cover a single shipment. Where the Insured makes regular shipments, it is customary to issue an Open policy. The policy does not provide any expiration date and is continuous until cancelled. (Open policies are in force today which were written 75 years ago.)

For the shipper, the Open policy is a very convenient device. He is automatically covered on any shipments he makes. While he is required to report any shipments as soon as possible, the insurance will be effective on any shipments made by him even if he forgets to make the proper declaration. Then again, the shipper does not have to arrange for insurance every time he plans to make a shipment, and is in a position in negotiating a price for his goods to know exactly what the insurance charges will be on such transaction.

There are two ways in which the Insured may report shipments made by him under his policy. If he is not required to furnish evidence of insurance to third parties, as is often the case with imports, he completes a short form declaration in which he sets forth the name of the vessel, the origin of the shipment, its destination, the nature and number of commodities, and the amount of insurance being effected. These declarations are forwarded to the Company, which bills the Insured once a month in accordance with the rates established in the policy.

In the majority of cases, particularly when exports are being made, the Insured will need to show his customer or the bank or other third parties that he is carrying insurance. This is accomplished under a special Marine policy or certificate which the Insured is empowered to issue and which gives all details of the shipment. The certificate or special Marine policy, as the case may be, is prepared in four copies, two of which are forwarded to the consignee or bank, while the remaining copies are retained by the shipper and the insurance Company.

Rates—Rates are determined by the underwriter, who is free to follow his judgment in the matter. Where shipments are made or imports received from various points, the policy contains a schedule of rates which is attached to the policy. Thus, shipments of a particular commodity to the United Kingdom may be rated at 11c per $100 of valuation, to Italy via the Italian Mediterranean ports not east of Sicily, 12½c; to Adriatic ports, 25c; to Cape Town, Johannesburg, Port Elizabeth, Durban and Natal, 35c, etc. Where several commodities differing in their susceptibility to loss are involved, separate rates will be established for each type of goods.

CARGO WAR RISK POLICY

AS INDICATED ABOVE, the perils of war are excluded under a Marine insurance policy, including collision of the vessel with floating mines even in time of peace. These risks may be insured and are usually written at the same time as the basic Marine policy, although in a separate policy.

The War Risk policy picks up practically all the war group perils excluded under the basic policy. In most respects other than perils covered, it is the same as the Marine policy which covers the basic risk. The War Risk policy differs from the basic Marine policy in that it may be cancelled upon 48 hours' notice, instead of the 30 days required for the basic policy; also in that there is no coverage prior to the loading of the cargo on the vessel, nor after 15 days after discharge of the cargo at the final port of destination. If the cargo is landed at a port for transshipment to another vessel overseas, the coverage is effective for 15 days after being landed, after which time it ceases until the merchandise is actually loaded on the new vessel.

HULL INSURANCE

AS POINTED OUT at the opening of this chapter, the basic Marine policy is the same for shipowner and shipper. When the policy covers the vessel itself, it is known as a Hull policy.

In addition to providing insurance on the ship, the owner is protected for his legal liability to others arising from collision of his vessel with another.

Different from the Cargo policy, which is almost always an Open Form, the Hull policy is generally written to cover a particular voyage or written for one year. The policy may contain a Trading Warranty, which restricts coverage while the vessel is within certain geographical limits.

The implied warranty of seaworthiness applies to Hull policies written on a voyage basis but not if written on a time basis. The latter type of policy may attach when the vessel is at sea, and to impose the warranty of seaworthiness on the shipowner might constitute a hardship. Under these policies, however, the Insured is expected to take all reasonable means to make the vessel seaworthy after she puts in at a port where repairs can be made.

The warranty of seaworthiness as regards a shipowner does not extend to the cargo. If cargo were shipped in such a state as to endanger the ship, the Hull policy would not be voided unless the Insured was aware of the dangerous condition in the goods and negligently allowed them to be loaded.

YACHT POLICY

A SPECIAL POLICY IS USED to insure pleasure craft like yachts, motorboats and sailboats. The policy covers the property of the boat owner and his liability for collision damages caused to other vessels. It may be extended to cover liability for other collisions and for injury to persons.

The policy describes the craft insured, and covers not only the hull but also its appurtenances — spars, sails, tackle, machinery, boats and furniture.

There are two forms under which the hull may be insured:

A Limited Hull policy will cover only against the perils of fire and lightning, or fire, lightning and theft.

The Full Marine policy covers the following perils:

Fire, lightning, explosion.

Explosion, bursting of boilers or breaking of shafts through latent defects in the hull or machinery. This is the coverage provided by the Marine policy under the Inchmaree Clause. (Discussed under Marine Cargo Policy—Hazards Covered—Latent Defects in Machinery, Hull, Appurtenances.)

Perils of the sea.

Theft of the entire boat and its equipment by persons making forcible entry.

Collision.

Conversion to his own use of the boat by its master or mariner.

When part of boat, its tackle or furniture is removed from the boat and is stored on shore, it is covered against fire only, and for not more than 50% of the amount of insurance applicable to the hull.

The policy also covers liability of the Insured for collision with other vessels, but not for collision damages caused to property other than boats. Liability for damages caused by the Insured's collision with bridges, piers, docks, wharves, buoys and other property may be added to the policy by a Protection and Indemnity Endorsement. This endorsement also covers the Insured's liability for bodily injury or death caused by the operation of the vessel.

The basic policy excludes the S. R. & C. C. perils and the F. C. & S. perils (discussed before). Coverage is specifically restricted to the waters described in the policy. The policy may not be written for more than one year, and usually stipulates certain months of the year during which the craft will be laid up.

The Yacht policy may be cancelled on 10 days' notice from either party to the other.

ALL RISK YACHT POLICY

Most companies also write an all-risk Yacht policy for risks which qualify for this broader coverage.

The policy covers all risks of physical loss or damage, excluding only certain stated perils. Generally, the exclusions are as follows:

Wear, tear, gradual deterioration, inherent vice;

Marine borers, vermin;

Loss caused by or resulting from ice or freezing while afloat;

Loss or damage to any spinnaker (sail) while racing;

Theft or mysterious disappearance of equipment or accessories unless there is visible evidence of forcible entry, or unless the entire Yacht is stolen.

FOR FURTHER READING

HUEBNER AND BLACK—Property Insurance
MAGEE AND BICKELHAUPT—General Insurance
MARINE INSURANCE—Practical Notes and Comments on Cargo Insurance
MEHR AND CAMMACK—Principles of Insurance
MOWBRAY AND BLANCHARD—Insurance
WINTER—History and Principles of Marine Insurance
WINTER—Marine Insurance

(See Reading List at End of Book)

CHAPTER 23

Negligence and Other Torts

A TORT MAY BE generally defined as a wrong committed by one person against another (other than a breach of contract) for which the law provides a civil remedy in the form of damages. Some examples of torts are assault and battery, trespass, conversion, defamation, and malicious destruction of property. In the main, such torts are of an intentional kind.

The most common form of a tort is the one committed unintentionally—the tort of negligence.

While there are several statutes which define negligence; e. g., wrongful death statutes, the Jones Act, automobile guest laws, dramshop liability statutes, etc., most of the law of negligence is common law rather than statutory. Its source is the reported opinions of courts that have decided similar points in the past rather than legislative enactment.

It is a firmly established rule of the common law that every person is required to conduct himself in such a manner as to avoid injuring either the person or the property of another.

Negligence may be defined as the "failure to exercise care, prudence and foresight such as is warranted by the circumstances" or "failure to do what a reasonable person would have done under the circumstances, or doing something which a reasonable man would not have done under the circumstances."

Even though a person has committed negligence or acted negligently to the injury of the person or property of another, he will not be held liable for the damages of the latter unless the negligence was the proximate cause of the damages.

It should be understood that it is not sufficient merely to show that an injury was caused by the actions of a second party. The mere fact that there was an accident does not in itself establish a presumption of negligence. The person claiming damages, in almost every instance, must *prove* the negligence of the other, and that the negligence was the direct or proximate cause of the injury or the damages. (A general exception to this rule is discussed later under Res Ipsa Loquitor.)

It is also important to understand that the question of whether there was negligence is a question of fact which is usually submitted to a jury. When the jury finds that there was negligence, the Court will almost always uphold the finding.

DEGREE OF CARE REQUIRED

The duty owed to different persons varies with the particular circumstances of the case. Thus, a person owes a greater degree of care to someone whom he has invited on his premises (an invitee) than he does to a trespasser. Many jurisdictions distinguish between the degree of care owed business visitors, referred to as invitees, and that which is due social guests, invitees. If his premises are readily accessible to children, he may be required to exercise greater care than otherwise. The degree of care required will also depend on the nature of the activities conducted by the individual or firm, and the type of product being handled.

Thus, a higher degree of care will be expected from one who keeps an explosive substance than from another who handles less dangerous objects. Similarly, a person who manufactures or sells an inherently dangerous item is expected to take more precautions to prevent its causing injury than he would if he were handling less dangerous objects. The degree of care expected in each instance is commensurate with the risk involved.

Attractive Hazard—As mentioned above, a person whose premises are readily accessible to children will be expected to take great care to avoid injury to the children. If there is something on the premises which will draw a child to investigate or use it, the owner of the property may be liable for the injuries sustained by the child, even though the item was entirely within the premises and the child trespassed on the property.

The attractiveness of the object, if above ordinary, is held to be an implied invitation to the child to enter the premises, and raises the status of the child above that of a trespasser. Swimming pools, wells, shafts, caves and similar facilities which have a strong attraction for children have been held to be "attractive nuisances" or "attractive hazards" and the owner charged with care in keeping children from coming to harm through such "attractions."

CONTRIBUTORY NEGLIGENCE

Even though a person can show that the negligence of another caused him damages, the second party may not be liable for the damages. In most states, a person who is claiming damages due to another's acts must himself be free of Contributory Negligence.

(This rule is modified in several jurisdictions, as outlined later under the separate states.)

Last Clear Chance—On the other hand, even where the injured party was guilty of Contributory Negligence, the defendant may be liable, if he had a "last clear chance" to avoid the accident. Such "last clear chance" may be held to override the plaintiff's Contributory Negligence.

Comparative Negligence—Eighteen states have enacted legislation modifying the strict requirement that a plaintiff be free of Contributory Negligence if he is to be permitted to recover damages.

ARKANSAS, COLORADO, HAWAII, IDAHO, MAINE, MASSACHUSETTS, MINNESOTA, MISSISSIPPI, NEW HAMPSHIRE, PUERTO RICO, RHODE ISLAND, VERMONT, WISCONSIN—The Comparative negligence statutes provide that a claimant's rights will *not* be extinguished by his contributory negligence, but only *diminished* in proportion to his contribution to the accident.

GEORGIA—Contributory negligence will defeat a plaintiff's right to recover if he could, by *ordinary* care, have avoided the consequences to himself of the defendant's negligence. In other cases however, the defendant is not relieved even though the plaintiff may have contributed to the injury sustained.

INDIANA, IOWA—The plaintiff does not have the burden of proving his freedom from contributory negligence. If the defendant does wish to rely on the negligence of the plaintiff as a defense, he shall have the burden of proving that the negligence of the plaintiff was the proximate cause of the injury or damage.

In the case of an action by a passenger against a common carrier, the defendant may plead and prove contributory negligence, and the plaintiff need not prove freedom therefrom. (IOWA only).

MARYLAND—In all actions to recover damages, for death, or injury to the person or property of an infant, by or on behalf of an infant, the negligence of the parent or other custodian of the infant shall not be imputed to the infant from the fact of such parenthood or custodianship.

NEBRASKA, OREGON, SOUTH DAKOTA—The contributory negligence of the plaintiff shall not bar recovery when his negligence was slight and the negligence of the defendant was gross in comparison.

RES IPSA LOQUITOR

Although the general rule is that the plaintiff must *prove* the negligence of the defendant, the occurrence of an accident under certain conditions is deemed to be prima facie evidence of negligence. This is known as the doctrine of "res ipsa loquitor"—the thing speaks for itself. Generally, this rule will apply when the thing that caused the accident was under the control of the defendant and the accident clearly of a kind that does not occur when proper care is exercised.

EXAMPLE: A building is destroyed by fire caused by sparks emitted from a locomotive or stationary engine. It is accepted that such fires will not result when due care is exercised.

The doctrine of "res ipsa loquitor" (the thing speaks for itself) is not invoked except when necessary evidence is absent or not readily available. Thus, after a train is derailed, it may not be possible to determine the cause of the accident. The injured parties are not burdened with proving the negligence of the railroad. The doctrine has the effect of justifying an inference of negligence, or in some jurisdictions, of establishing a presumption of this nature.

TORTS

A TORT IS A VIOLATION of another's natural right. As outlined above, most torts are committed unintentionally, as in the case of negligence which causes injury or damage. Examples of negligent torts would be failure to keep sidewalk in repair, negligence in the operation of a motor vehicle, malpractice by a physician, improper and unsafe maintenance of premises, etc. When a person has been injured or has suffered loss due to the negligent tort of another, the law recognizes the right of the injured party to redress (right of receiving compensation or money damages).

Liability insurance (to be discussed in Chapters 24 and 25) concerns itself with negligent torts. As will be shown, this form of insurance is designed to protect an individual or a firm from claims which may be brought against him for negligent torts. It is therefore important for the insurance man to have some understanding of the nature and extent of liability between persons, the restrictions and time limits on suits, and the liability of a person for the actions of others. Some of the more important statutes and practices on these matters are set down below under several headings. It should be stressed, however, that these are given in barest outline. The reader is therefore urged to check further into the laws of his state on any point made.

TIME LIMIT ON SUITS

Every state of the country places a limit on the time within which suits for damages must be commenced. These limits range from one year to six years. In many of the states, there is a difference in the time within which one may bring a suit to recover for personal injury and the time allowed for suits alleging property damage or wrongful death. Generally, the negligent act and the resulting injury occur simultaneously. It should be noted, however, that the time to commence a suit begins to run from the date of the injury, and not from the act of negligence, where these two do not coincide. Also, there are usually special statutes governing the time to sue for medical malpractice and for suits against municipalities. The chart reproduced below shows the limits applicable to all three types of actions in the different states.

LIMITATIONS

Time (in Years) Within Which Action Must Be Started

State	For Personal Injury	For Property Damage	For Wrongful Death
Alabama	1	1	2
Alaska	2	6	2
Arizona	2	2	2
Arkansas	3	3	3
California	1	3	1
Colorado	6	6	2*
Connecticut	2a	2a	2a
Delaware	2	2	2
District of Columbia	3	3	1
Florida	4	3	2
Georgia	2	4	2
Hawaii	2	2	2
Idaho	2	3	2
Illinois	2	2	2
Indiana	2	5	2
Iowa	2	5	2
Kansas	2b	2b	2
Kentucky	1	5	1
Louisiana	1	1	1
Maine	6‡	6‡	2
Maryland	3	3	3
Massachusetts	2	2	2†
Michigan	3	3	3
Minnesota	6	6	3*
Mississippi	6	6	6
Missouri	5	5	2
Montana	3	2	3
Nebraska	4	4	2
Nevada	2	3	2
New Hampshire	6	6	2
New Jersey	2	6	2
New Mexico	3	4	3
New York	3	3	2
North Carolina	3c	3c	2
North Dakota	6	6	2
Ohio	2	2	2
Oklahoma	2	2	2
Oregon	2	6	3*
Pennsylvania	2	6	1
Rhode Island	3	6	2
South Carolina	6	6	6
South Dakota	3	6	3
Tennessee	1	3	1*
Texas	2	2	2
Utah	4	3	2
Vermont	3	3	2
Virginia	2	5	2
Washington	3	3	3
West Virginia	2	2	2
Wisconsin	3**	6	3
Wyoming	4	4	2

* From time of negligence or injury causing death.

† Two years after cause of action accrues in motor vehicle accident cases.

** 6 years if 2-year notice of claim was served prior to July 1, 1959.

‡ 2 years where injury or damage caused by motor vehicle subject to supervision of Public Utilities Commission.

a From date when injury sustained or discovered or should have been discovered; otherwise not later than three years from date of act or omission.

b After act first causes substantial injury, or if fact of injury not reasonably ascertainable until after initial act after fact of injury becomes reasonably ascertainable, but in no event more than 10 years beyond the time of the act.

c Cause of action not readily apparent to claimant at time of origin deemed to have accrued at the time injury was discovered, or ought reasonably to have been discovered, whichever event first occurs; provided that in such cases the period shall not exceed 10 years from last act giving rise to claim.

Reprinted from "Statutes Affecting Liability Insurance" 15th Edition, December, 1971. American Insurance Association, N. Y., N. Y.

SUITS OF SPOUSE AGAINST SPOUSE

In 33 states, a spouse cannot sue a spouse in tort, i. e., sue for torts committed by the spouse. Two states make an exception to this rule for certain specific situations. In only 12 states are such suits permitted, while three states have no provision on this score.

ALABAMA, ARKANSAS, COLORADO, CONNECTICUT, NEVADA, NEW HAMPSHIRE, NORTH CAROLINA, NORTH DAKOTA, OKLAHOMA, SOUTH CAROLINA, SOUTH DAKOTA, WISCONSIN—Suits in tort of spouse against spouse are permitted.

ARIZONA, CALIFORNIA, DELAWARE, DISTRICT OF COLUMBIA, FLORIDA, GEORGIA, IDAHO, ILLINOIS, INDIANA, IOWA, KANSAS, MAINE, MARYLAND, MASSACHUSETTS, MICHIGAN, MINNESOTA, MISSISSIPPI, MISSOURI, MONTANA, NEBRASKA, NEW JERSEY, OHIO, PENNSYLVANIA, RHODE ISLAND, TEXAS, UTAH, VERMONT, VIRGINIA, WASHINGTON, WEST VIRGINIA, WYOMING—A spouse cannot sue a spouse in tort.

KENTUCKY—Suits of spouse against spouse are not permitted except that an administrator may sue a surviving spouse on behalf of children.

LOUISIANA—A spouse cannot sue a spouse in tort, but may sue the insurer of the spouse.

NEW MEXICO, OREGON, TENNESSEE—There is no statute on this question.

NEW YORK—A spouse may sue a spouse in tort. Under state law, however, no Liability policy will be held to provide coverage for such suits except if specifically endorsed on the policy by the Company.

GUEST LAWS

ALABAMA, COLORADO, FLORIDA, IOWA, KANSAS, MONTANA, TEXAS, VIRGINIA, WASHINGTON, WYOMING:

All of the above states have enacted laws which severely restrict persons who ride as guests in automobiles in their right to sue for injuries sustained by them. The exact terminology of these "Guest Laws" varies somewhat among the states, but their impact is fairly similar. In essence, these laws require as a minimum that the driver be guilty of gross negligence before a guest can take legal action against the driver to recover for injuries suffered while riding as a passenger in a private passenger automobile. Some "Guest Laws" are even more restrictive and permit a guest to sue only when the driver was intoxicated or guilty of "willful or wanton misconduct" or "reckless disregard of the rights of others."

A guest is usually defined as one who has not paid for his transportation, although the courts have on occasion interpreted the word more liberally in favor of the injured person. Thus, in specific cases, some court decisions have held that where the driver or owner of the automobile stood to benefit from the presence of his passenger, the passenger was not a guest and might therefore recover if ordinary negligence was the proximate cause of the accident. Generally, however, "Guest Laws" operate to restrict the right of suit of most ordinary passengers in privately owned automobiles.

GEORGIA—This state has no "Guest Law" but court decisions follow the principles of restricting the right of suit by guests in private passenger automobiles. The effect of these decisions in this state is to put guests on the same footing as in states where a "Guest Law" is on the statute books.

ARKANSAS, CALIFORNIA, OREGON—Guest laws apply not only to motor vehicles but also to aircraft and boats.

DELAWARE, IDAHO, ILLINOIS, INDIANA, MICHIGAN, NEBRASKA, NEVADA, NEW MEXICO, NORTH DAKOTA, OHIO, SOUTH CAROLINA, SOUTH DAKOTA, UTAH—Guest laws apply not only to motor vehicles but also to aircraft.

WASHINGTON—Suits by guest passengers may be brought only if the accident was intentional on the part of the owner or operator of the vehicle.

SURVIVAL OF ACTIONS AFTER DEATH

In practically every state, an action for personal injuries survives after the injured party has died. Similarly, if the defendant dies, the injured person's cause for action does not abate but continues against the deceased's personal representatives. A few states place a limitation on the type of damages that are recoverable in such instances or otherwise modify the right to continue such actions.

ALABAMA, ALASKA, COLORADO, IDAHO, ILLINOIS, KENTUCKY, MARYLAND, PENNSYLVANIA—In these states, while actions survive after death, an exception is made for actions for libel or slander, or damage to reputation.

ARIZONA—Action for personal injuries or wrongful death shall not abate by reason of death of defendant. Upon the death of the person injured, damages for pain or suffering of such injured person shall not be allowed. Every cause of action, except for breach of promise, seduction, libel, slander, separate maintenance, alimony, loss of consortium or invasion of the right of privacy shall survive the death of the person entitled thereto or liable therefor.

CALIFORNIA—When a person entitled to bring an action against another for bodily injury dies before judgment, the damages recoverable are limited to loss of earnings and expenses sustained or incurred prior to death, and shall not include damages for pain, suffering, disfigurement, or punitive or exemplary damages, nor damages for loss of prospective profits or earnings after date of death.

D. C.—In tort actions, the right of action shall be limited to damages for physical injury other than pain and suffering.

DELAWARE—Same as ALABAMA except that the law excepts actions for defamation, malicious persecution or upon penal statutes.

HAWAII—Same as ALABAMA except that the law excepts only actions for defamation and malicious prosecution.

INDIANA—All causes of action survive after death of person entitled to or liable to such action. When a person receives personal injuries by wrongful act of another and thereafter dies from causes *other* than said injuries, personal representatives may maintain action against wrongdoer, but shall be permitted to recover only the reasonable medical, hospital and nursing expense and loss of income of said injured person from date of injury to date of death.

KANSAS—Same as ALABAMA except that the law excepts actions for libel, slander, malicious prosecution or a nuisance.

LOUISIANA—The right to recover all damages other than to property, shall survive for a period of one year in favor of the children or spouse of the deceased, and in certain cases in favor of the brothers and sisters.

MASSACHUSETTS—In addition to actions which survive at common law, the following, among others, shall also survive: of tort for assault, battery or imprisonment or other damage to the person; for consequential damages arising out of injuries to the person and consisting of medical, nursing, hospital or surgical expenses incurred by spouse, parent or guardian; for damages to personal property.

MICHIGAN—All actions and claims survive death. Actions on claims for injuries which result in death shall not be prosecuted after death except pursuant to the wrongful death statute.

MINNESOTA—A cause of action arising out of an injury to the person dies with the person in whose favor it exists except as provided in the wrongful death statute. It also dies with person against whom it exists except that cause of action arising out of bodily injury or death caused by negligence of a decedent survives against his personal representatives.

NEBRASKA, NEW MEXICO, OKLAHOMA, WEST VIRGINIA—In addition to causes of action which survive at common law, the following among others shall also survive: for injuries to real or personal estate.

NEW JERSEY—In actions based on wrongful act, neglect or default of another, where death results from injuries for which the deceased would have had a cause of action if he had lived, the personal representative may recover all reasonable funeral expenses in addition to damages accrued during the lifetime of the deceased.

NEW YORK—An action may be brought or continued by or against the executor or administrator of the deceased, but punitive damages shall not be awarded nor penalties adjudged in any such action brought to recover damages for personal injury. Where injury causes death, damages shall be limited to those accruing before death and shall not include damages for or by reason of death, except that reasonable funeral expenses shall be recoverable.

NORTH DAKOTA—Same as ALABAMA except that the law excepts actions for breach of promise and alienation of affections, as well.

OREGON—Damages shall not exceed $25,000 and shall be limited to reasonable expenses paid or incurred for doctor, hospital or nursing services for the deceased and for his loss of earnings. Plaintiff may also recover a reasonable amount for attorney fees.

RHODE ISLAND—In addition to causes of action which survive at common law, causes of action for trespass and trespass on the case for damages to the person or to real and personal estate shall also survive. Recovery limited to actual damages sustained, without any vindictive or exemplary damages or damages for any alleged outrage to feelings of injured party.

TENNESSEE—Same as ALABAMA except that the law excepts actions for wrongs affecting character.

WASHINGTON—No personal representative shall be entitled to recover damages for pain and suffering, anxiety, emotional distress, or humiliation personal to and suffered by a deceased.

WYOMING—In action for personal injury damages, if person otherwise entitled thereto dies, recovery is limited to damages for wrongful death.

ACTIONS FOR WRONGFUL DEATH

In all states, personal representatives of a person killed by the wrongful act of another may maintain an action against the tortfeasor, the person who committed the tort. Some of the states have established a maximum limit recoverable for wrongful death, a few states also prescribe a minimum amount payable, and the limits applicable in the various states are set forth below. In those states which are not listed, there is no statutory maximum on the amount which may be recovered for wrongful death, where there are dependents, except that some states place a limit where there is no surviving spouse, or dependent children, or dependent next of kin.

It should be remembered that an action for wrongful death may be maintained separately from the one for personal injuries sustained by the person before his death. Even in the states which restrict or limit the right to sustain an action for personal injuries after one of the parties has died, the right to sue for wrongful death still exists.

COLORADO—The maximum recoverable for wrongful death is $45,000.

CONNECTICUT—Recovery is limited to damages plus medical, hospital, nursing and funeral expenses.

ILLINOIS—Where death occurred between July 14, 1955 and July 7, 1957, maximum recoverable is limited to $25,000; where death occurred after July 7, 1957, but before August 18, 1967, the maximum is $30,000; where death occurred after August 18, 1967, there is no maximum.

INDIANA—If no surviving spouse, dependent children, or dependent next of kin, damages limited to the total of the necessary and reasonable value of medical, hospital, funeral, legal and administrative service to deceased or his estate.

KANSAS—The maximum recoverable for wrongful death is $50,000.

KENTUCKY—A parent may recover in the case of a minor child's death for the loss of affection and companionship. Also that the personal representatives may recover for both wrongful death and personal injuries in the same action.

MAINE—Action by the deceased's personal representative for benefit of surviving spouse, children or heirs shall be brought within two years. Where deceased was a minor child at the time of injury, damages not exceeding $10,000 may be recovered by the parents for loss of comfort, society and companionship of said minor.

MASSACHUSETTS—The maximum recoverable for wrongful death is

$100,000, the minimum is $5,000. Damages for conscious suffering resulting from the same injury may be recovered as a separate amount. A special maximum of $4,000 applies to death due to a defective highway.

MISSOURI—The maximum is $50,000.

NEBRASKA—Action shall be brought for exclusive benefit of widow or widower and next of kin.

NEW HAMPSHIRE—Where the decedent has left neither a widow, widower, child, father, mother, grandfather or grandmother, damages shall not exceed $30,000; in all other cases, the damages shall not exceed $120,000.

OREGON—Recovery to be distributed one-half to spouse; one-half to dependents; if no surviving spouse, all to dependents; if no dependents, all to surviving spouse.

RHODE ISLAND—There is no maximum on recovery; the minimum is $5,000.

VIRGINIA—The maximum recoverable for wrongful death is $50,000, which is in addition to damages for solace up to $25,000, and up to $500 of actual funeral expenses and the actual cost of hospital, medical and ambulance services.

WEST VIRGINIA—Maximum is $10,000, except if pecuniary loss to distributees exceeds $10,000 in which case further damages not exceeding $100,000 as shall equal the financial loss sustained by the distributees. The personal representative shall also be entitled to recover reasonable funeral, hospital and medical expenses.

WISCONSIN—Judgment for damages for pecuniary injury and additional damages not exceeding $3,000 for loss of society and companionship may be awarded to spouse, unemancipated or dependent children or parents.

LIABILITY OF EMPLOYERS FOR NEGLIGENCE OF EMPLOYEES

(RESPONDEAT SUPERIOR)

All employers are obligated to protect the public from the wrongful acts of their employees. The courts hold an employer liable for the torts committed by his employees in the course of their employment.

At law, a Servant is anyone who for a lawful consideration undertakes to perform in a lawful pursuit at his Master's direction. Among the tests used in determining whether a Master-Servant relationship exists are: 1) the power to hire and discharge, and 2) the power to control the conditions of employment.

On the other hand, where the work is being done by one engaged for a fixed sum without reference to the hours or conditions of employment, and the principal exercises no direct control over the work, or the employment practices of the one engaged to render the service, it is usually held that no employer-employee relationship exists. It should be understood, however, that the question is often a close one.

A Master is not liable for the torts of his servant except when committed within the scope of the employment. Thus, if a porter pushing a hand truck down the street runs into a pedestrian, the employer will be liable for the injury, since it arose in the course of the employment.

On the other hand, if the porter left his truck to go across the street and got involved in a fight, the injuries he might cause would not be within the scope of his employment, and his employer would not be liable.

In many cases, the question becomes a close one. Thus, if a person was hired to keep order during a sale, and this employee became involved in a fight with an obstreperous customer, the question might be decided either way, depending on the individual circumstances of the case.

When an employee, in the course of his employment, commits a tort, *both* the employee and his employer may be sued. The plaintiff may satisfy his judgment against one or both. The employer may in turn sue the employee for indemnity against the liability to the third party from the employee's tort.

The points made above relate only to the question of an employer's liability for torts committed by his employees. When the employee is himself injured in the course of his employment, the liability of the employer to his *employee* is determined according to special Workmen's Compensation statutes (discussed in Chapters 30 and 31).

VICARIOUS LIABILITY

As mentioned before, a person is not generally held liable for the torts of another. A broad exception is made for employers whose employees commit a tort in the course of their employment.

In addition to the liability of employers for the torts of their employees, most states provide by statute that a person may be liable for damages caused by another's negligence in operating a motor vehicle. In some states, the rules have been extended to cover aircraft and boats as well as automobiles. The laws of the various states on this point take several forms. In some, minors who apply for a driver's license must have their application signed by a parent or both parents, and the parent is liable for the negligent torts of the minor. Many state statutes impose liability on the parents of any minor for the intentional, wilful or malicious damage to property done by such minor. (Most of these laws also provide that the parent may ask to have the license of the minor cancelled, after which he will no longer be liable for the minor's torts.)

Some state statutes state broadly that the owner of a motor vehicle is liable for damages caused by the negligence of anyone operating the vehicle with his permission, implied or expressed; in some cases, a limit is placed on such vicarious liability—to one form of vicarious liability, the operation of a motor vehicle by a minor.

Below are set down in brief outline the provisions of these vicarious liability statutes in the various states. The reader is urged in each case to make a more complete study of the statute in his own state.

ALABAMA—The parents of a minor under the age of 18 shall be liable up to $500 for damages caused by the minor to real or personal property. Court costs may be added to the award.

ALASKA—The application for an operator's license to be issued to any person under the age of 18 shall be signed by his parent or guardian. Any negligence of the minor while driving a motor vehicle shall be imputed to the person who signed the application who shall be jointly and severally liable for any damages caused by the negligence of the minor.

The owner of any watercraft is liable for injury or damage caused by the negligent operation of the craft by another who operates the watercraft with the owner's permission.

The parent or guardian of a minor who wilfully destroys or damages real or personal property may be held liable for such damages, up to $2,000.

ARIZONA—The provisions relating to the operation of a motor vehicle by a person under the age of 18 are the same as ALASKA above.

Liability for wilful misconduct of a minor is the same as ALASKA above except that the liability of the parent or guardian is limited to $500.

ARKANSAS—Same as ALASKA except that the liability for damages caused by a minor other than in a motor vehicle is limited to $300.

CALIFORNIA—In most instances, the application for an operator's license to be issued to a person under the age of 21 must be signed by the parent or guardian who then becomes jointly and severally liable for any damages caused by the minor. Liability under this section, except when the minor is acting as agent or servant of any person is limited to $15,000/30,000 and $5,000, which figures do not include punitive damages.

Owner of any watercraft being used with his permission by another is liable for injuries or death caused by the craft. Except when the liability arises out of agency or master and servant relationship, the limit recoverable is $10,000/20,000 and $5,000. Furthermore, a parent or guardian is liable up to $1,000 for the wilful misconduct of a minor in his care which results in injury to another or damage to property. In addition to all liabilities under these statutes, additional liability up to $15,000/30,000 may be assessed against a parent or guardian whose minor child under the age of 15 causes injury to person or property by the discharge of a firearm.

COLORADO—As respects motor vehicles, the law is similar to ALASKA above, except that the maximum age of the minor is 17. The parent or guardian of a minor who wilfully destroys or damages real or personal property, up to $1,000.

CONNECTICUT—Proof that a motor vehicle or watercraft was being operated by a spouse, parent or child of the owner of such vehicle shall raise the presumption that such was being operated with the permission of the owner. In any civil action brought against the owner of a motor vehicle for damages caused by the negligent operation of the vehicle, the operator, if other than the owner, shall be presumed to be agent and servant of the owner and operating same in course of his employment, and the defendant shall bear the burden of rebutting such presumption.

DELAWARE—Same as ALASKA above, except that the maximum liability for wilful damage to real or personal property (other than by motor vehicle or watercraft) is limited to $300.

DISTRICT OF COLUMBIA—Whenever any motor vehicle shall be operated by any person other than the owner with consent of latter, expressed or implied, operator, shall, in case of accident be deemed agent or owner, and proof of ownership of motor vehicle shall be prima facie evidence that person operated vehicle with consent of owner.

FLORIDA—Application for license by person under the age of 18—same as ALASKA above. Liability for negligent operation of a boat imposed on owner only if he is the operator or is present in the boat at the time of the accident.

GEORGIA—Every owner of a motor vehicle shall be liable for death, injury or damage resulting from negligence in the operation of the vehicle if it is being used in the prosecution of the business of the owner or is being operated for his benefit. As respects watercraft, the owner is liable if the craft is being used with his permission, implied or expressed. A parent or other person in loco parentis having custody of a minor under the age of 17 shall be liable for the wilful and wanton acts of said minor, resulting in death, injury or damage to the person or property of others.

HAWAII—As respects the license to operate a motor vehicle, the law is the same as ALASKA above except that it applies to any person under the age of 20.

IDAHO—Same as ARKANSAS except that there is also a statute which makes the owner of a motor vehicle liable for injuries or damages caused by any person operating the vehicle in the business of the owner or otherwise, by any person operating the vehicle with the permission, implied or expressed, of the owner.

ILLINOIS—Parent or legal guardian is liable for actual damages caused by the wilful or malicious acts of the minor, up to $500 for each person or entity, for each occurrence. The statute does not affect the right to recover damages in any other cause of action where the liability of the parent or legal guardian is predicated on a common law basis.

INDIANA—Same as ALASKA as respects motor vehicles. There is no statute relating to watercraft, but the liability of a parent for wilful or malicious or intentional acts of a minor under the age of 18 is limited to $750.

IOWA—In all cases where damage done by any car by reason of driver's negligence and car driven with the consent of the owner, latter shall become liable for such damage. A similar statute applies to watercraft. The parents of a minor child under the age of 18 shall be liable for damages to persons or property caused by unlawful acts of such minor, for not more than $1,000 for any one act nor more than $2,000 to the same claimant for two or more acts.

KANSAS—Every owner of a motor vehicle causing or knowingly permitting a minor under the age of 16 to drive the vehicle or who gives or furnishes a motor vehicle to such minor shall be jointly and severally liable with such minor for damages caused by his negligence.

The parents of a minor under the age of 18 who wilfully or maliciously damages property shall be liable, up to $1,000, for such damages except where the act of the minor is adjudged to have been the result of parental neglect, in which event the $1,000 limitation does not apply.

KENTUCKY—Same as ARIZONA above.

LOUISIANA—The owner of a watercraft shall be liable for any injury or damage caused by the negligent operation of the craft. The father, and after his death, the mother shall be responsible for damages caused by minor children residing with them.

MAINE—As respects motor vehicles and watercraft, the state provisions are similar to ALASKA above. Parents of any minor between the ages of 7 and 17 shall be liable up to $250 for injury to persons or damage to property wilfully or maliciously caused by the minor. The statute specifically stipulates that the minor is not relieved of personal liability for such damage or injury.

MARYLAND—As respects the license to operate a motor vehicle, the law is the same as ALASKA except that it applies to persons under the age of 21.

As respects damage or injury wilfully or maliciously caused by a minor, the judge may in his discretion award judgment against the parents of the minor.

MASSACHUSETTS—In all actions for personal injury, property damage or death arising out of a motor vehicle, evidence that the vehicle was at the time of the accident registered in the name of defendant as owner shall be prima facie evidence that it was being operated by and under control of a person for whose conduct the defendant was legally responsible. Parents of a minor under the age of 17 and over 7 shall be liable in a civil suit, up to $300, for the wilful act of such child which results in an injury or death of another person or damage to property.

MICHIGAN—Owner of vehicle shall be liable for negligent operation of the vehicle, but only if being driven with the implied or express permission of the owner. If the vehicle was being driven by a member of the immediate family of the owner, it shall be presumed that it was being driven with his consent.

MINNESOTA—Whenever a motor vehicle is operated by someone other than the owner, with consent of the owner, implied or express, the operator shall be deemed to be the agent of the owner. As respects watercraft, the law is similar to that of ALASKA above. The parent or guardian of a minor under the age of 18 who wilfully or maliciously causes damage to property or injury to persons shall be jointly and severally liable up to $100 with the minor for such damages.

MISSISSIPPI—As respects motor vehicles, the law is similar to that of ALASKA above, except that it applies to persons under the age of 17. Liability for damages caused by a minor other than in a motor vehicle follows the law in ARKANSAS.

MISSOURI—The parents of a minor against whom judgment has been rendered for damage to property shall be liable for payment of that judgment, up to $300, provided that the parent or guardian has been named as a party defendant in the action.

MONTANA—Same as ARKANSAS above.

NEBRASKA—The liability for damages caused by watercraft are the same as in ALASKA. The parents shall be jointly and severally liable for the wilful and intentional infliction of personal injury to any person or destruction of property occasioned by their minor or unemancipated child residing with them. In the event of personal injuries, damages are recoverable only to the extent of hospital and medical expenses incurred but not to exceed $1,000.

NEVADA—Same as ALASKA above, except that there is no statute relating to watercraft.

NEW HAMPSHIRE—Any parent or guardian or person having custody of a child found to be delinquent, and anyone else who contributes to his delinquency, may be punished by fine or imprisonment. In contempt proceedings the Court may require the parent to compensate any injured party for damages up to $500.

NEW JERSEY—A parent or guardian or other person having legal custody of an infant 16 years of age or under who fails or neglects to exercise reasonable control and supervision of the infant, shall be liable in a civil action for any wilful, malicious or unlawful injury or destruction by such infant, up to $250.

NEW MEXICO—Same as ALASKA above, except that the liability for non-vehicular damages is limited to $1,000.

NEW YORK—Same as IOWA except that the liability for non-vehicular or watercraft accidents is limited to $500.

NORTH CAROLINA—Same as NEW YORK above.

NORTH DAKOTA—Same as ARKANSAS above.

OHIO—Application for license to operate a motor vehicle subject to same requirements as in ALASKA above. As respects damages caused by a minor under the age of 18 other than in a motor vehicle, the parents are liable, up to $2,000, for the damages.

OKLAHOMA—Application for operator's license, same as ALASKA above, except that it applies to minors between the ages of 14 and 16. Provisions on watercraft also as under ALASKA. Liability for wilful damage caused by minors as under ALASKA except maximum liability is $1,500.

OREGON—In addition to any other remedies allowed by law, parents of a minor under the age of 18 shall be liable for damages not exceeding $300.

PENNSYLVANIA—As respects motor vehicles, the law is similar to the one in KANSAS. Every owner of a motor boat causing or knowingly permitting any person to operate the boat, and any person who leases or furnishes a motor boat to another person, shall be jointly and severally liable with such person for damages caused by the negligence of the person operating the boat.

Any parent whose child under the age of 18 is judged guilty of a wilful, tortious act shall be liable for such act up to $300 for loss or injuries sustained by one person or $1,000 regardless of the number of persons who suffer loss or damage.

PUERTO RICO—A driver's license may be issued to a person between the ages of 16 and 18 if the person under whose authority the minor may be, shall in a document presented to the Secretary of Public Works make himself liable for all damages the said driver may cause. The owner of a motor vehicle shall be deemed to have given permission to the operator of the vehicle to operate such vehicle. The father, and in the event of his death, the mother is liable for damages caused by minor children living with them. Liability shall cease when the liable persons prove that they employed all the diligence of a good father of a family to preclude the damage.

RHODE ISLAND—Same as ALASKA above, except that the liability of a parent for acts of a minor other than in vehicular or watercraft accidents is limited to $250.

SOUTH CAROLINA—Application for a driver's license subject to same requirements as in ALASKA above, except that the law applies to any unemancipated minor. Watercraft provisions similar to ALASKA. Parent is liable up to $1,000 for any unmarried minor under the age of 17 who maliciously and intentionally destroys, damages or steals property.

SOUTH DAKOTA—Any person or legal entity suffering damage to property through the malicious and wilful act of a minor under the age of

18 shall have a cause of action against the parents. Maximum liability is limited to $300.

TENNESSEE—The situation is very similar to that of ALASKA above, except that the liability of a parent for acts of his minor child other than in vehicle or watercraft accidents is limited to $2,500.

TEXAS—Application for a minor to operate a motor vehicle similar to ALASKA above. The parents of a child over the age of 10 and under the age of 18 are liable for actual damages, or $5,000, whichever is lower, plus court costs and reasonable attorney's fees for damages wilfully and maliciously caused by the minor.

UTAH—As respects operation of a motor vehicle or watercraft, similar to ALASKA above.

VERMONT—When an unemancipated minor under the age of 17 wilfully or maliciously damages property, the parent of the minor shall be liable for any amount not exceeding $250 for *each* of the children involved in the act.

VIRGINIA—Every owner of a motor vehicle causing or knowingly permitting a minor under 16 who is not permitted under the law to drive, and any person who furnishes a vehicle to such person, shall be jointly and severally liable with him for damages. The parent is liable up to $200 for damages to property caused by a minor under the age of 18.

WASHINGTON—The parent of a minor under the age of 18 who wilfully or maliciously destroys property shall be liable to the owner for damages in an amount not exceeding $1,000.

WEST VIRGINIA—Same as VIRGINIA above, except that the maximum liability is $300.

WISCONSIN—As respects license to operate a motor vehicle, the situation is similar to that in ALASKA. As respects wilful damages by minors, the law is similar to that of WASHINGTON above.

WYOMING—Same as WEST VIRGINIA above, except that the law applies to minors over the age of 10 and under the age of 17.

In a number of states, one who sells or distributes alcoholic beverages may be held liable for torts committed by an intoxicated individual to whom he has sold intoxicants.

FOR FURTHER READING

STATUTES AFFECTING LIABILITY INSURANCE—American Insurance Association, New York, N. Y. 15th Edition, December 1971.

This compilation is arranged by states and will provide the reader in any state with a concise digest of the statutes in his state relating to negligence and liability insurance. It will also provide a quick reference to the various statutes to which references are made by their exact number.

KULP AND HALL—Casualty Insurance

(See Reading List at End of Book)

CHAPTER 24

Public Liability Insurance

VARIOUS FORMS of Public Liability insurance have been designed to protect an Insured against many of the liabilities which face him in his business and personal life. It is important, however, to distinguish between an individual's legal liability and the coverage afforded by a particular Liability policy. Liability to another for one's acts or omissions may derive from a statute governing liability, or from the common law (doctrines based on past decisions), or from having undertaken a contractual obligation.

Whether the individual is covered against such liability, however, depends on the Liability policy he has purchased, its provisions, conditions and exclusions. For this reason, an insurance man, who wishes to advise his client properly, must be familiar with all of his Insured's legal obligations to others, and with the various Liability policies and endorsements which are available to protect against these hazards.

An analysis of an Insured's exposure to claims often reveals the need for protection under several Liability policies and special endorsements to these policies. In some cases, it may be found that the Insured faces liabilities which are not covered in any of the regular policies. Depending on the individual circumstances, it may be possible to arrange for coverage by special agreement with the insurance company.

This chapter will consider first some of the more important provisions which are common to most basic Liability policies. Each of the more widely sold Liability policies will then be analyzed separately to show how it meets specific needs and to point up the special characteristics and provisions which are unique to the particular form.

While Liability insurance forms are not uniform, most companies use policies which are fairly standard. There are some differences, however, among the forms used by different companies, and the reader should check his own Company's forms for possible variations.

WHAT IS COVERED

Most Liability insurance policies are divided into two separate sections—Coverage A for Bodily Injury Liability, and Coverage B for Property Damage Liability. Each coverage is separately rated, and different limits of liability may be afforded for each of these separate situations. Furthermore, the policy may be written under Coverage A only, without any protection against property damage liability under Coverage B.

Coverage A—Bodily Injury Liability—Under Coverage A, the Liability insurance policy undertakes to pay on behalf of the Insured all sums which the Insured becomes legally obligated to pay by reason of the liability imposed on him by law for bodily injury, including death, sustained by any person caused by an occurrence. The policy defines "occurrence" as an accident which results, during the policy period, in bodily injury neither expected nor intended from the standpoint of the Insured.

Coverage B — Property Damage Liability — Under this section, the Liability insurance policy undertakes to pay on behalf of the Insured all sums which the Insured shall become legally obligated to pay by reason of the liability imposed on him by law for damages to *tangible property* caused by an occurrence. As in the case of bodily injury, the word "occurrence" is defined to mean an accident which, during the policy period, results in such damage. Loss of use of property is included within the meaning of damages.

The policy provides coverage only for sums which the Insured becomes *legally obligated* to pay. There is no obligation on the Company to pay unless the Insured is held liable. The basic policy provides no coverage against liabilities for which the Insured is not obligated under the law; e. g., liabilities assumed by the Insured voluntarily, or damages which he feels morally obligated to pay.

While the Liability policy is responsible only for sums which the Insured is legally obligated to pay, bankruptcy or insolvency of the Insured will not relieve the Company.

Defense of Suits, Supplementary Benefits—All Liability policies provide for defending in the Insured's name any suits brought against him which allege injury or destruction. The Company will pay all costs of such defense, including the cost of investigating the claim, procuring of witnesses, etc.

The Company will defend any such suit brought against the Insured, even if false or groundless. However, the suit must be one which would constitute a claim under the policy, if it was successful. Thus, if the Insured had voluntarily assumed liability for an occurrence for which he was not liable under the law, the basic policy would not provide coverage, and the Company would not be required to defend a suit brought to enforce this assumed liability. Similarly, if an Insured had purchased Liability insurance only under Coverage A covering bodily injury, and a suit was brought against him for damage to property, the Liability insurance Company would not be required to defend such suit.

In addition, the Liability policy will pay all expenses incurred by the Company, all costs taxed against the Insured in any suit, and interest accruing after judgment has been entered. (The limit on such interest for which the Company is liable is discussed later under FOR HOW MUCH.)

The Liability policy will also pay all premiums on bonds required in the appeal of any suit and on bonds to release attachments. (The limit on the premiums for Release of Attachment Bonds also is discussed under FOR HOW MUCH.)

The policy will also reimburse the Insured for all reasonable expenses incurred by him at the Company's request; e. g., travel expenses, expenses in procuring witnesses, affidavits, evidence, etc. The policy will reimburse the Insured for any actual loss of wages or salary suffered by him because of his attendance at hearings or trials, but such payment shall not exceed $25 per day.

This provision is not specifically stated in the Liability policies of some companies, but the practical effect of all policies on this score is the same.

In addition, the Liability policy will pay all reasonable expenses incurred by the Insured at the time of an accident in furnishing first aid to others at the time of an accident for bodily injury to which the policy applies. Except for first aid, which is imperative at the time of the accident, an Insured is not to make any payments, incur any obligations or any expense unless authorized to do so by the Company.

Many policies also provide that the Company will service the Insured by inspecting the premises and suggesting improvements and changes which will tend to reduce accidents.

The policies of some companies do not contain this provision, but it is almost standard practice for insurance companies to make an inspection of the premises before accepting a risk and to check the premises regularly to determine what steps can be taken to minimize losses.

Medical Payments Coverage—Liability policies may be endorsed for an additional premium to cover the cost of medical expenses incurred by persons who suffer an accident on the Insured's premises or through other hazards described in the policy. This coverage is discussed fully below.

HAZARDS COVERED

While the word "occurrence" used in Liability policies is fairly broad, and is defined to include injurious exposure to conditions, it does not serve to bring within the coverage occurrences which do not result in bodily injury or property damage, e. g., libel, slander, false arrest, etc., situations for which Insureds are frequently held liable. Furthermore, the use of the word "accident" in the definition of "occurrence" is intended to denote the time of coverage and the application of the policy limits. Thus, in a situation involving a related series of events which are attributable to the same factor, the policy will cover only if the event occurs during the policy period. It is further intended that all the damage resulting from the same event be deemed one accident, and the policy limit applied to the total claims developed.

Many companies will, for an additional premium, extend the policy to cover *personal* injury rather than bodily injury. Under the endorsement, which is becoming standardized in most territories, personal injury coverage is extended to three separate groups of hazards with a special premium charge for each of these groups:

1. False arrest, detention or imprisonment, malicious prosecution.

2. Libel, slander, defamation of character or invasion of privacy.

3. Wrongful entry or eviction or other invasion of the right of private occupancy.

Medical Payments Coverage—The basic Liability policy is designed to cover the liability for which the Insured is legally liable and not obligations which he feels morally bound to pay, or which he assumes voluntarily. By special endorsement, however, it is possible to add to the Liability policy coverage for medical expenses incurred by members of the public who suffer an accident from a hazard described in the Liability policy. Under the Medical Payments coverage, these expenses are paid by the Company, even though the Insured is not liable for the accident.

Thus, assume a customer who comes into the Insured's store falls and injures himself. For the injured party to collect for his damages, it is necessary that he prove that the storekeeper's negligence was the proximate cause of the accident.

If the storekeeper is *not* held liable for the accident, his Liability policy will not be responsible for the damages. If, however, the policy had been endorsed with Medical Payments coverage, the customer's medical expenses would be paid by the Company, subject to the limits provided under the endorsement, as discussed below. These benefits will be paid, even though the storekeeper is not liable for the accident. (Medical Payments coverage, it can be seen, is not Liability insurance, but is really more akin to a separate Accident Reimbursement policy.)

The basic Liability policy does pay for any immediate medical and surgical expenses as are necessary at the time of the accident, and will defend the suit brought against the Insured, regardless of whether the Insured is ultimately held liable for the accident or not.

The Medical Payments coverage will pay all reasonable expenses incurred within one year of the date of the accident for necessary medical, surgical, dental, ambulance, hospital, professional nursing, and funeral services to each person who sustains bodily injury, sickness or disease caused by an occurrence, as defined, and arising out of the hazards described in the Liability policy.

Medical Payments Exclusions—The Medical Payments coverage is subject to the basic exclusions of the Liability policy to which it is attached. In addition, medical payments are not payable to the Insured, any partner, or any tenant or other person regularly residing on the premises, or any employee of the Insured or tenant while engaged in the employment of the Insured or the tenant.

Medical Payments are not payable to any other tenant of the premises, or any employee of such other tenant while engaged in the employment of such tenant on that part of the premises rented to the tenant.

Medical Payments are not payable to any person

—if benefits for the accident are payable under any Workmen's Compensation Law.

—while engaged in maintenance, alteration, demolition or new construction operations for the named Insured or for any lessee of the named Insured or any lessor of the premises.

—injured while practicing, instructing or participating in any physical training, sport, athletic activity or contents.

Medical Payments is often purchased by the larger business risk to improve the Experience Rating under the Public Liability insurance. It is felt that making available to potential claimants all the necessary medical services will hold down the frequency and severity of the suits brought.

Hazards Covered Under Separate Forms—Liability insurance is arranged under a basic unit or policy jacket which contains the elements common to all the various forms of coverage in this branch of insurance, and a large number of separate forms, or "coverage parts" which are adapted to the different types of risk that may be assumed.

Presently, there are 12 coverage parts: Owners, Landlords and Tenants Liability, Manufacturers and Contractors Liability, Comprehensive General Liability, Completed Operations and Products Liability, Owners and Contractors Protective Liability, Premises Medical Payments, Comprehensive Personal Liability, Farmers Comprehensive Personal Liability, Comprehensive Automobile Liability, Automobile Medical Payments, Uninsured Motorists Coverage and Garage Liability.

Any of the above coverages may be purchased separately or, in some instances, in combination with other insurance.

It is important to understand that each coverage is as separate from any other as though it were written in an individual policy. (The separate hazards are sometimes actually covered in separate policies.)

To understand any of the coverages, it is necessary to read it in conjunction with the basic unit which contains the provisions common to all Liability policies.

In this chapter, the section on HAZARDS NOT COVERED, which follows, will cover those exclusions which apply to all the usual Liability coverages. Chapter 25 will analyze some of the more popular forms of Liability insurance, and will take up separately the coverage provided under each of the policies. Any provisions or exclusions unique to a particular policy will be discussed under the respective form of Liability insurance.

HAZARDS NOT COVERED

Liability for Injuries or Death Covered Under Workmen's Compensation Law or Disability Benefits Law or Any Similar Law— Liability policies specifically exclude liability for bodily injury or death of any employee for which the Insured may be held liable under any Workmen's Compensation Law. The fact that an employer is obligated to his employee under a Workmen's Compensation Law is itself sufficient to exclude coverage for any claims arising out of injury to that employee, regardless of whether the employer did in fact carry Workmen's Compensation insurance.

The Liability policy does not cover any liability arising out of accidents suffered by such employees, regardless of to whom the liability exists. Thus, if an employee who is eligible for benefits under a Workmen's Compensation Law is injured while in his employer's business, and the employee's wife brings a suit against her

the Insured by independent contractors or for liability assumed by the Insured under an incidental contract.

War, Insurrection, Revolution, Etc.—The policy does not cover claims arising out of war, whether declared or not, civil war, insurrection, rebellion or revolution, or to any act or condition incident thereto.

Liability Arising Out of Alcoholic Beverages—The policy does not cover the liability of any person or organization engaged in manufacturing, selling or distributing or serving alcoholic beverages, or any owner of premises used for such purposes, for liability *by reason of any statute or ordinance* pertaining to the sale, gift or distribution or use of any alcoholic beverage (commonly referred to as dram shop ordinances). Furthermore, the policy will not cover such an Insured for liability arising out of the sale of liquor to a minor, or to a person under the influence of alcohol or which causes or contributes to the intoxication of any person. Nearly all states prohibit in some way the sale of liquor to minors or intoxicated persons.

Professional Service Exclusion—Liability policies covering physicians, dentists, beauty parlors, and similar professional services, specifically exclude bodily injury claims due to the rendering of any professional service, or the failure to render such service, unless specifically written to cover such hazards. The exclusion applicable to such risks is discussed more fully in Chapter 25 under the Owners' Landlords' and Tenants' Liability.

Nuclear Energy Liability—Under the law, an operator of a private reactor must provide security in an amount prescribed by the Atomic Energy Commission. The Nuclear Energy Liability policy which such operator provides includes as an Insured *anyone* responsible for a nuclear incident. All Public Liability, Personal Liability and Automobile Liability policies therefore exclude liability of the Insured for bodily injury or property damage claims when the Insured is covered as an (additional) Insured under any Nuclear Energy Liability policy. Commercial and industrial risks are also not covered under their Liability insurance policies for hazards which are intended to be covered under Nuclear Energy Liability policies.

Pollution—All Public Liability policies (except Personal and Professional Liability and policies issued to the oil industry) do not apply to bodily injury or property damage arising out of the discharge, dispersal, release or escape of smoke, vapors, soot, fumes, acids, alkalis, toxic chemicals, liquids or gases, waste materials or other irritants, contaminants, or pollutants into or upon land, the atmosphere or any watercourse or body of water; but this exclusion does not apply if such discharge, dispersal, release or escape is sudden or accidental.

In the case of risks in the oil industry, the exclusion applies *even if the occurrence is sudden and accidental.*

It can be seen that the intent of the exclusion is to eliminate coverage for steady (and presumably foreseeable) accretions of pollutants, but not situations which are unexpected, as for example, an explosion, or fire or other fortuitous event.

FOR HOW MUCH

Most Liability policies are written with two limits; e. g., $5,000/$10,000; $10,000/$20,000; $50,000/$100,000, etc. These limits are known as the upper and lower limits.

Under Coverage A, Bodily Injury Liability, the first limit is the limit *per person*—the maximum amount for which the Company is liable for injury to or death of one person. The second limit is the limit *per occurrence*—the maximum for which the Company is liable in any one occurrence, regardless of the number of persons injured or killed in the occurrence.

Thus, a policy with limits of $5,000/$10,000, usually referred to as 5/10 limits, will pay no more than $5,000 for injuries to one person. If two or more persons are injured or killed in the same occurrence, the policy will pay up to $10,000 for *all* persons injured in the accident.

In an occurrence in which more than one person is injured, the limit per person still applies, and the policy will not pay more than the "per person" limit to any one individual. Thus, assume two persons are injured in one accident caused by the negligence of an Insured who is carrying Liability insurance with limits of $5,000/$10,000. A is awarded $7,000; B is awarded $2,000. Even though there is $10,000 available for an accident in which two or more persons are injured, the policy will not pay more than $5,000 to A, since that is the policy's limit per person.

The policy limits are the maximums payable to all persons who may bring a suit against the Insured. Thus if, as a result of injuries to one person, an Insured is deemed liable to the injured person and for a separate amount to the injured person's spouse, the limit per person will apply to *all* claims arising from the accident to one person.

Under Coverage B, Property Damage Liability, the limit applies to all claims arising out of one occurrence. Under several forms of Liability insurance, the Property Damage coverage also includes an *aggregate* limit beyond which the Company is not liable for all claims arising out of all accidents within the policy year. Where a particular form of Liability insurance is subject to an aggregate limit, this fact will be pointed out in the analysis of the individual policy.

Defense of Suits, Supplementary Benefits—These benefits (discussed before under What Is Covered) are payable, regardless of their amount, over and above the limits of the policy.

EXAMPLE: A merchant carries a Liability policy with limits of $10,000/$20,000. A customer who comes into the store is injured and brings a suit against the Insured. The Liability insurance Company spends $1,800 to investigate the claim, procure witnesses and defend the suit in court. The claimant is awarded $13,000 plus $600 of court costs.

The Company under its policy pays $10,000 of the award (the full limit of liability per person) plus the $600 of court costs, despite the fact that it has already spent $1,800 to defend the case.

If, in this same case, the customer had required medical or surgical first aid at the time of the accident, the Company would pay the full cost of such first aid, in addition to all the sums listed above. If an appeal is taken and an Appeal Bond is required, the Liability policy will pay for the premium on such bonds. If the claimant secures an attachment of the Insured's property, and the Insured wishes to have this attachment released, he may be required to furnish a Release of Attachment Bond. The Liability insurance Company will pay the premium on such Release of Attachment Bond, but for no more than is required by its limit of liability. Thus, in the case under discussion, the company is liable for only 10/13th of the premium on the Bond to release the $13,000 attachment, since its liability for the accident is limited to $10,000.

The Liability policy is also liable for interest on judgments after entry. Here again, the policy is obligated to pay interest only on such portion of the judgment as is within the limit of the policy's liability. Thus, in the illustration above, the Company will pay only 10/13ths of such interest, since its policy limit for the particular accident is only $10,000.

Medical Payments Coverage Limits—Under Medical Payments coverage, the limit of liability is independent of the liability limits of the basic policy. The Medical Payments coverage is subject to two limits: The first limit is the limit per person; the second limit is the limit payable to all persons injured in a single accident.

Each person injured in one accident is entitled to collect up to the full limit per person. Assume the Medical Payments coverage added to a Liability policy is written with limits of $500/$10,000. If three persons are injured in the same accident, each is entitled to collect up to $500 for his medical expenses. No more than $10,000 is payable, however, to all persons injured in the same accident. Thus, if 25 persons were injured in one accident, each person could collect up to $500 for his medical expenses, but only $10,000 could be received by all 25 persons.

Medical expenses under the Medical Payments coverage are payable in addition to the cost of immediate medical and surgical first aid recoverable under the basic Liability policy.

Other Insurance—Unless otherwise stated, the Public Liability policy affords primary coverage. If there is other valid insurance available for the same loss, liability is determined in one of two ways. If all other insurance provides for contribution by equal shares, each policy is liable for an equal share of the loss until the amount of the lower policy (if the two are different in their limits) is exhausted. The remaining policy pays the excess of the loss, subject to its own maximum.

EXAMPLE: Assume the Insured has two Liability policies which are applicable to the same loss: Policy A with a limit of $30,000; and Policy B with a limit of $50,000. If the loss sustained is $70,000, both policies share in the first $60,000 of loss, and each pays $30,000. Policy A is thereby exhausted, and Policy B pays the additional $10,000 of the loss.

If any of the other insurance does not provide for contribution by equal shares, the policy pays that proportion of the loss that its applicable limit of liability bears to the total applicable limit.

EXAMPLE: Assume the same set of facts as in the EXAMPLE above, the policy would then pay 3/8 of the loss while the other insurance would pay 5/8.

WHO IS COVERED

The named Insured, if a corporation, is defined to include any officer, director or stockholder acting within the scope of his employment, or any partner, if the Insured is a partnership. Also, any person or organization (other than an employee of the Insured) with respect to real estate management for the named Insured.

Legal Representatives—If the named Insured dies during the policy period, the policy will automatically cover the Insured's legal representatives, and other persons having proper temporary custody of the named Insured's property until the appointment and qualification of a legal representative.

Additional Interests—Liability policies may be written without extra charge to cover any of a number of additional interests. Thus, Liability policies covering owners or lessees may include agents who operate or have care, custody or control of the property. Policies covering estates of deceased persons or trusts may include executors, administrators, trustees or beneficiaries.

A policy covering a lessee of land who has erected a building on the land may include the owner of the land under certain conditions, etc. Other additional interests may be added to Liability policies only by payment of an additional premium. Thus, a policy covering a lessee or tenant of a building or premises may be endorsed to cover owners, managers or operators of the property. Certain interests may not be added to a Liability policy. Thus, a contractor or subcontractor cannot be added to a policy covering an owner.

Right of Third Parties—While the Liability policy insures only those named or included in the policy as Insureds, any person who has secured a judgment against the Insured becomes entitled to recover under the policy.

WHERE COVERED

Liability policies generally cover accidents caused by the Insured's operations, even though they occur away from the premises designated in the policy. Most forms provide that the policy provides coverage only within the United States of America, its territories and possessions, and Canada. The policy is extended to cover international waters or air space, provided the bodily injury or property damage does not occur in the course of travel or transportation to or from any other country, state or nation. A policy which covers the Products Liability exposure also covers occurrences anywhere in the world with respect to bodily injury or property damage arising out of a product sold for use in the United States, its territories or Canada, provided the original suit for damages is brought within these areas.

RATES

There are several methods of rating Liability insurance and these will be described under the individual policies in Chapter 25.

Deductibles—Most forms of Liability insurance may be written with a Deductible provision. The Insured is granted a reduced premium, in return for which he agrees to contribute a stated amount to any loss. The Company is liable only for the excess of any loss over the amount of the Deductible. Deductibles range from $25 to $1,000.

Three-Year Policies—Most Liability forms may be purchased for a three-year period at a reduced rate. This feature is discussed under the separate policies in the next chapter.

Medical Payments Coverage—The rates for Medical Payments coverage depend on the nature of the Insured's operations. The rate for any risk is a percentage of the rate for the basic Liability policy to which this additional coverage is attached. Manual rates are shown for limits per person of $250, $500 or $1,000, and per accident, for limits of $10,000, $25,000 and $50,000. Other limits are available upon submission for rating. A 10% credit is granted if the Insured employs a licensed physician or graduate nurse who is in constant attendance at the premises.

INSURED'S STATEMENTS

The first page of the Liability policy contains the Declarations made by the Insured. These include the Insured's name, the exact location of the risk and the premises insured, a description of the operations conducted at the insured premises, and whether any insurance company has cancelled any similar insurance in the past period. By his acceptance of the policy, the Insured agrees that the statements in the Declarations are his agreements and representations, and that the policy is issued in reliance upon the truth of such representations.

INSURED'S DUTIES

Notice of Accident—The Insured is required to notify the Company or its agent of any accident as soon as practicable. The notice must contain sufficient information to identify the Insured, the time, place and circumstances of the accident, and the names and addresses of available witnesses.

Preventing Further Damages—In the event of an occurrence, the Insured is required to take all reasonable steps to prevent other bodily injury or property damage arising out of the same or similar condition. It is important that such steps, which are to be undertaken at the Insured's expense, are not recoverable under the policy. In this last respect, the Liability policy differs from Fire insurance, which will permit the Insured to recover the expenses he undergoes to save and preserve the property from further damage (discussed in Chapter 2 under REQUIREMENTS AFTER LOSS).

Notice of Claim or Suit—If a claim is made or a suit brought against the Insured, he must immediately forward to the Company every demand, notice, summons or other process received by him or his representative.

Cooperation with Company—The Insured is required to cooperate with the Company. If requested by the Company, he must attend hearings and trials and assist in effecting settlements, securing and giving evidence, and obtaining the attendance of witnesses. He must cooperate with the Company in its defense of the suit brought against him.

As discussed before, the Company will reimburse the Insured for all reasonable expenses he incurs, except for his loss of time. The Insured must not, however, assume any liability or settle any claim, except at his own expense, nor should he incur any expense except if authorized by the Company.

Inspection and Audit—The Insured agrees to permit the Company at any time during the policy period to inspect the premises and the operations being conducted. The policy stipulates that the Company's right to make such inspection shall not constitute an undertaking on behalf of the Insured to determine or warrant that the premises or operations being conducted therein are safe. Where the premium for a Liability policy is based on the Insured's payroll or receipts, the Company may examine and audit the Insured's records during the policy period and within one year after the termination of the policy.

Settlement of Claim—The Company reserves the right to investigate, negotiate and settle any claim or suit as it may deem expedient.

OTHER CLAUSES

Subrogation—See Chapter 2.

Cancellation—See Chapter 2.

Assignment—No Assignment of the policy will bind the Company unless it consents to the assignment. The policy does under given conditions cover the Insured's legal representatives (see WHO IS COVERED).

When Covered—Most Liability policies attach at 12:01 A. M. Contrast with the Fire insurance policy, which attaches at 12:00 Noon, Standard Time. Some companies' Liability policies attach at 12:00 Noon. It is important that the individual policy be checked to see what it provides on this score.

FOR FURTHER READING

ACKERMAN—Insurance
GEE—Agent's Casualty Guide
HEDGES—Practical Fire and Casualty Insurance
KULP AND HALL—Casualty Insurance
MAGEE AND BICKELHAUPT—General Insurance
MEHR AND CAMMACK—Principles of Insurance
MOWBRAY AND BLANCHARD—Insurance
RIEGEL, ROBERT and MILLER—Insurance Principles and Practices

(See Reading List at End of Book)

CHAPTER 25

Basic Public Liability Insurance Coverages

THE PRECEDING CHAPTER was devoted to general aspects of liability and to certain provisions of Liability insurance which are common to most Liability policies. This chapter will take up separately and analyze several of the more widely used Liability insurance coverages and show the specific type of risk for which each policy is designed and the nature of the hazards it covers. The discussion of any policy which follows should be read together with Chapter 24, as in each instance this chapter will concern itself only with the special provisions and features which are unique to the particular form.

OWNERS', LANDLORDS' AND TENANTS' LIABILITY INSURANCE

THE OWNERS', LANDLORDS' AND TENANTS' Liability coverage (commonly referred to as O. L. & T.) is designed to insure owners and lessees of buildings, vacant land, residences, mercantile premises of all kind, both wholesale and retail, and various types of service businesses and operations like amusement parks, bazaars, shows, banks, clubs, libraries, newsstands and similar occupancies of a non-manufacturing nature.

HAZARDS COVERED

The policy covers the ownership, maintenance or use of the premises. "Premises" is defined in the policy to include all buildings and structures on the premises and the ways immediately adjoining the designated premises.

The policy also covers all operations which are necessary or incidental to the Insured's operations. The policy will therefore cover accidents which occur not only on the Insured's premises but also those which occur away from the premises, provided they arise out of the Insured's regular operations. Thus, if the Insured's employee in making delivery of a product to a customer at his home injures someone, the policy will cover. Similarly, if coverage is provided under Coverage B for Property Damage Liability, any damage to the property of others in the course of such delivery would be covered.

Newly Acquired Premises—Automatic coverage is afforded for any other premises which the Insured acquires during the policy period, provided the Company is notified of such new locations within 30 days after the Insured acquires their ownership or control.

Newly Added Operations—Automatic coverage is afforded for additional or changed operations at the Insured's premises, provided the Company is notified within 30 days after the commencement of such new operations.

Grantor's Liability—The policies of some companies define "premises" to include also any premises which the Insured formerly owned and over which he has relinquished all ownership and control. Other forms bring such surrendered premises within the hazards defined in the policy.

Under either type of language, the Insured is covered under an existing Liability policy for liability that may be imposed on him for any premises relinquished by him, no matter how long ago. Thus, if after the Insured has sold a piece of property to another, an accident occurs due to a condition in the premises of which the new owner did not have an opportunity to learn, the former owner may be held liable for the damages caused.

The Liability policy covering an Insured for premises he owns will also cover him for any premises sold or relinquished by him. Where the policy of a particular Company is silent on this score, the Company will assume such liability without additional charge.

Grantor's Liability, as this coverage is known, is provided only under a policy which is in force at the time the accident occurs at the relinquished premises. If an Insured who has only one piece of property sells the property and cancels his Liability policy, he will not be covered for any liabilities that may be imposed on him arising out of premises he formerly owned.

Structural Alterations—The Owners', Landlords' and Tenants' Liability policy may be written to include or exclude liability arising out of structural alterations.

HAZARDS NOT COVERED

Assumed Liability—The policy excludes any liability assumed by the Insured under any contract or agreement. Coverage for such liabilities may be provided for under a separate division of the policy (discussed later under Contractual Liability). Exceptions are made for several types of incidental contracts, and the policy will apply to liability arising out of such an assumed liability. The policy defines "incidental contracts" to mean any *written:*

(1) lease of premises;

(2) easement agreement, except in connection with construction or demolition operations on or adjacent to a railroad;

(3) an undertaking to indemnify a municipality which is required by municipal ordinance, except in connection with work for the municipality;

(4) sidetrack agreement;

(5) elevator maintenance agreement.

Vehicles, Aircraft—The policy also excludes liability arising out of the ownership, maintenance, use, operation, loading or unloading of any automobile or aircraft owned or operated by or rented or loaned to the named Insured. Also excluded is liability arising out of any other automobile or aircraft operated by any person in the employ of the named Insured. An exception is made for the parking of an automobile on the insured premises even if by an employee of the Insured. Thus, coverage will apply in the case of risks like hotels, restaurants, clubs and others who may park customers' cars or provide parking facilities.

The definition of "automobile" in the policy specifically excludes certain types of mobile equipment and these do *not* fall within the exclusions enumerated. Mobile equipment falls into four basic groups:

(1) vehicles not subject to motor vehicle registration;

(2) vehicles maintained exclusively on premises owned by or rented to the Insured;

(3) vehicles designed for use principally off public roads (occasional operation on a public road, as for servicing or repair would not defeat coverage);

(4) a series of contractors' equipment powered by vehicles, e. g., power cranes, shovels, loaders, diggers, etc.

NOTE: A special exclusion applies to liability arising out of and in the course of *transporting* mobile equipment, and such is NOT covered under the Public Liability policy.

Watercraft—The policy does not apply to liability arising out of occurrences involving watercraft, but only when such accidents occur *away* from the premises insured. Accidents on the insured premises would be covered.

New Construction or Demolition Operations—The Owners',

Landlords' and Tenants' Liability policy excludes accidents arising out of new construction or demolition operations, including changing the size of or moving buildings or other structures. The exclusion applies whether the work is being performed by the Insured, his own employees, or by others under contract to the Insured, as in the case of an independent contractor.

Coverage for this hazard may be added to the policy under a Construction and Demolition Permit, for which an additional premium is charged.

For private and two-family dwellings, the exclusion applies only if the new construction is for the purpose of changing the use of the premises to other than one-or two-family dwelling occupancy. Otherwise, new construction, as if a wing is being added to a home, is covered.

Water Damage, Sprinkler Leakage—APPLICABLE ONLY IN GREATER NEW YORK—The Liability policy covering an apartment house risk in Greater New York *only* excludes liability for damage to property caused by the discharge, leakage or overflow of water or steam from within stated sources, or by the discharge of any substance from within an automatic sprinkler system, or by rain or snow admitted to a building interior in certain ways. The excepted risks are in the main three or four family dwellings, apartment and apartment hotels including Housing Projects, banks, buildings occupied by a single manufacturing tenant and buildings leased entirely to a single tenant for manufacturing or private warehousing. (The sources of water or steam enumerated and the definition of sprinkler leakage are those contained in the Water Damage and Sprinkler Leakage policies, discussed in Chapter 9.)

The exclusion applies *only* insofar as the loss occurs on or from premises owned by or rented to the named Insured, and injures or destroys buildings or property therein. Furthermore, the exclusion does not apply to operations performed for the Insured by independent contractors. Thus, if an Insured contractor is working at a building, and causes loss from one of the water sources enumerated before, the contractor's liability for such damage *is* covered, since the premises are not owned by or rented to the Insured. Similarly, if a tenant who sustains water damage arising from an operation being performed for his landlord by independent contractors, sues the landlord, the Liability policy of the landlord will respond, since the exclusion does not extend to operations being performed for the Insured by independent contractors. On the other hand, if a tenant suffers water damage and sues his landlord, the landlord's Liability policy will not cover, since the loss arose on and from premises owned by the Insured.

Even in Greater New York, on apartment risks (where this special exclusion applies), the policy specifically includes liability for damage to property caused by such water sources or sprinkler systems as respects loss due to fire. Thus if, as a result of a fire at an Insured's premises, the automatic sprinkler system opened, and water from the system flowed into a neighbor's premises, the Insured's liability for damages caused to the neighbor's property would be covered under the Insured's Liability policy. On the other hand, if there were no fire and the sprinkler system opened accidentally, the Insured's liability for damages caused a neighbor would not be covered.

This exclusion applies only to Coverage B — Property Damage Liability. If a person were *injured* by one of these perils, the policy under Coverage A would pay any sums which the Insured became legally obligated to pay for such bodily injuries.

Coverage for Property Damage Liability due to these water and sprinkler perils may be assumed by the policy for an additional premium. Protection against these hazards is often purchased in separate Water Damage and Sprinkler Leakage policies written to cover Liability Imposed by Law. The basic policy covers liability of the Insured for damage to the property of others; a special form and a higher rate applies where coverage is required to cover liability for damage to property in the Insured's "care, custody and control."

Professional Service Exclusion—Owners', Landlords' and Tenants' Liability policies written to cover a doctor's or dentist's office or a beauty parlor and similar premises contain a special exclusion not found in other policies of this kind. Under the terms of the exclusion, the policy does not cover bodily injury claims due to the rendering of any professional service, or the omission of such service. Risks of this kind must purchase separate Malpractice Liability to cover such claims.

Thus, if a dentist were to injure a patient while drilling his tooth, the patient might bring suit against the dentist alleging malpractice. No coverage for this type of claim is provided under an Owners', Landlords' and Tenants' Liability policy, and such suit would be defended and any judgment paid only under a Malpractice Liability policy.

It is also important to understand that the Malpractice Liability policy does not provide complete Liability protection for the professional person, since it does *not* cover the premises hazard. Thus, if a patient who had come into a doctor's office tripped over a loose rug or fell against the sterilizing equipment, his claims for bodily injury would *not* be covered under the doctor's Malpractice Liability policy, but would fall within the scope of the Owners', Landlords' and Tenants' Liability policy. It can be seen that a person in the professions listed before requires *both* forms of Liability insurance to be fully protected.

RATES

Rates for most Owners', Landlords' and Tenants' Liability policies are based on the following factors:

1. Territory.

2. Occupancy—Rates vary with the different types of occupancy or type of risk; e.g., apartment houses, dwellings, private residences, camps, clubs, hospitals, libraries, offices, schools, cigar stores, retail clothing stores, wholesale clothing stores, department stores, drug stores, etc.

How Premium Is Computed—The rate for an individual risk is based on the territory and the occupancy or type of risk, as outlined above. Various methods are used in this form of insurance to measure the size of the risk, and the manual lists alongside each classification the unit to which the rate applies. Below are listed the several ways in which risks are rated, with some examples of the kind of risks which fall into each group:

1. Area—The rate shown is applied to each 100 square feet occupied by the risk. This measure of exposure is used to rate most stores, physicians' and dentists' offices, colleges, churches, missions, settlement houses, riding clubs, buildings leased in entirety to others and used for manufacturing purposes, etc.

2. Receipts—for certain risks, the area or frontage would not give a true measure of the exposure, and these risks are rated on the basis of their receipts; e. g., horse shows, dog shows, dance halls, concessionaires, fairs, fireworks exhibits, etc.

3. Admissions—Certain risks are rated on the basis of the number of admissions; e. g., motion picture theatres, athletic exhibitions, automobile racing, automobile shows, etc.

4. Frontage—Vacant land, and risks like retail gasoline or oil supply stations when not operated by the Insured, are rated on the basis of frontage only.

5. Each—Certain risks are rated on the basis of a flat charge for each item covered; e. g., display booths, canoes, rowboats, parking meters, cigarette vending machines, newsstands, animals, etc.

Private dwelling, two-family, three-family and four-family dwellings are rated on the basis of a flat charge per dwelling. The basic rate includes grounds up to 50 acres. An additional charge is made for acreage in excess of 50 acres (see No. 6—Per Acre below).

NEW YORK CITY—Only private and two-family dwellings are rated on the basis of a flat charge per dwelling. Three-family and four-family dwellings are rated on the basis of area.

6. Per Acre—Certain risks are rated on the basis of a flat charge per acre. Cemeteries, and grounds of 1-2 family residences in excess of 50 acres are rated on this basis. Thus, where the grounds of a residence exceed 50 acres, a charge is made for each additional acre.

7. Per Pupil—Public schools, kindergartens, elementary and junior high as well as parochial schools are rated on the basis of the number of pupils.

8. Per Contestant—Risks like soap box derbies are rated on the basis of the number of contestants.

9. Per Mile—Streets are rated on the basis of a flat charge per mile.

10. Per Location, Per Day—Risks like conventions are rated on the basis of a flat charge per location for each day.

Policy Limits—Rates are quoted in the manual for Bodily Injury Liability with basic limits of $5,000/$10,000. For Coverage B (Property Damage Liability) rates are quoted for limits of $5,000 per accident.

The Insured may have the limits for Bodily Injury Liability or for Property Damage increased for a higher premium. The cost of higher limits decreases as the limits are increased. For example, for most risks, 10/20 limits cost only 16% more than the 5/10 basic limits. The additional cost for further increases is progressively lower. To increase limits from 10/20 to 25/50 costs only about 13% for most risks; the increase from 25/50 to 50/100 costs about 7% more, etc. Increases of limits under Coverage B follow a similar trend. To double the $5,000 per accident limit under Coverage B costs an additional 9%; for a 26% increase in premium, the basic $5,000 limit can be raised to $50,000, etc.

Three-Year Policies—Owners', Landlords' and Tenants' Liability policies (other than those subject to audit) may be written for three years. If the premium is paid in advance, the premium is three times the annual less 10%.

Whole Dollar Premium Rule—Discussed in Chapter 8 under OTHER FACTORS WHICH AFFECT FIRE INSURANCE RATES —Whole Dollar Premium Rule.

MANUFACTURERS' AND CONTRACTORS' LIABILITY INSURANCE

THE MANUFACTURERS' AND CONTRACTORS' LIABILITY POLICY is designed to cover all forms of manufacturing operations, and various types of service operations or contracting where construction, installation, repair, or maintenance work is done.

The Manufacturers' and Contractors' Liability policy is almost identical with the Owners', Landlords' and Tenants' policy discussed before. This section will treat only the differences between the two policies, and the reader should therefore read the remarks that follow, together with the analysis of the Owners', Landlords' and Tenants' policy and the preceding chapter, which discussed Features Common to Public Liability Policies.

HAZARDS COVERED

With two exceptions, the Manufacturers' and Contractors' Liability policy contains all the exclusions found in the Owners', Landlords' and Tenants' Liability policy. It also contains several special exclusions which are not found in the Owners', Landlords' and Tenants' policy.

Independent Contractors—The policy specifically excludes any liability arising out of work performed for the Insured by independent contractors other than maintenance, repairs and alterations which do not involve new construction or demolition. Coverage for such liability may be obtained by endorsement of the policy, but whether or not the Insured has availed himself of coverage for this hazard, the basic policy does not cover such liability.

New Construction and Demolition Operations—As regards Coverage A, Bodily Injury Liability, the Manufacturers' and Contractors' Liability policy does *not* exclude new construction or demolition operations, and will therefore be available for such claims, where the Owners', Landlords' and Tenants' Liability policy would not cover such liability.

If any construction or demolition is performed for the Insured by independent contractors, there will be no coverage for liabilities arising out of such operations, except if insurance is specifically purchased under the Independent Contractor Section of the policy (or in a separate Owners' and Contractors' Protective Liability policy, discussed later).

Newly Acquired Premises—The policy covers all newly acquired premises automatically, without notice to the Company.

Blasting and Explosion, Collapse, Excavation—While the basic

Manufacturers' and Contractors' Liability policy does not exclude the hazards of blasting and explosion, collapse and underground damage, these perils are not covered for certain classifications, unless specifically assumed by the Company for an additional premium. For these classifications, a special symbol is shown in the manual, and the rates for the basic coverage provide no coverage on the listed perils as respects Coverage B only (Property Damage Liability).

There are five types of symbol, each applicable to a different set of hazards, as follows:

c—Classifications so coded exclude coverage for Property Damage Liability arising out of the collapse of or structural injury to any building or structure due to grading of land, excavating, borrowing, filling, back-filling, tunneling, pile driving, coffer-dam work or caisson work, or to the moving, shoring, underpinning, raising or demolition of any building or structure, or removing or rebuilding of any structural support thereof.

d—Classifications so coded exclude coverage for Property Damage Liability arising out of injury to or destruction of underground property.

e—Classifications so coded exclude coverage for Property Damage Liability for injury to or destruction of property on or above the surface of the earth arising from a blowout or cratering of a gas or oil well.

u—Classifications so coded exclude coverage for Property Damage Liability for injury to or destruction of wires, conduits, pipes, mains, sewers or other similar property below the surface of the ground, arising from and during the use of mechanical equipment for the purpose of excavating or drilling in streets or highways, or injury to or destruction of property at any time resulting therefrom.

x—Classifications so coded exclude coverage for Property Damage Liability for injury to or destruction of property arising directly or indirectly from blasting or explosions however caused, other than explosions of air or steam vessels, piping under pressure, prime movers, machinery or power transmitting equipment.

FOR HOW MUCH

Rates are quoted in the manual for Bodily Injury Liability with basic limits of \$5,000/\$10,000. For Coverage B (Property Damage Liability), rates are quoted for limits of \$5,000 per occurrence. Differing from the Owners', Landlords' and Tenants' Liability, the limit for Property Damage Liability in the Manufacturers' and Contractors' policy includes an aggregate factor. Basic rates are quoted for limits of $5,000 for all claims arising out of one occurrence and, subject to this limit per occurrence, for an aggregate limit of $25,000 for all damages within the policy year.

Thus, under a Manufacturers' and Contractors' Liability policy with Coverage B (Property Damage) limits of $5,000/$25,000, the Company is not liable for more than $5,000 for all claims arising out of one occurrence. In any subsequent occurrence during the policy year, the limit of $5,000 per occurrence still applies, except that after the Company has paid out $25,000 *in the aggregate* for a series of occurrences, there is no further coverage under the policy.

RATES

Rates for Manufacturers' and Contractors' Liability insurance are based on the following factors:

1. Territory.

2. Nature of the Insured's operations; e. g., acid manufacturing, airplane manufacturing, armored car services, bag renovating bottling, cable installation, carpentry, concrete construction, express companies, exterminating vermin, gas distributing, grain elevator operation, etc.

How Premium Is Computed—The premium for a Manufacturers' and Contractors' Liability policy is not measured by the area or frontage of the Insured's premises, but on the basis of the Insured's payroll. The rate shown for a risk applies to each $100 of *annual* remuneration paid out by the Insured to his employees. The premium charged when the policy is written is arrived at on the basis of an estimate of the Insured's payroll for the twelve month period to come. At the end of the policy year, the Company makes an audit of the Insured's payroll figures to determine the payroll actually paid out by the Insured, and the final premium is computed on the basis of these figures.

If the final premium arrived at in this manner is larger than the deposit premium paid by the Insured at the inception of the policy, an additional premium is charged. If the Insured's deposit premium is larger than the final premium, he receives a return of the excess.

Governing Classification—Generally, the entire payroll of the Insured is considered as a unit under one classification, the Governing Classification. The Governing Classification is defined as the one which carries the largest amount of payroll, except for the Standard Exceptions (discussed later).

Thus, a clothing manufacturer may employ 60 sewing machine operators, 3 cutters, 6 finishers, 2 stock clerks, 2 shipping clerks, 1 porter, 1 foreman, and 1 inside salesman. The annual remuneration of *all* these employees is considered as one unit, and is multiplied by the rate for the Governing Classification; in this case, Clothing Manufacturing.

Except in the states listed below, only the first $300 of average weekly remuneration of an employee is considered in computing the premium for a Manufacturers' and Contractors' Liability policy, and any excess over $300 is disregarded. Thus, if an Insured employs three individuals at an average weekly wage of $350 each, and 10 employees who earn $60 each, the premium for the policy would be arrived at as follows:

3 employees at $300 per week	$ 900.00	
(Disregard wages over $300)		
10 employees at $60 per week	600.00	
Total Weekly Payroll	$ 1,500.00	
	× 52	weeks
Total Annual Payroll	$78,000.00	
× Rate for Risk, per $100 of Annual Payroll (Assume .08)	.08	per $100
	$ 62.40	Premium

Where board or lodging is furnished to an employee by the employer, a figure is included to represent the value of such services. Where an employee is compensated in whole or in part by bonuses or commissions, these amounts are included in the payroll for purposes of premium computation. Similarly, a figure is included to represent tips or gratuities received by an employee.

In arriving at a final premium for the policy, overtime wages are figured at straight time rates, provided the Insured's payroll records are kept in a manner that makes it possible to clearly ascertain the wages paid at overtime rates.

ARKANSAS, COLORADO, DISTRICT OF COLUMBIA, FLORIDA, GEORGIA, IOWA, KANSAS, LOUISIANA, MISSOURI, NEW YORK, OKLAHOMA, TENNESSEE—Only payroll in excess of $100 is disregarded.

TEXAS—Only payroll in excess of $200 is disregarded.

ARIZONA—Only payroll in excess of $1,000 per month is disregarded.

CALIFORNIA, DELAWARE, MINNESOTA, NEW JERSEY, PENNSYLVANIA, WISCONSIN—The entire payroll is considered.

Executive Officers, Owners, Partners—The payroll of all executive officers is included, subject to a minimum per officer of $50 and a maximum of $300 per week. If the Insured is a sole proprietorship or a co-partnership, the payroll for each Insured-owner or partner is fixed at the rate of $5,200 per annum.

ARKANSAS, COLORADO, DISTRICT OF COLUMBIA, FLORIDA, GEORGIA, IOWA, KANSAS, LOUISIANA, MISSOURI, NEW YORK, OKLAHOMA, TENNESSEE—The payroll of all executive officers is included, subject to a minimum per officer of $30 and a maximum of $100 per week. If the Insured is a sole proprietorship or co-partnership, the payroll for each Insured is fixed at the rate of $3,600 per annum.

Standard Exceptions—Clerical Salesmen, Collectors and Messengers—Outside. Payroll for these occupations is excluded in arriving at the premium for the policy, except for certain specific classifications stipulated in the Liability manual.

Excluded Occupations—The payroll of chauffeurs and drivers is excluded from the payroll used in arriving at the premium for the policy.

PRODUCTS LIABILITY—COMPLETED OPERATIONS

WHILE MOST BUSINESSES RECOGNIZE their responsibility for the safe maintenance of their premises and elevators, and for the actions of their employees, it is not as well understood that a manufacturer may be held liable for conditions in the goods he produces which cause injury to persons or damage to property.

It is true that the general rule of law is that a manufacturer is not liable to a purchaser with whom he does not deal directly. There are many exceptions, however, to this doctrine, and manufacturers have found themselves directly liable to the ultimate consumer of their product, even though it had passed through many hands after it was sold by them. Generally, exceptions to the rule of non-liability are made for products which are "inherently dangerous" and articles made for human consumption, like drugs and medicines.

It is important to understand that an article need not be of an explosive or poisonous nature to be held "inherently dangerous." Articles have been held to fall within the scope of the term when they "are reasonably certain to place life and limb in peril *when dangerously made.*" This last rule has been further extended by court decisions which have held that the very fact that a product causes serious injury demonstrates that it possesses the power to become dangerous if defectively made. Thus, liability has been assessed against manufacturers to remote purchasers with whom they never dealt or whom they never knew, for products like sofas, coats, perfumes, hearing aids, and similar articles in everyday use.

It should also be understood that a seller may be held liable for a defect in the goods he markets, even though the product is made up and packaged by a remote manufacturer and sold in the original sealed container. Although the retailer may himself do nothing to the product except turn it over to the purchaser, it is held that he makes an *implied warranty* that the goods are fit and proper for the purpose announced. The retailers' liability is even clearer, of course, if he makes any statement regarding the safe or adequate or effective nature of the product he merchandises.

HAZARDS COVERED

Products Liability insurance is designed to cover liability imposed on the Insured arising out of the handling or use or the existence of any condition in goods or products manufactured, sold, handled or distributed by the Insured, if the occurrence occurs *after* the Insured has relinquished possession thereof to others, and *away from the premises* owned, rented or controlled by the Insured. In a similar way, it covers operations of the Insured if the occurrence occurs after the Insured has completed the operation.

If the product has not been relinquished, or if the operation being performed by the Insured has not been completed, a claim for damages due to an accident would not come under the Products Liability policy, but would be covered under the Owners', Landlords' and Tenants' Liability policy or the Manufacturers' and Contractors' Liability policy, as the case may be.

EXAMPLE: A customer comes into the Insured's store to purchase a lawn mower. In the course of demonstrating the machine, the Insured's clerk injures the prospective buyer. This claim would come under the O. L. & T. Liability policy. Similarly, if the lawn mower was being demonstrated by the Insured on the customer's grounds, the accident would fall within the coverage of the O. L. & T. policy, since the product had not yet been relinquished by the Insured.

On the other hand, if the customer takes the lawn mower home, and, in the course of working with it, injures himself or someone else, and contends that the accident was due to a defect in the product, the claim would be due "to a condition in the goods sold by the Insured" and would therefore be excluded under the policy. Coverage for such liability must be provided under Products Liability insurance.

Whether the customer has actually paid for the product or taken legal title to the item will not matter as regards coverage under the policy. If the product has been *relinquished* by the Insured and is *away from the premises* insured, claims for liability arising out of the product will fall within Products Liability insurance. On the other hand, if the product has been purchased by the customer but not yet removed from the premises, an accident caused by the product will fall within the Liability policy.

Thus, if the same customer in the illustration had completed the purchase of the lawn mower and paid for it, and was carrying it out of the store when the blade fell out and injured him, the claim would be within the scope of the basic Premises portion of the policy, since the accident occurred *on* the insured premises.

Vending machines and any property rented to or located for use of others but not sold are not considered "goods" within the scope of Products Liability coverage, and liability arising from such property would be covered under the Premises portion of the Liability policy.

Restaurants, hotels, clubs, bars and grills, taverns and drug stores are *not* covered under the policy for liability arising out of the handling, use of or the existence of a condition in goods after they have been sold by the Insured, even though the accident occurs *on the premises.* Risks of this nature are therefore not covered under the Owners', Landlords' and Tenants' policy for liability arising from food, beverages or other products which are consumed *on the premises.*

Except for drug stores, this hazard is included in the Products Liability policy which, for these classifications, covers accidents arising out of products both *on and off the premises.* For retail drug stores, a special policy is used to cover the Products Liability exposure. This policy, the Druggists' Liability policy, is discussed later in this chapter.

Similarly, Products Liability insurance will cover a service business or contractor who installs equipment for all claims that may be brought for injuries or damages arising out of the equipment or the installation *after* the work is completed.

In most instances, if the Insured has completed his operations at a given location, but has not picked up his tools or other uninstalled equipment or abandoned or unused materials, an accident arising out of such tools or equipment is covered under the Products Liability insurance.

The Products Liability policy covers all accidents which arise during the policy period. It does not matter when the product was manufactured or when it was sold. If the Insured is carrying a Products Liability policy at the time when an accident is caused by a product, and he is held liable, the policy will cover, regardless of whether he was insured in another Company when the product was manufactured or sold, or even if he was not carrying any insurance for this hazard at that time.

WHERE COVERED

The Products Liability policy covers within the United States, its possessions and territories, and Canada and international waters and air space. It will also apply to injury or damage occurring anywhere in the world arising out of a product which is sold for use or consumption, within the United States, its territories or possessions, or Canada, provided the original suit for damages is brought within these territories.

HAZARDS NOT COVERED

Equipment Rented to or Located for Use by Others—In addition to the exclusions discussed in Chapter 24, Products Liability specifically excludes liability arising out of the equipment or other property rented to others or located for use by others but not sold. This exposure is covered under Owners', Landlords' and Tenants' insurance.

No coverage is afforded under the policy, even though the property is away from the premises, since such rented or located property is not considered as relinquished by the Insured. Thus, an Insured whose business is the renting out or locating on the premises of others of vending machines, juke boxes or other equipment of this kind, will not be covered under Products Liability insurance for accidents arising out of such equipment.

While the Owners', Landlords' and Tenants' policy will cover the Insured's liability for accidents arising out of such equipment, it will not apply to a condition in the product which the machine sells, *after* the customer has made his purchase. Liability for a condition in the food or other commodity which the machine dispenses will fall back under the Products Liability policy.

Damage to Property Out of Which Accident Arises—In addition, the Products Liability policy excludes under Coverage B (Property Damage Liability) injury to or destruction of goods, products or completed work out of which the accident arises. Thus, if the Insured sold a customer a machine which exploded and damaged property, and the explosion was held to be due to a defect in the product, the customer might be able to bring a claim against the Insured for the damages caused. The Products Liability policy, if coverage had been purchased under Coverage B, will cover the Insured's liability for the damage to the customer's property, but not for the damage to the machine itself out of which the accident arose.

Assumed Liability—The Products Liability policy excludes liability assumed by the Insured under any contract or agreement other than a warranty of goods or products.

Failure to Perform Function—The Products Liability policy does not apply to claims brought against the Insured for the failure of a product or work done to perform the function or serve the function intended by the Insured, if such failure is due to a mistake or deficiency in any design, formula, plan, specifications, advertising material or printed instructions prepared or developed by the Insured.

Withdrawal of Product (Sistership Liability)—Products Liability insurance does not apply to claims made because of the withdrawal, inspection, repair or replacement, or loss of use of the Insured's products if such products are withdrawn from the market because of known or suspected defects in the products.

It is important to understand that under the "Insured's Duties in the Event of Occurrence, Claim or Suit," the policy requires the Insured to promptly take at his own expense all reasonable steps to prevent other bodily injury or property damage from arising out of the same or similar conditions. If the Insured fails to make reasonable efforts to recall a product with a known or suspected defect, he might be found to have breached the contract and be without coverage on any claims developing out of such defective products.

FOR HOW MUCH

Under Coverage A, Bodily Injury Liability, the Products Liability policy contains *three* limits; e. g., $5,000/10,000/25,000. The first two limits are similar to those of other Liability policies, the first limit applying to all claims for injury to or death of one person; the second limit to all claims from any one occurrence, regardless of the number of persons injured in the occurrence. As in other Liability policies, the limit per occurrence is subject to the limit per person.

The third limit is an aggregate limit for all claims arising during any one policy year. Thus, assume a Products Liability policy is written with limits of $5,000/10,000/25,000. In any occurrence in which one individual is injured, the maximum for which the policy is liable is $5,000. If two or more persons are injured as the result of a single occurrence, the policy will pay for claims arising out of the occurrence up to $10,000, with not more than $5,000 for the injuries caused to any one individual injured in the occurrence. To any subsequent occurrences during the same policy year these limits will again be applicable, except that after the Company has paid $25,000 for all claims within the policy year, the policy will have been exhausted. The basic limits for Property Damage Liability in a Products Liability policy provide $5,000 for all claims in one occurrence, subject to a maximum of $25,000 for all claims *in the aggregate* during the policy year.

RATES

Rates for Products Liability insurance are based on the nature of the product handled by the Insured or the operations performed by him; e. g., advertising signs, air-conditioning equipment, automobile accessory stores, bars and grills, bottled soft drinks, etc.

Rates are provided in the manual for less than 200 risks, and any risk not classified must be submitted for rating. In addition, about one-third of the risks which are listed in the manual must also be submitted for rating.

How Premium Is Computed—There are three methods for computing the premium for Products Liability insurance, as follows:

1. Sales—This method is most commonly used, and applies to most manufactured products and to most mercantile establishments. The rate for the risk is applied to each $1,000 of gross annual sales during the policy period.

2. Receipts—This method of arriving at the premium is used for most contracting and service risks. It is similar to the basis described under "Sales," except that the rate applies to each $1,000 of annual gross receipts during the policy period.

3. Per Unit—Certain risks like flour manufacturers, sugar refiners, risks dealing in gas and gasoline products of various kinds, trailer manufacturers, rubber tires and inner tubes are rated on the basis of the number of units; e. g., per 1,000 lbs., per ton, per item, etc.

Regardless of which basis is used for computing the premium for a Products Liability policy, all premiums are subject to audit at the expiration of the policy period. The final premium is arrived at in the same way as for a Manufacturers' and Contractors' Liability policy.

CONTRACTUAL LIABILITY

As POINTED OUT in the discussion of the various forms of Liability insurance, Liability policies cover only the sums which the Insured becomes legally obligated to pay, or state specifically that they will exclude all liability assumed by the Insured under any contract or agreement.

Thus, a contractor may enter into an agreement with his principal, in which he undertakes to hold the principal harmless and indemnify him for any accidents arising out of the work being done for him. A member of the public who comes on the premises and who is injured may sue the contractor and the principal. If the principal is held to be liable to the claimant for his injuries, he will be in a position to shift this liability to the contractor who, under the terms of his agreement with the principal, agreed to hold him harmless and indemnify him for all such claims arising out of work being done at the premises.

The contractor has no Liability coverage for this liability under his regular Manufacturers' and Contractors' Liability policy covering Premises and Operations, since it is a liability he assumed under contract. The contractor's direct liability to the injured person, if he is held liable to him, *is* covered under his policy. (See exceptions to this requirement towards the end of this section on Contractual Liability.)

In addition to these more widely used forms of agreement, manufacturers, distributors, and retailers regularly assume all manner of liability under contracts they enter into in their business. Thus, contracts with burglar alarm companies generally require that the Insured assume liability for false arrest, if the keys to the premises are left with the alarm company. These assumed liabilities are often unknown to the individual or firm. For this reason, the insurance man who undertakes to give his clients competent and thorough advice will ask his Insured to submit to him for review all hold harmless agreements, bills of sale, purchase orders and similar contracts under which his client may have assumed liabilities.

A special form of Liability is used to cover liabilities assumed by an Insured under a contract or agreement, since the basic Owners', Landlords' and Tenants' Liability insurance specifically excludes such assumed liabilities. Exceptions are made in that policy for written agreements of certain stipulated kinds relating to the lease of premises, easement agreements, agreements required by municipal ordinance, sidetrack and elevator maintenance agreements, and these *are* covered in the policy, as discussed at the beginning of this chapter under OWNERS,' LANDLORDS' AND TENANTS' POLICY—HAZARDS NOT COVERED—Assumed Liability. Such agreements do not therefore require coverage under a Contractual Liability policy, but all others do.

WHAT IS COVERED

The Contractual Liability does not automatically cover all contracts which the Insured may have entered into or those which he will assume during the policy period. Each contract under which liability has been assumed by the Insured must be specifically designated, if coverage is to be available to the Insured. Except for a few types of contracts, which have been fairly standardized and are therefore familiar to the Company, each contract to be insured must be submitted to the Company which reviews its terms to determine the scope of the liability which has been assumed.

HAZARDS NOT COVERED

Liability to Employees—Under Coverage A (Bodily Injury Liability), the Contractual Liability excludes only those injuries for which the Insured is liable under a Workmen's Compensation Law (discussed in Chapter 24).

Liability for Property in Care, Custody, Control—Under Coverage B (Property Damage Liability), the policy excludes coverage for damage to property in the Insured's care (discussed in Chapter 24). An exception is made for certain classifications like the Sidetrack Agreement which has been standardized by the National Industrial Traffic League. Policies covering such agreements do *not* exclude liability for damage to property in the Insured's care, custody or control. They do, however, continue to exclude liability for damage to property owned, occupied or rented to the Insured.

Liability to a Person Not Party to Contract—The policy specifically excludes liability to a person who is not a party to the contract or agreement which is the subject of the insurance provided. This exclusion may better be understood in light of a specific example: The sewer authority of a city retained a contractor and entered into a contract with him under which he would bear the responsibility for any injuries or damage to property which arose in the course of this work. An accident occurred, but the injured person could not establish any negligence, either on the part of the sewer authority or the contractor. The claimant contended that the contractor had assumed liability for all accidents, *regardless of negligence,* that the contract as drawn was therefore for the benefit of the public, and that he was therefore entitled to recover for his injuries. This type of claim would be ruled out by this exclusion, since it was brought by a person who is not a party to the contract between the contractor and the city.

FOR HOW MUCH

Contractual Liability insurance is written with the same type of limits as are used in Manufacturers' and Contractors' Liability policies.

RATES

As mentioned above, rates are published for a very limited number of contracts. All other classifications and all risks which are not shown must be submitted for rating.

Three-Year Policies—Certain Contractual Liability policies are subject to audit. Where a policy is not subject to audit of premium, it may be written for three years at three times the annual rate less 10%.

OWNERS' AND CONTRACTORS' PROTECTIVE LIABILITY INSURANCE

(INDEPENDENT CONTRACTORS)

As a general rule of law, a person who hires an independent contractor is not liable for any damages or injuries caused to the public by the contractor. Similarly, a contractor who subcontracts to another a portion of the work he has undertaken is not liable for the acts or omissions of the subcontractor.

However, this general rule of law is modified by several important exceptions, and an owner or contractor can be held liable under given conditions for the acts of persons whom he engages to work for him, even though these individuals are independent contractors, and therefore not his employees. Thus, it is held that an individual or firm is not relieved of all responsibility when the work it lets out to an independent contractor is inherently dangerous, or is covered by statutes which call for certain safety devices and precautions. Similarly, when work is to be performed in a public place, under certain conditions, the person to whom the license has been issued cannot shift all responsibility to the independent contractor he may engage.

Furthermore, under many circumstances, an owner who employs an independent contractor may be held liable for injuries caused by the contractor, if he has been guilty of negligence. Thus, an owner who employs an incompetent contractor, or furnishes him with defective tools or materials or fails to instruct him properly, may be deemed liable for the damages caused. Where the owner (or principal) exercises any supervision over the work being performed for him by the contractor, or over the contractor's employees, his liability for accidents caused by the contractor may be even clearer.

Whether an owner (or principal) will be liable in a given case for injuries or damages caused by the independent contractor he has engaged will depend on all the circumstances of the individual situation. It can be stated quite broadly, however, that an owner is not relieved of the threat of legal suit and possible imposition of liability merely because he has engaged an independent contractor and does not himself perform any of the work. Where an individual's Liability insurance does not cover this hazard, special protection is available under an Owners' or Contractors' Protective Liability policy, or as a separate division of certain Liability policies.

The Manufacturers' and Contractors' Liability policy specifically excludes any liability with respect to which insurance is or can be afforded under this Independent Contractor Division of the policy. Insurance on such liability must be purchased under an Owners' and Contractors' Protective Liability policy. This form of Liability insurance will be analyzed in this section, which should be read together with Chapter 24.

An Owners', Landlords' and Tenants' Liability policy does *not* exclude operations performed for the Insured by independent contractors. An individual or firm insured under this form does not require any additional insurance to cover liability arising out of operations performed for him by independent contractors. Such operations will be covered, *except* if they involve new construction or demolition operations, including changing the size of or moving buildings or other structures. Liability arising out of such operations is specifically excluded under the Owners', Landlords' and Tenants' Liability policy.

The exclusion applies to work of this kind whether it is performed by the Insured himself, or by his employees, or by independent contractors. As discussed under that policy, coverage for this type of work may be provided under a Construction and Demolition Permit, for which an extra premium is charged.

If the work is being done by the Insured's own employees, the Construction and Demolition Permit is rated according to the applicable classification in the Manufacturers' and Contractors' manual. If, on the other hand, the work is being performed for the Insured by an independent contractor, the rates and rules of Owners' and Contractors' Protective Liability insurance apply.

HAZARDS COVERED

Owners' and Contractors' Protective Liability insurance is designed to cover liabilities arising out of work performed for the Insured by independent contractors.

It is important to understand that the Owners' and Contractors' Protective Liability policy does not duplicate in any respect the coverage provided under the Owners', Landlords' and Tenants' or Manufacturers' and Contractors' Liability policies. Thus, if an Insured who is erecting a building engages a contractor to do some part of the work, the Owners' and Contractors' Protective policy will cover the owner only for liability that may be imposed on him arising out of the work being performed by the independent contractor. He will have no coverage for any damages arising out of the work he is doing himself or which is being done by his own employees. For such protection, he must look to a Manufacturers' and Contractors' Liability policy.

Similarly, a person for whom a building is being erected by an independent contractor may insure under an Owners' and Contractors' Protective Liability policy the liabilities to which he is exposed for operations being performed for him by the independent contractor. He may have no coverage under this insurance for liabilities that may arise out of maintenance or use of the land or the portion of the structure which has been completed, and will require insurance for this hazard under the Owners', Landlords' and Tenants' Liability policy.

The Owners' and Contractors' Protective Liability policy also covers liability arising out of the omissions or supervisory acts of the Insured in connection with work performed for the Insured by independent contractors.

HAZARDS NOT COVERED

The Owners' and Contractors' Protective Liability is subject to the exclusions which are common to other Public Liability policies (discussed in Chapter 24). In addition, the policy specifically excludes liability which is or can be insured under the Products Liability policy. The Products coverage, which takes in occurrences arising after the operations have been completed or abandoned, is discussed above and should be read together with this section in order to understand exactly what is excluded from the Owners' and Contractors' Protective Liability policy.

Products Liability insurance covers occurrences which occur after the operations have been completed and/or abandoned. That policy states specifically that it does not include the pick-up and delivery and the existence of tools, uninstalled equipment and abandoned or unused materials. The Owners' and Contractors' Protective policy, which does not cover occurrences occurring after the operations are completed, does however cover such occurrences as arise after operations have been completed out of pick-up or delivery operations, or the existence of tools, uninstalled equipment and abandoned or unused materials. The coverage of the Owners' and Contractors' Protective policy can thus be seen to fit exactly into the perils omitted from the Products coverage.

Maintenance, Repairs or Alterations—The Manufacturers' and Contractors' Liability policy does cover maintenance, repairs and alterations which do not involve new construction or demolition, even if the work is performed for the Insured by independent contractors. The insuring clause of the Owners' and Contractors' Protective Liability specifically states that it does *not* cover maintenance, repairs or alterations other than new construction or demolition operations. The Owners' and Contractors' Protective policy thus fits perfectly into the gap in the Manufacturers' and Contractors' Liability policy, and no overlap of coverage is created.

FOR HOW MUCH

The Owners' and Contractors' Protective Liability policy is written with two limits on Bodily Injury (Coverage A) and two limits on Property Damage (Coverage B). The limits in each instance are applied as under the Manufacturers' and Contractors' Liability policy.

RATES

Rates for Owners' and Contractors' Protective Liability insurance are based on the following factors:

1. Territory.

2. Nature of the operation; e. g., atomic energy commission projects, building maintenance operations, building wrecking operations, construction operations, logging and lumbering, mining, etc.

How Premium Is Computed—The rate for an individual risk is based on the territory and the nature of the operation, as outlined above. There are two methods of measuring the extent of the risk, and the manual indicates alongside each type of risk the unit to which the rate applies. Certain risks are classified in the manual but must be submitted for rating, as must any risk which is not shown. Below are listed the two methods by which risks are rated, with some examples of the kind of risks which fall into each group:

1. Total Cost—The rate shown or assigned to the risk is applied to the total cost of all work let or sublet in connection with each specific project, including the cost of all labor, materials and equipment furnished, used or delivered for use in the execution of such work, whether furnished by the owner, contractor, or subcontractor, as well as all fees, allowances, bonuses or commissions, made, paid or due. The unit of exposure to which the rate is applied is each $100 of total contract cost. The rate decreases after the first $500,000 of contract cost, and then again, after the first $1,000,000 of contract cost. This method of rating is used for risks like building maintenance, building moving, construction operations, mining, etc.

2. Area—This method of rating is used for wrecking and demolition operations. The rate shown or assigned to the risk is applied to the total number of square feet of floor space of buildings or parts thereof to be demolished. The unit of exposure to which the rate is applied is each 100 square feet of area.

COMPREHENSIVE GENERAL LIABILITY POLICY

THE COMPREHENSIVE GENERAL LIABILITY POLICY is designed to afford business risks with all-inclusive General (non-Automobile)

Liability insurance in a single policy. Frequently, the Public Liability insurance is written together with all the Automobile Liability coverages in a single policy, the Comprehensive General-Automobile policy. The coverages under the package policy are identical with those to be discussed in this chapter and the section on Automobile Liability insurance.

What Is Covered—Discussed in Chapter 24 under WHAT IS COVERED.

HAZARDS COVERED

In essence, the Comprehensive General Liability policy combines all the various coverages that can be obtained under the several individual Liability policies. The insuring clause does not stipulate particular hazards out of which accidents must arise, but agrees to pay all sums which the Insured shall become legally obligated to pay as damages for accidents sustained by others, subject only to stated exclusions. Like most Liability policies, coverage is provided for Bodily Injury Liability under Coverage A; coverage for Property Damage Liability may be provided separately under Coverage B, or may be omitted entirely.

The Comprehensive General Liability policy provides coverage automatically for any new premises or hazards which develop during the policy period. The Insured is not required to give any notice of such new hazards.

The Comprehensive General Liability policy covers all such hazards without endorsement, and will also cover automatically any other property of this kind acquired or used by the Insured during the term of the policy.

A Comprehensive General Liability policy may be written to exclude Products Liability and Contractual Liability.

FOR HOW MUCH

The limits of a Comprehensive General Liability policy apply to all the hazards of the policy. It is not permissible to write the policy with different limits applying to the various hazards covered. Limits are applied in the same manner as under the separate policies, with an aggregate limit on those coverages to which this third limit applies under the separate policies; e. g., on Products Liability; and under Coverage B (Property Damage Liability) on Contractual and Protective Liability; and on a Manufacturers' and Contractors' policy.

RATES

The premium for a Comprehensive General Liability policy is

arrived at by adding all the separate premiums that would be developed under the Schedule policy.

How Premium Is Determined—The premium paid by the Insured is based on an analysis of the exposures existing at the time the policy is written. This premium is a deposit premium, and is subject to adjustment at the end of the policy year. At that time, an audit is made to determine the extent of the hazards that existed throughout the policy year, and the scope of any undeclared hazards that might have developed. The final premium is computed accordingly, on the basis of the actual protection received by the Insured.

If the final premium is larger than the deposit premium paid by the Insured at the beginning of the policy year, he is required to pay an additional premium; if his deposit premium exceeds the final premium, he receives a refund of the excess paid by him.

STOREKEEPER'S LIABILITY POLICY

RETAIL STORES MAY INSURE under the regular Owners', Landlords' and Tenants' Liability policy at the rates for their particular classification. In addition, most retail stores are eligible for a package Liability policy which combines several of the hazards covered under separate divisions of the Schedule policy. The policy may be written for any retail store except those of the kind listed below.

Ineligible Risks—

1. Stores whose mail order sales comprise more than 50% of their total volume.

2. Stores whose principal sales are of their own products manufactured at a separate location.

3. Stores or refreshment stands with automobile parking areas used for tray service.

4. Auction, chain stores of more than ten locations, department stores, cleaning and dyeing establishments, laundries, markets, and most five and ten cent stores.

5. Drug stores, barber shops, beauty parlors, hearing aid stores and optical establishments.

6. Stores selling food whose annual sales are over $500,000 and the area of whose premises is not under 3,000 square feet.

WHAT IS COVERED

The entire discussion in Chapter 24 of What Is Covered applies to the Storekeeper's Liability policy except for two differences:

1. The policy is not divided into separate coverages for Bodily Injury and Property Damage Liability.

2. Medical Payments coverage does not require any endorsement on the policy.

HAZARDS COVERED

The Storekeeper's Liability policy is essentially a combination of the following divisions of the Owners', Landlords' and Tenants' Schedule Liability policy.

1. Premises—Operations
2. Products
3. Contractual Liability
4. Owners' Protective Liability

The Storekeeper's Liability policy, in much the same way as the Comprehensive General Liability policy, omits some of the exclusions found in the basic policies covering the hazards enumerated above.

It is important to understand that the Storekeeper's Liability policy differs from the Comprehensive General Liability policy in that it does *not* provide automatic coverage for new operations and hazards which may develop during the policy period, except as stipulated in the policy. The Storekeeper's policy is a "package" policy which combines in the one contract several separate sets of hazards rather than a "comprehensive" policy which covers automatically all hazards which might develop during the policy term.

As respects the Insured's premises and operations, the Storekeeper's Liability policy affords essentially the same protection as the Owners', Landlords' and Tenants' Liability policy, except that the policy specifically includes incidental premises like parking lots where no charge is made, booths or exhibits at fairs or expositions, and, if not owned by the Insured, areas used for meetings or employee recreation.

The Storekeeper's Liability policy also grants automatic coverage on newly acquired premises. The policy is identical on this score with the Owners', Landlords' and Tenants' policy.

As respects the coverage for Products Liability, the Storekeeper's Liability policy provides essentially the same coverage as the Products Liability policy, except that there is no aggregate limit on this exposure.

As respects Contractual Liability, the Storekeeper's Liability provides much the same coverage as the Comprehensive General Liability policy. As under that policy, coverage is provided on liabilities assumed under any contract of the type defined.

As respects coverage on work performed for the Insured by independent contractors, the Storekeeper's Liability policy provides coverage for any liability that may be imposed on the storekeeper out of such operations. (This coverage is discussed in the preceding section under OWNERS' AND CONTRACTORS' PROTECTIVE LIABILITY INSURANCE.) Excluded from this coverage under the Storekeeper's Liability policy is only the use by independent contractors of vehicles under certain conditions (discussed later under HAZARDS NOT COVERED—Animals, Vehicles). With this one exception, the Storekeeper's Liability policy will cover any liability arising out of accidents caused by independent contractors. Thus, if the Insured engages an independent contractor to wax his floors, clean his windows, or do other repair or maintenance work, his Storekeeper's Liability policy provides him with coverage on liabilities arising out of such operations.

The Storekeeper's Liability policy covers the Insured's liability for bodily injury claims arising out of *escalators* at his premises, provided he owns, rents or controls only part of the building and does not operate, maintain or control the escalator.

Medical Payments Coverage—Medical Payments coverage is provided as part of the basic Storekeeper's Liability policy, and no endorsement of the policy is necessary. (This coverage is discussed fully in Chapter 24.)

Medical Payments insurance under the Storekeeper's Liability policy contains an aggregate limit of liability, a maximum on all claims which will be paid under this coverage during the policy year.

HAZARDS NOT COVERED

Liability of an Insured to His Employees—See Chapter 24.

Liability for Property in the Insured's Care—See Chapter 24. An exception is made for sidetrack agreements.

Automobiles, Aircraft, Watercraft—This exclusion is similar to the one in the other Public Liability policies (discussed in Chapter 24—HAZARDS NOT COVERED—Liability Arising Out of Automobiles, Aircraft, Watercraft).

The policy, however, does cover the use of watercraft by independent contractors.

Demolition of Any Building—The Storekeeper's policy differs from the O. L. & T. Liability policy as respects new construction. There is no exclusion of such operations and the policy will therefore cover new construction. The policy, however, does exclude accidents caused by the demolition of any building.

Products Liability — Completed Operations — As pointed out before, the Storekeeper's policy does include Products Liability. The policy has one special exclusion relating to gas for heat or power (other than gas in non-refillable aerosol cans) or heating or cooking appliances (other than portable camp stoves or blow torches) operated by gas or liquid fuel, and the installation, servicing or repair of such appliances.

The exclusion applies only to the Products hazard. Liability arising out of an accident after the product has been sold, caused by a condition in the product, or after the installation or servicing has been completed, would not be covered. On the other hand, if a gas product, or appliance using gas, causes an accident on the Insured's premises, the liability arising from such accident *would* be covered, since such accidents do not fall within the Products hazard.

For the same reason, if the Insured rents property to others, any liability arising out of such property would be covered, even though the product were one using gas, since rented property does not fall within the scope of Products Liability insurance.

Water Damage—Sprinkler Leakage—This exclusion is discussed at the beginning of this chapter under OWNERS', LANDLORDS' AND TENANTS' LIABILITY POLICY—HAZARDS NOT COVERED—Water Damage, Sprinkler Leakage.

Liability Arising Out of Alcoholic Beverages—In some states, persons engaged in the business of the sale, gift, or distribution of any alcoholic beverages are subject to special statutes imposing liability upon them. Any person or organization engaged in the business of manufacturing, selling, or distributing alcoholic beverages, or as owner or lessor of premises used for such purposes is not covered under this policy for liability imposed upon him by reason of any such statute or ordinance.

Medical Payments Coverage—The exclusions applicable to the Medical Payments coverage of the Storekeeper's Liability policy are discussed in Chapter 24.

FOR HOW MUCH

The Storekeeper's Liability policy differs from all Liability policies previously discussed in that it does not separate Bodily Injury Liability from Property Damage Liability. Under Coverage A of the policy, both forms of liability are covered.

Furthermore, the policy does not contain a separate limit for claims arising out of injuries to one person, with a second limit applying to accidents in which more than one person is injured. The basic policy is written with a limit of $10,000, which applies to all claims arising out of any accident, regardless of the number of persons injured in the accident. The same limit is also applied to all claims for liability for damage to property. The policy does not contain any aggregate limit on property damage claims payable within the policy year. Limit may be increased up to $100,000.

The basic policy includes Medical Payments coverage with limits of $250/10,000. The first limit applies to the medical expenses of each person in any accident; the second limit is the maximum amount payable to all persons in any single accident. The limit per accident is subject to the limit per person.

RATES

The rates for a Storekeeper's Liability policy depend on two factors:

1. Territory.

2. Nature of the Insured's business; e. g., art galleries, bakeries, bootblacking, hat cleaning or shoe repairing establishments, fruit or vegetable stores, etc.

How Premium Is Determined—The basic rates provide for $10,000 of insurance for bodily injury or property damage liability, and for $250 of Medical Payments coverage, with an aggregate limit of $10,000. Higher limits may be purchased for an increased premium. The rate shown for a particular risk is applied to the area, and no further charges are developed.

DRUGGISTS' LIABILITY POLICY

AS POINTED OUT in the analysis of the Owners', Landlords' and Tenants' Liability policy, when this policy is written for a drug store, it does not cover liabilities arising out of the handling, use of or the existence of a condition in goods after they have been sold by the Insured, even if the accident occurs on the premises. For risks of this kind, the Products exposure begins as soon as the product is sold.

While firms selling drug products to others for resale can insure under Products Liability policies, retail drug stores must cover this hazard under a special policy, the Druggists' Liability policy.

Druggists' Liability insurance provides complete Products Liability coverage for retail drug stores, and the policy follows the general rules and provisions of Products Liability insurance. This section will treat only those features of the Druggists' Liability policy which depart from the basic coverage of the Products Liability policy.

HAZARDS COVERED

The Druggists' Liability policy provides coverage along the lines of other Products Liability policies for damages arising out of the handling or use of or the existence of any condition in drugs, medicines or other goods or products prepared, sold, handled or distributed by the Insured at the premises, provided the injury occurs after the Insured has relinquished possession of such goods to others. The coverage applies whether the product is consumed on the Insured's premises or off the premises.

Insurance under the Druggists' Liability policy is provided on an "occurrence" basis.

Equipment Rented to or Located for Use by Others—The Druggists' Liability policy does not exclude liability arising out of property rented to others or located for use by others, as does the regular Products Liability policy. A druggist who has rented equipment to a hospital, or to a patient, is covered under the basic Druggists' Liability for accidents arising out of such equipment, without endorsement on his policy.

Assumed Liability—The Druggists' Liability policy covers the Insured's liability under a warranty of goods or products. It does not cover any other assumed liability. In this respect, it is somewhat more restricted than the basic Products Liability policy, which covers any liability assumed by the Insured other than liability of others.

HAZARDS NOT COVERED

In addition to the exclusions found in all Liability policies, the Druggists' Liability policy excludes damage to property out of which the accident arises. (This exclusion is identical with the one in Products Liability insurance.)

Violation of a Penal Statute or Ordinance—The Druggists' Liability policy specifically excludes injury, sickness, disease or death caused by the willful violation of a penal statute or ordinance committed by or with the knowledge or consent of the Insured or of a store manager employed by the Insured.

The exclusion would not operate if an employee, other than a store manager, were guilty of violating such statute.

FOR HOW MUCH

Limits under the Druggists' Liability policy are applied differently from those of the Products Liability policy. There is no distinction between accidents causing bodily injury to one person, or those in which more than one person is injured. The limit applies to all claims arising out of a single accident, regardless of the number of persons injured. The same limit applies to Property Damage Liability, which is part of the basic Druggists' Liability policy. The basic limit is $5,000 with an aggregate limit of $15,000 for all claims arising during the policy period, regardless of whether for bodily injury or property damage.

RATES

Rates are based on the territory in which the risk is located. There are only two rating territories for this form of Liability insurance. The entire country, including Puerto Rico, is rated together except for the following states, to which a higher rate applies: Alaska, California, Connecticut, Delaware, District of Columbia, Florida, Massachusetts, Missouri, New York, Tennessee.

Stores whose annual receipts are less than $50,000 are rated on the basis of a flat charge per store. Stores whose gross annual receipts are $50,000 or higher are rated on the basis of their receipts.

COMPREHENSIVE PERSONAL LIABILITY POLICY

THE COMPREHENSIVE PERSONAL LIABILITY POLICY is designed to insure in a single policy against liability for all non-business activities. In its general purpose, it is similar to the Comprehensive General Liability policy, which affords protection on practically all liabilities that arise out of a business occupation.

In the Comprehensive Personal Liability policy will be found not only the coverages available under separate Liability policies, but certain protection not offered under any of those policies.

WHAT IS COVERED

The entire discussion in Chapter 24 of What Is Covered applies to the Comprehensive Personal Liability except for two differences:

1. The basic policy is not divided into separate coverages for Bodily Injury and Property Damage Liability (discussed later).

2. Medical Payments coverage does not require any endorsement on the policy (discussed later).

HAZARDS COVERED

The Comprehensive Personal Liability policy agrees to pay all sums which the Insured shall become legally obligated to pay as damages because of bodily injury, sickness or disease, including death at any time resulting therefrom, sustained by any person, and as damages because of injury to or destruction of property, including the loss of use thereof.

Some examples of situations which could give rise to liability on the part of the Insured and which would be covered under the policy are: accidents on the premises; injury caused by an animal; the Insured's sport activities, personal acts, his boat, domestic servants, etc.

There is no stipulation that the loss must be "caused by accident." The limit of liability applies to each "occurrence." To illustrate the difference between the coverage under a policy covering liability on a "caused by accident" basis and an "occurrence" type insuring clause, assume the Insured who owns a private residence has a trash burner in his backyard in which he regularly burns materials which emit heavy smoke and soot. After a period of some weeks, his neighbor contends that the accumulation of soot has smudged his drapes and upholstered furniture. He sues to recover damages. This situation is clearly not an "accident" in that there was no sudden unexpected event but it is an "occurrence" which would fall within the policy.

The Comprehensive Personal Liability policy will cover all liability arising out of non-business pursuits and liabilities the Insured assumes under a contract relating to the premises. These provisions are discussed more fully below.

Persons Covered—The policy covers, in addition to the Named Insured, his spouse and relatives of either if resident in the Insured's household and any person under the age of 21 in the care of any Insured, so defined.

Severability of Interests—The insurance afforded applies separately to each Insured against whom claim is made. Thus, coverage will extend to one Insured under the policy bringing suit against a second.

EXAMPLE: John Doe is the Named Insured under a Comprehensive Personal Liability policy. His mother-in-law, Mrs. Smith, resides with him. She trips on a torn carpet in the hallway of the residence. If she brings a suit against her son-in-law, John Doe, his policy would respond. Similarly, if Mrs. Smith's dog bites her son-in-law and he sues her, *his* policy will cover her.

Medical Payments Coverage—As indicated, Medical Payments coverage is part of the basic Comprehensive Personal Liability policy, and no endorsement of the policy is required to provide this extra coverage. Medical payments are payable to any person who is on the premises with the permission of the Insured; also, to a person who is elsewhere than on the Insured's premises if his injuries arise out of the premises or a condition in the ways immediately adjoining. Also covered are medical expenses of any person injured by the Insured, or by a residence employee of the Insured who is engaged at the time in the Insured's employment, or by an animal belonging to the Insured; also the medical expenses incurred by a residence employee of the Insured who meets with an accident while engaged in the Insured's employment.

Differing from the Liability insuring clause (Coverage L), the Medical Payments coverage (Coverage M) does stipulate that the injury, sickness or disease must be caused by *accident.*

Medical Payments Exclusion—The exclusions which apply to the Medical Payments coverage of the Comprehensive Personal Liability policy differ somewhat from those which apply to Liability policies covering business enterprises and will be discussed under HAZARDS NOT COVERED.

Physical Damage to Property—The basic policy, under a separate section, Coverage N, provides coverage for damage to or destruction of the property of others, up to $250 (subject to exclusions discussed next under HAZARDS NOT COVERED), caused by the Insured or any member of his household who is related to him. Under this coverage, payment is made regardless of whether there was any negligence or fault on the part of the Insured or a member of the household. It is important to note that the coverage is extended to cover physical damage to property even if in the care, custody or control of the Insured.

Liability for Damage to Rented Premises or House Furnishings by Fire, Explosion, Smoke, Smudge.—The Comprehensive Personal Liability, like all Public Liability policies, does not cover the Insured's liability for physical injury to property in his care, custody or control (Discussed in Chapter 24 under HAZARDS NOT COVERED—Liability for Property In Insured's Care). The coverage for Physical Damage to Property, which is part of the basic policy, as discussed directly above, is limited to property of others, and does not extend to property owned by or rented to an Insured. (This exclusion will be discussed under HAZARDS NOT COVERED.) An Insured who rents premises from another might be held liable for damage to the premises or the furnishings. The basic policy provides coverage for liability of this kind when it arises from certain stipulated situations. It covers the Insured's liability for damage to premises or house furnishings used by or rented to him, if the loss arises out of fire, explosion, or from smoke or smudge from the sudden, unusual and faulty operation of a heating or cooking unit.

HAZARDS NOT COVERED

Business Pursuits—The insuring clause of the Comprehensive Personal Liability policy does not state specifically that it will cover only activities of a personal nature. This effect is achieved by the policy's exclusion of business pursuits of the Insured. The policy defines "business" to include trade, profession or occupation.

This exclusion does not apply to all injuries caused by an Insured while engaged in his business pursuits, but only to those which arise from activities which are part of business. Thus, if a boiler inspector, on his way to make an inspection, accidentally pokes his umbrella into the eye of a passerby, the Comprehensive Personal Liability policy would cover such occurrence, since the opening or carrying of an umbrella is ordinarily incident to non-business pursuits.

On the other hand, if this same inspector forgot to reopen a safety valve of a boiler, and an explosion ensued, the resultant damages or injuries would not be covered by the policy, since the accident came about as the result of an activity which is incident to a business pursuit.

A Comprehensive Personal Liability policy may be written to cover a residence with incidental office, professional, private school or studio occupancy. An additional premium is charged for such extension of the policy.

Accommodation of less than two roomers or boarders, or the renting of office, school or studio space is not deemed renting or business activity.

Professional Services—Like almost every Liability policy, the Comprehensive Personal Liability policy does not provide any coverage for liabilities which grow out of the rendering of any professional service or the omission of such service. This exclusion will apply even though the policy has been endorsed to cover an incidental office used for professional purposes.

Secondary Residences—Under the policy definition of "premises" (discussed later under WHERE COVERED), the Insured is covered for any residences where he or his spouse maintains a residence. The Insured is asked when he buys the policy to list all premises where he maintains a residence. An extra premium charge is made for each additional residence. If the Insured acquires an additional residence during the term of the policy, such premises would be covered without additional premium until expiration.

Residential Property Rented To Others—There is no coverage for any premises owned, rented or controlled by the Insured unless he or his spouse maintains a residence at the location. If the Insured owns a private or two-family dwelling which he rents to others, coverage for such premises must be endorsed on the policy for an additional premium. If he occupies a portion of a multiple dwelling (three families or more), coverage for the portions rented to others may be endorsed on his Comprehensive Personal Liability policy. In the case of a multiple dwelling, coverage for the portions other than those occupied by the Insured is provided in accordance with the provisions of the Owners', Landlords' and Tenants' Liability policy.

Automobiles—The policy does not cover liability arising out of the ownership, maintenance, operation or use of any automobile or midget automobile, or their being loaded or unloaded while away from the designated premises or the ways immediately adjoining.

In most territories, an endorsement is attached which excludes coverage for claims arising out of snowmobiles away from the Insured's premises.

An exception to this rule is made for automobiles used in the course of work by independent contractors engaged by the Insured for non-business operations, provided the vehicle is not owned by or hired by the insured. Thus, if the Insured were to engage an independent contractor to repair his roof, the Insured's policy will cover any liability of the *Insured* arising out of the contractor's use of an automobile in connection with this work, except one owned by or rented by the Insured

If a residence employee, while engaged in the Insured's employment, is injured by the Insured's automobile, the policy *will* cover the Insured's liability to his employee, except if the employee is eligible for Workmen's Compensation benefits.

War Hazard—With respect to liability assumed by the Insured, the policy does not apply to bodily injury and property damage due to war, whether declared or not, civil war, insurrection, rebellion or revolution or to any act or condition incident thereto.

Liability to Employees of the Insured—The Comprehensive Personal Liability policy does not exclude liability of the Insured to his employees, as do most other Liability policies. However, the policy does not cover the Insured's liability to an employee for whom benefits are payable or required to be provided under any Workmen's Compensation law, or a residence employee for whom the Insured has procured Workmen's Compensation insurance. The exclusion applies only if the employee is injured while in the course of his employment.

If the Insured employs residence employees who are not eligible for benefits under a Workmen's Compensation law, the Comprehensive Personal Liability policy will cover the Insured's liability to those servants. The Insured is asked at the time he buys the policy whether he has more than two full-time residence employees, and an additional charge is made for each employee in excess of two. Part-time employees are disregarded unless they work for the Insured at least 50% of the customary work week. As respects claims for bodily injury by residence employees, the policy will not cover such claims brought more than three years after the period for which the policy is written.

Liability Assumed Under Contract—The Comprehensive Personal Liability policy does not cover the Insured for any liability he assumes under an oral contract. It will cover any *written* assumption of liability; e. g., a contract relating to his premises, to his sports activities, as in the case of his renting a golf cart, his hiring a hall for a wedding reception, etc. An exception is made for property damage which arises from fire, explosion, smoke or smudge caused by the sudden and faulty operation of a heating or cooking unit, and the policy would *not* apply to any liability assumed for such situations. It will not, however, cover any assumption of liability in connection with his business pursuits, as this entire area is specifically excluded (discussed above under HAZARDS NOT COVERED—Business Pursuits).

Liability for Damage to Property Used or Controlled—The Comprehensive Personal Liability policy, like most other forms of Liability insurance, does not cover the Insured's liability for damage to property used by or rented to the Insured, any resident of the named Insured, or any tenant of the Insured. The policy does not cover the Insured's liability for damage to property in his care, custody or control, except for the limited coverage (to a maximum of $250) on loss to property of others caused by an Insured (discussed above under HAZARDS COVERED—Physical Damage to Property) and the special coverage to rented premises and house furnishings (discussed above under HAZARDS COVERED—Liability for Damage to Rented Premises).

The exclusion with respect to Property Damage Liability does not apply to damage caused *by* property. Thus, if the Insured lends a tool or residence equipment to a neighbor, and the neighbor is injured by the equipment and contends that his injuries were due to the Insured's negligence in lending him a defective tool, the policy would defend the suit and pay any liability assessed against the Insured.

Assault and Battery — The Comprehensive policy specifically excludes injury, sickness, disease, death or destruction caused intentionally by the Insured or at his direction. The exclusion applies only to intentional damage committed by a person over the age of 12.

Watercraft While Away from Premises—If the Insured owns or rents watercraft with an inboard motor exceeding 50 horsepower, or a sailboat 26 feet or more in overall length, the policy does not cover liability arising out of such craft or its being loaded or unloaded while away from premises.

Any watercraft powered by an outboard motor of more than 24 horsepower, while away from the premises, also falls within the exclusion. An insured who owns such watercraft at the policy inception must declare it when he buys the policy and pay an additional premium. If an Insured owns such motor and has declared it to the Company at policy inception, or has no such motors when he purchases the policy, he will be covered automatically until the expiration of the policy on any outboard motors he may acquire during the policy term.

Similarly, if an Insured who did not own such an outboard motor when he purchased the policy acquires one during the policy term, he will be covered automatically for such liability until the expiration of the policy.

Any craft, regardless of its size, is covered while on the premises. Thus, if the Insured had put his boat up for the winter in his garage and a neighbor's child investigating the craft was injured, any liability of the Insured for the accident would be covered. Similarly, if the Insured injured someone on his own private lake, the policy would cover, since the lake is on the premises, and the exclusion applies only to watercraft while away from the premises. In any event, the exclusion will not apply to any watercraft of any size, no matter where used by the Insured if he did not own or rent it.

As under the exclusion of automobiles, if a residence employee is injured during the course of his employment by the Insured's boat the policy provides coverage, except if the employee is covered by Workmen's Compensation insurance.

Aircraft—The Comprehensive Personal Liability policy does not apply to aircraft or the loading or unloading of such craft. Liability of the Insured to a residence employee is excluded only if the employee is engaged in the operation or maintenance of the aircraft, or if the employee is covered by Workmen's Compensation insurance.

Elevators—There is no exclusion under the policy of liability arising out of elevators. The Insured is asked, when he buys the policy, to declare any elevators, incinerators or escalators on the premises, and an additional premium charge is made for each such device. Any elevator acquired during the term of the policy would be covered without additional premium charge until the policy expiration.

Nuclear Energy—There is no coverage under the Liability section for bodily injury or property damage with respect to which an Insured is also an Insured under a Nuclear Energy Liability policy, or would be an Insured under such a policy except for its exhaustion of its limits of Liability.

Medical Payments Coverage—Medical expenses under Coverage B, Medical Payments coverage, are not payable to any Insured, as defined in the policy (discussed later under WHO IS COVERED).

Nor is there any coverage under this section of the policy for any person while engaged in the Insured's employment if the person is eligible for benefits under a Workmen's Compensation law. There is no coverage for medical expenses incurred by any person who resides on the premises, or is on the premises because of a business conducted on the premises. This exclusion does not apply to a residence employee.

Business is defined in the policy to include trade, profession or occupation. Thus, if a lawyer or doctor has his Comprehensive Personal Liability policy written to include professional occupancy, the policy will cover his liability (other than for malpractice) to the patients or clients who come on his premises to consult him. Such persons are not eligible, however, for Medical Payments benefits.

WHO IS COVERED

The Comprehensive policy includes as an Insured not only the person named in the policy but, if they are residents in the same household, the Insured's spouse, relatives of either, and any person under the age of 21 who is in the care of an Insured.

Relatives of the named Insured or his spouse are covered regardless of their age, provided they are residents in the same household.

Persons not related to the Insured who are members of his household are not covered under the policy. They may be added to the policy for an extra premium.

The policy also covers, as respects animals or watercraft which are owned by an Insured, any person or organization legally responsible for such property. The policy also includes as an additional Insured any employee who drives a farm tractor or trailer or self-propelled or motor or animal drawn farm implement while engaged in the Insured's employment.

WHERE COVERED

The word "premises" is defined broadly in the Comprehensive Personal Liability policy. It includes any premises where the Insured or his spouse maintains residence and all private approaches thereto, individual or family burial plots, and any other premises where the Insured is residing temporarily, provided the premises are not owned by or rented to an Insured, and vacant land other than farm property.

The policy also covers vacant land, including land on which the Insured is having a one- or two-family dwelling constructed, provided the work is being done by independent contractors, and the dwelling is not being built for resale or to order for someone else. If the Insured is doing the work himself, or is directly employing persons to do the work (not independent contractors), the policy requires endorsement to cover such operations. An additional premium is charged for such coverage. If a substantial portion of the work is being performed for the Insured by contractors, then the Insured may undertake a part of the work himself.

Business Property — The policy specifically excludes business property from the definition of "premises." Unless specifically endorsed, any property from which a business is conducted is excluded, as is any property rented in whole or in part to others except for the Insured's own residence if rented occasionally, or if a two-family dwelling which is usually occupied in part by the Insured, or garages which do not house more than three vehicles.

CANCELLATION

For restrictions on the Company's right to cancel personal policies, see Chapter 2—CANCELLATION.

RATES

Rates are based on the territory in which the residence is located. The additional coverages that may be added to the policy, like incidental office, professional private school or studio occupancy, are also rated on a territorial basis.

The rates for coverage on boats of a certain size, for private residence and two-family residences rented to others, for employer's liability, and for additional residences maintained by persons other than the named Insured or his spouse differ somewhat according to the territory in which they are located.

Three-Year Policies—Comprehensive Personal Liability policies may be written for three years at 2.7 times the annual premium, provided the entire premium is paid in advance.

Other Provisions—The policy is identical with other Liability insurance discussed in Chapter 24 as regards Notice of Claim, Co-operation by Insured, Action of Others Against Company, Cancellation and Subrogation.

Assignment—Like all other forms of insurance, assignment of the policy is not valid without the written consent of the Company. If the Insured dies, the policy is terminated except if within 60 days of the date of the Insured's death the Company is notified of a new Insured to be designated under the policy.

FARMER'S COMPREHENSIVE PERSONAL LIABILITY POLICY

MOST FARMERS CAN INSURE their liability for their personal and farming activities in a single inclusive form of Liability insurance—The Farmer's Comprehensive Personal Liability policy. Only the following classes of farms are not eligible for this form of protection:

1. Farms whose principal purpose is to supply commodities for manufacturing or processing by the Insured for sale to others. In this group will fall farms operated by creameries and dairies. Dairy farmers who do not manufacture or process are eligible for the policy, as are beef farmers who slaughter and dress their livestock, and vegetable farmers who bunch or crate vegetables and fruit.
2. Farms operating freezing or dehydrating plants, and poultry factories.
3. Farms whose principal business is the raising and using of horses for racing purposes.

The Farmer's Comprehensive Personal Liability is practically identical with the Comprehensive Personal Liability policy. The chief difference between the two policies is that the Farmer's Comprehensive policy includes coverage on farming operations as well as personal activities.

The Farmer's Comprehensive Personal Liability policy does not cover property damage arising out of any substance released or discharged from any aircraft. The policy also excludes punitive or exemplary damages on account of bodily injury to any insured farm employee employed in violation of law.

A special coverage is made available under the Farmer's Comprehensive. Under Coverage O of the policy, which is optional, the Insured may cover the death of any cattle, horse, or hybrid thereof, hog, sheep or goat owned by an Insured caused by collision of the animal with a motor vehicle, if such collision is not caused by any vehicle owned or operated by the Insured or his employee. The policy covers only collision on a public highway when the animal is not being transported.

NOTE: Farmer's Comprehensive Personal Liability insurance may also be written in a special package policy for farmers, the Farmowners-Ranchowners Policy Program (discussed at the end of Chapter 35).

PROFESSIONAL LIABILITY INSURANCE

AS POINTED OUT at the beginning of this chapter, the Owners', Landlords' and Tenants' Liability policy covering a doctor or dentist will cover liability arising out of the maintenance or use of the premises, but specifically excludes liability arising out of the rendering of a professional service or the omission of such service. It should be remembered that a risk of this kind, even when insured against Products Liability will be without coverage for most of its professional acts, since Products only applies to accidents which may occur away from the premises after the product has been relinquished (discussed above under PRODUCTS LIABILITY—COMPLETED OPERATIONS). Similarly, the Comprehensive Personal Liability policy, even when endorsed to cover incidental professional occupancy, will not cover liability arising from "malpractice." This hazard is specifically excluded from Public Liability policies covering a whole series of risks, among which are: Advertisers and Advertising Agencies; Army Post Exchanges; Baths; Barbers; Beauty Parlors; Cemeteries; Colleges; Data Processors; Dentists; Directors and Officers; Druggists; Exercise or Health Institutes; Hearing Aid Stores; Hospitals; Jewelry Stores; Mausoleums; Morticians; Opticians; Optometrists; Physicians; Preparatory Schools; Real Estate Agents; Sanitariums; Schools; Swimming Pools; Telephone Secretarial Services; Veterinarians and Veterinary Hospitals; etc.

All risks of this kind require a special form of Liability insurance, *in addition* to one which covers their premises.

Different forms of Professional Liability insurance are usually issued to the various professions. In some instances, the Professional Liability policy is known as an Errors and Omissions contract, but its intent is the same—to cover the exposure to claims arising out of the rendering or failure to render of a professional service.

In addition to the professions in which actual physical or mental injury may be caused to clients, certain other professions are exposed to claims for malpractice. Claims may be brought against lawyers, accountants, architects and similar professional persons for errors or omissions in their professional capacity. Professional

Liability policies are made available to such risks, and these policies provide essentially the same protection as is afforded under a Physicians', Surgeons' or Dentists' Professional Liability policy.

Professional Liability policies follow in the main along the lines of regular Public Liability insurance discussed in this and the preceding chapter. The insuring clause is adapted to cover the type of exposure which the particular profession presents. Thus, in the case of policies covering attorneys (discussed below), there is no reference to "accidents."

Most Professional Liability policies differ from the regular Public Liability forms in that they do not give to the carrier the option of defending a suit or settling. In the case of Professional Liability, the Company may not make a settlement with the claimant except with the written consent of the Insured.

Many larger employers provide medical and nursing services for their employees on the premises, and such Insureds will require protection under their Liability insurance for malpractice that may be alleged by an employee.

Because of the possibility of disagreement as to whether a claim develops out of the premises operation or the professional activities of an Insured, it is advisable, *wherever possible,* to arrange both coverages in one policy, or in the same company.

Below will be analyzed several of the more widely sold Professional Liability coverages. Since most of these policies follow along similar lines, the Physicians', Surgeons' and Dentists' Professional Liability Insurance policy will be discussed first, and any significant differences between this policy and other Professional Liability policies pointed out thereafter.

PHYSICIANS', SURGEONS' AND DENTISTS' PROFESSIONAL LIABILITY INSURANCE POLICY

While there are some differences in the forms written by American carriers, these are minor and this coverage can be discussed along the lines set down below. A considerable body of this insurance however is placed in the London market, and the Lloyd's policy does present some more important differences, which will be pointed out.

Coverage may be afforded to a physician practicing as an individual, or to a medical partnership or to a medical professional corporation. In each case, the policy pays all sums which the Insured becomes obligated to pay as damages because of injury arising out of the rendering or the failure to render of professional service which falls within the scope of the Insured's profession.

In the case of physicians or surgeons, it can be seen, a considerable area of potential liability may develop out of the failure to render professional service. It should be borne in mind that a medical practitioner may be held liable for not visiting a patient whom he has previously undertaken to treat and that there are limitations on the doctor's right to terminate his ministering to the sick person.

Like all Public Liability policies, coverage is afforded not only for the acts of the Insured but for employees or others acting under his instructions in the scope of their duties for whom the Insured may be held liable. This will include assistants, nurses, technicians, etc. When written for a partnership, the policy covers the acts of any individual for whose acts the partnership is liable.

As under other Public Liability policies, the Company is not only obligated to pay any claims developing out of the acts which are covered but also to defend any suit brought against the Insured, even if false, fraudulent or groundless (discussed in Chapter 24 under PUBLIC LIABILITY INSURANCE—WHAT IS COVERED—Defense of Suits, Supplementary Benefits).

It is important to bear in mind that the policy covers only such sums as the Insured becomes obligated to pay arising out of injury sustained *during the policy period.*

The policy is written with two limits: the first is the maximum amount which the Company is obligated to pay for damages arising out of any covered claim. The policy also carries an "aggregate limit" which is the maximum the Company is obligated to pay for all claims under the policy. Note that the "aggregate limit" is subject to the "each claim" limit in any individual case.

Lloyd's Policy—As was pointed out above, the American form of Professional Liability insurance covers any claims which arise out of injury *occurring* during the policy period, regardless of when the claim is actually made. The Lloyd's form seeks to avoid being faced with a long tail of developing claims out of occurrences alleged to have taken place years ago. It therefore requires that the *claim itself be made during the policy period.* When the coverage is first placed with Lloyd's, the inception date of the policy becomes the "Retroactive Date" and is used in all subsequent renewals with Lloyd's. The current policy covers any claim which is made *on or after this Retroactive Date.*

After a Lloyd's Professional Liability policy is cancelled or not renewed, there is a Discovery Period granted the Insured (similar to the Discovery Period in a Fidelity Bond, discussed in Chapter 14 under FIDELITY BONDS—WHEN COVERED—Discovery

Period). The Discovery Period under the Professional Liability policy is 36 months during which time there is coverage for any claims made against the Insured but *only* for injuries which occurred during the term of the policy, or more accurately, between the Retroactive Date and the termination of the policy.

The American form, it was pointed out above, covers any rendering or failure to render of a professional service. The Lloyd's form spells out in the schedule the specific procedures for which coverage is provided. Separate premium charges are specified for each of the described procedures, among which the following may be listed: prescribing or fitting contact lenses; hypnosis; treatment of alcoholism, drug addition or mental illness, certain X-ray procedures; 14 specified forms of surgery, etc. An exception to the delimiting of coverage to the scheduled procedures is made under the "Good Samaritan" clause, which extends coverage to the Insured for claims arising out of his rendering in good faith emergency medical care at the scene of an accident or medical emergency even though the treatment involved procedures not scheduled in the policy.

MISCELLANEOUS MEDICAL PROFESSIONAL LIABILITY POLICIES

Professional Liability insurance for miscellaneous professions of a medical or quasi-medical nature is provided by special endorsements to the Physicians', Surgeons' and Dentists' policy or the Druggists' policy, as the case may be.

Such insurance is offered to Blood Banks, Chiropodists, Chiropractors, X-Ray Laboratories, Opticians, Optometrists, Physiotherapists, Veterinarians, etc. Nurses may also purchase a Professional Liability policy which is drawn along the lines of the Physicians', Surgeons' and Dentists' policy.

LAWYERS PROFESSIONAL LIABILITY INSURANCE

The policy is very similar to the Physicians', Dentists' and Surgeons' Professional Liability (discussed above). It covers the Insured against liability for acts or omissions arising out of professional services performed for others in a professional capacity. It also applies to acts performed by persons for whom the Insured is legally liable.

Coverage A applies to individuals; Coverage B to partnerships. Under Coverage B, the policy affords protection to the partnership and its members. Automatic coverage is extended to newly added partnerships, and to all changes in the partnership. For an additional premium, it is possible to cover the *personal* liability of employees of the Insured.

The policy covers against acts or omissions of the Insured which occur during the policy period, regardless of when the claim is made, and also claims made during the policy period for acts which took place *prior* to the inception of the policy, provided that the Insured did not know, or could not reasonably have been expected to know that an act or omission had occurred which could be expected to result in a claim being made.

The policy excludes loss caused by any fraudulent act or omission committed by the Insured or an employee. If an Insured is a salaried employee, the policy does not cover claims made by his employer. There is no coverage for loss sustained by the Insured as the beneficiary or distributee of any trust or estate.

There is a special clause relating to the Insured's duties as an executor or administrator, guardian, trustee or similar fiduciary. The Insured's acts or omissions in the course of performance of his duties in such capacity are covered but only to the extent that such acts or omissions are those for which he would be legally responsible as an attorney for a fiduciary.

BEAUTY SHOP AND BARBER SHOP LIABILITY INSURANCE

The Liability Insurance policies covering beauty shops and barber shops are not standardized although there is sufficient agreement among the carriers on the basic provisions to make it possible to set down in outline a form which will be fairly close to the one in use in most such risks.

Different from the situation which prevails in other Professional Liability policies, underwriters usually prefer to write the Premises, Products and the Professional (malpractice) coverages, frequently in the one contract.

Where most Professional Liability policies do not cover property damage (this presenting no real exposure in the ordinary professional situation), Beauty Shop Liability policies do offer property damage liability (usually subject to a deductible) to cover claims for damage to customers' clothing and other property from spilled dyes or other coloring preparations.

Most Beauty Shop Liability policies cover any professional service while within the premises, resulting from any work, treatment or operation, or the use of any preparation or appliance in connection with the operation of a beauty shop, some define covered professional services, along the following lines: Permanent hair waving by any cold process, heating or steaming methods, whether heat or steam is generated by electricity, gas, or the use of machineless heat pads or sachets; hair cutting, styling, singeing, trimming, conditioning, dressing, shampooing, shampoo-tinting, bleaching, dyeing or coloring by liquid dyes, henna treatments or hair crayons; eyelash or eyebrow tinting or coloring by use of "Roux Lash and Brow Tint," "Spiro's Coloura," mascara or eyebrow pencils; eyebrow arching, tweezing and plucking; the removal of unwanted hair by shaving or the use of wax or a depilatory preparation; hair and scalp treatments; face and neck massaging; manicuring and pedicuring; marcel, finger and water waving.

In addition to the exclusions which are common to all Public Liability policies (discussed in Chapter 24 under PUBLIC LIABILITY INSURANCE—HAZARDS NOT COVERED), the Beauty Shop and Barber Shop policy contains several exclusions which develop out of the specialized function of such establishments, among which are:

- Face lifting, plastic surgery, the removal or attempted removal of warts;
- Any apparatus utilizing X-rays for the removal of unwanted hair;
- Use of flammable dry shampoo;
- Combustion or explosion or burning of combs or other articles of a flammable nature other than hard rubber combs;
- Chiropody;
- Services rendered in connection with exercising, slenderizing or reducing services;
- Any operator of a permanent waving machine who has not had certain stipulated periods of actual and practical experience in the operation of such equipment;
- Use or administration of any dye to eye lashes or eyebrows other than the preparations mentioned in the insuring clause (see above).

The policy is frequently written with a Deductible applicable to each occurrence.

MORTICIANS PROFESSIONAL LIABILITY INSURANCE

The Morticians Professional Liability policy is very similar to other Professional Liability policies except that in addition to covering, as the others do, claims for bodily injury, sickness, disease or death, the Morticians policy also spells out *mental anguish* as a possible cause of claim.

The policy is written in two separate sections:

Coverage A—applies to bodily injury, sickness, disease or death because of any professional malpractice, error or mistake in the embalming, handling, disposition, burial, disinternment or removal of any deceased human body or any conduct of any memorial service by the Insured, even though no human body is present, or because of any injury to, destruction of or interference with the right of burial of a deceased body.

Coverage B—applies to the destruction of or injury to urns, caskets, linings or fittings, casket cases, crypts, mausoleums or other facilities for the care or burial of a deceased body, belonging to others, but in the care, custody or control of the Insured.

DIRECTORS AND OFFICERS LIABILITY POLICY

The area of liability of corporate directors and officers continues to broaden with the growing precedent of cases holding such individuals liable for acts or omissions in their capacity as directors or officers. Stockholders bring suit for damages which they contend they have suffered as a result of acts or omissions of corporation officers and directors. Competitors can institute actions seeking redress for unfair competition, while Government agencies like the Securities and Exchange Commission or the Fair Trade Commission may also bring suit.

As a consequence, more and more corporations find that they are required to enter into agreements with their directors and officers to hold them harmless and reimburse them for any liability that may be imposed on them in their capacity as officers or directors.

The Directors and Officers Liability policy is designed to cover the officer or director, as well as the corporation for such liability. There is a very restricted market for this coverage in this country and a large proportion of the coverage is placed with underwriters at Lloyd's in London.

There is no standardization, but generally the policy is written under two separate sections:

Directors and Officers Liability Coverage—Pays on behalf of any person who is or may become a director or officer of the named corporation all sums which such individual may be called on to pay for claims which may be made against him for any wrongful act. Wrongful act is defined as any breach, neglect, error, misstatement, omission or other act committed or wrongfully attempted by the Insureds or alleged to have been committed solely by reason of their being directors and officers of the company.

Company Reimbursement Coverage—This section, also known as the Company Indemnification section, pays on behalf of the corporation all sums which each director and officer may be required to pay for wrongful act (as defined) and which such director and officer is entitled to receive by way of reimbursement or indemnification from the company. Such sums include not only damages but also costs, charges or expenses incurred in connection with the defense of any suit, action or proceeding or appeal to which the directors or officers may be a party or which they may be threatened with.

The policy contains exclusions which are designed for the type of risk being assumed, among which are:

Libel, slander;

Acts contributed to by the dishonesty of the Insureds;

Acts which result in profits or other personal advantage to which the Insured is not legally entitled;

Loss caused by the failure of the Insured to maintain insurance.

Directors and Officers Liability is written with a Deductible. Most commonly, the policy requires that the Insured retain 5% of *each and every loss*. This 5% retention must not be insured. In this way, the carrier can count on the Insured's involvement to some degree in each and every loss situation. An exception is made for policies with limits of over $1,000,000, and in such cases, the carrier may agree to delete the coinsurance requirement.

Extended Discovery Clause—It is provided that if the Insurance Company refuses to renew or cancels a Directors and Officers Liability Insurance policy, the Insured has the right to extend the coverage of the policy to be available to protect against losses which are discovered within 12 months of the termination of the policy, but which occurred during the term of the policy, i. e., before the termination or cancellation of the contract. For this extension, the Insured is required to pay an additional premium equal to 25% of the three-year premium.

The market for this coverage is rather circumscribed, but coverage may generally be obtained, subject to underwriting, by companies which are publicly owned and whose annual sales exceed $10,000,000, $5,000,000 in assets or with stockholders' equity in excess of $2,000,000.

Mini-D. & O. Insurance—There are several markets for Directors and Officers Liability for smaller firms, banks, savings and loan associations, etc. A New York-based carrier, which has led the field in providing this coverage for large public corporations, is now offering this coverage to public companies, regardless of their size.

DATA PROCESSORS ERRORS AND OMISSIONS INSURANCE

The explosive growth of the data processing industry has resulted in a steady increase in the number of service organizations and in the volume of such activity. These firms perform data processing services for others on a fee or contract basis. It should also be borne in mind that many large corporations which maintain their own data processing department frequently offer services to outside companies in order to reduce their operating costs. Such firms will, as respects these services, face the same liability as regular data processing service companies.

The policy follows the format of the usual Professional Liability policy in that it undertakes to pay all sums which the Insured shall become legally obligated to pay as damages on account of any claim arising out of any negligent act, errror or omission of the Insured in the performance of data processing services for others.

The policy is almost always written with a Deductible, usually $1,000 with respect to each and every claim.

In addition to the usual exclusions, the Data Processors Errors and Omissions policy excludes loss arising out of advice on methods, practices or procedures, or opinions on financial statements, the preparation of any income tax returns and liability for loss or damage to the property of others in the care, custody or control of the Insured.

Policy forms in this field are not standardized; some are written on the basis that they will cover claims for acts which occurred during the policy period; others, only for claims which are actually *made* during the policy period.

BLANKET CATASTROPHE EXCESS LIABILITY POLICY (UMBRELLA LIABILITY)

Blanket Catastrophe Excess Liability insurance, while not yet standardized as to form or rates, is being underwritten by more and more companies. Usually written with a large limit of liability, the policy covers as excess over the Insured's Liability policies such hazards as *are* covered under those policies, and closes the gap, subject to a few limited exceptions, on all other liabilities for which no coverage may be provided in his underlying policies.

The coverage is now written for commercial as well as personal risks. Each of these forms of Excess Liability (Umbrella) insurance is discussed briefly below. It should be understood that these coverages vary in some respects, as written by the companies in this field and that the discussion below follows the more general provisions of these contracts.

COMMERCIAL UMBRELLA POLICY

As indicated above, the Excess Liability policy is designed to provide coverage above a stated figure (akin to a Deductible). The Insured is required to carry underlying Liability coverage with minimum limits, generally: $100/300,000 on Bodily Injury, $100,000 on Property Damage, $100,000 on Automobile Liability, and generally, $100,000 on Employers' Liability and Bailees' Liability. The Umbrella Liability policy covers above these amounts. It also provides coverage on all but a few specified excluded exposures which are not covered under the usual standard Liability policy, but such coverage is subject to a stated retention (Deductible) by the Insured. Finally, the Umbrella Liability policy provides automatic replacement for underlying Liability which is reduced or exhausted by losses.

The policy provides coverage for the following classes of perils:

1) Personal injury, including death.

NOTE: This coverage is broader than the bodily injury protection afforded by the standard Public Liability policy and includes not only bodily injury but also mental injury; false arrest, wrongful eviction, malicious prosecution, discrimination, humiliation; libel, slander, defamation of character; invasion of the rights of privacy (except that which arises out of an advertising activity).

2) Property Damage.

NOTE: Different from the usual form of Liability insurance, the Umbrella policy does NOT exclude liability for property in the Insured's care, custody or control. It therefore covers his liability as bailee.

3) The policy covers "Advertising Liability" in a separate section. Generally, the coverage is divided into four sections:

a) Libel, slander or defamation of character;

b) Infringement of copyright, name of product or slogan;

c) Invasion of privacy;

d) Piracy or misappropriation of an idea under a contract.

The policy excludes obligations of the Insured under any Workmen's Compensation or Disability Benefits Act.

Most Umbrella policies exclude liability arising out of any aircraft, and limit coverage on watercraft liability to that which arises out of the use of boats below a stated size.

An important exclusion in some policies applies to errors or mistakes of a professional nature. The Umbrella policy which carries such an exclusion would not be available to cover over and above any Professional Liability that the Insured carried.

The policy excludes the claims made against the Insured for

replacing or repairing defective products sold, handled or manufactured by the Insured.

PERSONAL UMBRELLA POLICY

Like the Commercial Umbrella policy discussed above, the Personal Umbrella policy is designed to cover as excess over underlying Liability policies maintained by the Insured; in most companies, it is written as excess over Automobile Liability insurance with limits of $100/300,000 on bodily injury and $10,000 Property Damage, or $300,000 single limit coverage; Comprehensive Personal Liability insurance of $50,000; Watercraft Liability on boats over 26 feet in length of $100,000; Employers Liability of $100,000; and Aircraft Liability where applicable.

For Insureds engaged in the professions, the Umbrella Liability policy may provide excess coverage on Professional Liability over $100/300,000 in the basic policy (although some Companies exclude the Professional Liability exposure entirely).

The Personal Umbrella Liability policy covers above these amounts. It also provides coverage, subject to the specified exclusions, on all exposures which are not covered in the basic policies, subject to a minimum retention (Deductible), usually $5,000.

The policy excludes obligations of the Insured under any Workmen's Compensation or Disability Benefits Law. There is no coverage for liability the Insured assumes by contract for damage to property rented to, occupied or used by or in the care, custody or control of the Insured to the extent that the contract *broadens the Insured's statutory or common law* liability.

There is no coverage for liability for damage to aircraft or watercraft rented to or used by or in the care, custody or control of the Insured. The policy does not cover liability for acts by the Insured or by his direction which result in bodily injury or property damage.

Recently, many insurers offering Personal Umbrella Liability have begun to include Excess Major Medical Coverage. Like the rest of the coverage provided by Umbrella insurance, this section is subject to a large Deductible, usually at least $10,000.

FOR FURTHER READING

ACKERMAN—Insurance
GEE—Agent's Casualty Guide
KULP AND HALL—Casualty Insurance
MAGEE AND BICKELHAUPT—General Insurance
MEHR AND CAMMACK—Principles of Insurance
POLICY, FORM & MANUAL ANALYSIS SERVICE
RIEGEL, ROBERT AND MILLER—Insurance
SPELL—Public Liability Hazards

(See Reading List at End of Book)

CHAPTER 26

Automobile Liability Insurance Policy

AN INDIVIDUAL FIRM or corporation which owns or operates a motor vehicle is charged with the duty of maintaining and using the vehicle in such a manner as will avoid injuring others, or doing damage to their property. In the case of automobiles, more than in the use of other property, we have seen that a large area of liability may rest upon the owner of the vehicle for accidents caused by others who use his car (discussed in Chapter 23 under VICARIOUS LIABILITY).

As pointed out in the preceding chapters, Liability policies, whether purchased by individuals or businesses, specifically exclude accidents arising out of use of automobiles and their being loaded or unloaded, while such vehicles are away from the Insured's premises. Insurance to cover this form of liability is provided in the Automobile Liability policy. (In some instances, this insurance is added to other Liability policies, but the coverage is the same as under the separate policy.) While the Automobile Liability policy is not uniform, it has been very highly standardized and few significant differences will be found among the forms used by the various Companies. As will be explained later, Automobile insurance is written either under the older form, usually referred to as the basic policy, or under a newer form, the Family Automobile policy. This chapter and Chapter 27 analyze the basic Automobile Liability and Automobile Physical Damage policy. Any difference between these policies and the Family Automobile policy are pointed up in italics under the appropriate coverages.

Eligibility for Family Automobile Policy—The Family Automobile policy is available to cover four-wheeled private passenger automobiles, including station wagons and jeeps, utility auto and farm trucks with a load capacity of 1,500 pounds or less of the pick-up body, sedan delivery or panel type and trailers designed for use with private passenger automobiles. This policy is available only if such vehicle is owned by an individual or by a husband and wife. Other types of automobiles, i. e., automobiles owned by corporations or partnerships, trucks larger than those listed above public vehicles, etc., continue to use the older form of Automobile Liability policy.

WHAT IS COVERED

The Automobile Liability policy is identical with other Public Liability forms as to the sums it will pay. (See Chapter 24 under WHAT IS COVERED.) In addition, the policy will pay up to $100 towards the cost of any Bail Bond which the Insured may be required to post in the event of accident or violation of any traffic law. Like most other Liability forms, the Automobile policy may be broadened to cover the medical expenses incurred by certain individuals in an accident, regardless of whether the Insured was liable for the particular accident or not. The Medical Payments coverage in an Automobile Liability policy is specifically designed for this form of insurance, and differs in some important respects from the Medical Payments coverage available under Public Liability policies. It is discussed fully below under HAZARDS COVERED—Medical Payments Coverage.

The Automobile Liability policy does not cover damage to the automobile itself. Damage to or loss of the vehicle is covered under a special form of insurance, the Automobile Physical Damage or Material Damage policy. This coverage is discussed in Chapter 29.

Financial Responsibility Laws — Automobile Liability policies generally contain a provision which makes the policy conform to any Motor Vehicle Financial Responsibility Law of the state or province which is applicable to liability arising out of the automobile described in the policy. Under certain conditions, this provision of the policy may obligate the Company to pay for damages for which it would not otherwise be responsible. This provision of the policy is discussed towards the end of this chapter under FINANCIAL RESPONSIBILITY LAWS.

HAZARDS COVERED

The Automobile Liability policy covers only the sums which the Insured becomes legally obligated to pay for damages caused *by accident.* (This is true in all states of the United States and the provinces of Canada except Saskatchewan, where an injured person is entitled to benefits in almost every instance, regardless of whether the operator of the automobile was at fault. Currently, there is widespread discussion in this country of proposals to fundamentally revise the legal basis of liability in automobile accidents. These proposals and analyses of existing No-Fault laws in several states are discussed at the end of this chapter under MODIFICATIONS OF TORT LIABILITY SYSTEM.

Family Automobile Policy—*Under this form of policy, coverage is not restricted to "caused by accident" situations. The term "occurrence" is used and all liability imposed on the Insured would be covered except for bodily injury or property damage done intentionally by him or at his direction. It should be noted, however, that the Medical Payments coverage (discussed next) is still on a "caused by accident" basis, as is the coverage under the Uninsured Motorist coverage or under the New York Motor Vehicle Accident Indemnification Corporation, discussed later in this chapter.*

The difference between coverage on a "caused by accident" basis and an "occurrence" basis may be illustrated as follows: An Insured who resides in a row of attached houses is in the habit of running his motor for 10 minutes each morning to warm it up before driving. After a period of several weeks, a neighbor alleges that the exhaust fumes have made him ill (or damaged his shrubbery). A claim of this kind would come under an "occurrence" policy, but might be denied under a "caused by accident" policy, since an accident is generally held to be an event which is sudden and fixed in time.

Coverage is afforded for the ownership, maintenance or use of the automobile designated in the policy. The basic policy also provides several other coverages without endorsement, as follows:

1. Other Drivers and Interests—The Automobile policy covers not only the named Insured and spouse as Insureds but also any other person who operates the car with the Insured's permission (discussed later under Other Drivers and Interests — Omnibus Clause).

2. Drive Other Cars—The Automobile policy also covers, under stated conditions, the named Insured and his spouse while operating any other automobile (discussed later under Drive Other Cars).

Family Automobile Policy—*Drive Other Car coverage is afforded to all residents of the Insured's household.*

3. Temporary Substitute Automobile—The policy also covers an automobile substituted by the Insured for the one designated in the policy. (The conditions of this coverage will be discussed under Temporary Substitute Automobile.)

4. Newly Acquired Automobiles—Coverage is also afforded for automobiles acquired by the Insured during the term of his policy (to be discussed under Newly Acquired Automobiles).

The Automobile Liability policy will cover the Insured's liability to almost anyone except his own employees.

ALABAMA, ARKANSAS, CALIFORNIA, COLORADO, DELAWARE, FLORIDA, IDAHO, ILLINOIS, INDIANA, IOWA, KANSAS, MICHIGAN, MONTANA, NEBRASKA, NEVADA, NEW MEXICO, NORTH DAKOTA, OHIO, OREGON, SOUTH CAROLINA, SOUTH DAKOTA,

TEXAS, UTAH, VIRGINIA, WASHINGTON, WYOMING—These states have enacted statutes which restrict the liability of a motor vehicle owner to his guest passengers. (See Chapter 23 under Guest Laws.)
GEORGIA, WASHINGTON—These states follow a rule similar to the Guest Laws (discussed in Chapter 23 under Guest Laws).
NEW YORK—While there is no restriction on the right of a spouse to sue a spouse in tort, no Automobile Liability policy will be deemed to provide any coverage for such liability, unless specifically endorsed on the policy.

Loading and Unloading—The policy specifically sets forth in the Declarations that the use of the automobile includes its loading or unloading. It is not designed, however, to take the place of regular Liability insurance which covers the operations of a business.When an accident occurs during the course of delivery, the Automobile Liability policy will pay for the Insured's liability. There are many cases, however, in which it becomes difficult to determine the precise point at which delivery is completed.

Thus, if an Insured removes a product from his vehicle and sets it down on the street before it is carried into a customer's premises, it may be held that the unloading had been completed when the item was removed from the vehicle and set down. If then a passerby were injured in an accident arising out of the product on the sidewalk, the Automobile Liability policy might be held to be *in*applicable to the accident because the unloading had been completed. (It is possible, of course, that the Company which wrote the Public Liability policy might consider the accident to be one which *did* arise during the course of unloading the vehicle, and as such, not covered under its policy. To avoid any difficulty of this kind, it is therefore advisable that both the Public Liability and Automobile Liability policies be written in the same Company, whenever possible.)

Trailers—Except for substitute automobiles and newly acquired automobiles, which are covered under certain conditions, the Automobile Liability policy covers only the automobiles designated in the policy. If an Insured owns more than one car, he should designate them all in his policy. While the policy states that it will not apply while the automobile is being used for towing a trailer owned or hired by the Insured which is not covered by insurance in the same Company, it defines "automobile" to include any trailer designed for use with a private passenger automobile, provided it is not being used for business purposes with commercial vehicles. Such trailers are therefore covered automatically. Only a trailer of the commercial type need be specifically insured. There *is* a difference in the coverage afforded under the Medical Payments Coverage for different types of trailer (discussed later under Medical Payments Coverage).

Other Drivers and Interests (Omnibus Clause)—The Automobile Liability policy covers accidents arising out of the operation of the automobile not only by the Insured named in the policy or his spouse but also by any other person who uses the automobile with the Insured's permission. The other person or persons are automatically covered as additional Insureds under the policy, without notice to the Company. This coverage, sometimes referred to as the Omnibus clause, is part of the basic policy and requires no endorsement. The policy also covers as additional Insureds any organization legally responsible for the use of the described automobile.

Thus, if a person is driving his automobile in the course of his work, and he injures someone, the injured party may bring a suit against the owner of the automobile *and* the employer. Subject to its limits, the policy will cover the named Insured and also the *employer* to the extent that each or both is held liable for the accident.

Family Automobile Policy—*With respect to the insured automobile, every resident of the Insured's household is included as an Insured, even while driving without the permission of the Insured or his spouse. Furthermore, the policy covers the liability of any resident of the Insured's household arising out of the use of the automobile by others.*

Severability of Interests—The term "Insured' is used severally, and not collectively. The insurance afforded applies separately to each Insured under the policy. The exclusions and conditions of the policy are applied to each Insured under the policy as meaning only the Insured against whom claim is made. Thus, if an Insured named in an Automobile Liability policy is riding as a passenger in his own car while it is being driven by a friend, and an accident occurs, the named Insured might make claim against his friend, and the policy would respond to such action.

Family Automobile Policy—*The policy does not contain a Severability of Interest clause, but the same result is arrived at by a provision that the insurance afforded under the Liability section of the policy applies separately to each Insured against whom claim is made or suit instituted.*

Thus, assume John Doe owns and insures under one Family Automobile policy two cars, a Ford and a Plymouth. His brother, Fred, who lives with him (and is therefore an additional Insured under the policy) is driving the Ford and collides with his brother's second car, the Plymouth. If John sues Fred, Fred is protected under John's policy.

Other Drivers and Interests (Omnibus Clause) Exclusions—Coverage for others who drive the described vehicle is extended to almost every person and organization who might be held liable for an accident caused by the automobile, provided the automobile is being used with the permission of the named Insured or his spouse.

Family Automobile Policy—*Policy covers any resident of the Insured's household who uses the car, even without the permission of the named Insured or his spouse.*

Excluded is only a person or organization, or an agent or employee of either, who operates an automobile repair shop, public garage, sales agency, service station or public parking place, or an employee of the Insured who injures another of the Insured's employees while both employees are engaged in their employer's business.

An exception is made for any resident of the named Insured's household, for a partnership of which the named Insured or a member of his household is a partner, or to any partner, agent or employee of such a resident or partnership. Coverage is afforded such individuals and partnerships regardless of their business or occupation.

Drive Other Cars — When an Automobile Liability policy is written for an Insured who is an individual (not a corporation or partnership), the policy will also cover the Insured and his spouse while driving *any other automobile.* The Automobile Liability policy "follows" the Insured individual and his spouse. Similarly, the policy will cover any other person or organization legally responsible for the Insured's using of any other automobile, except one which is owned or hired by the person or organization.

Thus, assume an employer telephones one of his salesmen at his home and asks him to call on a customer. The salesman's wife has taken the family automobile, and the salesman borrows a neighbor's car. While en route to the customer's home, the salesman runs a pedestrian down. The injured person brings a suit against the salesman, his employer, and the owner of the car. The salesman's Automobile Liability policy will protect the salesman and the employer, to the extent that each is liable.

On the other hand, if the employer had furnished the salesman with a car for the trip, the employer would not be covered under his salesman's Automobile Liability policy, since the vehicle was owned by the employer.

Drive Other Car coverage in the Automobile policy is excess insurance over any insurance covering the borrowed automobile itself. Thus, in the illustration used above, the salesman who used his neighbor's automobile is covered as an additional Insured under any Automobile Liability insurance carried by his neighbor. The salesman's liability for the accident will therefore be covered under his neighbor's policy. The salesman's own policy will come into play only if the neighbor is not insured (and will protect the salesman and his employer, but *not* the owner of the loaned automobile), or if the limits of insurance in his policy are not adequate to pay for the liability imposed in the particular accident. In the latter instance, the salesman's policy will be excess insurance, i. e., it will pay only any sums in excess of the amount collectible under the neighbor's policy which covered the automobile.

Thus, if the neighbor who owned the car was carrying Automobile Liability with Bodily Injury limits of $10,000/20,000, and the salesman who borrowed the car was carrying a policy of similar amount, and the judgment awarded to the person run down by the salesman was $15,000, the neighbor's policy would pay its full limit, $10,000, and the salesman's policy would be called on to pay the excess of $5,000. If the award in this case was $5,000, the neighbor's policy would be liable for the entire loss.

In no event is Drive Other Car coverage extended to the use of automobiles which are furnished for the regular use of the insured or his spouse. (This is discussed later under Drive Other Car Exclusions.)

It is important to understand that Drive Other Car coverage is afforded only to the Insured, his spouse, or one legally responsible for the Insured's use of another vehicle. This coverage does not extend to others, even though they are members of the Insured's family and residents of his household.

Thus, the Insured's son is covered as an additional Insured under his father's policy while driving his *father's* car, as is any other person who operates the automobile with permission. The Insured himself and his spouse are also covered under the basic policy while driving any other automobile. The son, however, is *not* covered for his operation of any other automobile.

Coverage for such use of other automobiles by members of the Insured's family may be added to the policy under a Drive Other Car Endorsement, for an additional premium.

Drive Other Car coverage is afforded only in policies which cover an Individual Insured, and is not included in policies written in the name of a corporation, a co-partnership or an unincorporated association. If a Company furnishes an executive or other employee with an automobile which is owned and insured in the Company's name, the employee has no coverage under the policy for his use of any automobile other than the one described in the policy.

To an Automobile policy covering a corporation-owned vehicle,

Drive Other Car coverage may be added by endorsement, naming the executive (or other employee) for whose use the automobile is furnished. This will give to the named employee and his spouse coverage for driving other automobiles.

NOTE: This added coverage will not be needed by the executive if he or his spouse own and insure another private passenger automobile in their individual names, or in their joint names, as such policy will afford Drive Other Car coverage as part of the basic policy.

Family Automobile Policy—*Drive Other Car coverage is afforded any relative of the named Insured who is resident in the same household as respects any private passenger automobile not owned by the relative or not regularly furnished for the relative's use, provided the vehicle is not used in business. An exception is made if the automobile is used in the business of the named Insured, and coverage would extend to such activity. The Insured's spouse receives even broader protection under the policy (discussed under Drive Other Car Exclusions).*

Drive Other Car Exclusions—As respects the use of other automobiles, the intent of the policy is to cover only such automobiles as are not used regularly or frequently. The policy specifically excludes any other automobile owned by the Insured or a member of his household, as it is contemplated that such automobiles will be insured at the appropriate premium for the coverage. Also excluded is any automobile other than a temporary substitute automobile (discussed later under Temporary Substitute Automobile) owned by or furnished for regular use to the Insured or a member of his household other than a domestic servant.

The policy also excludes all automobiles used in the Insured's business or occupation other than private passenger vehicles. Also excluded is any accident arising out of the operation of an Automobile repair shop, public garage, sales agency, service station or public parking place.

Newly Acquired Automobiles—If the Insured or his spouse trades the automobile described in the policy for a different one, the newly acquired vehicle is automatically covered without notice to the Company. If the Insured or his spouse acquires a new car *in addition* to the one described in the policy, similar automatic coverage is extended to the new automobile, but only if the Company insures all the automobiles which were owned by the Insured on the date of delivery of the new automobile and provided notice is given to the Company within 30 days of the acquisition of the vehicle. No automatic coverage would extend, however, if the Insured's spouse who owns a car insured in another Company were to acquire an additional automobile. It can be seen that an Insured who has only one automobile will be covered under his policy for any additional automobile he acquires. If he has two or more automobiles when he takes possession of the new automobile, this last acquired vehicle is covered under the policy only if the first two cars were insured in the same Company. The Insured is required to pay an additional premium for the new automobile, as the hazard covered under the policy has been increased by the addition of a new vehicle.

Family Automobile Policy—*The Insured may give notice of a newly acquired automobile at any time during the policy period. The 30-day limit does not apply under this form, except if the Insured or his spouse owns more than one automobile eligible for Family Automobile coverage and these vehicles are not insured in the same company.*

Temporary Substitute Automobile—If the automobile described in the policy is withdrawn from service while it is being repaired or serviced, or during a period when it has been lost or wrecked, the Insured's Automobile Liability policy covers him for the use of any other automobile which he is using temporarily as a substitute for the withdrawn vehicle, provided the Insured does not own the automobile. No notice of the substitution is required, and no additional premium is charged.

Medical Payments Coverage—The basic Automobile Liability policy is designed to cover the liability which is imposed on the Insured by *law,* and not obligations which he feels morally bound to pay, or those which he assumes voluntarily. As under most Liability policies, however, Medical Payments coverage may be added, and the policies thereby broadened to cover medical expenses incurred by certain persons within one year from the date of the accident.

Subject to the limits established in the policy for this coverage, these medical expenses will be paid, regardless of whether the Insured was liable for the accident or not. (The general principles of this coverage are set forth in Chapter 24 under HAZARDS COVERED—Medical Payments Coverage.) Under the Automobile Liability policy, Medical Payments insurance provides coverage along three basic lines:

1. To *all* persons injured while in or upon the automobile or while alighting from the described automobile.

2. To the Insured and all members of his family who reside in his household who are injured while in or upon *any* automobile or

while being *struck* by an automobile provided the automobile is not owned by the Insured.

3. When the Insured or his spouse drives other cars, Medical Payments coverage will extend under certain conditions to persons injured in such cars (discussed next under Medical Payments — Drive Other Cars).

It is important to understand that accidents caused under any other circumstances do not come within the scope of the Medical Payments coverage. Thus, if the Insured runs a pedestrian down, the Medical Payments coverage does not apply to the accident as regards the pedestrian. The Insured may provide under the policy immediate medical and surgical first aid at the time of the accident, and the Company will reimburse the Insured for such expenses as he incurs to furnish this first aid. Outside of such first aid expenses, however, the pedestrian is not entitled to medical expenses except if he can establish the Insured's negligence in the accident and hold him liable for the damages caused him.

The Medical Payments coverage under an Automobile Liability policy will pay for medical expenses incurred by any person, including the Insured. In this respect, the coverage is broader than Medical Payments coverage under other Liability policies.

Medical expenses under the Medical Payments coverage are payable over and above any other recovery which the injured person may have from the Insured.

Medical Payments—Drive Other Cars—When Medical Payments coverage is purchased under an Automobile Liability policy, this coverage "follows" the Insured while driving or riding in other automobiles, subject to the Drive Other Car coverage provided in the basic policy. If the Insured or his spouse is actually driving the other automobile, or it is being operated on their behalf by a private chauffeur or servant, the Medical Payments coverage will be available to any person injured as a result of such operation. If the operation of the vehicle is under the Insured's direction, the Medical Payments coverage will be applied similarly. If an injury is caused by the Insured's occupancy of the car, as when he slams the car door on a passenger's finger, the Medical Payments coverage will apply.

Family Automobile Policy—*Coverage is afforded to occupants of a non-owned automobile even if driven by a relative who is resident in the same household as the Insured, or if driven on his behalf, or if the accident is caused by his occupancy of the vehicle.*

If, however, the Insured or his spouse is merely a passive occupant of the other automobile, and the accident does not arise out of their occupancy of the vehicle, Medical Payments will be available only to them, and not to any other occupants of the automobile.

It is important to understand that Medical Payments will "follow" an Insured only in such cars as are covered under Drive Other Car coverage of the policy. Thus, there is no Medical Payments coverage for other automobiles owned by the Insured or a member of his household, nor for any automobile furnished for the frequent use of the Insured or member of his household, since such automobiles do not fall within the Drive Other Car coverage.

For the same reason, Medical Payments coverage written on an Automobile Liability policy covering a corporation will not apply to any other automobiles, since the Drive Other Car coverage applies only to automobiles owned by individuals.

Medical Payments Exclusions—As pointed out above, Medical Payments coverage, insofar as it relates to the Insured and his spouse in other cars, is limited to automobiles to which Drive Other Car coverage applies. The policy also specifically excludes medical expenses incurred by an employee of an automobile agency, repair shop, service station, storage garage or public parking place if the accident arises out of such business pursuits, and if benefits are payable or required to be paid under any Workmen's Compensation Law. Similarly excluded is liability to any domestic employee injured in the course of employment by the Insured, if benefits are payable or required to be paid under any Workmen's Compensation Law, or liability of the Insured for any obligation for which he may be held liable under a Workmen's Compensation Law.

Family Automobile Policy — *Medical Payments protection does not extend to anyone in the automobile business who is injured in the course of his employment, and is entitled to Workmen's Compensation benefits.*

Medical Payments coverage will not be available to an Insured while towing a trailer for business purposes with an automobile not of the private passenger type, or a trailer which is an office, store or display trailer, or a trailer while it is being used as a home or residence, unless such trailer is described in the policy.

For a trailer to fall within the exclusion of "being used as residence," it must be parked off its wheels.

Family Automobile Policy — *Coverage is afforded for loss sustained in a trailer designed for use with a private passenger automobile, if not being used for business purposes.*

Uninsured Motorist Coverage—In all states, an endorsement has been made available under all Automobile Liability policies which provides protection to an Insured and all members of his family who are injured in an automobile accident with an uninsured motorist who is financially irresponsible and cannot pay damages as well as a vehicle on which there is insurance in force at the time of the accident but where the insurer is or becomes insolvent. By definition, "uninsured automobile" includes a "hit-and-run" car. The injured person is covered under this endorsement for such damages up to the limits required by the Financial Responsibility Law of his state (discussed in Chapter 28).

This coverage is also available in most states to individuals who do not own an automobile.

In order for the Insured to collect under the Uninsured Motorist Endorsement, it is necessary that he be legally entitled to damages, it being stipulated that if there is any dispute about the liability of the other party, the question be submitted to arbitration.

In most states, coverage is afforded only for bodily injury claims.

There are some differences in the coverage as among the various states, as shown in the chart on the following page. The coverage is available to the Insured or his spouse while riding in other cars. Also, to *any* person riding with the Insured or his spouse, or if using the insured automobile with permission of the Insured or spouse. If the injury caused by an uninsured motorist is sustained by the Insured or his spouse while riding in another car, and the other vehicle is insured under a Liability policy which is endorsed for Uninsured Motorist coverage, the endorsement of the injured person's policy does not apply.

CONNECTICUT, MAINE, MASSACHUSETTS, MINNESOTA (on private passenger cars and pick-up trucks), MISSOURI, NEW HAMPSHIRE, NEW YORK, NORTH DAKOTA, OREGON, PENNSYLVANIA, SOUTH CAROLINA, VERMONT, VIRGINIA, WEST VIRGINIA, WISCONSIN—The coverage is mandatory with no right of rejection.

ILLINOIS—The Insured may reject coverage if he has bought excess coverage under the No-Fault Law.

MARYLAND—There is no statute requiring the Insured to carry this coverage nor any obligation on the part of the insurer to make it available. Purchase of the coverage is entirely voluntary on the part of the Insured.

NEW JERSEY—Insured must elect to accept offer of coverage in writing.

ALL STATES OTHER THAN THOSE LISTED ABOVE—The carrier is required to make the coverage available, but the Insured may reject it.

Eight states extend the coverage to Property Damage as well as Bodily Injury Liability. In each instance, the Property Damage coverage is subject to a Deductible, as set forth:

MANDATORY UNINSURED MOTORIST COVERAGE

STATE	LIMITS	PROPERTY DAMAGE EXCLUSION	MAY INSURED REJECT COVERAGE	UNINSURED MOTORIST FEE	APPLICABLE WHERE INSURER INSOLVENT?	UNUSUAL FEATURES
Alabama	10/20		Yes †	None	No prov.	
Alaska	15/30		Yes	None	No prov.	
Arizona	10/20		Yes †	None	Yes	
Arkansas	10/20		Yes	None	Yes	
California	15/30		Yes	None	Yes	(b) (h)
Colorado	15/30		Yes †	None	No prov.	
Connecticut	20/40 (a)		No	None	Yes	(n)
Delaware	10/20/5	$250	Yes †	None	Yes	(a)
Florida	10/20		Yes †	None	Yes	
Georgia	10/20/5 (m)	$250	Yes †	None	Yes	(e) (h) (j) (w)
Hawaii	10/20		Yes	None	No prov.	
Idaho	10/20		Yes †	None	Yes	
Illinois	10/20		Yes (d)	None	Yes	
Indiana	15/30		Yes †	None	Yes	
Iowa	10/20		Yes †	None	Yes	(j)
Kansas	15/30*		Yes †	None	Yes	(n)
Kentucky	10/20		Yes †	None	Yes	(h) (q)
Louisiana	5/10		Yes	None	Yes	(n)
Maine	20/40		No	None	Yes	
Massachusetts	5/10 (w)		No	None	Yes	
Michigan	20/40		Yes †	$ 45	Yes	(o)
Minnesota	10/20 (a)		(p)	None	Yes	(v)
Mississippi	5/10		Yes †	None	Yes	(e) (j)
Missouri	10/20		No	None	Yes	
Montana	10/20		Yes †	None	No prov.	
Nebraska	10/20		Yes †	None	Yes	
Nevada	15/30		Yes †	None	Yes	(a) (h) (j) (q) (r)
New Hampshire	20/40 (a)		No	None	Yes	
New Jersey	10/20/5	$100	Yes (f)	$ 50	No prov.	
New Mexico	10/20/5	$250	Yes †	None	No prov.	
New York	10/20		No	None	No prov.	(h)
North Carolina	10/20/5 (k)	$100	Yes	None	Yes	(g) (k)
North Dakota	10/20		No	None	Yes	
Ohio	12.5/25		Yes †	None	Yes	(h)
Oklahoma	5/10 (r)		Yes †	None	Yes	(s) (t)
Oregon	10/20		No	None	Yes	(c) (h)
Pennsylvania	10/20		No	None	Yes	
Rhode Island	10/20		Yes	None	Yes	
South Carolina	10/20/5	$200	No	$ 100	Yes	(e) (g) (h) (j)
South Dakota	15/30		Yes †	None	Yes	
Tennessee	10/20		Yes †	None	Yes	(e) (q)
Texas	10/20		Yes †	None	Yes	
Utah	10/20		Yes †	None	No prov.	
Vermont	10/20		No	None	Yes	
Virginia	20/30/5 (a)	$200	No	$ 50	No prov.	(e) (g) (h)
Washington	15/30		Yes †	None	Yes	
West Virginia	10/20/5	$300	No	None	Yes	(e) (j)
Wisconsin	15/30		No	None	Yes	
Wyoming	10/20		Yes †	None	Yes	

*-Effective July 1, 1972.

†-If rejected, insurer need not offer coverage on renewal unless requested.

a-Insured may require limits equal to his liability limits.

b-Failure to file evidence of financial responsibility under Financial Responsibility Law creates rebuttable presumption that vehicle was uninsured.

c-Coverage not required in policy covering trucks of combined weight and load capacity of more than 6000 operated by employees covered by workmen's compensation.

d-When insured purchases excess coverage under no-fault law.

e-Arbitration provision prohibited.

f-Insured must elect to accept or reject offer of coverage in writing.

g-Insurer may defend uninsured motorist.

h-Also covers where insurer denies liability.

j-Requires contact in hit-and-run cases.

k-Person who carries liability limits of at least 15/30 is entitled to 15/30 coverage.

m-Insured vehicle and contents only.

n-Arbitration optional with insured.

o-All policies to contain notice that coverage was explained and that insured may reject.

p-Coverage may not be rejected for policies covering private passenger vehicles or pick-up trucks. May be rejected as to others.

q-"Uninsured motor vehicle" includes vehicle insured in lower limits.

r-Arbitration provision not binding on named insured or person claiming under him.

s-If agreement by arbitration is not reached within 3 months from demand for arbitration insured may sue tortfeasor.

t-Inapplicable to motor carriers whose drivers are covered by workmen's compensation.

v-Also requires offering of death, disability and medical payments coverage.

w-Insured may require higher limits.

DELAWARE, GEORGIA, NEW MEXICO—A $250 Deductible applies.
NEW JERSEY, NORTH CAROLINA—A $100 Deductible applies.
SOUTH CAROLINA, VIRGINIA—A $200 Deductible applies.
WEST VIRGINIA—A $300 Deductible applies.

Unsatisfied Judgment Funds—In the Canadian provinces listed below and the states which appear on the chart reproduced directly after this paragraph, persons who have secured judgments for injuries sustained in automobile accidents, but cannot collect for these damages from the person responsible, can collect the amount of their judgment from a special fund set up by assessment of all automobiles registered in the state.

ALBERTA, BRITISH COLUMBIA, MANITOBA, NEW BRUNSWICK, NEWFOUNDLAND, NOVA SCOTIA, ONTARIO, PRINCE EDWARD ISLE.

CHART II – UNSATISFIED JUDGMENT FUNDS

State	Administered by:	SOURCE OF FUNDS AND MAXIMUM ASSESSMENT			MAXIMUM PAYMENT		Deductible (D) or minimum (M)	Available to non-residents	Provision for settlement of claims
		Insurers (% of premium)	Insured owners	Uninsured owners	Hit & run cases	Others			
Maryland	Insurers	2%	No	No max.	15/30	15/30/5	$100 (D) P.D. only	Recip.	Yes
Michigan	State	No	$1	$45	20/40	20/40/10	$200 (D) P.D. only	Recip.	Yes
New Jersey	Insurers	½%(y)	No	$50	10/20	10/20/5	$100 (D) P.D. only	Recip.	Yes
New York	Insurers	(z)	No	No	10/20	10/20	None	Recip.	Yes
North Dakota	State	No	$1	$1	5/10	10/20	$300 (M)	No	No

y-Only if assessment on uninsured motorists is insufficient.

z-Motor Vehicle Indemnification Corporation supported entirely by insurers.

Motor Vehicle Accident Indemnification Corporation — NEW YORK—In this state, a special corporation has been established to pay claims of innocent victims of motor vehicle accidents within the state caused by uninsured motorists. Protection is extended to all residents of the state, whether they own an automobile or not. Examples of such accidents are : (1) uninsured out-of-town automobiles; (2) unidentified hit and run drivers; (3) uninsured New York automobiles; (4) stolen cars; (5) cars operated without their owner's consent; (6) insured automobiles involved in an accident to which their insurance does not apply; (7) unregistered automobiles. The law establishing the Motor Vehicle Indemnification Corporation makes it mandatory for all Automobile Liability insurance policies to include the Uninsured Motorist Endorsement, and the cost of this coverage is included in the Automobile Liability insurance premium. All Automobile Liability insurers in the state are assessed in proportion to their respective premium writings to support the Motor Vehicle Accident Indemnification Corporation.

Claims are made directly to the Corporation but are paid by the insurance company. Notice of accident must be given to the

Corporation within 90 days. The police, a judge, a justice of the peace, or the Commissioner of Motor Vehicles must be notified within 24 hours.

There is no coverage under the endorsement for property damage claims, and bodily injury recovery is limited to $10,000 per person; $20,000 for injury or death of two or more persons. The coverage does not extend to accidents occurring outside of New York State, nor to persons driving in violation of a suspension or revocation of their driving privileges, nor to accidents caused by vehicles owned by the United States Government, Canada, a state, a political subdivision or agency of any of these political entities, nor to injuries or death of an uninsured motorist or his spouse or claims of persons not liable under law as, for example, claims between husband and wife.

HAZARDS NOT COVERED

This section will discuss only those exclusions in the Automobile Liability policy which apply to all coverages under the policy. It is important to remember that special exclusions apply to some of the specific coverages under the policy. The exclusions applicable to the specific sections of the policy are discussed, in each instance, under the coverage itself. (See Trailers, Other Drivers and Interests Exclusions, Drive Other Cars Exclusions and Medical Payments Exclusions, discussed before.)

Public or Livery Conveyance—The Automobile Liability policy specifically excludes coverage under any of its provisions while the automobile is used as a public or livery conveyance. Any carrying of passengers for hire, or renting the automobile to others for their use, would operate to suspend coverage under the policy, unless such use was stated in the policy.

Car pools or other "share ride" arrangements such as are entered into by a group of employees riding to work are not deemed to be carrying passengers for hire, even though the passengers contribute to the expenses of the trip.

Liability Assumed by Contract—Like most other Liability policies, the Automobile Liability policy specifically excludes any liability which the Insured assumes under a contract or agreement.

Family Automobile Policy—*This exclusion is not applicable to the Family Automobile policy. Thus, under this policy, an Insured who owns and insures a vehicle of his own might borrow an automobile which is not insured. He may undertake to hold the owner of the borrowed vehicle harmless for any accident arising out of* *the use of the car. If he became involved in an accident, his own Automobile Liability policy, if on the Family policy form, would cover this assumed liability. By contrast, the basic Automobile Liability policy would not cover this assumption of liability. It is important to understand that the assumed liability may be oral or written.*

Liability of an Insured to His Employees—This exclusion is similar to the one found in most forms of Liability insurance (discussed in Chapter 24).

Domestic servants are specifically exempted from the exclusion unless they are entitled to benefits under a Workmen's Compensation Law. In other words, while injuries to other employees of the Insured are not covered under the Automobile Liability policy, domestic servants *are* covered unless they are entitled to benefits under a Workmen's Compensation Law.

The policy also excludes coverage for injuries to the Insured's domestic employees who are not eligible under a Workmen's Compensation Law, if Workmen's Compensation insurance has been provided for them.

Liability for Property in Insured's Care—In Automobile Liability insurance, coverage is almost always purchased to cover Bodily Injury Liability as well as Property Damage Liability, although each of these coverages is separate. Under Coverage B, which covers Property Damage Liability, the policy excludes property owned by, rented to, in charge of or transported by the Insured. This exclusion is similar to the one incorporated in most forms of Liability insurance. An exception is made for a residence or private garage which is not owned by the Insured, and liability for damage to such property is covered under the policy.

It is important to understand that this exclusion will apply whether the property is in the Insured's charge, as when he is carrying property of others, or is the property of a passenger. Thus, if the Insured has borrowed a radio which he is carrying in his car, and the car is rammed by another vehicle and the radio is damaged, he may be held liable to the owner of the set for the damage if it is proved that his negligence was the proximate cause of the accident. The Automobile Liability policy will not, however, cover such liability, since the property was being transported by the Insured. Similarly, if the Insured, in backing out of his garage, damages the home he owns or rents, the Automobile Liability policy would provide no coverage. With the exception of property owned by, rented to, in charge of, or transported by the Insured, the Automobile Liability policy, under Coverage B, will cover the Insured's liability for damage to property of any kind. An exception is made for damage to a residence or private garage or one which is in his care, and liability for such damage *is* covered.

This exclusion will also apply to property owned by, rented to, in charge of or transported by any person included as an Insured under the policy (see Other Drivers—Omnibus Clause). Thus, if the Insured lends his car to his sister, damage to the property of the sister is not covered, since she is driving the Insured's automobile with his permission and is therefore included as an additional Insured.

Automobile Death Indemnity—Total Disability Benefits—A policy of Automobile Liability covering a private passenger vehicle may be endorsed for an additional premium to provide certain direct benefits to the Insured and relatives who are residents of his household. Two optional coverages are available:

Coverage A—Automobile Death Indemnity: A payment of $5,000 or $10,000 will be made if an Insured under the endorsement dies as a result of an accident while in, on or entering into or alighting from an automobile, or being struck by an automobile if death occurs within 90 days of the accident, or within 52 weeks of the accident if the Insured was continuously disabled from the time of the accident to the date of death.

Coverages A and B—Provides in addition to the death indemnity described above for specified disability benefits for dismemberment, loss of sight, fractures and dislocations.

Nuclear Energy Liability—Discussed in Chapter 24 under PUBLIC LIABILITY INSURANCE—HAZARDS NOT COVERED—Nuclear Energy Liability.

FOR HOW MUCH

The Automobile Liability policy is written with separate coverage on Bodily Injury Liability and on Property Damage Liability. Limits for each coverage are set as under most other forms of Liability insurance. Like other Liability policies, the Automobile policy provides for supplementary benefits (discussed in Chapter 24).

Medical Payments Coverage Limits—As pointed out before, Medical Payments coverage may be added to Automobile Liability insurance. The limits are applied "per person," with no limit per accident. Each person injured in the accident is entitled to reimbursement for his expenses up to the Medical Payments coverage limit established in the policy, regardless of the number of individuals injured. Medical Payments coverage may be purchased with limits from $250 to $5,000.

As pointed out, Medical Payments are payable over and above any amount recovered by the injured person in his claim against the insured. Furthermore, Medical Payments are available in addition to any sums paid for immediate medical and surgical first aid as are necessary at the time of the accident. Thus, assume a guest passenger is injured in an automobile accident. He requires first aid and this is administered at the scene of the accident. He is then removed to a hospital. The cost of the first aid administered comes to $100, and this sum is recoverable under the basic Automobile Liability policy as one of the Supplementary Benefits available. While in the hospital, the passenger's medical bills come to $200, and he is reimbursed for these expenses under the Insured's Medical Payments Coverage.

If the passenger contends that the accident was due to the Insured's negligence, he may institute a suit against him (subject to any Guest Law that may be operative in his state, discussed in Chapter 23 under Guest Laws). The insurance Company will defend the suit and, if its Insured is held liable for the accident, will pay the passenger the amount awarded him by the court. This award will most likely include a sum to compensate the injured passenger for his medical expenses. He will be entitled to the entire amount awarded him by the court, even though it will allow him double compensation for the medical bills he had incurred. When Medical Payments coverage "follows" an Insured and his spouse into other cars, the coverage is excess over any other Medical Payments coverage which applies to the other car.

Other Insurance—See Chapter 2.

If the automobile described in the policy has been withdrawn from use by the Insured, due to its being serviced, and the Insured is using a substitute vehicle, the Insured's policy covers the substitute vehicle, but only as excess over any policy covering the automobile.

WHO IS INSURED

Other Drivers and Interests (Omnibus Clause)—Discussed before.

Right of Third Parties—See Chapter 24.

Legal Representatives—If the Insured dies within the policy period, the Insured's legal representatives and spouse, or resident of the deceased's household will be covered under the policy. Such representatives will be covered as the named Insured in the policy. In addition, any other person who has proper temporary custody of the automobile will be covered as an Insured until the appointment and qualification of legal representative. As respects the Medical Payments coverage, such person will be covered only while the automobile is actually used by him.

WHERE COVERED

The Automobile Liability policy applies only to accidents which occur within the United States of America, its territories and possessions, Canada and Newfoundland, or while the automobile is being transported between ports of these territories. For an additional premium, the policy can be endorsed to afford coverage to an Insured who plans to use his automobile outside of these territorial limits.

RATES

Premiums for private passenger automobiles are based on rating plans which differ somewhat among the states. In addition Companies within the state may follow one of several different rating plans. The reader is therefore urged to check rating practices within his state, and the particular insurer whom he represents.

Basically, almost all companies use a rating formula which comes under one of three plans. ARKANSAS, CONNECTICUT, KANSAS, KENTUCKY, NEW YORK, NORTH CAROLINA, SOUTH CAROLINA, TEXAS (with some modifications), VIRGINIA, PUERTO RICO (under an older version of the plan)—In these states, rates for Automobile insurance are based on the following factors:

Nine-Class Rating Plan—Rates are based on the following factors:

1. Territory in which the car is *principally garaged.* (The legal domicile of the Insured or the territory within which he may operate his automobile does not control the rating of the Automobile Liability policy.)

2. The use to which the car is put. The number of classifications as to use varies in the different plans but, in almost every instance, consideration is given not only to the purpose for which the vehicle is used, but also to the age of the owner or operator of the vehicle. Some classifications are further broken down into a distance factor.

When a risk is required to file a certificate to comply with an Automobile Financial Responsibility Law, the rates are surcharged (discussed later under Certified Risks Surcharge).

A rating plan in use in a few states classifies private passenger automobiles as follows:

Class 1A—(No Operator Under 25. No Business Use.)

The lowest rates are charged for this classification. To be eligible for this group, an automobile must satisfy *all* three of the following conditions:

1. The automobile must be owned by an individual or by individuals.

2. The automobile must not be required or customarily involved in the duties of the Insured in his business, profession or occupation, nor in the occupation of any other person who customarily uses the vehicle.

Using the car to travel to and from an Insured's place of business will disqualify the automobile from Class 1A.

3. There is no male operator of the automobile under the age of 25 who is a resident of the Insured's household or employed by the Insured as a chauffeur.

An automobile will not be disqualified from Class 1A (or Class 1B or Class 1C) by the Insured's permitting the car to be driven by a person under the age of 25, provided the person is not a resident of the Insured's household or employed by him as a private chauffeur.

All automobiles owned by clergymen are in Class 1A, unless they do not meet the age of driver requirement.

Class 1B—(No Male Operator Under 25. Limited Driving To Work.)

An automobile which meets all the requirements of Class 1A except that it is driven to and from work will fall into Class 1B, provided the one way mileage to or from work is less than 10 miles. This is the second lowest rate classification.

Class 1C—(No Male Operator Under 25. Unlimited Driving To Work.)

An automobile which meets all the requirements of Class 1A except that the one way mileage to or from work is 10 miles or more falls into Class 1C. The rates for this classification are the highest of all three in the Class 1 groups.

Class 3—(Business Use or Automobiles Not Individually Owned.)

This group is the next higher in rate after the 1A, 1B and 1C classes. Any automobile owned by a corporation, partnership, or association is assigned to this classification, regardless of the age of the operator. In addition, any automobile owned by an individual which is used regularly in a business, profession or occupation falls into this Class, provided there is no operator under 25 who is resident in the Insured's household or employed as a chauffeur.

NEW YORK—Class 3 is subdivided into two classifications:

Class 3 A—individually owned private passenger vehicles which are used in the regular course of business, but are not operated by any male driver under age 25.

Class 3 B—all private passenger vehicles owned by a corporation, co-partnership or unincorporated association.

Class 2A—(Males Under 25 Not Owners or Principal Operators, Males Under 25 Married.)

An automobile which is owned by a male under 25, or which is principally operated by such person, falls into this class, provided the owner or operator is *married.* If the male under 25 is not the owner or principal operator, as when the car is owned and principally operated by some one else in the household of which he is a member, the vehicle also falls into this class, even though the under age person is not married.

Class 2C—(Males Under 25, Unmarried, Owners or Principal Operators.) An automobile which is owned or principally operated by any unmarried male person under 25 falls in this class. This is the highest rated classification.

NEW YORK—If all the male operators of the automobile are not the owners or principal operators and are students resident at a school over 100 miles from the principal garaging location of the vehicle, the rate comes under a special classification—2B.

Special Farmer Classifications—A private passenger automobile owned by an individual which is principally garaged on a farm and is not used in going to or from any work other than farming qualifies for 1 AF, 2 AF or 2 CF, corresponding in each instance to the classification 1A, 2A or 2C, as the case may be, less a reduction from that classification.

NEW YORK—There is also a 2BF for farm vehicles which qualify under the conditions set forth above.

Good Student Credit—Some of the states which have approved the Nine-Class Rating Plan grant a 25% rate credit to Class 2A. 2AF, 2C or 2CF risks who meet the following requirements:

If the applicant is a *male* operator under the age of 25 and is:

1. at least 16 years of age;

2. in full time attendance at high school or college (but is not below his junior year in high school);

3. scholastically either on the "Dean's List" or other comparable honor roll, or ranks in the upper 20% of his class, or has maintained a "B" average, or a "3" average in schools using numerical grade points.

NEW JERSEY, NEW YORK—The credit is not applicable.

Driver Course Credit—A 10% credit is granted to an Insured in any Class 2 group who present satisfactory evidence that every operator in the household under 25 has successfully completed a driver education course sponsored by a recognized secondary school, college or university and conducted by certified instructors. In order to qualify, such course must have the official approval of the State Department of Education or other responsible educational agency, and must comprise not less than 30 hours of classroom instruction and 6 hours of actual driving experience, or an average of three clock hours per student for actual driving experience exclusive of observation time in the automobile and a minimum of twelve clock hours per student in a device which simulates practice driving, approved by the State Department of Education or other responsible educational agency.

CONNECTICUT—A course conducted by a full-time commercial driving school is acceptable.

NEW YORK—The discount is 15%. Furthermore, part of the required classroom instruction may be in the form of television instruction.

260 Class Rating Plans—Most of the states are now using a modified version of the 260-Class Rating Plan which went into effect a few years ago.

The following six states still use the older Plan.

ALABAMA, MARYLAND, MISSISSIPPI, OKLAHOMA, RHODE ISLAND, TENNESSEE (with some individual modifications).

All other states use the newer 260-Class Rating Plan.

The 260-Class Rating Plan incorporates 52 driver categories based on the age, sex and marital status of the drivers subdivided into five use categories, i.e., used for pleasure only, driven less than 10 miles one way to work, driven more than 10 miles to work, business use and farm use. Good Student Credits are also applicable in many states using the 260-Class Rating Plan.

Merit Rating Plans—In 45 states, most insurance carriers have introduced a rating plan which is designed to modify the rate for *private passenger* Automobile Liability, Medical Payments and Collision insurance based on the accident and violation experience of the individual Insured. The plan does not affect the rates for Comprehensive Physical Damage, Fire and Theft, or Uninsured Motorist coverages.

The modification, which ranges from a discount for a "clean" record to a series of extra charges for accidents and stipulated traffic violations for which the Insured was convicted, is based on the driving record of the Insured and the members of his household who operate the automobile. The merit rating plans affect only rates for private passenger insurance, but in the majority of the states, all convictions are tolled, even if they involve vehicles of a non-passenger type. As respects accidents, only those involving private passenger automobiles are counted.

Certain accidents are specifically excluded from the point system, and are not reflected in the Insured's rate. They are:

(1) If automobile is legally parked.

(2) If the Insured gets a judgment against the person responsible for the accident or is reimbursed by the other driver or his insurance company.

(3) If the Insured's car is struck in the rear by another and he is not convicted of any traffic violation as a result.

(4) If the driver of the other car involved in the accident is convicted of a moving traffic violation as a result of the accident, and the Insured operator is not convicted.

(5) If the Insured's automobile is damaged by a hit-and-run driver, and the accident is reported within 24 hours.

Except for NEW YORK, NORTH CAROLINA and TEXAS, which are discussed separately, all states follow one of two point schedules, assessing moving violations at 5 points, 3 points, 1 point; or 3 points, 2 points, 1 point. There is not complete uniformity as to the violations charged for, but in the main, they are grouped along these lines:

The maximum points (5 or 3, depending on the state) are applied for a conviction for driving while intoxicated or under the influence of drugs; homicide arising out of the operation of a motor vehicle; failure to stop and report when involved in an accident; driving while an operator's license has been revoked or suspended.

Second highest assessment develops from accumulation of points under a state point system or any series of violations which make it necessary to file proof of financial responsibility.

One point is assigned a conviction of a violation which calls for suspension or revocation of an operator's license or requires the filing of proof of financial responsibility as of the inception date of the policy. (On the chart that follows, the point system in each of the states is indicated.) It should be emphasized that there are important variations among the states on many of the features of the plan; the reader is therefore urged to check the rules applicable in his territory.

One point is assessed for each accident involving bodily injury or death, or property damage in excess of $100. In addition, one point is charged for two or more property damage accidents below $100.

In the majority of states, no discount will be granted on policies covering operators who have not been licensed throughout the experience period. The following chart indicates how each state treats this question.

The number of rating classes produced by the merit rating plans varies among the states, as does the range of discounts and surcharges. On the chart, the maximum credits and debits are shown.

State	Point Schedule Violations	Discount Experienced Drivers Only	Maximum Discount %	Maximum Surcharge %
Alabama	3-2-1	Yes	15	150
Alaska	3-2-1	Yes	15	150
Arizona	5-3-1	No	20	100
Arkansas	3-2-1	Yes	15	150
California	5-3-1	No	20	100
Colorado	3-2-1	Yes	15	150
Connecticut	3-2-1	No	15	150
Delaware	3-2-1	Yes	15	150
District of Columbia	3-2-1	Yes	15	130
Florida	3-2-1	Yes	15	150
Georgia	3-2-1	Yes	15	150
Hawaii	3-2-1	Yes	15	150
Idaho	3-2-1	Yes	15	150
Illinois	3-2-1	Yes	15	150
Iowa	3-2-1	Yes	15	130
Kansas	3-2-1	Yes	15	150
Kentucky	3-2-1	Yes	15	150
Maine	3-2-1	Yes	15	150
Maryland	3-2-1	Yes	15	130
Michigan	3-2-1	Yes	15	150
Minnesota	3-2-1	Yes	15	150
Mississippi	3-2-1	Yes	15	150
Missouri	3-2-1	Yes	15	150
Montana	3-2-1	Yes	15	150
Nebraska	3-2-1	Yes	15	150
Nevada	3-2-1	Yes	15	150
New Jersey	3-2-1	Yes	15	150
New York	3-2	Yes	10	150
North Carolina	8-6-3-1	Yes	10	150
North Dakota	3-2-1	Yes	15	150
Ohio	3-2-1	Yes	15	150
Oklahoma	3-2-1	Yes	15	150
Oregon	3-2-1	Yes	15	150
Pennsylvania	3-2-1	Yes	15	150
Rhode Islan	5-3-1	No	15	100
South Carolina	3-2-1	Yes	15	150
South Dakota	3-2-1	Yes	15	150
Texas	4-1	No	20	100
Utah	3-2-1	Yes	15	150
Vermont	3-2-1	Yes	15	150
Virginia	3-2-1	Yes	10	150
Washington	3-2-1	Yes	15	150
West Virginia	3-2-1	Yes	15	150
Wisconsin	3-2-1	Yes	15	150
Wyoming	3-2-1	Yes	15	150

NEW YORK—In addition to the penalties for violations discussed above, three points are charged for criminal negligence in the operation of a motor vehicle resulting in death. Two points are assessed for bodily injury or property damage caused while driving at excessive speed.

The experience period ends on the last day of the *fourth* month preceding the month in which the policy attaches.

An exception is made for certain situations in which the driver is responding to emergency situations.

NORTH CAROLINA—In this state, a special point schedule applies to convictions, ranging from eight points down to one. Furthermore, speeding in excess of 55 miles per hour but not above 75 miles per hour assesses one point, as does following too closely, driving on the wrong side of the road, or any conviction for a moving violation after the first, even if such does not fall into the list of stipulated violations. Additionally, three points are assigned for hit and run driving which results in property damage, reckless driving, passing a stopped school bus, illegal passing or driving over 75 miles per hour.

TEXAS—As indicated on the chart above, there are only two conviction groups. Four points are assessed for driving while under the influence of liquor or drugs, failing to stop after an accident, negligent homicide, aggravated assault arising out of operation of a motor vehicle or any violation in connection with a motor vehicle which is punishable as a felony. There is a wider range of accidents for which no points are charged; the minimum amount of property damage for which a point is charged is $20.

MASSACHUSETTS—The accident-free motorist will receive a 2% annual reduction in premiums for every year, cumulatively; for each chargeable accident, a surcharge of 10% will be applied. There is no penalty for traffic violations of any kind.

A "chargeable" accident is one which results in bodily injury or property damage resulting in a claim being paid or a reserve being set aside.

Modified 260-Class Plan—ALASKA, ARIZONA, CALIFORNIA, COLORADO, DISTRICT OF COLUMBIA, DELAWARE, FLORIDA, GEORGIA, IDAHO, ILLINOIS, INDIANA, MAINE, MASSACHUSETTS, MICHIGAN, MINNESOTA, MISSOURI, MONTANA, NEBRASKA, NEVADA, NEW HAMPSHIRE, NEW MEXICO, NORTH DAKOTA, OHIO, OREGON, SOUTH DAKOTA, UTAH, VERMONT, WASHINGTON, WEST VIRGINIA, WISCONSIN, WYOMING, PUERTO RICO—In these states, a modification of the 260-Class Plan has been introduced which reflects the experience of the past two and a half years with the original plan. The primary change which results in a reduction in the number of rate classes is a limit on the categories for youthful drivers. The modified plan has only two classes for such drivers, i. e. 1) pleasure or farm and 2) drive to work or use in business.

Certified Risks Surcharge—When a risk is required to file a certificate of insurance in order to comply with a Financial Responsibility Law (discussed later in this chapter), a surcharge is added to the rate. The surcharge is a percentage of the manual rate, and depends on the reason which made it necessary to file a certificate, as follows:

50%—If due to a conviction for drunken driving, failing to stop and report when involved in an accident, or homicide or assault arising out of the operation of a motor vehicle.

25%—If due to a conviction for speeding or reckless driving which results in an accident.

5%—For any other reason.

Increased Limits—Rates in the Automobile Liability manual are shown for limits of $10,000/20,000 on Bodily Injury and $5,000 on Property Damage Liability in states which require these or higher limits. In all other states, basic limits of $5,000/10,000/5,000 are shown. These limits may be increased for an additional premium. As in all Liability insurance, the extra premium for increased limits decreases as the amount of coverage is increased. There are several Increased Limits tables. One widely used table gives a factor of 1.15 for increasing basic limits of $5,000/10,000 to $10,000/20,000. To increase the limits from $10,000/20,000 to $25,000/50,000, the factor is 1.19; to increase to $50,000/100,000, the factor is 1.30, etc.

Multi-Car Discount—In almost every instance, if an individual or an individual and his spouse own more than one private passenger automobile which is insured under the same policy, the rate for each automobile not classified as being used in business, is discounted.

In the states which use the 260-Class Rating Plan, the discount is a secondary factor reflected in the Safe Driving Insurance Rating Plan. In the other states, the discount is a flat percentage.

Fleet Rates—An Insured who owns five or more automobiles may insure them under a Fleet policy. A reduction in premium is granted for each automobile above five so insured. The amount of the credit increases with the number of automobiles insured under the plan.

Whole Dollar Premium Rule—discussed in Chapter 8 under OTHER FACTORS WHICH AFFECT FIRE INSURANCE RATES —Whole Dollar Premium Rule.

INSURED'S STATEMENTS

The first page of the Automobile Liability policy contains the Declarations made by the Insured. These include the Insured's name, his address, occupation, and the place where the automobile will be principally garaged. The policy also sets forth a complete description of the automobile, its make, model, year of manufacture, and identification number. (The Company may waive the description of the automobile.) The Insured is required to state whether during the past year any insurance Company had cancelled any policy of similar insurance. The policy also contains a statement that the named Insured is the sole owner of the described vehicle except for its being encumbered by a mortgage, under a conditional bill of sale, etc. By his acceptance of the policy, the Insured agrees that the Declarations made by him are his agreements and representations and that the policy is issued in reliance on the truth of such representations.

INSURED'S DUTIES

Notice of Accident—See Chapter 24.

Notice of Claim or Suit—See Chapter 24.

Cooperation with Company—The obligation on the part of the Insured to cooperate with the Company is identical with that stated in other Liability policies. This requirement falls on the named Insured and any other person who is included as an Insured because he operates the described automobile with the named Insured's permission. Certain obligations are also placed on the injured person, and these are discussed directly below.

Medical Reports—Proof—The injured person or someone on his behalf is required as soon as is practicable to give written proof of claim to the insurance Company. The Company may require such statement to be made under oath. He is also required to execute authorization to enable the Company to obtain medical reports and copies of records, and to submit himself to physical examination by physicians selected by the Company when and as often as the Company may reasonably require.

Payment for Services to Others—The Company has the option of paying the injured person or any person or organization which rendered services to him; e. g., a physician, hospital, ambulance service, nurses, etc. Payment by the Company to one who rendered services to the injured person will reduce the amount payable for the claim.

FINANCIAL RESPONSIBILITY LAWS

The Automobile Liability policy generally includes a provision which states that the insurance afforded will comply with the provisions of any Motor Vehicle Financial Responsibility Law of the state which applies to liability arising out of the automobile described in the policy. In all states except New Hampshire, when an Insured has become subject to the Financial Responsibility Laws of his state, the policy's liability to third parties is absolute. Thus, even though the Insured has voided his policy by false statements, or has breached its conditions or has failed to cooperate with the Company, the policy must pay, subject to its limits. The Company, when it has paid a claim under such circumstances, is entitled to reimbursement from its Insured.

Subrogation—The Automobile Liability policy contains a provision which is similar to the subrogation clause found in practically every form of property and liability insurance. The policy specifically states that the Insured is to do nothing after a loss that will prejudice his insurance Company's right of subrogation against third parties.

WHEN COVERED—The Automobile Liability policy attaches at 12:01 A. M.

CANCELLATION

The Automobile Liability policy may be cancelled by the Insured at any time by his surrender of the policy or by his mailing written notice to the Company or to the agent of the date when he wishes the cancellation to be effective. When the Insured requests cancellation of the policy, the cancellation is effected short rate (discussed in Chapter 2).

Cancellation by the Company—While most Casualty insurance policies provide for the Company's right to cancel the policy at any time subject to stipulated minimum periods of notice, the carrier's right to cancel an Automobile Liability policy in all states except those set down below has in recent years been made subject to considerable limitations. There are variations among the states as to the type of vehicle which is protected by anti-cancellation provisions but for the most part, they apply to vehicles of the private passenger type which are not used for private or public livery, and in many instances, which are not regularly used in the Insured's business.

ALABAMA, HAWAII, INDIANA, MAINE, MARYLAND, NEBRASKA, NEW MEXICO, OKLAHOMA, UTAH, VERMONT, WYOMING—No anti-cancellation statutes have been enacted in these states.

While provisions vary among the states, the anti-cancellation statutes or guidelines address themselves in the main to the procedures that need to be followed if the Company would cancel a new risk it has written, and those which are applicable to cancelling a policy during its term, but after it has been in force for certain minimum periods.

The legislatures of the majority of states have fixed statutory guidelines for the cancellation and non-renewal of Automobile insurance policies. In most states, after a policy has been in effect for a stipulated number of days, which varies among the states from 55 to 90, or effective immediately if the policy is a renewal, the Company may not exercise its right to cancel insurance except: For non-payment of premium for the policy or an installment; or if the driver's license or motor vehicle registration of the named Insured, or of any operator who resides with the named Insured in the same household or customarily operates an automobile insured under the policy, has been suspended or revoked.

There is increasing uniformity among the states with respect to statutes governing the cancellation and non-renewal of Automobile insurance. However, the situation is a changing one and special attention should be given to the specific requirements and procedures in each state.

The various statutes specify the types of policies and risks to which the cancellation and non-renewal laws apply (Generally all Automobile policies written on private passenger or pick-up type automobiles).

The statutes also indicate the initial number of days, generally 60, during which a policy may be cancelled for any reason. They set forth precise reasons for which a policy may be cancelled thereafter and, in some states, set limitations on non-renewal.

TEXAS—In addition to non-payment of premium and revocation or suspension of license, reasons which apply in most states, the law forbids cancellation because of a driver's age.

There are also statutory requirements with respect to giving notice of cancellation or non-renewal. Common requirements are 20 days for notice of cancellation except for non-payment which is 10 days, and 20 or 30 days notice for non-renewal. Practically all states require companies to give reasons with notice or on request if the policy is cancelled. There are fewer provisions for reasons for non-renewal. Some states have made provisions for hearings at the request of the insured as a final protection for the insured whose insurance has been cancelled or not renewed.

Cancellation When Certificate Has Been Filed—When a certificate of financial responsibility has been filed under a policy, the Company is usually required to give notice of cancellation not only to the Insured but also to the agency which administers motor vehicles in the state.

Suspension of Insurance—Many Insureds lay up their automobiles for several months of the year. An Automobile Liability policy may be suspended by the Insured, who will receive a return premium on a pro rata basis, subject to the following conditions:

1. No credit will be allowed for any suspension which is for less than 30 consecutive days.

2. Regardless of the period or periods during which the policy has been suspended, the Company will be entitled to retain not less than the short rate premium for 60 days.

NEW YORK—The registration certificate and the plates of the vehicle must be surrendered to the Motor Vehicle Bureau on or before the date of suspension. The Motor Vehicle Bureau furnishes a special receipt, the FS-6, which must be turned over to the insurance company before they will suspend the insurance coverage.

Assignment—No assignment of the policy will bind the Company unless it has consented to the assignment. The policy does cover the Insured's legal representatives or other persons who have proper temporary custody of the car.

MODIFICATIONS OF TORT LIABILITY SYSTEM AS A BASIS FOR COMPENSATING AUTOMOBILE ACCIDENT VICTIMS

As discussed in Chapter 23 on NEGLIGENCE, a person injured by another must at law establish that his injuries were due to the second party's negligence. In most states, he must also be in a position to show that he did not himself contribute to the accident. Even in states which do not follow this principle strictly (discussed in Chapter 23 under CONTRIBUTORY NEGLIGENCE—Comparative Negligence), the doctrine of fault underlies any compensation due the victim.

For a number of years, this approach to compensating victims of automobile accidents has called forth considerable criticism. It is contended by some that it is entirely unrealistic in most automobile accidents to try to pinpoint fault of one party or the other, involving as they do two or more high-speed motor vehicles where a fraction of a second determines the difference between safety and injury or death. The tort liability system, it is maintained, must as a consequence work unfairly, compensating some inadequately and rewarding others unnecessarily. Critics of the present system also contend that it serves to clutter the courts to the point where the victim of an accident faces delays of three years and longer before he can recover damages and that a substantial portion of the damages paid does not benefit the injured person but is consumed in legal fees, expenses of investigation, court costs, etc. Lastly, it is suggested that the present system exerts a powerful temptation on both parties to distort the facts, exaggerate claims and perjure themselves.

For some forty years (since the exhaustive 1932 Report of the Committee to Study Compensation for Auto Accidents published by the Columbia University Council for Research in the Social Sciences), suggestions have been proposed to modify or entirely discard the tort liability system in favor of a direct compensation approach.

The last few years have brought forth several proposals along these lines, some seeking to "scrap" the tort liability system entirely, others merely to modify it. Several of the large automobile insurance writers have experimented with Automobile Liability insurance which offers some direct first-party indemnity to accident victims.

In addition, the legislatures of practically every state have been examining the structure of the present tort system and giving consideration to modifying it to some extent. The Federal Government which has completed the most exhaustive study of the operation of the present Automobile insurance system has concluded that the needs of the American public are not being adequately served.

The Department of Transportation (DOT) under whose auspices the study was made finds that the system is expensive, that a large percentage of injured persons do not collect any compensation for their losses, that even when settlements are made, they are not always equitable in that they overcompensate for minor injuries or undercompensate for more serious injuries, that settlements are based on vague considerations, etc.

At the root of the problem, it is contended, is the necessity to establish who is at fault before the injured party can recover.

The National Association of Insurance Commissioners, in a resolution adopted in mid-1971 concurred in the position arrived at by the Department of Transportation and urged all the states to adopt some form of No-Fault plan providing for prompt payment of economic losses incurred in automobile accidents.

Some form of No-Fault legislation has been enacted in six states. In two other states, No-Fault coverage must be offered *as an option* with all Automobile Liability policies covering a motor vehicle registered or principally garaged in the state.

While there are differences among the provisions of the several No-Fault statutes, they all address themselves to providing indemnity for medical expenses incurred as a result of an accident on a *first-party* basis. They also make provisions for reimbursement for loss of wages during periods of disability.

Generally, a person recovering first party benefits is precluded from pleading or introducing into evidence in a tort action those damages for which compensation benefits are available, whether or not such benefits are actually recoverable.

AUTO NO-FAULT AND FIRST PARTY BENEFIT LAWS

(Compiled by American Insurance Association, 1972)

Part A

STATE	VEHICLES INCLUDED	TORT EXEMPTION		
		PAIN AND SUFFERING	BODILY INJURY	PROPERTY DAMAGE
DELAWARE	All	None	Damages for which compensation is available (or would be except for deductibles) may not be proved in tort action	Damages for which compensation is available (or would be except for deductibles) may not be proved in tort action
FLORIDA	Private passenger only	Recoverable only if medical exceeds $1,000 or injury consists of disfigurement, serious fracture, loss of member, permanent injury, permanent loss of a body function or death	Exempt from liability to extent benefits are payable (or would be but for exclusions or deductibles) unless action for pain and suffering is maintainable	Owner exempt from liability for damage to motor vehicle subject to Act (except parked vehicle) unless damage exceeds $550
ILLINOIS	Private passenger only	Recovery may not exceed one-half of medical if total is $500 or less and amount of medical exceeding $500	First party benefits subtracted from tort recovery	None
MASSACHU–SETTS	All as to p.d. Private passenger only as to b.i.	Recoverable only if medical exceeds $500 or injury causes death, dismemberment, disfigurement, loss of sight or hearing or consists of a fracture	Exempt from liability to extent of first party benefits	Persons subject to law exempt from liability for damage to vehicle to which Act applies; insurer must make available collision and limited collision coverage
OREGON	Private passenger only	None	None	None
PUERTO RICO	All	Recoverable if in excess of $1,000	Tortfeasor relieved from liability to extent of no-fault benefits except where damages exceed $2,000	None

	Part B						
STATE	FIRST PARTY BENEFITS				CREDIT AGAINST TORT RE–COVERY	INSURER SUBRO–GATED	COLLATERAL BENEFITS
	MEDICAL	FUNERAL	WAGES	LOSS OF SERVICES			
DELAWARE	$10,000/20,000 overall max. on first party benefits	$2,000 max.	$10,000/20,000 overall max. on first party benefits		Yes	Yes	No provision
FLORIDA	$5,000 overall max. on first party benefits	$1,000 max.	100% of loss of income and earnings unless benefits are not includable for income tax, in which event 85%, plus expenses incurred for services; $5,000 overall max. on first party benefits		Yes	Yes	Benefits primary except workmen's compensation credited
ILLINOIS	$2,000 max. per person for medical and funeral		85% of loss of income as result of total disability; max. $150 per week for 52 weeks	Max. $12 per day for 365 days	Yes	Yes	Benefits paid regardless of collateral sources except workmen's compensation or federal employment
MASSACHU-SETTS	$2,000 overall max. on first party benefits		75% of loss of wages less amount received under wage continuation program; $2,000 overall max. on first party benefits	Payments made to non-family members; $2,000 over all max. on first party benefits	Yes	Yes as to b.i. No subrogation for p.d. except where commercial vehicle is involved	Person entitled to workmen's compensation benefits not entitled to first party benefits
OREGON	$3,000	None	70% of loss of income; 14 day waiting period; max. $500 per month, 52 weeks	Expenses incurred after 14 days; max. $12 per day, 52 weeks	No provision	Yes	Benefits primary as to insured and family, but workmen's compensation and medical and disability benefits deductible; excess as to guests and pedestrians
PUERTO RICO	Unlimited	$500	50% of salary (max. $50 per week) for first 52 weeks; $25 for next 52 weeks; 15 day waiting period	No benefits to housewife	Yes	No	Deductible, with certain exceptions

As respects payment for "pain and suffering" there is considerable variation among the plans.

The more important provisions of the No-Fault laws of the six states which have enacted such legislation are shown on pages 486 and 487 in chart form.

Pain and Suffering—As indicated above, the provisions relating to recovery for pain and suffering differ substantially among the states.

DELAWARE—The Delaware Motorists Protection Act permits the injured party to sue for pain and suffering despite the medical coverage of the act.

FLORIDA—An injured person may sue for pain and suffering provided medical benefits authorized by the act exceed $1,000; there is a permanent injury or loss of a bodily function or certain types of fracture to a weight-bearing bone; or injury is the proximate cause of death.

ILLINOIS—When no serious disability results and medical expenses are under $500, payment for pain and inconvenience may not exceed 50% of the medical expenses. When medical expenses in a non-permanent injury exceed $500, payment for pain and inconvenience may equal 100% of the medical expenses *over $500.* In all cases of death, permanent disfigurement, dismemberment or permanent disability, the accident victim may seek damages to cover these serious losses, in addition to the basic medical expenses and wage loss indemnities covered under the basic law.

MASSACHUSETTS—No suit may be instituted against the owner or operator of a motor vehicle which causes injury until the full $2,000 available under the basic law has been collected or the injured party has been unable to collect the stipulated wage loss benefits. A claimant is barred from suing for pain and suffering unless medical expenses exceed $500 or the injury results in death, disfigurement, loss of sight or hearing, or a fracture.

OREGON—The No-Fault Law does not limit the right of an injured party to sue for tort liability.

No-Fault Protection (Optional)

MINNESOTA—Minnesota insurers must offer on an *optional* basis supplementary to any Automobile policy covering any vehicle registered or principally garaged in the state No-Fault first party coverages. The Insured must have the right to buy at least $2,000 in Medical Payments, $60 per week of Disability benefits and $10,000 Accidental Death benefits. The right of an injured party to institute a suit for tort liability is not affected. The Insured may accept or reject any of these coverages.

SOUTH DAKOTA—The provisions of the No-Fault Law are essentially the same as in MINNESOTA. As respects recovery for loss of wages, the benefits of $60 per week are payable only beginning with the 15th day of disability, and for a maximum of 52 weeks.

FOR FURTHER READING

ACKERMAN—Insurance
GEE—Agent's Automobile Guide
HEDGES—Practical Fire and Casualty Insurance
HUEBNER AND BLACK—Property Insurance
KULP AND HALL—Casualty Insurance
MAGEE AND BICKELHAUPT—General Insurance
MEHR AND CAMMACK—Principles of Insurance
POLICY, FORM & MANUAL ANALYSIS SERVICE
RIEGEL, ROBERT AND MILLER—Insurance Principles and Practices

(See Reading List at End of Book)

CHAPTER 27

Commercial and Other Automobile Liability Policies

COMMERCIAL AUTOMOBILES

MOTOR VEHICLES of the truck type, including truck tractors, delivery sedans and automobiles with pick-up bodies are classified as Commercial Automobiles. Included in this classification are also private passenger automobiles which have been altered and adapted to the carrying of merchandise or products. Liability insurance covering a commercial vehicle is essentially the same as the coverage provided for a private passenger automobile, and this section on Commercial Automobiles should therefore be read together with Chapter 26.

The policy covering a commercial vehicle contains the same exclusions as are found in insurance covering a private passenger automobile. There is no coverage while the vehicle is used as a public or livery conveyance, and such automobiles are considered separately as Public Automobiles (discussed in the section that follows).

The basic policy covering a commercial vehicle does *not* provide any Drive Other Car coverage. Such coverage may be provided for an additional premium. An additional premium is also required for insurance on all trailers and tractors.

An exception is made for commercial vehicles with a load capacity of not more than 1,500 lbs. and for private passenger automobiles which have been altered by the attachment of a platform or box or by the structural alteration of the exterior of the body. If such vehicles are not used for wholesale or retail delivery, coverage on trailers applies as under a private passenger automobile and Drive Other Car coverage is provided.

A further exception is made in the case of vehicles of the kind described above even if used for delivery. Trailer coverage and Drive Other Car coverage will apply to such commercial automobiles if owned by cabinet makers, carpenters, electricians, interior decorators, masons, painters, paper-hangers, plumbers, repair and service contractors and vehicles used in connection with radio repair and household furniture installation and repair.

Like most forms of Liability insurance, the Automobile Liability policy does not cover the injury to or destruction of property owned by, rented to, in charge of or transported by the Insured. Coverage for damage to property being carried on the vehicle must be provided under an Inland Marine policy, as discussed in Chapter 21.

The Automobile Liability policy covering a commercial automobile used for the transportation of gasoline or oil contains a special exclusion, in that it does not cover accidents resulting from the erroneous delivery of gasoline for oil, or oil for gasoline, or from the delivery of gasoline or oil into the wrong receptacle, if the accident occurs after operations have been completed at the place of occurrence thereof.

Medical Payments coverage is available under Liability policies covering commercial automobiles. It should be remembered, however, that the medical payments are not available to any person to whom benefits are payable under a Workmen's Compensation Law. Since the individual operating a truck is usually an employee covered by a Workmen's Compensation Law, and since passengers are relatively rare in such vehicles, it can be seen that for many commercial automobiles Medical Payments coverage will afford comparatively limited coverage. On the other hand, sole proprietors and partners who personally operate trucks will be covered under the Medical Payments coverage, since they are not employees eligible for benefits under a Workmen's Compensation Law.

RATES

The rate for a commercial automobile depends on the following four factors:

1. Use

All risks are assigned to one of five classifications, depending on the purpose to which the vehicle is put; e. g., ambulances, garbage trucks, bakers, butchers, carnivals, concrete mixers, egg dealers, fruit, vegetable or poultry dealers, newspaper delivery, retail department stores, road contractors, etc.

Truckmen who haul goods for others are rated separately (discussed later under Truckman Rule).

2. Size

Commercial vehicles which are not required to be registered with the state are rated on the basis of the load capacity of the vehicle—CA if the load capacity is not over 9,500 lbs., CB if over 9,500.

With certain few exceptions, all other commercial automobiles are rated according to the weight of capacity shown for the vehicle on the registration certificate for the state in which they are principally garaged, as follows:

ALABAMA, GEORGIA, KENTUCKY, MISSOURI, TENNESSEE—If the *gross vehicle weight* is not over 18,000 lbs.—CA; if over 18,000 lbs. CB.

ARIZONA, CALIFORNIA, COLORADO, DISTRICT OF COLUMBIA, FLORIDA, HAWAII, MICHIGAN, MINNESOTA (urban trucks), NEVADA, OHIO, WYOMING—If the *net vehicle weight* (unladen weight) is not over 9,500 lbs.—CA; if over 9,500 lbs.—CB.

ARKANSAS, IDAHO, ILLINOIS, INDIANA, KANSAS, MISSISSIPPI, MONTANA, NEBRASKA, NORTH CAROLINA, OREGON, VIRGINIA, WASHINGTON, WISCONSIN—If the *gross vehicle weight* is not over 20,000 lbs.—CA; if over 20,000 lbs.—CB.

CONNECTICUT, DELAWARE, IOWA, MAINE, MINNESOTA (except urban trucks which are rated according to the net vehicle weight table), NEW HAMPSHIRE, NEW JERSEY, NEW YORK, NORTH DAKOTA, RHODE ISLAND, VERMONT, WEST VIRGINIA—If the *gross vehicle weight* is not over 19,500 lbs.—CA; if over 19,500 lbs.—CB.

LOUISIANA—If the *gross weight per load carrying axle* is not over 14,000 lbs.—CA; if over 14,000 lbs.—CB.

MARYLAND, NEW MEXICO, SOUTH DAKOTA—If the *chassis weight* is not over 7,500 lbs.—CA; if over 7,500 lbs.—CB.

OKLAHOMA, PENNSYLVANIA, UTAH—If the *gross vehicle weight* is not over 21,000 lbs.—CA; if over 21,000 lbs.—CB.

PUERTO RICO—If the *load capacity* is not over two tons—CA; if over two tons—CB.

SOUTH CAROLINA—If the *load capacity* is not over 10,000 lbs.—CA; if over 10,000 lbs.—CB.

In addition, all dual rear axle trucks are rated CB, as are all trucks equipped to haul trailers. Special rules apply to tank trucks equipped to carry water or petroleum.

3. Territory

Rates vary with the territory in which the vehicle is principally garaged.

4. Radius of Operations

An increase in rate applies to all commercial automobiles which are customarily operated beyond a 50-mile radius from the limits of the city or town in which the automobile is principally garaged.

For purposes of determining whether a risk is subject to the surcharge, the radius of operations is based on the limits of the *city or town* in which the automobile is principally garaged, and not the rating territory into which the risk falls. Thus, a vehicle may be principally garaged in a territory which includes an entire county, and the rate will be based on the rate for that county. Even though the vehicle does not travel outside of the county, its operation may extend beyond a radius of 50 miles from the limits of the *town* in which the risk is located, and the surcharge will be applied.

Truckmen Rule

Truckmen who haul or transport merchandise or property for others are divided for rating purposes into two groups:

Local Truckmen—All truckmen whose operations are customarily confined within a 50-mile radius of the limits of the city or town in which the automobile is principally garaged are classed as Local Truckmen.

Rates are determined according to the four factors for commercial automobiles outlined above, except that all Local Truckmen are rated as Class 3 risks. As respects territory, Local Truckmen are not rated according to the place where the vehicle is principally garaged, but according to the highest rated territory within a 50-mile radius of the city or town in which the automobile is principally garaged. (An exception is made for Local Truckmen who never travel into the highest rated territory.)

Gross Receipts Basis—Local Truckmen who own or operate 10 or more commercial automobiles and have been in business for at least 15 months may have their insurance written on a gross receipts basis. The premium paid at the inception of the policy is based on an estimate of the gross receipts to be realized during the policy period. At the expiration of the policy, an audit is made of the Insured's records to ascertain his total gross receipts during the policy period. The final premium is based on the Insured's actual receipts. A return premium is allowed, or an additional premium charged, as the individual case requires.

Long Haul Truckmen—Any truckman who does not come within the Local Truckman classification is classed as a Long Haul Truckman. Rates for risks of this kind depend on the distance regularly traveled from the point at which the load is placed on the truck to the farthest point to which the Insured transports the load or operates his equipment. There are three groups:

1. Commercial automobiles operated over 50 miles but not over 100 miles.

2. Commercial automobiles operated over 100 miles but not over 300 miles.

3. Commercial automobiles operated over 300 miles.

Gross Receipts Basis—Long Haul Truckmen may also have their insurance written on a gross receipts basis. The rules are similar to those for Local Truckmen except that the ownership or use of *five* long haul trucks or tractors makes a risk eligible for this form of policy.

Whole Dollar Premium Rule—Discussed in Chapter 8 under

OTHER FACTORS WHICH AFFECT FIRE INSURANCE RATES —Whole Dollar Premium Rule.

INSURANCE REQUIRED OF FRANCHISED CARRIERS

Common carriers and contract carriers who transport property in interstate or foreign commerce for hire are required to carry Automobile Liability insurance. Exempted from this requirement are only carriers whose vehicles are used exclusively in carrying newspapers, or livestock, fish or agricultural products. The minimum limits that must be carried are $25,000 per person, and from $100,000 to $300,000 per accident, depending on the type of limit. $10,000 of Property Damage Liability insurance must also be maintained. The carrier is required to file a certificate of insurance with the Interstate Commerce Commission.

If the policy for which a certificate has been issued is cancelled, notice of not less than 30 days must be given by the insurance Company to the Interstate Commerce Commission. Every policy for which a certificate is required must also include an endorsement similar in scope to the one required by the Interstate Commerce Commission on Cargo Liability policies (discussed in Chapter 21).

The requirement for Automobile Liability insurance is not to be confused with insurance to cover a truckman's liability to his customers, which is also made mandatory on common carriers.

In addition to the requirements imposed on interstate carriers by the Interstate Commerce Commission, practically every state makes Automobile Liability insurance compulsory on most carriers of property for hire. Carriers are required to maintain insurance which in every instance is at least as high in amount as required by the Interstate Commerce Commission.

In a few instances, the limits required of carriers vary with the weight of the truck. In some states, higher limits are required of haulers who carry explosives, petroleum products, combustibles, etc. Carriers of livestock and agricultural products are usually exempted from the requirement.

PUBLIC AUTOMOBILES

THE BASIC AUTOMOBILE Liability policy provides no coverage while the automobile is used as a public or livery conveyance. Any vehicle so used is insured according to the rules and rates of the Public Automobile section of the Automobile manual, under a policy which specifically includes use of the car as a public or livery conveyance. The policy is identical with the one used to insure private passenger automobiles except for several special provisions which are discussed below.

Any vehicle used to carry passengers for a charge falls within the Public Automobile designation, which is divided into the following groups:

1. Airport Bus.

2. Apartment House, Apartment Hotel, Camp, Country Club, Department Store, Golf Club, Hotel and Real Estate Development Bus.

3. Cemetery Bus.

4. Charter Bus. A public automobile of any type with a seating capacity in excess of eight passengers excluding the driver, used for special trips for touring, picnics, outings, games and similar uses.

5. Church Bus.

6. Civic, Charitable and Welfare Organization Bus. An automobile of any type used by American Legion, Boy Scout, Red Cross or other civic or welfare organization in connection with the activities of the organization for special trips for touring, picnics, outings, games and similar uses, and not used to pick up, transport and discharge passengers along a route.

7. Club Livery Automobile. A public livery of any type with a seating capacity not in excess of eight passengers excluding the driver, the use of which is limited by written contract with a designated club to provide a regular transportation service to members and guests, and incidental private livery.

8. General Passenger Service Bus.

9. Limited Passenger Service Bus. An automobile of any type used in the business of transporting to and from work employees of one or more employers.

10. Private Livery Automobile. A public automobile of any type with a seating capacity not in excess of eight passengers excluding the driver, rented only from a garage or the residence of the named Insured with the named Insured or an employee of the named Insured in attendance as chauffeur, for use in connection with social functions, funerals, touring and similar purposes.

11. Public Livery, Taxicab. The maximum seating capacity of a Public Livery automobile is the same as for Private Livery automobiles, outlined above. The Insured, or an employee, must be in attendance as a chauffeur. The automobile cannot be used to pick up, discharge and transport passengers along a route.

12. School Bus.

13. Sightseeing Bus. Separate rates are applicable to sightseeing buses with seating capacity of 60 or less and those with larger capacity, and for those whose radius of operation is confined to a 15-mile radius of the city in which the vehicle is principally garaged as opposed to those who exceed this distance.

14. Spare or Substitute Bus.

15. Star Mail Route Bus. This classification includes an automobile of any type operated under a Star Route Service contract for the transportation of mail and parcel post to and from post offices and railroad stations, and used at the same time to transport passengers for a charge.

Passenger Hazard—The Automobile Liability policy covering a public automobile may be written at a reduced premium to exclude liability to any person in or upon, entering or alighting from the automobile.

The passenger hazard may not be excluded from Drive-Yourself Automobiles.

Property of Passengers Hazard—The basic Automobile Liability policy covering a private passenger automobile specifically excludes liability for damage to property owned by, rented to, in charge of or transported by the Insured. The Liability policy covering a Public Automobile, however, does include, under the Property Damage Section, coverage for liability to passengers for loss or damage to their property carried in the insured automobile. Such coverage is afforded under a Public Automobile policy covering all public automobiles except a Drive-Yourself Automobile.

Compulsory Insurance for Public Carriers of Passengers—Under the Federal Motor Carrier Act, every common or contract carrier who transports passengers for hire in interstate commerce is required to carry Automobile Liability insurance. The minimum amount of insurance that must be carried varies with the seating capacity of the vehicle, as follows:

Seating Capacity	Bodily Injury Limits	Property Damage Limits
1- 7	$25,000/100,000	$10,000
8-12	25,000/150,000	10,000
13-20	25,000/200,000	10,000
21-30	25,000/250,000	10,000
31 and over	25,000/300,000	10,000

As with freight carriers, a certificate of insurance must be filed with the Interstate Commerce Commission. Furthermore, 30 days' notice must be given to the Commission when a policy is cancelled. The policy for which a certificate has been filed must also contain an endorsement prescribed by the Commission which is similar in its scope to the one required of freight carriers on their Cargo Liability policy (discussed in Chapter 21).

Insurance Required of Intrastate Carriers—In most states, motor carriers that transport passengers for hire within the state are subject to regulation by some state agency—the Public Service Commission, Public Utilities Commission, Bureau of Motor Vehicles, Board of Railroad Commissioners, etc. Carriers that come under the jurisdiction of the state are required by the state to carry Automobile Liability insurance of prescribed limits. There is little standardization among the various states as to the amount of insurance required.

In almost every instance, the amount of Bodily Injury Liability insurance required is $5,000 per person; the per accident limit varies with the seating capacity of the vehicle.

CONNECTICUT, MISSOURI—The minimum limit per person is $15,000.

ILLINOIS, KANSAS, LOUISIANA, MICHIGAN, MINNESOTA, OHIO, WISCONSIN—The minimum limit per person is $10,000.

MONTANA—School districts owning and operating their own buses are required to carry insurance with limits of $7,500/50,000.

NEW MEXICO—The minimum limit per person is $7,500.

NEW YORK—The limit per person on vehicles whose seating capacity is less than 8 is $10,000.00. On vehicles whose capacity is 8 or more, $10,000 is the minimum limit per person. For vehicles which require a license from the Public Service Commission, minimum limits for vehicles operated outside of New York City is $25,000/300,000. Vehicles which operate within New York City must maintain insurance with limits of not less than $50,000/100,000.

SOUTH CAROLINA—The minimum limit for bodily injuries to one person is $10,000.00. For injuries to all persons in any one accident, the limit runs from $30,000.00 to $100,000.00 depending on capacity.

VIRGINIA—The minimum limit is $10,000 per person. For school buses, the limits are $15,000/100,000.00.

The state agency administering intrastate passenger carriers requires notice (usually 30 days) before any policy may be cancelled. In addition, the policy is required to have attached to it an endorsement similar to the one required by the Interstate Commerce Commission of interstate common and contract carriers (discussed in Chapter 21).

NON-OWNED AUTOMOBILES EMPLOYERS' NON-OWNERSHIP LIABILITY INSURANCE

AS POINTED OUT in Chapter 23, under Master and Servant Rule, an employer is charged with the duty of protecting the public from coming to harm through the acts of his employees. Usually when an employee in the course of his work causes an accident, the injured person will bring a suit against the employee *and* the employer. The courts may find the employer liable jointly with the employee, and the plaintiff may satisfy the judgment against one or both.

When a firm or corporation owns and operates private passenger, commercial or public automobiles, it usually provides Automobile Liability insurance to cover accidents arising out of the use, maintenance or operation of the vehicles. It is important, however, to understand that liability may also be imposed on the business because of accidents caused by *non-owned* automobiles.

Thus, if an employee drives his *own* car in the course of his business or occupation, and becomes involved in an accident, the employer may be held liable for the accident caused by the employee. Countless privately owned automobiles are operated in employer's business by salesmen, route men, inspectors, repair and maintenance men, testers, etc.

Even where an employee's work does not call for regular use of an automobile, the employer may ask him to make an occasional pickup or delivery or a special call on a customer. An accident which arises out of such a trip may impose liability on the employer just as when it arises from an automobile regularly driven by a salesman or route man, or other employee whose duties involve the regular use of an automobile. The employer may be held liable for an accident caused by an employee who was operating his own car (or a borrowed car) even though the employer was completely unaware of the action, and had not authorized the employee to make use of such automobile.

If the employee carries Automobile Liability insurance covering the vehicle owned by him, his employer will be protected under the policy as an additional Insured. However, it may develop after the accident that the limits of liability in the employee's policy are not high enough to meet a large claim. An employer may take steps to satisfy himself that any of his employees who drives an automobile in the course of his work does carry Automobile Liability insurance. Even though he has determined that an Automobile Liability policy was issued to his employee, he cannot be certain that the Insured will keep the policy in force continuously by meeting his premiums when due. Furthermore, despite the fact that the premiums have been paid, the circumstances may be such at the time of the accident that the Insured has suspended his insurance by breaching a warranty or condition of the policy, or voided it by misrepresentation.

Employers' Non-Ownership Liability insurance is designed to give an employer full protection on any liability that may be imposed on him by reason of the operation in his business of non-owned automobiles. The basic coverages of the policy are those of regular Automobile Liability insurance, and the Employers' Non-Ownership policy is written by attaching an endorsement to the basic policy. Discussed below are only such provisions of the policy which differ from the standard Automobile Liability policy discussed in Chapter 26.

HAZARDS COVERED

The Employers' Non-Ownership Liability policy covers two types of motor vehicles used in the Insured's business, as listed below. Such vehicles are covered only when not owned in whole or in part, or hired or leased by, or loaned to, or registered in the name of the insured, or by a partner of an insured partnership. The types of non-owned vehicles covered are:

1. Automobiles of the private passenger type.
2. Commercial automobiles, provided their operation is only occasional and not frequent.

When the use in the Insured's business of non-owned commercial automobiles is frequent, the policy may be endorsed, for an additional premium, to cover such operations.

The policy covers any vehicles of the kind outlined above. The Insured is not required to itemize the automobiles, nor is he limited to any stipulated number of automobiles.

The Employers' Non-Ownership Liability policy does not apply to automobiles hired or leased by the Insured. Where an employee hires a car, as is done frequently by salesmen who travel to a distant point by plane or train and then hire an automobile from an automobile renting service, such use would be covered, unless the vehicle were hired in the employer's name.

HAZARDS NOT COVERED

With only a few differences, the exclusions found in Automobile Liability policies apply to Employers' Non-Ownership Liability insurance. The Non-Ownership policy will cover the towing of any trailer not owned or hired by the Insured.

WHO IS INSURED

Under the Employers' Non-Ownership Liability policy, there is coverage only for the employer who is named as Insured. The entire Other Drivers and Interests provision (Omnibus clause) of the basic Automobile Liability policy is deleted.

An exception is made for Non-Ownership Liability policies covering a corporation. Such policies do cover without additional charges the liability of an executive officer for the operation in the business of any automobile which is insured under the policy (non-owned automobiles). In other words, the corporation is protected for any liability that it may face from the operation *by* an executive officer of non-owned automobiles, since the officer is an employee of the corporation.

The policy is further extended to cover the executive officer as an additional insured. If he is held personally liable as an officer of the corporation for an accident caused by another employee operating a motor vehicle in the business of the corporation, his liability is also covered under the policy. With this one exception, the Non-Ownership Liability policy provides insurance only for the named Insured.

It is important to understand that a Non-Ownership Liability policy does not cover the liability of the employee. If such employee becomes involved in an accident, his employer may be joined in the suit, but the employee himself will almost always be held primarily liable. For *his* liability, he will find no protection under his employer's Non-Ownership Liability policy.

FOR HOW MUCH

Employers' Non-Ownership Liability acts as excess insurance over any other valid and collectible insurance under which the named Insured is entitled to collect. Thus, assume a salesman who operates his own automobile in his work is insured under a policy with Bodily Injury limits of $20,000/40,000, and his employer carries Employers' Non-Ownership Liability insurance with limits of $100,000/300,000. While traveling for the firm, the salesman becomes involved in an accident. The injured person brings a suit against the salesman and his employer. He is awarded $60,000.

The salesman's Automobile Liability policy will have to pay $20,000, its full limit for injuries to one person; the Employers' Non-Ownership policy will be called on only for the amount by which the loss exceeds the salesman's policy and will, in this case, pay $40,000. On the other hand, if in a similar situation, the liability for the accident had come to $10,000, the salesman's policy would have paid the entire loss.

RATES

Rates for Non-Ownership Liability depend on the type of individuals covered and, in some instances, on the territory in which the user of the automobile makes his headquarters. For purposes of rating, all persons who come under a Non-Ownership Liability policy fall into one of two groups:

Class 1 Persons—This class includes all *outside* officers and employees whose usual duties involve the use in the Insured's business of motor vehicles (of the type described before under Hazards Covered).

Also, all other officers and employees whose usual duties involve the use of a motor vehicle and who either receive a specific operating allowance for their use of the vehicle, or whose salary, commission or terms of employment contemplate the use of a motor vehicle.

Also all direct agents and representatives who as far as the business of the Insured is concerned are the exclusives agents of the Insured and whose duties involve the use of motor vehicles in the Insured's business.

Class 2—This class includes all other officers and employees not included in Class 1.

Class 2 includes only employees, while Class 1 includes employees and certain other "persons."

The rate for a Class 1 employee depends on the territory of his headquarters; for Class 2 employees, no territorial distinction is made.

Specific and Blanket Basis—A Non-Ownership Liability policy may be written on a specific basis or a Blanket basis. A specific policy covers only the persons mentioned by name in the policy. Policies of this kind must cover some Class 1 employees. If the employer wishes to insure only Class 2 employees, the policy must cover all such employees, and the policy is rated like a Blanket policy.

Blanket Non-Ownership Liability insurance covers all use of non-owned automobiles. The Insured is not required to designate the individuals by name, and is afforded automatic coverage on all such persons, whether they were in his employ when the policy was issued or came into his organization thereafter.

The premium for the Blanket policy is based on the number of Class 1 and Class 2 employees who are in the Insured's employ when the policy is written. At the end of the policy period, or more frequently if the Company requests, an audit is made to ascertain the number of persons of each class who were actually in the Insured's employ during the term of the policy. The earned premium is computed, and the Insured receives a return premium, or pays an additional premium, as may be warranted by the facts.

Whole Dollar Premium Rule—Discussed in Chapter 8 under OTHER FACTORS WHICH AFFECT FIRE INSURANCE RATES—Whole Dollar Premium Rule.

MISCELLANEOUS NON-OWNERSHIP LIABILITY

NON-OWNERSHIP LIABILITY insurance is available also to private individuals for their liability for the non-business use of non-owned automobiles. Such insurance is also available to clubs, department stores, hotels, theatres and similar organizations who require insurance against liabilities arising out of the operation by their employees of customers' cars.

As outlined above, Non-Ownership Liability insurance does apply to commercial automobiles, but only when their use is occasional and not frequent. When an individual or a business engages an independent contractor who does operate commercial vehicles in the course of the work being performed, the individual or firm may require Non-Ownership Liability—Independent Contractors insurance to cover liability arising out of such operations.

HIRED CARS

AN INDIVIDUAL or a business may be held liable for accidents arising out of automobiles which are not owned by the individual or business, or any of its employees. A situation of this kind may develop when automobiles are hired, either with or without a driver, and an accident is caused by an operator while on his employer's business. As pointed out previously, the employer may be held jointly liable with the operator for damages inflicted or caused.

An individual Insured who rents or hires motor vehicles is not insured under his regular Automobile Liability policy for accidents arising out of such vehicles, if the automobile is hired as part of the frequent use of hired automobiles, or furnished for his regular use. The Drive Other Car Coverage specifically limits the operation of hired cars to such as are not regularly hired. Even if not used frequently, a hired automobile is not covered if used in the Insured's business, unless it is a private passenger automobile and is actually operated by him, his spouse, a chauffeur or a servant.

In any event, there is no coverage for the use of other automobiles under any Automobile Liability policy except when the named Insured is an individual. (The scope of Drive Other Car coverage is discussed fully in Chapter 26.)

A Non-Ownership Liability policy will cover an Insured for the use of non-owned vehicles by his employees in his business. It will not apply, however, to vehicles hired by the Insured, even if their hire is not frequent or regular.

A business which hires automobiles will be covered as an additional Insured under the Automobile Liability policy, which covers the owner of the vehicle. It may be, however, that the owner of the vehicle is not insured, or not properly or adequately covered. To be fully protected against any liability that may arise from hired automobiles, the individual or firm which hires automobiles requires Hired Car insurance.

Hired Car coverage is usually written by endorsement of the regular Automobile Liability policy. It covers the Insured for the liability which may be imposed on him arising out of automobiles whose complete supervision, direction and control rests with him. Hired Car coverage does not apply to any automobile which is owned by, or registered in the name of, the named Insured, or an executive officer or partner of the Insured. Nor does it apply to any automobile owned by, or registered in the name of an employee or agent of the Insured who is granted an operating allowance of any sort for the use of such automobiles.

Hired Car coverage may be purchased on a Specified Automobile basis or on a Cost of Hire basis.

Specified Automobile Basis—This method is suitable for Insureds who hire automobiles on a long term basis. The vehicles to be covered are specified in the policy, and there is no coverage for vehicles other than those insured. The rates used for the hired automobiles insured specifically are the same as though the Insured owned the vehicles. If the rate for the automobile, as based on the use to which the Insured puts it, is higher than the rate that would apply to the owner of the vehicle, the owner of the vehicle is covered along with the Insured who hires it. Contrariwise, if the rate for the Insured is lower than would be applicable to the owner, the interest of the owner is not covered under the policy.

Cost of Hire Basis—This method is better suited to Insureds who hire automobiles for temporary periods and cannot determine in advance how many automobiles they may hire during the policy period. It is not available however to risks engaged in local or long haul trucking operations or to moving van associations and risks in the freight forwarding business.

The policy automatically covers all automobiles and trailers hired by the Insured. Under policies written on this basis, the interest of the owner may not be included. Rates are based on the cost of hire of the automobiles, which includes wages paid to the chauffeurs who operate the automobile, whether these are the Insured's own employees or are chauffeurs furnished with the hired automobiles. The wages of chauffeurs to be included in figuring the cost of hire includes their actual remuneration, and all commissions, bonuses, overtime wages, food and lodging and any other compensation, subject to a maximum of $100 per week for each chauffeur.

Hired Car coverage is excess insurance over any other valid and collectible insurance under which the Insured is entitled to collect. (In this respect, the policy is identical with Employers' Non-Ownership Liability insurance.)

COMPREHENSIVE AUTOMOBILE LIABILITY POLICY

Larger risks frequently insure their automobile exposures under the Comprehensive Automobile Liability policy, which affords broader protection for a very nominal additional cost. The policy covers the Insured's liability arising out of any automobile. An estimated premium is projected based on the owned vehicles, hired cars, employer's non-ownership liability and independent contractors which the Insured is likely to use during the policy period. The advance premium is composed of these individual charges. The policy is audited annually and the premium adjusted on the basis of the exposures that actually developed during the policy period.

The policy coverage is not restricted to the cars enumerated in the questionnaire which the Insured submits with his request for insurance. Subject to stipulated exclusions, the policy covers any unknown, unratable automobile exposure.

Comprehensive General Liability insurance is available in combination with the Comprehensive Automobile Liability policy under a single policy, the Comprehensive Public Liability policy.

GARAGE INSURANCE

SPECIAL FORMS OF INSURANCE have been devised to meet the Liability insurance needs of businesses which sell or service automobiles. The Garage Insurance policy provides coverage on most of the hazards that risks of this kind face in the everyday conduct of their business.

These Garage policies are available to any automobile dealer, Automobile repair shop, service station, storage garage, and to machinery and implement dealers and repair shops.

MISSISSIPPI—This coverage is compulsory.

GARAGE LIABILITY POLICY

THE GARAGE LIABILITY policy is essentially an Owners', Landlords' and Tenants' Liability policy adapted to the specialized needs of

Automobile risks. There are many important differences, however, between the two policies, and these are pointed out below.

Like the Owners', Landlords' and Tenants' policy, the Garage Liability policy is a schedule policy with coverage available separately for different sets of hazards. The policy may be written in one of two ways, depending on the nature of the risk to be insured. The "Garage Operations Hazard," which is basic to the policy, is extended to take in the Automobile hazard in one of the following two ways:

1. Automobile Hazards 1—covers all automobiles, or
2. Automobile Hazards 2—covers only automobiles not owned or hired by the Insured.

Dealers, whether franchised or non-franchised, and dealers in equipment and implements must insure the automobile exposure under Automobile Hazard 1; service stations, repair shops and garages must insure this exposure under Hazard 2. Where a risk of this latter kind also owns or leases automobiles, it must insure such vehicles under the regular rates and rules applicable to private passenger or commercial vehicles, as the case may be.

Automobile Hazards 2 is designed for risks where the exposure is limited to automobiles stored or serviced. Risks which own or rent automobiles can purchase the coverage they require under Automobile Hazards 1, except that Hazards 1 only covers for purpose stated in the policy, where Hazards 2 provides protection for limited personal use of the vehicles of the Insured.

It will be noted that both forms of the policy, except as they apply to owned automobiles, are identical as to the hazards covered, and apply to the premises maintained and all operations necessary or incidental thereto.

Both apply to Premises and Operations and differ only as to the kind of automobiles covered.

WHAT IS COVERED

The Garage Liability policy is divided into three parts, as follows:

Part I — Coverage A — Bodily Injury
B — Property Damage

Part II — Expenses for Medical Services
Coverage C — Automobile Medical Payments
D — Premises Medical Payments

Part III — Garage Keepers' Legal Liability
Coverage E — Fire and Explosion
F — Theft

G — Riot and Vandalism
H — Collision or Upset.

The Insured may at his option purchase insurance under any of the available coverages. Different limits of liability may be afforded under the various coverages, each of which is separately rated.

Coverage A—Bodily Injury Liability—See Chapter 24.

Coverage B—Property Damage Liability—See Chapter 24.

Coverage C—Automobile Medical Payments —This coverage is discussed below under HAZARDS COVERED

Coverage D—Premises Medical Payments

Part III—Coverage E, F, G and H are discussed at the end of Chapter 29 under Garage Keepers' Legal Liability Insurance.

HAZARDS COVERED

Like an Owners', Landlords' and Tenants' Liability policy, the Garage policy covers the ownership, maintenance and use of the premises and all operations necessary or incidental to such operations.

The policy covers not only the premises occupied by the Insured at the time the policy is issued, but any premises which he may acquire during its term. Contrast with the Owners', Landlords' and Tenants' policy, under which the Company must be notified of newly acquired premises within 30 days.

To be covered under the policy, the premises must be used for the purposes of an automobile dealer, repair shop, service station, storage garage or public parking place, or for operations necessary or incidental to such operations. Many garages and service stations use a portion of the premises for other business or trade. If there is any doubt as to whether a particular operation being conducted at the Insured's premises is incidental to the garage risk, it should be discussed with the Company, which can issue an endorsement and explicitly bring the portion of the premises within the coverage of the policy.

Where the Owners', Landlords' and Tenants' Liability policy excludes accidents arising from vehicles while away from the premises, the Garage Liability policy specifically includes the ownership, maintenance or use of automobiles in connection with the Insured's operations.

Automobile Hazards 2 covers the use in the garage business of the Insured of any automobile which is not owned or hired by the named Insured, a partner of the Insured, or a member of the household of any such person.

Automobile Hazards 1 will cover the occasional use for other business purposes of any automobile which is owned by the Insured or is in his charge. Also, if used principally for business, the occasional use of the vehicle for pleasure is also covered.

Thus, the Insured may use an automobile or truck owned by his garage in another business, or on a farm he operates, or lend a friend an automobile for use in his business, and such vehicles will be covered, if not used regularly in such operations. The Garage Liability policy also covers any automobile owned by the named Insured in connection with his garage operations, which is used for pleasure (non-business purposes) by the named Insured, a partner, an executive officer if the Insured is a corporation, or a member of the household of any such person.

The policy also covers any automobile furnished for the regular use of any other person or organization. Such protection is afforded without additional premium charge to the extent of *one automobile* for each officer of a corporation Insured or the spouse of such officer, or for each partner or spouse. For each additional vehicle furnished for the use of such individuals, an additional premium is charged.

"Automobile" is defined in the policy to mean a land motor vehicle, trailer or semi-trailer, other land equipment capable of moving under its own power, and equipment for use with such vehicles. The policy will therefore cover motorcycles, motor scooters, etc. Also included is animal drawn equipment.

Products Liability—The Garage Liability policy does not exclude Products Liability—accidents arising out of the handling or use of or the existence of any condition in goods or products manufactured, sold, handled or distributed by the Insured (discussed in Chapter 26 under Products Liability). This coverage is part of the basic contract, and is not subject to any aggregate limit (as under Products Liability written under other Public Liability policies).

The Garage Liability policy therefore covers without endorsement accidents arising out of defective parts sold or distributed or faulty work done by the Insured.

Thus, if the Insured's employee improperly mounted a wheel on a customer's car, and an accident resulted from the faulty work, after the car was no longer in the Insured's possession, the garage might be held liable for the accident, and such liability would be covered under the Garage Liability. If, on the other hand, the Insured was road-testing the automobile on which he had just mounted a wheel or new tire, there would *not* be any coverage for an accident to the customer's automobile because the policy does not apply to property in the care, custody or control of or being transported by the Insured or property as to which the Insured is for any purpose exercising physical control. This exclusion and others which relate to the Products Liability coverage are discussed later in this section under HAZARDS NOT COVERED—Products Liability.

The policy does not cover injury *to* the goods or products. This exclusion is discussed later under HAZARDS NOT COVERED—Products Liability.

Expenses for Medical Services—Like the Automobile Liability policy covering a private passenger automobile, the Garage Liability policy contains a separate coverage under which the Insured can purchase insurance to cover the medical expenses of any person who sustains an injury while in or upon, entering or alighting from an automobile which is insured under the policy (discussed in Chapter 26 under Automobile Medical Payments). This is Section I of the policy.

The Insured may also buy Automobile Medical Payments *and* Premises Medical Payments coverage under Sections I & J.

The Premises Medical Payments coverage is identical with the Medical Payments coverage available under an Owners', Landlords' and Tenants' Liability policy, discussed in Chapter 24.

Under the Premises Medical Payments coverage, the named Insured or a partner or an employee is specifically excluded. By contrast, the Automobile Medical Payments coverage follows the coverage afforded under Automobile policies and does not exclude the named Insured. It should be remembered, however, that Medical Payments benefits are not available to any employee of the Insured or any person to whom benefits are payable under any Workmen's Compensation Law. The Insured, if an individual, or a partner of a co-partnership, will be covered under Automobile Medical Payments, but not the officer of an insured corporation, since he is an employee.

HAZARDS NOT COVERED

Liability of an Insured to His Employees—See Chapter 24.

Elevators—Elevator Liability coverage is included in the basic policy. A charge is made only for inspections required by law which are made by the insurance company.

An additional premium is payable for escalators and for elevators in automated parking facilities which are operated by electronic devices and park automobiles without a driver at the wheel.

Liability Assumed Under Contract—Like most other Liability forms, the Garage Liability policy covers only sums for which the Insured becomes legally obligated, but not liability which he may assume under a contract. The Garage Liability policy, however, specifically provides coverage on the Insured's liability arising out of a warranty of goods or products, even though such warranty is a liability assumed by the Insured. It also covers the liability the Insured assumes under certain stipulated types of agreement (discussed in Chapter 25 under OL & T Liability insurance—HAZARDS NOT COVERED—Assumed Liability).

Thus, assume the Insured changes the oil in a customer's automobile but fails to replace the drain plug properly. After the customer has driven the car for some distance, the plug is shaken loose, all the oil leaks out of the crankcase, and the engine is badly damaged. In such situations, the garage is generally considered as having made an implied warranty that its work and products will be satisfactory, and it is likely that it will be held liable to the customer for the damage to the automobile. The Garage Liability policy *does* cover this liability. It is not, however, responsible for the oil which is lost.

Products Liability—When insurance is provided under Property Damage Liability, the Garage Liability covers the Insured's liability for accidents which damage property. There is no coverage, however, for injury to or destruction of goods or products manufactured, sold, handled or distributed, or work completed by or for the named Insured, out of which the accident arises. In the "crankcase" loss used as an illustration, there would be no coverage for the loss of the plug itself or the oil which the Insured had used to fill the crankcase, since these are products handled by the Insured.

In a similar way, assume the automobile dealer sells a defective tire to a customer. After being driven for a few miles, the tire blows out and the car runs into a telegraph pole and is badly damaged. The Garage Liability policy will cover the Insured's liability to the customer for the damage to his car, but not for the tire itself, since the tire was a product sold by the Insured. (See Deductible provision, discussed later under FOR HOW MUCH—Deductible.)

If, in the illustration used above, the accident occurred before the Insured had turned the automobile over to the customer, the policy would *not* cover. (This exclusion is discussed below under Liability for Property In Insured's Care.)

Liability for Property In Insured's Care—Like practically every form of Liability insurance, the Garage Liability excludes liability for damage to property owned by or rented to the Insured, or property in charge of or transported by the Insured. This exclusion is eased as respects Property Damage and liability for damage to property is covered when it arises from any elevator for which insurance is afforded under the policy.

A special exception is spelled out in the policy also as respects any servicing hoist, and the Insured's liability for damage to property in his care, custody or control arising out of such servicing hoist *is* covered.

The Insured's liability for damage to property in his charge due to collision or upset, as well as to fire, explosion, theft, riot and vandalism may be covered under Parts K-1, K-2, K-3 and K-4 of the policy (discussed in Chapter 29 under Garage Keepers' Legal Liability insurance)

Public or Livery Conveyance—As under the Automobile Liability policy, there is no coverage for accidents caused while the automobile is being used as public or livery conveyance. The Garage Liability policy also excludes accidents caused while the Insured is *carrying property* for a charge.

The policy may be endorsed for an additional premium, to cover the renting of automobiles or trucks as private or commercial livery. The Garage Liability policy cannot be written to cover public livery automobiles or taxicabs.

Liability to Employees—Discussed in Chapter 24 under HAZARDS NOT COVERED—Liability of Insured to Employees Engaged in His Business.

Racing or Speed Contest — There is no coverage for claims arising out of an automobile which is operated in any prearranged or organized racing or speed contest.

Expenses for Medical Services (Medical Payments)—There is no coverage for medical expenses incurred by an employee of the Insured who is injured in the course of employment. Nor to the expenses of any person injured while occupying or being struck by an automobile while *away from the premises.* The coverage is also not available for the medical expenses of any person engaged in structural alteration, new construction or demolition operations or of anyone injured in such situations when being performed by independent contractors.

There is no coverage under the *Expenses for Medical Services* section for bodily injury arising out of elevators unless the named Insured does not operate, maintain or control such elevators. Also excluded from coverage is bodily injury due to war, whether declared or not, civil war, insurrection, revolution or any act incident thereto.

Rented Automobiles—With one exception, the Garage Liability policy specifically excludes the Insured's liability arising out of automobiles which he rents to others. An exception is made for an automobile rented to salesmen for use principally in the Insured's business.

It is fairly common in the automobile business for automobile dealers to rent a car to a salesman for demonstration purposes, and any liability imposed on the Insured for accidents caused by such automobiles would be covered under the policy. On the other hand, if the Insured rents automobiles to a customer, there is no coverage under the policy unless endorsed. The exclusion applies only to *rented automobiles.* If the garage *lends* an automobile to a customer while his own car is being repaired, the Garage Liability policy would apply to such automobile. However, if a charge is made for the rental of the substitute vehicle, the policy ceases to cover.

The Garage Liability policy may be endorsed, for an additional premium, to cover automobiles rented to customers while the customers' automobiles are temporarily left with the Insured for servicing, repair or for sale. This extension of the policy is available only under policies written under Division 1.

Haulaway, Tank Trucks, Tank Trailers, Tractors — Haulaways (vehicles used to transport automobiles), tank trucks, tank trailers and tractors used in connection with such vehicles, if owned, hired or held for sale by the Insured, are not insured under the Garage Liability policy while away from the premises except if they are being delivered, demonstrated or tested.

It is important to understand that such vehicles are excluded only if they do not fall within any of the conditions designated. Thus, if the Insured does not own or hire the vehicles and is not holding them for sale, the policy will cover. If such vehicles are on the Insured's premises, they will be covered, even though the Insured owns or hires them or is holding them for sale. Regardless of where they are located and despite the fact that the Insured owns such vehicles, they will be covered if they are being delivered, demonstrated or tested.

Structural Alterations, New Construction or Demolition Operations—The Garage Liability policy specifically excludes accidents caused by independent contractors who are engaged by the Insured to make structural alterations or new construction or perform demolition operations for the Insured, unless notice is given to the

Company within 30 days of the commencement of such operations.

If the Insured is making alterations or doing construction himself or with his own employees, accidents arising out of such work are covered. If he engages independent contractors to do work other than of the type specified, he is covered for any liability that may be imposed on him for accidents arising out of such operations. Thus, if he hires independent contractors to do painting, waxing, cleaning, delivering and similar work, he is covered under his Garage Liability policy for accidents arising out of such operations.

Coverage for the excluded types of independent contractor operations is available under an Owners' and Contractors' Protective Liability policy, discussed in Chapter 25.

Aircraft—Watercraft—The Garage Liability policy specifically excludes accidents arising from any aircraft, or for watercraft when away from the premises.

FOR HOW MUCH

As respects the application of the various limits in the policy, the Garage Liability policy is similar to other Liability forms discussed in Chapter 24. Under the Medical Payments coverage, there is no *per accident* limit, even when written to cover Premises—Operations.

As pointed out before, the Garage Liability policy covers the Products hazard as part of the basic Garage Operations hazard. The limits applicable to accidents arising out of a condition in goods is therefore the same as for any other liabilities covered under the policy without any aggregate limit of liability, as is found in other Products Liability insurance.

Deductible — A $100 Deductible is applicable to the coverage afforded by the policy for property damage to any automobile arising out of work performed on such automobile by the Insured.

Supplementary Payments — Like all Liability policies, the Garage Liability policy provides for defense and supplementary payments. The policy will also pay the cost of Bail Bonds required of the Insured because of accident or traffic law violation, up to $250. Also, the policy will pay up to $25 per day for expenses incurred by the Insured because of his attendance at trials or hearings. Different from other Liability policies, the Garage Liability policy will cover the Insured's actual loss of wages or salary during such appearances.

Other Insurance—If the Insured has any other insurance against a loss covered under his Garage Liability policy, the policy will pay only such proportion of the loss as the limits of liability in the policy bear to the total limits of liability in all insurance which is valid and collectible.

WHO IS COVERED

Other Drivers and Interests (Omnibus Clause)—As under the basic Automobile Liability policy, coverage is included for the use of insured automobiles not only by the named Insured but also by any other person or organization legally responsible for the automobile while it is being driven with the Insured's permission. Such persons are covered as additional Insureds under the policy.

The Garage Liability policy also covers as an additional Insured any partner, employee, director or stockholder while acting within the scope of his employment, and any person who has a financial interest in the business of the named Insured.

The policy does not cover any person as an additional Insured while driving an automobile owned by him or by a member of his household, except for the named Insured, even if being used on garage business. Thus, if a partner operates an automobile which is owned by him or by a member of his family, his *personal* liability will not be covered under the Garage Liability policy. It is important to understand that any liability imposed on the *garage* because of the operation of such privately owned automobiles in the garage's business will be covered under the Garage Liability policy. The *personal* liability of the partner, in this situation, however, must be covered by an individual Automobile Liability policy covering the owner of the automobile.

It is interesting to note, too, that the garage is not covered as an additional Insured under the policy covering the owner of the automobile, since garages are specifically excluded from coverage as additional Insureds under a policy covering a private passenger automobile (discussed in Chapter 26 under HAZARDS COVERED —Other Drivers and Interests—Omnibus Clause).

Right of Third Parties—See Chapter 24.

Legal Representatives—The Garage Liability policy is identical with other Liability forms (see Chapter 25) except that 60 days is allowed for notice to the Company.

WHERE COVERED

Coverage is afforded only for accidents which occur within the United States of America, its territories or possessions, or Canada.

RATES

Rates for Garage Liability insurance vary with the territory in which the risk is located. The rates shown are applied to each $100 of the Insured's annual payroll. For purposes of rating policies written under Division 1, the Insured's payroll is divided into three classes:

Class (a)—This class includes all office employees whose duties are confined exclusively to work of a clerical nature.

Class (b)—This class includes all proprietors, officers, salesmen, general managers, service managers, and chauffeurs. The payroll of all such persons (except inactive officers) is taken at a fixed figure of $2,000 per annum.

If an employee devotes part of his time to office work and has other duties on the Insured's premises, his entire payroll is assigned to Class (b).

Class (c)—This class includes all employees who do not fall within Class (a) or Class (b). In this group will be rated the payroll of all regular employees who are engaged in duties in and around the automobiles serviced, stored or repaired.

Except for those persons whose payroll is taken at a flat figure of $2,000 under Class (b) above, the portion of an employee's payroll which exceeds an average weekly maximum of $100 is omitted, provided the Insured's payroll records are kept in such a manner as makes it possible to determine the excess.

The rates for Class (a) are the lowest. Class (c) rates are approximately four times as high; the rates for Class (b) are the highest, approximately three times as high as for Class (c).

Policies written under Division 2 are rated in the same manner as Division 1 policies except that there is no separation of payroll, all of which is considered as a unit.

Risks with a payroll of $30,000 or more are experience rated.

Whole Dollar Premium Rule—Discussed in Chapter 8 under OTHER FACTORS WHICH AFFECT FIRE INSURANCE RATES—Whole Dollar Premium Rule.

AUTO INSURANCE (ASSIGNED RISK) PLANS

ALTHOUGH AUTOMOBILE Liability insurance is not compulsory for private passenger automobiles (except in Delaware, Florida, Massachusetts, New York, North Carolina, Puerto Rico, and in several other states, for minors), it has long been accepted that owners and operators of motor vehicles should be encouraged to provide protection for injuries or damages they may cause while operating a vehicle on the public streets and highways. Furthermore, Financial Responsibility Laws which have been enacted in almost every state make it virtually impossible for many persons to own or operate a motor vehicle without insurance. We have seen, too, that most carriers of passengers or freight for hire are required to carry Automobile Liability insurance.

In the ordinary conduct of its business, an insurance Company is free to refuse a risk which does not meet with its underwriting standards. It can therefore come about that an individual or a firm which wishes to carry or is required to carry Automobile Liability insurance may be unable to obtain it. In order to make such insurance available to bona fide applicants and to distribute these risks equitably among all companies licensed to write Automobile Liability insurance, every state has enacted special statutes setting up Assigned Risk Plans.

While there are some minor differences in the administration of these statutes, they generally empower the Insurance Commissioner or Superintendent to approve a plan for the distribution of automobile risks among all carriers licensed to write Automobile Liability insurance in the state.

Any eligible risk which cannot procure Automobile Liability insurance in the usual fashion may apply to the Assigned Risk Plan, (known as Automobile Insurance Plans in some states) which will assign a Company to write the risk. The risk is required to complete an application in which he certifies that he has made efforts within the 60 days immediately preceding to obtain insurance and has been refused.

Risks are distributed according to a formula which is designed to allot to each Company an amount of Assigned Risk business which is in proportion to the amount of their net premiums for directly written Automobile Bodily Injury Liability business in the state.

The Plans are administered by a Manager and a Governing Committee which is made up of representatives of the following groups and classes of insurance companies:

Insurance Services Office
Mutual Insurance Rating Bureau
National Association of Independent Insurers
All other capital stock insurance companies
All other non-stock insurance companies.

Limits of Liability—A company to which an automobile risk is assigned under an Assigned Risk Plan is not required to issue the coverage under the Family Automobile policy, and may offer only the basic policy. When the plans were first established they were required to provide no more than the minimum limits stipulated under the Financial Responsibility Law of the state where the risk was located. If the Insured drove into states with higher limits under the Financial Responsibility Law than were in effect in his home state, he could obtain higher limits from the Plan. In such cases, however, the higher limits applied only while he was actually within the neighbor state.

EXAMPLE: A New York applicant to the New York Automobile Insurance Plan will be furnished with limits of $10/20,000 and $5,000, the Financial Responsibility requirements of New York. If the Insured drives through or into Connecticut, he may apply for limits of 20/20 on bodily injury, since these are the minimum limits required under the Connecticut law. The policy will provide 10/20 limits throughout except when the Insured is actually in Connecticut, when the higher limits will apply. The extra premium charge is computed as 75% of the premium ordinarily charged for the additional limits.

Assigned Risk Plan facilities in an increasing number of states now provide Medical Payments coverage in addition to Liability coverages.

In a growing number of states, the Assigned Risk Plan has been mandated to provide limits in excess of the state's Financial Responsibility Law. In some, the extra coverage is being granted voluntarily by the member companies even though there has been no legislation requiring the broadening.

CONNECTICUT, FLORIDA, KANSAS, KENTUCKY, LOUISIANA, MASSACHUSETTS, MICHIGAN, MINNESOTA, MISSOURI, NEW HAMPSHIRE, NEW JERSEY, NEW YORK, NORTH CAROLINA, RHODE ISLAND, SOUTH CAROLINA, VERMONT, WEST VIRGINIA—Limits which exceed the state's Financial Responsibility Laws are available through the Plans on an optional basis.

Further broadening of the facilities of the Plans have been put into effect which now offer Physical Damage and Collision coverages in the following states:

ARIZONA, ARKANSAS, COLORADO, CONNECTICUT, DELAWARE, FLORIDA, HAWAII, ILLINOIS, INDIANA, IOWA, KANSAS, LOUISIANA, MAINE, MARYLAND, MICHIGAN, MINNESOTA, MISSOURI, NEW HAMPSHIRE, NEW JERSEY, NEW MEXICO, NEW YORK, OHIO, RHODE ISLAND, VERMONT, WEST VIRGINIA.

Eligible Risks—There is a growing trend to broadening the eligibility of automobile owners for coverage through the Automobile Insurance Plans.

This easing of eligibility requirements is now in effect in the following states:

ALABAMA, ARIZONA, CALIFORNIA, COLORADO, CONNECTICUT, DELAWARE, DISTRICT OF COLUMBIA, FLORIDA, GEORGIA, HAWAII, ILLINOIS, INDIANA, IOWA, KANSAS, LOUISIANA, MAINE, MARYLAND, MICHIGAN, MINNESOTA, NEW HAMPSHIRE, NEW JERSEY, NEW MEXICO, NEW YORK, NORTH CAROLINA, OHIO, OREGON, PENNSYLVANIA, RHODE ISLAND, SOUTH CAROLINA, TENNESSEE, TEXAS, VERMONT, VIRGINIA, WEST VIRGINIA.

Ineligible Risks—Some states still spell out a number of factors which will render an applicant ineligible; principally, being engaged in an illegal enterprise, or having been convicted of a felony within 36 months preceding the date of application.

Initial Payment with Application—In almost every instance, the applicant is required to make some payment with his application. In the majority of the states, an investigation fee, usually $5, must be paid with the application, and this fee is credited towards the first premium, if and when the policy is issued.

In every instance, some payment is required with the application—generally a fixed amount.

DISTRICT OF COLUMBIA, PENNSYLVANIA, PUERTO RICO—A deposit of 30% is required on all private passenger automobile applications.

GEORGIA, KENTUCKY, MASSACHUSETTS, SOUTH CAROLINA, TENNESSEE, TEXAS, VIRGINIA, WASHINGTON—The full annual premium is required on all applications for insurance on private passenger automobiles.

OREGON—A $40 per car deposit is required.

Rate Surcharges—The provisions for surcharge of risks which are assigned by the Plan vary among the states. The most usual practice is to write any risk which has no record (clean business) at the regular manual rates without surcharge. If the applicant has been involved in a single accident or convicted of one minor infraction, a surcharge of 10% is made on public passenger and long-haul trucking risks; 25% on all others. If the applicant has been convicted of a serious offense, or has been involved in two or more accidents, or convicted of two or more offenses, the surcharge is 35%. A similar surcharge is also made of any risk which is required to file proof of financial responsibility, regardless of convictions or accidents.

FOR FURTHER READING

ACKERMAN—Insurance

BURNSIDE—New and Broader Garage Liability Insurance

CHART ANALYSIS OF AUTOMOBILE ASSIGNED RISK PLANS—American Insurance Association

GEE—Agent's Automobile Guide

HEDGES—Practical Fire and Casualty Insurance

MEHR AND CAMMACK—Principles of Insurance

POLICY, FORM AND MANUAL ANALYSIS SERVICE

RIEGEL, ROBERT AND MILLER—Insurance

(See Reading List at End of Book)

CHAPTER 28

Compulsory Insurance and Financial Responsibility Laws (Motor Vehicle)

EVERY STATE of this country and every province of Canada has enacted some type of Financial Responsibility Law in connection with the right to own and operate motor vehicles. These laws, also known as Safety Responsibility Laws, are designed to protect the public against drivers and owners of automobiles who are financially unable to pay for injuries or property damage they may cause.

SECURITY-TYPE LAWS

The following analysis of Security-Type Laws is quoted, with permission, from Rough Notes Policy, Form and Manual Analysis Service. For chart Analysis of Financial Responsibility Laws, reprinted with permission of the American Insurance Association, see pages 520-21.

FIFTY STATES, the District of Columbia and ten Canadian provinces have Security-Type laws that prohibit anyone involved in any accident from driving unless he can show he can pay damages. These laws are largely based on a model safety responsibility law, Act IV of the Uniform Vehicle Code. The laws function as follows, with some variations effected by individual state legislatures:

Accidents—Administrative officers responsible for enforcing the laws require sufficient security to satisfy any judgment from a vehicle operator involved in an accident resulting in bodily injury or in damage to property in excess of minimum indicated in chart. They may also, at their discretion, require proof of financial responsibility for a period of one year following the accident.

Security is usually not required when the insurance Company of the operator or owner of the vehicle furnishes a notice FS-1 (SR-21) stating that an acceptable amount of Automobile Liability insurance was in effect at the time of the accident. Operator's license is suspended when the operator is unable to furnish security or proof of financial responsibility. Such suspension continues until security or proof is filed or until one year after the accident, if no action is brought.

Convictions—The Bureau of Motor Vehicles or similar authority may suspend the operator's license and vehicle registration certificates of any person convicted for offenses under the motor vehicle laws of the state. Suspension follows manslaughter, intoxication, fleeing scene of accident and frequent reckless driving. Suspension is ended only when an individual is able to give proof of financial responsibility for the future. This can be done by an insurance company filing SR-22, proof of Automobile Liability insurance.

Judgments—When a driver fails to satisfy judgments within a specified period for bodily injury or property damage, his operator's license and registration certificates are suspended by the commissioner or other responsible person. Suspension continues until the obligation is paid and proof of financial responsibility is given for the future.

Proof of Financial Responsibility is usually evidenced by: Certificate of an insurance company, certifying that it has issued an Automobile Liability policy; Bond of a Surety company; receipt of the state treasurer for a deposit of a specified amount of cash or securities. Almost all of the states require proof of ability to pay any judgment up to $10,000 for one person or $20,000 for all persons killed or injured in a single accident and $5,000 for property damage. (See charts on following pages for requirements of individual states.)

COMPULSORY LAWS

The subject of compulsory Automobile Liability insurance has been a controversial one for many years. There are compelling arguments both in favor of it and against it. One of the fundamental arguments against it is that it would be unnecessary if the Financial Responsibility Laws were properly enforced. Be that as it may, compulsory laws, applicable to all vehicles are in force in four states or territories; some form of compulsory insurance affecting only stated situations is in effect in four other states. We present herewith a digest of those laws because of their effect upon financial responsibility requirements:

Connecticut. Vehicles (other than farm vehicles) owned by minors cannot be registered without proof of financial responsibility. No driver under the age of 18 may operate a motor vehicle unless it is insured.

Delaware. Every owner must carry liability insurance for bodily injury, death or property damage of at least $25,000.

Florida. Every owner of a motor vehicle must carry insurance which qualifies under the state's Financial Responsibility Act.

Illinois. A firm in the business of leasing trucks must submit a photocopy of the policy covering its vehicles, unless it has qualified as a self-insurer.

Maryland. Proof of financial responsibility must accompany the application of any minor for a driving license, and must be maintained until age 21.

Massachusetts. The law applies to all owners of motor vehicles registered in the state and all vehicles operated within the state for more than 30 days in any year. Guest coverage is excluded. Operation of a vehicle without the required proof punishable by fine of $100 to $500 or imprisonment of one year.

New York. Applicable to all owners of motor vehicles registered in the state and to all owners and operators of motor vehicles used in the state, resident and non-resident. Coverage is prescribed by regulation. Territory affected is the entire United States and Canada. A policy need not be coterminous with a vehicle registration. Before a motor vehicle can be registered in the state, the owner must produce proof of insurance. The insurance company issues a two-part Insurance Identification Card which certifies that an Automobile Liability policy has been issued to the Insured. This card, the FS 20, is valid for twelve months. A new card is issued upon renewal of the policy.

The Insured is required to carry his ID Card in the motor vehicle at all times, as well as the time when registration procedure is put into effect. Failure to produce the ID Card is considered presumptive evidence that the vehicle is uninsured, and subjects the owner to heavy fine.

North Carolina. Applicable to all owners of motor vehicles registered in the state. Required coverage is in accordance with proof of financial responsibility as defined in the Financial Responsibility Law. Territory affected is the entire United States and Canada. A policy need not be coterminous with a vehicle registration. The owner must file a Certificate of Insurance. The owner of a motor vehicle registered in the state who operates or permits operation without financial responsibility in effect is guilty of a misdemeanor.

Puerto Rico. Applicable to all owners of motor vehicles registered in Puerto Rico. Coverage is prescribed by statute and the territory affected is Puerto Rico.

ANALYSIS OF LAWS RELATING TO AUTOMOBILE INSURANCE

(Compiled by the Law Department, American Insurance Association)

Chart I – Financial Responsibility and Related

November 1971 (Corrected 1/72)

State	Liability limits	Compulsory liability insurance	No fault or first party benefits	Uninsured motorist coverage (M-Mandatory; R-Subject to rejection)	FINANCIAL RESPONSIBILITY LAWS: Scope (P–Proof; S–Security; Sat.–Satisfaction. Figures indicate number of years proof required)			Accidents								Supplementary laws
					Accidents	Convictions	Judgments	Minimum property damage	Requires security (S), proof (P); from driver (D), owner (O)	Regardless of fault? (ss)	Applicable by reciprocity to accidents in other states?	Insurance in effect: Information required in accident report?	Insurance in effect: Notice or verification required from insurer? (* - Only if policy not in effect)	Other exemptions: 1. Parked car; 2. Car stopped, standing or parked; 3. Certain motor carriers; 4. Certain publicly owned vehicles.	Unusual provisions	
Alabama	10/20/5			R	S	P - 3	Sat. & P - 3	$50	S - D & O	Yes	Yes	Yes	Verif.	1,3,4		
Alaska	15/30/5			R	S & P - 3	P - 3	Sat. & P - 3	$200	S & P - D (v)	Yes	Yes	Yes	Verif.*	1,4(s)	(gg)	
Arizona	10/20/5			R	S & P - 3	P - 3	Sat. & P - 3	$100	S & P - D & O	Yes	Yes	Yes	Verif.*	2,3,4(r) (s)		
Arkansas	10/20/5			R	S	P - 3	Sat. & P - 3	$100	S - D & O	Yes	Yes	Yes	Notice (o)	1,3,4(r)		
California	15/30/5			R	S (y)	P - 3	Sat. & P - 3	$200	S - D & O (y)(v)	No	No	Yes	Verif.*	1,4(r)	(aa)	IMP
Colorado	15/30/5			R	S (uu)	P - 3 (dd)	Sat. & P - 3	$100	S - D & O (uu)	No	Yes	Yes	Verif.*	1,4	(hh) (oo)	
Connecticut	20/40/5	(b)		M	S	P - 3	Sat.	$400	S - D & O	No	Yes	Yes	Verif.*	1,3,4(p) (r)		
Delaware	10/20/5 †	Yes	See Chart II	R	S	P - 3	Sat. & P - 3	$100	S - D & O	Yes	No	Yes	Notice	1,3,4	(ff)	
Dist. of Col.	10/20/5			No prov.	S	P - 3	Sat. & P - 3	$100	S - D & O	Yes	Yes	Yes	Verif.	1,3,4(r)		
Florida	10/20/5	Yes	See Chart II	R	S & P - 3	P - 3	Sat. & P - 3	$200	S & P - D & O	Yes	Yes	Yes (m)	Verif.*	1,4	(xx)	
Georgia	10/20/5			R	S & P-1 (tt)	P - 1 (tt)	Sat.	$100 (f)	S & P - D & O	Yes	Yes	Yes	Notice	1,3,4	(hh)	
Hawaii	10/20/5			R	S	P - 3	Sat. & P - 3	$100	S - D & O	Yes	No	No	Notice	1,3,4	(gg)	
Idaho	10/20/5			R	S (y)	P - 3	Sat. & P - 3	$100	S - D & O (y)	Yes	Yes	Yes	Notice	1,4		
Illinois	10/20/5		See Chart II	R(ll)	S	P - 3	Sat. & P - 3	$250	S & P - D & O	Yes	Yes	Yes	Verif.*	1,3,4	(pp)	
Indiana	15/30/10			R	S & P - 1 (d)	P - 3	Sat. & P - 3	$100	S & P - D & O (x)	Yes	No	Yes	Notice	3	(xx)	
Iowa	10/20/5			R	S	P - 3	Sat. & P - 3	$100	S - D & O	Yes	No	Yes	Verif.*	2,3,4		
Kansas	15/30/5*			R	S & P - 3	P - 2	Sat. & P - 2	$100	S - D & O	Yes	Yes	Yes	Verif.*	1,3,4	(vv)	
Kentucky	10/20/5			R	S	P - 3	Sat. & P - 3	$100	S - D & O	Yes	No	Yes	Verif.*	1,4		
Louisiana	5/10/1			R	S	P - 3	Sat. & P - 3	$200	S - D & O (n)	Yes	Yes	Yes	Verif.*	1,3,4 (mm)	(hh)	
Maine	20/40/10			M	S & P (a)	P - 3	Sat. & P - 3	$200	S & P - D & O	No	Yes	Yes	Verif.*	3,4		
Maryland	15/30/5			No prov.	S		Sat.	$100	S - D & O	No	Yes	Yes	Notice	1(r)		UJ3
Massachusetts	5/10/5	Yes	See Chart II	M	(ee)		Sat. (P. D.)		(ee)							
Michigan	20/40/10			R		P - 3	Sat. & P - 3									UJ4
Minnesota	10/20/5		OFP1	(bb)	S	P - 3	Sat. & P - 3	$100	S - D & O	No	Yes	Yes	Verif.*	2,4(r)	(gg)	
Mississippi	5/10/5			R	S & P - 3	P - 3	Sat. & P - 3	$100	S & P - D & O	Yes	Yes	Yes	Verif.*	1,4		
Missouri	10/20/2			M	S	P - 3	Sat. & P - 3	$100	S - D & O	Yes	Yes	Yes	Verif.*	1,3,4		
Montana	10/20/5			R	S	P - 3	Sat. & P - 3	$250	S - D & O	Yes	Yes	Yes	Verif.*	1,3,4		
Nebraska	10/20/5			R	S & P - 3	P - 3	Sat. & P - 3	$100	S & P - D & O	Yes	Yes	Yes	Verif.*	1,4	(l) (qq)	
Nevada	15/30/5			R	S (y)	P - 3	Sat. & P - 3	$250	S - D & O (y)	Yes	Yes	Yes	Verif.*	1,4		
New Hamp.	20/40/5		FP	M	S & P - 3	P - 3 (d)	Sat. & P - 3	$50	S & P - D & O	No	Yes	Yes	Verif.	4		
New Jersey	10/20/5			R	S	P - 3	Sat. & P - 3	$200	S - D & O	Yes	Yes	Yes	Verif.*	1,3,4(s)	(z)	UJ2
New Mexico	10/20/5			R		P - 3	Sat. & P - 3	$100							(hh)	
New York	10/20/5	Yes		M	S		Sat.	$200	S - D & O	Yes	Yes	Yes	No	3,4	(gg)	IC
North Carolina	10/20/5	Yes		R	S (e)		Sat.	$200	S - D & O	No (e)	Yes	Yes	Verif.*	1,3,4(rr)	(gg) (hh)	
North Dakota	10/20/5			M	S (h) P	P - 3	Sat. & P - 3	$100	S (h) or P - D	No (h)	Yes	No	Notice	2,4	(gg) (h)	UJ1
Ohio	12.5/25/7.5			R	S	P - 3	Sat. & P - 3	$100	S - D & O	Yes	Yes	Yes	Notice	1,4	(l)	
Oklahoma	5/10/5			R	S & P - 3 (t)	P - 3	Sat. & P - 3	$100	S & P - D & O (t)	Yes	Yes	Yes	Verif.*	1,3,4	(qq)	
Oregon	10/20/5		See Chart II	M	P - 5	P - 5	Sat. & P - 5	$200	P - D & O	Yes	Yes	Yes	Verif.*	1,3,4		
Pennsylvania	10/20/5			M	S	P - 3	Sat. & P - 3	$100	S - D & O	Yes	Yes	Yes	Verif.*	1,4		
Puerto Rico		Yes	See Chart II	No prov.												
Rhode Island	10/20/5	(c)		R	S	P - 1	Sat. & P - 1	$150	S - D & O	Yes	Yes	Yes	Verif.*	2.4		
South Carolina	10/20/5			M	S & P - 3	P - 3	Sat. & P - 3	$100	S & P - D & O	Yes	Yes	Yes	Verif.*	1,3,4	(nn) (hh)	
South Dakota	15/30/10		OFP2	R	S	P - 3	Sat. & P - 3	$100	S - D & O	Yes	Yes	Yes	Verif.*	1,3,4		
Tennessee	10/20/5			R	S & P - 3	P - 3	Sat. & P - 3	$200	S & P - D & O	Yes	Yes	Yes	Verif.*	1,3,4	(l) (qq)	
Texas	10/20/5			R	S & P - 5	P - 5	Sat. & P - 5	$250	S & P - D & O	Yes	Yes	Yes	Verif.*	1,3,4(jj)	(ii) (hh)	
Utah	10/20/5			R	S	P - 3	Sat. & P - 3	$100	S - D (v)	Yes	Yes	Yes	No	1,4(r)(s)		
Vermont	10/20/5			M	S & P - 3 (j)	P - 3	Sat. & P - 3	$100(j)	S & P - D	(j)	(ww)	Yes	Verif.*	1	(gg) (j)	
Virginia	20/30/5			M	S	P - 3	Sat. & P - 3	$50	S - D	No	No	Yes	Notice	1,3,4(i)	(f)	
Washington	15/30/5			R	S & P - 3	P - 3	Sat. & P - 3	$100	S & P - D & O	Yes	Yes	Yes	Verif.*	1,4	(gg)	
West Virginia	10/20/5			M	S	P - 3	Sat. & P - 3	$100	S - D & O	Yes	No	Yes	Verif.*	1,4	(aa)	
Wisconsin	15/30/5		OMP	M	S	P - 3	Sat. & P - 3	$200	S - D & O	Yes	Yes	Yes	Verif.* (kk)	1,3,4		
Wyoming	10/20/5			R	S	P - 3	Sat. & P - 3	$250	S - D & O	Yes	Yes	Yes	Notice	1,4		

*—Effective July 1, 1972.

†—$25,000 single limit under compulsory law, plus $5,000 for damages to property other than motor vehicle.

a—Security and proof requirement may be waived 6 years after accident. Proof requirement may be waived 3 years after request for compliance if security filed.

b—Vehicles owned by minors cannot be registered unless proof filed; minors under 18 may operate only insured vehicles.

c—Minors owning motor vehicles must furnish proof before registration.

d—Requirement of proof discretionary.

e—Appeal to court automatically stays suspension, and court may exempt motorist not at fault.

f—Where damage is less than $300, security not required in behalf of non-resident except on request.

h—Adjudication of responsibility required as prerequisite to security.

i—Person whose proof furnished by employer.

j—Security required only if operator is convicted as a result of accident. No property damage minimum if convicted.

k—In case of unique hardship Commissioner may dispense with release.

l—Minimum security $500 on bodily injury.

m—Motorist completes and returns SR-21 form mailed by F.R. Division.

n-Registration of owner not suspended where under law owner is not legally liable.

o—Insurer must pay $5 filing fee if SR-21 not filed within 50 days after accident.

p—Car stopped at stop sign or light, or where other person convicted.

q—Inapplicable to person who was unable to procure insurance because of race or color.

r—Person who has received payment for his damages.

s—Operator employed by owner.

t—In hardship cases court may modify extent of compliance with security requirement, and in that event proof is required.

u—If insurer of any operator settles, all operators deemed released.

v—Owner subject to law if employer of driver. In that event registration of employer suspended.

w—Privilege to drive as chauffeur in course of employment not suspended.

x—Discretionary as to owner.

y—When license restored after lapse of 1 year without suit, proof must be given for 3 years.

z—Non-owner subject to requirements may operate vehicle when owner has furnished proof.

aa—Applicable only to accidents on streets and highways.

bb—Mandatory for private passenger vehicles; may be rejected as to others.

dd—Requires showing of insurance after suspension for accumulation of points.

ee—In action against nonresident, plaintiff may move for security.

ff-Commissioner may issue limited license or registration when necessary for occupation or livelihood.

gg—Law affects driving licenses only, not registrations.

hh—$10 fee on reinstatement of license.

ii—Minimum security $200.

jj—Car stopped at traffic signal.

kk—As respects permission, insurer may correct report only by filing affidavit within 30 days after receipt.

ll—When insured purchases excess coverage under no-fault law.

mm-Where operator of other vehicle is convicted of drunk driving, negligent injury or negligent homicide.

nn-Minimum security $250.

oo—Request for hearing stays suspension.

pp—Minimum security $250.

qq—$25 fee on filing proof.

rr—Commissioner may exempt person where another person involved has been convicted.

ss—U.S. Supreme Court (Bell v. Burson, 91 Supr. Ct. Rep. 1586) held that state must provide forum for determination whether there is reasonable possibility of judgment.

tt—Also requires showing of insurance after minor violations. Second time proof required it shall be maintained for 3 years.

uu—Also requires showing of insurance in effect at time of deposit.

vv—$25 fee on reinstatement after suspension for failure to deposit security.

ww—License suspended for failure to furnish proof required because of accident in another state.

xx—$5 on reinstatement of license.

UJ1-Unsatisfied Judgment Fund, state operated, effective 7/1/47; assessment on all motorists (Maximum $1); applies to b.i. judgments, including hit-and-run cases, obtained by residents, $300 deductible.

UJ2—Unsatisfied Claim and Judgment Fund, insurance company operated, effective 4/1/55; assessment on uninsured motorists (maximum $50) and on insurers (maximum 1/2 of 1% of premium); applies to b.i. and p.d. claims, including b.i in hit-and-run cases, of residents and (non-residents, subject to reciprocity); $100 deductible from p.d. claims.

UJ3—Unsatisfied Claim and Judgment Fund, insurance company operated, effective 6/1/59; assessments on insurers (maximum 2% of premium) and remainder on uninsured motorists; applies to b.i. and p.d. claims, including b.i. in hit-and-run and insolvency cases, of residents (and non-residents, subject to reciprocity); $100 deductible.

UJ4—Accident Claims Fund, state operated, effective 1/1/66; assessment of $45 on uninsured motorists; $1 on others; applies to p.d. in excess of $200 and b.i., including b.i. in hit-and-run cases.

IC—Motor Vehicle Indemnification Corporation, insurance company operated and supported, pays to limits of 10/20 b.i. claims of "qualified persons" (Persons not covered under u.m.c.) resulting from accidents caused by financially irresponsible motorists, including hit-and-run and disclaimer cases. Effective 1/1/59. Also provides that where owner or operator of motor vehicle involved in b.i. accident fails to produce proof of financial security with 48 hours any peace officer may impound vehicle or owner shall cause vehicle to be stored until final disposition of claim. Prior liens not affected.

IMP—Vehicle involved in accident must be stored until owner or operator complies with financial responsibility law.

OFP-1—No policy shall be issued with respect to any automobile registered or principally garaged in the state unless coverage is made available for accidental death benefits of at least $10,000 for the named insured, indemnity of at least $60 per week for at least 52 weeks while the named insured is prevented from performing the usual duties of his regular occupation, and medical payments coverage of $2,000 per person; if injured person not gainfully employed, weekly indemnity reduced by 50%; insured may accept in writing all or any of the coverages.

OFP-2—No policy shall be issued with respect to any automobile registered or principally garaged in this state unless coverage is made available for accidental death benefits of at least $10,000 for the named insured. Indemnity of at least $60 per week after 14 days, for at least 52 weeks while the named insured is prevented from performing the usual duties of his regular occupation, and medical payments coverage of $2,000 per person; if injured person not gainfully employed, weekly indemnity reduced by 50%; insured may accept in writing all or any of the coverages.

FP Policy covering private passenger car shall, unless person has equivalent coverage, include medical payments coverage of at least $1,000.

OMP-Requires $1,000 medical payments coverage unless rejected. (Effective 5/18/72).

Rhode Island. Owners of motor vehicles who are under 21 must furnish proof of financial responsibility with limits of $10/20,000-$5,000 in order to register the vehicle.

FOR FURTHER READING

AUTOMOBILE LIABILITY SECURITY LAWS OF THE UNITED STATES (Individual pamphlets for each of the states of the United States and the provinces of Canada)—American Insurance Association.

KULP AND HALL—Casualty Insurance

POLICY, FORM & MANUAL ANALYSIS SERVICE.

(See Reading List at End of Book)

CHAPTER 29

Automobile Physical Damage Insurance

IT IS OBVIOUS that every automobile owner is exposed to the threat of loss by fire, theft, lightning, windstorm, flood, malicious mischief, collisions in which no other person is at fault, and countless other perils.

Special forms of insurance are made available to cover the hazards that face automobile property. These policies which cover physical damage to automobiles are written as a separate contract, or in a Combination policy with the Liability coverages. It is important to understand that there is no coverage for any loss or damage to the vehicle itself unless such coverage is specifically provided in the policy.

An automobile may be insured against loss or damage due to certain specific perils, i. e., fire, theft, windstorm, earthquake, explosion, etc. These perils are usually grouped together under individual coverages, some of which may be purchased alone, while others are made available only in combination.

Most commonly, however, Physical Damage insurance on vehicles, particularly of the private passenger type, is purchased under a Comprehensive Physical Damage policy, which provides insurance on an "all-risk" basis. This policy will be analyzed below, after which the various specific coverages will be outlined.

Family Automobile Policy—See *Eligibility for Family Automobile Policy,* discussed at beginning of Chapter 26.

MASSACHUSETTS—The Family Automobile policy is not available.

COMPREHENSIVE PHYSICAL DAMAGE INSURANCE

(Material Damage Policy)

EACH AUTOMOBILE to be covered is listed in the policy, and is fully described. In addition, the Insured is required to set forth certain facts regarding the purchase and ownership of the vehicle (discussed later under Insured's Statements).

Equipment—The policy covers not only the described automobile but also the equipment of the vehicle and any other equipment which is permanently attached.

Sound Reproducing or Recording Equipment—The policy does not cover loss or damage to any device or instrument for the recording or reproduction of sound *unless it is permanently installed in the automobile,* nor any tape, wire, record, disc or other medium for use with such equipment.

Coverage for stereo tapes may be purchased for an additional premium. The endorsement, *Limited Insurance for Certain Sound Reproducing or Recording Tapes,* affords protection against theft or accidental loss of or damage to the tapes (including wires, record discs or other media) subject to a maximum of $200 in any one loss. Coverage applies only to tapes owned by the Insured (or a relative who is a resident of his household) if the loss occurs while the tapes are in the car owned by the Insured or his wife or in a vehicle being used by them temporarily while their own is being repaired.

Newly Acquired Automobile—If the Insured or his spouse acquires an automobile to replace the one insured in the policy, the automobile is automatically covered, provided the Company is notified within 30 days. If he or his spouse acquires a new car in addition to the one described in the policy, similar automatic coverage is extended to the new automobile, but only if the Company insures all the automobiles which were owned by the Insured or his spouse when the new automobile was acquired.

Family Automobile Policy—*Notice of the acquisition of a new vehicle may be given at any time during the policy period.*

Loss of Use by Theft—Rental Reimbursement—The Comprehensive Physical Damage policy will also pay, when the insured vehicle has been stolen, for the expenses incurred by the Insured in renting a substitute vehicle. This coverage will be discussed under HAZARDS COVERED—Loss of Use by Theft—Rental Reimbursement.

General Average and Salvage Charges — The Comprehensive Physical Damage policy covers all general average and salvage for which the Insured may become liable. (These coverages are discussed in Chapter 22.)

Rented or Borrowed Utility Trailer—Under the Family Automobile policy, such equipment is insured subject to a maximum limit of $500. The policy will not cover a trailer owned by the Insured unless it is declared in the policy.

Family Automobile Policy—*Robes, Wearing Apparel, Personal Effects—The Family Automobile policy provides $100 of coverage on robes, wearing apparel and other personal effects which are damaged or destroyed by fire and lightning while in any automobile owned by the Insured.*

HAZARDS COVERED

The Comprehensive Physical Damage policy does not enumerate the perils which are insured against. Coverage is provided on an "all-risk" basis against all direct and accidental loss of or damage to the automobile except when caused by perils which are specifically excluded. Like all "all-risk" insurance, the policy specifically excludes certain perils, and these are discussed later under HAZARDS NOT COVERED. In addition, the basic insuring clause stipulates that there is no coverage for loss caused by any of the following:

1. Collision of the automobile with another object.

Collision and Upset insurance is an optional coverage. No coverage is provided under the basic Comprehensive Physical Damage policy for collision losses, whether with another automobile or with a stationary object. (For several exceptions, see Breakage of Glass, Etc., below.)

2. Upset of the automobile.

3. Collision of the automobile with a vehicle to which it is attached.

Certain types of loss are specifically excepted from the meaning of the words "collision or upset." These exceptions do, therefore, fall within the coverage of the Comprehensive Physical Damage policy. They are discussed directly below, under Breakage of Glass and Loss by Missiles, Falling Objects, Vandalism, Etc.

While the policy is very broad in its scope, it is intended to cover only *accidental* loss. There would be no coverage for losses caused *deliberately*, as when an Insured who has locked himself out of his automobile breaks a window in order to gain access to the vehicle.

Family Automobile Policy—*Since the Family Automobile policy covers "owned" automobiles as well as "non-owned" automobiles, all the coverages applicable to the insured vehicle will be available to the Insured on any automobile which he uses, but only for non-owned vehicles of the private passenger type which are not furnished for his regular use and only if such vehicle is not insured. If the non-owned vehicle is insured but with a deductible which is higher than the one provided in the Insured's own policy, he can look to his policy for the difference in the deductible.*

Breakage of Glass and Loss by Missiles, Falling Objects, Vandalism, Contact With Animals, Etc.—The insuring clause of the Comprehensive Physical Damage coverage of the policy specifically excludes loss caused by collision or upset of the vehicle. All other accidental loss or damage is covered, except for several minor exclusions (discussed later).

It is important to understand, however, that certain types of loss are specifically omitted from the meaning of the words "collision or upset." Any peril which is so excepted would therefore fall within the coverage of the basic policy. Thus, the policy stipulates that any breakage of glass shall not be deemed to be a loss by collision. If a vehicle is involved in a collision, and the radiator and grill are damaged and several windows are broken, the Comprehensive Physical Damage policy *will* cover the windows, even though the breakage resulted from a collision. However, the damage to the radiator and grill will *not* be covered.

The following perils are specifically enumerated in the policy as losses which are *not* deemed to be loss by "collision or upset":

1. Breakage of glass
2. Missiles and falling objects
3. Fire, explosion
4. Windstorm, hail, water, flood, earthquake
5. Vandalism, riot, civil commotion
6. Theft.

Family Automobile Policy—*The policy also covers damage due to contact with animals or birds.*

Any loss caused by one of these enumerated perils is covered under the Comprehensive Physical Damage section, whether it involves a collision or not. Thus, if a tree falls over on an automobile, the loss is covered under the Comprehensive Physical Damage policy, since it was caused by a falling object. On the other hand, if the automobile runs into a tree, there would be no coverage, since the loss was caused by collision with another object.

The question of whether a particular loss is due to collision or to one of the excepted perils is often a close one, but it is generally held that if the proximate cause of the loss was one of perils specifically mentioned in the policy as "not deemed to be collision or upset," the loss is covered.

Thus, if vandals deliberately released the brakes of an automobile and allowed it to run downhill, and it crashed into a pole and was wrecked, the loss would be considered as caused by vandalism and not by collision. As such, it would be covered under the Comprehensive Physical Damage policy. Similarly, if an automobile is stolen, and is wrecked by the thief in a collision, the loss would be considered a loss by theft, and would fall within the Comprehensive Physical Damage policy.

Loss of Use by Theft—Rental Reimbursement—If an insured vehicle is stolen, the Company will pay for the vehicle or for damages done to the vehicle during the theft. In addition, the policy will also reimburse the Insured for the expense he incurs in renting a substitute automobile or taxicabs, up to $5 a day. The maximum recovery for rental reimbursement is limited to $150 or the actual cash value of the stolen automobile, whichever is less.

The Insured is not entitled to reimbursement for any expenses he incurs before 72 hours after the theft has been reported to the police *and* the insurance Company. Furthermore, he is not entitled to reimbursement for any expenses he incurs after the date on which the whereabouts of the automobile becomes known to the Insured or the Company, or after the Company has paid the Insured for the automobile.

EXAMPLE: An automobile is stolen during the night of June 2. The Insured reports the loss to the insurance Company and the police at 9:00 A. M. on June 3. He hires a substitute vehicle from an automobile rental agency on June 3 at the rate of $8 per day. The Company will pay him $5 (the maximum under the policy) for each day after 9:00 A. M. on June 6 for his rental expenses. If the automobile is still undiscovered 30 days later, on July 6, and the loss has not been paid by the Company, the Insured is not entitled to any further reimbursement for loss of use, since he will have received $150, the maximum payable under this coverage.

On the other hand, if the automobile is discovered on June 10, even though it is recovered in a condition unfit for use, the Company is not required to pay any further rental reimbursement after the date of the discovery of the automobile. In no event, however, is the Insured entitled to receive reimbursement for loss of use by theft which exceeds the actual cash value. Thus, if the stolen vehicle at the time of the loss was worth only $100, the maximum recoverable for rental of a substitute vehicle would be $100.

The reimbursement for loss of use is payable *in addition* to the indemnity for the automobile itself. Thus, if in the illustration just used, the Insured had received $150 for rental of a substitute automobile, and the stolen vehicle was never recovered, he would then receive indemnity for the automobile itself. No deduction from the settlement would be made for the money already paid out for rental reimbursement.

No reimbursement is made except for expenses actually incurred by the Insured. Generally, the Company will ask for receipts or other verification of the money paid out by the Insured for renting a substitute automobile or taxicabs.

Reimbursement for loss of use is available only after the automobile has been *stolen*. There is no similar reimbursement for hiring a substitute vehicle when the insured automobile is damaged or destroyed by any other peril.

Family Automobile Policy—*The Loss of Use by Theft coverage is considerably broader under the Family Automobile policy. Reimbursement will be made at the rate of $10 per day, subject to a maximum of $300, not only for the cost of hiring a substitute automobile but for all transportation expenses. Indemnity becomes payable beginning within 48 hours after the loss is reported to the Company and the police, and is payable until the Company pays for the loss or the automobile is returned to use.*

Indemnity for loss of use is payable in addition to the actual cash value of the automobile, if the vehicle is not recovered.

Loss of Use By Perils Other Than Theft—Rental Reimbursement—In some 35 states, the policy may be extended to provide rental reimbursement when the vehicle is withdrawn from use because of a collision or other peril which is covered under the Comprehensive Physical Damage policy.

The limit of liability is the same as outlined directly above under *Family Automobile Policy*. Reimbursement will be made for the cost of renting a substitute automobile, but such charges will not include mileage charges.

HAZARDS NOT COVERED

The Comprehensive Physical Damage coverage has several exclusions which will be discussed in this section. Collision and Upset are *not* among the perils enumerated in the exclusions, but these important hazards are eliminated in the insuring clause. (See discussion of this important point under HAZARDS COVERED in the preceding section.) In addition, the Comprehensive Physical Damage coverage specifically excludes the following perils:

Public or Livery Conveyance—Policy specifically excludes coverage under any of its provisions while the automobile is used as a public or livery conveyance. Any carrying of passengers for hire, or renting the automobile to others for their use would suspend coverage under the policy, unless such use is stated in the policy. Car pools and other "share the ride" arrangements, even though the passengers contribute to the expense, are not considered carrying passengers for hire.

Wear and Tear, Freezing, Mechanical Breakdown, Etc. — The policy does not cover any loss which is due and confined to wear and tear, freezing, mechanical or electrical breakdown or failure, unless such damage is the result of other loss covered under the policy.

To be excluded, the loss must be due and confined to one of the listed perils. Thus, damage to the radiator of the car by freezing would not be covered. However, if a fire broke out in the wiring of the automobile and it became impossible to move the car, as a result of which the radiator was damaged by freezing, the loss would be covered, since the freezing would be due to another loss which is covered under the policy.

Damage to Tires—The policy specifically excludes any damage to tires unless caused by fire or stolen, or unless such damage occurs at the same time and from the same cause as other loss which is covered under the policy.

Thus, if vandals slash the tires of an automobile, there is no coverage under the policy. On the other hand, if the vandals also damage the windows of the automobile or the engine, the entire loss would be covered. Similarly, if an explosion damages the tires of an automobile and the body, the damage to the tires would be covered, since it was coincident with other loss under the policy.

Family Automobile Policy—*The policy will pay for damage to tires by vandalism or malicious mischief whether or not it occurs at the same time as other loss covered by the policy.*

War, Invasion, Insurrection, Etc.—There is no coverage under the policy for loss due to war, whether declared or not, nor for loss due to civil war, insurrection, rebellion or revolution or to any act or condition incident to such events or to confiscation by duly constituted governmental or civil authority.

Radioactive Contamination—The policy excludes loss due to radioactive contamination.

NEW YORK—This exclusion is not applicable.

Loss Due to Conversion, Embezzlement, Etc. — The policy excludes loss due to conversion, embezzlement or secretion by any person in lawful possession of the automobile under a bailment lease, conditional sale, mortgage or other encumbrance.

Loss to Automobile Subject to Undeclared Bailment Lease, Mortgage, Etc. — The Insured is required to declare in the policy any encumbrance to which the automobile is subject or to which it becomes subject during the term of the policy on his automobile (discussed later under Insured's Statements). If he fails to disclose the existence of such encumbrance, there is no coverage under the policy for any loss.

Family Automobile Policy—*Under this form, is it not necessary* *to report the existence of a bailment lease, conditional sale, purchase agreement, mortgage or other encumbrance.*

Illicit Trade or Transportation—Some Companies incorporate an exclusion of loss or damage to the vehicle while it is being used in any illicit trade or transportation.

FOR HOW MUCH

Comprehensive Physical Damage policies covering an automobile may be written in one of two ways, each of which is discussed directly below: (1) Actual Cash Value basis, or (2) Stated Amount basis. (In addition, a third form of policy is made available by some companies, and this alternate method of insuring is discussed after the more usual forms.)

It is important to understand that the Company's liability under either of the basic forms is limited to the actual cash value of the automobile. Furthermore, the Company has the option of paying for the loss in cash, or making the repairs or replacement, or of taking all of the automobile or any part of it at the agreed price.

When an Insured becomes entitled to reimbursement for loss of use of an automobile after it has been stolen, these expenses are payable in addition to the indemnity for the vehicle itself.

Actual Cash Value Basis—Under this form, no dollar amount of insurance is stipulated. The words "actual cash value" are inserted in the policy under the heading "Limits of Liability." The described vehicle is insured for the amount of its actual cash value at the time of the loss.

Stated Amount Basis—Under the Stated Amount form, a dollar amount of insurance is given alongside each insured vehicle. As in any other form of property insurance, the Company is never liable for more than the amount of insurance in its policy.

But it is important to understand that the Company is not *necessarily* liable for the amount stated in the policy. Regardless of the amount for which the policy is written, the Company is not liable for more than the actual cash value of the automobile at the time of the loss. While the Company will not knowingly insure a vehicle for more than its actual cash value, it is not obligated to pay more than the actual cash value, even if the amount stated in the policy is higher.

Deductible—The Comprehensive Physical Damage policy may be written with a $50 Deductible. This is frequently insisted upon by underwriters for older vehicles, or where the automobile is not garaged. Under this form, which is written at a substantial reduction in premium, the Insured is called upon to contribute the first

$50 in any loss, with the Company liable only for the excess, if any, over the Deductible. The Deductible does *not* apply, however, to losses by fire, lightning, transportation, or theft, larceny, robbery or pilferage occasioned by the taking of the entire automobile.

Thus, if an automobile insured under a $50 Deductible Comprehensive Physical Damage policy is stolen, the Company will pay the loss in full. If the vehicle is stolen, and subsequently recovered after it has been stripped of its equipment, or is in a damaged condition, the loss will also be paid in full, since it was occasioned by the taking of the entire automobile. On the other hand, if the radio of a car is removed by thieves who do not take the automobile itself, the settlement is subject to the application of the Deductible.

Valued Monthly Reduction Basis—This form is the same as the Stated Amount form discussed directly before, except that, in the event of a *total* loss, the Company will pay the amount stated in its policy, less a stipulated percentage for depreciation since the date of the policy. The percentage to be deducted is 1½% of the original amount of the policy per month.

Other Insurance—See Chapter 27.

WHERE COVERED

The policy applies only to accidents which occur within the United States, its territories and possessions, Canada and Newfoundland, or while the automobile is being transported between ports of these territories. For an additional premium, the policy can be endorsed to cover outside of these territorial limits.

RATES

Private Passenger Vehicles—Rates for Comprehensive Physical Damage insurance on private passenger automobiles depend on the following factors:

1. Territory—Rates vary with the territory in which the automobile is principally garaged.

2. Make, Year, Model of Automobile—The Automobile manual lists each make of automobile, broken down into the year of its manufacture. Further breakdown is made for the various models and body types, and a rating symbol assigned to each type of car; e. g.:

AMERICAN MOTORS

Body Type	Symbol
1971-6 Gremlin	
46-0 Sed 2 dr (2 pass)	3

	BUICK	
1971-8	Sportswagon	
43436	Sta Wag 4 dr 2S	4
	DODGE	
1971-6	Dart	
LL 41	Sed 4 Dr.	3
	FORD	
1971-8	Maverick	
	Sed 2 Dr	3

For the Stated Amount policy, rates are shown for each $100 of insurance. For the Actual Cash Value policy, the manual shows the *premium* for each of the various rating symbols. However, in rating this form of policy, a third rating factor comes into play—the age of the car. After the two rating factors enumerated above have been taken into account, the premium for any automobile insured on the Actual Cash Value form is further subdivided into one of the following four age groups:

Age	Definition
1	All automobiles of the current model year
2	All automobiles of the first preceding model year
3	All automobiles of the second preceding model year
	All other automobiles

The premium for any vehicle is somewhat lower in each higher age group, since the car's value decreases with its age, and the Company's risk is correspondingly less.

Fleet Rates—Where an Insured operates five or more automobiles (or other self-propelled units) for business purposes, and the entire fleet is under one ownership, special Fleet rates are made available. Automobile Fleet policies are written only on the Stated Amount basis.

Commercial Automobiles—In rating commercial automobiles, the radius of the vehicle's operation is taken into account. Rates are promulgated for three classes; Local hauling, up to 50 miles; intermediate hauling, over 50 but not over 150 miles; long distance hauling, over 150 miles.

Insured's Statements — The Comprehensive Physical Damage policy contains the same declarations as are required in the Automobile Liability policy. In addition, the Insured is required to disclose any encumbrance on the automobile. If any such encumbrance has not been disclosed, the policy does not cover. (See HAZARDS NOT COVERED—Loss to Automobiles Subject to Undeclared Bailment Lease, Mortgage, Etc.)

INSURED'S DUTIES

Notice of Accident—Insured is required to notify Company or its agent in writing as soon as practicable, with sufficient information to identify the Insured, the time, place and circumstances of accident, and names and addresses of available witnesses.

Notice of Claim or Suit—Insured must immediately forward to Company every demand, notice, summons or other process received by him or his representatives.

Cooperation with Company — Insured is required to cooperate with Company, and if requested by Company, must attend hearings and trials and assist in effecting settlements, securing and giving evidence, and obtaining the attendance of witnesses.

OTHER CLAUSES

Appraisal—See Chapter 2.

Subrogation—Contains Subrogation clause similar to that found in practically every form of Property and Liability insurance. The policy specifically states that the Insured is to do nothing after a loss that will prejudice his insurance Company's right to subrogation against third parties.

Cancellation—The cancellation provisions of the Comprehensive Physical Damage policy are the same as in the Automobile Liability policy. There is no provision, however, for suspending this form of insurance.

Assignment—No assignment of the policy will bind the Company unless it consents to the assignment.

Family Automobile Policy — *In the event of the death of the named Insured, the surviving spouse will be continued as the named Insured. The policy covers the Insured's legal representatives while they are acting in the scope of their duties, and also covers any person having proper temporary custody of an owned automobile until such legal representatives have been appointed and qualified.*

When Covered—The Comprehensive Physical Damage policy attaches at 12:01 A. M.

COLLISION INSURANCE

AS MENTIONED BEFORE, the Comprehensive Physical Damage policy specifically omits from its coverage loss due to collision or upset of the vehicle. Damage through collision is, of course, one of the most frequent sources of loss that faces automobile property. This hazard may be insured against separately under Collision or Upset insurance, which is made available as one of the coverages, Coverage E, of an Automobile policy.

When Collision or Upset coverage is purchased, it is subject to the basic provisions and exclusions of the Automobile Physical Damage policy, as mentioned. This section, which will analyze the Collision coverage, should therefore be read together with the entire section on the Automobile Physical Damage policy.

Family Automobile Policy—See *Eligibility for Family Automobile Policy,* discussed at beginning of Chapter 26.

HAZARDS COVERED

Under the Collision coverage, the Company undertakes to pay for direct and accidental loss of or damage to the automobile caused by collision of the automobile with another object or by upset of the automobile. It can be seen that this coverage fills precisely the gap in the insurance provided by the basic Comprehensive Physical Damage policy. When Collision insurance is added to a Comprehensive Physical Damage policy, the automobile owner is provided with virtually all-risk insurance, subject to the exclusions outlined before under Hazards Not Covered.

Collision insurance is not to be confused with Property Damage Liability insurance. Collision insurance is direct Property insurance carried by an automobile owner on his vehicle and, as such, it will indemnify him for any damage to his car which is due to collision or upset. The element of fault or liability does not enter into the question.

Contrariwise, Property Damage Liability insurance will pay all sums which the Insured becomes legally obligated to pay *to others* for the damage he does to their property with his automobile.

Thus, if Smith carries Collision insurance and becomes involved in a collision with another automobile driven by Jones, Smith can collect for the damage to his *own* car under his Collision insurance.

If it can be proved that the collision was the result of Jones' negligence, Smith's insurance company can be reimbursed for the payment it has made to its Insured. If it turns out that the collision was due to Smith's negligence, the Collision insurance Company must still pay Smith for the damages to his car, even though it cannot expect any reimbursement.

As regards the damages to Jones' car, Jones may endeavor to prove that the accident resulted from Smith's negligence. In this case, Smith's Automobile *Liability* policy will defend him and pay any sums which he is held liable for.

NOTE: If an automobile is involved in a collision with a second car, and both automobiles are insured in the same Company, the Deductible clause is waived, and the loss is payable in full.

Drive Other Cars—The Collision insurance policy is similar to the Automobile Liability policy on this score (discussed in Chapter 26 under HAZARDS COVERED—Drive Other Cars).

FOR HOW MUCH

Collision insurance is always written on the Actual Cash Value basis. While this coverage may be written without a Deductible, it is almost always written with some Deductible. The most common Deductible is $50, although the policy may provide for a Deductible of $25, $50, $75, $100, $150, $250 or $500.

80% Collision Form (80-20 Form)—Under this form, the Deductible is not a flat sum deducted from each loss. The Insured bears 20% of any collision loss, while the Company pays the other 80%.

It is further provided that the maximum which an Insured can be called on to pay in any single loss is $50. Thus, if the collision damage came to $80, the Company would pay $64; on a $200 loss, the Company would pay $160; on losses of $250 or over, the Insured would pay $50 and the Company would pay the balance.

ILLINOIS, KANSAS—This form is not available in these states.

Convertible (Retention) Insurance—Under this form, the Insured obtains Full Coverage Collision insurance (without Deductible). The premium paid for this policy is usually 50% of the premium that would ordinarily be charged for Full Coverage Collision insurance. If no claims are made by the Insured, no additional premium is charged. If, however, a claim for collision damage is presented, regardless of how slight, the Insured is required to pay an additional premium, which is usually equal to the initial premium paid at the inception of the policy.

MAINE, MICHIGAN, MISSISSIPPI, NEW HAMPSHIRE, NEW YORK, NORTH CAROLINA, PENNSYLVANIA, VIRGINIA—This form of Collision insurance is not available in these states.

RATES

Private Passenger Automobiles—Rates for Collision insurance on private passenger automobiles are based essentially on the same factors as those used for rating Comprehensive Physical Damage insurance (discussed earlier in this chapter) and for Automobile Liability (discussed in Chapter 26 under RATES).

Driver Course Credit—discussed in Chapter 26 under RATES—Driver Course Credit.

Good Student Credit—A credit on the rates for Physical Damage insurance and for Collision insurance is granted for students who achieve certain scholastic standing (discussed in Chapter 26 under RATES—Good Student Discount).

Multi-Car Discount—The rules for discounting Collision policies covering individuals who own more than one private passenger vehicle which are insured in the same policy are similar to those which are applied to Automobile Liability insurance (discussed in Chapter 26 under RATES—Multi-Car Discount). In Collision insurance, the discount is 10%.

Bumper Discount—In most states, a discount of 10% on the premiums for Collision insurance is granted on 1972 model automobiles which meet Federal bumper standards established by the Department of Transportation. The standards require that the bumper be able to withstand a crash into a fixed barrier at five miles per hour and rear bumpers able to withstand a 2½ mile per hour impact without damage to safety related equipment such as hood, trunk and door latches; headlights; fuel system and cooling systems.

Merit Rating Plans—In the majority of states, a merit rating plan has been introduced which modifies the premium for Automobile Liability, Medical Payments and Collision insurance. These plans are discussed in Chapter 26 under RATES — Merit Rating Plan. The system is *not* applicable to Comprehensive Physical Damage coverage.

Commercial Automobiles—The premium for Collision insurance on a commercial vehicle is based on the following factors:

1. The territory in which the vehicle is principally garaged.

2. The age of the vehicle—For commercial vehicles, there are only two age groups, depending on whether the vehicle was purchased new more than 18 months prior to the inception of the policy, or not.

3. Radius of operations—Discussed under RATES—Commercial Automobiles.

Suspension of Insurance—Many Insureds lay up their automobiles for several months of the year. The policy may be suspended by the Insured, who will receive a return premium on a pro rata basis, subject to the following conditions:

1. No credit will be allowed for any suspension of less than 30 consecutive days.

2. Company will be entitled to retain no less than the short rate premium for 60 days, regardless of period or periods during which policy has been suspended.

Whole Dollar Premium Rule—Discussed in Chapter 8 under OTHER FACTORS WHICH AFFECT FIRE INSURANCE RATES—Whole Dollar Premium Rule.

SPECIFIED PERILS AUTOMOBILE INSURANCE

AS MENTIONED at the opening of this chapter, automobiles, particularly of the private passenger variety, are most commonly insured on an "all-risk" basis under a Comprehensive Physical Damage policy. It is possible, however, for a somewhat lower premium to insure only against specified perils. In some instances, as in the case of older automobiles, the companies may not wish to issue Comprehensive policies and will confine themselves only to Specified Perils insurance.

The specified perils are generally grouped together under separate coverages, as outlined below. Each of these coverages is made available in a regular Automobile policy, which is subject to the same general provisions and exclusions as the Comprehensive Physical Damage policy discussed in the earlier portion of this chapter.

FIRE, LIGHTNING, TRANSPORTATION INSURANCE

Under this coverage (Coverage F), the described vehicle is insured against the following perils:

Fire, Lightning, Smoke and Smudge—The policy will pay for accidental loss or damage to the automobile by fire or lightning. Also, for damage by smoke or smudge due to the sudden, unusual and faulty operation of any fixed heating equipment serving the premises in which the automobile is located.

Transportation—The policy will also pay for all accidental loss or damage to the automobile caused by the stranding, sinking, burning, collision or derailment of any conveyance in or upon which the automobile is being transported on land or on water.

THEFT INSURANCE

Theft insurance on automobiles is written as a separate coverage under the Automobile policy (Coverage G) and is separately rated, but it is written only in conjunction with the Fire insurance on the same vehicle. Under this coverage, insurance is afforded for all loss of or damage to the automobile caused by theft, larceny, robbery or pilferage.

There is no coverage for attempted theft. Thus, if an auto thief breaks a car window in order to gain access to the vehicle, but is frightened off before completing the theft, the Theft policy does not cover the loss. (Such loss *would* be covered under the Comprehensive Physical Damage policy.)

Theft insurance on an automobile is written in one of two ways:

1. Theft (Deductible Form)—The Insured must contribute $25 to each loss, except if occasioned by the taking of the entire automobile, in which case, the loss is paid in full.

2. Theft (Broad Form)—Under the Broad Form policy, no Deductible applies to any loss, whether occasioned by the theft of the entire vehicle or otherwise.

WINDSTORM, EARTHQUAKE, EXPLOSION, HAIL OR WATER DAMAGE INSURANCE

Under this section of the policy (Coverage H), insurance is provided for all accidental loss or damage to the vehicle by windstorm, hail, earthquake, explosion. Damage by rain, snow or sleet whether driven by the wind or not is specifically excluded.

COMBINED ADDITIONAL COVERAGE

Under this section of the policy (Coverage I), insurance is afforded for all the perils of Coverage H (outlined directly above) plus riot or civil commotion, the forced landing or falling of any aircraft or of its parts or equipment, flood or rising waters, and the external discharge or leakage of water. Loss by vandalism and malicious mischief is also covered, subject to a $25 Deductible.

TOWING AND LABOR COSTS

Under this coverage (Coverage J), the Insured will be reimbursed for the towing and labor costs necessitated by the disablement of the insured automobile. These expenses are payable only up to $25 for each disablement, and only when the labor is performed at the place of disablement.

There is no coverage for replacement of parts. Only labor and towing charges are covered.

CALIFORNIA—Not available under the Standard Policy.

GARAGE KEEPER'S LEGAL LIABILITY INSURANCE

A GARAGE OR REPAIR SHOP or parking lot in whose custody customers leave their cars is a bailee and, as such, may be held liable for loss of or damage to the property bailed to him. The Garage Insurance policy under Sections K-1, K-2, K-3 and K-4 is made available to cover some of the liability that faces garages, repair shops and parking lots for damage to their customers' property.

These coverages must be distinguished from the Garage Liability insurance provided under Section G—Bodily Injury Liability and H—Property Damage Liability (discussed in Chapter 27), which cover the liability of a garage to third parties, but like most Public Liability policies, do not apply to losses for property which is in the care, custody or control of an Insured. The Garage Keeper's Legal Liability, a bailee's form, closes this gap in the Garage Liability policy.

WHAT IS COVERED

The Garage Keeper's Legal Liability policy covers the Insured's *liability* for automobiles which he has accepted for safekeeping, storage, service or repairs when such are lost or damaged by certain perils specified in the policy. The policy does not extend to vehicles which are being road tested for appraisal or demonstrated for sale. It is important to understand that the policy is not "all-risk" but covers only for stipulated losses. Also, that it is not a policy covering customers' goods like some forms of bailee insurance but a *liability* policy which covers only when the Insured is liable for the loss.

If a customer's automobile is damaged by a peril covered in the policy, and if the Insured is *held liable* for the damage, the policy will pay. On the other hand, if the loss is not held to be one for which the Insured is liable, there is no coverage, even though the damage was due to one of the perils described in the policy.

It is equally important to be clear on the fact that the policy does not cover *all* of the Insured's liability for damage to customers' cars, but only for such damages as are caused by a peril insured against. Thus, assume a flood damaged a garage and several of the customers' automobiles stored therein, and that the garage was held liable for failing to protect the automobiles by removing them to a higher floor. The Garage Keeper's Legal Liability policy would not cover the Insured's liability for this loss, since the policy does not specify flood as a peril insured against. (In this respect, the Garage Keeper's Legal Liability policy is similar to the Cargo Liability policy discussed in Chapter 21.)

It is also important to understand that a garage or service station cannot rely on its customers' Automobile insurance. If a customer's automobile is damaged while it is in the custody of a garage or repairman, and it can be proved that the loss was due to the negligence of the bailee, the customer can look to the garage for compensation for the damages. If the customer carries insurance on his automobile and collects under his policy, the insurance Company, after it has paid the loss, can move against the garage for reimbursement.

Loss of Use by Theft—The policy covers loss or damage to the customer's automobile. If insurance is purchased against Theft, the policy will also pay for the customer's loss of use when the automobile is stolen.

Defense of Suits—Supplementary Benefits—These benefits are payable, regardless of their amount over and above the limits of the policy.

HAZARDS COVERED

Fire and Explosion—Under this coverage, K-1, the Insured's liability for loss or damage to customers' property is covered when arising from fire or explosion. There is a specific exclusion of loss due to explosion of tires.

Theft—Under this coverage, Coverage K-2, the Insured's liability for theft is covered but only if the entire automobile is stolen. There is no coverage for theft of parts of the automobile, or for pilferage.

The policy does not exclude dishonesty of the Insured's employees. It is important to understand, however, that it covers only theft. Whether the taking of an automobile by an employee is a theft will depend on the construction given to the word "theft" in a particular jurisdiction. If the act is held to be conversion or embezzlement, there will probably be no coverage under the policy.

Riot, Civil Commotion, Vandalism, Malicious Mischief—Under Coverage K-3, the policy will cover liability of the Insured for damage to customers' cars when arising from these four perils. The coverage for Malicious Mischief or Vandalism is subject to a Deductible of $25, while the Riot and Civil Commotion insurance is full coverage (without Deductible).

Collision or Upset—Coverage K-4 will cover the Insured's liability for damage to automobiles and other property customarily left in the custody of a garage by collision or upset. It is written subject to a Deductible of $50 or $100, which applies to each separate accident. As respects damage to property other than automobiles, the policy will not cover for more than $5,000 in any one loss.

Loss of use is covered under Coverages K-2 and K-4, but not K-1 or K-3.

HAZARDS NOT COVERED

Employee Dishonesty—The policy does not cover fraudulent, dishonest or criminal acts committed by the Insured, a partner or member of a firm, or by an employee while working or otherwise, and whether acting alone or in collusion with others.

Close questions arise under the policy in cases where an employee who is delivering an automobile to a customer decides to take a "joy ride." It is sometimes contended that the act does not constitute a theft since the employee had every intention of delivering the car to its rightful owner. On the other hand, in many states, the unauthorized use of a motor vehicle constitutes a felony, and as such, would be excluded from coverage.

Liability for Loss of Robes, Wearing Apparel, Personal Effects, Etc.—The policy covers the Insured's legal liability for loss of or damage to automobiles, but not to robes, wearing apparel or other personal effects, or merchandise of any description.

Liability for Loss of Automobiles Owned by Insured, Employees, Etc. — Only liability for automobiles owned by others is covered. There is no coverage for any automobile owned by the Insured, or any employee of the Insured, or any member of the Insured's family, unless a charge has been made for such vehicles. If the Insured is a partnership, the exclusion extends to any partner or member of the partner's family; if a corporation, there is no coverage for any automobile owned by an officer of the corporation or his family. An auto in the Insured's custody for demonstration or sale is not covered.

Liability Assumed Under Contract—The policy covers such liability of the Insured as arises from the usual conduct of his business, but not for additional liability he may assume by special agreement with his customers, nor for any liability that he may face for faulty workmanship.

Thus, a garage might advertise that it protected its customers against loss by fire and theft. By virtue of this agreement, it might be held liable for a fire or theft, even though it had not contributed in any way to the loss by its negligence. Such assumed liability would not be covered under the Garage Keeper's Legal Liability policy.

Elevator Liability—There is no coverage for loss arising out of the use of any elevator or service hoist.

Racing Contest—There is no coverage while an automobile is being operated in any organized racing or speeding contest or in practice therefor.

War, Revolution Risks—The policy excludes loss due to war, insurrection, rebellion or revolution.

Radioactive Contamination—Loss due to radioactive contamination is not covered.

Defective Parts—There is no coverage for defective parts, accessories or materials furnished or to faulty work performed on an automobile, out of which loss arises.

FOR HOW MUCH

Each separate location at which the Insured storages or services automobiles is individually enumerated in the policy. Alongside each location, the Insured is required to indicate the maximum number of automobiles that will be stored. The limit of liability for each individual location is based on the number of automobiles which the Insured indicates he will store at the particular location.

Pro Rata Liability (Coinsurance)—The policy contains a clause which stipulates that the Company will not be liable for a greater proportion of the amount for which it would otherwise be liable than the amount of automobiles stated in the policy bears to the number actually stored on the date of the loss.

Thus, assume an Insured's policy states that he will store not more than 50 cars. The maximum limit of liability for this number of automobiles is $15,000. Assume further that a fire breaks out at his premises and does $600 of damage to three automobiles and that the Insured is found liable for the damages. On the date of the loss, it develops that the Insured was storing 60 automobiles instead of the 50 declared in his policy. The policy is liable only for 5/6 of the loss, arrived at as follows:

$$\frac{\text{Maximum Number of Automobiles Stated in Policy}}{\text{Number of Automobiles Actually Stored on Date of Loss}} = \frac{50}{60} = \frac{5}{6}$$

It can be seen that this clause imposes upon the Insured the requirements of a 100% Coinsurance clause, and is actually more stringent. In the event of a total or near-total loss, the Insured will still receive only a fraction of the amount of insurance being carried.

Thus, assume that in the illustration used above the Insured suffers a loss of $20,000 and is found liable for the loss. Under the Garage Keeper's Legal Liability policy, the Insured would not receive 5/6 of his loss, as he would under a 100% Coinsurance clause, but only 5/6 of the amount for which the policy would otherwise be liable—5/6 of $15,000, or $12,500.

An Insured may increase the limits under his policy. This will automatically increase the number of cars permitted under the policy.

Deductibles—As pointed out before, the Collision coverage and the Vandalism and Malicious Mischief coverage are subject to Deductibles.

FOR FURTHER READING

ACKERMAN—Insurance
GEE—Agent's Automobile Guide
HEDGES—Practical Fire and Casualty Insurance
KULP AND HALL—Casualty Insurance
MAGEE AND BICKELHAUPT—General Insurance
MEHR AND CAMMACK—Principles of Insurance
POLICY, FORM AND MANUAL ANALYSIS SERVICE

(See Reading List at End of Book)

CHAPTER 30

Workmen's Compensation and Employers' Liability Insurance

TODAY, EVERY STATE in the country has on its statute books special laws designed to afford immediate medical and surgical assistance to workers injured in occupational accidents. In addition, the statutes provide financial compensation to the worker for his loss of earnings if he is disabled as a result of such injuries and death benefits to his widow and children if the injury is fatal. In all states, the Workmen's Compensation Law also includes coverage for occupational and radiation diseases, and workers are entitled to compensation for disability arising from such diseases as well as for occupational injuries.

While there are important differences in the provisions of the Workmen's Compensation Laws of the separate states, one principle is basic to all statutes—that the economic burden of occupational injuries shall be charged in part, at least, to the cost of production, and not borne entirely by the worker.

Present-day Workmen's Compensation Laws have evolved steadily over a period of many years. Originally, a worker who was injured in the course of his employment could collect for his injuries only if he could prove that they resulted from the negligence of his employer, and that he himself had been free of contributory negligence.

In actuality, the injured worker was often in a worse position than a member of the general public who wished to bring a suit for damages. For one thing, he was reluctant to sue his employer, particularly if his injuries were not too severe and he wished to continue in the employ of the same employer. If he did decide to institute a suit, he often found himself defeated by the cost of retaining counsel and procuring witnesses and evidence to sustain his action. Even when the negligence of the employer was indicated, it was often extremely difficult to prove this contention by evidence, particularly since the most valuable witnesses were likely to be fellow-employees who were loathe to testify against their employer.

Over and above these practical considerations which stood in the way of a successful suit by an employee, there were available to any employer several special defenses. Like any other defendant in a negligence action, he could contend that he had been free of negligence or that the plaintiff had contributed to the accident by his own active negligence (Doctrine of Contributory Negligence). The employer could also plead that the employee had been injured through the active negligence of a fellow employee (Fellow-Servant or Fellow-Worker Rule) or that the injured employee, when he accepted the job, had assumed the risks of the occupation and had taken them into account in arriving at a fair rate of pay (Doctrine of Assumption of Risk). Under each of these defenses, the employer could contend that he should not be held liable for any damages to the injured employee.

Towards the end of the 19th century, with the development of large-scale heavy industry, the number of industrial accidents increased and many of the states began to enact Employers' Liability Acts which modified and, in some instances, repealed the Fellow-Servant Rule and the Assumption of Risk Doctrine. In some instances, the defense of Contributory Negligence was also softened, and the less harsh comparative negligence rule was substituted (discussed in Chapter 23 under Contributory Negligence).

Despite the improvements made in the worker's position by these socially-minded statutes, he might still require years of expensive litigation before he could recover for his injuries and loss of time. During such periods, he often found it necessary to go without proper medical attention because he was unable to meet the costs. It became apparent that worth-while progress would be achieved if compensation for occupational accidents was removed from the arena of negligence and fault, if all injuries received prompt medical attention, and the worker was assured of some indemnity for his loss of earnings without recourse to court action.

Present-day Workmen's Compensation statutes, while differing among the states, all reflect this changed attitude towards industrial accidents. Through the operation of these laws, the cost of work accidents is levied upon the industry, where it occurs, rather than upon the worker, his family, or the general public. In the over-all picture, the employee, the employer and the general public benefit. The severity of occupational disability is lightened by prompt and adequate medical and surgical treatment. The aggregate cost of compensation for industrial disability is further reduced by the elimination of many of the legal fees and court actions that formerly attended these cases, and court calendars are freed of most of the employee-employer actions which formerly crowded them.

Finally, procedures such as Experience Rating and Retrospective Rating in Workmen's Compensation insurance encourage employer interest in safety measures which will prevent or lighten the severity of industrial accidents.

DIFFERENCES AMONG STATE WORKMEN'S COMPENSATION STATUTES

For chart Analyses by states of Workmen's Compensation benefits and requirements, see pages 548-554.

Except for special acts relating to maritime workers and Federal employees, all Workmen's Compensation benefits are administered on a state level. Each of the states, the District of Columbia, Puerto Rico, the Virgin Islands, Guam and each province of Canada has its own fairly extensive laws governing compensation for occupational disability, and there are significant differences among the various statutes. All of the Canadian provinces, as well as Puerto Rico and the Virgin Islands, operate such laws through a monopolistic State Fund system. Canada has also enacted the Canadian Merchant Seamen Act to apply to employees of Canadian registered ships. Canadian government employees receive benefits under the Government Compensation Act administered by the Department of Labour. On a Federal Government level, there is the Federal Employees' Compensation Act for Government Employees, the Merchant Marine Act of 1920 for seamen, and the United States Longshoremen's and Harbor Workers' Compensation Act for longshoremen and harbor workers injured on vessels. The War Hazards Compensation Act covers employees of contractors working for the Federal Government when injuries to such employees result from acts of war, or if imprisonment results from their employment on overseas bases. Many states provide coverage for civil defense and other volunteer workers, such as volunteer firemen.

This chapter will touch on some of the general principles which are basic to all compensation laws and will point up some of the more important variations among the different states. It should be stressed that the analysis omits from consideration many factors of importance to an understanding of the Workmen's Compensation Laws of any state. It is therefore recommended that the reader consult a more comprehensive analysis of the statutes of his own state.

LIABILITY REGARDLESS OF FAULT

One of the most important features of Workmen's Compensation Laws is that employees are made eligible for benefits, regardless of whether the employer was guilty of negligence or not. With some minor exceptions, all that is required to establish the worker's right to compensation is that the injury he sustains shall arise *out of and in the course of* his employment. (Under elective type laws, discussed below, this principle is not as completely established, but an employer who elects to stay outside the field of the Workmen's Compensation Law finds himself seriously impeded in defending against a suit by an employee.)

In all states, coverage extends to benefits for occupational diseases. Questions of the employer's negligence, the employee's contributory negligence, the negligence of a fellow-servant, the employee's assumption of risk—all these issues are set aside and compensation becomes payable as a matter of right to an employee who sustains an occupational injury.

Usually the statutes provide certain situations in which a worker's injuries are not compensable. Thus, in New York, there are five such situations in which an award for compensation may be denied:

1. If the injury was caused solely by reason of the employee's intoxication.

2. If the injury arose in the course of work absolutely forbidden by the employer.

3. If the worker wilfully injured himself.

4. If the worker was engaged in illegal employment.

5. If the worker was injured while trying to injure a fellow-worker or other person. (This restriction is often applied in connection with accidents arising out of horseplay or practical jokes, when benefits are denied to the injured worker who *instigated* the horseplay or joke which gave rise to his injury. On the other hand, an employee injured at work through horseplay instigated by others would be entitled to benefits.)

In all such cases, the employer has the burden of proving that the accident was caused by one of these causes. Doubts are usually resolved in favor of the claimant.

It was pointed out above that injuries, to be compensable, must arise out of and during the course of employment. It is not sufficient that the employee is injured while he is working. The injury must also arise out of the work. Thus, death benefits under a Workmen's Compensation Law were recently denied to the widow of a taxi driver who had been fatally shot while driving a passenger who had a personal grudge against him and had sworn to kill him. While the driver had been killed during the course of his employment, it was held that the shooting did not arise out of the employment, since it was the result of a personal feud between the men. Contrariwise, if

(Continued on page 555)

WORKMEN'S COMPENSATION
BENEFITS FOR PERMANENT AND TEMPORARY TOTAL DISABILITIES
January 1, 1972

JURISDICTION	LIMITATIONS ON PERMANENT TOTAL					LIMITATIONS ON TEMPORARY TOTAL					NOTATIONS
	MAXIMUM PERCENT OF WAGES	MAXIMUM WEEKLY PAYMENT	MINIMUM WEEKLY PAYMENT	TIME LIMIT	AMOUNT LIMIT	MAXIMUM PERCENT OF WAGES*	MAXIMUM WEEKLY PAYMENT	MINIMUM WEEKLY PAYMENT	TIME LIMIT	AMOUNT LIMIT	
ALABAMA	65 [10]	$55.00*	$ 15.00	550 weeks	$22,000	65	$55.00*	$15.00[1]	300 weeks	$16,500	Increases to $60 and max. total of $24,000 on 7/1/72
ALASKA	65	82.55	25.00[1]	Life		65	127.00	25.00[1]	Disability	17,000	Disfigurement maximum, $3,500.00
ARIZONA	65	150.00[2]	32.50	Life		65	150.00[2]	32.50	433 weeks	65,000	
ARKANSAS	65 [26]	49.00	10.00			65 [26]	49.00	10.00	450 weeks	19,500	Disfigurement maximum, $3500
CALIFORNIA [37]	65	70.00	20.00	Life*		61-3/4	105.00	33.25	240 weeks [20]		60% maximum after 400 weeks.
COLORADO [15]	66-2/3	64.75 [21]	13.00	Life*	20,267	66-2/3	64.75	13.00	Disability	20,267	50% increase in compensation where employer has failed to comply with insurance provisions. 50% decrease in compensation where injury results from failure to obey safety regulations or from intoxication.
CONNECTICUT	66-2/3	95.00[19]	20.00	Life	25	66-2/3	95.00[19]	20.00	Disability		
DELAWARE [34]	66-2/3	75.00	25.00[1]	Life		66-2/3	75.00	25.00[1]	Disability		
DIST. OF COLUMBIA	66-2/3	70.00	18.00[1]	Life		66-2/3	70.00	18.00[1]	Disability	24,000 [18]	
FLORIDA [33]	60	56.00	12.00[1]	Life		60	56.00	12.00[1]	350 weeks	19,600	
GEORGIA	60	50.00	15.00	400 weeks	18,000	60	50.00	15.00	400 weeks	18,000	
GUAM	66-2/3	56.00	28.00[1]	Life	20,000	66-2/3	56.00	28.00[1]	Disability	20,000	Disfigurement maximum, $3,500.
HAWAII	66-2/3	112.50*	18.00*	Life	35,100 [14]	66-2/3	112.50 [35]	18.00[1]	Disability	35,100 [13]	Director may order payment of $150 per month for attendant, paid from special fund.
IDAHO	60-90	71.08*	53.31*	Life		60-90	71.08*	53.31*	Disability		Based on State avg. wage, plus 7% per child, max. 90%=$106.62, min. 45%=$53.31.
ILLINOIS	65-80*	85.00	31.50	Life	30,250*	65-80	109.00	31.50	8 years		Limited to amount if death had resulted. Pension thereafter.*Based upon number of dependents.
INDIANA	60	60.00[6]	21.00[1]	500 weeks*	30,000	60	60.00[6]	21.00[1]	500 weeks	30,000	Additional benefits from second injury fund.
IOWA	66-2/3	59.00	18.00[1]	500 weeks		66-2/3	64.00	18.00[1]	300 weeks		Weekly compensation based upon 50% of state average wage, annually.
KANSAS	60	56.00	7.00	415 weeks	23,240	60	56.00	7.00	415 weeks	23,240	
KENTUCKY [22]	66-2/3	60.00	27.00	425 weeks	25,500	66-2/3	60.00	27.00	425 weeks	25,500	Disfigurement benefits.
LOUISIANA [29]	65	49.00	10.00[1]	500 weeks	24,500	65	49.00	10.00	300 weeks	14,700	
MAINE [23]	66-2/3	78.00				66-2/3	78.00				Disfigurement benefits, $5,000 max. [23A]
MARYLAND [17]	66-2/3	85.68	25.00[1]		45,000	66-2/3 [27]	85.68 after first 42 days @ $55.00	25.00[1]	208 weeks		If permanent disability exceeds 50% of the body as a whole, employee is entitled to additional compensation for the full disability from the "Subsequent Injury Fund" after completion of payments by the employer.

MASSACHUSETTS [16A]	66-2/3	77.00*	20.00[3]	Life	20,000	66-2/3	77.00*	20.00[3]	Disability	20,000	$6.00 additional each wholly dependent but not to exceed weekly wage. Combined total compensation for total and partial disability not to exceed $20,000.
MICHIGAN [24]	66-2/3	79.00*	27.00	Disability [16]	(16)	66-2/3	79.00*	27.00	Disability		$6 add. for ea. dependent up to 5, max. $108.
MINNESOTA [36]	66-2/3	80.00	17.50	Life	(14)	66-2/3	80.00	17.50	350 weeks	28,000	Additional $5,000 allowable in certain cases. Disfigurement benefits.
MISSISSIPPI	66-2/3	40.00	10.00*	450 weeks [9]	15,000 [9]	66-2/3	40.00	10.00*	450 weeks [9]	15,000 [9]	Less in partially dependent cases. $2,000 disfigurement maximum.
MISSOURI	66-2/3	60.00	16.00	300 weeks [7]		66-2/3	70.00	16.00 [1]	400 weeks	28,000	$2,000 disfigurement maximum.
MONTANA	66-2/3	60.00*	34.50	500 weeks [31]	30,000	66-2/3	80.00	45.00	300 weeks	24,000	Reducing schedule if less than 5 children.
NEBRASKA	66-2/3*	62.00*	40.00 [1]	Life [8]		66-2/3*	62.00	40.00 [1]	300 weeks [8]	18,600	45% after 300 weeks, maximum $47.00 minimum $36.00 (or actual wages if less.)
NEVADA	90	67.16 [12]		Life		90 [12]	103.85		100 months	45,000	Additional allowance for constant attendant if necessary. $50.00 a month.
NEW HAMPSHIRE	66-2/3	92.00	20.00 [1]	(*)		66-2/3	92.00	20.00 [1]	(*)		After six successive years of payment, additional payments may be made only on order of the commissioner upon application by the employee and to the employer. If employer objects, medical panel provided for.
NEW JERSEY	(17)	101.00*	15.00	450 weeks*		(17)	101.00	15.00	300 weeks		After 450 weeks at reduced rate, if employed; at full rate if not rehabilitable.
NEW MEXICO*	60	57.00	28.50 [1]	500 weeks	28,500	60	57.00	28.50 [1]	500 weeks	28,500	10% additional compensation payable by employer for failure to provide safety devices.
NEW YORK [28]	66-2/3	80.00	20.00 [1]	Life		66-2/3	95.00	30.00 [1]	Disability		Additional compensation for vocational rehabilitation.
NORTH CAROLINA	60	56.00	20.00	400 weeks*	20,000*	60	56.00	20.00	400 weeks	20,000	In cases of paralysis from a brain or spinal injury, or loss of two limbs or eyes, payments may be extended for the life of the claimant and the total may exceed $20,000.

*See Notations column.

1 Actual wage if less.

2 No actual limit in computing average monthly wage. All wages in excess of $1,000 per month excluded.

3 Actual wage if less, but not under $10.00 for work week of 15 hours or over.

4 Disability extending beyond period compensated from second injury fund.

5 Actual wage if less, but in no case less than $20.00.

6 Plus $3 per dependent, max. of 5 dependents.

7 50% thereafter but not less than $20.00 or more than $40.00 for life.

8 Reduced amounts after 300 weeks.

9 Plus rehabilitation allowance, maximum $160 for 104 weeks.

10 Percentage increased 5% each, for dependent wife and children. Maximum 65%, wife and children.

11 May not exceed actual wage.

12 65 per cent of average monthly wage plus an additional 15% for each dependent not to exceed 90%; for temp. total % of $500, for perm. total % of $416.

13 Same rate of compensation thereafter from special fund. Disfigurement maximum $15,000.

14 Old age and survivors insurance benefits credited on compensation after $25,000 has been paid.

15 Disfigurement maximum $1,000.

16 Persons receiving less than benefits provided after 1955 receive difference in amounts from second injury fund.

16A If no benefits paid prior to final decision of claim, award shall be based upon benefits in effect at time of decision instead of date of injury. Max. wkly. goes to $80 on 11/1/72.

17 Maximum not to exceed 66-2/3 per cent of average industrial wage determined annually (as of 1/1/72).

18 Does not include rehabilitation allowance.

19 66-2/3% of average production wage determined annually by Labor Commissioner, plus $5 for each dependent but not to exceed 50% of benefit or 75% of wage. 10/1/71.

20 Within period of 5 years from date of injury.

21 If employee is receiving social security benefits for disability, compensation may be reduced by 50% of such payments.

22 Maximum shall not exceed 55% of 85% of average weekly state wage; minimum shall be 25% of 85% of same, promulgated annually by Workmen's Compensation Board as of Jan. 1, 1972.

23 Maximum not to exceed 66-2/3% of state average weekly wage fixed by Maine Employment Security Commission, as of 6/1/71. Benefits shall be adjusted annually to maintain constant ratio to wage at time of injury.

23A Added benefits during rehab.—$35 weekly.

24 All benefits adjusted to average state wage.

25 Additional allowance of $5 per dependent child but not to exceed 50% of benefit or 75% of average weekly wage but may exceed 66-2/3% of annual average production wage. Retroactive benefit increases provided for cases prior to 1953 and 1969, and prospectively for cases after 1969. Benefits also adjusted annually based on cost of living.

26 Compensation increased 15% if disability due to employer's violation of safety regulations.

27 Based upon State's average weekly wage computed annually.

28 Supplemental retroactive benefits payable in permanent total disability cases before 1960, maximum weekly benefit $50. Payments made from Reopened Cases Fund.

29 After December 31, 1969 maximum weekly benefit is increased to $49.

31 Board may order further benefits in hardship cases where necessary.

33 During training and rehabilitation in use of artificial members, maximum of 40 weeks.

34 Supplemental benefits payable in permanent total disability cases prior to 1970 from 2nd Injury Fund up to maximum of $75 or pro-rata share thereof.

35 10% penalty added for failure to pay compensation within 10 days if uncontroverted.

36 Supplemental benefits payable in permanent total disability cases after 104 weeks up to $60 max. wkly from Special Comp. Fund.

37 Benefits are effective April 1, 1972.

WORKMEN'S COMPENSATION
BENEFITS FOR PERMANENT AND TEMPORARY TOTAL DISABILITIES
January 1, 1972

JURISDICTION	LIMITATIONS ON PERMANENT TOTAL					LIMITATIONS ON TEMPORARY TOTAL					NOTATIONS
	MAXIMUM PERCENT OF WAGES	MAXIMUM WEEKLY PAYMENT	MINIMUM WEEKLY PAYMENT	TIME LIMIT	AMOUNT LIMIT	MAXIMUM PERCENT OF WAGES*	MAXIMUM WEEKLY PAYMENT	MINIMUM WEEKLY PAYMENT	TIME LIMIT	AMOUNT LIMIT	
NORTH DAKOTA	55*	64.00*		Life		55	64.00*		Disability		55% of state's average weekly wage, determined annually. Plus $5.00 for each child under 18. Max. not to exceed weekly take-home pay after taxes of $104 for 1971.
OHIO	66-2/3	77.00	49.00[1,9]	Life		66-2/3	77.00*	35.00[1]	Disability	10,750	During first 12 weeks of temporary total disability, max. compensation is $84.00.
OKLAHOMA	66-2/3	50.00	20.00[1]	500 weeks	25,000	66-2/3	60.00	20.00[1]	300 weeks		Disfigurement $3,000 maximum.
OREGON	55	62.50	40.00	Life		90	85.00*	50.00+	Disability		Reducing schedule if less than 6 children. +Or 90% of wage, if less.
PENNSYLVANIA	66-2/3	60.00	35.00[11]			66-2/3	60.00	35.00			
PUERTO RICO[19]	66-2/3	28.86	11.54	Life		66-2/3	45.00	10.00	312 weeks		Additional benefits in specific cases such as for vocational rehabilitation or constant companion at not more than $30 a month. Disfigurement $3,000 max.
RHODE ISLAND	66-2/3*	75.00	30.00	Life 12	(12)	66-2/3	75.00	30.00	Duration 12	(12)	Additional benefit of $6.00 per week each dependent but total shall not exceed his average weekly wage nor 60% of average state wage, computed annually (9/1/71)
SOUTH CAROLINA	60	50.00	5.00	500 weeks	12,500	60	50.00	5.00	500 weeks	12,500	
SOUTH DAKOTA	66-2/3	56.00	27.00[1]	Life*	78,000	55	56.00	27.00[1]	312 weeks	15,600	After 300 weeks, maximum $15.00 per week. Minimum $12.00
TENNESSEE	65	55.00	15.00[4]	550 weeks	22,000	65	55.00	15.00[4]			After 400 weeks $15.00 per week, or actual wage if less but not less than $15.00. Disfigurement benefits.
TEXAS	60	49.00	12.00	401 weeks	19,649	60	49.00	12.00	401 weeks	19,649	
UTAH	60*	54.00[2]	29.00[1]	Life*	24,648[6]	60	54.00[2]	29.00[1]	312 weeks	24,648	After 260 weeks 45% plus $5.00 for a dependent wife and $5.00 for each dependent minor under 18 up to four such children. Disfigurement benefits.
VERMONT	66-2/3	65.00[5]	31.00[1]	330 weeks	23,430	66-2/3	65.00[5]	31.00[1]	330 weeks	23,430	
VIRGINIA[26]	60	62.00	14.00	500 weeks	31,200	60	62.00	14.00	500 weeks	31,200	Disfigurement benefits.
WASHINGTON[22]	60-75	112.00*	50.00+	Life			112.00*	50.00+	Disability		Additional allowance for constant attendant, if necessary $258.00 per month. Reducing schedule if less than 5 children. +Min. $74 if married.
WEST VIRGINIA[23]	66-2/3	77.55	26.00	Life		66-2/3	77.55	26.00	208 weeks	15,130	
WISCONSIN	70	90.00	14.00	Life		70	90.00	8.75	Disability		Additional compensation for vocational rehabilitation. 14
WYOMING		79.38*		Life		66-2/3	79.38	43.38	Disability	12,000	Plus $7.50 for each child (no limit)3. Aggregate sum for children $10,000.

FEDERAL EMPLOYEES' COMPENSATION ACT	75[18]	479.71*	74.51[1]	Life		75	479.71*	74.51[1]	Disability		Additional allowance of $300.00 per month for constant attendant if necessary.
LONGSHOREMEN AND HARBOR WORKERS' ACT	66-2/3	70.00	18.00[1]	Life		66-2/3	70.00	18.00[1]	Disability	24,000[7]	
ALBERTA	75	95.20	40.00[1,25]	Life		75	95.20	40.00[1]	Disability		75% of maximum earnings of $6,600 per year.
BRITISH COLUMBIA	75	109.62	38.22[1]	Life		75	109.62	36.57[1]	Disability		75% of maximum earnings of $7,600 per year.[15]
MANITOBA	75	115.38	35.00[1,16]	Life		75	115.38	35.00[1]	Disability		75% of maximum earnings of $8,000 per year.
NEW BRUNSWICK	75	101.00	25.00[1]	Life		75	101.00	30.00[1]	Disability		75% of maximum earnings of $7,000 per year.
NEWFOUNDLAND	75	101.00	30.00[1]	Life		75	101.00	30.00[1]	Disability		75% of maximum earnings of $7,000 per year.[27]
NOVA SCOTIA	75	101.00[21]	35.00[1]	Life		75	101.00	35.00[1]	Disability		75% of maximum earnings of $7,000 per year.
ONTARIO	75	101.00	40.39	Life		75	130.00	40.00[1]	Disability		75% of maximum earnings of $9,000 per year. Disfigurement benefits.
PRINCE EDWARD ISLAND	75	86.54	25.00[1]	Life		75	86.54	25.00[1]	Disability		75% of maximum earnings of $6,000 per year.
QUEBEC[13]	75	86.54	35.00	Life		75	86.54	35.00	Disability		75% of maximum earnings of $6,000 per year.[24]
SASKATCHEWAN	75	95.20	40.00[17]	Life		75	95.20	40.00[1]	Disability		75% of maximum earnings of $6,600 per year.[8]
CANADIAN MERCHANT SEAMEN COMPENSATION ACT	75	86.54	35.00[1]	Life		75	86.54	35.00[1]	Disability		75% of maximum earnings of $6,000 per year.

*See notations column.

[1]Actual wage if less.

[2]$5.00 additional for dependent wife and $5.00 for each dependent child under 18, up to four such children. Supplemental benefit of $44 wkly. payable to all permanent total disability cases, from special fund.

[3]Court will supervise disbursement of fund for children.

[4]Actual wage if less but with a minimum of $12.00.

[5]Maximum not to exceed 1/2 of average industrial wage determined annually or $65 (as of 7/71) Additional amount of $3.50 per week for each dependent child under 21.

[6]Employees tentatively found permanently and totally disabled referred to rehabilitation program. If employee has cooperated, cannot be rehabilitated and has exhausted benefits, then maximum of $54.00 per week is paid by special fund upon termination of payments by employer and carrier until employee's death.

[7]Plus rehabilitation allowance.

[8]Board has discretion to choose the 12 months in the preceding 3 year period most advantageous to workmen for computation of his earnings.

[9]Actual wage if less, but not under $10.00 for work week of 15 hours or over.

[11]Actual wage if less but in no case less than $22.00.

[12]Disability extending beyond 500 weeks or $32,500 paid from second injury fund. Maximum weekly benefit not to exceed 60% of state average weekly wage computed annually on September 1. Added benefits to dependents excepted from 60% maximum. Employee paid compensation for 3 months or more shall be evaluated for rehabilitation services.

[13]Beginning September 30, 1965, benefit increases varying from 1.1-40% for awards made from September 1, 1931 and January 1, 1965 will be paid existing cases.

[14]Compensation reduced 15% for employee's failure to use safety devices.

[15]Applicable to all cases prior to January 1, 1965. Benefits to be increased annually by 2% increase in Consumer Price Index. Maximum wage rate to be adjusted according to annual gross earnings of workmen. Increased benefits payable prospectively.

[16]Minimum benefits of $150 per month increased retroactively to August 5, 1959.

[17]Minimum benefits increased retroactively as of July 1, 1965.

[18]Maximum is based upon grade 15 of Gen. Schedule Classification Act ($33,260) minimum upon grade 2 ($5,166) as of 1/9/72. Benefits to be increased annually by 3% increase in Consumer Price Index after 1967.

[19]Compensation doubled if disability due to employer's violation of safety or health law or regulation.

[21]Extra allowance of $100 monthly for attendant, if needed.

[22]Max. not to exceed 75% of state's average monthly wage of $646 = $112 max. wkly.

[23]Maximum not to exceed 55% of state's average weekly wage - 7/1/71.

[24]Beginning January 1, 1970, benefits shall be increased annually by 2% increase in Consumer Price Index. Increased benefits payable prospectively.

[25]Increase in minimum benefits made retroactive to existing cases. Alberta is paying same from Gen. Revenue Fund.

[26]Failure to pay compensation within 2 weeks after due, 20% penalty added.

[27]Ceiling may be increased annually by $1,000 when 20% of claimants earn over $7,000 in excess thereof and not less than 45% earn more than maximum.

WORKMEN'S COMPENSATION — FATAL INJURIES

Benefits for Widows and Children — January 1, 1972

JURISDICTION	MAXIMUM BURIAL ALLOWANCE	MAXIMUM[1] PERIOD	MAXIMUM PER WEEK		MAXIMUM AMOUNTS[2]		MINIMUM PER WEEK WIDOW ONLY	PERCENTAGE OF WAGE		
			WIDOW ONLY	WIDOW PLUS CHILDREN	WIDOW ONLY	WIDOW PLUS CHILDREN		MAXIMUM	WIDOW ONLY	ONE CHILD ONLY
ALABAMA	$800	400 weeks	$ 44.00	$ 44.00	$17,600	$17,600	$15.00[4]	65	35	35
ALASKA[55]	1,000	Not Specified	127.00	127.00	20,000	(55)	45.00	65	35	35
ARIZONA	800	Not Specified	80.77[13]	153.69[13]	(3)	(3)		66-2/3	35	25
ARKANSAS	750	Not Specified	49.00	49.00			10.00	65[59]	35	50
CALIFORNIA	1,000	Not Specified	87.50	87.50	20,000	23,000	25.00	61-3/4		
COLORADO	500	312 weeks[22]	64.75	78.25[42]	20,267	24,492	13.00	66-2/3	66-2/3	66-2/3
CONNECTICUT	1,000	Not Specified	95.00[41]	95.00[41]				66-2/3	66-2/3	66-2/3
DELAWARE e	700	400 weeks[5]	56.25	90.00	15,000		15.00	80	50	50
DISTRICT OF COLUMBIA	400	Not Specified	36.75	70.00	(3)	(3)	9.45[4]	66-2/3	35	35
FLORIDA	500	350 weeks	56.00	56.00	15,000	15,000	12.00[4]	60	35	25
GEORGIA[28]	750	400 weeks	31.45	31.45	12,500	12,500	12.00[4]	(23)	(23)	(23)
GUAM	600	Not Specified	29.40	56.00[14]	20,000	20,000	29.40	66-2/3	35	35[7]
HAWAII	1,500	Not Specified[25]	84.38	112.50	(26)	35,100[26]	15.00	66-2/3	50	40
IDAHO[62]	750	500 weeks[5]	53.31	71.08	26,655		53.31	60	45	30
ILLINOIS	1,250	Not Specified	61.00	71.00	18,000	25,200	32.50	80	65	70
INDIANA	1,500	500 weeks	60.00	60.00	30,000	30,000	21.00	60	60	60
IOWA[28]	500	300 weeks	56.00	56.00			18.00[4]	66-2/3	66-2/3	66-2/3
KANSAS	750	Not Specified	56.00	76.00	18,500	25,000	56.00	60	60	60
KENTUCKY[50]	500	400 weeks	54.00	54.00	21,600	21,600	27.00	66-2/3	66-2/3	66-2/3
LOUISIANA[32]	1,000	500 weeks	49.00	49.00	22,500	22,500	12.50[4]	65	32-1/2	32-1/2
MAINE[51]	1,000	Not Specified[18]	78.00	78.00				66-2/3	66-2/3	66-2/3
MARYLAND[59/63]	b 750	500 weeks	85.68	85.68	27,500	27,500	25.00[4]	66-2/3	66-2/3	66-2/3
MASSACHUSETTS f	1,000	400 weeks[5]	45.00	(6)	14,000	16,000[29]	45.00			
MICHIGAN	750	500 weeks	75.00	104.00[52]	37,500	52,000	27.00	66-2/3	66-2/3	66-2/3
MINNESOTA	1,000	Not Specified	80.00	80.00	35,000	35,000	17.50	66-2/3	40	45
MISSISSIPPI	350	450 weeks	40.00	40.00	15,000	15,000	10.00	66-2/3	35	25
MISSOURI	800	Not Specified	70.00	70.00	22,500	22,500	16.00	66-2/3	66-2/3	66-2/3
MONTANA[60]	500	600 weeks	37.00	60.00	22,200	36,000	34.50	66-2/3	50	55
NEBRASKA	1,000	325 weeks[1]	62.00	62.00	20,150	20,150	40.00[4]	66-2/3	66-2/3	66-2/3
NEVADA[31]	c 650	Not Specified	38.65	(31)	(3)	(3)		90	50	30
NEW HAMPSHIRE	a 1,000	341 weeks	67.00	67.00	22,847	22,847	20.00[4]	66-2/3	66-2/3	66-2/3
NEW JERSEY[61]	750	450 weeks[5]	101.00	101.00			15.00	70	50	50
NEW MEXICO[30]	750	500 weeks	48.00	48.00	24,000	24,000	24.00	60	40	25

NEW YORK[16]	750	Not Specified	48.00	80.00	(3)	(3)	12.00	66-2/3	40	30
NORTH CAROLINA[53]	500	350 weeks	56.00	56.00	20,000	20,000	20.00	60	60	60
NORTH DAKOTA[58]	500	Not Specified	25.00	64.00	(3)	(3)	25.00	(58)		
OHIO	750	Not Specified	56.00	56.00	17,000	20,000[40]	40.25	66-2/3	66-2/3	66-2/3
OKLAHOMA	a 1,000	Pay in lump sum			14,000	25,000[20]				$14,000
OREGON	600	Not Specified	25.36	94.62	(3)	(3)	25.36			
PENNSYLVANIA	750		39.00	60.00			25.50	66-2/3	51	32
PUERTO RICO	a 300	540 weeks[46]	23.09[47]	28.86[47]	(3)	(3)	11.54	85	50	60
RHODE ISLAND	1,250	500 weeks	70.33	(34)	32,500	(34)	30.00	66-2/3	66-2/3	66-2/3
SOUTH CAROLINA	400	350 weeks	50.00	50.00	12,500	12,500	5.00	60	60	60
SOUTH DAKOTA	a 1,000	Not Specified	(44)	(44)	25,000	35,000	10.25	66-2/3	66-2/3	(44)
TENNESSEE	500	Not Specified	47.00	47.00	18,800	18,800	15.00[4]	65	50	50
TEXAS	500	360 weeks	49.00	49.00	17,640	17,640	12.00	60	60	60
UTAH	1,000	312 weeks	50.00	65.00[12]	15,787	20,280	27.00	60	60	60
VERMONT[57]	500		65.00	65.00			27.00	60	50	55
VIRGINIA	500	400 weeks	62.00	62.00	24,800	24,800	14.00	60	60	60
WASHINGTON	800	Not Specified	112.00	112.00[8]	(3)	(3)	42.69	70	60	62
WEST VIRGINIA	1,200	Not Specified	20.77	(9)	(3)	(3)	20.77			
WISCONSIN[27]	750	1000 weeks	64.29	(10)	25,714[10]	(10)	10.00	50[19]	50	50
WYOMING	d 600	Not Specified	34.62	(11)	13,000	23,000	34.62			
FEDERAL EMPLOYEES'[56]	800	Not Specified	282.00	480.00	(3)	(3)	44.70	75	45	35
LONGSHOREMEN'S ACT	400	Not Specified	36.75	70.00	(3)	(3)	9.45[4]	66-2/3	35	35
ALBERTA	g 450	Not Specified	24.62	(48)	(3)	(3)	24.62			
BRITISH COLUMBIA	g 350	Not Specified	31.70	(15)	(3)	(3)	31.70			
MANITOBA	g 350	Not Specified	27.69	115.38	(3)	(3)	27.69	75[38]	75[38]	75[38]
NEW BRUNSWICK	g 500	Not Specified	23.08	101.00	(3)	(3)	23.08	75[9, 36A]	75[9, 36A]	75[9, 36A]
NEW FOUNDLAND	g 300	Not Specified	27.69	101.00	(3)	(3)	27.69	75[37]	75[37]	75[37]
NOVA SCOTIA	g 400	Not Specified[48]	26.54	101.00	(3)	(3)	26.54	75[36]		
ONTARIO	g 400	Not Specified	40.38	173.08	(3)	(3)	40.38	100[38A]	100[38A]	
PRINCE EDWARD ISLAND	g 400	Not Specified[48]	23.08	86.54	(3)	(3)	23.08	75[37A, 39]	75	75
QUEBEC[49]	g 600	Not Specified	23.08	86.54	(3)	(3)	23.08	75[37B]	75[37B]	75[37B]
SASKATCHEWAN	g 350	Not Specified	36.40[17]	126.80	(3)	(3)	25.41[17]	100[38]	100[38]	100[38]
CANADIAN MERCHANT SEAMEN COMPENSATION ACT	400	Not Specified	23.08	86.54	(3)	(3)	23.08	75[37A]	75[37A]	75[37A]

[a]If no dependents.
[b]Amount in excess thereof must be approved by Commission.
[c]Additional amount for transportation of deceased and accompanying person within the U.S.
[d]Employer may agree to other arrangements.
[e]Supplemental benefits payable from 2nd Injury Fund in death cases prior to 1970 up to maximum $75 or pro-rata amount thereof.
[f]Employee found dead on job case is presumed compensable.
[g]Additional allowance for transportation of body.

1. Benefits are generally payable to the widow until remarriage and to children until specified age, but not in excess of amounts stated in law. A few laws provide lump sums payable to widow upon remarriage. In some jurisdictions benefits continue for a longer period when there are children or incapacitated dependents.

2. Total maximum payments computed where not stipulated by law. Disability payments deducted in all laws, except those of Arizona, Arkansas, California, Delaware, District of Columbia, Federal Employees' Compensation Act, Florida, Longshoremen's Act, Michigan, Mississippi, Missouri, Nevada, New York, North Dakota, Oregon, Washington, West Virginia, Wisconsin, Wyoming.

3. No limit.

4. Actual wage, if less. (Some states have minimum regardless of wage—examples, Massachusetts and Tennessee).

5. Thereafter to children until specified age. Age 18 in New Jersey and Pennsylvania but at reduced rate in Pennsylvania. In New Jersey, after 450 weeks amount reduced by amount of widow's earnings.

6. Add $6.00 for each child under 18 or over said age if mentally incapacitated.

7. Where sole survivor is child 35 per cent, 15 per cent additional for each additional child up to limit of 2/3 of average weekly wages.

8. $8.61 first child, $7.23 second child, $5.36 each additional child, with maximum for widow and children $63.80 per week.

9. $20.77 for widow and $5.77 for each child under 18 or until 22 if a full-time student. In case of invalid child, $8.20 as long as child is an invalid.

10. $6.78 per week is payable for each child until age 16, from children's fund.

11. $34.62 for widow plus $6.92 for each child, $10,000 maximum for children.

12. $50.00 plus $3.60 for each dependent child, up to 4, at the time of death.

13. In computing average monthly wage, all wages in excess of $1,000.00 per month excluded.

14. 15 per cent additional for each child up to total of 2/3 of "average weekly wages."

15. $10.50 to $13.25 for each child under 21 if attending school. If invalid, payment continued to recovery. Increased death benefits retroactive to those prior to 1/1/65, and prospective to annual increases of 2% in Consumer Price Index.

16. Maximum benefits computed on $455 per month. Supplemental retroactive benefits payable to widows for death cases prior to 1960, max. wkly. benefit $30 from Reopened Cases Fund.

17. Reverts to $17.31 when widow reaches age 70.

18. From date of accident.

19. Aggregate amount calculated on basis of 70 per cent of average weekly wage. Weekly installments payable 50 per cent of average weekly wage.

20. Single payment of sum to heirs at law. Death more than 5 years after accident conclusively presumed non-compensable.

21. Additional amount payable $10.38 for each child. (See Footnote 37).

22. Not applicable where there are partially dependent persons.

23. 85 per cent of compensation for total disability. Applicable to weekly benefit only. Where there are no dependents, compensation shall cover reasonable expenses of last sickness, and burial expenses not to exceed $500.

24. $5.77 for each child under 18, with parent.

25. If a widower, until remarriage, if a dependent child, until age 18 or duration of dependency, or until age 20 if a full-time student and unmarried.

26. Aggregate of disability and death benefits, except as in note 25.

27. In cases where there are no dependents, employers may be required to pay to state treasury up to $11,000.

28. Covers hospital, doctor, ambulance and special nursing. Maximum weekly benefit based upon 46% of state's average weekly wage computed annually.

31. Reduced benefits if beneficiary a non-resident alien. Add $11.60 per each dependent child.

32. Benefits payable to dependents, only if death follows accident within 2 years. After Dec. 31, 1969 max. wkly. benefit is increased to $49.

33. Not less than $19.00.

34. Add $6.00 for each dependent child but total not to exceed employee's average weekly wage. Dependents benefits are in addition to aggregate total of $32,500.

35. Maximum earnings not to exceed $4,200.

36. Maximum earnings not to exceed $6,000 per annum.

36A. Maximum earnings not to exceed $5,500 in 1969; thereafter, $6,000.

37. Maximum earnings not to exceed $6,000 per annum.

37A. Maximum earnings not to exceed $4,500 per annum.

37B. Maximum earnings not to exceed $6,000.

38. Maximum earnings not to exceed $6,600 per annum. Maximum compensation to dependents not to exceed workmen's average earnings.

38A. Maximum earnings not to exceed $7,000.

39. Board may waive 75% maximum of $6,000 annual salary, where required.

40. $1,000 additional for each child under 18 and spouse up to $3,000.

41. 60% of average production wage, to be determined annually by Labor Commission—$84.00 as of October 1, 1970.

42. $4.20 per week for each child up to 3 children.

43. $23.07 for widow plus $8.69 for each dependent child.

44. 66⅔% of average weekly wage of deceased plus $3.45 per week for each child under 18.

45. $19.62 for widow plus $10.40 for each child.

46. No limit if beneficiaries are widow, father, mother, child or concubine, except, in case of death or remarriage of widow or concubine. Dependent children until age 18, or, while studying, until 25. Parents or beneficiaries of a lower category to receive no more than $9,000 maximum based upon degree of consanguinity.

47. If necessary and upon request, Administrator may make advance payment at death of worker: $500 to widow, $50 to each dependent child. Maximum $1,100. Compensation doubled if death due to employer's violation of safety or health law or regulation.

48. The Board may, in its discretion, pay compensation to a child who is continuing his education to the age of 21.

49. A dependent child is paid compensation so long as he is attending school regularly otherwise the age limit is 18.

50. Maximum shall not exceed 50% of 85% of average weekly state wage ($51 for 1971); minimum shall be 25% of 85% of same; shall be promulgated annually by Board. Payment to dependent child enrolled in educational institution continued until age 25, otherwise, age 20.

51. Maximum not to exceed ⅔ of state's average weekly wage as computed by Maine Employment Commission = $73.00 as of 6/1/70. Employer must pay additional $1,000 to next of kin.

52. Payment to dependent children may continue until age 21 or cease after 16 if self supporting for 6 months.

53. In no-dependency death cases, benefits payable to next of kin.

54. Plus $7.00 for each dependent child. Also, a lump sum of $300.00 to widow plus $100 for each child, $600.00 maximum.

55. Payments to children until age 19 or over 19 if a student; $10,000 lump sum to spouse upon remarriage; total maximum limit not applicable in case of physically disabled spouse, incapable of self-support.

56. Payments to student children continue until age 23 or marriage. Upon re-marriage of widow, lump sum of 24 monthly payments, excluding amounts on account of other dependents.

57. Maximum weekly benefit shall equal 50% of state annual average weekly wage as of 7/1/70. Increased to $61 maximum weekly and $31 minimum. Payments continue until age 62, remarriage or death of widow; 330 weeks to a child; 264 weeks to parent, grand-parent, grand-child, brothers or sisters.

58. Add $5.00 weekly per each dependent child; also a lump sum of $300

the shooting had developed out of an argument over the fare or some other situation relating to the work of driving a cab, the driver's injuries or death would very likely have been deemed compensable.

In many instances, the question becomes a close one. Thus, where an employee is injured while going to or returning from work or during lunch hour while on his employer's premises, the question of compensation will depend on the individual circumstances and whether the facts lead to the conclusion that the accident arose out of and during the course of the employment. Generally, the Laws do not cover employees before or after working hours or before or after leaving their employer's premises, if they have a fixed place of employment, such as an office or factory. However, the broad coverage of these Laws is underlined by cases which have awarded benefits to employees for falls in the street, traffic accidents, stray bullets, fainting, dizziness and epileptic fits where an employee falls on the job, injuries sustained during employer-sponsored picnics and during lunch or recreation hours while on the employer's premises with his consent.

On the other hand, if an employee does not have a fixed place of employment, as in the case of a traveling salesman, the Law would cover him from the time he left home to call on a customer until he returned home, or to some other point not related to his work. In this area there are cases where an employee may be required to work at a remote location and maintain temporary living quarters at such location. An accident may occur to such employee while away from his job location, during his leisure hours, or while engaged in some recreational activity. Benefits have been paid for such accidents on the rationale that they arise as an incident of employment.

Where employers pay their employees' expenses of transportation to and from the job site, accidents which occur while the employee is so engaged are compensable.

Benefits have been awarded in some instances where an employee sustains an accident while engaged in an activity *not* connected with his employment but which is construed as promoting the good will and interest of the employer.

In cases where an employee is injured in an assault on him by an employer or supervisor, the employee usually has the choice of claiming benefits under the Law, or bringing a suit against his employer, since the assault could be construed as having severed the employer-employee relationship. If, however, an employee is assaulted by a *fellow-employee* in the course of employment, such injuries are covered by the Law and there is no right of action against the employer.

Controversies arise in accidents where it is contended that an employee was injured while violating work rules laid down by his employer. This is not a bar to benefits, and claims are not rejected where work is performed in a forbidden manner. Furthermore, benefits are afforded for injuries in a legitimate employment even though the employee's employ may be prohibited by the State Labor Law because of age, sex or other conditions, e. g., minors illegally employed receive benefits.

Employees frequently engage in sport activities sponsored by their employers, and injuries sustained in such activities are generally considered compensable under the Law.

It should be noted that in the main, Workmen's Compensation statutes provide benefits for *accidental* injuries and *accidental* death. As might be expected, a question frequently arises as to whether a particular occurrence constitutes an "accident." The courts have generally held that an accident is an untoward event which is not expected or designed. In this light, an unusual injury resulting from the ordinary strain of an employee's work has been construed as an accident compensable under the law, as has the aggravation of a previously existing disease or condition. Thus in recent years, heart attacks have been held to be compensable when it can be shown that they were brought on by unusual stress, strain or tension resulting from the employee's work. The law also provides that "accident" includes a deliberate and wilful act of a third party.

EXCLUSIVE LIABILITY OF EMPLOYER

It can be seen that the Workmen's Compensation Law of any state provides extremely valuable protection to those workers who fall within its scope. On the other hand, in return for being held liable to his employees for every occupational accident, the employer receives assurance that his liability will be limited to the benefits spelled out in the law, provided he has complied with the security provisions of such law. Where the employer has so complied, the employee must accept the benefits, and cannot sue the employer at law, regardless of the employer's negligence. The employer's liability under the Workmen's Compensation Law is spoken of as "exclusive" and "in place of all other liability to such an employee, his spouse, dependents, or anyone otherwise entitled to recover damages."

An employee injured through the apparent negligence of a fellow-employee has no right to sue the fellow-employee for damages and is entitled only to the benefits provided by the Workmen's Compensation Law. Situations of this kind often arise when employees are injured while being driven to work by a fellow-employee.

It should be understood that the employer's liability is exclusive only for such injuries or diseases as are compensable under the Workmen's Compensation Law. If a particular accident or occupational disease does not come under the Workmen's Compensation Law, the employee retains the right to instigate a suit at common law alleging negligence on the part of the employer. In such a suit, the employer would have recourse to his normal common law defenses. This distinction between an employer's *statutory* liability under Workmen's Compensation Laws and his common law *negligence* liability to his employees for situations which do not fall within these Laws should be clearly understood. The Standard policy provides coverage against both the employer's statutory liability under the Workmen's Compensation Law of his state *and* against his negligence liability (discussed later in this chapter under WHAT IS COVERED).

On the other hand, under most state laws, if the employer is not insured as required by Law, an injured employee has the right to sue his uninsured employer, who, under these circumstances, is not permitted to use his common law defenses in defending himself against such suit. In such situations, the employee also has the option of claiming the regular benefits spelled out in the law, which must be paid by the uninsured employer.

NEW YORK: An Uninsured Employers' Fund pays the benefits if it is determined that an uninsured employer has no assets to meet his obligation; however, the Fund is not available for any damages awarded to an employee who elects to sue his uninsured employer.

RIGHT OF ACTION OF EMPLOYEE AGAINST THIRD PARTIES

As pointed out before, an employee whose injury falls within the Workmen's Compensation statutes must accept the benefits provided in the law and cannot sue his employer. Wives (or husbands) periodically endeavor to bring a suit against an employer on the ground that as a result of the industrial accident in which their spouse was injured they have been deprived of his (or her) services. This is known as "loss of consortium." Such suits are usually unsuccessful, it being held that the benefits spelled out under the Workmen's Compensation Law are the sole remedy provided for industrial accident or death. A successful suit of this nature, it is maintained, would be contrary to the intent of the Workmen's Compensation Law which is designed to avert any common law actions. If a suit of this kind were in fact successful, the employer would be protected under a separate section of the Workmen's Compensation, Coverage B (which will be discussed later in this chapter).

It should be understood, however, that there is nothing in Workmen's Compensation Laws to prevent a covered employee who is entitled to benefits, and may in fact be receiving such benefits, from bringing a suit against a *third* party whose negligence he alleges caused the accident.

EXAMPLE: A worker is employed as the driver of a truck for a contractor who makes street repairs. While on the job, an overhead high voltage wire belonging to a utility company falls on the truck, and the driver is severely injured by electric shock. The worker is entitled to the benefits spelled out in the Workmen's Compensation Law and cannot sue the contractor. He can, however, institute a suit against the utility company as a third party and endeavor to prove that its negligence was the proximate cause of his injury.

The right of an injured employee to sue a third party who is not connected with the employment is stipulated in the Workmen's Compensation statutes of all but three states. The laws usually place some limit on the employee's right to recover from the third party, so that he cannot collect from both his employer and the third party wrongdoer. When an employee's injury is caused by a third party, it is provided that the employer remain directly and primarily responsible for all Workmen's Compensation and medical benefits to the same extent as though no third party were involved. By virtue of this provision, when it develops that a third party has no assets from which the injured employee can recover, his employer remains fully responsible for the benefits.

NOTE: A fellow employee is not a third party and a worker does not have the right to sue a fellow-employee for damages.

This is accomplished in one of several ways. In some states, the employer (or the insurance carrier) who is responsible to the employee takes over the employee's right against the third parties. Provision is made for the employer (or the carrier) to pay over to the employee any excess it collects over the sums it has paid to the injured employee. Other states provide that the employee may proceed against the third party even though he has accepted benefits under the Workmen's Compensation Law. If the worker recovers in his suit against the third party, after his net recovery (expenses deducted) has been computed, he must reimburse the self-insured employer or the insurance carrier for the Workmen's Compensation benefits received by him. Thus, in such states, an employee could collect more than his benefits under the Law by recovering higher damages from a third party.

The most common form of statute provides that the worker can *either* sue the third party or elect to take the benefits of the Workmen's Compensation Law of his state.

ALABAMA, ARKANSAS, CALIFORNIA, CONNECTICUT, GEORGIA, IOWA, KANSAS, KENTUCKY, LOUISIANA, MONTANA, NEBRASKA, NEVADA, NEW JERSEY, RHODE ISLAND, TENNESSEE, WISCONSIN—In these states, the worker can collect Compensation benefits and proceed against the third party wrongdoer.

ILLINOIS, PENNSYLVANIA, VIRGINIA—A claim for Workmen's Compensation benefits transfers to the employer the employee's right of action against third parties.

NEW HAMPSHIRE, OHIO, WEST VIRGINIA—The statutes have no provision on the right to sue third parties.

NEW YORK—Employee may claim benefits under the Workmen's Compensation Law and may, at the same time, institute an action against a third party. The suit must be commenced before six months after the first award of compensation, or one year after the date of the accident, whichever is *earlier*. In any case, where an employee sues a third party, the Law provides that he will never be left with less than the benefits to which he is entitled in the Law. It is provided that if the employee does collect less in his suit than the benefits to which he is entitled under the Law, the employer must pay the difference. On the other hand, while the Law provides for reimbursement of an employer out of any damages received by the employee from a third party, it is possible for the employee to collect damages in excess of those spelled out in the Law. If an employee who has instituted a suit against a third party decides to settle the suit for an amount which is *less* than the benefits spelled out in the Workmen's Compensation Law, he must obtain the written consent of his employer to such settlement in order that he remain eligible for a deficiency payment from his employer. Such consent is not required however if a compromise order has been obtained from a judge of the court in which the action is pending. Once an employee commences suit against a third party, he is not permitted to settle the suit without permission of his employer. Settlement without such permission deprives the employee of any deficiency compensation.

Three states have enacted amendments to their Workmen's Compensation laws which liberalize the statutes in the employee's favor:

ARKANSAS, WISCONSIN—The employee is entitled to ⅓ of the net recovery from the third party. Above the ⅓, the employer (or the carrier) is entitled to the balance up to the point where he is reimbursed. The excess over this amount goes to the employee.

NEW YORK—If the employee fails to start an action against a third party within the prescribed time limit, the employer is subrogated to the rights of the employee, and the cause of action is thus assigned to the employer. Then the employer has the right to sue the third party and, if the employer's recovery (less expenses) from the third party exceeds the compensation payments he made to the employee, he must give two-thirds of such excess to the employee. However an employee does not lose his right of action against the third party unless his employer notifies him at least 30 days before the expiration of the time limit stated above that his failure to institute action against the third party will operate as an assignment of his cause of action to his employer.

A recent development in third party accidents is known as "Third Party Over" or "Liability Over" suits. This arises when an employee sues a third party and the third party contends that the employee's accident was caused by the primary and active negligence of the employee's own employer, and not by the negligence of the third party.

Generally, the third party impleads the employer in the original suit by the employee, and contends that judgment should be against the employer. The employer then becomes a defendant in the suit and the court is called on to decide whether judgment should be entered against the employer, the third party, or both. Any liability assessed against the employer is covered under the Employers' Liability section of the Workmen's Compensation and Employer's Liability policy rather than under the Public Liability policy (discussed later in this chapter under WHAT IS COVERED—Coverage B — Employers' Liability Section). Such third party suits and "Liability Over" suits are also permitted under the United States Longshoremen's and Harbor Workers' Act. The negligence liability of a third party is covered of course by a Public Liability policy.

COMPULSORY AND ELECTIVE TYPE LAWS

The Workmen's Compensation laws of the separate states and the provinces of Canada divide themselves almost equally into one of two groups—Compulsory or Elective Laws.

Compulsory Laws—With the exception of those states enumerated below under Elective Laws, every state has in effect a Compulsory Workmen's Compensation Law. In such states, every employer who falls within the scope of the law must provide the benefits stipulated in the law and penalties are established for non-compliance.

Elective Laws—Under the elective type of law, an employer covered by the law has the right to accept application of the law or may elect to reject the law without becoming subject to penalty. If, however, an employer who is engaged in work covered by the law elects to reject it, and an employee is injured in the course of his employment, the injured worker may institute a suit against his employer and, in such case, the employer is stripped of the three common law defenses that would otherwise be available to him: Contributory Negligence of the Injured Employee, Negligence of a Fellow-Servant, and Assumption of Risk. A few states go even further and provide that a presumption of the employer's negligence be set up in all occupational injuries. As a result of the harsh penalties that may attend rejection of the law, most employers accept its application, and rejection is practically inoperative.

WHO IS COVERED

No Workmen's Compensation Law covers every employer and type of employment. In almost every jurisdiction, farm labor, domestic employment, and employees of religious, charitable and nonprofit educational institutions do not come within the law. In addition, many states make their law applicable only to establishments which employ a minimum number of employees, while in others, the law applies only to those engaged in hazardous or specifically listed occupations. Here are given in outline the different requirements in separate states. It should be emphasized that there are exceptions and special provisions applicable in the different states, which the reader should check by referring to an analysis of his own state's laws for complete information.

It will be noted that the laws fall into two broad groups—compulsory and elective.

A compulsory law requires that every covered employer accept the act and pay the compensation specified.

An elective type law gives the employer the option of accepting or rejecting the law. If he rejects, he is stripped of his common law defenses (assumption of risk by the employee, contributory negligence and negligence of fellow employees). In most states, workers in excepted or excluded employment may be brought under the Act voluntarily; in some jurisdictions, such action must be consented to by the employees.

COMPULSORY TYPE LAWS

ALASKA, CALIFORNIA, CONNECTICUT, DISTRICT OF COLUMBIA, HAWAII (industrial employment only), IDAHO, IOWA, MARYLAND, MINNESOTA, NEW HAMPSHIRE, NEW YORK (see below), OREGON, PUERTO RICO, UTAH, WISCONSIN—The Law applies to all employers, regardless of the number of employees.

ARIZONA, DELAWARE, MICHIGAN, OHIO, FLORIDA—The law applies to employers of 3 or more employees.

ARKANSAS, VIRGINIA—The law applies to employers of 5 or more employees.

GUAM—The Law applies to all employers of 6 or more employees.

MASSACHUSETTS, RHODE ISLAND—The Law applies to all occupations listed as "hazardous" with four or more employees.

ILLINOIS, MONTANA, NORTH DAKOTA, WASHINGTON, WYOMING—The Law applies to all employers in occupations listed as "hazardous."

MISSISSIPPI—The Law applies to all employers of eight or more employees.

NEVADA—The Law applies to all employers of two or more employees.

OKLAHOMA—The Law applies to all employers of two or more employees in "hazardous" occupations.

NEW YORK—The Workmen's Compensation Law enumerates over 500 occupations which are classified as hazardous. An employer who is conducting any such occupation for profit, and employs even one worker, must insure or self-insure the payment of benefits for *all* of his employees. This same requirement will apply to any other employer conducting any operation for profit, including certain farmers as specified below. Non-profit enterprises (including religious, charitable or educational institutions), with at least one employee, must also insure or self-insure all of their employees other than domestics, but in such organizations the Law excludes priests, ministers, rabbis and Christian Science readers, and also teachers and non-manual workers. The only domestic employees who are required to be insured in New York are those who are employed by the *same employer* for at least 48 hours a week. All other domestic workers are excluded from the Law unless voluntarily insured by their employer. Also excluded are private chauffeurs except in New York City and municipal employees not engaged in operations specifically listed as hazardous. New York has a separate compensation law for volunteer firemen called "The Volunteer Firemen's Benefit Law."

The Law also excludes baby-sitters; minors 14 years of age or older engaged for casual work in and about owner-occupied one-family residences or on premises of non-profit, non-commercial organizations—provided the work does not require the use of power-driven machinery; any casually employed person (in non-recurring employment) engaged by the owner of a one-family owner-occupied residence to perform yard work, household chores, painting or repairs; members of amateur athletic activities operated on a non-profit basis, such as Little League teams sponsored by local merchants—provided such persons are not otherwise employed by the sponsor.

The Law requires that all farm labor be insured as of April 1st of any year by a farmer who in the preceding calendar year paid all his farm laborers *cash* wages of $1,200 in the aggregate. Note that the value of food and lodging that may have been furnished the laborer is excluded. Furthermore, all commercial lumbering operations must be insured at all times, regardless of the number of employees involved or the wages paid out.

ELECTIVE TYPE LAWS

ALABAMA—The Law applies to employers of eight or more employees.

COLORADO—The Law applies to all employers of four or more employees.

GEORGIA—The Law applies to all employers of ten or more employees.

INDIANA, MAINE, NEBRASKA, NEW JERSEY, PENNSYLVANIA, SOUTH DAKOTA, WEST VIRGINIA—The Law applies to all employers, regardless of the number of employees.

KANSAS—The Law applies to all employers of three or more employees in "hazardous" employment.

KENTUCKY, TEXAS, VERMONT—The Law applies to all employers of three or more employees.

MISSOURI—The Law applies to all employers of seven or more employees.

LOUISIANA—The Law applies to all employers in "hazardous" employment.

NEW MEXICO—The Law applies to all employers of four or more employees in "extra-hazardous" occupations.

NORTH CAROLINA, TENNESSEE—The Law applies to all employers of five or more employees.

SOUTH CAROLINA—The Law applies to all employers who have fifteen or more regular employees.

Longshoremen's and Harbor Workers' Act—This law applies

to all such employees in maritime employment on navigable waters of the United States including drydocks. It does not cover masters and members of crews of vessels.

EXCLUDED EMPLOYMENTS

Certain types of employment are specifically exempted from the Workmen's Compensation Law of almost every state. Subject to the exceptions enumerated next, agricultural workers, domestic workers and casual workers are not entitled to coverage under Workmen's Compensation Law.

CALIFORNIA—Domestic workers who work for one employer for more than 52 hours in one week come within the law as do gardeners who are employed by one employer for more than 44 hours a month.

CONNECTICUT, KANSAS, NEW JERSEY, OHIO—No exception is made for domestic workers, who are subject to the provisions of Workmen's Compensation Law of the particular state. However, Connecticut excludes any person performing any type of service in or about a private dwelling when not employed more than 26 hours a week.

NEW YORK—Domestic workers who work for the same employer for 48 hours a week or more in cities or villages with a population of 40,000 or more come under the law. Similarly, private or domestic chauffeurs who are employed in cities with a population of 2,000,000 or more are under the law.

Maritime Employment—The state Workmen's Compensation Laws do not cover workers in maritime employment. Masters and members of crews of vessels are subject to Admiralty jurisdiction under the General Maritime Law. Admiralty jurisdiction covers navigable waters and seamen are subject to a Federal Law called the Jones Act—also known as the Merchant Marine Act of 1920. Under the Jones Act, seamen receive the benefits of the Federal Employers' Liability Act which basically applies to interstate railroad workers. Masters and members of crews of vessels file their claims in the Admiralty Court with the procedure analagous to an Employers' Liability action. It is permissible to write coverage for crews of vessels under the Standard Workmen's Compensation and Employers' Liability policy under one of the following alternative forms of coverage:

Coverage I: Pays Workmen's Compensation benefits if the employer is held to have such liability. If the employer is not liable, then the policy agrees to pay damages.

Coverage II: Offers a settlement of claims strictly on the basis of the statutory benefit provisions of the Workmen's Compensation law of any one state, which has been preselected by the employer. If such offer is rejected, the only recourse left is for negligent damages.

A policy providing either coverage must have attached to it

two endorsements: Amendments to Coverage B endorsement and the Voluntary Compensation endorsement. The employer has the option of including or excluding coverage for liability for (a) transportation, wages, maintenance and cure; or (b) injury by disease. These coverages are subject to a standard limit of liability of $5,000 for any one employee or $10,000 for any one accident, but higher limits may be purchased.

NEW YORK—The claimant and the employer may collectively waive admiralty rights and accept an award under the Workmen's Compensation law.

Longshoremen injured on vessels and drydocks are covered by the United States Longshoremen's and Harbor Workers' Compensation Act, which is a compulsory law administered by the Bureau of Employees' Compensation of the United States Department of Labor. The insurance required under this act is written under the standard Workmen's Compensation and Employers' Liability policy, to which is attached the United States Longshoremen's and Harbor Workers' Compensation Act Endorsement. This endorsement provides for a standard limit of $100,000 per accident (or in the aggregate for disease) for such employees under Coverage B, Employers' Liability. Higher limits of $500,000 or $1 million may be purchased. There is no limit of liability on such policies under Coverage A, Workmen's Compensation insurance, and all payments required under this Federal Act are covered without limitation. The Bureau of Employees' Compensation of the United States Department of Labor also administers another special statute, the Federal Employees' Compensation Act, which covers civil employees of the Federal Government. This Act also covers all private employment in the District of Columbia and employment outside the United States by contractors at United States military bases.

Longshoremen often perform their operations both on vessels and on land or docks in loading and unloading work. It is important to note that the Federal Act covers only accidents occurring on vessels. Consequently, longshoremen injured on land or docks are covered under the state's Workmen's Compensation Law rather than by the Federal Act. Questions often arise as to whether the Federal Act or the particular state law applies. To be covered under the Federal Act, it must be shown that the accident occurred on navigable waters, that the employment was maritime (on water, or while loading, unloading or repairing vessels or scows) *and* that the accident is one excluded by state law, i.e., not on something securely fastened to land as a floating shop, floating clubhouse or on a dock.

To obtain complete coverage, an employer of longshoremen must have his Workmen's Compensation policy specifically provide coverage under any applicable state laws as well as under the Federal Law. The Act specifies that the insurance which is required may be written by any carrier qualified to write insurance under the New York Workmen's Compensation Law.

The benefits provided by the Federal Law as respects indemnity are based on a schedule; medical expenses are paid without limit; the waiting period is three days, with this period covered retroactively after 28 days. Employees under this Law also have the right to sue third parties (discussed above under RIGHT OF ACTION OF EMPLOYEE AGAINST THIRD PARTIES).

OCCUPATIONAL SAFETY AND HEALTH ACT OF 1970 (OSHA)

With the exception of the special areas of employment described directly above, the regulation of Workmen's Compensation insurance is left to the separate states.

The Federal Government has become directly involved in protecting the safety and health of workers in *all* industries through the enactment of the Occupational Safety and Health Act of 1970 (Williams-Steiger Bill).

The law requires employers to provide a safe place, free of health hazards, to employees. Almost every business, even those with only a single employee, is subject to the law, although amendments are now under consideration which would exempt employment with 25 or less workers. The proposed amendments would also delay for one year compliance with the law on the part of employers of 100 or less employees, and would provide technical help to these smaller firms to help them come into compliance.

While present law applies to all firms, regardless of their size (an estimated 5 million firms employing some 60 million workers), the House of Representatives has amended the Labor Department's budget for 1973 to bar payment to inspectors who enter the plants of employers who have less than 25 employees.

The employer must obey detailed and fairly complicated standards set forth in a 248 page booklet which was developed through the joint efforts of the National Fire Protection Association, the American National Standards Institute and the American Council of Government Industrial Hygienists.

Standards are established in all aspects of industrial safety (e.g. size of ladders, protective screening against atomic radiation, safety nets for bridge builders) and a deadline for correction of any defect is set by inspectors who check on plants throughout the country. A fine of up to $1,000 may be levied for each day beyond the deadline when compliance is not secured.

Machinery for appeal from the decision of the inspectors who work for the Labor Department, which administers the Act, may be taken to an independent agency—the Occupational Safety and Health Review Commission which has three members appointed by the President. A Commission decision may be appealed to a Federal Court of Appeals.

The law applies in all states, the District of Columbia, Puerto Rico, the Virgin Islands, American Samoa, Wake, Outer Continental Shelf Lands, Johnston Island and the Canal Zone.

State and municipal workers are excluded from coverage as are all working conditions protected under other Federal occupational and safety health laws, such as the Federal Coal Mine Health and Safety Act and the Atomic Energy Act of 1954.

VOLUNTARY COVERAGE

As pointed out, no state law brings *all* employment within its scope. In practically every case, all or most of such exempted employment may be brought within the coverage of the Workmen's Compensation Law by voluntary action on the part of the employer. In a few states, the otherwise exempted employees must consent to being brought under the law but, generally, such choice is left to the employer. If an employer voluntarily brings his exempt establishment under the Workmen's Compensation Law, the workers become eligible for benefits on the same basis as workers in covered employment, and the employer is secure against common law suits by his employees. In most states, when a non-covered employer wishes to bring his employment under the Workmen's Compensation Law on a voluntary basis, the only action necessary is his applying for and receiving a policy of Workmen's Compensation insurance. Procurement of Workmen's Compensation insurance usually acts as an election to be covered by the law.

Insurance men in states which have elective type Workmen's Compensation Laws should be clear on the difference between voluntary coverage and elective coverage. In practically every state, certain types of employment are exempt. Thus, in Alabama, the law is elective as to all establishments having eight or more employees, which means that while such employer is subject to the law, he has the right to elect not to come under the law. Consequently, if he elects not to come under the law, he is not held in violation of the law and is not subject to penalties for non-compliance. However, if a worker in his plant is injured, and sues him at law, the employer is stripped of his usual defenses.

On the other hand, if this employer had only seven employees, he would not come under the law, and would not be stripped of his defenses in an action by an injured employee. This employer could, however, *voluntarily* come under the law and provide insurance for his workers. In such event, an injured worker would not have to prove his employer's negligence in order to receive the benefits provided in the law, and the employer would not be open to suits by the employee, since such voluntary coverage would give the employer the benefit of the "exclusive liability" provisions of the law.

Independent Contractors—Generally, an independent contractor does not come within the scope of the law, since he is not considered an employee. Thus, a building owner who engaged an independent contractor to make repairs is not liable to the contractor under the Workmen's Compensation Law. This differs from the situation where a contractor engages a subcontractor (to be discussed later).

It often becomes a close question whether an individual was acting as an independent contractor or was actually employed by the principal. Generally speaking, the deciding factor is not so much the express contract between the parties as the degree of control exercised by the principal over the conditions of employment. An independent contractor usually supplies his own materials and equipment and is paid a lump sum instead of by the day, week or month. He is generally responsible only for the final result achieved, and is not subject to discharge as in an employment contract.

As indicated above, an independent contractor does not come within the scope of the law, and the Standard Workmen's Compensation policy which insures only employees does not extend to injuries sustained by independent contractors. If an alleged independent contractor makes a claim for benefits, and is held to be an employee, the policy will cover and the insurance carrier will be liable, regardless of whether premium was paid for the person in question. Examples of persons whose status has been subject to controversy and who have been held to be employees are commission salesmen and so called "side-line" salesmen, who handle several lines of merchandise of different concerns, entertainers, installers, construction workers and truck drivers.

While the person who engages an independent contractor may not be liable to the contractor, it is very important that he satisfy himself that the contractor has provided for the payment of Workmen's Compensation benefits to his (the contractor's) employees. The laws of most states specifically provide that the principal will be responsible for injuries to employees of the contractor. Many state laws provide that if a contractor engages a subcontractor who is not carrying Workmen's Compensation insurance, the principal contractor will be held liable for the payment of benefits to employees of the uninsured subcontractor who are injured in the course of their employment. This obligation of a contractor is automatically insured under the Standard Workmen's Compensation and Employers' Liability policy. Contractors are required to furnish to their insurance carriers Certificates of Insurance covering each of their subcontractors. If an uninsured subcontractor is disclosed upon audit of the contractor's books, an additional premium is charged. It is therefore important that contractors make certain that any subcontractors they engage are properly insured.

While the law extends to employees of uninsured subcontractors this additional protection, it does not affect other rights and obligations. Thus, the uninsured subcontractor is nevertheless an uninsured employer in violation of law. The injured employee of the subcontractor has the right to sue the principal contractor as a third party.

METHODS OF COMPLYING WITH WORKMEN'S COMPENSATION LAWS

With the few exceptions listed below, the Workmen's Compensation Laws of every state and the provinces of Canada not only make the employer liable to his employees, but also require that he take steps to guarantee the payment of the stipulated benefits. Compliance with the law calls for the purchase of a standard Workmen's Compensation insurance policy, or for self-insurance.

GUAM, NEVADA, NORTH DAKOTA, PUERTO RICO, TEXAS, WASHINGTON, WYOMING, ALBERTA, BRITISH COLUMBIA, MANITOBA, NEW BRUNSWICK, NOVA SCOTIA, ONTARIO, PRINCE EDWARD ISLAND, QUEBEC, SASKATCHEWAN—Self-insurance is not permitted.

LOUISIANA—Employer is not required to provide insurance or security.
NEW HAMPSHIRE—Employer may insure or furnish proof of financial security.

Methods of Insuring—In the majority of the states, the employer may comply with the law by providing a standard Workmen's Compensation insurance policy in any approved private carrier. State-managed insurance funds for the writing of Workmen's Compensation insurance (called State Funds) exist only in the following states:

ARIZONA, CALIFORNIA, COLORADO, IDAHO, MARYLAND, MICHIGAN, MONTANA, NEW YORK, OKLAHOMA, OREGON, PENNSYLVANIA, UTAH—The employer may purchase Workmen's Compensation insurance from a private carrier, or from the State Fund which operates in competition with the private carriers. All of these states permit self-insurance.

NEVADA, NORTH DAKOTA, OHIO, WASHINGTON, WEST VIRGINIA, WYOMING—Workmen's Compensation must be purchased from the State Fund, except that OHIO and WEST VIRGINIA permit self-insurance.

PENALTIES FOR FAILURE TO COMPLY WITH LAW

With few exceptions, every state makes failure to furnish the required insurance punishable by a fine and, in some cases, by imprisonment. In addition, the majority of states provide that an employer who has failed to provide the required insurance will be liable for suit by his employee with defenses abrogated.

MAINE—No provision on this score.

CALIFORNIA, COLORADO, IDAHO, NEW MEXICO, WISCONSIN, WYOMING, ALBERTA, NOVA SCOTIA—In addition to other penalties provided in the law, a non-complying employer may be restrained from continuing in business.

In some states, such as New York, if the uninsured employer is a corporation, its executive officers are held personally responsible for the failure to comply.

NEW YORK—The Law provides for fines up to $500 plus an assessment of up to $1,650 for the benefit of the Uninsured Employers' Fund plus an additional $25 for each ten consecutive days of violation.

WHAT IS COVERED

Under the Workmen's Compensation Law, an injured worker becomes entitled to medical, surgical, hospital and nursing care. In all states except those listed below, the worker is entitled to unlimited medical care.

Medical Benefits—Injured workers are entitled to medical, surgical, hospital and nursing care. These benefits usually include X-rays, medical specialists, artificial limbs, and appliances, and drugs. While a few states give the employee a free choice of physician, in most states it is provided that the employer must provide the medical treatment so that the employer retains the right to designate the physician who is to provide treatment.

In all states except those listed below, the worker is entitled to unlimited medical care.

ALABAMA, COLORADO, GEORGIA, IOWA, KANSAS, KENTUCKY, LOUISIANA, MONTANA, SOUTH DAKOTA, TENNESSEE, VIRGINIA, WEST VIRGINIA—A statutory limit is set on the extent of medical care to which an employee is entitled. In some of these states, a top dollar limit is stipulated; in others a maximum time period beyond which no benefits will be paid.

Occupational Disease Coverage—An occupational disease is an injury or disease due to causes and conditions characteristic of and peculiar to a particular trade, occupation, process, or employment—but it excludes ordinary diseases to which the general public is exposed. The statutes of the various states vary considerably as respects occupational diseases.

ALABAMA, ARIZONA, ARKANSAS, COLORADO, GEORGIA, IDAHO, IOWA, KANSAS, LOUISIANA, MONTANA, NEW MEXICO, NORTH CAROLINA, OKLAHOMA, SOUTH DAKOTA, TENNESSEE, TEXAS, VERMONT, WYOMING, SASKATCHEWAN—The law enumerates certain diseases or groups of diseases which are compensable.

ALASKA, CALIFORNIA, CONNECTICUT, DELAWARE, DISTRICT OF COLUMBIA, FLORIDA, HAWAII, ILLINOIS, INDIANA, KENTUCKY, MAINE, MARYLAND, MASSACHUSETTS, MICHIGAN, MINNESOTA, MISSISSIPPI, MISSOURI, NEBRASKA, NEVADA, NEW HAMPSHIRE, NEW JERSEY, NEW YORK, NORTH DAKOTA, OHIO, OREGON, PENNSYLVANIA, PUERTO RICO, RHODE ISLAND, SOUTH CAROLINA, UTAH, VIRGINIA, WASHINGTON, WEST VIRGINIA, WISCONSIN, ALBERTA, BRITISH COLUMBIA, MANITOBA, NEW BRUNSWICK, NEWFOUNDLAND, NOVA SCOTIA, ONTARIO, PRINCE EDWARD ISLAND, QUEBEC—The law covers all occupational diseases.

Silicosis is usually compensable on a more limited basis than other occupational disabilities, and the reader is urged to check his own state law on his score.

Diseases Caused By Ionizing Radiation—In all states except those listed below, loss due to ionizing radiation is covered on the same basis as any other occupational disease.

ALABAMA, ARIZONA, IOWA, MAINE, MONTANA, NEW HAMPSHIRE, NORTH CAROLINA, SOUTH DAKOTA, TENNESSEE—Only partial coverage is afforded for loss due to ionizing radiation.

Extra Legal Medical Coverage—In many of the states which place a top limit on the amount of medical expenses for which an employer is liable under the Workmen's Compensation Law, an Insured-employer may purchase Additional or Extra Legal Medical Benefits Coverage. This extra protection is purchased by attachment of the Standard Additional Medical Coverage endorsement; which provides for an additional limit of $10,000 on medical expenses for each employee. Higher limits are available.

Indemnity for Loss of Time—Over and above the medical, surgical, hospital and other expenses for care and rehabilitation to which the worker is entitled, he is also eligible for indemnity for his loss of earnings during a period of total or partial disability. The law of each state fixes a percentage of the worker's regular weekly wage, subject to a minimum and maximum per week. In addition, some statutes provide a maximum period during which indemnity is payable, and a maximum dollar amount. The limitations in each state on indemnity for permanent total disability and for temporary total disability are shown on the charts reproduced on pages 548-551.

Waiting Period—While medical care payments begin at the time of accident, in all jurisdictions, indemnity for loss of time does not begin until a stipulated number of days of disability have passed. In practically every case, the law provides further that benefits will be paid for the waiting period if the disability continues past a given number of days, known as the retroactive period. While there is little standardization as regards the retroactive period, the majority of states provide for a seven-day waiting period. (Under the United States Longshoremen's and Harbor Workers' Compensation Act and the Federal Employees' Compensation Act, the waiting period is three days.)

ALASKA, CONNECTICUT, DELAWARE, DISTRICT OF COLUMBIA, MARYLAND, MINNESOTA, MISSOURI, OREGON, PUERTO RICO, RHODE ISLAND, UTAH, WASHINGTON, WISCONSIN, WYOMING, BRITISH COLUMBIA, NOVA SCOTIA—The waiting period is three days.

HAWAII—The waiting period is two days.

ILLINOIS—The waiting period is six days.

MASSACHUSETTS, MISSISSIPPI, NEVADA, NORTH DAKOTA, OKLAHOMA—The waiting period is five days.

ALBERTA, MANITOBA, NEWFOUNDLAND, ONTARIO, PRINCE EDWARD ISLAND, SASKATCHEWAN—The waiting period is one day.

NEW BRUNSWICK—The waiting period is four days.

Scheduled Awards—The laws of every state provide statutory maximum amounts for certain specified permanent injuries, like the loss of an arm, one hand, a thumb, one foot, the hearing of one ear, etc.

Permanent Total Disability—In the majority of the states, a worker who is permanently disabled becomes entitled to benefits for life. Generally, the loss of both hands, both feet or both eyes, or of any two such members is regarded as permanent disability.

Death Benefits—When a worker is fatally injured in a compensable accident, funeral benefits are defrayed to a certain extent through the payment of a funeral benefit in the amount specified in the law, and his widow and children become entitled to benefits.

Dependency benefits are usually paid to the widow for the remainder of her life or until she remarries and to the children until each reaches the age of 18. In some states, a lump sum is paid to the widow at the time she remarries. These benefits are subject to maximums and minimums as shown on the charts reproduced on pages 552-553.

Status of Benefits—Workmen's Compensation benefits are tax exempt; they are also exempt from creditors' claims and from levy, execution or attachment. They are not reduced by nor do they pro-rate with other benefits received from Life insurance, Accident and Sickness insurance or medical care insurance or benefits received under Social Security. They are not assignable by the beneficiary.

EMPLOYER'S DUTIES

Report of Injury by Employer—In every state, an employer is required to report injuries sustained by his employees in the course of their employment. The report must be made to the state agency, board, or commission which administers the law. The majority of the states impose the requirement of reporting only for injuries which cause disability of stipulated duration—one day, three days, seven days, or 14 days. Penalties are stipulated for failure to report as required. These range from $25 to $1,000.

ALABAMA, BRITISH COLUMBIA, DISTRICT OF COLUMBIA, GUAM, IDAHO, ILLINOIS, INDIANA, MINNESOTA, MISSOURI, NEW YORK, NORTH DAKOTA, OHIO, OKLAHOMA, UTAH, WYOMING—Maximum fine for failure to report is $500.

ALABAMA, ALBERTA, DELAWARE, HAWAII, MISSOURI, PENNSYLVANIA, PRINCE EDWARD ISLAND—Failure to report is also punishable by imprisonment.

Keeping of Accident Reports—

ALABAMA, ALASKA, ARKANSAS, COLORADO, CONNECTICUT, DELAWARE, DISTRICT OF COLUMBIA, FLORIDA, GEORGIA, GUAM, HAWAII, IDAHO, INDIANA, IOWA, KENTUCKY, MASSACHUSETTS, MICHIGAN, MISSISSIPPI, PUERTO RICO, BRITISH COLUMBIA, NEW HAMPSHIRE, NEW JERSEY, NEW YORK, NORTH CAROLINA, NORTH DAKOTA, OHIO, OKLAHOMA, SOUTH CAROLINA, SOUTH DAKOTA, TEXAS, UTAH, VERMONT, VIRGINIA, WISCONSIN—The employer is required to keep records of work accidents sustained by his employees.

Report of Injury by Employees—The Workmen's Compensation Law of many states also requires that the employer be given notice of an accident by the employee within a stipulated time, such as within 30 days after accident.

NEW YORK—While an employee is required to give notice of an injury within 30 days, he has 90 to report an occupational disease. There is an absolute time limit of two years for filing a claim after an accident or death.

NORTH DAKOTA, OHIO, PUERTO RICO, WEST VIRGINIA — No provision for notice to employer.

MINORS UNDER WORKMEN'S COMPENSATION LAWS

While a minor who is legally employed does have the power to enter into a valid contract of employment, his somewhat restricted legal powers have brought it about that the Workmen's Compensation statutes expressly bring minors under their scope. In all but four states, a minor, whether employed legally or illegally, comes within the protection of the Workmen's Compensation Laws.

OKLAHOMA, VERMONT, WEST VIRGINIA—In these states, a minor who is *illegally* employed is not covered under the Workmen's Compensation Act but can sue his employer at common law.

It is important to understand that in the Employers' Liability section of the Workmen's Compensation policy (discussed later in this chapter under WORKMEN'S COMPENSATION AND EMPLOYERS' LIABILITY INSURANCE POLICY—Coverage B—Employers' Liability Section) there is no coverage for liability on account of injury to anyone employed in violation of law with the employer's knowledge.

In many states, additional protection is placed around a minor who is illegally employed, and such minors are entitled to increased benefits under the law, as outlined below. The additional benefit for the illegally employed minor is not insurable, and must be paid by the employer. Furthermore, most states give consideration to the future earning capacity of a minor and base benefits to be paid on such projected earnings.

ALABAMA, ARKANSAS, FLORIDA, INDIANA, MARYLAND, MASSACHUSETTS, MISSISSIPPI, NEW HAMPSHIRE, NEW JERSEY, UTAH, PUERTO RICO—The minor is entitled to twice the benefits spelled out in the law.

ILLINOIS—If the minor is under 16, he is entitled to 50% extra benefits.

INDIANA—If the minor is under 17, he is entitled to double compensation.

MICHIGAN, NEW YORK, PUERTO RICO—The minor is entitled to double compensation, if under 18.

MISSOURI, PENNSYLVANIA (if under 18)—The minor is entitled to 50% additional compensation.

NEVADA—$300 to $2,000 payable into the State Fund.

OREGON—25% additional compensation, to a maximum of $500, is payable into the State Fund.

RHODE ISLAND—Entitled to triple compensation.

WASHINGTON—50% additional compensation is payable into the State Fund.

WISCONSIN—Illegally employed minors are entitled to two or three times the regular compensation benefits.

EXTRA-TERRITORIAL PROVISIONS

It frequently happens that an employee who is hired in one state is injured in another. This situation arises not only with employees who travel from state to state but also those who are injured in foreign countries, as in the case of salesmen and technicians who travel in foreign countries and employees of contractors who work in such countries. In such cases, the question frequently arises as to which state law is applicable. This can be of considerable importance where there is a difference in the level of benefits in the two states. Most Workmen's Compensation statutes are extra-territorial in their scope, and will pay benefits for accidents which occur in other states. It is usually provided, however, that to qualify for benefits, the contract of hire must have been made in the state where benefits are being claimed.

When questions develop regarding extra-territorial accidents, the claim and premium procedures are controlled by principles enunciated in court decisions. Thus, benefits have been awarded when the employment is transitory, temporary, incidental and controlled from the home state. On the other hand, benefits have been denied in the home state and the accident attributed to the state in which it occurred where the employment was a fixed location (as in construction work), or where supervision was exercised from a fixed or permanent location, such as branch headquarters.

An employee may file a claim and collect benefits in one state and then find that he can present a claim in a second state. This is permitted in many states, but in such cases, the second state must take credit for any benefits paid by the first state.

All States Endorsement—A Workmen's Compensation policy issued to cover under the law of a specific state does not insure claims alleged under the law of another state. An employer whose operations make him subject to the law of another state should have an All States endorsement attached to his policy.

GENERAL AND SPECIAL EMPLOYERS

IT FREQUENTLY happens that employees are loaned by one employer to another. If the employee is injured, a problem arises as to which employer is liable for the benefits. This is sometimes a difficult and perplexing problem to resolve, despite the general rule of placing liability on the employer to whom the employee was loaned. In some cases of this type, both employers are held jointly liable and are required to share between them liability for the benefits to which the injured employee is entitled. Some of the important features which are taken into account in adjudicating this question are: With whom the specific contract of hire was made, if the actual work being performed was a specialty of one of the employers; which employer actually controlled the work, etc. It is sometimes held that a loaned employee has the choice of making claim against either employer if the contract of hire is dual in nature and the work and supervision common to both employers. If such an employee makes claim against one employer, the courts have ruled that he cannot sue the other employer for damages.

SECOND INJURY FUNDS

A worker who has lost a hand, or foot or eye in an industrial accident or otherwise may suffer another such loss as a result of a subsequent industrial accident. He may thereby become totally or permanently disabled, and the amount of Workmen's Compensation benefits to be paid will be considerably increased when the worker receives full benefits for the combined disabilities. For this reason, employers might be reluctant to employ partially disabled workers. To avoid such situations and to limit the employer's liability in such cases, every state (with four exceptions) has enacted into law provisions for a second injury fund, so that the employer will pay only for the last injury.

In these states, a worker suffering a second loss of a member is compensated on the basis of his entire permanent disability following his second injury without regard to his pre-existing physical disability. His employer, however, has a limited liability following the second injury, because these Second Injury Funds either pay the difference between the cost of the partial and permanent or total disability or reimburse the employer for all compensation payments beyond a specified period. For example, an employer in New York is responsible for only the first 104 weeks of compensation benefits following a second injury.

The Second Injury Fund is supported either by assessments levied on all insurance companies writing Workmen's Compensation or, in some states, by the employer paying stipulated sums into the fund when a worker without dependents is fatally injured on the job.

GEORGIA, LOUISIANA, NEVADA, VIRGINIA—No Second Injury Fund has been set up in these states. The employer in whose employment a worker sustains a second injury is generally liable for the total disability which results from the second injury.

In some states, other Special Funds have been established to make payments when compensation claims are reopened after extended periods of time have elapsed, or to assist in meeting the cost of vocational rehabilitation of injured workers.

WORKMEN'S COMPENSATION AND EMPLOYERS' LIABILITY INSURANCE POLICY

WORKMEN'S COMPENSATION STATUTES of every state not only broaden an employer's liability to his employees, but require him to take concrete steps to guarantee that the benefits promised under the law will actually be available to an employee who becomes eligible to receive them. Every state requires the employer to buy a policy of Workmen's Compensation insurance from an insurance Company or a State Fund, or to self-insure. (Five states and all the provinces of Canada do not sanction self-insurance, as previously discussed.)

It is important to understand that self-insurance is a positive act on an employer's part, which calls for his complying with certain definite requirements of the agency which administers the Workmen's Compensation Law. In all instances, an employer who wishes to self-insure must satisfy the agency on his financial ability to meet his obligations under the law In most of these states, he must also furnish some form of security, such as cash, deposit of securities or a Surety Bond, to guarantee his promise to pay the benefits. (Deposits of cash or securities are not tax deductible, whereas insurance premiums are a deductible business expense.)

A self-insurer must also make provision for furnishing his employees with medical attention, must file reports with the State Workmen's Compensation agency, and perform many of the services which are normally furnished by an insurance Company. As might be expected, self-insurance, where permitted under state law, is generally suitable only for the exceptionally substantial employer with a very large working force. The great majority of employers secure compliance with the law by purchasing a Workmen's Compensation insurance policy in a private insurance carrier or in the State Fund. Thus, in New York, less than 200 are self-insured but these employers average 2,700 employees per risk.

The Workmen's Compensation policy used in all states, except the six monopolistic State Fund states, is a standard form used without deviation. This standard policy, analyzed next, provides both Workmen's Compensation Insurance and Employers' Liability insurance. Its language is such that it reads into the policy contract the applicable Workmen's Compensation Laws and the company manuals governing the insurance. Consequently, state modifying endorsements are not necessary. This Standard policy is thus used with few, if any, endorsements and is arranged in the same form as other liability policies used on a national basis. This policy provides automatic Workmen's Compensation and Employers' Liability insurance for all operations of the insured employer within the scope of any state law specified in the policy in its Declarations.

WHAT IS COVERED

The standard Workmen's Compensation insurance policy is divided into two separate and distinct coverages, as shown in the following analysis of the four Insuring Agreements:

Insuring Agreement I

Under Coverage A, the policy covers the employer's legal obligations under the Workmen's Compensation Law.

Under Coverage B, the policy covers the employer's legal liability for damages to his employees for those situations which are *not* covered under the Workmen's Compensation Law.

Coverage A — Workmen's Compensation Section — The policy provides that all the Workmen's Compensation statutes of the states designated in the Declarations shall become part of the policy, exactly as if they had been reproduced in full in the policy. Under Coverage A of the policy, the insurance Company undertakes to cover the employer's entire obligation under the Workmen's Compensation Law, including any obligation placed upon him by such law with respect to that employer's uninsured subcontractors. As will be pointed out under FOR HOW MUCH, the policy covers the obligation in full, without stipulating any dollar amount or maximum limit of liability for Workmen's Compensation benefits. Thus, the Insured receives under Coverage A automatic state-wide coverage for all operations and locations which are under any state law specified in the Declarations. This applies to all locations and operations, even if unmentioned in the Declarations, or if unknown or undisclosed to the insurance carrier when the policy was issued, *except* those which are otherwise insured or self-insured or specifically excluded by endorsement.

The basic policy insures the employer's obligations only under the law of the state listed in the Declarations. An employer whose operations may subject him to the Workmen's Compensation Law of another state may add coverage for the state by endorsement, or may have the All States endorsement added to his policy (discussed above under EXTRA-TERRITORIAL PROVISIONS—All States Endorsement).

Coverage B — Employers' Liability Section — As was pointed out in the preceding chapter, the Workmen's Compensation Law makes the employer (or his insurance carrier) liable to the employee for almost every type of occupational injury. In no state, however, does the law cover every situation in which an employee may seek to recover damages from his employer for conditions arising out of and in the course of employment.

An accident or disease may not be compensable under the law and thus the employee is quite free to institute a suit against his employer. Since Coverage A of the Workmen's Compensation policy covers only the employer's obligations under the Workmen's Compensation statutes, the employer would find no protection under the policy for such situations. His Public Liability policy, moreover, would afford him no protection either for this situation, since all Liability policies specifically exclude the liability of an Insured to his employees (discussed in Chapter 24).

To close this gap in an employer's protection, there has been added to the Workmen's Compensation insurance policy a second Insuring Agreement—Coverage B, which covers any legal liability of an employer to pay damages to his employees on account of bodily injury or disease not within the Workmen's Compensation statutes of his state. To be included under Coverage B, however, bodily injury or disease incurred by an employee must arise out of and in the course of employment. It should be noted that the exclusion in the Liability policies now applies only to injuries arising out of and in the course of employment. Illustrations of the protection coming under this section of the policy, Coverage B, would be, in addition to disease, third-party-over cases, loss of hearing in some states, loss of consortium, maritime accidents and those in necessary or incidental operations in states not mentioned in Coverage A and not covered by the Workmen's Compensation laws of such other states. This coverage is limited to employment in those states for which the policy provides Workmen's Compensation coverage or in operations necessary or incidental thereto. Coverage B provides world-wide coverage, making the territorial scope of the policy consistent with the Public Liability policy on this score. The coverage is limited however to citizens of the United States or Canada while they are temporarily outside their own country, provided the injuries they sustain arise out of operations in a state designated in the policy Declarations. There is no coverage therefore for a foreign national working at a location in his own country. Also excluded is coverage for any suit brought in a foreign jurisdiction or to enforce a foreign judgment (other than Canadian).

It is important too to emphasize that Coverage B is strictly a legal liability coverage and actions under such coverage are always subject to the rules of negligence. Furthermore, whereas the insurance carrier's liability under Coverage A is unlimited, there is a specific limit on the liability under Coverage B as will be explained under FOR HOW MUCH.

Insuring Agreement II

Defense, Settlement, Supplementary Benefits—The policy covers not only the employer's liability under the Workmen's Compensation Law, Coverage A and the employer's common law liability under Coverage B, but also provides further that the Company will defend him against any claim, suit or proceeding instituted by an employee, pay all expenses thus incurred, and will provide the supplementary payments usual in other forms of Liability insurance.

The obligation to defend the employer, pay the cost of investigations, and the other supplementary payments promised apply to both Coverage A and Coverage B of the policy. Defense is provided even if the suit is groundless, false or fraudulent, and the carrier has the right to investigate, negotiate and settle any claim or suit. The Insured will be reimbursed for all reasonable expenses he incurs at the carrier's request, except for his loss of earnings.

Insuring Agreement III

Definitions—The basic definition stipulates that the words "workmen's compensation law" as used in the policy mean the Workmen's Compensation Law and any Occupational Disease Law of any state specified in the Policy Declarations. The effect of this definition is most important since it reads into and makes part of the policy contract, as though it were printed therein, the entire Workmen's Compensation Law of any state mentioned in the Policy Declarations. This definition excludes the United States Longshoremen's and Harbor Workers' Compensation Act. Coverage under that Act would have to be specifically endorsed on the policy by means of the standard "United States Longshoremen's and Harbor Workers' Compensation Act Endorsement."

The definitions also distinguish between bodily injury due to "accident" and bodily injury due to "disease," so that a single injury cannot be deemed to fall within both causes. As in the Public Liability policy, it is provided that under Coverage B, assault and battery are deemed an accident unless committed by or at the direction of the Insured.

Insuring Agreement IV

Application of Policy—This agreement states that the policy applies only to accidents occurring during the policy period. As to disease, it is stated that the policy applies only if the last day of the last exposure in the employment of the Insured occurred during the policy period.

Conditions—As in other policies covering liability, the Workmen's Compensation policy includes conditions which govern the relationship between the Insured and the Company and also serve to explain the application of the Insuring Agreements, to wit:

Inspection and Audit—The Company and any rating organization are given the right to inspect any operation covered by the policy and to make audit examination of all the Insured's records so as to be able to determine the correct premium due. These rights apply not only during the policy period but for three years after its termination. The Company making an audit has the right to examine all payroll books, general ledger, disbursements, vouchers, contracts, tax reports and any other records which will yield information on the remuneration paid employees.

The provision governing inspections stipulates that no liability to make an inspection is imposed on the Company and that the Company makes no warranty as to the safety of the operations or equipment of the Insured.

Premium Determination—The Company has the right to compute the premium in accordance with the Manual for Workmen's Compensation and Employers' Liability insurance and all rating plans. This condition has the effect of making the Manual and the rating plans part of the policy. The Insured must maintain payroll and other records and make them available to the Company.

Partners or Joint Ventures—This condition excludes coverage for operations of an individual partner which are not operations of the partnership as a whole.

WHO IS COVERED

Since the Workmen's Compensation insurance policy covers the employer's entire obligation under the law, it covers his liability to any employee who comes under the law. Except in those states which provide that only certain classes of employees are subject to the law, the Workmen's Compensation policy covers *all* employees of an insured employer, including any who are hired during its term.

As a general rule, it is not permissible to have one Workmen's Compensation policy cover more than one legal entity, except when the same individuals have a majority interest in more than one business. When such common ownership does exist, combining insurance in one policy may result in important savings in premium costs.

HAZARDS NOT COVERED

Since the Workmen's Compensation policy covers the employer's entire liability under the Workmen's Compensation Law, no exclusions from such laws are stated in the policy. The policy does not cover more than the law provides under Coverage A and, if a particular accident is not compensable, the policy does not cover it under Coverage A. Such an accident, however, may be covered under Coverage B if it arises out of and in course of employment (discussed above) and if the Insured in an action for negligence is held legally liable for the occurrence.

Locations Not Described—The policy specifically excludes, from both Coverages A and B, operations conducted at any workplace not described in the Declarations, if the Insured has other insurance for such operations, or is self-insured. Otherwise, undisclosed locations would be automatically covered if they had not been specifically excluded by endorsement.

Domestic or Agricultural Employees—Unless specifically stated in the Policy Declarations or required by law, the policy does not apply under Coverage A or B to domestic or agricultural employments. An Insured who conducts an operation covered by the Workmen's Compensation Law, e.g., a factory, does not have his insurance extended to a farm he may own, or to his domestic servants, unless he elects to do so, or the law requires the insurance of farm or domestic employees.

NEW YORK—See exception for this state discussed earlier in this chapter under WHO IS COVERED.

Assumed Liability—Coverage B of the policy relates to Employers' Liability, which does not come under the Workmen's Compensation Law (discussed under WHAT IS COVERED). There is no coverage, however, for any liability ASSUMED by the Insured under any contract or agreement. This provision does not however exclude coverage for warranties made by the Insured as to the quality of the work done by him. Such warranties are not deemed to be contracts and are therefore not excluded from the Employers' Liability section of the Workmen's Compensation policy. It will be recalled that General Liability policies generally exclude this type of warranty (discussed in Chapter 25 under OWNERS', LANDLORDS' AND TENANTS' LIABILITY POLICY—HAZARDS NOT COVERED). This section of the Workmen's Compensation policy, it can be seen, closes an important gap in the Insured's coverage.

Punitive Damages, Illegal Employment—Earlier in the chapter, there was discussion of MINORS UNDER WORKMEN'S COMPENSATION LAWS. It was pointed out that many states impose a penalty on employers who employ minors illegally. The extra compensation for which an employer becomes liable in such cases is *not* covered under the Workmen's Compensation policy. Furthermore, under Coverage B—Employers' Liability, there is no protection extended an employer who is sued at common law by a minor whom he has knowingly employed in violation of law.

FOR HOW MUCH

There is no dollar limit upon the Company's liability under Coverage A of a Workmen's Compensation policy. The policy covers the full liability of the employer under the law. This includes the cost of medical, surgical, hospital, nursing and similar services, as well as the weekly indemnity prescribed under the law. It also covers funeral expenses when a worker is fatally injured, and the compensation payable to his widow and other dependents. Where the law covers the cost of furnishing artificial appliances (as it does in all states except Nebraska), the policy will cover such expenditures.

Under Coverage B, the policy does provide for a limit of liability. The rates shown in the manual provide for a standard limit of $100,000 for each accident involving one or more employees. This limit is also aggregate limit by state for all damages on account of disease. (These limits may be increased for a higher premium.) This limit applies to policies which are not written on a voluntary compensation basis.

In connection with operations which are covered on a voluntary compensation basis, the manual rates include Coverage B coverage with a limit of $5,000 for all damages arising out of bodily injuries or death of one person, and subject to this limit per person, to a total limit of $10,000 for damages or death of two or more persons in any one accident.

MASSACHUSETTS, MISSOURI—The policy provides full coverage on Coverage A as well as Coverage B.

NEW YORK—As discussed before, the New York Workmen's Compensation Law covers all occupational diseases. The employer's complete liability for such diseases is therefore covered under Coverage A of the policy.

There are situations, however, where an employee may be taken sick with a condition which is not considered an occupational disease but which the employee contends was due to his employer's negligence. Thus, a worker contracts a respiratory ailment and alleges that it was due to his being compelled to work in damp or draughty surroundings. An illness of this kind is not an "occupational disease" and will not be compensable under the Workmen's Compensation Law. The worker is therefore free to sue his employer at law. Coverage B of the policy expressly covers legal liability for such disease.

Under the New York Amendatory endorsement which must be attached to every policy which provides insurance under the New York law, Coverage B is unlimited for accidents or disease in connection with employees working in operations which are subject to the New York law. For employees *not* subject to this state's law (like maritime work) the basic limit for Coverage B is $100,000 for each accident and $100,000 in the *aggregate* for disease. Limits of $500,000 or $1,000,000 are available for higher premiums.

HOW PREMIUM IS COMPUTED

The rate for Workmen's Compensation insurance is based on the nature of the Insured's operations, and varies with the hazards of the work. The premium is based on the amount of payroll expended by the Insured and is arrived at by multiplying the rate shown in the manual by the amount of the entire remuneration, subject to certain maximums, special charges, discounts and exceptions discussed below. The rates shown in the manual apply to each $100 of remuneration, regardless of the length of time during which the payroll was expended. Thus, the premium charge for a payroll of $10,000 expended during one month is the same as for a $10,000 payroll paid out over a 10-month period. If the rate in a given state for the manufacture of wood alcohol is 6.54, and the insured has ten employees who earn $60 per week each, the basic premium for the policy is arrived at as follows:

Weekly remuneration	$ 600.00
× 52 weeks	52
Total annual remuneration	$31,200.00
× rate per $100	6.54
Annual premium	$ 2,040.48

If the policy is issued for a short term, or in the event of cancellation, the manual rate will be charged on the amount of payroll expended from the effective date of the policy to such termination date. However, if the policy is cancelled by the Insured (except when retiring from business covered by the policy), the standard Short Rate cancellation table will apply to the premium computation.

Payroll in Excess of $300 per Week—Except in the states listed next, all payroll of employees, which is in excess of an average of $300 per week for the time they are employed, is disregarded in the computation of the premium for Workmen's Compensation insurance, provided the Insured segregates the payroll records of such employees. (The method of calculating is discussed more fully in Chapter 25 under MANUFACTURERS' AND CONTRACTORS' LIABILITY—RATES—Governing Classification.)

FLORIDA, LOUISIANA, MISSOURI, OKLAHOMA—Only payroll in excess of $100 per week is disregarded.
TEXAS—Only payroll in excess of $200 per week is disregarded.
CALIFORNIA, DELAWARE, MINNESOTA, NEW JERSEY, PENNSYLVANIA, WISCONSIN—The entire payroll is considered.

Board, Lodging, Services—Bonuses, Commissions and Tips—The money value of board, rent, housing, merchandise, credits, and services of any kind received by an employee as compensation for his services is included in the remuneration used for determining Workmen's Compensation premiums. Where an employee is compensated in whole or part by bonuses, commissions or tips, these are included in the remuneration on which the premium for the policy is based. Remuneration also includes vacation pay, sick pay, holiday pay, all piece work earnings, and any money received under incentive or profit-sharing plans.

FLORIDA—Pure gratuities and voluntary profit-sharing are not included in determining an employee's remuneration.

NEW YORK—Meals are valued at $1 per day. Lodging (when merely a place to sleep) is valued at $3.50 per day; an apartment or private dwelling at its actual cash value. The actual amount of tips is disregarded, but wages of such employees will not be taken at less than $15 per week.

Overtime Pay—If the Insured keeps his payroll records in such a manner that it is possible to determine separately the remuneration earned at regular rates of pay and the extra remuneration for overtime work, the extra pay for overtime will be disregarded in arriving at the remuneration on which to base the premium for Workmen's Compensation insurance. Thus, assume a worker works 48 hours in one week. For the first 40 hours he is paid at the rate of $1.50 per hour. For the last 8 hours, he receives time and a half, at $2.25 per hour. For purposes of determining the amount of remuneration to be charged for, all the hours worked are figured as though they had been compensated for on straight time, i. e., 48 hours at $1.50 per hour.

NOTE: The rule for computation of overtime pay is applied before the Payroll Limitation rule discussed above.

Payroll of Executive Officers—The payroll of all executive officers is included in arriving at the premium, subject to the same rules which apply to the payroll of regular employees (discussed under Payroll in Excess of $300 per Week).

CALIFORNIA—Maximum for executive officers is $12,000 per year.

COLORADO—The maximum is $3,600.

DELAWARE, MINNESOTA, PENNSYLVANIA, WISCONSIN—The maximum is $100 per week.

NEW JERSEY—The maximum is $200 per week.

NEW YORK—All executive officers of corporations are automatically covered under the policy by law, except those in religious, charitable, educational, municipal and war veteran corporations. These may be voluntarily insured. The maximum payroll for premium computation purposes is $300. The minimum individual remuneration taken for any executive officer is $50 per week and this minimum is also applied to officers who serve without pay. Inactive officers are included at $100 per annum.

Partners— In those states in which partners are subject to the Workmen's Compensation Law, or in which partners may elect to come under the law, the payroll of each partner for premium determination is fixed at $5,200 per annum.

UTAH—The payroll of partners is fixed at $400 per month.

Per Capita Premiums—Certain few classifications are rated on a per capita basis instead of on the basis of payroll. This procedure is followed in the case of inservants, outservants, private chauffeurs and occasional servants. The "occasional servant" per capita rate applies when a servant is employed one-half (or less) of the customary full time hours.

NEW YORK—The premium for part-time janitors is a "per location" charge; for volunteer firemen it is based on the population of the area served; for building wrecking, on the cubic contents of the building being demolished.

Governing Classification—The rate used for any risk is based on the classification in the manual which best describes the activities of the Insured, known as the "Governing Classification." The payroll of all employees of an Insured (with certain exceptions to be discussed below) is included in the Governing Classification. Thus, the Governing Classification for a shoe manufacturer is "Shoe or Boot Mfg." and it includes the payroll of the machinists, porters and other employees, even though they may not be engaged in the actual making of shoes. If an employer conducts separate enterprises and his operations are described in the policy by two or more classifications, the Governing Classification is the one which develops the largest amount of payroll, and such Governing Classification would then apply to the payroll of miscellaneous employees, such as elevator operators and maintenance men.

Standard Exceptions—For purposes of rating, four classes of employees are considered separately. These special classifications, outlined below, are known as Standard Exceptions:

(a) Clerical Office Employees—whose duties are confined exclusively to office work performed in buildings or floors separate from the plant where other operations are performed or in departments separated by structural partitions from all other work places of the Insured.

(b) Draughtsmen—whose duties do not expose them to the operative hazards of the employer's business.

(c) Outside Salesmen, Collectors or Messengers—whose activities are conducted principally away from the premises of the employer and who do not deliver the merchandise handled by the Insured.

(d) Drivers, Chauffeurs and Their Helpers—whose principal duties are performed upon or in connection with vehicles, or who use bicycles on their employer's business.

The payroll of employees who come within the Standard Exceptions, as outlined, is not included with that of the employees engaged in the employer's regular business. Each of the Standard Exceptions are rated separately, but the Standard Exception Classifications are not considered in determining the Governing Classification of the risk.

Exceptions in Construction or Erection Work—If a construction or erection risk includes separate and distinct operations; e.g., masonry, plastering, carpentry, each separate type of work is subject to a separate classification and rate. In order to obtain the separate rating, however, the employer must maintain separate payroll records for each operation. If such separate payroll records are not maintained, the entire payroll is assigned to the highest rated classification applicable to any part of the job.

Constant Charges—There are two constants in the form of separate, additional premium charges applicable to Workmen's Compensation policies which develop a premium of less than $500.00. A Loss Constant is applied first; after the premium *including* the Loss Constant has been determined and Expense Constant is applied. The rules governing the application of these Constants are set down below.

Loss Constant—It has been found that the loss ratio on a policy which develops a lower premium is higher than on larger premium policies. To offset this higher loss factor, a Loss Constant is added to all policies with an annual premium of less than $500.00. The Loss Constant which is usually between $5.00 and $20.00 varies by Manual classification and is shown on the state rate pages. Only one Loss Constant is charged on each policy and in no event is a Loss Constant added which will serve to increase the premium beyond $500.00. Thus if the addition of the Loss Constant would cause the premium to exceed $500.00, only so much of the Loss Constant is charged as will bring the premium to $500.00.

EXAMPLES:

a. Premium under $500:

Policy Premium (excluding Expense Constant)	=	$265
Loss Constant	=	17
Premium *before* consideration of Expense Constant	=	$282

b. Premium near $500:

Policy Premium (excluding Expense Constant)	=	$490
Loss Constant	=	17
		$507

Only $10.00 of the Loss Constant is charged making the premium $500 instead of $507 shown in example b.

c. Premium $500 or more: No Loss Constant is charged:

NEW YORK—On multiple classification policies, the Loss Constant for the policy is one which corresponds to the classification (including Standard Exception classifications) which develops the largest premium.

Expense Constant—After the policy premium *including the Loss Constant* has been determined, the Expense Constant is considered. This charge is made to offset the higher *expense* factor on policies with premiums under $500. The Expense Constant does not vary by classification but depends on the premium bracket in which the particular policy falls.

1. For a policy premium (including the Loss Constant) under $200, the Expense Constant charge is $15 except that the total premium including the $15 Expense Constant is not permitted to exceed $210.

EXAMPLES:

a. Premium (including Loss Constant)	under $200:	=	$140
	Expense Constant	=	15
	Total Premium	=	$155
b. Premium (including Loss Constant)	near $200:	=	$198
	Expense Constant	=	15
	Total Premium	=	$213

Only $12 of the Loss Constant is charged making the final premium $210 instead of the $213 shown in example b.

2. For policy premiums (including the Loss Constant) from $200 to $500, the Expense Constant is $10 unless the addition of the $10 Expense Constant would increase the premium more than $500 in which case the total premium is limited to $500.

EXAMPLES:

a. Premium (including Loss Constant)	between $200 and $500:	=	$345
	Expense Constant	=	10
	Total Premium	=	$355
b. Premium (including Loss Constant)	near $500:	=	$495
	Expense Constant	=	10
	Total premium	=	$505

Only $5 of the Expense Constant is charged making the total premium $500 instead of the $505 shown in example b.

On any policy where the premium including the Loss Constant is $500 or more, no Expense Constant is charged.

Audit Premiums—The entire rating manual is made part of the policy contract, just as though it were actualy printed in the policy. It is thus stipulated that the final earned premium will be based on the rules, classifications, rates and rating plans set forth in the manual. Since there is no way to know the precise payroll that will be expended during a policy year, the policy is written for a deposit premium based on an *estimate* of the Insured's payroll. At the end of the policy year, the insurance Company makes an audit of the Insured's payroll records. If the final earned premium based upon audit is larger than the deposit premium paid at the inception of the policy year, the Insured is required to pay the difference; if such final premium is less than the deposit premium paid, the Company refunds the excess. When the annual premium is less than $750, audits are usually made once every three years, with premiums for the intervening years based on payroll statements prepared by the Insured. If the premum is more than $750, annual audits are made.

The company and any rating organization are given the right to audit and examine all records, ledgers, contracts and tax reports which might have any bearing on the premium or the remuneration of employees. This right applies throughout the policy period and within three years after its expiration.

Interim Premium Adjustments—Larger risks may be written subject to more frequent audits of premium, and this procedure is almost standard on construction risks. Under this plan, the deposit premium required of the Insured is less than the estimated premium for the full year, and his payroll records are audited semi-annually, quarterly or monthly. Below are shown the minimum deposit premiums which are required on each type of policies subject to interim premium adjustment.

Monthly audit ....Not less than 25% of the annual premium
Quarterly audit ....Not less than 50% of the annual premium
Semi-annual audit...Not less than 75% of the annual premium

Under any policy subject to interim audits, the Deposit Premium shall not be less than $100 and the Insured is required to make periodic premium payments when each interim audit is made. Where interim audits are made, the Deposit Premium is credited only to the final audit.

Minimum Premiums—A minimum premium is established for each classification in the manual. Except when the policy is cancelled before its expiration, the minimum premium will be retained even though remuneration actually paid out by the Insured would develop a smaller premium. Only one minimum premium applies to each policy. Where a policy is subject to more than one classification, the highest minimum premium applies.

NEW YORK: The minimum premium under multiple classification policies is that which corresponds to any classification (including Standard Exception classifications) which develops the largest premium.

Premium Discount—To reflect the lower expense in the handling of larger risks, a discount is allowed on the portion of the premium which exceeds $1,000. The discount increases as the premium increases. A separate scale of discount percentages is applied to premiums written in stock carriers and non-stock carriers, and the percentages vary among the states. In practically all states, the Premium Discount is based on the total premium for all states covered by the policy; and the Premium Discount thus applies on an interstate basis. For each state, however, a different percentage of discount is applicable to the portion of the premium developed for that state.

Experience Rating—To encourage employers to decrease the frequency and severity of industrial accidents, most states have in effect a method of rewarding better than average risks and penalizing those whose accident ratio is poorer than average. The ratings are computed by the state rating organizations which maintain detailed records of the loss experience of all risks eligible for experience rating. The individual employer's loss experience is measured against the average for his industry, and a factor called an Experience Modification is developed. This factor is used to modify the premium which the risk develops at manual rates during the ensuing policy year. The Experience Modification is expressed as a decimal, e. g., .75 would produce a 25% credit, 1.30 would produce a charge of 30%.

In this way, the employer with a superior accident ratio enjoys a reduced premium; the employer whose accident morbidity is high pays a higher premium for insurance. Since the promulgation of Experience Modifications is a comparatively involved procedure, and since the loss experience of a smaller risk in any given year is not as conclusive as that of larger employers, Experience Rating is not applied except where the premium exceeds a minimum figure. While there are a few variations, in practically all states to be eligible for Experience Rating, a risk must have developed a premium which averages $750 for the last two or three years of the experience period. One year of experience will qualify a risk, provided the premium for that year was at least $1,500.

The year immediately preceding the current policy period is usually omitted in the Experience Rating of risks. A risk which is large enough to qualify for Experience Rating is automatically subject to the plan. The Insured does not have to elect to come under Experience Rating, nor can he decline to have the modification applied.

Interstate Experience Rating—If a risk conducts operations in more than one state, the Experience Rating Plan is automatically applied on an interstate basis, if the risk qualifies for Experience Rating in any one of the states in which it has operations. Thus a single Experience Modification will be calculated and applied to the entire manual premium for such interstate risk.

CALIFORNIA, DELAWARE, NEVADA, NEW JERSEY, NORTH DAKOTA, OHIO, OREGON, PENNSYLVANIA, WASHINGTON, WEST VIRGINIA, WYOMING—Interstate rating does not apply.

RETROSPECTIVE RATING

Retrospective Rating—Plan D:—The Experience Rating Plan is compulsory for all risks which meet its qualifications but the Experience Rating Modification is based upon past losses incurred during the experience period. Another rating plan, on an optional basis, is available to risks of a larger premium size. This is the Retrospective Rating Plan which provides for the adjustment of the premium for a current policy on the basis of the losses incurred during the term of that specific policy. Thus an Insured may elect application of the Retrospective Rating Plan in order to obtain a reflection of favorable losses developed under the current policy as compared with unfavorable losses incurred during the experience period used by the Experience Rating Plan. It is also possible that when the Retrospective Rating Plan is applied to a policy, the resulting Retrospective Premium would be higher on account of unfavorable losses. The Retrospective Rating Plan is always applied to a policy to modify the premium which is produced by the application of the Experience Rating Modification. Consequently, when a risk qualifies for Experience Rating, the premium for the current policy is modified to reflect the debit or credit resulting from Experience Rating. Then, if such standard premium is sufficiently large, the risk has the option of applying the Retrospective Rating Plan. Upon such election, the Experience Rating premium will then be adjusted on the basis of the losses incurred during the term of that current policy.

To qualify for retrospective rating, a premium of $1,000 per year is required for application of the Tabular Plans A, B, C and J, while an annual premium of $5,000 is required for Plan D. The distinction between these Plans will be explained later.

NEW YORK—The qualification for all Plans is $7,500 annual premium.

The Retrospective Rating Plan is a form of cost plus insurance because it attempts to charge a premium based upon the actual cost of insuring a risk by computing the incurred losses, and adding thereto the operating expenses and taxes paid by the carrier. The Premium Discount rule explained previously does not apply to any policy under the Retrospective Rating Plan because the factors in that Plan automatically reflect the effect of the Premium Discount rule. When a policy is subject to retrospective rating, the final premium is held between a predetermined maximum premium and a predetermined minimum premium which the Insured selects in advance based upon the size of the standard premium. The variation in the final retrospective premium for the policy depends primarily upon the losses which had been incurred during that policy term. Regardless of the premium computation basis which is selected, the formula for determining the final Retrospective Premium is always as follows:

Retrospective Premium = [Basic Premium + (Standard Premium × Excess Loss Premium Factor × Loss Conversion Factor) + (Losses × Loss Conversion Factor)] × Tax Multiplier.

The foregoing elements in the formula are included for the following purposes:

Basic Premium covers insurance carrier expenses, other than taxes, and also acquisition, audit, administration and profit or contingencies.

Standard Premium is the premium at manual rates as modified by any experience modification.

Excess Loss Premium Factor establishes a limit such as $10,000 as the maximum at which any single loss will be included in the retrospective rating premium computation. The carrier pays the full loss but the loss is limited in the formula to the selected loss limitation. Thus the impact on final premium of a single large loss is lessened.

Loss Conversion Factor is a factor for claim adjustment expenses.

Losses are those incurred during the policy term but which will be included in the above formula at not more than the preselected loss limitation.

Tax Multiplier is included to cover the premium taxes which the carrier must pay.

In all cases the premium resulting from the formula will not exceed the preselected maximum premium, nor be less than the predetermined minimum premium.

Within the scope of the Retrospective Rating Plan there are other optional Tabular Plans, so called because the factors used in the Retrospective Premium formula are based upon tables published in the Plan. Tabular Plans may be used only for Workmen's Compensation insurance on an intrastate or interstate basis:

PLAN A—The minimum premium is less than the standard premium but the maximum premium will not exceed the standard premium. For example, the minimum premium range may be from about 85% of the standard premium for smaller risks to 25% for large risks with a premium of about $400,000.

PLAN B, which is frequently used, provides for a minimum less than standard premium and a maximum over standard premium. The minimum premium varies from about 65% for smaller risks with a maximum premium of 170% for such risks, and about 110% maximum for large risks.

PLAN C does not have any minimum premium but does provide for a maximum premium so that the minimum would depend only upon incurred losses and the application of the formula. The maximum premium ranges would be the same as in Plan B.

PLAN J is used for large risks and provides for a narrower range of minimum and maximum premium ratios as compared with Plan B. For example, the range of maximum premiums in Plan J is between 130% and 105% and it also provides for a narrower range of minimum premiums.

In addition to the Tabular Plans explained above, Retrospective Rating PLAN D may be applied without using tables. In such instances, each element of the retrospective rating formula is determined on the basis of the individual risk, subject to approval of the rating organization governing the states covered by the policy. PLAN D without tables is suitable for large risks with premiums in excess of $25,000 annually and it may apply on an interstate or intrastate basis. Also, the same rating may include Workmen's Compensation insurance in combination with other third party liability lines or automobile physical damage, burglary and glass coverages.

The Retrospective Rating Plan may also be applied to a risk on a three-year basis, at the option of the insured, provided that the same insurance carrier writes the successive annual policies. The same options are available on a three-year basis as for a single year. The three-year plan involves lower basic premium factors than a one-year plan and with losses spread over three years, a single unfavorable year could be offset by better experience in the other years.

In all cases, the option to elect the Retrospective Rating Plan must be made in advance of the effective date of the policy. This Plan gives an employer the advantage of obtaining the benefit of lower loss ratios during the term of a policy because the final retrospective premium is based principally on incurred losses with a relatively small charge for the operating expenses of the carrier.

Three Year Fixed Rate Policies—In all states except CALIFORNIA, it is optional, by agreement between the carrier and the Insured, to issue any policy with an estimated annual premium of less than $200 for a period of three years on a fixed manual rate basis. When such policy is issued, the manual rates in effect on the policy's inception date will remain applicable throughout the term of the policy, regardless of any general revision in the rate schedule which may be promulgated. The Deposit Premium is computed by applying the manual rate to the three year estimated payroll. The regular Loss Constant is applied but only one $15 Expense Constant is charged if the three year premium is paid in advance; two $15 Expense Constants if the three year premium is paid in three equal annual installments. Thus the Insured receives a $30 discount for paying the entire three year premium in advance or a $15 discount for installment payments. The final earned premium determination may be deferred until the end of the three year term. If a three year fixed rate policy is cancelled by the Insured, other than when he is retiring from business, the final earned premium is computed on a pro rata basis and a flat penalty added to the earned premium (in lieu of a short rate calculation).

INSURED'S DUTIES

Policy Declarations—The policy contains the following Declarations, called Items, which are statements the Insured makes to the Company:

Item 1. Name, address and legal status (whether an individual, partnership, corporation or some other type of entity such as association or a fiduciary).

Item 2. The policy period.

Item 3. The states in which Coverage A is to apply are listed.

Item 4. The premium computation is set forth in this Item, as explained previously.

Item 5. The limit of liability for Coverage B.

The policy stipulates that the statements in the Declarations are the Insured's agreements and representations and that the policy is issued in reliance thereon.

Notice of Accident—See Chapter 24 under INSURED'S DUTIES.

Notice of Claim or Suit—See Chapter 24 under INSURED'S DUTIES.

Subrogation—See RIGHT OF ACTION OF EMPLOYEES AGAINST THIRD PARTIES.

Cancellation—The Company may cancel the policy at any time, as may the Insured. The policy conforms to the Workmen's Compensation Law of the individual state as regards cancellation. Usually, the Company must give at least ten days' notice to the Insured *and* to the agency which administers Workmen's Compensation.

NEW YORK—Notice to the Insured must be delivered to him in person or by registered mail. The cancellation cannot take effect until at least ten days after the notice is received and date stamped in the Workmen's Compensation office in Albany. If an employer has canceled his Workmen's Compensation insurance without replacing it, and an employee sustains an accident after the date of the cancellation for which the employer does not have assets to pay, such claim is covered by the Uninsured Employers' Fund. This fund is administered by the Workmen's Compensation Board.

If the Company cancels, the cancellation is effected pro rata. If the cancellation is at the request of the Insured, the cancellation is effected at short rates, except if the Insured is retiring from business, in which case the cancellation is made on a pro rata basis.

NEW YORK—If the Company cancels, or if the Insured requests cancellation when he is retiring from business, the cancellation is made on a pro rata basis, but the earned premium shall not be less than the pro rata portion of the minimum premium. If the cancellation is made at the Insured's request when he has completed the work covered by the policy but is not retiring from business, the earned premium, exclusive of the Loss and Expense Constant, shall be adjusted pro rata but the Constant shall be adjusted at short rates, and the earned premium including such Constant at short rates shall not be less than the short rate percentage of the minimum premium.

Assignment—No assignment of the policy will bind the Company except when it has given its consent.

When Covered—Workmen's Compensation policies attach at 12:01 A. M., Standard Time, at the address of the Insured, as stated in the policy. This avoids dispute as to the time coverage attached when the employer operates in different time zones.

Claims for disease under Coverage B must be brought within 36 months after the end of the policy period.

UNITED STATES LONGSHOREMEN'S AND HARBOR WORKERS' COMPENSATION ACT

AS MENTIONED in the preceding chapter, a special Federal Compensation Law applies to maritime workers other than masters and members of the crews of vessels. The line between maritime employment and work on land is sometimes hard to draw, as when an employee working on land is thrown onto a ship or into the water, or when an employee is injured while going from ship to shore, but the following general rules may be applied to such situations.

Although the individual states include in their domain all their waters, including the ocean which bounds them up to the three-mile limit, jurisdiction over all navigable waters is granted to the Federal Government. All maritime employees except members of crews of vessels, come under the jurisdiction of the United States Longshoremen's and Harbor Workers' Compensation Act, with respect to injuries sustained by them in the operation or maintenance of vessels or in loading or unloading work while on vessels. If such employees are injured on land or docks while loading or unloading vessels, they are subject to the state Compensation Laws.

A special Workmen's Compensation Act of the U. S. Government covers the majority of maritime workers other than masters and members of the crews of vessels. This act, known as the Longshoremen's and Harbor Workers' Act, covers all injuries or death sustained by employees on the navigable waters of the United States or any dry dock. Since these injuries do not come under the state Workmen's Compensation Laws, the standard Workmen's Compensation insurance policy does not apply to an employer's liability for such accidents. To provide insurance to employers for their liability under the Longshoremen's and Harbor Workers' Act, a special endorsement is used with the standard Workmen's Compensation policy. In most states, there is an additional premium charge for insurance under this Federal Act because it provides benefits which are usually higher than those under the state laws. Stevedoring concerns require insurance under both the state and Federal laws.

FOR FURTHER READING

ACKERMAN—Insurance
ANALYSIS OF PROVISIONS OF WORKMEN'S COMPENSATION LAWS AND DISCUSSION OF COVERAGES—Chamber of Commerce of the United States
DIGEST OF WORKMEN'S COMPENSATION LAWS IN THE UNITED STATES AND TERRITORIES—American Insurance Association
GEE—Agent's Casualty Guide
GUIDE TO STATE DISABILITY BENEFITS LAWS
HEDGES—Practical Fire and Casualty Insurance
HOBBS—Workmen's Compensation Insurance
KULP AND HALL—Casualty Insurance
MAGEE AND BICKELHAUPT—General Insurance
MEHR AND CAMMACK—Principles of Insurance
MOWBRAY—Insurance
POLICY, FORM AND MANUAL ANALYSIS SERVICE
RIEGEL, ROBERT and MILLER—Insurance
WRIGHT—Subrogation Under Workmen's Compensation Acts

(See Reading List at End of Book)

CHAPTER 31

Disability Insurance

HOSPITALIZATION AND MEDICAL CARE INSURANCE—DISABILITY BENEFITS INSURANCE
INSURANCE AGAINST LOSS OF TIME THROUGH DISABILITY
(Accident and Health Insurance)

THE MOST VALUABLE economic asset owned by most people is, of course, their earning power. Becoming disabled by an accident or illness is therefore one of the most serious hazards that faces producing people, for it threatens the foundation on which their financial stability depends. The problem is usually aggravated by the fact that heavy medical or surgical expenses must be met at the same time as income is cut off. Accident and Health insurance developed out of the very fundamental need to be protected, in part at least, against the economic consequences of disability.

The need for this protection varies for different individuals. Where some can face protracted periods without steady income, others will find themselves in serious difficulties after a comparatively short time, while for some, any curtailment of regular income produces immediate strain.

To meet these varying needs, there are available a very wide variety of policies and plans. Numerous Casualty companies, Accident and Health carriers, Life insurance and fraternal organizations offer different forms of Disability insurance, and no two plans are exactly the same. While considerable standardization is being developed in certain provisions of Accident and Health policies, no "standard policy" exists, and the various benefits offered in any one policy are practically always different in some respects from those offered in a second policy.

This chapter will discuss the broad aspects of Accident and Health insurance and will analyze the more typical policy in use. It should be remembered, however, that a complete analysis of any Disability insurance policy can be made only by a study of the actual policy.

TYPES OF ACCIDENT AND HEALTH INSURANCE

Most insurance against disability will fall into one of the following broad groups:

1. Commercial Accident and Health Insurance.
2. Industrial (Weekly Premium) Accident and Health Insurance.
3. Non-cancellable Accident and Health Insurance.
4. Limited Type Accident and Health Insurance.
5. Group and "Wholesale" or "Franchise."
6. Fraternal Accident and Health Insurance.
7. Disability Provisions in Life Insurance Policies.

Each of these types of Accident and Health insurance will be commented on separately.

"UNIFORM" AND "STANDARD" PROVISIONS

About 1914, various states began to pass what are known as "Standard Provisions" laws, to secure uniformity in policy conditions and operating procedures in Accident and Health policies. While these Standard Provisions were uniform at the start, the laws were changed in details as they were adopted, and have been amended in some states from time to time.

In 1950, the National Association of Insurance Companies drew up a model set of "Uniform Provisions" to replace the old "Standard Provisions," and adoption by all states was urged. All states except Minnesota and Missouri have either enacted these provisions into law or will accept and approve them for use in their jurisdiction.

Some of the more common Uniform Provisions are:

Entire Contract: Changes—It is stipulated that the policy and the riders and endorsements and other attached papers constitute the entire contract. No changes in the policy shall be valid unless approved by an executive officer and endorsed on the policy. No agent has authority to change or modify the policy in any way or to waive any of its provisions.

Time Limit on Certain Defenses—After the policy shall have been in force for two years, no statement made by the Insured in his application (except fraudulent misstatements) shall be invoked to void the policy or to deny a loss incurred from disability commencing after the expiration of the two-year period.

Grace Period—After the payment of the first premium, a grace period shall be granted for the payment of all premiums. On weekly premium policies, the grace period is seven days; on monthly premium policies, 10 days; on all other policies (quarterly, semi-annual and annual), the grace period is 31 days.

NOTE: Ordinarily, when an insurance company reserves the right to refuse renewal of a policy, it must give the Insured at least 30 days' notice of its intention not to renew.

Reinstatement—If a renewal premium is not paid within the time granted, the subsequent acceptance of the premium by the company or an agent authorized to receive such premium, without requirement of an application for reinstatement, shall reinstate the policy. If the company or the agent does require an application for reinstatement and issues a conditional receipt for the renewal premium being tendered, the policy will be reinstated only after approval of such application by the company; or if the company fails to notify the Insured of its disapproval of his application for 45 days after the issuance of the conditional receipt.

The reinstated policy will cover claims arising only from accidental injury which occurs after the date of the reinstatement; in the case of sickness, only such conditions which begin more than ten days after such date.

Any period accepted in connection with a reinstated policy shall be applied towards the period for which the premium was not paid, but in no event to any period more than 60 days prior to the date of the reinstatement.

COMMERCIAL ACCIDENT AND HEALTH INSURANCE

OF THE SEVERAL TYPES of Disability insurance offered to individuals, the most popular policy is of the Commercial type. This policy provides comparatively broad coverage, and is sold largely to individuals in the less hazardous occupations. Premiums are payable annually, semi-annually or quarterly. Policies may be written to cover only against disability resulting from accidents, or for both accidental injury and sickness. For purposes of illustration, this section will discuss a policy covering *both* types of hazard—an Accident and Health policy. Where a policy is purchased to insure only against the risk of accidents, the provisions discussed below relating to sickness do not appear.

WHAT IS COVERED

Indemnity for Loss of Time—Most Accident and Health policies provide a series of benefits, as will be outlined next. The most important of these benefits is the weekly or monthly indemnity promised for the Insured's loss of time from his work. The basic Insuring Clause provides that if the Insured is disabled (as defined in the policy) he will receive a stipulated sum each week, or each month, during the continuance of the disability.

Policies vary widely not only as to the amount of indemnity they will pay but also as to the length of time during which benefits will be paid. Thus, one policy may be written to pay the stipulated indemnity for life, another will pay for no more than 52 weeks, or 104 weeks, or 60 months, etc. Furthermore, the same policy may offer longer indemnity for disability resulting from an accident than for disabling illness. Indemnity may be paid for life on disabilities caused by accident, with sickness benefits usually limited to one year, or two years, etc.

Accidental Death Provisions—Principal Sum—Most policies provide that the Insured's beneficiary will receive a lump sum payment if the Insured dies as the result of an accident. Some companies provide a stipulated accidental death benefit, depending on the amount of weekly or monthly indemnity; others permit the Insured to choose the amount of death benefit.

There is no provision for death benefits if the Insured dies other than by accident.

Dismemberment or Loss of Sight Provisions—Capital Sum—Many policies provide that the Insured will receive a lump sum if he suffers the loss of certain designated members of his body, or the loss of sight as the result of an accident. A table in the policy enumerates the amount payable for various dismemberments. Payments are shown as based either on the Principal Sum or on the weekly indemnity. Below is reproduced a fairly typical schedule of Death, Dismemberment or Loss of Sight provisions:

For Loss of Life	The Principal Sum [Line (a) above]
For Loss of	A Sum Equal to Weekly Indemnity for
Both Hands or Both Feet or Sight of Both Eyes	208 Weeks
One Hand and One Foot	208 Weeks
Either Hand or Foot and Sight of One Eye	208 Weeks
Either Hand or Foot	100 Weeks
Sight of One Eye	65 Weeks
Thumb and Index Finger of Either Hand	52 Weeks

The specific sums are payable in addition to any weekly indemnity which may have been paid to the Insured up to the date of the dismemberment.

If the Insured loses both hands, or both feet, or the sight of both eyes, he is usually granted the option of taking the lump sum stipulated in the schedule, or of continuing to receive the Weekly Indemnity as long as he lives.

Elective Indemnity for Specific Accidents—Some policies provide that for certain other accidents, dislocations or fractures, the

Insured will be entitled to a choice of the stipulated Weekly Indemnity or of designated lump sum payments.

Double Indemnity for Specific Accidents—Some policies provide that accident benefits will be paid at twice the usual rate if the Insured meets with an injury under certain stated conditions; e. g., while riding as a passenger on a common carrier, or in a passenger elevator, or if struck by lightning, etc.

Hospital Benefits—Many policies offer additional benefits if the Insured is confined to a hospital. These benefits take different forms. In some policies, the weekly indemnity is increased during hospital confinement; in others, all hospital expenses up to a stated maximum are paid, while some waive the elimination period (discussed under WHEN COVERED), if the Insured is confined to a hospital.

Surgical Indemnity Provisions—The policy usually includes a schedule of lump sum payments which will be paid to an Insured if he is compelled to undergo any of a designated list of surgical operations. Benefits are usually expressed as fractions or multiples of the Weekly Indemnity, ranging from 20% for some types of treatment to 400% for others; or the policy may contain a schedule of stated amounts for various types of operations.

Nursing Benefits—Some policies provide that the additional indemnity will be paid for each day during which the Insured continues under the care of a nurse at home or in a hospital.

Blanket Medical Expense Benefits—Some policies offer to pay the cost of all medical, surgical, hospital and nursing care up to a stated maximum. These benefits are generally confined to disabling injuries and do not apply to illnesses.

Non-Disabling Injuries—A small additional benefit is offered in many policies to pay for the medical expenses incurred by the Insured in non-disabling injuries.

HAZARDS COVERED

Total Disability—The benefits promised in the policy are payable if the Insured, during the term of the policy, becomes wholly and continuously disabled as the result of an accident or illness. The disability must result directly and independently of all other causes.

Policies differ as to their definition of the term "disability." Where the indemnity is promised for a relatively short period, as one year or less, disability is usually defined as the Insured's inability to perform each and every duty pertaining to his occupation,

Policies in which the indemnity extends over longer periods usually define disability as the Insured's inability to perform each and every duty pertaining to his occupation during the first twelve months, after which his condition must be such as to make it impossible for him to engage in each and every occupation for employment or profit.

Total loss of sight in both eyes is usually taken to constitute total disability.

Accidental Bodily Injury — Accidental Means — Some policies cover only bodily injuries which are caused "directly, solely and independently of all other causes by external, violent and accidental means." Other policies insure against "accidental bodily injuries." Strictly construed, the first language is somewhat more restrictive, as it is held that the *means* which led to the injury must be accidental, i. e., unexpected, happening by chance.

Thus, if the Insured, voluntarily trying to move a piece of furniture, ruptures a blood vessel, the injury would not have been caused by accidental means, since no violent, external, accidental means intervened to cause the injury. Such loss would be held covered under policies covering "accidental bodily injury." Of recent years, the area between these two types of language has been narrowed considerably by court decisions and by the deletion of the words "external and violent" from the insuring clause of many "accidental means" policies.

Partial Disability—The basic insurance afforded under Accident and Health policies revolves about total disability. Most policies of the Commercial type also provide some indemnity for partial disability. Partial disability is defined as the inability to perform one or more important duties pertaining to the Insured's occupation. Indemnity is usually provided only for partial disability resulting from accident, and only when such partial disability follows a period of total disability. Indemnity is usually payable at the rate of 50% of the total disability benefits, and for no more than 26 consecutive weeks.

HAZARDS NOT COVERED

The exclusions vary among different policies. Practically every policy specifically excludes claims arising from:

1. Suicide, or attempts at suicide or injuries intentionally self-inflicted.
2. Acts of war, or while the Insured is in the armed forces.
3. Sickness contracted while the Insured is outside of the United States, its possessions or Canada.

4. The Insured's travel on any aircraft other than as a fare-paying passenger on a regularly scheduled passenger flight over an established route between regular airports within the United States of America or Canada. Policies differ on this score, with some extending the permitted radius to include Mexico; others take in all of North America, including 50 nautical miles off the mainland, etc. Some policies are broad enough on this score to cover all flying accidents provided the Insured was not involved in any duties relating to the plane.

5. Hernia is generally excluded, although some policies provide limited coverage for claims due to this condition.

Excluded Conditions—In addition to the exclusions listed above, which are practically standard in all policies, some forms also exclude mental or nervous infirmities, tuberculosis, venereal diseases, etc.

Loss While Engaged in Committing Felony—Many policies contain a provision which excludes any loss if the contributing cause was the Insured's committing of a felony or his being engaged in an illegal act.

Loss While Intoxicated or Under Influence of Narcotics—In a similar vein, some policies state that the Company will not be liable for loss which occurs while the Insured is intoxicated or, except when administered on the advice of a physician, when under the influence of narcotics.

WHEN COVERED

The policy attaches at 12 o'clock Noon Standard Time, at the residence of the Insured. Different from Property insurance policies, the policy is issued in consideration of the premium and is therefore not in effect until the first premium has been paid. The initial premium covers a given period, usually one year, although policies are sometimes written for a six-month period or a three-month period. The insurance ceases at the end of the period, except when a grace period is provided (discussed later). Provision is made for the renewal of the policy by payment of further premiums, but such renewals are at the option of the Company, which may refuse to accept any renewal premium. (Some policies contain a Cancellation clause, later discussed under CANCELLATION.)

If the Company refuses to renew a policy, this does not affect the Insured's right to benefits on any claim which originated before the renewal date. Thus, assume the Insured purchased a policy promising $100 of monthly indemnity for five years on disabling injuries. The policy was dated February 1, 1953, and an annual premium paid to February 1, 1954. On October 1, 1953, the Insured suffers an accident. He receives indemnity at the rate of $100 for the months of October, November, December and January. On February 1, 1954, the renewal date, the Company does not renew the policy. The Insured is nevertheless entitled to continue receiving indemnity during each month of the continuance of his disability up to 60 months.

NEW YORK—Any Accident and Health policy issued after July 1, 1959, in which one-third or more of the total premium is allocable to hospital, surgical or medical benefits, is guaranteed renewable after it has been in force for two years.

Age Limits—Most policies stipulate that coverage will terminate when the Insured attains a given age.

Grace Period—Discussed under UNIFORM AND STANDARD PROVISIONS at the beginning of this chapter.

Pre-Existing Conditions—As pointed out, the policy covers only for accidents sustained or diseases contracted while the policy is in force. There is no coverage for conditions which existed prior to the date on which the policy attached.

Incontestable Clause—Recently, more and more policies are incorporating a special clause which sets a time limit on a Company's defense for a pre-existing condition. The clause provides that any claim which begins more than three years after the policy has been in force shall not be denied on the ground that the condition had existed prior to the issuance of the policy. Some policies provide that no claim shall be invalidated because of any statements in the application.

Probationary Period—To be protected against liability for conditions which may already have been contracted by the Insured when he purchases a policy, many companies include a "probationary period" as regards illnesses. A stipulated number of days must elapse after the policy is purchased before there is any coverage for illnesses. There is no Probationary Period for coverage on accidents.

Elimination Period—Waiting Period—To eliminate small claims and reduce the cost of insurance to the policyholder, most policies contain a Waiting Period, also known as an Elimination Period. It is expressly provided that no indemnity will be paid for the first days of any disability. Waiting Periods vary from three days to as much as 90 days. Often, the Waiting Period for sickness is longer than for disability caused by accidents.

Waiting Periods are not to be confused with Probationary Periods (discussed directly above). The Probationary Period is effective only when the policy is first purchased, and acts to exclude completely any claims which originate during the period. Waiting Periods apply to all claims, no matter when they originate and, like a Deductible clause, act to make the Insured carry part of each loss himself.

Reinstatement After Lapse—As pointed out above, Accident and Health policies are written for stipulated periods, and may be renewed for further periods by the payment of a renewal premium. Different from policies in the property insurance field, no new policy or certificate is issued to effect renewal. The payment of the renewal premium and its acceptance by the Insured is sufficient to carry the policy for a further period.

On the other hand, if a renewal premium is not paid on its due date, or within the grace period that may be allowed by the policy, the policy lapses, and all protection ceases. The Company may consent to reinstate a lapsed policy. Usually, the Insured is required, at the time of application for reinstatement, to complete a form giving information on his state of health. Most policies provide that, after they have been reinstated, there will be a new Probationary Period of 10 days on sickness, and no indemnity will be paid for any sickness which originates within these 10 days. No Probationary Period applies to accidents.

FOR HOW MUCH

As pointed out at the beginning of this chapter, Accident and Health policies differ very widely as to the amount of the benefits, the duration of indemnities, and the extra features that may be offered.

Under most conditions, the Insured will receive the stipulated benefits in full. He will not suffer any reduction in benefits because he is entitled to Workmen's Compensation, veteran's benefits, or any other benefits. Furthermore, an Insured who collects under his Accident and Health policy for an injury he has sustained may still institute a suit against a third party whose negligence was the cause of the accident.

Accident and Health policies do not contain a Subrogation clause, and the Company which pays benefits under an Accident and Health policy is not entitled to reimbursement from any recovery its Insured may have against third parties. For all practical purposes, the Accident and Health policy is akin to a Valued Policy—the Insured will receive the promised benefits under any and all conditions, if he becomes disabled within the meaning of the policy.

There are, however, several clauses in some Accident and Health policies which may act to modify the amount of benefits which an Insured will receive, and these are discussed next.

Accumulations—Some policies provide that certain indemnities shall be increased for each year that the policy is renewed and continued in force without lapse. Thus, each year 10% may be added to the Principal Sum and the Dismemberment indemnities until a stated maximum is attained. Other policies (usually the Non-Cancellable forms, discussed separately) may grant a 10% increase in indemnity for loss of time if the premium prior to the disability was paid annually, 5% if paid semi-annually.

Pro-Rating for Change to More Hazardous Occupation—Some policies provide that if the Insured changes to a more hazardous occupation than the one stated in the policy, or if he is injured while doing any act or thing pertaining to any occupation so classified, the Company will pay only such portion of the indemnities provided in the policy as the premium paid would have purchased at the rate for the higher rated occupation. It is expressly stipulated that there will be no reduction in benefits if the accident arises out of the Insured's ordinary duties around his residence, or while engaged in recreation.

EXAMPLE: A bookkeeper buys a policy providing for $100 of monthly income in the event of disability. He pays an annual premium of $40. Some time later, the Insured changes his occupation to that of house painter. The premium for the same amount of indemnity in this more hazardous classification would be $60. If the Insured is injured, he will be entitled to receive only 40/60ths, or ⅔ of the indemnities—$66.67 per month.

Benefits are reduced only if the Insured is injured. There is no pro-rating of benefits if the Insured becomes disabled as a result of illness.

Pro-Rating with Other Insurance—Some policies provide that the Insured must notify the Company if he purchases any additional Disability insurance. If he fails to do so, the policy will pay only such portion of the promised indemnity as that indemnity bears to the total amount of indemnity promised in all policies.

EXAMPLE: The Insured buys an Accident and Health policy in the Ajax Casualty Co., which provides for $100 of monthly income in the event of disability. The policy contains a Pro Rating clause of the type under discussion. Some time later, he buys a similar policy from the Solid Casualty Co. He does not inform the Ajax of the addition to his disability insurance program. In the event of his becoming disabled, the Ajax policy will pay only $50 a month, which is arrived at as follows:

$$\frac{\text{Amount of Benefits Promised in Ajax Policy} = \$100 \text{ per month}}{\text{Total Indemnity Promised in Both Policies} = \$200 \text{ per month}} = \frac{1}{2}$$

Limit on Total Indemnity—Some policies provide that if the total indemnity promised in all policies in the same Company exceeds a stated amount, the excess insurance will be void.

Reduction for Misstatement of Age—A provision in some policies provides that if the Insured had misstated his age when he purchased the policy, the benefits to which he will become entitled will be reduced to the amount which the premium paid would have purchased at the correct age.

Confining Clause—Some policies contain a clause which states that full indemnity will be paid for disabling illnesses which confine the Insured continuously within doors. If the Insured is disabled but able to leave such confinement, benefits are reduced or are payable for shorter periods.

INSURED'S DUTIES

Application—The Insured is required to submit a written application for an Accident and Health policy. The application, or a copy of it, is usually attached to the policy, and becomes part of the contract. Most policies provide further that no statement of the policyholder which does not appear in the application shall be used to void the policy or in any legal proceeding.

While the exact form of the application is not standardized, all companies ask substantially the same questions. The Insured is required to give certain personal data, details of his physical condition, his insurance history, including any claims submitted, his occupation, and the facts concerning other Disability coverages which he has in force.

Notice of Claim—The policy provides time limits within which the Insured must give notice of the different types of claim that develop under his policy. Notice of an accident or illness must be given within 20 days, or as soon thereafter as is reasonably possible. Some policies also require immediate notice of accidental death. The Company must be furnished with data sufficient to identify the Insured. The policy provides further that a claim shall not be invalidated because the Insured fails to give notice within the prescribed time, if it can be shown that it was not possible for him to have given such notice.

Proof of Loss—Proofs of loss for claims covering indemnity for loss of time must be filed by the Insured within 90 days after termination of the period for which benefits are being claimed. On claims for dismemberment, hospital, medical reimbursement and other benefits, proof must be filed within 90 days of the date of loss.

Time to Bring Suit—The Insured cannot institute a suit under the policy before 60 days have elapsed from the filing of proof of loss, nor after three years. These time limits are considered extended if the law of the state in which the Insured resides allows a longer period.

Medical Examination—Autopsy—The Company may ask the Insured to submit himself to a medical examination as often as is reasonable and, where not prohibited by law, may perform an autopsy in case of death.

WHEN LOSS IS PAYABLE

The policy provides that indemnity for specific losses, like dismemberment, shall be paid within a definite number of days. Most policies stipulate that such losses shall be paid immediately upon receipt of proof of loss. When the Insured becomes entitled to indemnity for loss of time, it is provided that he need not wait until the termination of his disability, but shall receive such indemnities periodically, usually every four weeks.

CANCELLATION

As discussed under WHEN COVERED, Accident and Health policies are written for a definite period, and may be renewed for additional periods with the Company's consent. (Non-Cancellable forms are discussed separately later.) The Company cannot cancel the policy during the term for which the premium has been paid. Some policies do, however, contain a cancellation privilege. Under such policies, the Company may cancel the policy at any time by giving five days' written notice to the Insured. A pro rata return premium is given the Insured for the unearned term. As under a policy which the Company refuses to renew, the cancellation of a policy does not prejudice any claim which has already originated (discussed under WHEN COVERED).

NEW MEXICO, OHIO—Company may cancel only at end of period for which premium has been paid.
NORTH CAROLINA—Notice of cancellation of between 30 days to 2 years is required.

Cancellation by Insured—There is no provision for the Insured's cancelling a policy except, under the old Standard Provisions, if the Insured changes to an occupation classified as less hazardous than the one stated in his policy, he may request cancellation of his policy and refund of the unearned premium. Under the new Uniform Provisions (optional), the Company may agree to reduce the rate, and refund the excess unearned premium.

INDUSTRIAL (WEEKLY PREMIUM) ACCIDENT AND HEALTH INSURANCE

THIS FORM OF INSURANCE is usually sold to individuals who are engaged in the more hazardous types of employment. Premiums are payable more frequently than on Commercial Accident and Health policies, usually weekly or monthly, and the benefits are somewhat more restricted. Since individuals insured under Industrial policies are usually covered by Workmen's Compensation laws, Industrial policies are often written on a non-occupational basis, to cover only for such disabilities as are not compensable under the Compensation statutes. In all other respects, the Industrial policy is similar to the Commercial policy analyzed in the preceding section of this chapter.

NON-CANCELLABLE ACCIDENT AND HEALTH INSURANCE

AS POINTED OUT BEFORE in the discussion of Commercial Accident and Health insurance, even when the policy does not grant the Company the right to cancel a policy, the Company has the option of refusing to renew a policy at the expiration of the period for which it is written. Such policies may not be labelled as "Non-Cancellable" in most jurisdictions.

An increasing number of companies now make available Accident and Health insurance which grants the *Insured* the right to renew the policy at his sole option until he attains a stated age, usually 60 or 65. These plans are generally sold only to the least hazardous occupations; e. g., professionals, executives and white collar workers. Underwriting standards are usually stricter than for other types of coverage, and a medical examination is almost always required.

GUARANTEED RENEWABLE ACCIDENT AND HEALTH INSURANCE

LIKE NON-CANCELLABLE Accident and Health insurance, this form of Disability insurance is renewable by the Insured at his sole option (usually up to a stipulated age), but the Company reserves the right to modify the premium on any anniversary of the policy but only for the entire class of Insureds and only when it can demonstrate that its losses on this class are excessive.

LIMITED TYPE ACCIDENT AND HEALTH INSURANCE

NUMEROUS FORMS of Accident policies and some Accident and Health policies are offered which provide coverage for specific types of loss. Travel policies are sold to cover only for accidents sustained in automobiles, or railroads or airplanes or other common carriers. Some of these policies are issued only for a specified trip (as in the case of Aviation policies offered at airports) or for a limited number of days. Policies are also issued to cover only against specified diseases, like poliomyelitis.

HOSPITAL, SURGICAL AND MEDICAL CARE POLICIES

THE MOST WIDELY SOLD policy offering protection for limited situations is the Hospitalization or Hospital Expense policy. This form of insurance may be written to cover an individual, or a husband and wife, or the entire family group. It is very widely sold on a group basis to cover all members of an employed group, and often their families.

Coverage is provided while the Insured is necessarily confined to a legally constituted hospital. No indemnity for loss of time is included, and the policy pays only a stipulated sum between $5 and $10 for each day that the Insured stays in the hospital. Where the policy covers a family, somewhat lower benefits are usually paid to the wife and children.

In the Hospital policies offered by private carriers, the Insured receives the cash benefits directly, dependent only upon his being confined to the hospital. Throughout the country, there are also non-profit plans, commonly known as Blue Cross plans. These plans do not promise any cash payments to the Insured. They are organized in conjunction with a group of cooperating hospitals in the community, which agree to furnish certain types of accommodations to the insured members. The insurance plan pays the hospital directly.

Under both types of Hospital Plan policies, provision is also made for the payment of certain miscellaneous expenses which an Insured may incur in a hospital. These are spelled out in the policy, and usually include use of the operating room, anaesthetics, X-rays, laboratory fees, drugs, dressings, etc. A maximum on such miscellaneous benefits is set in the policy, usually expressed as a multiple of the daily benefits; e. g., five times the daily benefit, 10 times the daily benefit, etc. Some policies limit the total of such expenses to a stated maximum, like $250 or $500, etc.

Under most Hospitalization policies, the Insured may also provide for stipulated indemnities for surgical expenses. The amount of benefits is listed in a schedule which is similar to the one found in regular Accident and Health policies (discussed under WHAT IS COVERED).

In some policies, the Insured may also purchase Medical Care reimbursement, and will be entitled to payment for medical expenses, other than surgery, which he incurs while confined to the hospital.

NEW YORK—Every policy providing hospital, surgical, or medical benefits must be guaranteed renewable after it has been in force two years.

MAJOR MEDICAL EXPENSE INSURANCE
(Catastrophe Medical Expense Insurance)

THE SHARP INCREASE in the cost of hospital, medical and surgical expense has given rise to a form of insurance which is designed to cushion the financial impact of the more severe illness or accident. The coverage proceeds on the premise that many individuals and families who can budget for the more routine expenses of medical attention would be deeply burdened by the expenses associated with a long and serious illness or accident. To this end, the policy usually contains a relatively large deductible, and the Company's liability begins only after the Insured has incurred expenses equal to the Deductible (discussed later under FOR HOW MUCH—Deductible).

In addition, almost all Major Medical Expense policies provide for some participation on the part of the Insured in the medical expenses incurred, even when those exceed the Deductible. This feature is discussed later under FOR HOW MUCH—Coinsurance.

It should be remembered that there is no standardized Major Medical Expense insurance, and that a staggering variety of policies are offered by Casualty insurers, Accident and Health companies and Life insurance carriers, and that new forms are constantly being developed and issued. In addition to policies offered to individuals and family groups, almost every company in the field writes Major Medical Expense on a group basis, for employer-employee groups and for associations of various kinds. Hundreds of thousands of workers are covered under Major Medical Expense policies negotiated on their behalf by trade unions with employers and trade associations.

In this section, we shall endeavor to point up the basic features which are common to most Major Medical Expense insurance policies. The reader is urged to check carefully any individual policy which is being considered.

WHAT IS COVERED

While there are exceptions in many Major Medical policies (some of which are discussed later under FOR HOW MUCH), the general intent of most policies of this kind is to cover all medical expenses whether incurred in or out of the hospital without any specific limitation on such charges. Also included are expenses incurred for ambulance, nursing and other health services, and almost always, the cost of drugs prescribed by a medical practitioner. While specific limitations are few, it is fairly common to find an "inside limit" on hospital room and board charges, and sometimes on surgery expense. (Discussed later under FOR HOW MUCH—Inside Limits.)

HAZARDS COVERED

Generally, the policy does not enumerate the medical conditions for which coverage is provided, and all medical expense which meets the Deductible is considered as "covered expenses." Almost all policies do NOT cover expenses incurred for dental care. Some do provide that expenses incurred for the repair of sound teeth injured in an accident will be covered.

Most policies limit coverage for mental and nervous infirmities, some providing only for such expense as is incurred in conditions of this kind in a legally constituted hospital. Policies differ widely on this last score, some providing that out-of-hospital psychiatric care will be covered for a specified limit per treatment with an overall maximum per year. Usually, policies written on a Group basis are more liberal in covering mental or emotional disturbances.

HAZARDS NOT COVERED

In addition to the exclusion of dental care and the limitations on treatment of mental or emotional infirmities (discussed under HAZARDS COVERED), most policies contain the following exclusions:

War—Expenses incurred as a result of war, or injury or sickness sustained while serving in the armed forces are usually excluded.

Workmen's Compensation—Accidents or illnesses which are compensable under a state Workmen's Compensation Law or a Federal statute governing industrially connected illness or disability are excluded.

Government Hospital Treatments—The policy does not apply to expenses incurred for treatment in Federal Government or Veterans' hospitals.

Cosmetic Surgery—Cosmetic or plastic surgery are excluded. Some policies cover such surgery when necessitated by an accident.

Pregnancy—Most policies exclude expense in connection with childbirth. Frequently, the policy will consider as covered expense the costs involved in Caesarian section or other medical attention required where such involves abnormal delivery situations.

FOR HOW MUCH

Deductible—As indicated at the opening of this section on Major Medical Expense insurance, the intent of the policy is to cover the larger, catastrophe-type illness or accident. This is accomplished by incorporating a Deductible in the policy, and no indemnity is payable for any expenses incurred until they exceed the maximum.

Deductibles range from $50 to $1,000 (and higher in some instances). In Individual (non-group) policies, the Deductible is usually at least $300 and, more commonly, $500 or more. Some policies base the Deductible on the earnings of the Insured, with a higher Deductible applicable to those who earn more.

It is important to understand that the stipulated Deductible must be reached within a stated period. Some policies provide a 90-day period to accumulate the Deductible, others provide four months, six months, or even the calendar year. Obviously, a policy which allows 90 days to accumulate the Deductible is likely to be called on less to pay indemnity than one which provides a calendar year for accumulating the same sum. Thus, with a $500 90-day Deductible, an Insured could spend almost $2,000 in the year without incurring the $500 within any 90-day period. A policy with the same dollar Deductible which provides a year to accumulate would be called to pay (or contribute to) $1,500 of the $2,000 expended.

Coinsurance—With a few exceptions, all Major Medical Expense policies contain a Coinsurance clause which provides that the Insured will self-insure a percentage of the covered charges. The Company usually undertakes to pay 75% or 80% of the covered expenses which exceed the Deductible. Some carriers pay 75% or 80% of the first $5,000 of covered charges which exceed the Deductible, and then pay 100% of any excess over the first $5,000. In this way, the Insured's contribution is more limited than it would be in a policy with a straight Coinsurance feature.

Time Limit on Claims—Almost all policies limit the period for which expenses will be paid on a single illness or accident. A common time limit is two years, although many policies will pay up to three years.

Lifetime vs. Per Cause Maximum—All policies carry a maximum limit on the sums which an Insured can recover under the policy. The maximum may relate to all claims presented under the policy throughout its lifetime of the contract, or to the expenses incurred for a single condition—a per cause maximum. Under a per cause maximum, the Insured may recover the policy amount for each separate, unrelated illness, or accident.

WHO IS INSURED

Major Medical policies are sold to individuals, or to family groups. A policy issued to a family will cover husband, spouse and all children until they attain a stated age. Some policies provide that children are covered until they attain age 19, or while they are full-time students and unmarried, until they attain the age of 23.

WHEN COVERED

Some Major Medical policies are renewable each year at the Company's option. Others are issued on a guaranteed renewable basis, except that renewal may be exercised only until the Insured attains a stated age, usually 65. A growing number of policies in the field are renewable throughout lifetime. This last type usually reduces or restricts benefits payable after age 65.

RATES

There is no standardization of rates. Premiums are payable annually, semi-annually or quarterly. Some companies will accept monthly premiums. It is fairly common under policies which are renewable at the Insured's option to provide that the premium may be changed by the Company on any anniversary of the register date of the policy.

GROUP ACCIDENT AND HEALTH INSURANCE

GROUP ACCIDENT AND HEALTH plans are in wide use today in industries throughout the country. These plans are sold to an individual employer or, in states where the law permits, to employers in a trade association, or to all members of a trade union, members of certain professional societies, like physicians who are enrolled in a local medical society, lawyers who are members of a bar association, or a county lawyers' association, etc.

Under these Group plans, a master policy is issued to the employer, or union or association. Each individual Insured receives a certificate setting forth in outline the benefits of the plan which are more fully enunciated in the master policy. Most Group policies are written on a non-occupational basis, and do not cover any injuries which are compensable under the Workmen's Compensation laws of the particular state.

It is usually required that a minimum percentage of all employees in an insured plant come under the plan. The employer may pay the entire premium, or may require contributions from the employees.

The Company cannot cancel coverage as to any individual employee as long as he continues in the employment covered, or in the trade union or professional association. It does, however, reserve the right to refuse to renew the entire contract.

NEW YORK—Any worker who has been covered for three months or more under a Group policy becomes entitled to convert from the Group plan to an individual policy when his employment is terminated, for whatever reason. There is no age limit on this right, and the policy may not exclude any pre-existing condition.

The policy offered the retiring employee must provide at least $10 per day for hospital room and board, up to 21 days; at least $100 of hospital expense benefits; and at least $200 of surgical expense benefits.

If a worker who is insured under a Group policy which also covers his dependents dies, the insured dependents become eligible to convert the insurance on them to an individual policy. Furthermore, when the child of a worker insured under a Group policy reaches the age at which he is no longer covered by the family policy, he becomes entitled to receive an individual policy from the Company, regardless of his physical condition.

WHOLESALE OR FRANCHISE INSURANCE

Where the number of employees is not large enough for a true Group policy, or where more flexibility in the range of benefits offered is desired, individual policies may be issued, individually underwritten. Usually a minimum of five is required. The term "Wholesale" is usually used by Life agents, and "Franchise" by Casualty agents.

Such policies offer about the same coverages as Group, but at a slightly higher premium. Usually, they may be continued as individual policies on termination of employment or eligibility.

FRATERNAL ACCIDENT AND HEALTH INSURANCE

MANY FRATERNAL ORGANIZATIONS provide disability benefits to their members. Most of these plans are now underwritten by regular insurance carriers, or are set up with special reserves, like self-insurance. Plans of this kind are therefore practically identical with the Group plans described before. Under some of the older plans, no separate reserves or outside underwriting is provided, and the benefits which a member is eligible to receive are part of his membership and are paid out of the general treasury or by assessment of the members.

DISABILITY PROVISIONS IN LIFE INSURANCE

ALMOST EVERY LIFE insurance carrier will, for a small additional premium, attach to a Life insurance policy a Waiver of Premium Disability clause. If the Insured is disabled by injury or illness, the Company agrees to waive all further premiums on the policy as they fall due during the continuance of the Insured's disability. Disability must be total and permanent, but it is expressly provided that, if the Insured has been totally disabled for a given period, usually six months, his disability will be presumed to be total.

Total disability is usually defined as the inability of the Insured to engage in any occupation for remuneration or profit, although a somewhat less restrictive clause is found in the policies of several companies. Thus, one Company requires only that the Insured be unable to engage in his occupation or any occupation for which he was trained; a second Company will consider as eligible for disability benefits any Insured who, as a result of injury or illness, has suffered reduction in his earnings to 25% or less of his average earnings prior to his disability.

A smaller number of companies also offer to pay the Insured a stipulated monthly income during the continuance of his disability. The income is set as a percentage of the face amount of the policy. Thus, the 1% Monthly Income clause will pay $10 monthly for each $1,000 of Life insurance; some policies pay $7.50 for each $1,000; some pay $5. Recently, a modification of the Disability Income provision has been introduced by several Life insurance companies. It is further provided that, if the Insured's disability continues to age 65, the face amount of the policy will be paid him in cash.

DISABILITY BENEFITS LAWS

UNDER THE UNEMPLOYMENT INSURANCE LAWS of the country, most workers are afforded some income protection during periods of unemployment. However, to be eligible for these benefits, the worker must be "ready, willing and able" to work. He therefore cannot receive these benefits if he is disabled. If his disability arose out of and during the course of his employment, he may, of course, be entitled to Workmen's Compensation benefits, but no protection extends to "off-the-job" disability, except as may have been provided under private insurance plans or employee welfare plans.

As was pointed out in the preceding chapter, under Group Accident and Health Insurance, an increasing number of employers in recent years have installed plans which give their employees some indemnity for loss of time through non-occupational disability. Such plans are completely voluntary on the part of the employer, or are entered into as a result of collective bargaining between employer and employees, or their trade union. Where such Group Disability plans are in effect, the worker has some protection against all possible threats to his income producing power; i. e., his inability to work because he has no work, or because he is disabled on the job, or off the job.

The past decade has seen very extensive discussions in many states of *compulsory* plans covering employees against non-occupational illnesses and accidents. To date, five states have enacted such Disability Benefits Laws, which became effective as follows:

Rhode Island	1943	New York	1950
California	1946	Hawaii	1970
New Jersey	1949	Puerto Rico	1971

How Administered—The Disability Benefit Law is administered under the State Unemployment Insurance agency except for New York where the Workmen's Compensation Board has jurisdiction and Hawaii whose Department of Labor and Industrial Relations administers the Act.

WHAT IS COVERED

The benefits afforded and the method of administering the law vary in the four states, but the basic purpose in each instance is the same—to provide cash payments to workers who are unable to work because of illness or accident which is *not* connected with their employment.

Differing from Workmen's Compensation benefits, and from most private plans of Disability insurance, the Disability Benefits Law does not provide for the payment of medical expenses of any kind (with an exception in California). The worker is entitled only to stipulated weekly payments during temporary periods of disability.

While the several states all address themselves to the problem of providing some indemnity to workers during temporary periods of non-occupational disability, there are considerable differences in the provisions among the states. On the pages that follow, a chart analysis of the first four enacted Disability Benefits Laws is set forth. The two most recently enacted laws are discussed briefly after the charts.

COMPARATIVE ANALYSIS
STATE DISABILITY BENEFITS LAWS

	NEW YORK	NEW JERSEY	CALIFORNIA	RHODE ISLAND
Name of Program	Disability Benefits	Temporary Disability Benefits.	Unemployment Compensation Disability Benefits.	Temporary Disability Insurance.
Type of Law	Competitive between state fund and private plans—employer must choose.	Competitive between state fund and private plans—former automatic if latter not elected by employer and majority of employees.	Competitive between state fund and private plans—former automatic if latter not elected by employer or with his consent, and by employee.	Monopolistic state fund — no private plans allowed in substitution.
Approach Used	Employer required to provide benefits — like Workmen's Compensation but employees share cost.	Tax supported state fund provides benefits — like Unemployment Compensation but private plans may be substituted.	Tax supported state fund provides benefits — like Unemployment Compensation but voluntary (private) plans may be substituted.	Tax supported state fund provides benefits — like Unemployment Compensation.
Types of Private Plans	Insured and self-insured plans equalling or exceeding statutory requirements and continuation of certain other existings plans.	Insured and self-insured plans equalling or exceeding state fund standards, and continuation of certain other existing plans.	Insured and self-insured plans exceeding state fund standards.	None.
Limitations Upon Right to Establish Private Plans	None.	None if private plan does not exclude any class of employees, determined by age, sex, race, or wages.	Must not result in substantial "adverse selection" against state fund. Voluntary plans must meet each of three tests based upon distribution of employees by sex, age, and amount of wages received, to be approved under this provision.	———
Contributions Began	January 1, 1950.	June 2, 1948, for employees. January 1, 1949, for employers.	May 21, 1946.	June 1, 1942.
Benefit Payments Began	July 1, 1950.	January 1, 1949.	December 1, 1946.	April 1, 1943.
Federal Unemployment Trust Fund Monies Used	None available for disability benefits.	$50 million.	$103 million authorized, $70.2 million drawn down.	$29 million.
Employee Contributions	Maximum of ½% of first $60 of weekly wages.	½% of first $3,600 of annual wages.	1% of first $7,400 of annual wages.	1% of first $4,800 of annual wages.

	NEW YORK	NEW JERSEY	CALIFORNIA	RHODE ISLAND
Employer Contributions Required	Balance of Cost.	¼% of first $3,600 of annual wages if in state plan; balance of cost, if any, in private plan.	None.	None.
Experience Rating of Contributions to State Fund	The net effect of competitive premium rates will be substantially the same as the results of experience rating.	Yes, employer's share only (between ¾% and 1/10%).	No.	No.
Employers Covered	Employers of 1 or more (4 or more domestics) on each of 30 days in one calendar year.	Employers of one or more paying wages of $1,000 or more per year—same as Unemployment Compensation.	Employers of 1 or more with $100 payroll in any calendar quarter—same as Unemployment Compensation.	Employers of 1 or more on any day—same as Unemployment Compensation.
Employees Excluded	Farm laborers, day students, casual employees, railroad and government employees, and certain others.	Farm laborers, domestic servants, students, employees of certain non-profit organizations, railroad and government employees, and certain others.	Domestic servants, certain casual employees, employees of certain non-profit organizations, railroad, and government employees, real estate salesmen and certain others.	Farm laborers, domestic servants, students, employees of certain non-profit organizations, railroad and government employees, and certain others.
Religious Exemptions	None.	Christian Scientists, etc., may apply for exemption.	Christian Scientists, etc., may apply for exemption.	Christian Scientists, etc., may apply for exemption.
Statutory Eligibility Requirements	Generally four consecutive weeks of covered employment, not necessarily with current employer.	17 weeks of work or earned wages of $1,350 or more in covered employment during base year. Week counted when wages from one employer were $15 or more.	Earnings in base year of $300 in covered employment.	20 weeks of work or $1,200 of wages in covered employment during base year. Week counted when wages were $20 or more.
How Benefits Are Computed	½ of average weekly wage in preceding 8 weeks, subject to maximum.	⅔ of average weekly wage in base year, subject to maximum. Same as Unemployment Compensation benefits.	Depends upon wages in highest quarter of base year. Benefits exceed those for Unemployment Compensation.	55% of average weekly wage in base year, subject to maximum. Same as Unemployment Compensation.
Minimum Weekly Benefits	$20, or average weekly wage whichever is less.	$10.	$25.	$12.
Maximum Weekly Benefits in State Plan	$65.	50% of average weekly wage in covered employment ($69 for 1970).	$87 plus $12 per day for first 20 days of hospital confinement.	50% of average weekly wage in covered employment ($56 for period 7/1/67 to 6/30/70), plus $3 per dependent up to $12.
Maximum Duration	26 weeks.	26 weeks.	26 weeks.	26 weeks.
Waiting Period	7 days for each disability.	7 days for each disability, but if benefits payable for 3 consecutive weeks, retroactive benefit paid for first 7 days.	7 days for each disability. None if hospitalized.	7 days for each benefit year.

Maternity Benefits	No.	Yes. Eligibility limited to 4 weeks prior to and 4 weeks following birth.	No.	Yes, limited to 14 weeks.
Duplication of Benefits With Workmen's Compensation	Not eligible for any period for which Workmen's Compensation (other than permanent partial benefits for a prior disability) is paid or payable.	Not eligible for any period for which Workmen's Compensation (other than benefits for a permanent disability previously incurred) is paid or payable.	Not eligible for any period for which Workmen's Compensation (other than benefits for a permanent disability) is paid or payable unless Workmen's Compensation is less than disability; in that case the difference is payable.	Eligible up to a combined benefit of 85% of average weekly wage but not more than $67 total per week exclusive of dependents' benefits.
Effect of Continued Pay from Employer During Disability	None if voluntarily provided by employer, otherwise generally disqualifies for benefits.	Reduces benefits if total of benefits and sick pay would otherwise exceed regular wages.	None on hospital benefits. Combined benefits and sick pay cannot exceed regular wages.	None—benefits and sick pay may be received simultaneously.
Benefits for Disabled Unemployed Financed By	Assessments of insurance companies, self-insurers, state insurance fund and existing plans in amount needed to restore fund balance to $12,000,000.	State plan, which may assess private plans for pro rata share of excess of cost over interest on $50 million of initial fund. Assessment limited to .02% of taxable wages.	State plan, by means of separate account credited each year with .12% of taxable wages, such amounts being obtained from private plans by assessment.	State plan.
Administrative Assessments Against Private Plans	Administrative costs of program assessed against carriers in proportion to taxable wages; no limit.	Added administrative costs attributable to private plans assessed against plans in proportion to taxable wages; limit of .02% of taxable wages.	Added administrative costs attributable to private plans assessed against plans in proportion to taxable wages; no limit.	——
Administrative Agency	Workmen's Compensation Board.	Department of Labor and Industry, Division of Employment Security.	Department of Employment.	Department of Employment Security.
Citation	Workmen's Compensation Law, Art. 9 (§§200-242).	Title 43, Ch. 21, Art. 2 (§§43:21-25 to 43:21-56), RS 1937, as amended.	Unemployment Insurance Code, Div. 1, Part 2 (§§2601-3271).	Title 28, Chs. 39—41, General Laws 1956.

Note: Hawaii and Puerto Rico have enacted Cash Sickness legislation just recently. Details will be incorporated herein when applicable and available. Source of this information is the Life Insurance Association of America. 70-1.

Hawaii—The law applies to all workers except government employees, domestics, agricultural employees, newsboys under the age of 18 and family employment.

To qualify for benefits, a worker must have at least 14 weeks of prior employment and must have earned at least $400 during the four calendar quarters preceding his disability. He must also be under the care of a licensed physician.

Benefits which begin with the 8th day of disability are equal to 55% of the employee's average wage but subject to the maximum payable for Unemployment insurance. Benefits are paid for 26 weeks.

Employers may comply with the law through insurance or self-insurance. The plan is financed jointly by employer and employee, with the maximum payment from the employee limited to ½ of 1% of his weekly wage. A maximum on the base used for calculating the employee's contribution is established—121% of the Department of Labor's published Average Weekly Wages.

Puerto Rico—Coverage may be afforded under the Government plan or under a private plan, which may be insured or self-insured. If the employer wishes to establish a private plan to which his employees will be asked to contribute, he must obtain the consent of the majority of his employees.

The maximum wage base for computing the tax is $7,800 annually per employee. A tax of 1% is imposed on the employer, minus the ½ of 1% which is taxed on an employee's wages, subject to a maximum of 75¢ per week.

Maximum weekly benefits are $78 per week, except for agricultural workers for whom a $20 maximum is set. Benefits are not payable beyond 26 consecutive weeks. No benefits are payable for the first seven days of disability except if the worker is hospitalized during the first three days of his disability in which case benefits are paid from the first day.

FOR FURTHER READING

ACCIDENT AND HEALTH INSURANCE PRIMER—**Health and Accident Underwriters' Conference**
ACKERMAN—**Insurance**
FAULKNER—**Health Insurance**
HANDBOOK OF ACCIDENT AND HEALTH INSURANCE—**The National Underwriter Company**
HEDGES—**Practical Fire and Casualty Insurance**
KULP AND HALL—**Casualty Insurance**
MEHR AND CAMMACK—**Principles of Insurance**
OSLER—**Guide to Health Insurance**
POLICY, FORM AND MANUAL ANALYSIS SERVICE
RIEGEL, ROBERT and MILLER—**Insurance**

(See Reading List at End of Book)

CHAPTER 32

Miscellaneous Forms of Insurance

COMPREHENSIVE GLASS POLICY

ALTHOUGH GLASS INSURANCE is most usually purchased to cover damage to plate glass, and the policy is commonly referred to as the Plate Glass policy, the Comprehensive Glass policy may be used to cover almost every type of glass, including art glass, stained glass, structural glass, leaded glass, mirrors, Thermopane, barber poles, burglar alarm foil, plexiglass, tropical doors, windows and shutters, glass of special manufacture, etc. The Comprehensive Glass policy is also used to cover residence glass. In most states, residence glass may also be insured by endorsement on a Fire insurance policy covering the residence (discussed later).

Neon Signs, Fluorescent Signs and Lamps—The Comprehensive Glass policy may also be written to cover neon signs, fluorescent signs and lamps.

WHAT IS COVERED

Except for larger risks and for glass in residences, each item of glass (often referred to as a "light" of glass) is separately described in the policy schedule which enumerates the kind of glass, its size, and position in the building. Lettering and ornamentation may be covered under the policy as separate items.

Blanket Policies—A Glass policy may be written without a schedule of the pieces of glass to be insured. The Insured files a schedule with the Company, when the policy is applied for, of all glass to be covered (other than glass in two special classes). Automatic insurance is then afforded on any newly installed glass, provided the Company is notified within 60 days of the installation.

The glass in private residences occupied by not more than four families or private apartments may be insured without scheduling of the individual panes covered. All permanently fixed glass is covered for a flat premium, with a limit of $50 on any one plate of glass or glass object. On certain stipulated types of glass, such as multiple plate insulating units, radiant heating panels, conservatory or green house glass, chandeliers or light fixtures, jalousies, louvres or shutters, Venetian type doors or windows, stained or leaded glass, glass bricks or shingles or other structural glass, the limit is $50 *per occurrence.*

Repairing or Replacing Frames—In addition to covering the described glass, the Comprehensive Glass policy will also pay up to $75 at each separate location for repairing or replacing frames encasing insured glass when damage to the glass makes it necessary to repair or replace the frames.

Boarding Up Openings—The policy will also pay up to $75 at each separate location for the cost of installing temporary plates or boarding up openings when made necessary by unavoidable delay in replacing or repairing insured glass.

Removing Obstructions—The policy will also pay up to $75 at each separate location for the cost of removing obstructions made necessary in replacing insured glass which has been broken or damaged.

HAZARDS COVERED

The Comprehensive Glass policy provides virtually all-risk coverage and insures all breakage, subject to the two exclusions discussed under HAZARDS NOT COVERED. The policy also covers damage by chemicals accidentally or maliciously applied.

The Glass policy covers damage or breakage arising from vandalism and malicious mischief, but only if such actions actually break the glass. Thus, scratching of a glass by a person acting maliciously would not be covered. As noted directly above, malicious damage by acids or chemicals *would* be covered.

While the policy is very broad as respects breakage, it does not cover scratching or other marring of glass, unless occasioned as part of breakage or as a result of acids thrown accidentally or maliciously.

HAZARDS NOT COVERED

Fire—There is no coverage for loss caused by fire.

War, Invasion, Etc.—The policy does not cover loss caused by war, whether declared or not, invasion, civil war, insurrection, rebellion or revolution, or to any act or condition incident to any of these perils.

Nuclear Energy—Discussed in Chapter 3 under HAZARDS NOT COVERED—Nuclear Perils.

Cracked Glass Endorsement—If a pane of glass is damaged by a crack or a small hole at the time the insurance is applied for, the Company will attach a special endorsement—the Cracked Glass Endorsement (Cracked Light Endorsement). The location and extent of the crack is shown on the endorsement by diagram, and the policy excludes liability for the existing crack or its extension.

FOR HOW MUCH

As stated at the beginning of this chapter, Glass policies usually enumerate each piece of glass insured. No dollar amount is shown alongside the described items, which are insured for their actual cash value, plus the cost of labor, at the time of loss, but for not more than the cost to repair or replace. Lettering and ornamentation, which may be insured under a Glass policy, are insured for a specific amount in dollars.

As discussed under What Is Covered—Repairing or Replacing Frames, Boarding Up Openings, Removing Obstructions—the basic policy sets $75 as the limit of its liability for each of the three additional expenses covered. This limit may be increased by endorsement.

As in most other Property insurance policies, the Company has the option of paying for the loss in cash, or repairing or replacing the damage. In actual practice, the companies usually exercise their option to replace and have their own glaziers make the repairs. Any glass which is salvageable belongs to the insurance Company.

When neon signs or fluorescent signs or lamps are insured under a Glass policy, the coverage is written subject to a 100% Coinsurance clause and, usually, with a Deductible.

RATES

Rates for Glass insurance depend on four factors:

1. Type of Glass—All insurable glass is graded into one of six classes.

2. Position in Building—Different rates apply to exterior glass, interior glass, glass on grade floors, glass above grade floors, etc.

3. Size of Glass.

4. Territory.

Term Policies—Residence glass may be insured on a three-year basis at 2.7 times the annual rate.

Residence glass may also be insured by endorsement of a Fire insurance policy in all states, except those enumerated below. When so written, the Glass coverage may have the same term as the Fire insurance policy—one year, three years or five years. When written for five years, the rate for Glass insurance is 4.4 times the annual rate, if paid in advance.

ARIZONA, HAWAII, INDIANA, MINNESOTA, MISSISSIPPI, NEW JERSEY, NEW YORK, NORTH CAROLINA, PENNSYLVANIA, VIRGINIA, WISCONSIN.

Glass insurance cannot be written by endorsement of a Fire insurance policy.

Minimum Premiums—The minimum premium is $15.00 except in New York where the minimum is $10.00.

Whole Dollar Premium Rule—discussed in Chapter 8 under OTHER FACTORS WHICH AFFECT FIRE INSURANCE RATES —Whole Dollar Premium Rule.

INSURED'S DUTIES

Notice of Loss—The Insured is required to give notice of loss to the Company as soon as practicable.

Proof of Loss—The Company may request the Insured to file proof of loss on forms provided by them. In actual practice, since the companies customarily make replacements, no proof of loss is necessary.

OTHER PROVISIONS

Reinstatement After Loss—After a loss, and when the glass has been replaced, the policy is automatically restored and full coverage continued without any additional premium.

Cancellation—See Chapter 2.

Assignment—Assignment of the policy does not bind the Company unless it consents to the assignment. If the Insured dies or is adjudged bankrupt, the policy will cover the Insured's legal representatives, provided notice of the death or bankruptcy of the Insured is given to the Company within 60 days.

Subrogation—See Chapter 2.

Regulation—Much of the Glass insurance of the country is written by carriers which are members of the National Bureau of Casualty Underwriters, which promulgates rates and forms for the coverage.

Time of Policy—The Comprehensive Glass policy attaches at 12:00 o'clock Noon, Standard Time.

BOILER AND MACHINERY INSURANCE
(POWER PLANT INSURANCE)

ALTHOUGH ONE ORDINARILY thinks of Explosion insurance in connection with high pressure steam boilers, the Boiler and Machinery policy is actually used to cover almost every kind of equipment for containing pressure or generating or transmitting power. An idea of the wide variety of pressure vessels and machinery that can be covered may be had from a listing of some of the schedules that attach to the basic policy. These schedules are grouped below under the two broad headings which give the Boiler and Machinery policy its name.

Boiler and Pressure Vessels

Auxiliary Piping
Cast Iron Boilers
Fire Tube Boilers
Fired Vessels
Refrigerating Systems
Residence Boilers and Vessels
Unfired Vessels
Water Tube Boilers

Machinery

Air Conditioner Units
Centrifugal or Rotary Pumps and Compressors
Deep Well Pump Units
Electric Generators
Electric Motors
Fans and Blowers
Gear Wheels and Enclosed Gear Sets
Internal Combustion Engines
Reciprocating Pumps and Compressors
Shafting
Steam Turbines
Transformers
Water Turbines

It is obvious that many of the objects listed differ greatly from one another in their nature and in the hazards to which they are exposed, and that different insurance coverages are required for the different equipment. This is accomplished by adapting the basic Boiler and Machinery policy to the specific kind of equipment by an endorsement built around the class of object insured.

The basic Boiler and Machinery policy will be analyzed next. This analysis will be followed by an outline of the more widely used schedules which are attached to the policy. After these Direct Damage coverages have been discussed, a brief review will be given of several indirect coverages in this field.

BOILER AND MACHINERY POLICY
WHAT IS COVERED

GENERALLY, EACH OBJECT to be insured is listed and described in the appropriate schedule attached to the policy. The policy may be written without itemizing each object; a group description is stated in the policy, and all objects within that class are covered. Only objects in use or connected ready for use are covered, except for the automatic coverage extended to newly acquired objects (see Insuring Agreement VI).

The basic policy contains six Insuring Agreements:

I. **Loss on Property of Insured.**

II. **Expediting Expenses**—The policy will pay the reasonable extra cost of temporary repair and of expediting the repair of the Insured's damaged property. Under this Insuring Agreement, the Company's liability is limited to $1,000 or the amount of loss under Insuring Agreement I, whichever is less.

III. **Property Damage Liability**—Under this section, the policy will pay all sums which the Insured becomes legally obligated to pay to others for damage to their property. This coverage is identical with that provided under Coverage B of a Public Liability policy, discussed in Chapter 24.

IV. **Bodily Injury Liability**—Under this section, the policy will pay all sums which the Insured becomes legally obligated to pay to others for bodily injury, sickness or death caused by an accident, as defined. This coverage is identical with that provided under Coverage A of a Public Liability policy, discussed in Chapter 24.

V. **Defense, Settlement, Supplementary Payments**—Under this section, the policy will defend suits brought against the Insured and pay Supplementary benefits similar to those available under Liability policies (discussed in Chapter 24).

VI. **Automatic Coverage**—Coverage is afforded automatically on all newly acquired installed objects, including objects at newly acquired locations, unless such period is specifically extended by the Company. Notice of such acquisitions must be given within 90 days.

Repair and Replacement—Coverage is available in all companies to cover the replacement value of the Insured's property (discussed under FOR HOW MUCH—Repair and Replacement). Many companies include this coverage as one of the Insuring Agreements in their basic policy, usually as Insuring Agreement II.

Inspection Service—One of the most valuable features of Boiler and Machinery insurance is the regular inspection service which the Company provides to all Insureds. Through these periodic inspections, many dangerous conditions in the equipment are detected before they can result in an accident. This service is included in the premium charged for the policy.

HAZARDS COVERED

Unless written on the Limited Coverage Form, the policy covers the sudden and accidental breakdown of the object, or part of the object, which arises out of physical damage to the object which necessitates repair or replacement of the object. Also included are losses due to strikes, riot, civil commotion, sabotage, vandalism and malicious mischief.

HAZARDS NOT COVERED

War Damage Exclusion—There is no coverage for any loss caused directly or indirectly by hostile or warlike action, including action in combating or defending against an actual, impending or expected enemy attack by any military, naval or air forces of any government or authority which maintains or uses military, naval or air forces. The policy also excludes actions taken by an agent of any such government or authority, and losses caused by insurrection, rebellion, revolution, civil war or usurped power, or confiscation by order of any government or civil authority.

Nuclear Energy Exclusion — The policy does not cover loss, whether it be direct or indirect, proximate or remote from any accident caused by nuclear reaction, nuclear radiation or radioactive contamination.

Fire—As respects damage to the Insured's property (Insuring Agreement I), there is no coverage for loss caused by fire or any means used to extinguish fire. (Such loss would be covered under a Fire insurance policy.) It is important to understand that this exclusion takes in losses by fire even when caused by an insured accident, despite the fact that in such a case the accident is the proximate cause of the loss. Where an accident causes a fire, the Boiler and Machinery policy covers only the damage done by the explosion, while the Fire policy covers the damage by fire.

Strikes, Riot, Civil Commotion, Vandalism, Malicious Mischief—As mentioned under HAZARDS COVERED, the policy covers as "accident" these listed perils. Sabotage by an enemy agent would fall within the War Exclusion, and would *not* be covered, but similar acts by an employee or other person not an enemy agent would fall within the scope of the coverage.

It should also be remembered that the coverage against vandalism and malicious mischief in a Boiler policy affords protection only against such acts which cause an accident as defined in the policy. Any act of a vandal other than of this kind would not be covered. The coverage dovetails with the Vandalism and Malicious Mischief Endorsement available with the Fire insurance policy, which specifically excludes explosion caused by vandalism or malicious mischief.

Combustion Explosion Outside of Object—The policy will not pay for loss caused by a combustion explosion outside of the insured object, even though the explosion was set off by an accident to an insured object. Thus, if an insured boiler explodes, all direct damage to the Insured's property will be covered. If the explosion in turn sets off a tank of combustible fuel oil, there is no coverage for the damage done by the explosion of the tank.

Indirect Loss—The basic policy does not cover loss caused by interruption of business or manufacture, or from lack of power, light, heat, steam, or refrigeration, or any other indirect result of an accident. These losses require separate coverage under one of several endorsements to be discussed towards the end of this chapter.

Limited Coverage—A Boiler and Machinery policy may be written on a Limited Coverage basis. The policy is then limited to the sudden and accidental tearing asunder of the object caused by the pressure of water or steam within the object. Cracking, leakage, or the malfunction of any safety device or protective device is specifically excluded from the coverage. (When the equipment to be insured is very old or poorly maintained, the Company may offer an applicant for insurance only Limited Coverage.)

FOR HOW MUCH

The amount of insurance in a Boiler and Machinery policy is the limit "per accident." There is no Coinsurance clause in the policy, and the Insured is free to carry any amount of insurance he chooses. The policy provides that losses under the individual Insuring Agreements will be paid in the order in which these coverages are enumerated in the policy. Thus, assume an Insured purchases a Boiler and Machinery policy with a limit per accident of $50,000. In an explosion of an insured object, $45,000 of damage is done to the Insured's own property and an additional $1,000 is paid under Insuring Agreement II for expediting expenses. A neighbor whose building was damaged by the blast brings a suit against the Insured to recover for his loss. Only $4,000 is available under the policy for this liability, since $46,000 has already been paid out under Insuring Agreements I and II.

Repair and Replacement Coverage—The basic policy covers on an "actual cash value basis" (discussed in Chapter 2 under FOR HOW MUCH). An endorsement to the Boiler policy is available for an additional premium under which the Insured will be indemnified on a replacement basis, without deduction of depreciation. A policy, so endorsed, will pay replacement cost not only for the insured object, but also for any real or personal property damaged in a covered loss. It is stipulated, however, that an Insured must actually make the replacement if he would collect on a replacement basis.

Some Companies make this coverage part of their basic policy, including it as an additional Insuring Agreement. The coverage and the premium charges are identical under the endorsement, or the Insuring Agreement.

Other Insurance—Bodily Injury—As pointed out before, Insuring Agreement IV of the policy covering Bodily Injury Liability is optional. If this coverage is purchased under a Boiler policy, it acts as excess coverage only over any other insurance covering the loss.

Other Insurance—Property Damage Liability—As respects liability for damage to the property of others, the Boiler and Machinery policy which covers this hazard under Insuring Agreement III contributes with any other insurance covering the Insured's liability for such damage.

RATES

Rates depend on the object insured. If a limit higher than $25,000 is required, the rate shown in the manual is increased by an Excess Limit factor, except where an object is not subject to catastrophe hazard, like residence boilers. A location charge is added to make up the rate, and this charge depends on the limit per accident for which the policy is written, ranging from $15 in a policy with a limit of $5,000 to $450 for a limit of $2,000,000.

Three-Year Policies—The manual rates for Boiler and Machinery insurance are shown for three-year policies. The three-year premium can also be paid in annual installments of 33⅓%. An extra charge of 5% of the entire three-year premium is made for policies paid in installments.

Premium Discount—On that portion of the premium for a three-year policy which exceeds $3,000, a 25% discount is allowed. On one-year policies, the premium in excess of $1,000 is so discounted. On policies issued for a term of more than one year, but not exceeding two years, the premium discount applies to the portion of the premium which exceeds $2,000.

Deductibles—Coverage on the Insured's property (Insuring Agreement I) may be written subject to a Deductible clause. A single deductible may apply to all objects, or different deductibles made applicable to the various objects insured. In a loss involving two or more insured objects with different deductibles, the highest deductible will apply.

There is also available a *disappearing deductible.* Under this type of clause, the deductible decreases as the loss increases until at a pre-selected point there is no deductible.

INSURED'S DUTIES

Inspection—The Company is permitted at all reasonable times to inspect any insured object and the premises. For the Insured's obligation to keep the insured objects in safe condition, see CANCELLATION—Suspension.

Notice of Loss—The Insured must give notice of any loss as soon as practicable. He is also required to give notice of any claim made against him and to forward every summons or other process served upon him.

CANCELLATION

The policy contains the standard Cancellation clauses of most Property insurance policies, except that the Company must give ten days' notice of its intention to cancel.

Suspension—As pointed out under Inspection, the Insured is required to permit inspection to be made as often as is reasonable. If the Company's inspector discovers a dangerous condition in an insured object, he may immediately suspend coverage on that object by mailing or delivering a written notice to the Insured.

OTHER PROVISIONS

Subrogation—See Chapter 2.
Assignment—See under Comprehensive Glass policy.
Regulation—See under Comprehensive Glass policy.
Time of Policy—The policy attaches at Noon, Standard Time.

BOILER SCHEDULE

(FIRED VESSELS AND ELECTRIC STEAM GENERATORS) WHAT IS COVERED

THE BOILERS and other apparatus of this class are described in the schedule under definition of "object." It is stipulated that the object includes the complete boiler or apparatus described and that part of any apparatus under pressure which is within the setting or furnace of any object, any indirect water heater which does not form part of a water storage tank and which is installed outside the object, if such heater is directly in the boiler water circulation, and the inter-connecting piping, including valves and fittings thereon, between parts of the object.

Boiler Piping—The piping which contains steam or vapor generated in whole or in part in the object, if said piping is on the premises of the Insured, or between separate premises of the Insured, and feed piping and condensation piping of certain description is also covered under the policy.

Furnace Explosion—Explosion from within the furnace of an insured object may be covered under the policy, in which case the word "Included" is inserted under the column headed by "Furnace Explosion" and the type of fuel used shown. (This coverage duplicates in large measure the Explosion coverage of the Extended Coverage Endorsement, which excludes only the explosion, rupture or bursting of steam boilers, steam pipes, steam turbines, steam engines, or fly-wheels but *not* the explosion of accumulated gases or unconsumed fuel from within a fire-box or combustion chamber. The Boiler policy is broader than the Extended Coverage endorsement, since the latter will cover only the Insured's property or property on his premises for which he may be liable. The Boiler policy provides legal liability coverage for damage to adjoining properties.)

ELECTRICAL MACHINES SCHEDULE

WHAT IS COVERED

THE SCHEDULE PROVIDES that the object described shall include the complete apparatus, together with any belt wheel, rope wheel, coupling, gear or magnetic brake mechanism on its shaft or frame, and any gear set with its bearings and shafts built into the frame of a motor or into a casing integral with a part of a motor. Any motor with a specified capacity of not more than 100 horsepower also includes the complete mechanism used exclusively to start, stop or control the said motor, including all electrical conductors connecting such equipment with said motor.

REFRIGERATING SYSTEMS SCHEDULE

WHAT IS COVERED

THE SCHEDULE DESCRIBES separately the equipment covered, if of the Compression type, and the equipment of the Absorption type.

Contamination—Rates shown in the manual provide coverage for loss by ammonia contacting or permeating property for an amount not in excess of $1,000.

Water Damage—The basic policy contains a limitation of $1,000 for damage by water. This limit may be increased for an additional premium.

RESIDENCE BOILER SCHEDULE

RESIDENCE BOILERS may be insured under one of two forms. The broader form of coverage is available to any dwelling with not more than 30 rooms, provided no merchandise is sold, or not more than three rooms used for professional purposes. This coverage is essentially the same as provided for commercial boilers (discussed under BOILER SCHEDULE) except that no Bodily Injury Liability insurance is afforded.

The policy is written on a Blanket basis to cover all boilers, including hot air furnaces and stoves, hot water heaters, and other objects in the residence. As under commercial Boiler insurance, periodic inspection service is furnished as part of the premium.

Residences which do not contain more than 12 heated rooms are also insurable under a special Residence policy, which is written at a lower premium and covers only direct property damage caused by explosion of boilers, hot air furnaces and water heaters, including furnace explosion. The policy does not cover cracking, bulging or burnout, and no inspection service is furnished. (This limited form of Boiler insurance is fairly similar to the explosion coverage under the Dwelling Building(s) and Contents Broad Form or the Dwelling Building(s) Broad Form or Special Form discussed in Chapter 3.)

NON-OWNERSHIP EXPLOSION INSURANCE

THIS FORM OF BOILER and Machinery insurance affords coverage for loss on property of the Insured and for his liability to others for damage to their property in his care, custody or control, resulting from an explosion of boilers, pressure vessels or machinery *not owned* by, or leased by, or actually under the control of the Insured.

INDIRECT DAMAGE COVERAGES

CONSEQUENTIAL DAMAGE

COUNTLESS INDUSTRIES and merchants depend on continuous refrigeration or uninterrupted heat to keep their products from spoiling. Many industrial processes must continue to their end without interruption if deterioration or spoilage is to be avoided. For such firms, interruption of power or of light may result in large scale loss.

The Boiler and Machinery policy provides insurance only for *direct* damage done by the accident. If the Insured's goods or other property are not directly damaged, but spoil because of the failure of refrigeration or heat or power, the loss is considered "indirect" or "consequential" and the regular policy does not cover. (For a more complete discussion of a similar situation under Fire insurance policies, see Chapter 7 under Consequential Loss Clauses.)

This indirect, consequential risk of spoilage through failure of equipment can be insured under an endorsement to the Boiler and Machinery policy. This coverage can be written separately, but is almost always written only in conjunction with insurance on direct damage. The endorsement—Consequential Damage Endorsement—obligates the Company to pay the Insured for loss caused by spoilage from lack of power, light, heat or steam or refrigeration which results from an accident to any object described in the Boiler and Machinery policy.

Coverage is afforded for loss to the Insured's property, for the Insured's liability to others for spoilage of their property in his care, and for the expense to reduce loss. The endorsement contains the exclusions found in the basic Boiler policy (discussed under HAZARDS NOT COVERED).

It is important to be clear on the fact that the policy covers only spoilage due to the failure of an object which is caused by an accident as defined in the schedule applicable to the particular equipment. Thus, if an Insured were to load a refrigerator excessively and the equipment did not maintain a temperature low enough to prevent spoilage of the product, there would be no coverage, since there had been no accident to the equipment within the definition stated in the schedule. Similarly, if the door of a refrigerator opened accidentally during the night, or if sufficient ventilation was not maintained, the resulting spoilage would not be covered.

Consequential Damage insurance under a Boiler policy is a separate coverage, with an individual limit of liability. Rates are shown in the manual per $1,000 of insurance.

USE AND OCCUPANCY INSURANCE

(BUSINESS INTERRUPTION INSURANCE)

THE EXPLOSION of a pressure vessel or the failure of other equipment in a plant frequently causes interruption of business or manufacture. The Boiler and Machinery policy will cover the direct damage to the property, but not the loss caused the Insured by his inability to continue operations. This indirect, consequential loss requires separate insurance, and is effected by attaching a Use and Occupancy endorsement to a Boiler policy.

As in the case of Consequential Damage insurance, the policy will pay for loss due to interruption only if it results from an accident to an object designated in the basic policy. Use and Occupancy insurance in Boiler and Machinery coverages is available under one of several forms. Most frequently, this coverage is provided under one of the following two forms:

Actual Loss Sustained—The Company is liable only for the actual loss sustained by the Insured during the period in which operations are suspended. The policy is written with a maximum *Daily* Indemnity and a Limit of Loss for the entire accident. The form contains a Coinsurance clause similar to the one used in Business Interruption Fire insurance.

The Insured is granted a choice of Coinsurance percentages—25%, 35%, 50%, 70%, 80%, 90% or 100%. In Boiler and Machinery insurance, the Coinsurance clause is applied somewhat differently than in Fire insurance covering this hazard. Whether the Coinsurance requirements have been complied with is determined according to the following formula:

$$\frac{\text{Maximum Daily Indemnity in Policy}}{\text{Coinsurance \%} \times \dfrac{\text{Total Net Profits, Fixed Charges and Expenses as Would Have Been Earned in the Month in Which Loss Occurs}}{\text{Number of Working Days in Month}}}$$

Valued Form—The majority of Use and Occupancy insurance under the Boiler and Machinery policy is written under a Valued Form. The Insured sets a Limit of Loss for the policy and a Daily Indemnity. In the event of a total loss necessitating a complete suspension of business resulting from an accident to an insured object, the Company becomes liable for the full Daily Indemnity for each day in which operations are suspended. In the event of a partial suspension of business, the loss is adjusted on the basis of the Daily Indemnity promised in the policy. The Insured is not required to prove that he did actually sustain a loss of this amount.

OUTAGE INSURANCE

IN CERTAIN SITUATIONS, an accident to an insured object would not result in suspension of business, but the Insured would be put to increased expenses in order to continue operating. Thus, the burning out of an electrical machine may make it necessary for the Insured to hire substitute facilities at an increased cost; the explosion of a boiler of a steam locomotive used by the Insured on his plant grounds may necessitate the hiring of trailer trucks; the failure of a generator may put the Insured to the expense of bringing in outside power, etc. The Use and Occupancy forms discussed before will not meet these increased expenses.

Outage Insurance is available to cover these situations, although the market for this coverage is rather limited. Under this form of insurance, a specified amount of indemnity is paid for each *hour* during which a specified object is out of commission due to an accident. It can be seen that Outage insurance is akin to Extra Expense insurance under a Fire insurance policy (discussed in Chapter 7). Outage insurance must be written in conjunction with direct damage coverage on the objects. The policy contains three limits: 1) a limit per hour, 2) a limit per day, and 3) a limit per object.

FOR FURTHER READING

ACKERMAN—Insurance
GEE—Agent's Casualty Guide
HEDGES—Practical Fire and Casualty Insurance
KULP AND HALL—Casualty Insurance
MAGEE AND BICKELHAUPT—General Insurance
POLICY, FORM & MANUAL ANALYSIS SERVICE
RIEGEL, ROBERT AND MILLER—Insurance

(See Reading List at End of Book)

CHAPTER 33

Types of Insurers

THE BULK OF INSURANCE carried by individuals and firms is purchased from organizations whose business it is to provide protection for a premium. Some insurance is also purchased from individuals and, in certain industries, arrangements have been made to exchange insurance protection. Each of these types of insurance will be commented on separately below.

MUTUAL INSURANCE

A mutual insurer is a corporation which is owned by its Insureds. Every policyholder is a member of the Company and is entitled to vote at any regular or special meeting of the Company, in much the same way as the stockholders of an ordinary corporation. Usually, each Insured has one vote which he may exercise in person or by proxy. In most states, the charter or by-laws of the Company may also be drawn to distribute voting privileges among the member-policyholders on the basis of the amount of insurance held by each, or the amount of premiums paid by each, or in any manner approved by the Insurance Department.

As a part owner of the Company, each Insured is entitled to share in any profits earned by the Company. Excess earnings, if any, are returned to the member-Insured in the form of a refund on his premium, commonly referred to as a "dividend."

On the other hand, if the premiums collected by the Company are not adequate to meet the losses and expenses incurred, each Insured may be required to contribute towards the Company's loss for the period. This assessment that may be required of a policyholder in a mutual Company is also referred to as his "contingent liability." Under most conditions, a mutual Company may by contract agree with its policyholders to limit their contingent liability to a flat sum, or one additional annual premium, or two premiums, or five premiums, etc.

In most states, a mutual Company may also write policies which are completely non-assessable. The Insurance Department of the state imposes special requirements on such carriers as to their surplus. Thus, in New York, any mutual carrier may apply for approval of non-assessable policies, provided it maintains a surplus which, together with its unearned premium reserve, is at least equal to the minimum capital required on organization of a capital stock Company, plus a deposit of at least $250,000.

Since the policyholders of a mutual Company "participate" in the Company's surplus, this form of insurance is known as "participating" insurance although, strictly, a non-mutual Company may also write participating policies and offer its Insureds "dividends."

Mutual insurance carriers fall into three broad groups:

1. Local or County Mutuals—generally organized in a single county or township to insure local property owners. These Companies are usually operated on a purely assessment basis, and require only a small advance premium at the time the policy is issued.

2. Factory Insurance Mutuals—a group of older Fire insurance mutuals which write only the larger superior-construction risks.

3. Regular Fire and Casualty Mutuals—which operate in much the same manner as stock companies, charging a standard or near-standard premium.

CAPITAL STOCK COMPANIES (STOCK COMPANIES)

A capital stock insurance Company (stock Company) is a corporation operated by individuals who contribute capital in the hope of earning a profit through the sale of insurance protection. The stockholders elect the directors, direct the Company's operations, and share in any profits earned. While mutual carriers in the Property insurance field far outnumber the capital stock Companies, the latter write about 75% of the Fire and Casualty insurance of the country. This is in sharp contrast with the Life insurance business, where mutual Companies, although less in number, write the bulk of the Life insurance in force.

RECIPROCALS (INTER-INSURANCE EXCHANGES)

As in the case of a mutual Company, the policyholders in a Reciprocal Exchange (Reciprocal) are both Insured and insurer. There are no stockholders. The Reciprocal is not incorporated, but is actually an aggregation of individuals, firms and business corporations which *exchange* insurance on one another.

Each member assumes a fraction of the coverage on every other member. Profits earned by the Reciprocal Exchange are distributed among the members in the form of premium refunds (dividends) in the same manner as in the mutual carriers. The actual exchange of insurance is effected through an attorney-in-fact, appointed by the members and empowered on their behalf to bind them to one another.

Some Reciprocal Exchanges are organized by a particular industry and confine their activities to this industry, while others offer insurance to the general public.

ASSOCIATIONS (DOMESTIC LLOYDS)

This type of organization is formed by a number of unincorporated individuals who are associated together and are authorized to operate an insurance business. Each individual agrees to accept for himself only a portion of the risk. These associations are patterned on the famous Lloyds of London, and are sometimes referred to as domestic Lloyds.

STATE INSURANCE FUNDS

In various states, special insurance funds have been set up by the state to provide insurance. The state acts as insurer, collecting premiums or taxes from the public and offering protection against specified hazards. Most usually, the State Fund is empowered to write only Workmen's Compensation insurance, or Workmen's Compensation and Employer's Liability insurance. In four states, as discussed in Chapter 31, Disability Benefits insurance is also written by the State Fund.

When the Law provides that a given form of insurance must be procured only through the State Fund, the Fund is spoken of as "monopolistic"; when the Fund operates alongside private carriers, the operations are described as "competitive."

DOMESTIC, FOREIGN AND ALIEN INSURERS

An insurer which is domiciled within a state is, as respects that state, a domestic carrier. All carriers which are incorporated or organized outside of the state are "foreign" insurers, while those domiciled outside of the United States are "alien" insurers.

REINSURANCE

INSURANCE CARRIERS have long understood the importance of spreading their risks, and have therefore avoided accepting a heavy concentration of liability in one area, or on a single Insured's operations, or one type of risk. To further protect themselves against catastrophe losses, the Companies commonly reinsure—transfer a portion of the risk they have assumed to other carriers.

This practice enables them to offer an Insured larger amounts of insurance than they would otherwise issue, and also permits them to stabilize their operations by divesting themselves of risks which they do not consider it wise to retain.

The Company which undertakes to protect the Insured is called the *ceding* carrier, because it gives up a portion of its risk to another carrier, known as the *assuming* carrier. For its reinsuring part of the risk, the assuming carrier receives a premium from the ceding carrier. Reinsurance is purchased either from special Reinsurance Companies (Excess Companies) or from regular Companies which transact an insurance business with the public and also reinsure other Companies.

It is important to understand that the Insured has no part in the reinsurance transaction which is effected without his knowledge or consent. If he suffers a loss under his policy, it is to the Company which issued his policy that he will look for recovery. After it has paid the loss to its Insured, the ceding carrier turns to the assuming carrier for reimbursement, according to the terms of the reinsurance contract between them.

TYPES OF REINSURANCE AGREEMENTS

Facultative Basis—Under this method, each risk is specifically reinsured under a separate agreement. Since individual transactions are required, the Facultative method is somewhat cumbersome and, as a result, a more efficient method of handling reinsurance has been evolved. This method is discussed directly below.

Treaty Basis—Under this method, the ceding carrier enters into a contract with one or more assuming Companies to assume automatically a certain portion of all the business it writes for the public. The ceding Company periodically informs the Reinsurance Company on a special form, called a "borderaux," of all the transactions it has entered into. There are two broad types of Treaty Reinsurance:

1. Excess Cover—the Reinsurer is liable only for such portion of any loss as exceeds a stated amount, or a stated percentage. The ceding insurer pays all losses up to that amount.

2. Quota Share—The assuming Company accepts a fixed percentage of every risk underwritten by the ceding carrier and, regardless of the size of the loss, pays the stipulated percentage.

RETROCESSION

A reinsurance Company may find itself carrying too much liability and turn to another reinsurer to assume part of its liabilities. This is known as retrocession.

SELF-INSURANCE

GENERALLY, an individual or firm that wishes to insure its property or its liability to others turns to a risk-bearing institution—an insurance Company. In some forms of insurance, particularly Workmen's Compensation insurance, there is considerable self-insurance in effect. A self-insurer does not transfer the risk to an outside carrier, but sets up its own reserves to provide for losses. Usually, some form of excess insurance is purchased from an insurance carrier to cover losses which exceed a stated maximum, and the self-insurer bears only the portion of any loss which falls below this figure.

There are two broad types of excess insurance. In Property insurance, the self-insurer will buy *excess of loss* coverage to be protected against catastrophe losses. Thus, a large manufacturer with numerous plants in different parts of the country might purchase Fire insurance on each plant with a Deductible of $100,000. Any loss which does not reach $100,000 is self-insured, and the manufacturer must meet such loss from his own reserves. If a loss exceeds this figure, the insurance Company will be liable for the excess.

Where *frequency* of loss is a factor, as in Workmen's Compensation benefits, excess insurance may also be procured on a stop-loss indemnity basis. The employer is liable under this form of excess insurance for all losses in the policy year until they aggregate the figure set in the excess policy. Once he has paid out to his employees benefits which total the stop-loss figure, the insurance Company must meet all further losses within the policy period.

It is important to differentiate between being self-insured and not carrying insurance. If a merchant does not carry Fire insurance on his stocks, he is, of course, himself assuming the risk of loss, but this is not self-insurance. Self-insurance is a *positive* act —that of actually setting aside reserves to meet anticipated losses. In order to be sound, a fairly accurate estimate must be made of the frequency and severity of losses that may be expected. The uninsured owner faces financial ruin if he sustains a serious loss; the properly established program of self-insurance should be able to weather such situations without undue strain.

When the form of insurance being self-insured is statutory, the state agency administering the coverage usually requires proof of financial responsibility from the risk, and may also ask for other guarantees in the form of a Bond or security.

MASS MERCHANDISING

Life insurance, disability, hospital and medical care and major medical insurance have been sold on a group basis for many years. Recently, the mass marketing approach has been extended to several other branches of the insurance business.

For the most part, the group approach is now being used to market personal automobile, Homeowners policies and insurance on private watercraft.

The insurance companies require a minimum participation of 1,000 Insureds; some set 5,000 as a minimum. A discount is usually allowed from the rates which are used for individual policies of the same kind.

FOR FURTHER READING

ACKERMAN—Insurance
HEDGES—Practical Fire and Casualty Insurance
KULP AND HALL—Casualty Insurance
MOWBRAY AND BLANCHARD—Insurance
RIEGEL, ROBERT AND MILLER—Insurance

(See Reading List at End of Book)

CHAPTER 34

Personal Multiple Peril Policies

DURING THE PAST 20 YEARS, the insurance industry has introduced a series of package policies which incorporate both the Direct Damage (first party) and Liability (third party) coverages. As a result of economies in handling, these policies usually develop lower premiums than the separate policies which they replace, and frequently provide broader protection than was formerly available.

This chapter will analyze the various Homeowners policies which have all but replaced individual policies for owners of private residences. Chapter 35 will discuss package policies which have been made available to business risks.

HOMEOWNERS PACKAGE POLICIES

THE SERIES of Homeowners package policies, available to owners of private dwellings, and in some cases, to tenants, group together coverage on the dwelling, the household contents, and the liability of the Insured.

Some of these policies are based on an indivisible premium, while others allow some flexibility in packaging the individual coverages. In every instance, the Insured realizes a savings over the cost of comparable coverages purchased individually.

While there are several independent filings for home owners, most of the package policies for home owners are written under one of five forms—Homeowners 1, 2, 3, 4 and 5. These policies replace an earlier group of policies for home owners—The Homeowners A, Homeowners B, Homeowners C, and the Comprehensive Dwelling policy, which are available only in a few states.

HOMEOWNERS POLICIES 1, 2, 3, 4 AND 5

The Homeowners 1, 2, 3, 4 and 5 Policy Program was first developed in 1959, as an improvement over the original Homeowners A, B and C program. The first major revision of the 1959 program has been made in 1968 after several years of careful review by insurance companies and agents' groups. The purpose of the new revision is to update the coverage of the Homeowners Program to reflect more flexible coverage needs for the changing conditions in modern living and indications for the future. Another purpose of this revision is to clarify certain provisions of the forms, and to arrange the format of the policy to give the Insured a better understanding of his policy.

One of the five forms is attached to the Homeowners basic policy jacket to effect the coverage the Insured elects to carry. All forms, except for Form 4 which covers contents only, have an identical structure, covering as follows:

Section I—Coverage	A—Applies to the dwelling.
	B—Applies to appurtenant structures on premises other than the dwelling.
	C—Applies to unscheduled personal property.
	D—Applies to additional living expense.
Section II—Coverage	E—Applies to Personal Liability.
	F—Applies to Medical Payments to Others.

Except for Form 4, which covers contents, the Homeowners forms are available only to owner-occupied one- or two-family dwellings.

NOTE: In a number of states eligibility for Homeowners policies may be extended to owner-occupied three- and four-family dwellings. Special rules apply to this coverage.

WHAT IS COVERED

The forms differ among themselves primarily in the extent of the perils covered under Section I. The Liability insurance afforded under Section II is identical under all forms.

Coverage A—Dwellings—Under this item, the policy covers the dwelling described in the policy, the fixtures, equipment used in maintenance of the building, outdoor equipment on the premises, or while temporarily off the premises, and all materials and supplies in use for construction, repair, or alteration of the dwelling. The policies are very close in scope to the Dwelling Form discussed in Chapter 3.

Coverage B—Appurtenant Structures—The Insured may apply up to 10% of the amount of insurance to the dwelling to cover structures on the premises, other than the dwelling and additions in contact with the dwelling. The coverage is similar to the insurance on outbuildings afforded under the Dwelling Form, discussed in Chapter 3.

Coverage C—Unscheduled Personal Property—Like the Household Contents Form (discussed in Chapter 3), all personal property—such as is usual to a dwelling occupancy—is covered. The coverage is divided into two parts: On Premises and Off Premises. On premises, the policy covers property owned by the Insured and all members of his household, and the property of guests while on the portion of the premises occupied exclusively by the Insured. Off premises, the policy covers personal property of the Insured and members of his family, guests in a temporary residence of the Insured, and property of servants who are actually engaged in the service of the Insured while such property is in the custody of the servant, or in a residence temporarily occupied by the Insured.

Coverage D—Additional Living and Rental Value Expense—The coverage is identical with that afforded under Dwelling Building(s) and Contents Broad Form, discussed in Chapter 5. The amount of coverage applicable under this section differs under the Homeowners 1 and the other Homeowners policies, as will be pointed out later under FOR HOW MUCH. Included in this section is any loss of the rental value of any portion of the described premises rented to others or held for rental as, for example, a second apartment in a two-family dwelling, a private garage, or other outbuildings rented to others, etc.

Coverages E and F—Personal Liability and Medical Payments to Others—All the Homeowners forms provide coverage which is similar to Comprehensive Personal Liability policy, including Medical Payments to Others coverage. (See Chapter 25.)

PROPERTY NOT COVERED

The policies do not cover:

Animals, birds or fish.

All motorized vehicles, except those vehicles used for the service of the premises and not licensed for road use

Aircraft

Property of roomers and boarders not related to the Insured

Property carried or held as samples or for sale or for delivery after sale; business property while away from the premises

Property rented or held for rental to others by the Insured

Property separately described and specifically insured in whole or part by any other insurance.

CALIFORNIA—Outdoor radio and television antennas, including their lead-in wiring, masts and towers are not covered for the perils of windstorm and hail.

The policy excludes any sound recording or reproducing device or instrument which is operated by power from an automobile electrical system, and any tape, wire, record, disc or other medium for use with this device while any of this property is in a motor vehicle.

Loss arising from theft of a credit card is not covered under the basic policy, unless a special endorsement is purchased for an additional premium.

NEW YORK—In the counties of New York, Kings, Queens, Bronx, Richmond, Nassau, Suffolk, Westchester, Rockland and Putnam, the policy does not cover Theft Away from the Premises, unless a special endorsement is purchased. This endorsement needs supplementing by a second, if coverage is to be afforded to theft from an unattended automobile or watercraft.

Trees, Shrubs, Plants and Lawns—These classes of property are covered against the perils of fire, lightning, explosion, riot, civil commotion, vandalism, malicious mischief, theft, aircraft, or vehicles not owned or operated by an occupant of the premises on all Homeowners forms.

When Premises Are Rented to Others—When the portion of the dwelling customarily occupied exclusively by the insured is rented to others the policy does not apply to the following property as to the peril of theft:

Money, bullion, coin collections or bank notes

Securities, accounts, bills, deeds, evidences of debt, letters of credit, notes other than bank notes, passports, railroad and other tickets, stamps and stamp collections

Jewelry, watches, necklaces, bracelets, gems, precious and semi-precious stones, articles of gold and platinum, or any article of fur or trimmed with fur

Loss caused by a tenant or his employees, or members of his household.

FOR HOW MUCH

Money, Stamps, Etc.—The policy will not pay more than $100 for loss of money, bullion, numismatic property and bank notes; $500 on securities, accounts, bills, deeds, evidences of debt, letters of credit, notes other than bank notes, passports, railroad and other tickets and stamps, including philatelic property; $1,000 on manuscripts.

Watercraft—$500 on watercraft, including their trailers, furnishings, equipment.

HOMEOWNERS POLICY 1—BASIC FORM

HAZARDS COVERED

In addition to the Personal Liability coverage afforded in all

Homeowners forms—discussed under WHAT IS COVERED, Sections E and F—the Homeowners 1 covers:

All perils of the Fire insurance policy (See Chapter 2).

All perils of the Extended Coverage endorsement (See Chapter 5).

All perils of the Vandalism and Malicious Mischief endorsement (See Chapter 5).

Theft—Defined as an act of stealing. In this respect, the coverage is similar to the PERSONAL THEFT POLICY, which does not include mysterious disappearance as an insured peril, as the BROAD FORM THEFT POLICY does. (Both policies are discussed in Chapter 10.) In other respects, the Theft coverage is closely related to the Broad Form Theft policy, except that the Homeowners policy does *not* exclude property in the mails, and does not limit loss from premises, like cleaners and laundries, to the perils of robbery and burglary.

Glass Breakage—Any glass which constitutes part of the insured dwelling is covered, including glass in storm windows and storm doors. Note that this coverage applies to any breakage, whether or not caused by one of the perils covered in the particular Homeowners policy. There is no coverage, however, if the dwelling has been vacant for more than 30 consecutive days before the breakage.

HAZARDS NOT COVERED

Since the Homeowners forms attach to the Fire insurance policy, the basic exclusions of the Fire policy are applicable to the insurance afforded under the Homeowners forms. Specifically eliminated by a provision in the Homeowners form are the exclusions of loss by theft and suspension of insurance (discussed in Chapter 2 under HAZARDS NOT COVERED and WHEN COVERED).

Unoccupancy—If the property is vacant beyond 30 consecutive days, there is no coverage for loss by vandalism and malicious mischief, or for glass breakage.

Theft Exclusions—There is no coverage for theft committed by an Insured, or for loss in a dwelling under construction, or loss of a precious or semi-precious stone from its setting, or loss arising from theft of a credit card.

War Risks—The exclusion on this score of the basic Fire policy is applicable to the Homeowners policies. In addition, the policy incorporates the broader War Risks exclusion of the Extended Coverage Endorsement (discussed in Chapter 5 under EXTENDED COVERAGE ENDORSEMENT—HAZARDS NOT COVERED).

Seizure Under Quarantine—All the Homeowners forms exclude loss caused by seizure or destruction under quarantine or Custom's regulations, confiscation by order of any government or public authority, risks of contraband, or illegal transportation or trade.

Nuclear Perils—Discussed in Chapter 3 under HAZARDS NOT COVERED.

Flood, Water Damage — Discussed in Chapter 5 under EXTENDED COVERAGE ENDORSEMENT—Exclusions Applicable to All Perils.

Enforcement of Local or State Ordinance—All of the Homeowners forms exclude coverage loss necessitated by the enforcement of a local or state ordinance regulating the construction, repair or demolition of a building or structure.

Earthquake or Earth Movement—Homeowners policies also exclude loss resulting from earth movement, including earthquake, volcanic eruption, landslide, etc.

NOTE: The policy may be extended by endorsement to cover the perils of Earthquake and Volcanic Eruption.

Power, Heating or Cooling Failure—Consequential loss to property is excluded, unless such loss results from physical damage to power, heating or cooling equipment on premises caused by an insured peril.

Watercraft Exclusion—Section E of the policy which applies to Personal Liability and Medical Payments specifically excludes coverage for liability arising out of watercraft powered by an inboard motor exceeding 50 horsepower or by an outboard motor (or combination of motors on a single craft) of 25 horsepower or more. Also excluded is coverage for liability arising out of a sailing vessel 26 feet or more in length. Coverage for the liability arising from *outboard* motor powered craft may be written under the policy for an additional premium if such motors are declared in the policy.

Snowmobiles and other Recreational Vehicles—There is no coverage under the Liability section for claims arising out of snowmobiles owned by the Insured for bodily injury or property damage occurring away from the insured premises.

Automobiles, Aircraft—There is no coverage under the Liability section of the policy for bodily injury or property damage arising out of any aircraft or any motor vehicle owned or operated by, or rented or loaned to an Insured if the accident occurs away from the premises. The policy does *not* exclude such losses arising from golf carts while being used for golfing purposes and to any recreational motor vehicle on the residence premises.

Professional Services—The policy does not apply to liability arising out of the rendering or the failure to render of any professional service.

Business Pursuits—The policy does not apply to business pursuits of the Insured except such activities as are incidental to non-business pursuits. (This exclusion is discussed more fully in Chapter 25 under COMPREHENSIVE PERSONAL LIABILITY POLICY—HAZARDS NOT COVERED—Business Pursuits).

Other Premises—The policy does not apply to any premises owned, rented or controlled by an Insured, unless these are insured under the policy.

Intended Result—The policy does not cover bodily injury or property damage which from the viewpoint of the Insured is intended or expected.

FOR HOW MUCH

As pointed out at the beginning of this chapter, a central idea of most Homeowners policies is the indivisible premium. The Insured elects an amount of coverage on the dwelling structure — $8,000 is the minimum under the form—and the amounts of coverage under the other sections of the policy are related to this amount, as follows:

• Coverage B—Appurtenant Structures—10% of amount on dwelling.

• Coverage C—Personal Property—50% of amount on dwelling. 10% of the amount of Coverage C applies away from premises, as under any Household Contents form (See Chapter 3), but in any event, not less than $1,000 is available for such off premises losses.

NOTE: This amount of insurance may be increased or decreased to as little as 40%. The off-premises limit may also be increased.

NOTE: An Insured who maintains an incidental office, private school, or studio at the premises is required to increase from 50% to at least 60% the coverage on contents under Coverage C. An exception is made if the Insured gives music or dancing lessons, and has made no physical alteration to the premises for this purpose, and employs no assistants.

• Coverage D—Additional Living Expense—including Rental Value—up to 10% of the amount of insurance on the dwelling.

• Coverage E—Personal Liability—$25,000.

• Coverage F—Medical Payments—$500 per person; $25,000 aggregate limit.

Trees, Shrubs, Plants and Lawns—Coverage on any one tree, shrub, or plant is limited to 5% of the amount of insurance on the dwelling, or $250, whichever is less.

Money—Coverage on money, bullion, bank notes and coin collections is limited to $100.

Accounts, Bills, Deeds, Etc.—A limit of $500 applies to losses involving accounts, bills, notes other than bank notes, passports, railroad, airline, theatre, and other tickets, securities, stamps, and stamp collections.

Jewelry, Furs—Coverage on jewelry, watches, necklaces, bracelets, gems, precious and semi-precious stones, gold, platinum, furs and articles trimmed with fur are covered against all perils insured against, except that no more than $500 will be paid for loss by *theft* in the aggregate for all items, in any one occurrence.

NEW JERSEY—Theft coverage is extended to an aggregate of $500 on jewelry and $500 on furs.

NEW YORK—Policies issued in counties of Bronx, Kings, Nassau, New York, Putnam, Queens, Richmond, Rockland, Suffolk and Westchester have limitation in the aggregate of $250 on jewelry and furs by theft.

Manuscripts—Coverage is limited to $1,000.

Watercraft—A $500 aggregate limit is applicable to watercraft, including their trailers, furnishings, equipment and outboard motors.

Trailers—Coverage is also limited to $500 on trailers.

Deductibles—The 1968 Homeowners Program contemplates the use of only one Loss Deductible clause. For Forms 1, 2, 3 and 4 this clause is a $50 deductible applicable to all losses covered under the policy. The deductible is a disappearing deductible. Under the provision when the loss is between $50 and $500, the Company absorbs more and more of the deductible. On any loss over $50, but less than $500, the Company is liable for 111% of the loss in excess of $50 (i. e., if the loss is $100, the Company pays $55.50 and the Insured, $44.50).

In a number of states where the "all peril" $50 Deductible Clause has not been approved, other combinations or variations of the Windstorm and Hail Deductible Clause No. 1 and the Other Perils Deductible Clause No. 2 used under the old Homeowners Program will continue to be used. In most of these states the Windstorm and Hail Deductible is mandatory or automatic, while the Other Perils Deductible may usually be "bought back" for an additional premium charge.

The deductible does not apply to Additional Living Expense or the Fire Department Service Charge.

Replacement Cost Coverage—All Homeowners policies incorporate a Replacement Cost section, applicable to buildings and outbuildings. This basis of recovery is identical with the Replacement Cost coverage discussed in Chapter 5 under DWELLING BUILDING(S) AND CONTENTS—BROAD FORM—FOR HOW MUCH.

Inflation Guard Endorsement—For an additional premium, the policy may be endorsed to provide that the amounts of insurance under each of the four coverages of Section I shall increase *automatically* at the rate of 1% per quarter for the first thirty months of the policy period followed by a final increase of 2% at the end of the 33rd month. Note that the percentage increase is based on the original amount of insurance in force when the policy attaches.

Breakage of Glass—Policy limits to $50 recovery for any one loss under this peril.

Damage to the Property of Others—Under this extension of the policy, the Insured is covered to a maximum of $250 in any one occurrence for loss or damage to property of others which is in his custody. There is no coverage however for loss caused intentionally by an insured under the policy who has attained the age of 13, or to property owned by or rented to an Insured, a tenant of the Insured or any resident of his household.

Fire Legal Liability—The Liability section of the policy is extended to cover the Insured's liability for damage to the insured premises and house furnishings arising from fire, explosion, or smoke or smudge caused by sudden, unusual and faulty operation of any heating or cooking unit.

WHERE COVERED

The Homeowners policy covers the buildings and personal property of the Insured while on the premises and subject to the limitations described in this section—AWAY FROM PREMISES—while off premises.

Away from Premises—As pointed out under Coverage C, at the opening of this chapter, the Insured may apply up to 10% of the amount of insurance on contents to cover similar property while elsewhere on the described premises. In this respect, the coverage is similar to the Away from Premises coverage of the Household Contents Form and the Dwelling Building(s) and Contents Broad Form and Special Form—all discussed in Chapters 3 and 5. Under the Homeowners forms, however, coverage is world-wide, and

$1,000 of insurance is granted as a minimum under this provision, even if this should exceed 10% of the insurance on the dwelling.

With respect to provisions applicable only to the peril of theft, Homeowners Form 1 does not cover loss *away from the premises* under the following situations:

Unoccupied Dwelling—Any dwelling or premises owned, rented or occupied by the Insured unless the insured is temporarily residing there.

Unattended Motor Vehicles—Except for a public conveyance, there is no coverage for theft of property while unattended in or on any motor vehicle or trailer, unless as a result of forcible entry into the vehicle while all doors, windows or other openings are closed and locked, and there are visible signs of such forcible entry on the exterior of the vehicle. However, property stolen from a vehicle when the insured is required to leave the keys with a bailee, such as a parking garage, is covered.

Unattended Watercraft, Watercraft and Trailers — Property left in an unattended watercraft is also not covered unless taken by forcible entry into a locked compartment with visible signs of such entry upon the exterior.

Watercraft, their furnishings, equipment and outboard motors and trailers off-premises are not covered if stolen.

SUPPLEMENTARY COVERAGES

Automatic Removal—A new coverage in the 1968 Homeowners Program provides coverage in all forms for unscheduled personal property at both locations when the Insured moves from the described premises to another location within the Continental U. S. or Hawaii. Coverage is pro rata at each location to the total value of such personal property. This coverage applies only for a period of 30 days.

Debris Removal—See Chapter 3—Provisions Common to the Various Forms—HAZARDS COVERED.

Fire Department Service Charge—The Homeowners policy covers for an amount up to $250 for the Insured's liability under contract or agreement for fire department charges where a fire department is called to the premises because of a fire in, on or exposing the Insured's property.

OPTIONAL COVERAGES

The outline of the Homeowners Forms analyzed the basic policy as respects the coverages which are mandatory.

There is a whole series of Optional Coverages which are offered under the Homeowners policies, and below are listed some of the more widely used endorsements adding such additional protection:

a) **Credit Card and Depositors Forgery**—By endorsement, the Homeowners Policy may be extended to cover loss from credit card forgery, depositors forgery and acceptance of counterfeit currency. The endorsement also covers court costs and attorney's fees incurred by the Insured or his bank in connection with credit card or depositors forgery. These costs are payable over and above the limits of liability stated in the endorsement. There is a $50 limit on loss due to counterfeit currency in any one transaction, subject to an aggregate limit of $100. The coverage against Depositors Forgery is very similar to the commercial form of this insurance discussed in Chapter 15 under DEPOSITORS FORGERY BOND, *except* that there is no coverage for forged instruments used in the Insured's business pursuits.

b) **Glass Coverage**—The policy may be endorsed to cover scheduled articles of glass.

c) **Theft From Unattended Vehicle**—The policy may be extended to cover theft from an unattended vehicle or watercraft.

d) **Earthquake Coverage**—The policy may be extended to cover the peril of earthquake.

e) **Demolition, Increased Cost** — Like most policies covering property, the Homeowners forms cover on an actual cash value basis. An Insured may be living in a dwelling of a construction which could not be utilized in rebuilding after a loss due to the operation of zoning laws. (This entire question is discussed at the end of Chapter 8 under CONTINGENT LIABILITY FROM OPERATION OF ZONING OR BUILDING LAWS). Coverage for the increased cost of reconstruction may be provided by endorsement of a Homeowners Policy.

f) **Increased Limits on Specific Coverages**—In addition to the added coverages which are outlined above, it is permissible to increase the limits on certain features of the Homeowners, as follows:

1) Appurtenant Structures—Increased Limit, 2) Additional Living Expense—Increased Limit, 3) Fire Department Service Charge, 4) Money and Securities, 5) Secondary Residence Limit, etc.

Physicians, Surgeons, Dentists and Veterinarians may have their Homeowners policy extended to cover their professional instruments, medicines, drugs and books against the peril of theft while away from their premises.

HOMEOWNERS FORM 2—BROAD FORM

THIS ANALYSIS of Homeowners Form 2—Broad Form will point up only the differences between the form and Homeowners Form 1—Basic Form, which was discussed in the preceding section of the chapter. It should be read together with the analysis of the Homeowners Form 1 and the general comments on all the Homeowners forms, which preceded that section.

HAZARDS COVERED

The Homeowners Form 2—Broad Form adds to the coverage of the Homeowners Form 1 all the perils assumed under the Dwelling Building(s) and Contents Broad Form. (See Chapter 5.)

Smoke—The policy covers sudden and accidental damage from smoke, whether from a heating or cooking unit, or otherwise. Smoke from fireplaces is covered. Excludes only agricultural smudging or industrial operations.

Electrical Appliances—Accidental injury to electrical appliances, devices, fixtures and wiring, (except tubes, transistors and similar electronic components) is covered.

Explosion—The coverage includes all explosion, as well as the sudden and accidental tearing asunder, cracking, burning, or bulging of a steam or hot water system. (See DWELLING BUILDING(S) AND CONTENTS BROAD FORM—HAZARDS COVERED.)

Glass Breakage—The Homeowners Form 2 does not contain a $50 limit on loss to glass.

Theft—Property in a vehicle which is stolen and not recovered within 30 days is covered in Homeowners Form 2.

FOR HOW MUCH

Additional Living Expense—Under the Homeowners Form 2, the Insured may apply up to 20% of the amount of insurance on the dwelling to cover Additional Living Expense.

WHERE COVERED

Theft Coverage Extension — In the analysis of Homeowners Form 1 under WHERE COVERED—Theft from Unattended Motor Vehicles and Unattended Watercraft, it was pointed out that there was no coverage for theft from an unattended motor vehicle or watercraft, except if as the result of forcible entry. This exclusion carries over into Homeowners Form 2—Broad Form. The policy may be endorsed for an additional premium to waive these two exclusions. (This endorsement is not available under Homeowners Policy Form 1.)

Physicians, Surgeons, Dentists and Veterinarians Away from Premises Coverage—When a Homeowners Form 2 has been endorsed with a Theft Coverage Extension for a physician, surgeon, dentist or veterinarian, the Insured may broaden his policy to cover theft of instruments, apparatus, medicines, drugs or books, including the bag, kit or instrument case while away from the Insured's dwelling or office.

HOMEOWNERS FORM 3—SPECIAL FORM

WHILE THE Homeowners Form 3 in the 1968 Homeowners Program is still called the Homeowners Special Form, it is no longer used in conjunction with Homeowners Form 4 as previously done. The new Homeowners Form 3 covers the Dwelling, Appurtenant Structures and Additional Living Expense on an all-risk basis, and Unscheduled Personal Property on a broad form named peril basis.

HAZARDS COVERED

Coverage for the Dwelling and Appurtenant Structures and Additional Living Expense is virtually identical with the Dwelling Building(s) Special Form—HAZARDS COVERED and HAZARDS NOT COVERED—analyzed in Chapter 5.

FOR HOW MUCH

The amounts of coverage applicable to the several classes of property are the same as under the Homeowners Form 2.

HOMEOWNERS FORM 4 CONTENTS—BROAD FORM

HOMEOWNERS FORM 4 applies only to personal property. It may be purchased by: 1) A tenant of a dwelling or apartment; or 2) the owner-occupant of a dwelling, or in an apartment house, not eligible for any other Homeowners form.

WHAT IS COVERED

The Homeowners Form 4 covers the same classes of property as Contents coverage of the other Homeowners forms. The policy includes coverage against breakage of glass, but this does not apply in the same way as under Homeowners Form 2 (discussed under HAZARDS COVERED, to follow).

Building Additions and Alterations—A tenant who is insured under a Homeowners Policy 4 may apply up to 10% of the amount of insurance on his contents to cover improvements and building additions and alterations.

HAZARDS COVERED

The policy is virtually identical with the Homeowners Policy 2—Broad Form. As respects glass, the policy does not cover on the all-risk basis of Form 2, but only against the perils specified in the policy.

FOR HOW MUCH

The Homeowners Form 4 is written for a minimum amount of $4,000 on Coverage C—Unscheduled Personal Property. This amount may be increased by endorsement, but not reduced. Coverage away from premises is 10% of Coverage C, but not less than $1,000. The limit on Additional Living Expense is 20% of the amount of contents.

Replacement Cost Coverage—The Homeowners Form 4, which is applicable only to contents, does not cover on a Replacement Cost basis, since contents are never covered other than on an "actual cash value" basis—replacement cost *less* depreciation.

HOMEOWNERS POLICY 5—COMPREHENSIVE FORM

THIS POLICY provides all-risk insurance on dwellings and contents.

HAZARDS COVERED

As respects the dwelling structures and the appurtenant outbuildings, the coverage is virtually the same as that of the Dwelling Building(s) Special Form (discussed under HAZARDS COVERED and HAZARDS NOT COVERED—analyzed in Chapter 5). The Contents coverage follows the Personal Property Floater, analyzed in Chapter 18. There are several differences between these policies, and these follow.

PROPERTY NOT COVERED

The Homeowners Form 5 excludes all motorized vehicles, except those used for service of premises, aircraft, birds, animals and fish, property of roomers and boarders not related to the Insured, samples, property rented to others, and property pertaining to the Insured's business when away from the premises.

Boats and Trailers—The policy does provide limited coverage on boats and trailers (discussed under FOR HOW MUCH).

Breakage of Fragile Articles—The exclusion of breakage of eyeglasses, glassware, statuary, marbles, bric-a-brac, porcelains, and similar fragile articles is the same as under the Personal Property Floater, but the list of excepted perils are: Fire, lightning, windstorm, hail, smoke (other than agricultural smudging or industrial operations), explosion, riot, civil commotion, falling aircraft, vehicle collision, vandalism and malicious mischief, collapse of a building or any part thereof, earthquake, water not otherwise excluded, theft or attempted theft, or sudden and accidental tearing asunder, cracking, burning or bulging of a steam or hot water heating system.

FOR HOW MUCH

The minimum amount of insurance required under the Dwelling coverage for Homeowners Form 5 is $15,000. All other minimum limits for coverage are the same as Homeowners Forms 2 and 3.

Jewelry, Furs—As in the other Homeowners forms, coverage on unscheduled jewelry, watches, furs, etc., is limited to $500 in the aggregate for the peril of theft. However, differing from the other forms, this limited coverage is not applicable to losses by the following perils:

Fire and lightning

Windstorm, hail, smoke, explosion, riot, civil commotion, aircraft or other falling objects, vehicle collision

Vandalism and malicious mischief

Collapse of a building.

Boats—Coverage up to a maximum of $500 in the aggregate is afforded on watercraft, their trailers, furnishings, equipment and outboard motors, but on a named perils basis only. The policy covers against the following perils:

Fire and lightning

Explosion, smoke, riot, civil commotion, aircraft and other falling objects

Vandalism or malicious mischief, collapse of a building, theft, and collision, upset or overturning of land vehicles.

Deductibles—The Homeowners Form 5 makes the Deductible Clause incorporated in the policy mandatory. Furthermore, the amount of the Deductible is $100. In the case of the $100 Deductible, the Company is liable for 125% of the loss in excess of $100. When the loss exceeds $50, the Deductible no longer applies. The rules permit the reduction of the Homeowners 5 Deductible to $50 in most states, for an additional premium charge.

CONDOMINIUM PROPERTY INSURANCE

Cooperative ownership of apartment buildings has been known in this country for many years. Because of the income tax advantages it offers, this form of ownership has spread very widely since the end of World War II. Tenants of a cooperative commonly speak of their "owning" their apartment, but in a strict legal sense, they are tenants under a proprietary lease granted them by virtue of their ownership of stock in the corporation which owns and operates the building.

As a "cooperator," the owner of stock in a cooperative building insures his personal property in much the same manner as any other tenant. The corporation requires insurance on the building —liability, workmen's compensation and allied lines which does not differ substantially from the coverages an individual owner would purchase.

The recent period has seen the spread of a new form of ownership of apartments, which until recently was not known in the continental United States. The laws of most states now provide for a form of ownership in which each individual actually owns the unit he occupies in *fee simple absolute.* Under a condominium, as it is known, the unit owner has exclusive ownership of his own unit, like the owner of a private residence. He shares with all other unit owners the "common elements"—the land, entrances, exits, hallways, passageways, fire escapes, elevators, heat, light and power facilities, yard and roof facilities, water supply, etc. Each unit together with its common interest constitutes *real property.* (A condominium need not be an apartment building; it can include buildings of almost every description, e.g., office, mercantile, shopping centers, etc.)

The owner of a unit in a condominium is not involved in a common mortgage, as in a cooperative apartment; he arranges his own financing in accordance with his individual preference, or may own his unit outright.

While there are some differences in the various states in the laws governing condominiums, they all provide that the proceeds of insurance be used as promptly as possible to make repairs or reconstruction after a loss. Such repairs are to be undertaken by the Board of Managers, or other individual designated as insurance trustee, except that in most jurisdictions, it is further stipulated that when the damage exceeds 75% of the property and at least 75% of the unit owners decide not to have the repairs made, that the property shall become subject to an action for partition at the suit of any unit owner. The proceeds of the sale of the property are divided among the unit owners in proportion to their respective common interests.

A special Condominium Property Endorsement is used for such property, under the terms of which the Board of Managers or other Agent is designated to act as Insurance Trustee for the unit owners collectively. Any loss to the building property or the personal property pertaining to the service of the building is adjusted with and payable to such Trustee on behalf of all the unit owners. Each owner is free of course to insure his own unit as he sees fit.

The Improvements and Betterments clause of the usual Fire insurance policy applies only when the Insured is not the building owner (discussed in Chapter 3—WHAT IS COVERED—Improvements and Betterments). Since the unit owner in a condominium is actually an owner of the unit he occupies, the value of any improvements and betterments he makes to his unit should be added to the value of the entire property and insured as such. For an individual owner who wishes the additional security of carrying insurance on his own interest, a special endorsement is provided. The Condominium Property Owner's Contingent Insurance Building Additions and Alterations Endorsement covers the Insured's interest in building additions and alterations to an amount which is in excess of any recovery for the benefit of the Insured as owner of a unit of the condominium from any insurance covering the interests of the owners of the condominium collectively.

FOR FURTHER READING

GEE, HAROLD F.—Personal Lines Insurance
POLICY, FORM AND MANUAL ANALYSIS SERVICE

(See Reading List at End of Book)

CHAPTER 35

Commercial Multiple Peril Policies

SPECIAL MULTI-PERIL POLICY PROGRAM

Almost every non-manufacturing business risk (commercial and institutional) is eligible for a form of package insurance which incorporates into a single policy most of the coverages of property and casualty hazards otherwise available in separate contracts. The Special Multi-Peril Program offers the packaged coverages at a discount.

Seven classes of risk are now offered SMP programs:

- Apartment House Program
- Institutional Program
- Motel-Hotel Program
- Office Program
- Mercantile Program
- Processing or Service Program
- Industrial Program

Each of the above programs contains specific features which are designed for the class of property to be insured. In the main, though, the coverage under all the programs is similar enough to be treated as a whole.

GENERAL PROVISIONS OF SPECIAL MULTI-PERIL POLICY

The several package programs all utilize the same manual of rules and rates. A single policy "jacket" to which may be attached a series of forms and endorsements gives the program flexibility to meet the insurance needs of different types of enterprise.

As indicated, most of the coverages which the industry has made available separately are offered in the package policy. The most important exceptions are insurance on the automobile exposures and suretyship, for which separate policies may still be required. (Some of the features of the coverages in these two excepted fields are however included in the SMP policy, i.e., Employer's Non-Ownership Automobile Liability insurance and Garage

Keepers' Legal Liability and Fidelity insurance. All other automobile and surety exposures require separate policies.)

MANDATORY COVERAGES

The Special Multi-Peril policy must include coverage on property and liability exposures. If the Insured who occupies the premises is also owner of the building, both the building and contents must be insured. A whole series of optional coverages are available, and these will be discussed below under OPTIONAL COVERAGES.

Similarly, under the Liability section, certain coverages are basic while others may be added at the option of the Insured. The insuring clause of the Liability section provides that it is mandatory to provide bodily injury and property damage insurance on all "General Liability" hazards provided by the policy except "with respect to optional coverages."

WHAT IS COVERED

Buildings—In addition to affording coverage on the building, Coverage A also applies to building service equipment owned by the Insured and used for the maintenance and servicing of the building, all while at the described premises. Such property will include floor coverings fastened to the floor or walls, mirrors, air conditioning, domestic appliances, fire extinguishing equipment, outdoor equipment, etc.

Personal Property—The basic policy covers *business* personal property of the Insured like furniture, fixtures, equipment and supplies which are not otherwise covered under the policy and property of others held by the Insured for which the Insured is liable.

Lawns, Trees, Shrubs and Plants—Limited coverage is afforded on this class of property, as discussed below under FOR HOW MUCH.

Debris Removal—Discussed in Chapter 3 under PROVISIONS COMMON TO THE VARIOUS FORMS—Debris Removal Clause.

Valuable Papers and Records—Limited coverage is extended to cover the extra expense incurred to reproduce accounts, drawings, card index systems and other business records which are destroyed while on the premises (discussed later under FOR HOW MUCH).

Improvements and Betterments—Discussed in Chapter 3 under BUILDINGS AND CONTENTS FORM—WHAT IS COVERED—Building Coverage.

EXTENSIONS OF COVERAGE

Household and personal effects in living quarters occupied by the Insured, an officer, director or stockholder of the Insured, or relatives of any of these individuals are covered only up to $100 on the effects of any one individual, with a maximum limit of $500 on the entire loss to such property.

The policy does not cover crops and lawns. On trees, shrubs and plants, unless held for sale, the policy limits coverage on any one such item to $250, with a maximum of $1,000 on all loss to such property.

There is no coverage on property of tenants or guests, except in so far as the extension of coverage provides to household and personal effects of an officer, director, stockholder of the Insured, or a relative of any of the foregoing (discussed directly above).

Valuable papers and records consisting of books of account, manuscripts, abstracts, drawings, card index systems, film, tape, disc, drum, cell and other magnetic recording or storage media for electronic data processing are covered only to a maximum of $500.

NOTE: The coverage on valuable papers in the basic policy differs from the virtually all-risk Valuable Papers policy discussed in Chapter 13. In the Special Multi-Peril policy the perils covered are only those which are provided by the basic policy. It is possible however by endorsement to provide the broader all-risk coverage on scheduled items as well as on a blanket basis.

The Insured may apply up to 10% of the amount of insurance on the described building to cover new additions, new buildings and new structures on the described premises which are intended for occupancy similar to that of the described location. This coverage which is limited to a maximum of $25,000 ceases 30 days after construction begins.

The policy covers up to a maximum of $1,000 on Extra Expense (discussed in Chapter 7 under EXTRA EXPENSE).

PROPERTY NOT COVERED

Certain types of property are specifically not covered under the policy, to wit:

Animals, pets;

Automobiles, trailers and semi-trailers, except motorized equipment not licensed for use on public thoroughfares and operated principally on the Insured's premises; aircraft; watercraft including motors, equipment and accessories (except rowboats and canoes while out of the water and on the described premises);

Outdoor swimming pools, fences, piers, wharves, docks, beach or diving platforms or appurtenances, retaining walls unless such items are specifically insured;

Outdoor signs, unless specifically endorsed;

Foundations—Discussed in Chapter 3 under BUILDING AND

CONTENTS FORM—PROPERTY NOT COVERED—Foundation Exclusion Clause.

HAZARDS COVERED

The Special Multi-Peril policy is written on a named-perils basis. It covers against the perils of:

Fire, Lightning (the perils of the Standard Fire Insurance policy).

Windstorm, Hail, Explosion, Riot, Riot Attending A Strike, Aircraft, Vehicles, Smoke (the perils of the Extended Coverage Endorsement discussed in Chapter 5).

NOTE: The Smoke provisions are considerably broader than under the Extended Coverage Endorsement. The policy covers any sudden and accidental damage by smoke other than from agricultural smudging or industrial operations.

Consequential Loss—Discussed in Chapter 3 under HOUSEHOLD CONTENTS FORM—HAZARDS COVERED—Consequential loss.

Liability Coverages—As mentioned at the opening of this Section, coverage is afforded in the one contract for both property (first party)—and liability (third party). The Liability coverages, which make up Section II of the policy, are closely patterned on the Public Liability coverages discussed in Chapter 25 under OWNERS', LANDLORDS' AND TENANTS' LIABILITY INSURANCE, except that the policy is a single limit contract providing a set amount of insurance for both bodily injury and property damage claims. In this respect, the policy is similar to the Comprehensive Personal Liability or the Storekeepers' Liability, both of which are analyzed in Chapter 25. Provision is made for excluding product liability and medical payments coverage. Otherwise, the Liability section covers all the general liability exposures of the average risk.

HAZARDS NOT COVERED

Ordinance Regulating Construction—As discussed in Chapter 7 under DEMOLITION INSURANCE, local or state ordinances sometimes prohibit the construction or repair of buildings except in a more expensive manner than was used in the original structure. The policy does not cover any loss occasioned by such ordinance.

Electrical Apparatus Clause—The policy does not cover electrical injury or disturbance caused by electrical currents artificially generated unless fire or explosion ensues, and then only for the loss by such fire or explosion.

Earthquake, Landslide, Etc.—Discussed in Chapter 5 under DWELLING BUILDING(S) AND CONTENTS—BROAD FORM —HAZARDS NOT COVERED—Earthquake, Landslide or Other Earth Movement.

Water Exclusion Clause—Discussed in Chapter 5 under EXTENDED COVERAGE ENDORSEMENT—HAZARDS NOT COVERED—Water Exclusion Clause.

Liability Exclusions—Under the Liability portions of the policy, the basic exclusions of the regular Public Liability forms are incorporated (discussed in Chapter 24 under PUBLIC LIABILITY INSURANCE — HAZARDS NOT COVERED — and Chapter 25 OWNERS', LANDLORDS' AND TENANTS' LIABILITY POLICY —HAZARDS NOT COVERED).

WHERE COVERED

Property Outside Buildings—The policy covers property while within the described locations and when within 100 feet in the open.

Off Premises Coverage—In addition to coverage on the building structures described in the policy, and on the personal property as set forth above, the Special Multi-Peril policy provides coverage for business personal property (other than stock or merchandise) while removed for purposes of cleaning, repairing, reconstruction or restoration, up to 2% of the buildings and contents coverage, but not to exceed $5,000. This extension does not apply to property in transit.

FOR HOW MUCH

Trees, Shrubs, Plants—As mentioned before under WHAT IS COVERED, the policy affords limited coverage on trees, shrubs and plants. No single tree, shrub or plant is insured for more than $250 including cost of removal of debris in connection with loss to such property. The maximum payable in any event for all loss in a single occurrence is $1,000. Furthermore, such coverage is afforded only for loss by fire, lightning, explosion, riot, civil commotion or aircraft.

Coinsurance Clause—A coinsurance percentage is stipulated on the first page of the policy. This application of such clause is discussed in Chapter 3 under FOR HOW MUCH—COINSURANCE CLAUSE.

Replacement Cost Coverage—The Special Multi-Peril Policy is a cash value form, except that losses to building structures which do not exceed $1,000 are covered on a replacement cost basis (without deduction for depreciation). This small loss waiver of the actual cash value indemnity basis of the policy is part of the basic contract. Full Replacement Cost coverage is available by endorsement (discussed in Chapter 5 under DWELLING BUILDING(S) AND CONTENTS—BROAD FORM—FOR HOW MUCH—Replacement Cost Coverage).

Deductible Clauses—There are two Deductibles available under the Special Multi-Peril Policy. The first Deductible clause applies to windstorm and hail losses to buildings, structures and personal property in the open; Loss Deductible Clause #2 to all other perils. Both Deductibles exclude losses of $50 or less. If a loss exceeds $500, the Deductible is not applicable. If the loss is between $50 and $500, the Insured is entitled to receive 111% of the amount by which the loss exceeds $50.

HOW POLICY IS WRITTEN

The Commercial Property Coverage forms and All-Risk contents coverage on processing and industrial risks may be written in one of two ways—on a reporting or a non-reporting basis. The non-reporting policy is subject to coinsurance.

OPTIONAL COVERAGES

As mentioned at the opening of this section on the SMP policy, each of the programs packages certain mandatory coverages under Section I (Property Coverage) and Section II (Liability Coverage). A series of endorsements is available under these two sections, and two additional sections offered on an optional basis—Section III—Crime Coverages and Section IV—Boiler and Machinery.

SECTION I—PROPERTY COVERAGE

All-Risk Insurance—The coverage on buildings, office, institutional and commercial property may be broadened to insure on an all-risk basis. There is also available to builders insurance under an All-Risk Builders Risk form.

Sprinkler Leakage—A sprinklered risk may by endorsement add coverage against loss by sprinkler leakage. (This insurance is discussed in Chapter 9.)

Optional Perils Endorsement—This endorsement broadens the basic policy to include the following perils:

Breakage of Glass (subject to a limit of $50 per plate; to $250 per occurrence).
Falling Objects
Weight of Snow, Ice, Sleet
Water Damage
Collapse

These perils are discussed in Chapter 5 under DWELLING BUILDING(S) AND CONTENTS—BROAD FORM.

Additional Coverage Endorsement (only available under Mer-

cantile Program)—This endorsement adds to the basic policy the following perils:

Vandalism and Malicious Mischief
Sprinkler Leakage
Falling Objects
Weight of Ice, Snow, Sleet
Collapse of Building
Premises Burglary or Robbery

Other Endorsements—Coverage may be added to the basic policy under any of the following endorsements, among others:

Replacement Cost Coverage—Buildings and certain classes of eligible personal property may be covered on a replacement cost basis, replacing the "actual cash value" basis of the policy (discussed in Chapter 2 under FOR HOW MUCH).

Household and Personal Property—Such property may be covered under the policy by endorsement.

Outdoor Signs Endorsement—Such items may be covered against the perils of Fire and the Extended Coverage Endorsement (discussed in Chapter 5) subject to a Deductible of $50 applicable to the perils of windstorm and hail.

Fine Arts Endorsement—Coverage on such property may be added on an all-risk basis, similar to the insurance afforded under a Fine Arts Floater (discussed in Chapter 17 under FINE ARTS FLOATER).

Camera Property—Coverage on such property, similar to that afforded under a Camera Floater, may be endorsed (discussed in Chapter 17 under CAMERA FLOATER).

Musical Instruments Floater—The coverage on such property available by endorsement is similar to the Musical Instrument Floater (discussed in Chapter 17).

Time Element Coverages—Coverage against loss due to interruption under a series of endorsements is available, e. g., Gross Earnings Endorsement, Loss of Earnings Endorsement, Extra Expense Endorsement, Tuition Fees Endorsement, Loss of Rents Endorsement, etc.

Accounts Receivable Insurance—This coverage (discussed at the end of Chapter 13) may be added to the policy by endorsement.

SECTION II—LIABILITY COVERAGE

Comprehensive General Liability—The Liability coverage of the basic policy may be broadened to cover on a Comprehensive General Liability basis (discussed in Chapter 25).

Premises Medical Payments Insurance—Medical Payments insurance (discussed in Chapter 24 under PUBLIC LIABILITY INSURANCE—WHAT IS COVERED—Medical Payments Coverage) may be added to the policy.

Personal Injury Liability Endorsement—Coverage may be added to the policy under one or more of the following sources of claims:

False arrest, detention or imprisonment, or malicious prosecution;

Libel, slander, defamation or violation of right of privacy;

Wrongful entry or eviction or other invasion of private occupancy.

Employer's Non-Ownership Automobile Liability—This coverage, which is discussed in Chapter 27 under NON-OWNED AUTOMOBILES — EMPLOYER'S NON-OWNERSHIP AUTOMOBILE LIABILITY INSURANCE, may be added to the basic policy for risks which are exposed to such claims.

Tourists Court Endorsement—Under the terms of this endorsement, risks of this kind may modify the basic policy to provide coverage against claims arising out of the use of saddle animals and watercraft, and to *exclude* professional liability (malpractice).

Garage Keeper's Legal Liability Insurance—This coverage may be added to the policy. (It is discussed fully in Chapter 29 under GARAGE KEEPER'S LEGAL LIABILITY INSURANCE).

There are also a series of exclusionary endorsements which modify or limit the coverage, among which are the following:

EXCLUSION of completed operations and products; of logging and lumbering operations; of laundry and dry cleaning damage; of inmates or persons being cared for in institutions; explosion, collapse and underground property damage, etc.

SECTION III—CRIME COVERAGES

An optional section, Section III, is available to add coverages on the crime exposures of a risk. Known as the Comprehensive Crime Coverage Form, this endorsement incorporates into the policy the following coverages:

Blanket Fidelity insurance (Blanket Position or Primary Commercial Blanket) (discussed in Chapter 15)

Loss Inside Premises
Loss Outside Premises
Money Order and Counterfeit Paper Currency
Depositors Forgery

The policy may also be endorsed with the Blanket Crime Coverage Form or a Public Employees Blanket Coverage Form.

SECTION IV—BOILER AND MACHINERY COVERAGES

Under Section IV, the policy may be extended to cover loss due to an accident involving boilers and machinery. These coverages are discussed in Chapter 32.

WHEN COVERED

Term of Policy—The new policy may be written only for a three-year term. The premium may be paid annually under the terms of the Deferred Premium Payment Plan.

RATES

Minimum Premiums—For the mandatory coverages under Section I (Property Coverages), the minimum premium is $100 for most risks. When an endorsement is attached to the policy, the minimum premium is $6 per endorsement.

Deductibles—The policy is subject to a mandatory Deductible of $50, although this may be amended by endorsement to $250, $500 or $1,000 with rate credits granted for the use of these higher Deductibles.

The Deductible does *not* apply to losses by fire or lightning (the perils of the Standard Fire Insurance policy).

OFFICE PERSONAL PROPERTY FORM

Many business risks are eligible for recently introduced all-risk insurance. The Office Personal Property Form is available to any business or professional *office* which is not connected with a mercantile, non-manufacturing or manufacturing occupancy. Thus, the office of an insurance agent, lawyer, accountant, real estate broker, and similar occupancies which do not manufacture or service or trade in merchandise are eligible. On the other hand, the Office Personal Property Form is not available to offices of a department store, the clerical department of a factory, etc. The policy is not offered to doctors, dentists or clinics.

WHAT IS COVERED

The Office Personal Property Form covers all office contents such as are usual to the occupancy of an office. This includes furniture, fixtures, equipment and supplies.

Property of Others—The policy may be extended, at the option of the Insured, to cover personal property of others while in the care, custody or under the control of the Insured, and while on the described premises. The maximum available for such loss is $2,000, or 2% of the amount of insurance applicable to personal property under the policy, whichever is less. There is no coverage on furs, jewelry, watches and similar property.

Trees, Shrubs, Plants—These classes of property are covered against the perils of fire, lightning, explosion, riot, civil commotion and aircraft for a maximum of $1,000 in any single occurrence. No more than $250, including debris removal, is available on any single item.

Improvements and Betterments—If the Insured is a tenant, the policy covers his interest in such property, subject to the conditions of the Tenant's Improvements and Betterments clause, discussed in Chapter 3.

Damage to Premises—If the Insured is the owner of the building or the equipment pertaining to the service of the building or is liable for such property, the policy covers damage caused by theft or attempted theft. There is no coverage for loss to glass which constitutes a part of the building except for glass building blocks, or for fire or explosion.

Debris Removal—This coverage is discussed in Chapter 3 under Debris Removal.

Money, Stamps—The Insured may apply up to $250 in any one occurrence for loss of currency, money or stamps on the premises, or while such property is being conveyed outside the premises by the Insured or an employee of the Insured.

Personal Effects—The Insured may apply up to $500 to cover loss of personal effects of the Insured, partners or employees when loss occurs on the premises. No more than $100 of this amount is available for loss of the property of any one individual.

Valuable Papers and Records—Subject to a maximum limit of $500 in any one occurrence, the policy will pay for the extra expenses incurred by the Insured in reproducing books of account, manuscripts, drawings, card index systems and other business records when such are damaged by a peril insured against in the policy.

General Average and Salvage Charges—Discussed in Chapter 22.

PROPERTY NOT COVERED

Stock, Samples—The Office Personal Property Form does not cover stocks of merchandise, nor materials and supplies entering into their manufacture, storage or sale, nor salesman's samples.

Accounts, Bills, Bullion, Notes, Etc.—There is no coverage for bullion, notes, securities, deeds, accounts, bills, evidences of debt, letters of credit, or tickets. (Money and Stamps coverage is limited, as shown under WHAT IS COVERED—Money, Stamps.) Records are covered, subject to the limitation discussed under FOR HOW MUCH—Records.

Steam Boilers — There is no coverage for damage to steam boilers, steam pipes, steam turbines or steam engines against loss by bursting, rupture or explosion of such objects (other than explosion of accumulated gases or unconsumed fuel within a fire box or combustion chamber; machinery against loss by rupture, bursting or disintegrating of rotating or moving parts caused by centrifugal or reciprocating force). Note that damage to other types of property *would* be covered against these same perils.

Signs—Except for loss by fire, lightning and the perils of the Extended Coverage Endorsement (discussed in Chapter 5) and leakage or accidental discharge from an automatic sprinkler system, the policy does not cover loss to neon or automatic or mechanical electrical signs.

HAZARDS COVERED

The Office Personal Property Form is written on an all-risk basis, and all loss is covered except if caused by one of the stipulated perils excluded in the policy (see HAZARDS NOT COVERED, next).

HAZARDS NOT COVERED

Unexplained Loss, Mysterious Disappearance—Except when in the custody of a carrier or other bailee for hire, there is no coverage for unexplained loss or mysterious disappearance, nor for inventory shortages.

Theft from Unattended Automobile—The policy does not cover theft from an unattended automobile, unless the vehicle or a compartment is broken into forcibly and evidence of such forcible entry left on the vehicle. An exception is made for loss from carriers or bailees for hire.

Fraudulent Scheme—There is no coverage for any fraudulent scheme, trick, device or false pretense practiced upon the Insured, or upon any person to whom the property may be entrusted except a carrier for hire, nor for any act of this kind done *by* an Insured or at the instigation of the Insured, partner, officer, director or trustee of the Insured, or any person to whom the property may be entrusted, other than a carrier for hire.

Delay, Loss of Market—The policy does not cover loss due to delay, loss of market, interruption of business, or any other consequential loss.

Jewelry, Watches, Furs—Jewelry, watches, furs, precious and semi-precious stones and metals are not covered.

Vehicles, Aircraft, Watercraft—All vehicles except for motorized equipment not licensed for operation on public roads and used only on the insured premises are excluded.

Glass, Statuary, Bric-a-brac—Loss by breakage of this type of property and "other articles of a fragile or brittle nature" is covered only against such loss arising from fire and lightning (the perils of the Fire Insurance policy), windstorm, hail, explosion, riot, civil commotion, aircraft, vehicles and smoke (the perils of the Extended Coverage Endorsement), Vandalism and Malicious Mischief and leakage from fire protective systems like sprinklers, etc. This limitation does not apply to lenses or to containers for property held for sale.

Explosion—There is no coverage for steam boilers, steam engines, steam pipes and steam turbines damaged by bursting, rupture, cracking or explosion which originate in the equipment.

Water Damage Exclusion—Loss from stipulated sources of water is excluded, as discussed in Chapter 5 under EXTENDED COVERAGE ENDORSEMENT—HAZARDS NOT COVERED.

Wear, Tear, Depreciation, Etc. — The policy does not cover change in flavor, odor, texture or finish; evaporation, shrinkage or loss of weight; dampness or dryness of atmosphere; freezing; extremes or changes in temperature; corrosion, contamination; marring or scratching; gas or smoke from agricultural or industrial operations; smog; latent defect; mechanical breakdown or derangement; moths, vermin, inherent vice, wear and tear or deterioration *unless* caused by an insured peril.

Earthquake—The policy does not cover loss caused by earthquake or other earth movement, except if fire, explosion or smoke ensues, in which case the policy will cover the ensuing loss. The exclusion does not apply to property in transit.

Damage Due to Being Worked On—There is no coverage for loss to property from being worked upon or in course of installation, except with respect to ensuing loss caused by or resulting from fire, explosion, water damage not otherwise excluded, smoke or vehicles.

War Risks, Nuclear Perils—The policy excludes the war perils enumerated in the Fire insurance policy (see Chapter 2 under

HAZARDS NOT COVERED), and the war-like acts and nuclear perils excluded under the Extended Coverage Endorsement (discussed in Chapter 5).

Order of Civil Authority—See Chapter 2.

Rain, Snow, Sleet—The policy does not cover damage to property in the open by rain, snow or sleet except if such loss occurs while the property is in the custody of a carrier for hire.

FOR HOW MUCH

Records—Except for the limited extra expense in reproducing valuable papers and records (discussed under WHAT IS COVERED—Valuable Papers and Records), the Office Personal Property Form, like other forms covering offices, the policy limits recovery for loss of books of record, manuscript, drawings, card index systems and other office records to the cost of blank books, blank cards and other material—plus the actual cost of labor in transcribing or copying such records. If film is lost or damaged, recovery is limited to cost of unexposed film.

Money—See under WHAT IS COVERED—Money—previously discussed.

Property of Others—The policy will cover to the extent of the Insured's liability for damage to the property of others, but not exceeding its actual cash value.

Improvements and Betterments—Discussed in Chapter 3 under BUILDING AND CONTENTS FORM—WHAT IS COVERED—Tenant's Improvements and Betterments Form.

Deductible—A $100 Flat Deductible applies to all losses under the Office Personal Property Form, *except* to loss by fire, lightning or the perils of the Extended Coverage Endorsement (discussed in Chapter 5). The Deductible *does* apply, however, to loss by windstorm or hail to property outside of building. In addition to the excepted perils listed in the preceding sentence, the deductible does *not* apply to loss by vandalism and malicious mischief, leakage from sprinkler systems, burglary, robbery, collision, or overturn of a vehicle.

Coinsurance Clause—A Coinsurance clause with a percentage of not less than 80% is required under all Office Personal Property Form policies.

WHERE COVERED

Property Outside Buildings—Discussed in Chapter 3.

Off Premises Clause—The policy covers up to 10% of its amount on property away from the insured premises, while anywhere within the Continental United States, or while in transit in Canada. This extension of coverage does not apply to any premises owned, leased, operated or regularly used by the Insured.

OTHER CLAUSES

The policy contains a Waiver of Inventory of Undamaged Property clause, Breach of Warranty clause, Liberalization clause, Subrogation clause, and permits to the Insured, as are usual to the Fire forms, discussed in Chapter 3.

RATES

The policy premium is based on the Insured's Fire Contents rate, to which is added a loading charge, which decreases with the size of the risk. The minimum premium per policy is $25, regard less of its term.

COMMERCIAL PROPERTY COVERAGE

IN MOST STATES, the Commercial Property coverage offers all-risk insurance to a wide variety of non-manufacturing risks. Certain classes for which special Inland Marine contracts are available (e.g., Furriers Block, Jeweler's Block, Camera Dealers Floater, Musical Instrument Dealers Policy) are not eligible. Certain types of risks —like restaurants, florists and theatres—are specifically ruled ineligible, and no Insured who is engaged *primarily* in a bailee, installation, repair or service station operation may purchase the policy.

Where this type of work is only incidental to the Insured's business, and the value of the bailed property does not exceed 10% of the total property, a risk not otherwise ineligible may procure insurance under the Commercial Property coverage.

Furthermore, an extension of the policy in most states has brought within the eligible group risks which engage in manufacturing on an incidental basis, where not more than 25% of annual sales develop from the sale, lease, rental or use of products which the Insured manufactures.

WHAT IS COVERED

Merchandise, Furniture, Fixtures — Policy covers all personal property usual to the Insured's business.

Tenant's Improvements and Betterments — Under a separate section, the policy may be written to cover the Insured's interest in improvements and betterments made by an Insured who is a tenant, provided such property is not subject to legal removal by him. For limit of coverage, see under FOR HOW MUCH—Tenant's Improvements and Betterments.

Property of Others—The policy may be extended, at the option of the Insured, to cover personal property of others while in the care, custody or under the control of the Insured, and while on the described premises. The maximum available for such loss is $2,000 or 2% of the amount of insurance applicable to personal property under the policy, whichever is less.

Damage to Premises — Discussed previously under OFFICE PERSONAL PROPERTY FORM—WHAT IS COVERED—Damage to Premises.

Debris Removal—Discussed in Chapter 3 under Debris Removal.

PROPERTY NOT COVERED

Accounts, Money, Securities, Etc.—The Commercial Property coverage does not cover accounts, bills, currency, deeds, evidences of debt, money and securities (uninsurable property under the Fire policy discussed in Chapter 2 under PROPERTY NOT COVERED) nor stamps, bullion, notes, letters of credit and tickets.

Property Sold Under Conditional Sale Agreement—There is no coverage for property sold by the Insured under conditional sale, trust agreement, installment payment or other deferred payment plan, after delivery to customers.

Vehicles—The policy does not cover automobiles, motor trucks, trailers, semi-trailers, motorcycles, motorscooters, similar vehicles licensed for road use, watercraft while afloat or aircraft. An exception is made for motorcycles or motorscooters, or trailers designed for use with private passenger vehicles for general utility purposes, when such are held for sale or sold but not delivered.

Trees, Lawns—There is no coverage for trees, lawns or growing crops.

Steam Boilers—Discussed in preceding section under OFFICE PERSONAL PROPERTY FORM—PROPERTY NOT COVERED—Steam Boilers.

Signs — Neon, automatic and electric signs are covered only against the perils of fire, lightning, windstorm and hail (other than to property in the open) explosion, riot, civil commotion, aircraft, vehicles and smoke (the perils of the Extended Coverage Endorsement) and leakage and accidental discharge from sprinkler systems.

Machinery—The policy does not cover loss to machines and machinery by rupture, bursting or disintegration of their rotating or moving parts resulting from centrifugal or reciprocating force.

Glass Breakage—Glass, glassware, statuary, bric-a-brac, porcelains and other articles of a fragile nature are covered only against the perils of fire, lightning, the perils of the Extended Coverage Endorsement, vandalism and malicious mischief, or leakage from sprinkler systems. This limitation does *not* apply to bottles or similar containers of property held for sale by the Insured, or sold but not delivered, nor to lenses of photographic or scientific instruments.

Animals—Animals, birds and fish are covered only if held for sale, or sold but not delivered, and then only for loss by fire, lightning, the perils of the Extended Coverage Endorsement, vandalism and malicious mischief, and the accidental leakage of a sprinkler system.

Shrubs and Plants—This property is covered subject to the same conditions as animals.

HAZARDS COVERED

The Commercial Property coverage is written on an all-risks basis, and all loss is covered, except if caused by one of the stipulated perils excluded in the policy (see HAZARDS NOT COVERED, next).

HAZARDS NOT COVERED

The exclusions of the Commercial Property coverage are almost identical with those of the Office Personal Property Form, discussed in the preceding section, with these two differences:

• The Water Exclusion is repeated, but the Commercial Property coverage policy also excludes damage to property in the open (other than in the custody of a carrier for hire), by rain, snow or sleet.

• The wear and tear exclusion is stated somewhat differently. The Commercial Property coverage excludes loss due to inherent vice, wear and tear, marring or scratching, gradual deterioration, moths, vermin, dampness or dryness of the atmosphere, changes in temperature, rust or corrosion.

FOR HOW MUCH

Records—See OFFICE PERSONAL PROPERTY FORM—FOR HOW MUCH—Records.

Tenant's Improvements and Betterments—Recovery for such

property is subject to the conditions of the Tenant's Improvements and Betterments clause, discussed in Chapter 3.

Furs—Furs and fur garments are covered only up to $1,000 in any one loss. This limitation does not apply to loss by fire, lightning, the perils of the Extended Coverage Endorsement, vandalism and malicious mischief, and the accidental discharge of a sprinkler system.

Jewelry—The policy limits to $1,000 recovery for any one occurrence involving jewelry and watches, watch movements, jewels, pearls, precious and semi-precious stones, gold, silver, platinum and other precious alloys or metals. This limitation does not apply to any watch or jewelry valued at $25 or less, nor in any event to loss by fire, lightning, the perils of the Extended Coverage Endorsement, vandalism and malicious mischief, and the accidental leakage from a sprinkler system.

Patterns, Dies, Molds, Etc.—The Insured cannot recover more than $1,000 for any loss involving patterns, dies, molds and forms.

Deductible—A $100 Deductible applies to losses by all perils, except fire, lightning, the perils of the Extended Coverage Endorsement (other than windstorm or hail to property in the open), vandalism and malicious mischief, leakage from sprinkler systems, burglary or robbery, loss to property while in the custody of a carrier for hire, or loss resulting from collision or overturn of a motor vehicle.

Coinsurance—A Coinsurance clause, with a percentage of not less than 80%, is required on all Commercial Property coverage policies.

WHERE COVERED

The Commercial Property coverage policy covers only within the 50 states of the United States, the District of Columbia, and in transit between such places and Canada.

Property Outside Buildings—The insured premises includes the area within 100 feet of the building.

Property in Mails—There is no coverage on property from the time it passes into the custody of the Post Office.

Waterborne Property—The policy does not cover property while waterborne, except while on ferries incidental to other modes of transportation.

OTHER CLAUSES

The Commercial Property coverage contains a Waiver of Inventory of Undamaged Property clause, Breach of Warranty clause, Liberalization clause, Subrogation clause, and Permits to the Insured, as are usual to the Fire Forms, discussed in Chapter 3.

Impairment of Recovery—As respects property on the insured premises, the policy will not be impaired by the Insured's releasing third parties in writing prior to a loss. As respects property in transit, permission is given to the Insured to accept such released bills of lading as are usually issued by carriers.

MANUFACTURER'S OUTPUT POLICY

The Commercial Property coverage program, discussed above, offers all-risk insurance to non-manufacturing risks. A special policy, the Manufacturer's Output policy, is available to risks whose principal activity is manufacturing, processing or assembling. Originally developed for the larger risk, the recently lowered minimum premium requirements have rendered it useful for a wide variety of medium-size industrial risks, e. g., bakeries, bottling plants, printers, ice cream plants, etc., and almost all processors and assemblers.

WHAT IS COVERED

Personal Property of Insured—The policy covers all personal property (not real property) owned by the Insured.

Improvements and Betterments—The policy does not cover buildings owned by the Insured, but does apply to improvements and betterments to buildings not owned by him. The basis of adjustment for such property is discussed below under FOR HOW MUCH—Improvements and Betterments.

Personal Property of Others—The Insured's interest in and legal liability for personal property of others in his custody is covered. Furthermore, the policy specifically covers personal property of others in his custody which the Insured has agreed to insure, or which the Insured has sold but agreed to insure during the course of delivery, or which the Insured is installing for a purchaser and for which he is responsible until the installation is accepted by the purchaser.

PROPERTY NOT COVERED

The policy specifically excludes:
Currency, money, notes, securities
Growing crops or standing timber
Animals
Aircraft or watercraft

NOTE: There is no exclusion of automobiles, as such. The coverage afforded on such property is discussed below under HAZARDS NOT COVERED—Collision Damage to Vehicles.

Property sold under conditional sale, trust agreement, installment payment or other deferred payment plan.

Property while covered under import or export Ocean Marine policies.

NOTE: If the property is not covered under Ocean Marine insurance, the Manufacturer's Output policy does provide coverage until the property is loaded on board a vessel or aircraft; on imports, the policy begins to cover from the point the property is discharged from the vessel or aircraft.

General Average and salvage charges are covered under the Manufacturer's Output policy on waterborne shipments, to the extent that such are covered under the policy.

HAZARDS COVERED

The Manufacturer's Output policy covers on an all-risk basis, subject only to the stated exclusions.

HAZARDS NOT COVERED

The Manufacturer's Output policy specifically excludes the following perils:

Hostile or Warlike Action—The policy excludes a broad area of perils associated with war and enemy acts (discussed in Chapter 17 under PERSONAL FLOATERS—Exclusions Common to All Personal Floaters).

Seizure or destruction under quarantine or customs regulations, or confiscation by order of any government or public authority. Risks of contraband or illegal trade.

Infidelity of Employees—The policy excludes loss or damage by employees of the Insured, or any partners in a co-partnership.

Infidelity of Independent Contractors—The policy also excludes loss or damage by a proprietor, partner, director, trustee or elected officer of any entity engaged by the Insured to render any service in connection with property insured under the policy.

NOTE: Loss caused by an employee of such entity engaged by the Insured is NOT excluded unless the employee is an officer, director or trustee.

Earthquake, Flood—The Manufacturer's Output policy excludes loss or damage caused by or resulting from earthquake or flood. Certain specific classes of property are exempted from these exclusions, and *are* covered when damaged by earthquake or flood. The earthquake and flood exclusion does NOT apply to:

salesmen's samples, patterns, dies

cameras and equipment, scientific instruments and other similar

property of a mobile nature not intended for sale
property in due course of transit, imports, exports
property in custody of processors
automobiles, rolling stock

NOTE: Aircraft and watercraft are excluded entirely (discussed above under PROPERTY NOT COVERED).

Rupture or Bursting of Steam Boilers, Etc.—This exclusion is very similar to the one spelled out in the Extended Coverage Endorsement (discussed in Chapter 5—Explosion Provisions).

Electrical Apparatus Clause—(discussed in Chapter 3 under FIRE FORMS—HAZARDS NOT COVERED—Electrical Apparatus Clause).

Damage Due to Process—discussed in Chapter 10 under FURRIERS' CUSTOMERS POLICY—HAZARDS NOT COVERED—Damage Due to Process.

Dampness of the Atmosphere, Extremes of Temperature—The policy does not cover loss or damage resulting from dampness or dryness of the atmosphere, extremes of temperature, shrinkage, evaporation, loss of weight, rust, contamination, change in flavor or color or texture or finish UNLESS such loss is caused by one of the following specified perils: fire, lightning (the perils of the Standard Fire policy), windstorm, hail, explosion, riot, civil commotion, aircraft, vehicles other than transporting conveyances (the perils of the Extended Coverage Endorsement, except for smoke), vandalism, malicious mischief, theft or attempted theft, casualty occurring to a vessel or other vehicle used in transporting the property.

NOTE: Loss by dampness, dryness, extremes of temperature and the other excluded perils is covered if arising from one of the exceptions spelled out above. Losses of this kind arising from vehicles are covered, except if the vehicle is the one used to convey the damaged property. On the other hand, if the transporting vehicle itself sustains a casualty which results in a loss (not otherwise excluded by the policy), such loss is covered.

Collision Damage to Vehicles—Under PROPERTY NOT COVERED, discussed above, it was pointed out that there is no exclusion of automobiles, although aircraft and watercraft are not covered. There is no coverage however for loss or damage to vehicles caused by collision or overturn, except for the ensuing fire.

Delay, Loss of Market, Loss of Use

Wear, Tear, Gradual Deterioration

Inherent Vice, Moths, Vermin

Inventory Shortage—The policy does not cover unexplained loss, mysterious disappearance, or loss or shortage disclosed on taking inventory.

WHERE COVERED

Insured's Manufacturing Premises—The Manufacturer's Output policy does not cover any property while on any premises used by the Insured for manufacturing purposes, unless such premises are specifically endorsed on the policy. An exception is made for licensed automobiles owned by the Insured and such are covered even while on the Insured's manufacturing premises, subject to the limitation on collision losses, discussed above under HAZARDS NOT COVERED—Collision Damage to Vehicles.

Territory—Policy covers within the continental United States or Alaska, in Canada, and in transit between places in these areas. There is no coverage however on waterborne shipments to and from Alaska, or via the Panama Canal.

FOR HOW MUCH

Actual Cash Value—Loss or damage is adjusted on the basis of actual cash value, except that improvements and betterments are valued at replacement cost if actually replaced within two years from date of loss. Patterns and dies are similarly valued at replacement cost, if actually replaced; if not, then at cash value. Accounts, manuscripts, mechanical drawings and other records and documents are valued at blank value, plus the cost of transcribing.

Limits of Liability—Separate limits of liability are established on:

a) property at any one location
b) property on any one conveyance
c) in any single disaster, regardless of the number of locations or conveyances involved
d) for loss due to flood
e) on property at any convention or fair.

HOW INSURANCE IS WRITTEN

Reporting Form—The Manufacturer's Output policy is a continuous contract, without expiration date. The Insured is required to furnish monthly reports of all property at risk under the policy as of the last business day of each month. Such reports must be filed within sixty days after the close of the month. Furthermore, once during each calendar year, the Insured is required to furnish a report of the values at risk by location, and the values in transit.

Other Insurance—The Insured may, with the permission of the Company, carry other insurance applicable to the property insured under the policy. The Insured is then bound to keep the other insurance in force, and the Manufacturer's Output policy is liable only for the excess of any loss which is covered under the other policies.

An interesting feature of the policy is its provision for advancing to the Insured as a loan the amount that would have been collectible under the Manufacturer's Output policy except for the "Other Insurance" section of the policy. The Insured is required to repay such loan or advance only to the extent that he recovers from the other insurance.

OTHER PROVISIONS

Cancellation—The policy may be cancelled by the Insured or the Company, but either party must give at least 90 days' notice to the other.

Notice of Loss—Proof of Loss—discussed in Chapter 17 under PERSONAL FLOATERS—REQUIREMENTS IN CASE OF LOSS.

Sue and Labor—discussed in Chapter 17 under PERSONAL FLOATERS—REQUIREMENTS IN CASE OF LOSS.

Carriers or Bailees—discussed in Chapter 17 under PERSONAL FLOATERS—REQUIREMENTS IN CASE OF LOSS—Benefit of Insurance.

Appraisal—discussed in Chapter 2 under REQUIREMENTS AFTER LOSS—Appraisal.

Misrepresentation and Fraud—discussed in Chapter 2 under INSURED'S DUTIES AND OBLIGATIONS—Moral Duties—Concealment, Fraud. In addition, the Manufacturer's Output policy stipulates that wilful under-reporting of values at risk shall be construed as an attempt to defraud the Company.

FARMOWNERS-RANCHOWNERS POLICY PROGRAM

The Farmowners-Ranchowners Policy program offers in one policy Property and Liability insurance coverages for farm or ranch property. Almost every type of farm or ranch may be covered except:

Farms whose principal function is the supplying of commodities for manufacturing or processing by the Insured for sale to others, e.g., creameries and dairies or dairy farms operating freezing or dehydrating plants or poultry factories. Dairy farms as such are NOT excluded from the program.

Farms or ranches engaged principally in the raising of horses for racing or show purposes.

Vacant farms or ranches.

Mobile homes, trailer homes, house trailers or their contents may be written under the Program but only for certain coverages.

WHAT IS COVERED

Six classes of property may be insured under the Farmowners-Ranchowners Program, as follows:

Coverage A—Dwelling

Coverage B—Unscheduled Personal Property (Household)

Coverage C—Additional Living Expense

Coverage D—Scheduled Farm Personal Property

Coverage E—Unscheduled Farm Personal Property (on a blanket basis)

Coverage F—Barns, Buildings, Structures and Additional Dwellings

HAZARDS COVERED

Insurance on physical property may be written in one of six ways, each of which is outlined below:

(1) Form FR-1 Basic Form—Coverage against the property enumerated above under Coverages A, B and C is provided against the following specified perils:

Fire, lightning, removal (perils of the Fire policy)

Windstorm, hail, explosion, riot, civil commotion, vehicles, aircraft, smoke (perils of the Extended Coverage Endorsement)

Vandalism and malicious mischief

Theft

(2) Form FR-2 Broad Form—Form FR-2 adds to the coverages of FR-1, the following perils:

Breakage of glass

Falling objects; weight of ice, snow or sleet; collapse of buildings

Sudden and accidental tearing asunder of heating systems and appliances

Accidental discharge of water or steam

Freezing of plumbing, heating systems and appliances

Sudden and accidental injury from electrical currents

(3) FR-4 Contents Broad Form—Form FR-4 covers unscheduled personal (household) property including the Insured's interest in building additions and alterations and additional living expense against the same perils as Form FR-2 described immediately above (This is basically a Tenants policy).

(4) Form FR-6 Scheduled Farm Personal Property—Form FR-

6 covers *scheduled* farm personal property against the perils covered under the Basic Form, FR-1, plus the following additional perils:

Collision, Upset or Overturn
Electrocution of livestock

(5) Form FR-7 Unscheduled Farm Personal Property—Form FR-7 covers on a *blanket* basis (where permitted) against the perils of Form FR-6 above.

(6) Form FR-8 Barns, Buildings, Structures and Additional Dwellings—Form FR-8 covers the enumerated classes of property against the perils of the Basic Form, FR-1, except for Theft.

As mentioned above, the Farmowners-Ranchowners Program also offers insurance against liability.

Form FR-9 Liability Coverages—Under Coverage G—Personal Liability, the policy provides the coverage of the Public Liability policy (discussed in Chapter 24).

Coverage H—Medical Payments (discussed in Chapter 24 under HAZARDS COVERED—Medical Payments Coverage).

FOR HOW MUCH

The Program provides that the coverages be written with certain stated minimum limits under the separate sections:

Coverage A—Dwelling—Type A—$12,000; Type B—$10,000; Type C—$8,000.

Coverage B—Unscheduled Personal Property—50% of limit on Coverage A—Dwelling.

Coverage C—Additional Living Expense—10% of limit on Coverage A—Dwelling.

Coverage E—Farm Personal Property (Blanket)—$15,000 minimum.

There are also minimum limits applicable to Coverages D and F, but these vary somewhat, depending on the amount of insurance written on Coverage E.

Deductibles—The Property coverages are subject to a $100 flat Deductible under all of Section I except Additional Living Expenses and Fire Department Service Charge.

Optional Deductibles of $250 or $500 are available, as above. An optional $250 Deductible applicable only to the peril of theft is available.

The limit on money, bullion, securities, numismatic property, accounts, bills, deeds, evidences of debt, letters of credit, notes, passports, railroad and other tickets, stamps and stamp collections may be increased by endorsement.

OPTIONAL COVERAGES

Property Damage Coverages—The coverage under this Section may be amended as follows:

Additional Living Expense—The limit in the basic policy may be increased.

Building Additions and Alterations—The limit in the basic policy may be increased.

Unscheduled Personal Property—The limit in the basic policy may be increased, decreased or the coverage eliminated entirely.

Scheduled Personal Property—Subject to certain exceptions, coverage may be provided on *all-risk* basis.

The following coverages may be added to the policy by endorsement:

a) Credit Card and Depositors Forgery

b) Earthquake

c) Fire Department Service Charges

d) Glass Coverage to cover scheduled items of glass

e) Inland Marine Coverage on farm personal property, agricultural machinery, livestock and other property.

Liability Coverages—The following coverages may be added to the Liability section of the policy by endorsement:

a) Additional residence premises rented to others.

b) Business pursuits of the Insured other than businesses of which he is the sole owner.

c) Custom farming. Incidental custom farming is covered under the basic Liability section; where such activity is more than incidental, coverage may be provided by endorsement.

d) Employers liability.

e) Farms rented by the Insured to others or held by him for rental or sale are not covered under the basic Liability section of the policy, and must be declared and specifically insured.

f) Liability coverage for outboard motors of more than 25 horsepower or other watercraft not covered under the basic policy may be insured against liability claims by endorsement.

WHEN COVERED

The Farmowners-Ranchowners policy attaches at 12 o'clock noon (Standard Time). When the policy is written to replace insurance which expires at 12:01 A. M. (Standard Time), the policy may be endorsed to attach on such exposures at 12:01 A. M. (Standard Time). No additional charge is made for this endorsement of the policy.

FOR FURTHER READING

GEE, HAROLD F.—Personal Lines Insurance
POLICY, FORM & MANUAL ANALYSIS SERVICE

FOR FURTHER READING

Author—Title—Year of Publication—Publisher

ACKERMAN, S. B.—Insurance (1951)—The Ronald Press Co.

BARBOUR, ROBERT P.—Agent's Key to Fire Insurance (1949)—The Spectator Co.

BURNSIDE, O. S.—New and Broader Garage Liability Insurance —Hartford Accident and Indemnity Co.

CRIST, G. W. JR.—Corporate Suretyship (1950)—McGraw-Hill Book Co.

CROUCH, IRVIN E.—Use and Occupancy or Business Interruption Insurance (1947)—Aetna Insurance Co.

DAYNARD, HAROLD S.—Paths and Bypaths of Inland Marine Insurance (1949)—Insurance Advocate, New York City.

DEMAREST, EUGENE E.—Know Your Fire Insurance and Extended Coverage (1951)—Canyon Press.

FAULKNER, EDWIN J.—Accident and Health Insurance (1960) —McGraw-Hill Book Co.

GEE, HAROLD F.—Agent's Automobile Guide (1971)—The Rough Notes Co., Inc.

GEE, HAROLD F.—Agent's Casualty Guide (1972)—The Rough Notes Co., Inc.

GEE, HAROLD F.—Broad Form Crime Insurance Primer (1963)—The Rough Notes Co., Inc.

GWERTZMAN, MAX J.—Law of Transportation Insurance in Its Relation to Transportation Insurance (1950)—The Macade Press, Larchmont, N. Y.

HEDGES, J. EDWARD—Practical Fire and Casualty Insurance (1961)—The National Underwriter Co.

HOBBS, CLARENCE W.—Workmen's Compensation Insurance (1939)—McGraw-Hill Book Co.

HUEBNER, S. S., and BLACK, KENNETH JR.—Property Insurance (1957)—D. Appleton-Century Co.

KLEIN, HENRY C.—Business Interruption Insurance (1964)—The Rough Notes Co., Inc.

KULP, C. A. and HALL, J. W.—Casualty Insurance (1968)—The Ronald Press.

LAVINE, A. LINCOLN—Manual of Commercial Law (1948) —Prentice-Hall, Inc.

LUCAS, JULIAN—The Standard Fire Insurance Policy of the State of New York (1932)—Pennsylvania Fire Insurance Co.

MACKALL, LUTHER E.—Surety Underwriting Manual (1972) —The Rough Notes Co., Inc.

MAGEE, JOHN H. AND BICKELHAUPT, DAVID L.—General Insurance (1970)—Richard D. Irwin, Inc.

MAURICE, STEWART—Checks Payable to Fictitious Payees—Insurance Society of New York, Readings in Insurance No. 21.

MEHR AND CAMMACK—Principles of Insurance (1972)—Richard D. Irwin, Inc.

MORTIMER, WILLIAM—Adjusting Practices, Inland Marine and Transportation Insurance (1951)—Transportation Service Co.

MOWBRAY, ALBERT H. and BLANCHARD, RALPH H. and WILLIAMS, C. ARTHUR—Insurance (1968)—McGraw-Hill Book Co.

OSLER, ROBERT W.—Guide to Health Insurance (1972)—The Rough Notes Co., Inc.

RIEGEL, ROBERT AND MILLER, JEROME S. — Insurance Principles and Practices (1966)—Prentice-Hall, Inc.

RODDA, WILLIAM H.—Marine Insurance: Ocean and Inland (1970)—Prentice-Hall, Inc.

SPELL, REGINALD V.—Public Liability Hazards (1956) — The Rough Notes Co., Inc.

WINTER, WILLIAM D.—Marine Insurance (1952)—McGraw-Hill Book Co.

WINTER, WILLIAM D.—History and Principles of Marine Insurance (1945)—Insurance Society of New York.

WRIGHT, WILLIAM B.—Subrogation under Workmen's Compensation Acts (1949)—Central Book Co., New York, N. Y.

OTHER BOOKS AND SERVICES

Title—Publisher

POLICY, FORM AND MANUAL ANALYSIS SERVICE (Monthly)—The Rough Notes Co., Inc.

AUTOMOBILE ASSIGNED RISK PLANS, CHART ANALYSIS OF—American Insurance Association.

AUTOMOBILE LIABILITY SECURITY LAWS OF THE UNITED STATES—American Insurance Association.

LIABILITY INSURANCE STATUTES AFFECTING (By States) —American Insurance Association.

MARINE INSURANCE—Practical Notes and Comments on Cargo Insurance (1951)—Insurance Company of North America.

WORKMEN'S COMPENSATION LAWS—(1972), ANALYSIS OF PROVISIONS OF—Chamber of Commerce of The United States.

WORKMEN'S COMPENSATION LAWS IN THE UNITED STATES AND TERRITORIES, DIGEST OF—American Insurance Association.

Index

Page

ACCIDENT AND HEALTH INSURANCE 596-620
Accidental Death Provisions 599
Accidental Means 601
Accumulation of Indemnity 605
Age Limits 603
Age, Misstatement of, Effect 606
Aircraft Provisions 602
Application 606
Autopsy 607
Blanket Medical Expense Benefit.... 600
Bodily Injury, Accidental 601
Cancellation 607
  By Insured 607
Capital Sum 599
Change of Occupation 605
Claim, Notice of 606
Commercial Policies 598
Confining Clause 606
Disability-Benefits Laws
  See Disability Benefits Insurance
Disability Provisions, Life Insurance 615
Dismemberment Provisions 599
Double Indemnity 600
Elective Indemnities 599
Elimination Period 603
Entire Contract 597
Felony, Loss While Engaged in Committing 602
Franchise Insurance 614
Fraternal Policies 614
Grace Period 597
Group Policies 613-614
Guaranteed Renewable 608
Hazards Not Covered 601
Hospital Benefits 600
Hospital Expense Policies 609-610
Incontestable Clause 603
Industrial Policies 608
Intoxicated, Loss Committed While 602
Lapse 604
Limit on Total Indemnity 606
Limited Type of Policies 608-609
Loss of Time Indemnities 598-599
Loss, When Payable 607
Major Medical Expense Insurance 610-613
Medical Examination 607
Narcotics, Loss While Under Influence 602
Non-Cancellable 608
Non-Disabling Injuries 600

Page

Non-Reduction of Benefits 604
Nursing Benefits 600
Other Insurance, Pro Rating 605
Partial Disability 601
Pre-Existing Conditions 603
Principal Sum 599
Probationary Period 603
Proof of Loss 606
Pro Rating of Benefits 605
Reinstatement 598, 604
Suit 607
Surgical Indemnity Provisions 600
Time Limit on Certain Defenses 597
Total Disability 600
Types of 597
Uniform Standard Provisions 597
Waiting Period 603
When Covered 602

ACCOUNTS RECEIVABLE POLICY 204

ACCRUED CHARGES
  See under Inland Marine, Bailees Customers Form, also under Furriers Customers Policy

ACTUAL CASH VALUE
In Fire Insurance Policy 37

ADDITIONAL LIVING EXPENSE 81, 114

AGREED AMOUNT, BUSINESS INTERRUPTION 100

AIRCRAFT AND VEHICLES
Extended Coverage Endorsement 75
Objects Falling from Aircraft 75

ALL RISK INSURANCE
  See Inland Marine Insurance

ALTERATIONS AND REPAIRS
Fire Forms 55
Sprinkler Leakage Policy 136
Water Damage Insurance 141

ANTI-COINSURANCE LAWS,
  See Valued Policy Laws

APPORTIONMENT CLAUSE
In Extended Coverage Endorsement 70

APPRAISAL
Fire Insurance 42

ASSIGNMENT
Fire Insurance Policy 38

INDEX

Page

AUTOMOBILE INSURANCE (ASSIGNED RISK) PLANS 513-516

Distribution of Risks 514
Eligible Risks 515
Ineligible Risks 515
Limits 514-515
Medical Payments 515
Payment of Premium, with Application 516
Physical Damage 515
Purpose of 513-514
Surcharges 516

AUTOMOBILE INSURANCE,
See
Automobile Liability Policy
Automobile Physical Damage Insurance, Collision Insurance

AUTOMOBILE LIABILITY POLICY, 455-484

Assigned Risk Plans, See Automobile Insurance (Assigned Risk) Plans
Assignment 484
Assumed Liability, Exclusion 469
Automobile Death Benefit 471
Buses 494-495
Cancellation 482-484
  State Statutes Affecting 482
  When Certificate of Financial Responsibility Filed 483
Caused by Accident 456
Commercial Automobiles 489-493
Comprehensive Automobile Liability Policy 503
Compulsory Insurance..493, 495, 518-522
  State Requirements 496
Cooperation with Companies 481
Drive Other Cars 457, 460-462
  Drive Other Car Endorsement 461
  Excess Coverage 461
  Exclusions Under 462
  Individually Owned Cars Only 461
  Insured and Spouse 462
  Medical Payments 464
Employees, Liability to 470
  Domestic Servant, Exception 470
Employer's Non-Ownership Liability 496-500
  Blanket Basis 500
  Commercial Vehicles, Frequent Use 498
  Excess Coverage 499
  Limits 499
  Rating 499-500
Family Automobile Policy 456-470
  Eligibility for 455
Fleet Rates 480
Franchised Carriers, Insurance Required 493
Garage Liability, See Garage Liability Insurance
Gasoline, Erroneous Delivery of 490
Hazards Covered 456

Page

Hazards Not Covered 469
Hired Car Coverage 501-503
Insolvent Insurer 466
Legal Representatives 472
Limits 471, 480
  Increased 480
Livery, Exclusion of 469
Livery, Private 494
Loading and Unloading 458
Medical Payments 463-464
  Driving Other Cars 464
  Exclusion Under 465
  Limits 471
Medical Reports 481
Miscellaneous Forms 501
Motor Vehicle Accident Indemnification Corporation....468-469
Motor Vehicles Financial Responsibility Laws..456, 481, 517-522
Newly Acquired Automobile 462
Nine Class Plan 473-476
Non-Ownership Liability—Independent Contractor Coverage..501
Nuclear Energy Liability 471
Occurrence 457
Omnibus Clause 459
Other Insurance 472
Passenger Hazard Exclusion 495
Passenger Property, Exclusion of 495
Property in Insured's Care 470
  Of Additional Insured 471
  Garage, See Garage Keeper's Legal Liability Insurance
Public Automobiles 493-496
Public Conveyance Exclusion of 469
Rating of 473-480
  Certified Risks Surcharge 479
  Commercial Auto 490-492
  Driver Course Credit 475-476
  Farmer Classifications 475
  Fleet Rates 480
  Good Student Credit 475
  Increased Limits 480
  Merit Rating Plans 476-479
  Modified 260-Class Plan 479
  Multi-Car Discount 480
  Nine-Class Rating Plan 473-476
  260-Class Rating Plan 476
Services to Others, Payment for 481
Severability of Interests 459
Statement by Insured 480-481
Subrogation 482
Substitute Automobile, See Temporary Substitute Automobile
Suspension of 483
Taxicabs 494
Temporary Substitute Automobile 463
Territorial Limits 473
Third Parties, Rights of 401, 472
Time of Policy 482
Tort Liability, Modification of....484-488
  Comparison Charts 486-487

Page
Pain and Suffering 488
Trailers 458
Truckmen Rule 492
Exception to Classification as.......... 489
Gross Receipts Basis 492
Local Truckmen Rule 492
Long Haul Truckmen 492
Uninsured Motorist Coverage 465-468
Property Damage 466
Unsatisfied Judgment Funds 468
Whole Dollar Premium Rule......126, 480

AUTOMOBILE PHYSICAL DAMAGE INSURANCE 523-542
Comprehensive Physical Damage, See Comprehensive Physical Damage Insurance
Garage Keeper's Legal Liability Insurance, See Garage Keeper's Legal Liability Insurance

AVERAGE CLAUSE
See Coinsurance

BAILEE,
See Inland Marine Insurance
Assumed Liability of 294
Definition of 292
Liability of 293, 328-329
Limitation on 294, 331

BAILMENT,
See Inland Marine Insurance
Gratuitous 292
Mutual Benefit 293

BAILORS POLICIES
See Individual Policies Under Inland Marine Insurance, e.g. Garment Contractors' Floater, Jewelers' Block Policy, Installment Sales Form, Salesmen's Floater, etc.

BANKERS' BLANKET BOND NO. 24
Cancellation 239
Carrier, for Hire 239
Armored Car 239
Court Costs, Attorney's Fees 239
Credit Card Exposure 237
Deductibles 241
Discovery Period 240
Fidelity Insuring Clause 235
Forgery Insuring Clause 236
Furnishings, Fixtures, Loss to 235
Hazards Not Covered 236-237
In Transit Insuring Clause 237-238
Nominees of Bank 238
Premises Insuring Clause 235
Property Covered, Types of 234
Not Enumerated 239
Rating of 240
Retroactive Extension 239
Securities Insuring Clause 236
Teller's Shortages 237

Page
Term of 239
What Is Covered 234

BEACH PROPERTY INSURANCE POOLS 131-133

BEAUTY SHOP AND BARBER SHOP LIABILITY 448-449

BILL OF LADING
See Under Transportation Insurance

BINDER
Fire Insurance 44

BLANKET CRIME POLICY 245-246

BLANKET POLICY 51
Pro-Rata Distribution Clause, Fire Insurance 51

BLANKET POSITION BOND
Cancellation 226
Collusion Losses 224
Inventory Shortage 225
Maximum Amount 225
Minimum Amount 225
Rating of 225-226
Experience Credits 226
Reinstatement after Loss 226
Superseding Commercial Blanket Bond 224
Unidentifiable Employees, Loss By 223

BOILER AND MACHINERY INSURANCE
"Accident" Defined 626
Automatic Coverage 626
Bodily Injury Liability 626
Boiler Schedule 630-631
Business Interruption Insurance, See Use and Occupancy Insurance 633-634
Cancellation 630
Civil Authority 627
Civil Commotion 627
Consequential Damage 632-633
Contamination, Limit on 631
Deductibles 629-630
Defense, Supplementary Benefits.......... 626
Electrical Machine Schedule 631
Expediting Expenses 626
Explosion Outside of Object 628
Fire 627
Furnace Explosion 631
Under Extended Coverage 631
Indirect Loss 628
Inspection Service 626, 630
Liability Coverages 626
Limited Coverage 628
Limits 628
Non-Ownership Explosion Insurance 632
Notice of Loss 630
Nuclear Energy Exclusion 627
"Object" Defined 630

Page
Other Insurance 629
Outage Insurance 634-635
Piping, Boiler 631
Premium Discount 629
Property Damage Liability 626
Property of Insured 626
Rating of 629
Refrigerating Systems Schedule 631
Repair and Replacement
Coverage 626, 628
Residence Boiler Coverage 632
Riots 627
Sabotage 627
Strikes 627
Suspension 630
Three-Year Policies 629
Types of Equipment Covered 625
Use and Occupancy 633-634
Actual Loss Sustained Form 634
Valued Form 634
Vandalism and Malicious Mischief 627
War Damage, Exclusion of 627
Water Damage Limit 632

BONDS
See Fidelity Bonds, Surety Bonds

BROAD FORM PERSONAL THEFT POLICY 143-153
See Also Personal Theft
Policy 153-155
Away From Premises 147
Limitation on Coverage 147
Blanket, 100%, Coverage 150
Boarding House, Use
of Premises 146-147
Boats, Limitation on 149
Damage, By Theft or
Attempt at 144
Death of Insured 146
Deductible Clause 149
Depository, Public Warehouse 146
Divided Coverage 150
Examination Under Oath 151
Geographical Limits 147
Guest Property 144
Hazards Covered 144
Hazards Not Covered 145
Jewelry, Furs, Limitation on 148
Larceny 144
Laundry, Cleaner, Dyer, Tailor,
Presser, Theft From 148
Mails, Property in 147
Minimum Premiums 153
Money, Limitation on 148
Mysterious Disappearance 144
Notice of Loss 151
Other Insurance
On Not Owned Property 149
On Scheduled Property 148-149
On Unscheduled Property 149
Other Occupied Residence 147
Pair and Set Clause 149
Physicians, Surgeons, Dentists
Outside Coverage 151

Page
Premises Defined 146
Proof of Loss 151
Rating of 152-153
Regulation of 152
Reinstatement After Loss 152
Removal of Insured 147
Rented Premises 144
Exclusion of Money, Securities,
Stamps, Jewelry, Watches 144
Secondary Residence 147
Securities, Limitation on 148
Servants 148
Settlement of Loss, With Others 152
Specified Articles 150
Statements, by Insured 151
Suit 151
Theft from Premises 146
Theft Defined 144
Three-Year Policies 153
Vandalism and Malicious
Mischief 144-145
What Is Covered 143

BROAD FORM STOREKEEPERS POLICY 198-200

BUILDER'S RISK
See Buildings in Course of
Construction

BUILDING AND CONTENTS FORM .. 53

BUILDINGS IN COURSE OF CONSTRUCTION
Fire Insurance 63
Rent Insurance 109

BURGLARY INSURANCE
See Open Stock Burglary Policy
Mercantile Safe Burglary.
See Also Under Broad Form
Personal Theft Policy

BUSINESS INTERRUPTION INSURANCE, FIRE 90-103
Actual Loss Sustained 96-98
Agreed Amount Forms 100
Coinsurance Clause 98-99
Contingent Business Interruption
Forms 102
Earnings Insurance 100
Effect on Credit 91-92
Electronic Data Loss 94
Expiration, Effect of 93
Extended Period of Indemnity 98
Extra Expense Combined 113
Gross Earnings Form 94-95
Hazards Covered 92
Hazards Not Covered 96
Interruption by Civil Authority 94
Measure of Loss 93
Need for 90
Payroll, Ordinary 95-96
Premium Adjustment Forms 101
Salvage 94
Stock, Finished 93-94

Page

Stock, Time to Replace 93
Tuition Fees Insurance 103
Types of 94-95

CAMERA INSURANCE 271

CANCELLATION

Accident and Health Insurance, Commercial 607
Automobile Insurance 482-483
Bailee's Customers Form 298
Bankers' Blanket Bond No. 24 239
Fidelity Bonds 216
Fire Insurance 43-44
Flat 128
Interstate Commerce Commission 338, 496
Marine Insurance 369
Mortgagee, Notice to 58
Parcel Post Insurance 351
Transportation Insurance, Carrier's.. 338
Transportation Insurance, Shippers.. 347
Workmen's Compensation 593-594

CARGO INSURANCE (Ocean)

See Ocean Marine Insurance

CARGO LIABILITY

See Motor Truck Merchandise Floater-Carrier's Form

CARGO WAR RISK POLICY 370

CARRIER, COMMON

See Under Transportation Insurance

CERTIFICATES

Furriers Customers Policy 303

C & F 354

CHARGE CARD ISSUERS BOND.... 241

CHURCH THEFT POLICY 202

C. I. F. 355

CIVIL AUTHORITY

Business Interruption 94
Loss by, Fire Insurance 36
Rent Insurance 106
Transportation, Common Carrier 329

CIVIL COMMOTION 74-75

CIVIL WAR

Loss by, Fire Insurance 36

CLOTHING, RISKS, CONSEQUENTIAL LOSS CLAUSE 116-117

COINSURANCE CLAUSE

Anti-Coinsurance Laws 67-68
Business Interruption 98-99
Extended Coverage Endorsement 71
Fire Insurance 47-51

Page

Garment Contractors Floater 311
Major Medical 612
Marine Policy 365
Monthly Limitation Forms 107-108
No Coinsurance Form 100
Open Stock Burglary 161-163
Rent Insurance 107
Sprinkler Leakage Policy 138
Transportation Floater 336
Water Damage Insurance 141

COLD STORAGE LOCKER BAILEE FLOATER 304-305

COLLAPSE 79

COLLATERAL, IN BONDS 252, 256

COLLISION (AUTOMOBILE) INSURANCE

Contrasted With Property Damage Liability 534
Convertible Insurance 535
Deductible, in 535
Eighty Percent (80%) Collision Form 535
Hazards Covered 534
Rating of 535-537
Bumper Discount 536
Commercial Vehicles 536
Credits 536
Multi-Car Discount 536
Suspension of Insurance 536

COMMERCIAL AUTOMOBILES....489-493

See Automobile Liability Policy

COMMERCIAL BLANKET BOND

Collusion Losses 224
Minimum Amount 225
Rating of 225-226
Reinstatement After Loss 227
Superseding Blanket Position Bond 224

COMMERCIAL PROPERTY COVERAGE 672-676

COMPREHENSIVE DISHONESTY, DISAPPEARANCE AND DESTRUCTION POLICY 243-245

COMPREHENSIVE GENERAL LIABILITY POLICY 426-428

See Also Public Liability Insurance

Limits 427
Rating of 427-428

COMPREHENSIVE GLASS POLICY 621-624

All-Risk Coverage 622
Blanket Policies 621
Boarding Up Openings 622
Chemical, Damage by 622
Cracked Glass Endorsement 623
Fire, Exclusion of 622
Neon Signs 621

Page
Non-Accidental Breakage 622
Options, of Company 623
Rating of 623
Regulation of 624
Reinstatment After Loss 624
Removing Obstructions 622
Repairing Frames 622
Scheduling of Glass 621
Scratching, Marring 622
Term Policies 623
Types of Glass Covered 621
Vandalism and Malicious Mischief 622
War, Invasion, Exclusion of 622

COMPREHENSIVE PERSONAL LIABILITY POLICY 434-443
See Also Public Liability Insurance

Aircraft 440
Assault and Battery 439
Assignment 443
Assumed Liability 439
Automobiles 438
Domestic Servant, Injury by 438
Business Pursuits 436-437
Contractual Liability 439
Elevator Liability 440
Employees, Liability for 438
Medical Payments,
Accident, Caused by 436
Basic Policy 435, 441
Workmen's Compensation Coverage 441
Nuclear Exclusion 441
Occurrence Basis 435
Office, Incidental 437
Physical Damage to Property 436
Fire, Explosion, Smoke or Smudge, Liability for 436
Premises 442
Business Property 442
Temporary Residence 442
Vacant Land 442
Professional Services 437
Property in Insured's Care 439
Rating of 442
Rented to Others, Property 437
Secondary Residences 437
Severability of Interests 435
Snowmobiles 438
Three-Year Policies 442
War Exclusion 438
Watercraft, Away From Premises.... 440
Who Is Covered 441

COMPREHENSIVE PHYSICAL DAMAGE INSURANCE 523-533
Actual Cash Value Basis 530
All-Risk Basis 525
Collision, Exclusion of 525
Upset, Exclusion of 525
Animals, Contact with 526
Civil Commotion 526
Collision, See Collision Insurance

Page
Conversion, Exclusion 529
Cooperation With Company 533
Deductible 530-531
Embezzlement, Exclusion of 529
Equipment of Automobile 524
Explosion 526
Falling Objects 526
Family Auto Policy 523-530
Fire 526
Forms of Policy 530
Freezing 528
General Average 524
Glass, Breakage 526
Hail 526
Hazards Covered 525
Hazards Not Covered 528
Illicit Trade 530
Illicit Transportation 530
Livery, Public 528
Mechanical Breakdown 528
Missiles and Falling Objects 526
Mortgage, Undeclared 529
Newly Acquired Automobile 524
Additional Automobile 524
Notice of Replacing Vehicle 524
Notice of Accident 533
Notice of Claim 533
Radioactive Contamination 529
Rating of 531-532
Fleet Rates 532
Private Passenger 531-532
Radius of Operations 532
Rental Reimbursement........527-528
Other Perils 528
Theft 524, 527
Riot 526
Salvage 524
Stated Amount Basis 530
Statements of Insured 532
Suit 533
Tapes and Tape Players 524
Territorial Limits 531
Theft, Loss of Use 524, 527
Tires, Damage to 529
Undeclared Bailment Lease 529
Utility Trailer, Rented or Borrowed 524
Valued Form, Monthly Reduction Basis 531
Vandalism 526
War, Exclusion of 529
Wear and Tear, Exclusion of 528
Windstorm 526

COMPREHENSIVE 3-D
See Comprehensive Dishonesty, Disappearance and Destruction Policy 243-245

COMPULSORY INSURANCE
Automobiles,
Private Passenger 518-522
Common Carriers,
Cargo 337
Interstate 493
Intrastate Carriers 496

INDEX

Page

Passenger Carriers 495
State Requirements 496

CONCEALMENT,
See Also Misrepresentation
Marine Insurance 368
Of Material Fact 28

CONDOMINIUM PROPERTY INSURANCE 657-658

CONSEQUENTIAL LOSS ASSUMPTION CLAUSE, FIRE INSURANCE
Clothing Risks 116-117
Cold Storage Risks 115-116
Household Contents Form 62

CONSEQUENTIAL LOSS, FIRE
See Business Interruption Insurance and Rent Insurance

Contingent Liability From Operation of Building Laws 117-118
Demolition Cost Insurance 118
Fire Department Charges 119
Increased Cost of Construction Endorsement 118-119

CONSEQUENTIAL LOSS, GARMENT CONTRACTORS FLOATER 309-310

CONSTRUCTION
Permit, Liability Insurance 407

CONTINGENT BUSINESS INTERRUPTION 102
Off-Premises, Power Light, Heat 102

CONTINGENT LIABILITY FROM OPERATION OF BUILDING LAWS 117-119

CONTRACT 27-29
General Rules of 27
In Insurance 28

CONTRACTORS EQUIPMENT FLOATER 325

CONTRACTUAL LIABILITY INSURANCE 420-422
Assumed Liability 421
Hazards Not Covered 422
Hold Harmless Agreements 421
Liability to a Person Not Party to a Contract 422
Liability to Employees 422
Liability for Property in Care, Custody, Control 422
Rating of 422
What Is Covered 421

CREDIT CARD FORGERY BOND 232-233
Under Homeowners Policies 652

Page

CRIME COVERAGES,
See Under Individual Policies; Broad Form Personal Theft, Open Stock Burglary, Robbery, Money and Securities Broad Form Policy, etc.
Package Policies,
See Storekeeper's Burglary and Robbery Policy, Office Burglary and Robbery Policy, etc.

DATA PROCESSORS E&O 452

DEDUCTIBLE CLAUSE
Auto Collision 535
Auto Comprehensive Physical Damage 530-531
Boiler and Machinery 629-630
Broad Form Personal Theft Policy.. 149
Commercial Property Coverage 675
Disappearing 127
Dwelling 127
Dwelling Broad Form 83
Dwelling Special Form........ 86
Fidelity Bonds 217
Fire Insurance (Excess of Loss) 127
Franchise (Disappearing) 127
Franchise (Marine) 367
Garage Keepers Legal Liability..540, 542
Garage Liability 511
Homeowners Policies 649, 656
Jewelers Block 320
Major Medical 612
Office Personal Property Form 671
Personal Property Floater 288-289
Public Liability Insurance 401
Special Multi-Peril Policy 667
Vandalism and Malicious Mischief 76-77
Windstorm and Hail 72-73

DEFERRED PAYMENT MERCHANDISE FLOATER,
See Installment Sales Form Under Inland Marine Insurance

DEMOLITION COST INSURANCE, FIRE 117-119

DEPARTMENT STORE FLOATER 348

DEPOSITORS FORGERY BOND
Bank as Additional Insured 231
Branch Office Endorsement 232
Hazards Covered 229
Incoming Check Endorsement 231
Liability at Bank 228
Other Insurance 231
Personal Account Forgery 231

DEPRECIATION 37
See Also Actual Cash Value

DIRECTORS AND OFFICERS LIABILITY 450-451
Company Reimbursement Coverage 451
Extended Discovery Period 451
Mini D&O 451

INDEX

Page

DISABILITY BENEFITS INSURANCE
Administration of ... 616
Benefits Under ... 616
Chart Analysis of State Disability Benefits Laws ... 617-619
Disability Benefits Laws ... 615
Hawaii ... 620
Puerto Rico ... 620
What Is Covered ... 616

DISABILITY INSURANCE
See Accident and Health

DISCOVERY BOND ... 227

DISCOVERY PERIOD
See Under Fidelity Bonds, Also Under Money and Securities Broad Form

DRUGGISTS LIABILITY POLICY 432-434
Assumed Liability ... 433
Equipment Rented to or Located for Use by Others ... 433
Hazards Covered ... 433
Limits, Single ... 433-434
Occurrence Basis ... 433
Rating of ... 434
Violation of Penal Statute or Ordinance ... 433

DUTIES, INSURED'S
Fire Insurance ... 40

DWELLING BUILDINGS & CONTENTS BROAD FORM ... 77-83

DWELLING BUILDINGS SPECIAL FORM ... 84-86

DWELLING FORMS, MULTIPLE PERILS
See Homeowners Policies

EARNINGS INSURANCE ... 100

EARTHQUAKE
Broad Form Dwelling ... 80

ELECTRIC ARCING ... 73

ELEVATOR COLLISION INSURANCE ... 396

EMPLOYEE DISHONESTY,
See Also Fidelity Insurance
Furriers Customers Policy ... 301
Jewelers Block Policy ... 316

EMPLOYER, LIABILITY FOR EMPLOYEE ... 382-383

EMPLOYER'S LIABILITY
See Workmen's Compensation Insurance

EMPLOYER'S NON-OWNERSHIP LIABILITY INSURANCE ... 496-500
See Also Under Automobile Liability Insurance

ENEMY ATTACK
Loss by, Fire Insurance ... 36

Page

EXAMINATION UNDER OATH
Fire Insurance ... 42

EXCEPTED PROPERTY
In Fire Insurance ... 40

EX DOCK, NAMED PORT OF IMPORTATION ... 354

EXPENSE TO REDUCE LOSS
Business Interruption Insurance ... 94

EXPLOSION
See Also Boiler and Machinery Insurance
Dwelling Broad Form ... 78
Extended Coverage ... 74
Fire Insurance Policy
Furnace Explosion ... 74
Inherent Explosion ... 60
Vandalism and Malicious Mischief Endorsement ... 76

EX POINT OF ORIGIN ... 354

EXTENDED COVERAGE ENDORSEMENT ... 69-75
Apportionment Clause ... 70-71
Deductible Clause ... 72-73
Hazards Not Covered ... 69-70, 71-72

EXTRA EXPENSE INSURANCE ... 111-112
Business Interruption, Combined 113-114

FAIR ACCESS TO INSURANCE REQUIREMENTS (FAIR) PLANS ... 129-131

FAMILY FORGERY BOND ... 232

FARM EQUIPMENT FLOATER ... 325

FARMER'S COMPREHENSIVE PERSONAL LIABILITY POLICY ... 443
See Also Public Liability Policy, Comprehensive Personal Liability Policy
Animal Collision ... 443
Ineligible Risks ... 443
Substance Discharged from Aircraft 443

FARMOWNERS-RANCHOWNERS POLICY PROGRAM ... 680-683

F. A. S. ... 354

FEDERAL CRIME INSURANCE ... 184-185
Cancellation ... 185
Commercial Coverages ... 185
Deductibles ... 185
Residential Coverages ... 184

FIDELITY AND SURETY BONDS,
See Also Fidelity Bonds, Surety Bonds
Differences Between Bonds and Insurance ... 206-208

Page

General Principles of 206
Obligee 207
Principal 207
Surety 207

FIDELITY BONDS 208

Amount of Loss 214
Automatic Coverage on
  Terminated Employees 223
Blanket Position Bond, See Blanket
  Position Bond. See Also Comprehensive Dishonesty, Disappearance, and Destruction Policy
Cancellation, of Bond 216
Cancellation, on Dishonest
  Employee 211, 226
Continuous Term 216
Cooperation With Company 216
Deductibles 217
Depositors Forgery Bond 228-232
Discovery Bond 227
Discovery Period 212
Employee, Previously Cancelled 211
Hazards Covered 209
Indemnity Against Loss Under
  Prior Bond 213
Inventory Shortage 215, 225
Non-Accumulation of Liability 215
Notice of Loss 216
Other Insurance 215
Ownership of Property 209
Penalty of 214
Proof of Loss 216
Rating of 217
  Deductibles 217
  Experience Rating 217
  Term Policy 217
Regulation of 216
Salvage 215
Standardization of 216
Suit 216
Superseded Suretyship 213
Territorial Limits 215
Types of 219
  Blanket Bonds, See Blanket
  Position Bond, Primary
  Commercial Blanket Bond
  Bankers Blanket Bond
  Individual Bond 219
  Name Schedule Bond 220
  Position Schedule Bond 220-223
What Is Covered 209
When Loss Must Be Discovered 212
When Loss Must Occur 212
Who Is Covered 210

FINANCIAL INSTITUTIONS, BONDS

Forms of 233

FINANCIAL RESPONSIBILITY LAWS

  See Motor Vehicle Financial
  Responsibility Laws
Bond, Required Under 264

Page

FINE ARTS INSURANCE 273-274

Hazards Not Covered 273
  Breakage of Fragile Articles 273
  Damage Due to Process 273
  Packing 274
  Property on Exhibition 274
Newly Acquired Property 273
Pair and Set Clause 274
Valued Basis 274

FIRE DEPARTMENT CHARGES FIRE INSURANCE 119

FIRE INSURANCE POLICY 30-45

Actual Cash Value 37
Additional Living Expense 114
Anti-Coinsurance Laws 67
Appraisal 42
Assignment 38
Average Clause 47
Binders 44
Breach of Warranty Clause 56
Builder's Risk Reporting Form 63
  Completed Value 63
Building and Contents Form 53
Building Coverage 53
Buildings in Course of
  Construction 63
Business Interruption Insurance
  See Business Interruption
  Insurance, Fire
Cancellation 43-44
Coinsurance Clause 47-51
Concurrency 45
Consequential Loss Clauses
  Change in Temperature 62
  Clothing Risks 116-117
Contents Coverage 53
Control of Property Clause 57
Debris Removal 46-47
Dwelling and Contents Form 60
Dwelling Building(s) and
  Contents Broad Form 77-83
Dwelling Building(s)
  Special Form 84-86
Dwelling Form 60
Electrical Apparatus Clause 47
Electrical Apparatus
  Lightning Deductible 61
Examination Under Oath 42
Excepted Property 40
Excluded Hazards 36
Fair Access to Insurance
  Requirements (FAIR) Plans 129-131
Fire Department Charges 119
Fire Forms 46
For How Much 37
Foundations Exclusion Clause 55
Hazards Covered 30
Hazards Not Covered 36
Hostile Fire 31
Household Contents Form 61-63
Improvements & Betterments 53-54

Page

Increase of Hazard 40
Inherent Explosion 60
Insurable Interest 38
Insured's Duties and
  Obligations 40, 55, 61
  Warranties 57
Liberalization Clause 47
Loss Payable Clause 59
Market Value Clause 115
Mortgagee, Benefits of 58
  Obligations Imposed on 59
Mortgagee Clause 57-59
New York Form 30
No Abandonment 38
Non-Concurrency 45
Nuclear Perils 47
Off-Premises Extension 54
Other Insurance 45
Outbuilding Coverage 60
Personal Property of Others 54
Power Failure Loss Clauses 115-116
Proof of Loss 41
Property Outside Buildings 55
Pro Rata Distribution Clause 51
Pro Rata Liability 39
Proximate Cause 31
Rates, See Rates,
  Fire Insurance
Records, Reproduction of 119
Reduced Rate Contribution Clause.. 47
Rent Insurance 60, 81, 104-109
Replacement Cost Coverage 51-52
Requirements After Loss 40
Selling Price Clause 114-115
Standardization of 30, 46
Subrogation 43, 57
Text of Standard Fire Insurance
  Policy of New York 32-35
Time of Policy 43
Trees, Plants, Shrubs 61, 82, 85
Uninsurable Property 40
Vacancy and Unoccupancy 40, 56
Valued Policy and
  Anti-Coinsurance Laws 65-68
Valued Policy Laws 65-67
Waiver of Inventory
  And Appraisement Clause 52
Where Covered 39
Who Is Insured 39
Work and Materials Clause 55-56

FLOATERS, COMMERCIAL, OWNER'S FORMS
  See Individual Policies Under
  Inland Marine Insurance, e.g.
  Garment Contractors' Floater
  Jewelers' Block Policy
  Installment Sales Form
  Salesman's Floater
  Contractors' Equipment Foater

FLOATERS, PERSONAL
  See Under Inland Marine
  Insurance

FLOOD INSURANCE 87-89

Page

F. O. B. SHIPMENTS 340, 354

FORGERY
  See Depositors Forgery Bond
  Family Forgery Bond
  See Also Under Bankers'
  Blanket Bond No. 24

FORM, FIRE INSURANCE 46

FORTUITOUS EVENT 27
Marine Insurance 360

FRANCHISE CLAUSES
Marine Insurance 367

FRAUD
Fire Insurance 40
Marine Insurance 368

FREE OF PARTICULAR AVERAGE 365-366

FUR INSURANCE, PERSONAL 270

FURRIERS CUSTOMERS POLICY,
  See Under Inland Marine
  Insurance

GARAGE KEEPER'S LEGAL LIABILITY INSURANCE,
  See Also Garage Liability
  Insurance
Assumed Liability 541
Civil Commotion 540
Coinsurance Clause 542
Collision 540
Deductible Clause 540, 542
Defective Parts 541
Defense, Supplementary Benefits 540
Elevators and Hoists 541
Employee Dishonesty 540
Explosion 540
Fire 540
Liability Coverage Only 539
Location, Specified 542
Need For 539
Owned Automobiles 541
Personal Effects 541
Pro Rata Liability 542
Racing Contests 541
Radioactive Contamination 541
Riot 540
Theft Coverage 540
  Entire Automobile, of 540
Upset 540
Use, Loss of by Theft 540
Vandalism and Malicious Mischief.. 540
War Exclusion 541
Wearing Apparel, Loss of 541

GARAGE LIABILITY INSURANCE 503-513
  See Also Garage Keeper's Legal
  Liability
Aggregate Limit, Absense of 511

INDEX

Page

Aircraft Exclusion 511
Alterations, Structural 510-511
Assumed Liability 508
Damage to Property Out of Which
  Accident Arises 508
Deductible 511
Elevators 507
Eligible Risks 504, 505
Family Cars, Non-Business Use 506
Faulty Work, Liability for 506
Haulaway, Tank Trucks, etc. 510
Hoist, Servicing 509
Independent Contractors 511
Legal Representatives 512
Livery Purpose 509
Loaned Automobile 510
Medical Services, Expenses for 507, 509
  Auto Medical Payments 507
  Combined Auto and Premises
    Medical Payments 507
Non-Incidental Operations 506
Omnibus Clause 512
Other Insurance 511-512
Products Liability 506, 508
Property In Insured's
  Care 508-509
  See Also Under Collision Liability
  See Also Garage Keeper's Legal Liability Insurance
Racing or Speed Contest 509
Rating of 512-513
Rented Automobiles 510
Supplementary Payments 511
Territorial Limits 512
Trailers 510
Warranty of Goods 506
Watercraft Exclusion 511

GARMENT CONTRACTORS FLOATER 306-314
  See Under Inland Marine Insurance

GENERAL AVERAGE 355-356

GENERAL PROPERTY FORM 53

GLASS,
  See Comprehensive Glass Policy
Dwelling, Broad Form 79
Under Vandalism and Malicious
  Mischief Endorsement 76

GROSS EARNINGS,
  See Business Interruption Insurance

GUEST LAWS 378-379

HIRED CAR COVERAGE,
  See Under Automobile Liability Insurance

Page

HOMEOWNERS POLICIES 642-656
Homeowners 1, 2, 3, 4, and 5 642
Homeowners 1—Basic Form 645-652
Homeowners 2—Broad Form 653-654
Homeowners 3—Special Form 654
Homeowners 4—Contents
  Broad Form 654-655
Homeowners 5—Comprehensive
  Form 655-656
Coverages E and F 644

HOSPITALIZATION INSURANCE 609-610

HULL INSURANCE 370

ICE, SNOW, SLEET 78

IMPLEMENT DEALERS FLOATER 324

IMPROVEMENTS AND BETTERMENTS
Building and Contents Form 53-54
Condominium Property 658
Dwelling Broad Form 81

INCREASE OF HAZARD
In Fire Insurance 40
Under Mortgage Clause 58

INDEPENDENT CONTRACTORS LIABILITY INSURANCE
  See Owners and Contractors Liability Insurance

INDIRECT LOSS, FIRE
  See Business Interruption Insurance
  See Also Rent Insurance

INHERENT VICE 267, 329

INLAND MARINE INSURANCE
  See Also Transportation Insurance
Additionally Acquired
  Property 270, 272
(Newly Acquired Property) 273
All Risk Basis 267
Bailees' Customers Form 295-299
  Accrued Charges 295
  Adjustment of Loss 298
  All-Risk Form A 299
  Cancellation 298
  Hazards Covered 296-297
  Hazards Not Covered 297
  Limits of Liability 298
  Notice of Loss 298
  Premium 298
  Property Covered 295
  Property Not Covered 295-296
  Suit, by Insured 298
  Time of Policy 299
  Transit Coverage 296, 297
Benefit of Insurance 269

INDEX

Page

Blanket Insurance 271, 272
Cameras and Camera Equipment.... 271
Cold Storage Locker Bailee
  Floater 304-305
Contractors' Equipment Floater 325
Exclusions, Common to Floaters...... 267
Farm Equipment Floater 325
Fine Arts 273-274
Floor Plan Merchandise Policy 323
Furriers Customers Policy 299-304
  Accrued Charges 300
  Certificates, by Insured 303
  Eligible Risks 300
  Employee Dishonesty 301
  Excess Legal Liability 302
  Guarantee of Work, Liability of.. 301
  Hazards Not Covered 301
  Limit of Liability 302
  Premium 303
  Process, Damage Due to 301
Garment Contractors Floater 306-314
  All-Risk 310-311
  Bill of Lading, Released 313
  Coinsurance Clause 311
  Consequential Damage 309
  Consequential, Full Range of
    Size and Colors 310
  Contractor's Premises 307
  Explosion 309
  Hazards Covered, Premises 308
  Hazards Not Covered 310
  Optional Additional Coverages 309
  Other Insurance 313
  Premises Excluded 307
  Premium Determination 314
  Reporting Form 312
  Strikes, Riots, Malicious Mischief 309
  Theft Coverage 309
  Time of Policy 313
  Transit Coverage 307, 308
  Unnamed Contractors 311-312
  Water Damage 308
  What Is Covered 306
Implement Dealers Floater 324
Insects, Vermin 267, 282
Installation Floater 323-324
Installment Payment of Premiums.. 269
Installment Sales Form 322-323
  Dual Interest Form 322
  Limits of Liability 323
  Open Form 323
  Single Interest Form 322
  Single Interest, Uncollectible
    Amount 323
Jewelers Block Policy 314-322
  Adjustment of Losses With
    Others 320
  Application for 320
  Breakage, Fragile Articles 317
  Carriers, Type Covered 318
  Corrosion, Dampness 316
  Deductible 320
  Delay, Loss of Market 316
  Dishonesty of Insured,
    Employees 316

Page

  Earthquake 316
  Exhibition, Property on 319
  Express Shipment 318
  Fire, Exclusion 317
  Flood 316
  Furniture, Fixtures, Machinery,
    Tools 315
  Improvements and Betterments.... 315
  Insured's Duties 320
  In Transit Coverage 318
  Inventory Shortage 317
  Limits, Various 319
  Loan Receipt 321
  Mail, Property in 318
  Money 315
  Patterns, Molds, Models,
    Dies 315
  Pledged Articles 319-320
  Process, Damage Due to 316
  Property Not Covered 315
  Protective Devices 320
  Records, Maintenance of 320
  Show Cases, of Insured 318
  Show Cases, Other Premises 319
  Subrogation 321
  Term of Policy 321
  Theft, Damage by 315
  Vehicles, Unattended 318
  What Is Covered 314
Marine Definition 266
Minimum Premiums 269
Musical Instruments 271-272
Nuclear Exclusion 267
Origin of 266
Pair and Set Clause 271, 274, 286
Parcel Post, See Parcel Post
  Insurance
Personal Articles Floater 270
Personal Effects Floater, See Under
  Personal Effects Floater
Personal Furs 270
Personal Jewelry 270-271
Personal Property Floater, See
  Under Personal Property Floater
Processors' Floaters 304
Registered Mail, See Registered
  Mail Insurance
Requirements in Case of Loss 268-269
Salesmen's Floater 324
Scheduling of Items Insured 268, 286
Stamp and Coin Collections 272
Sue and Labor 269
Territorial, World-Wide 268
Transportation, See Transportation
  Policy. See Also Under Individual
  Inland Marine Policies
Unscheduled Personal Property
  Floaters 275
  See Under Personal Effects
  Floater, Personal Property
  Floater
Valued Forms 268
War Risk Exclusions 267

Page

Wear and Tear 267
Wedding Present Floater 291

INNKEEPERS LIABILITY POLICY 202

INSTALLATION FLOATER 323-324

INSTALLMENT PAYMENT PLANS
See Under Form of Insurance

INSTALLMENT SALES FORM 322-323
See Under Inland Marine Insurance

INSURABLE INTEREST 27, 38
When Must Exist 38

INSURED
In Fire Insurance Policy 39

INSURERS, TYPES OF 636-641
Alien Insurer 638
Assessability 636-637
Capital Stock Company 637
Contingent Liability, Policyholder.... 636
Dividends 636
Domestic Insurer 638
Foreign Insurer 638
Inter-Insurance Exchange 637
Lloyds, Domestic 638
Mutual Carrier 636-637
Reciprocal Exchange 637
State Insurance Funds 638

INSURRECTION
Loss by, Fire Insurance 36

INTERSTATE COMMERCE COMMISSION ENDORSEMENT 337, 493

INTERSTATE LOCATIONS, FIRE INSURANCE 124

INVENTORY
Fire Insurance 41
Sprinkler Leakage 138

JEWELERS' BLOCK POLICY,
See Under Inland Marine Insurance 314-322

JEWELRY INSURANCE, PERSONAL 270-271

LABOR ORGANIZATION BOND 242

LEASEHOLD INTEREST INSURANCE 109-111

LIABILITY INSURANCE,
See Public Liability Insurance Also Individual Liability Policies e.g. Owners, Landlords and Tenants Schedule Liability Policy, Manufacturers' and Contractors' Liability Insurance, Comprehensive General Liability Policy, Comprehensive Personal Liability Policy, Automobile Liability Policy

Page

LIBERALIZATION CLAUSE 47

LIGHTNING 30

LIMITATIONS, STATUTE OF....376-378

LOSS OF TIME INSURANCE,
See Accident and Health

LOSS PAYABLE CLAUSE, FIRE INSURANCE
Contrasted With Mortgagee Clause 59

MAJOR MEDICAL EXPENSE INSURANCE (CATASTROPHE MEDICAL EXPENSE INSURANCE) 610-613
Coinsurance 612
Cosmetic Surgery 612
Deductible 612
Government Hospital Treatment 611
Hazards Covered 611
Hazards Not Covered 611
Lifetime Maximum 613
Per Cause Maximum 613
Pregnancy 612
Rates 613
Time Limit on Claims 612
War 611
What Is Covered 611
When Covered 613
Who Is Insured 613
Workmen's Compensation 611

MALICIOUS MISCHIEF,
See Vandalism

MALPRACTICE
See Professional Liability Insurance

MANUFACTURERS' AND CONTRACTORS' LIABILITY INSURANCE 411-415
See Also Public Liability Insurance
Audit Premium 413
Blasting, Explosion, Collapse, Excavation 411-412
Eligible Risks 411
Excluded Occupations 415
Executive Officers, Payroll of 414-415
Governing Classification 413-414
Independent Contractors 411
See Also Owners and Contractors Protective Liability
Construction Permit 424
Limits
Aggregate 412-413
New Construction, Demolition 411

Page
Newly Acquired Premises 411
Owners, Payroll of 414-415
Partners, Payroll of 414-415
Payroll Basis 413-414
Rating of 413
Standard Exceptions 415
X. C. U. Classifications 412

MANUFACTURER'S OUTPUT POLICY 676-680
Actual Cash Value 679
Cancellation 680
Collision Damage to Vehicles 678
Dampness of Atmosphere 678
Delay, Loss of Market 678
Earthquake 677
Extremes of Temperature 678
Flood 677
Hazards Covered 677
Hostile or Warlike Action 677
Improvements and Betterments 676
Infidelity of Employees 677
Infidelity of Independent
Contractors 677
Insured's Manufacturing Premises.... 679
Inventory Shortage 678
Limits of Liability 679
Other Insurance 679
Personal Property of Insured 676
Personal Property of Others 676
Process, Damage Due to 678
Property Not Covered 676
Reporting Form 679
Steam Boilers, etc. 678
Territory 679

MARINE INSURANCE 353-372
See Also Transportation, Inland Marine Insurance

Background of 353
Cargo Policy 357
Abandonment 367
"All Other Perils" 359
All Risk 362
Assailing Thieves 359
Barratry 359
Cancellation 369
Coinsurance 365
Constructive Total Loss 367
Dampness-Breakage 360
Deviation 364
Duties, Insured's 368
Explosion 360
Fire 359
Franchise Clause 367
Fraud, Concealment 368
Free of Capture, Seizure 361
Free of Particular Average 365-366
Freight Charges 356, 357
General Average 355-356
Hazards Covered 358-359
Hazards Not Covered 360
Import Duties 357
Inchmaree 360
Jettison 359

Page
Latent Defects 360
Liability of Shipowner 353
Loss of Market 361
Machinery 367
Marine Extension Clauses 363
Memorandum Clauses 366
No Deviation 364
On Deck Shipments 363
Open Policy 369
Optional Perils 360
Other Insurance 368
Particular Average 365
Perils of the Sea 358-359
Perils on Land 360
Prompt Attachment, Warranty 364
Rating of 369-370
Reporting Shipments 369
Sabotage 362
Seaworthiness, Implied 363
Strikes, Riots, Civil Commotion .. 361
Subrogation 368
Sue and Labor 358
Under Deck Shipments 363
Valuation of Goods 365
Warehouse to Warehouse 362
War Risk 370
What Is Covered 357

MARKET VALUE CLAUSE, FIRE INSURANCE 115

MASS MERCHANDISING 641

MASTER AND SERVANT RULE 382
Automobile Liability, in 496-497

MATERIAL FACT 28
Concealment of 28
Increase of Hazard 40
Marine Insurance 368

MERCANTILE ROBBERY 172-178
Custodian Defined 174
Damage to Property and Premises .. 174
Failure to Maintain Protection 174
Hazards Covered 172
Home of Custodian 176
Infidelity of Employees 175
Kidnapping Coverage 173
Premises 175
Rates 177-178
Credits 178
Minimum Premium 178
Show Window Robbery 173
What Is Covered 172

MERCANTILE SAFE BURGLARY 166-170
Actual Cash Value 168
Blanket Insurance 170
Burglary, Defined 167
Damage to Property 167
Fire, Caused by 168
Hazards Covered 167
Money, Contrast With Open
Stock Burglary 166
Pledged Articles 169

Page

Profits Insurance 168-169
Rating of 169-170
Credits 170
Minimum Premiums 170
Term of Policy 170
What Is Covered 166

MINIMUM PREMIUMS,
See Under Form of Insurance

MISCELLANEOUS MEDICAL PROFESSIONAL LIABILITY 447

MISREPRESENTATION,
See Also Concealment 28

MONEY AND SECURITIES BROAD FORM POLICY 187-194
Additional Locations, Automatic Insurance 190
Blanket Policy 192
Cooperation With Company 192
Damage to Premises 187
Discovery of Loss 189
Dishonesty, Employee 189
Existing Insurance 192
Fire 189
Hazards Covered 188
Hazards Not Covered 189
Home of Messenger 190
Inside Premises 190
Locked Cash Drawer, Cash Box or Register 189
Loss In Exchange or Purchase 189
Messenger 190
Money and Securities 187, 188
Night Depository 190
Notice of Loss 192
Nuclear Perils 189
Other Insurance 191
Other (than Money and Securities) Property Coverage 188
Outside Premises 189-190
Pledged Articles 191
Proof of Loss 192
Property Not Covered 187
Rating of 193-194
Credits 193-194
Minimum Premiums 194
Records of Insured 189
Salvage 191
Schedule Policy 192
Securities, Negotiation of 192
Superseded Insurance 189
Vending Machine 189
War Risks 189

MORTGAGEE CLAUSE, FIRE INSURANCE 57-59
Immunity to Acts of Mortgagor 58

MORTICIANS PROFESSIONAL LIABILITY 449-450

MOTOR TRUCK MERCHANDISE FLOATER—CARRIER'S FORM....333-339

Page

Cancellation of 338
Coinsurance 336
Collision 334
Compulsory Insurance 337
Cooperation By Insured 338
Hazards Covered 333-334
Hazards Not Covered 335
ICC Endorsement 337
Limits of Liability 336
Other Insurance 337
Premium Determination 338
Terminal Coverage 334
Theft 334

MOTOR VEHICLE FINANCIAL RESPONSIBILITY LAWS 456, 481, 517-522
Accidents 517
Chart Analysis, All States 520-521
Compulsory Laws By States 518-519, 522
Convictions 518
Judgments 518
Proof, Methods of Furnishing 518
Purpose of 517
Security Type Laws 517

MULTIPLE PERIL COMMERCIAL POLICIES 659-683
Boiler and Machinery Coverage 667
Commercial Property Coverage 672-676
Comprehensive Crime Coverage 666
Farmowners-Ranchowners Policy Program 680-683
Manufacturer's Output Policy....676-680
Office Personal Property Form....667-672
Special Multi-Peril Program 659-667

MULTIPLE PERIL DWELLING POLICIES 642-656
See Homeowners Policies

MUSICAL INSTRUMENTS 271-272

NEGLECT OF INSURED,
See Also Negligence
Fire Insurance 36

NEGLIGENCE 373-388
As Proximate Cause of Damages 373
Attractive Hazard, Attractive Nuisance 374
Common Law Doctrine 373
Comparative Negligence Rule 375
Contributory Negligence 374
Definition of 373
Degrees of Care Required 374
Attractive Hazard 374
Invitee 374
Trespasser 374
Employer, Liability for Employee 382-383
Fact, Question of 374
Guest Laws 378-379
Last Clear Chance 375
Master and Servant Rule 382

Page
Res Ipsa Loquitor 375
Respondeat Superior Rule 382-383
Spouse vs. Spouse, Suits of 378
Survival of Actions
After Death 379-381
Time Limit on Suits,
by States 377-378
Torts, Definition of 376
Negligent 376
Unintentional 376
Vehicle Owner, Liability of 383
Vicarious Liability 383-388
Wrongful Death, Actions for 381-382

NEW ENGLAND FIRE INSURANCE POLICY
NEW YORK STANDARD FIRE INSURANCE POLICY
See Fire Insurance Policy

NO ABANDONMENT
In Fire Insurance 38
Marine Insurance 367

NO BENEFIT TO BAILEE,
See Inland Marine Insurance—Benefit of Insurance

NON-OCCUPATIONAL DISABILITY INSURANCE
See Disability Benefits Insurance

NON-OWNERSHIP (AUTOMOBILE) LIABILITY
See Under Individual Liability Policy; Owners, Landlords and Tenants, Manufacturers, Comprehensive Personal, Druggists, Professional, etc.
See Also Under Automobile Liability Insurance 496-500

NOTICE OF LOSS
See Under Form of Insurance

OCCUPATIONAL SAFETY AND HEALTH ACT (OSHA) 565-566

OCEAN MARINE 353-372
See Marine Insurance

OFFICE BURGLARY AND ROBBERY POLICY 200-202
Eligible Risks 200
Hazards Covered 201
Ineligible Risks 200-201
Rating of 202
Theft Coverage 201
What Is Covered 201

OFFICE PERSONAL PROPERTY FORM 667-672

OPEN POLICY
Fidelity Insurance 216

Page
Marine Insurance 369
Parcel Post 351

OPEN STOCK BURGLARY POLICY 156-166
Actual Cash Value 160
Additional Locations, Automatic
Coverage 160
Assignment 166
Burglary, Defined 157
Change In Condition of Risk 159
Coinsurance Clause 161-163
Coinsurance Limit 162
Jewelry, Exception From 162-163
Consequential Loss—Clothing
Risk 161
Cooperation With Company 163
Damage 156
Disappearance 158
Fire 158-159
Fur Articles 159
Hazards Covered 157
Hazards Not Covered 158
Infidelity of Employees 158
Insured's Statements 163
Inventory, After Loss 163
Jewelry, Limit on 161
Notice of Loss 163
Nuclear Perils 160
Other Insurance 163
Ownership of Property 156
Property of Others 156
Pledged Articles 161
Premises 160
Inspection of 163
Maintenance of 163
Profits Insurance 161
Proof of Loss 163
Rating of 164-165
Credits 165
Records of Insured 159
Reduction in Amount 164
Regulation of 166
Reinstatement After Loss 164
Robbery of Watchman 157
Salvage, to Insured 160
Show Cases 160
Storekeeper, See Also Storekeepers' Burglary and Robbery Policy
Suits 164
Theft Endorsement 157-158
Vandalism and Malicious Mischief.. 159
War Hazards 158
What Is Covered 156
Where Covered 160

OTHER INSURANCE
See Under Form of Insurance

OWNERS AND CONTRACTORS PROTECTIVE LIABILITY INSURANCE 423-426
Independent Contractor,
Liability for 423
Limits 426

Page

Maintenance, Repairs or Alterations ... 425
Pick Up of Tools ... 425
Premises-Operations, Exclusion ... 424
Rating of ... 426

OWNERS', LANDLORDS' AND TENANTS' SCHEDULE LIABILITY INSURANCE ...404-410
See Also Public Liability Insurance
Assumed Liability ...405-406
See Also Contractual Liability Insurance
Construction and Demolition Permit ...406-407
Grantor's Liability ... 405
Hazards Covered ... 404
Hazards Not Covered ... 405
Incidental Contracts ... 406
Limits ... 410
Loading, Unloading of Vehicles... 406
New Construction, Demolition Operations ...406-407
Newly Acquired Premises ... 405
Newly Added Operations ... 405
Premises-Operations Coverage ... 404
Professional Services, Exclusion of ... 408
Purpose of ... 404
Rating of ...409-410
Area ... 409
Frontage ... 409
Premium Bases ... 409
Sprinkler Leakage, Exclusion of ... 407
Storekeepers, See Storekeeper's Liability Policy
Structural Alterations ... 405
Three-Year Policies ... 410
Vehicles, Aircraft ... 406
Excepted Mobile Equipment ... 406
On Premises Accidents ... 406
Watercraft Exclusion ... 406
Water Damage, Exclusion of ... 407

PARCEL POST INSURANCE ...348-351
Cancellation ... 351
Consignment ... 349
Hazards Covered ... 349
Insurance With Post Office Required ... 350
Limit of Liability ... 350
Open Form ... 351
Postal Regulations, Compliance ... 349
Property Not Covered ... 349
Requirements on Addressing, Labeling, etc. ... 349
Subrogation ... 350
Transients, Shipments to ... 350
What Is Covered ... 348

PARTICULAR AVERAGE ... 365

PARTNERSHIP BOND ... 241

Page

PAYMASTER ROBBERY POLICY
See Also Robbery Insurance
Broad Form Policy ...182-184
Absent Custodian ...182-183
Employee Dishonesty ... 183
Loss in Exchange or Purchase ... 183
Employees, Robbery of ... 180
Inside and Outside Coverages ... 180
Non Payroll Funds ... 180
Rating ... 182
What Is Covered ... 179

PERSONAL ARTICLES FLOATER ... 270

PERSONAL EFFECTS FLOATER..275-279
Breakage Exclusion ... 276
Deductible Clause ... 278
Domicile of Insured ... 276
Exclusion of Theft, Larceny ... 278
Hazards Not Covered ... 276
Jewelry and Furs Limitation ... 276
Loss Payable ... 279
Persons Insured Under ... 278
Property Not Covered ... 275
Reinstatement After Loss ... 278
Schools, Dormitories, Fraternity, Sorority, Premises ... 277
Storage, Property in ... 277
Term Policy, Not Available ... 278
Theft From Unattended Automobile ... 277
Trailer Home, Contents ... 278
What Is Covered ... 275

PERSONAL INJURY LIABILITY ... 392

PERSONAL LIABILITY,
See Comprehensive Personal Liability Insurance, Schedule Personal Liability Insurance, Farmer's Comprehensive Personal Liability Policy

PERSONAL PROPERTY FLOATER ...279-291
Boats ... 288
Breakage, Fragile Articles ...281-282
Damage by Pets ... 283
Damage Due to Process ... 282
Dampness of Atmosphere or Extremes of Temperature ... 282
Declarations of Insured ... 285
Deductible Clauses ...288-289
Furs, Unscheduled ...281, 287
Hazards Not Covered ... 281
Insects, Vermin ... 282
Jewelry, Unscheduled ...281, 287
Mechanical Breakdown ... 282
Money and Securities ...281, 286
Non Reduction After Loss ... 291
Other Insurance ... 289
Pair and Set Clause ...286
Premiums, Factors ... 290
Property Not Covered ... 280

Page

Property of Others ... 284
Scheduling Property ... 285, 286
Secondary Residence ... 284, 288
Servants, Personal Property of ... 284
Term Policies ... 290
Water Damage Exclusion ... 283
Wear, Tear ... 282
What Is Covered ... 279
  Real Property ... 280
  Vandalism and Malicious Mischief 280

PERSONAL THEFT POLICY ... 153-155
Automobile, Theft From ... 154
Mysterious Disappearance ... 153

PHYSICIANS', SURGEONS' AND DENTISTS' PROFESSIONAL LIABILITY ... 445-447
Lloyd's Policy ... 446-447

POWER FAILURE OR CONSEQUENTIAL LOSS PROVISIONS ... 115-116

POWER PLANT INSURANCE,
  See Boiler and Machinery Insurance

PREMIUM ADJUSTMENT FORMS
Business Interruption Forms ... 101
Rent Insurance ... 109

PROCESSORS FLOATERS ... 304

PRODUCTS LIABILITY— COMPLETED OPERATIONS
Assumed Liability ... 418
  See Also Contractual Liability Insurance
Consumption Articles ... 415
Damage to Property Out of Which Accident Arises ... 418
Druggists, See Druggists Liability Policy
Equipment Rented to or Located By Others ... 418
Failure to Perform Function ... 418
Hazards Covered ... 416
  Special Classifications ... 417
Implied Warranty of Fitness ... 416
Inherently Dangerous Articles ... 415
Liability of Manufacturer ... 415
Liability of Seller ... 415
Limits, Under ... 419
Rating of ... 420
Relinquishment, Importance of ... 416
Sistership Liability ... 419
When Accidents Must Occur ... 416
Withdrawal of Product ... 419

PROFESSIONAL LIABILITY INSURANCE
Beauty Shop, Barbers ... 448-449
Data Processors ... 452
Directors & Officers ... 450-451

Page

Lawyers ... 447-448
Miscellaneous Medical ... 447
Morticians ... 449-450
Physicians, Surgeons and
  Dentists ... 445-447
  Lloyd's Policy ... 446-447
Risks Requiring ... 444

PROOF OF LOSS
  See Under Form of Insurance

PRO RATA DISTRIBUTION CLAUSE, FIRE INSURANCE ... 51

PRO RATA LIABILITY
Fire Insurance ... 39
Garage Keepers Legal Liability ... 542

PROTECTED TERRITORY ... 123

PROTECTION OF PROPERTY
After Loss, Fire Insurance ... 41

PROTECTIVE LIABILITY,
  See Owners and Contractors Protective Liability Insurance

PROXIMATE CAUSE
In Fire Insurance ... 31
Negligence ... 373

PUBLIC EMPLOYEES BOND ... 259-260

PUBLIC LIABILITY INSURANCE 389-403
Additional Interests ... 400
Alcoholic Beverages, Liability ... 397
Appeal Bonds, Premiums ... 391
Assignment ... 403
Audit ... 403
Auto, Aircraft, Watercraft Exclusion 396
Basic Policy Jacket ... 393
Bodily Injury Coverage ... 390
Care, Custody or Control
  Exclusion ... 395
  Elevator Liability, Exception ... 395
Claim, Notice of ... 402
Completed Operations Liability,
  See Products Liability Insurance
Comprehensive General Liability,
  See Comprehensive General Liability Policy
Contractual Liability,
  See Contractual Liability Policy
Cooperation With Company ... 402
Court Costs ... 391
Coverage Parts, Separate ... 394
Deductibles ... 401
Defense, Supplementary
  Benefits ... 390, 399
  False, Groundless Suits ... 390
Elevator Collision Insurance ... 396
Employees, Exclusion of ... 395
  See Workmen's Compensation Insurance
  Comprehensive Personal
    Liability Policy ... 438
  Domestic Servant ... 438-439

Page

Farmer's Liability
See Farmer's Comprehensive Personal Liability Policy
First Aid, Under 391
Hazards Not Covered 394
Workmen's Compensation, Exclusion Under 394
Independent Contractors,
See Owners and Contractors, Liability Insurance
Inspection of Premises 403
Interests of Judgments 391
Legal Representatives 400
Liability and Coverages, Distinction 389
Liability, Sources of 390
Assumed 390
Imposed By Law 390
Limits Under 398
Per Occurrence 398
Loss of Earnings, Insured's 391
Malpractice Exclusion 397
Medical Payments
Coverage 391, 392
Exclusions 393
Limits 399
Rates 401
Notice of Accident 402
Nuclear Energy Liability 397
Occurrence
Caused by 390
Defined 390, 392
Other Insurance 400
Personal Injury Liability 392
Personal Liability,
See Comprehensive Personal Liability Insurance, Schedule Personal Liability Insurance
Pollution Exclusion 397
Preventing Further Damages 402
Products Liability Insurance,
See Products Liability Insurance
Professional Liability,
See Professional Liability
Professional Service Exclusion 397
Property Damage, Coverage 390
Property in Care, Custody or Control 395
Elevator Liability, Exception 395
Physical Damage to Property 436
Rating 401
Release of Attachment Bonds, Premiums 391
Repeated or Continuous Exposure 392
Settlement of Claim 403
Standardization of 389
Statements, By Insured 402
Storekeeper's Liability Policy,
See Storekeeper's Liability Policy
Territorial Limits 401
Third Parties, Rights of 401
Time of Policy 403

Page

War, Insurrection, Revolution, Exclusion 397
Witnesses, Expense of 391
Workmen's Compensation, Exclusion Under 394

PUBLIC OFFICIAL BOND 260-261

RAILWAY EXPRESS TRANSIT POLICY 348

RATE REGULATION
Fire Insurance 121-133

RATES, FIRE INSURANCE
Approved Roofs 123
Beach Property Insurance Pools 131-133
Civil Disorder Loadings 128
Coinsurance, Effect of 127
Consent to Rate Laws 131
Construction 123
Deductibles, Effect of 127
FAIR Plan 129-131
Vandalism and Malicious Mischief 131
Flat Cancellation 128
General Class 122
Installment Payment, Term Premiums 125
Interstate Locations 124
Loss Constant Rating Factor 128
Minimum Premiums 125-126
Protected Territory 123
Rating Organizations, Fire 121-122
Reduction, Broker's Duty 124
Reduction in Amount, Pro Rata 128
Regulation of 121
Schedule 123-124
Specific 123-124
Term Policies 125
Whole Dollar Premium Rule 126

REBELLION
Loss By, Fire Insurance 36

RECORDS, REPRODUCTION OF, FIRE 119

REDUCED RATE CONTRIBUTION CLAUSE,
See Coinsurance Clause

REDUCTION OF POLICY AMOUNT 128

REGISTERED MAIL INSURANCE 351

REINSURANCE 638-640
Facultative Basis 639
Retrocession 639-640
Treaty Basis 639

REMOVAL
Of Property for Preservation 39

RENT INSURANCE 104-109
Annual Rental Forms 105
Buildings in Course of Construction 109

INDEX

Page

Coinsurance Clauses 107
Dwelling Policy 60, 81, 108
Extended Coverage 105
Extension of Fire Policy 105
Hazards Covered 105-106
Hazards Not Covered 106
Interruption by Civil Authority 106
Lease Effect on Rent Insurance 104
Monthly Limitation Forms 107-108
Premium Adjustment Form 109
Seasonal Property 108-109
Vacant Premises, Coverage on 106

REPLACEMENT

In Fire Insurance 37

REPLACEMENT COST COVERAGE 51-52
Dwelling Broad Form 82-83

REPORTING POLICIES

Buildings in Course of Construction 63
Garment Contractors Floater 312
Rent Insurance 109

REQUIREMENTS AFTER LOSS

In Fire Insurance 40

RES IPSA LOQUITOR 375

RESIDENCE CONTENTS BROAD FORM 4

See Homeowners Package Policies

RESPONDEAT SUPERIOR RULE .. 382-383

Automobile Liability, in 496-497

RETROSPECTIVE RATING

Plan D 590-592
Plans A., B., C., J. 591-592

REVOLUTION

Loss By, Fire Insurance 36

RIOT

Definition of 74
Extended Coverage 74
In Fire Insurance Policy 37

RISK OF LOSS 28

ROBBERY INSURANCE 172-185

See Paymaster Robbery and Mercantile Robbery. See Also Money and Securities Broad Form Policy

Blanket Policy 176
Custodian, Defined 174, 181
Janitor, Porter, Watchman, Exclusion of 174, 181
Damage, By Robbery or Attempt 174
Dishonesty of Employees 175, 183
Hazards Covered 172-174
Hazards Not Covered 174
Home of Custodian 176

Page

Inside Premises 175
Kidnapping 173
Mercantile Robbery Policy 172-178
Messenger, Defined 174
Designation of 176
Outside Premises 175
Ownership of Property 172
Protection, Failure to Maintain 174
Rating of 177-178
Reinstatement After Loss 177
Robbery, Defined 172-173
Show Window 173, 176
Open for Business Requirement 174

SAFE BURGLARY,

See Mercantile Safe Burglary

SAFETY RESPONSIBILITY— MOTOR VEHICLES,

See Motor Vehicle Financial Responsibility Laws

SALESMEN'S FLOATER 324

SELF-INSURANCE 640

SELLING PRICE CLAUSE

Fire Insurance 114-115

SMOKE

Extended Coverage Endorsement.... 73

SONIC BOOM 74

SPECIAL MULTI-PERIL POLICY PROGRAM 659-667

SPECIFIED PERILS AUTO 537-538

SPOUSE VS. SPOUSE, SUITS OF 378

SPRINKLER LEAKAGE INSURANCE 134-139
Alarm Clause 139
Alterations and Repairs 136
Coinsurance Clause 138
Consequential Losses 139
Hazards Covered 135
Hazards Not Covered 135
Inventory, Waiver Clause 138
Limits 138
Loss, Source of 134
Tanks, Damage By 135
Vacancy and Unoccupancy 136
Watchman Clause 139
What Is Covered 136-137
Where Covered 137

SPRINKLER LEAKAGE LEGAL LIABILITY POLICY 408

STAMP AND COIN COLLECTIONS 272

STANDARD FIRE INSURANCE POLICY,

See Fire Insurance Policy

Page

STATUTE OF LIMITATIONS 377-378

STOREKEEPER'S BURGLARY AND ROBBERY POLICY 194-198
Burglary of Merchandise 196
Damage to Premises 196
Dishonesty, Employees 197
Home of Messenger 196
Inside Premises, Robbery 195
Jewelry, Limitation on 196
Kidnapping 195
Limit Under Insuring Agreements.... 197
Additional Units 198
Messenger, Limitation on 195
Night Depository, Theft From 196
Other Insurance 198
Rating 198
Robbery, Outside Premises 195
Safe Burglary 195-196
Term of Policy 198

STOREKEEPER'S LIABILITY POLICY 428-432
See Also Public Liability Policy
Alcoholic Beverage Dispensers 431
Autos, Aircraft, Watercraft 430
Contractual Liability 429
Demolition 430
Hazards Covered 429
Hazards Not Covered 430
Ineligible Risks 428
Limits, Single 431-432
Medical Payments, Basic Policy 430
Products Liability in Basic Policy 429, 431
Gas Appliances, Exclusion 431
Rating 432
Water Damage—Sprinkler Leakage.. 431

SUBROGATION
Fire Insurance 43, 57
Inland Marine Insurance, See Under Individual Floaters
Marine Insurance 368
Parcel Post Insurance 350

SUE AND LABOR,
See Under Inland Marine Insurance Form and Under Marine Insurance

SUIT
See Under Form of Insurance

SURETY ASSOCIATION OF AMERICA 216, 240

SURETY BONDS
See Also Fidelity and Surety Bonds
Bid Bonds 257
Collateral 252, 256
Contract Bonds 256-258
See Also Performance Bonds

Page

Court Bonds 247-256
Administrator's Bond 249
Appeal Bond—Plaintiff's 253-254
Assignee's Bond 252
Attachment Bond 252
Bankruptcy, Bond in 251
Certiorari Bond 254
Civil Arrest Bond 254
Claimant's Bond 254
Cost Bonds 254
Counter Replevin Bond 255
Deceased Persons, Miscellaneous Bonds 249
Defendant's Bonds 254-256
Distraint for Rent Bond 253
Defendant's Bond 255
Executor's Bond 249
Fiduciary Bonds 248-252
Guardian Ad Litem Bond 250
Guardian Bond 250
Incompetents, Bonds in Estate of 251
Indemnity to Sheriff Bond 253
Injunction Bond 253
Injunction, Bond to Dissolve 255
Joint Control 249
Mechanics Lien 256
Minors, Bonds in Estates of 250
Open Default Bond 255
Penalty, Set by Court 248
Plaintiff's Bonds 252-254
Premiums Payable 248
Probate Bonds 248-252
Receiver's Bond 251
Release of Attachment Bond 254
Removal Bond 254
Replevin Bond 253
Stay of Execution Bond 255
Term of Bond 248
Trustee's Bond 251
Trust Estates, Bonds in 250
Writ of Replevin 253
Financial Responsibility— Motor Vehicle Bonds 264
Joint Control 249
License and Permit Bonds 259
Litigation Bonds 252-256
Collateral 252
Lost Instrument Bond 263
Miscellaneous Bonds 263-265
Performance Bond 257-258
Completion Bond 258
Construction Contract Bond 258
Labor and Material Payment Bond 258
Maintenance Bond 258
Supply Contract Bond 258
Public Employees Bond 259-260
Public Official Bond 260-261
Retained Percentage 256
SBA Surety Bond Guarantee Program 258-259
U. S. Government Bonds 261-263
Alcohol Products Bonds 262
Alien or Immigration Bonds 262

Page

Custom House Bonds ... 262
Income Tax Bonds ... 262
Internal Revenue Bonds ... 262
Intoxicating Liquor Bonds ... 262
Varieties of ... 247
Workmen's Compensation Bonds ... 263

SURVIVAL OF ACTIONS AFTER DEATH ... 379-381

THEFT
In Fire Insurance ... 36
Under Vandalism and Malicious Mischief Endorsement ... 76

THREE FOURTHS LOSS CLAUSE, FIRE INSURANCE ... 50

THREE FOURTHS VALUE CLAUSE, FIRE INSURANCE ... 50

TIME LIMIT ON SUITS ... 376

TIME OF POLICY
See Under Form of Insurance

TITLE, CHANGE IN
See Assignment Under Mortgagee Clause ... 59

TORT LIABILITY MODIFICATION IN AUTO ACCIDENTS
Comparison Charts ... 486-487
Pain and Suffering ... 488

TORTS ... 376
See Under Negligence

TRANSIT
Bailees' Customers Form ... 296, 297
Garment Contractors' Floater ... 307
Jewelers' Block Policy ... 318

TRANSPORTATION
See Also Under Inland Marine Insurance, See Also Transportation Policy
Carriers, Defined ... 327-328
Carrier's Form, See Motor Truck Merchandise Floater
Civil Aeronautics Board ... 331
Common Carrier ... 327
Compulsory Insurance ... 332
Initial Carrier Liability ... 329
Liability of ... 328
Liability, Limitation on ... 331
Regulation of ... 331-332
Warehouseman, Liability as ... 330
Compulsory Insurance ... 332, 337
I.C.C. Endorsement ... 337
Contract Carrier ... 328
Delivery ... 330
Designated Carriers, Effect on Title ... 340
F. O. B. ... 340, 354
Fraudulent Delivery ... 331
General Principles ... 339

Page

Interstate Commerce
Cancellation to ... 337
Commission ... 331-332
Compulsory Insurance ... 332, 337
Shipment Different From Instructions, Effect on Title ... 340
Shipper's Forms—
See Transportation Policy—Shipper's Form, See Also Parcel Post Insurance
Title, When Passes ... 339, 354
Ascertained Goods ... 340
F. O. B. Shipments ... 340
Unascertained Goods ... 340
Transit, Duration of ... 330-331, 354, 362

TRANSPORTATION POLICY— SHIPPER'S FORM ... 341-348
Alcoholic Beverage Limitation ... 344
All Risk Endorsement ... 342
Cancellation ... 347
Endorsement C ... 343-344
Form A ... 343
Form B ... 343
Geographical Limits ... 343
Hazards Covered ... 341
Hazards Not Covered ... 342
Hazards of Transportation ... 342-343
Invoice Value ... 344
Labels Clause ... 345
Limit of Liability Aggregate ... 344
Machinery Clause ... 344
Non-Standardization of ... 341
Notice of Loss ... 347
Other Insurance ... 345
Owner's Trucks Forms ... 343-344
Premium Determination ... 346
Proof of Loss ... 347
Property Not Covered ... 341
Subrogation Under ... 347
Impairment of Carrier's Liability 345
Suit Under ... 347
Valuation ... 344
What Is Covered ... 341

TRIP TRANSIT INSURANCE ... 348

TUITION FEES INSURANCE ... 103

UMBRELLA LIABILITY ... 452-454
Commercial ... 453
Personal ... 454

UNINSURABLE PROPERTY
In Fire Insurance Policy ... 40

UNINSURED MOTORIST COVERAGE ... 465-468

UNOCCUPANCY
In Extended Coverage ... 71
In Fire Insurance ... 40, 56

UNPROTECTED TERRITORY ... 123

UNSATISFIED JUDGMENT FUNDS .. 468

Page

VACANCY AND UNOCCUPANCY

Extended Coverage 71
Fire Insurance 40, 56
Sprinkler Leakage Insurance 136
Vandalism and Malicious Mischief Endorsement 76
Water Damage Policy 140

VALUABLE PAPERS POLICY 203-204

VALUED POLICY LAWS 65-68

VANDALISM

Deductible 76-77
Dwelling-Broad Form 78
Vandalism and Malicious Mischief Endorsement 75-76

VEHICLE, DAMAGE BY

Extended Coverage Endorsement.... 75
Owned or Operated by Insured or Tenant 75

VEHICLE OWNER, LIABILITY OF 383

VICARIOUS LIABILITY..........383-388

WAREHOUSEMAN'S LIABILITY POLICY 203

WARRANTY 29

Sprinkler Leakage, Alarm or Watchman 139

WATER DAMAGE INSURANCE 139-142

Broad Form—Dwelling 79
Chemical Refrigerant Leakage 142
Coinsurance 141
Deductible Clause 142
Hazards Covered 139-140
  Rain or Snow 140
  Tanks, Damage by 140
  Water or Steam Discharge 139-140
Hazards Not Covered 140
  Aircraft in Motion 140
  Alteration and Repairs 141
  Vacancy and Unoccupancy 140
Underground Water Supply Mains and Fire Hydrants 142

WATER DAMAGE LEGAL LIABILITY POLICY 408

WATER EXCLUSION CLAUSE

Extended Coverage 70

WEDDING PRESENTS FLOATER 291

WELFARE AND PENSION PLAN BOND 242

WHOLE DOLLAR PREMIUM RULE 126

WINDSTORM

Deductible Clause 72-73
In Extended Coverage Endorsement 71-72

Page

WORKMEN'S COMPENSATION AND EMPLOYERS' LIABILITY INSURANCE 544-595

Accident, Notice of 572
Accident Reports, Keeping of 572
Agricultural Employees 581
All States Endorsement 574
Application of Policy 579
Assumed Liability 581
Assumption of Risk Doctrine 545
Audit Premiums 587
  Interim Premium Adjustments.... 588
Benefits Under 555, 569-572
Board, Lodging, Services 583
Bonuses, Commissions and Tips 583
Cancellation 593-594
Chauffeurs 585
Clerical Employment 585
Collectors 585
Complying With, Methods of 568
Compulsory Laws 560, 561-562
Conditions 579
Construction, Erection Work 586
Contributory Negligence 545
Course of Employment 547, 555-556
Covered Employees 561-563
Death Benefits 552-554, 571
Defense, Supplementary Benefits 578-579
Definitions 579
Disability Benefits 548-551
Domestic Employees 581
Draughtsmen 585
Drivers 585
Elective Laws 560, 562
Employer's Duties 572
Employer's Liability Section 577-578
Excluded Employments 563
Exclusive, Liability of Employer 556-557
Executive Officers 584
Expense Constant 586-587
Experience Rating 589
  Interstate 589
Extra Legal Medical Coverage 570
Extra Territorial Provisions 573-574
Failure to Comply With, Penalties.. 569
Fatal Injuries, Benefits By States 552-554
Fellow Servant Rule 545
General and Special Employers 574
Governing Classification 585
Illegal Employment of Minors 573, 581
Independent Contractors 567-568
  Principal, Liability of 567
Inspection and Audit 579
Ionizing Radiation, Diseases Caused By 570
Laws, Workmen's Compensation 544-575
  Basic Principle of 544
  Evolution of 544-545
  Purpose of 544
Liability Regardless of Fault 546-547, 555-556

INDEX

Page

Limit, Under Coverage A 581
Limit, Under Coverage B.................. 582
Locations, Not Described 580
Longshoremen's and Harbor
  Worker's Act....562, 564-565, 594-595
Loss Constant 586
Loss of Time Indemnities 570
Maritime Employment 563-565
Medical, Surgical Care 569
Messengers 585
Minimum Premiums 588
Minors, Under 572-573
  Illegally Employed 573
Occupational Disease Coverage 570
Occupational Safety and
  Health Act 565-566
Overtime Pay 584
Partners 580, 584
Payroll Base, Premium 582-583
  Excess of $300 Per Week 583
Per Capita Premiums 584
Policy Coverage 575-582
Premium, Computation of 582-589
Premium Discount 588
Punitive Damages 581
Report of Injuries, Employee's 572
Report of Injury, Employer's 572

Page

Retrospective Rating 590-593
  Plan D 590-592
  Plans A, B, C, J 591-592
Salesmen, Outside 585
Scheduled Awards 571
Second Injury Funds 574-575
Securing of Benefits 555, 569-572
Self-Insurance 575-576
Standard Exceptions 585
States, Differences Among 546
Third Party Actions 557-560
  Differences, Among States 559
Three Year Fixed Rate Policies 592-593
Total Disability, Benefits
  By States 548-551, 571
United States Longshoremen's and
  Harbor Worker's Compensation
  Act 562, 564-565, 594-595
Voluntary Coverage 566
Waiting Period 571
Workmen's Compensation Section.... 577

WRONGFUL DEATH, ACTION FOR 381-382

YACHT INSURANCE 371-372

All Risk Policy 372